D1144794

pling, ratio
 sampling.

whose business o
s and decision
ocedures and r
his book at
uide and r

——— –

AANE, \
le

ELEMENTARY SAMPLING THEORY

ELEMENTARY SAMPLING THEORY

Taro Yamane

Department of Economics
New York University

PRENTICE-HALL, INC., *Englewood Cliffs, N. J.*

PRENTICE-HALL INTERNATIONAL, INC., London
PRENTICE-HALL OF AUSTRALIA PTY. LTD., Sydney
PRENTICE-HALL OF CANADA, LTD., Toronto
PRENTICE-HALL OF INDIA (PRIVATE) LTD., New Delhi
PRENTICE-HALL OF JAPAN, INC., Tokyo

Current printing (last digit): 10 9 8 7 6 5 4 3 2 1

PREFACE

The rapid development of sampling techniques in recent years has brought about their increased application to problems in economic research, business, industry, agriculture, and many other fields. In order to keep abreast of these developments, undergraduate courses in sampling theory are gradually becoming part of business and economics curricula.

A number of excellent texts have been written, but these books are very often too advanced for undergraduate business or economics students with an ordinary mathematics and statistics background.

While teaching sampling theory in the economics department of San Diego State College, I developed an extensive set of notes in order to fulfill my students' need of a simpler text. These notes have been revised and expanded into the present book, which is aimed at undergraduate business and economics majors (juniors and seniors with at least one course of basic statistics), and is intended to be used as the text for a one-semester course in elementary sampling theory.

The text has been divided into three parts. The first part (Chapters 1–4) comprises the introductory material and explains basic concepts of sampling theory. The first part also reviews such topics as expectation, variance, and estimation. The second part (Chapters 5–8) presents basic techniques of sampling theory, including random sampling, stratified random sampling, systematic sampling and, cluster sampling. The third part (Chapters 9–14) considers extensions of basic and special techniques, including cluster sampling with probability proportional to size, three-stage cluster sampling, stratified cluster sampling, ratio estimates, and replicated sampling.

Instructors may wish to consider only the new sampling concepts in the first part—omitting the discussion of expectation, variance, and estimation—and proceed directly to the second part. Most of the applied techniques are to be found in part three, and it is important to plan the course so as to allow sufficient time to cover this section.

Because of the usual classroom time limitations, I feel that the emphasis should be on a theoretical understanding of sampling theory rather than on a drill in the solution of practical problems. One of the aims of this book is to provide the student with a certain amount of technical theory so as to enhance his understanding of sampling theory. Acquiring the knack of reading and manipulating formulas will probably be of more lasting value because it will provide the student with a strong basis for later studies. However, since it is recognized that most students will be users of sampling techniques rather than theoretical statisticians, the text contains only simple theoretical derivations—the more involved derivations have been placed in appendices at the end of each appropriate section. Those students interested in rigorous proofs will find advanced references listed at the end of each chapter. As a further assist to students who are not particularly strong in mathematics, numerous hypothetical examples have been completely worked out. The student may thus actually "see" the mechanics of the theories.

The nontechnical material (such as making questionnaires, how to partition an area into segments, how to handle nonresponse, and many other topics which are important for practical work) has not been included. Those persons who have had experience in designing sample surveys know that a large amount of institutional knowledge is necessary to plan surveys. These and similar practical and institutional problems are also not discussed. However, suggestions for additional readings in theory and nontechnical problems have been given in the Notes and References at the end of each chapter. The business and economics students usually have no trouble understanding nontechnical material, and they are strongly urged to seek and read these materials because of their importance when conducting actual surveys. It is hoped that the background acquired with this text will enable them to place the discussions and the additional readings in their proper perspective.

It is hoped that the important aspects of standard basic sampling theory, the work of many pioneering statisticians in the field of sampling theory, have been covered. References to these scholars have been made throughout the text and I would like to express my indebtedness to all these men. I would also like to express my appreciation to Professors Adam Gifford, Denis A. Flagg, Kozo Yamamura, and the other members of the Department of Economics at San Diego State College, for giving me the opportunity to teach this course and providing the necessary facilities for the completion of the manuscript. I am also indebted to Professors Francis M. Ponti of Drexel Institute of Technology and John J. Chai of Syracuse University for their many helpful suggestions. Thanks are also due to the Department of Economics at New York University for providing the time and facilities to complete this project. Last—but not least—my special thanks to Miss Naoko Okubo for her excellent job of typing the entire manuscript.

New York   TARO YAMANE

CONTENTS

CHAPTER 1

Introduction

1.1 Introduction

Surveying the popularity of candidates at election time is a familiar problem. A sample of voters (say, from New York City) is selected by a certain method, and the preference of voters in New York City (the population, or, universe) for a certain candidate is estimated. This process of selecting a sample to infer the characteristics of the population is a process constantly going on in almost every phase of our daily activities. Some other examples are as follows:

(1) The Bureau of Census selects samples to obtain information on employment, income distribution, education, and various other characteristics of the population.

(2) Industrial firms select samples from their production process to check product quality.

(3) Opinion survey organizations, such as Gallup's American Institute of Public Opinion, select samples to estimate opinions concerning specific issues (such as abolishing the death penalty, forecasting elections, etc.).

(4) Survey research centers use sampling procedures to collect economic data. The Survey Research Center of the University of Michigan collects data on consumer finances which include such things as data on liquid assets, savings, plans and expectations regarding savings and liquid assets, etc.

(5) Market research organizations use sampling extensively to investigate consumer preferences of products, effectiveness of advertisements, etc.

(6) Sampling is used in agriculture for crop estimation and forecasting; and in forestry to estimate amounts of timber, etc.

(7) Sampling is used in accounting to investigate such problems as the age of accounts, booking and clerical errors, inventories, etc.

1

(8) Sampling is used by the armed forces to check the quality of various products it purchases.

(9) Sampling is used by medical doctors and scientists to check the effectiveness of new types of medicine, or to gather data concerning, for example, the coincidence of lung cancer and smoking.

In spite of the fact that most of our knowledge is obtained through a sample that is selected from a population, not much thought was given in the past to the method and theory of selecting the sample or to the problem of evaluating the sampled data. However, paralleling the general development of statistical theory, sampling theory has developed rapidly since the 1940's. This branch of statistics is mainly concerned with the method and theory of selecting samples, the use of sample data to estimate the characteristics of the population (such as the average, total, or proportion), and the evaluation of these estimates.

Those who participated in the development of the various sampling procedures were seeking ways of selecting a sample that would satisfy the following criteria: (1) the sample represents the population; (2) the estimates of the population characteristics (such as the average, total, or proportion) obtained from the sample are precise and we may measure their reliability; (3) the cost of selecting the sample is small. For example, when selecting a sample of voters in New York City, the sample should be representative of all the voters in the city and not just a certain group. The result (for instance, the proportion of people in favor of fluoridation) obtained from the sample should be close to the true proportion, and we should be able to state the reliability of the sample estimate. For obvious reasons, we wish the cost of conducting such a survey to be small.

Our problem in this book will be to investigate various methods of sampling that will give us the desired results with required reliability at minimum cost; or maximum reliability with a given cost. To achieve this purpose, we shall first (in Chapters 2-4) define new terms—such as *frame, universe, precision, reliability*— and also briefly review such concepts as *expectation, variance,* and *confidence interval.*

Then (in Chapters 5-8), we shall discuss four basic sampling procedures: *simple random sampling, stratified random sampling, systematic sampling,* and *simple cluster sampling.* In Chapters 9-12, we shall extend our discussion of cluster sampling to *multistage cluster sampling,* and finally (in Chapters 13-14), we shall briefly discuss various other special sampling procedures.

Sampling, as previously mentioned, is used in a very large number of ways, and we shall give illustrations of its uses as the discussion develops. However, before starting our discussion of the frame and universe, let us mention several sampling procedures that were used mainly in the 1930's to gain a better historical perspective.

1.2 Various sampling procedures

We may say to start with, that there are two kinds of sampling methods. One is *probability sampling* and the other is *nonprobability sampling*. Probability sampling (a term due to Deming, 1950) is a sampling process where each unit is drawn with known probability. This is the method we shall be discussing in detail later on. It is the method that has developed most rapidly since the 1940's and has, for all practical purposes, replaced the nonprobability method of sampling.

The nonprobability method of sampling is a process whereby probabilities cannot be assigned to the units objectively, and hence we cannot determine the reliability of the sample results in terms of probability. Examples of nonprobability sampling used extensively in the 1920's and 1930's are the *judgment sample, quota sample,* and the *mail questionnaire.*

Judgment sampling is a sampling process whereby an expert selects a representative sample according to his expert subjective judgment. For example, a teacher may be asked to select 10 students from a group of 200 students for purposes of estimating the average grade of all the students. She may select 10 students which she thinks are representative of all the students, according to her own expert subjective judgment. If a second teacher is also asked to select 10 students, she will probably select a different group of 10 students, and it is probable that no two experts will agree on what is representative.

When the sample is selected according to an expert's subjective judgment, there is no objective way of evaluating the results, since the reliability of the results depends on the expert's subjective judgment, and not on objective criteria, such as probability theory.

It should be noted, however, that we do not mean to imply that judgment sampling is a bad sampling procedure. In some cases one may have to use it, the results may be good, and the procedure may be economical. For example, an expert may select a sample of wheat off the top of a large pile to check its quality. It may be physically impossible to select a random sample from somewhere inside the pile. However, from long experience, the expert may know various facts about the wheat; perhaps, that it is usually of uniform quality. In this case, a small judgment sample selected from the top of the pile may be sufficient to provide the necessary information concerning the wheat.

The quota sample is a variation of the judgment sample in that it provides more explicit instructions concerning what to select. In order to estimate the average weight of sixth graders in a school of 10 classes where each class is of about equal size, the surveyor may specify that the interviewer select 6 students from each class. The surveyor may further specify that 4 students should be boys and 2 be girls, if that is the approximate ratio of boys and girls in each class, but may leave it up to the interviewer as to how these boys and girls are to be selected. We may say that the interviewers are given definite quotas to fulfill, and these quotas are determined to a certain extent by the population characteristics so that the quota sample will be representative of the population.

This quota sample method was widely used in the 1930's and 40's for election forecasts, public opinion polls, and market research surveys. The names of Elmo Roper and George Gallup are probably familiar to those who recall the presidential election forecasts since the middle of the 1930's. To obtain a representative sample of voters, the U.S. may first be divided into a number of geographic regions. Then, a certain number of voters are selected from each of these regions, in proportions perhaps equal to those of the census population. The number of voters in each region may be further classified as to sex, age, income, education, etc., and the interviewers will be assigned quotas based on these characteristics. The actual selection of individuals is usually left to the discretion of the interviewers.

As demonstrated, quota sampling does not base its selection procedures on probability theory, and hence does not provide a means of objectively assessing the precision and reliability of the estimates. It is, furthermore, subject to the bias of the interviewer—since he is allowed to decide who shall be interviewed—and the degree of bias cannot be objectively measured. The terms precision and bias will be explained more fully later in Chapter 5, but for the moment it will suffice if they are interpreted in a common sense manner. The rapid development of various probability sampling procedures has provided many better means of sampling and, as a result, quota sampling is rapidly losing favor.

The mail questionnaire sampling procedure was also used extensively in the 1920's and 30's, and is still widely used in many surveys because of its low cost and ease of administration. Whether or not this is a nonprobability sampling procedure depends on the method of selecting the sample. If the sample is selected in a manner similar to, say, the quota sampling method, and is not based on probability theory, it is a nonprobability sampling procedure. If the selection is based on probability theory, and the precision and reliability of the estimates may be objectively calculated, it becomes a probability sampling procedure.

A well-known example (in the 1920's and 30's) of a nonrigorous use of the mail questionnaire procedure is the Literary Digest poll. It mailed as many as 10 million ballots to forecast presidential elections, and in some cases the error of the forecast was as small as 2% (1932), while in other instances it was as much as 19% (1936). This large error caused many to lose faith in this kind of sampling procedure. A major cause of this error was the large percentage of nonresponse.

The principal objection to a mail questionnaire procedure is the bias caused by nonresponse. In some Literary Digest polls, only about 20% answered the questionnaire. Various proposals have been made to counteract this problem. One suggestion is to combine the mail questionnaire and personal interview procedures, proposed by Hansen and Hurwitz (1946). Hansen and Hurwitz proposed to mail questionnaires "in excess of the number expected to be returned, and to follow up by enumerating a sample of those that do not respond to the mail canvass." Various other studies concerning the problem of nonresponse and which may be of interest to the reader are given in the references at the end of this chapter. It is a problem that plagues not only the mail questionnaire sampling procedure, but also the probability sampling procedures. It is, however, most prominent in the mail questionnaire procedure, and in most cases makes it impossible to objectively assess the precision and reliability of the survey results.

However, when the surveyor is sure of a very high response, the mail questionnaire procedure may be very effective. For example, the surveyor may be interested in obtaining information about steel companies. Questionnaires may be sent to a sample of steel companies, and the surveyor may be sure that he will get a 100% response. In such instances, the mail questionnaire may be a suitable sampling procedure.

The defects of nonprobability sampling were soon recognized by statisticians, and efforts were made to conduct surveys using probability sampling techniques during the latter half of the 1930's and 40's. Late in the 1930's, members of the Bureau of Agriculture and the Bureau of Census used probability sampling techniques for various regional surveys. In the 1940 population census, the Bureau of Census selected a 5% sample from the population, and this was an important innovation in census work. These 5% of the people were asked additional questions during the census, and quick preliminary estimates of characteristics of the whole population were obtained from this sample. P.M. Hauser, who was a member of the Bureau of the Census at that time (1941), wrote:

"It is to be hoped that the use of sampling techniques in the 1940 Census will serve as a precedent for future censuses, and that new extensions and use of sampling methods will follow to the benefit of not only professional statisticians and social scientists, but also to the benefit of governmental and private consumers of statistics and to the public at large."*

Shortly thereafter, in 1943, the Bureau of Agricultural Economics decided to engage in a major reform of sampling surveys based on probability sampling. The Bureau of Agricultural Economics and the Statistical Laboratory at Iowa State College (now Iowa State University) started work on what is known as the Master Sample, which was to cover the entire country.

This work soon attracted the attention of the Bureau of Census and, in

*Hauser, P. M. (1941). The use of sampling in the census. J. Am. Stat. Assoc., Vol. 36. 369–375.

1945, it cooperated with the Bureau of Agricultural Economics to develop the Master Sample. As a result, the scope of the Master Sample (which was originally designed for agricultural surveys) was enlarged to represent the entire population.

In 1954, the Bureau of Census introduced an enlarged and improved sample to be used as a general purpose sample.

This sequence of developments since the latter part of the 1930's has led to the firm installment of probability sampling procedures in Government statistical work.

Efforts to use probability sampling methods were, of course, not confined to the Government, although theirs was a major contribution. As the examples in Section 1.1 show, probability sampling procedures are widely used in industry, business, public opinion polls, and various other areas, and have at present pretty well replaced the above mentioned nonprobability sampling procedures.

1.3 Advantages of sampling

Before starting our discussion of sampling techniques based on probability sampling, let us briefly consider one more preliminary matter—namely, the advantages of sampling. Why do we use sampling?

Most of the advantages are obvious. The first and most apparent is that it is cheaper to obtain information from a sample than from an entire population.

Another advantage is that it gathers information more quickly. For example, the compilation of a population census may take a year or so. In this particular case, a sample may be taken along with the population census, and preliminary estimates of the population characteristics (such as the ratio of male to female, increases or decreases in population, etc.) may be obtained in a very short time, say, in two or three months.

A third advantage is that more comprehensive data may be obtained. This is because a small sample may be thoroughly investigated whereas, for a large population, this may be impossible or too costly. As mentioned in the previous section, sampling procedures were first introduced in the 1940 population census, and a 5% sample was selected so that additional information might be obtained. These additional questions, which were thought suitable for sampling, were asked in the course of the general canvass. Questions relating to origin of parents, native language, social security coverage, military status, family size, and occupation were among those that were asked.

A fourth advantage is that it obtains data that could not possibly be available otherwise. For example, if testing the life of light bulbs, a manufacturer surely will not burn out all of the bulbs to gather data. A doctor will not drain all of the blood out of a patient in order to check his blood type.

Finally, as mentioned in the previous section, we may obtain a measure of reliability for the sample results. This point will be explained in Chapter 4.

Notes and References

There are a number of excellent books on sampling theory which are of an advanced nature and require varying degrees of mathematical proficiency. We shall, however, limit the references to mainly six books which are usually available in most libraries, and also are of a level accessible to students in business, economics, and other branches of the social sciences. These six books are as follows:

Cochran, W. G. (1963). *Sampling Techniques* (2nd ed.). New York: John Wiley & Sons, Inc.

Hansen, M. H., Hurwitz W. N., and Madow W. G. (1953). *Sample Survey, Methods and Theory*. Vol. I, *Methods and Applications;* Vol. II, *Theory*. New York: John Wiley & Sons, Inc.

Deming, W. E., (1950). *Some Theory of Sampling*. New York: John Wiley & Sons, Inc.

Deming, W. E., (1960). *Sample Design in Business Research*. New York: John Wiley & Sons, Inc.

Kish, L., (1965). *Survey Sampling*. New York: John Wiley & Sons, Inc.

Yates, F., (1960). *Sampling Methods for Census Surveys* (3rd ed.). New York: Hafner Publishing Co., Inc.

Other books will be mentioned as the occasion arises.

References to articles will also be made, but will be confined mainly to those found in the Journal of the American Statistical Association, which can probably be found in most libraries.

A difficulty the student will encounter when reading these references will be the difference in notation. Cochran and Yates use the "y" notation, whereas Deming and Hansen, Hurwitz, and Madow use the "x" notation. For example, Cochran uses $\bar{Y}$ for the population mean, whereas Hansen, Hurwitz, and Madow use $\bar{X}$. As can be seen, sampling theorists do not usually use Greek letters for population parameters (such as μ for the population mean). The notation in this book follows mainly the Hansen, Hurwitz, and Madow notation, but deviates from it in certain cases. It is suggested that the reader learn the notation in this book prior to reading the references.

When making references, we shall write Cochran (1963) to refer to Cochran's book of 1963. Four sources for advanced references are the bibliography at the end of Yates (1960) and Kish (1965), and the references at the end of every chapter of Cochran (1963), and Stephan and McCarthy (1958).

Stephan, F. J., and McCarthy, P. J. (1958). *Sampling Opinions: An Analysis of Survey Procedure*. New York: John Wiley & Sons, Inc.

1.1–1.3 Additional general readings for Sections 1.1–1.3 may be found in the following books: Deming (1950), pp. 9–15. Cochran (1963), Sections 1.1, 1.2, 1.4,

1.5. Yates (1960), Chapter 1. Deming (1960), Chapter 2. Slonim (1960), Preface, Chapter 1.

Slonim, M.J. (1960). *Sampling in a Nutshell*. New York: Simon and Schuster, Inc.

Additional references concerning master sample, mail questionnaires, non-response, etc., are as follows:

Roper, E. (1940). "Sampling Public Opinion," *J. Am. Stat. Assoc.*, Vol. 35, 325–334.

Stephan, F. F., Deming, W. E., and Hansen, M. H. (1940). "On the sampling procedure of the 1940 population census," *J. Am. Stat. Assoc.*, Vol. 35, 615–630.

Hauser, P. M. (1941). "The use of sampling in the census," *J. Am. Stat. Assoc.*, Vol. 36, 369–375.

King, A. J., and Jessen, R. J. (1945). "The master sample of agriculture," *J. Am. Stat. Assoc.*, Vol. 40, 38–56.

Hansen, M. H. and Hurwitz, W. N. (1946). "The problem of nonresponse in sample surveys, "*J. Am. Stat. Assoc.*, Vol. 41, 517–529.

Politz, A. and Simmons, W. (1949). "An attempt to get the 'not at homes' into the sample without call backs," *J. Am. Stat. Assoc.*, Vol. 44, 9–31.

Politz, A. and Simmons, W. (1950). Note on "An attempt to get the 'not-at-homes' into the sample without call backs," *J. Am. Stat. Assoc.*, Vol. 45, 136–137.

El-Badry, M. A., (1959). "A sampling procedure for mailed questionnaires," *J. Am. Stat. Assoc.*, Vol. 51, 209–227.

Hansen, M. H., Hurwitz, W. N., Nisselson, H., and J. Steinberg, (1955). "The redesign of the census current population survey," *J. Am. Stat. Assoc.*, Vol. 50, 701–719.

Stephan, F. F., (1948). "History of the uses of modern sampling procedures," *J. Am. Stat. Assoc.*, Vol. 43, 12–39.

The mathematically advanced references are as follows:

Sukhatme, P. V. (1954). *Sampling Theory of Surveys with Applications, Ames, Iowa:* Iowa State University Press.

Hansen, M. H., Hurwitz, W. N., and Madow, W. G. (1953). *Sample Survey Methods and Theory*. New York: John Wiley & Sons, Inc., Vol. II.

CHAPTER 2

Expected Values and Variances

Before proceeding into the discussion of sampling theory proper, there are several preliminaries that need to be considered. As our discussion of sampling theory develops, we shall be discussing various ways of estimating the mean and variance of the population. These means and variances will appear in various forms. They will, however, derive from a common theoretical basis. Hence, to understand the variations of these formulas for the mean and variance, we need a knowledge of the underlying theory of the basic case. In this chapter, we shall discuss the basic ideas of the mean value and variance of a variable which will provide part of the theoretical background for our subsequent discussion. Those who are familiar with these concepts may skip this section and proceed to the next chapter without loss of continuity.

2.1 All possible samples

In all branches of statistics—whether it be sampling theory, regression analysis, or quality control—we usually select samples from the population and investigate the characteristics of the sample statistics to infer about the population. It is therefore imperative, as a first step, that we understand clearly how the samples are selected, and how many can be selected from the population. We learn in elementary statistics that there are two basic ways of selecting samples; one is to select samples with replacement, and the other is selecting them without replacement. The number of possible samples that can be selected will differ, depending on the method of selection used.

As a starting point of our discussion of expected values and variances, let us review the results concerning the number of possible samples of size n that may be selected from a population of size N.

In elementary statistics, we learn that given N students, there are N^n

possible ways of selecting a sample of n students with replacement. For example, given $N = 3$ students—A, B, and C—there are $N^2 = 3^2 = 9$ possible ways of selecting samples of $n = 2$ students. In tabular form, this may be shown as

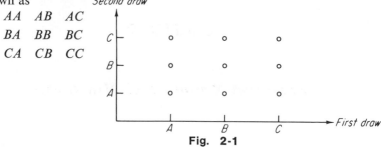

$$\begin{array}{ccc} AA & AB & AC \\ BA & BB & BC \\ CA & CB & CC \end{array}$$

Fig. 2-1

It may also be shown graphically, as in Fig. 2-1. The graph is a 2-dimensional sample space and each point is a sample point showing a sample of size $n = 2$. There are $3^2 = 9$ sample points.

We also learn in elementary statistics that there are

(1) $$\binom{N}{n} = \frac{N!}{n!(N-n)!}$$

possible samples of size n that can be selected from a population of size N without replacement and when the order is not considered. Let us explain this formula with our illustration. Since sampling is without replacement, there are $N = 3$ choices for the 1st draw and $N - 1 = 2$ choices for the 2nd draw. Hence, there are

$$N(N-1) = 3(3-1) = 6$$

possible samples which may be shown as

$$\begin{array}{ccc} .. & AB & AC \\ BA & .. & BC \\ CA & CB & .. \end{array}$$

But note that AB and BA are the same sample, except that the order of A and B differ. Similarly for AC and BC. As shown, there are $2! = 2$ ways of ordering $n = 2$ elements. Hence, when the order is disregarded, there will be

$$\frac{N(N-1)}{n!} = \frac{3(3-1)}{2!} = 3$$

possible samples. This may be shown as follows:

$$\begin{array}{ccc} .. & AB & AC \\ .. & .. & BC \\ .. & .. & .. \end{array}$$

If we have a population of $N = 5$ and samples of size $n = 3$ are selected, there are

$$N \times N \times N = N^3$$

possible samples when sampling with replacement. When sampling without replacement and when the order is considered, there are

$$N(N - 1)(N - 2) = 5(5 - 1)(5 - 2) = 60$$

possible samples. There are $n! = 3! = 6$ different ways of ordering $n = 3$ elements. Hence, when the order is disregarded, there will be

$$\frac{N(N - 1)(N - 2)}{n!} = \frac{5(5 - 1)(5 - 2)}{3!} = 10$$

possible samples.

In general, when the population is of size N, samples of size n are selected without replacement, and the order is disregarded, there are

$$\frac{N(N - 1)(N - 2) \ldots (N - n + 1)}{n!}$$

possible samples. It can easily be shown by algebraic manipulation that

$$\frac{N(N - 1)(N - 2) \ldots (N - n + 1)}{n!} = \frac{N!}{n!(N - n)!}$$

which is usually expressed as equation (1) above.

Example. Suppose there are $N = 5$ students. How many possible samples of size $n = 2$ students can we select when sampling without replacement?

$$\binom{N}{n} = \binom{5}{2} = \frac{N(N - 1)}{n!} = \frac{5 \times 4}{2!} = 10$$

Problems

1. Given $N = 10$ students, how many ways are there of selecting a basketball team of $n = 5$ students?

2. There are 2 tables seating 3 and 4 guests, respectively. How many different ways are there of dividing the 7 guests into two groups?

3. Given choices of 3 meats, 4 vegetables, 2 soups, and 3 kinds of bread, a student is asked to select 1 meat, 2 vegetables, 1 soup, and 1 kind of bread. How many choices does he have?

4. Show by algebraic manipulation that

$$\frac{N(N - 1)(N - 2) \cdots (N - n + 1)}{n!} = \frac{N!}{n!(N - n)!}$$

2.2 Probability of selecting a sample of size n

Having found the number of possible samples of size n that may be selected from a population of size N, let us now consider the following three questions: (i) what is the probability of selecting a sample of size n; (ii) what is the probability that a certain member of the population will be in the sample; (iii) what is the probability that a certain member of the population will be selected on the mth draw? By using the answer to the first question, we may define a simple random sample. The answers to the other two questions will be used later.

(i) *What is the probability of selecting a sample of size $n = 2$ from a population of $N = 5$?*

Let us start out with the simple case. We know that the probability of selecting $n = 1$ letter (say A) from $N = 5$ letters (A, B, C, D, and E) is $1/N$.

The probability of selecting a second letter (B, for instance) from the remaining $N - 1 = 5 - 1 = 4$ letters is $1/(N - 1)$.

Since the draws are random, the probability of selecting a sample A, B, in that order, is

$$\frac{1}{N} \cdot \frac{1}{N-1}$$

However, we consider sample BA to be the same as AB. There are $n! = 2!$ ways of permuting A, B. Hence, the probability of selecting a sample AB where the order is disregarded is

(1) $$\frac{1}{N} \cdot \frac{1}{N-1} \cdot n! = \frac{1}{5} \cdot \frac{1}{4} \cdot 2! = \frac{1}{10}$$

The student will have already noticed that the probability of $1/10$ corresponds to the result we obtained in the previous section where there were

$$\binom{N}{n} = \binom{5}{2} = \frac{5!}{2!3!} = \frac{5 \times 4}{2} = 10$$

different ways of selecting a sample of size 2.

Combining this result with equation (1) above, we find that for $n = 2$

$$\frac{1}{N} \cdot \frac{1}{N-1} \cdot n! = \frac{1}{\dfrac{N(N-1)}{n!}} = \frac{1}{\binom{N}{n}}$$

We can easily reason that this process is applicable to a sample of size n. Hence, we conclude that: given a population of size N and a sample of size n, there are $\binom{N}{n}$ different ways of selecting the sample and the probability of selecting a given sample of size n is

$$\frac{1}{\binom{N}{n}}$$

Using this result, we may now define the terms *simple random sampling* and *simple random sample*. Simple random sampling (also known as random sampling) is a method of selecting *n* units out of *N* such that every one of the $\binom{N}{n}$ samples has an equal chance of being selected, and the sample thus selected is called a simple random sample.

If we let $n = 1$, then

$$\binom{N}{n} = \binom{N}{1} = N$$

which means that the probability of selecting a sample of size $n = 1$ is $1/N$.

From this, we can say that random sampling is a method of selecting *n* units out of *N* such that each unit has an equal chance of being drawn at each draw. Hence, the probability of the first unit being drawn is $1/N$; the probability of the second unit being drawn is $1/(N-1)$, and so forth. When sampling with replacement, it is clear that the probability will always be $1/N$.

Example 1. Suppose there are $N = 7$ boys from which $n = 5$ are to be selected to form a basketball team. What is the probability of selecting the $n = 5$ tallest boys? The probability is

$$\frac{1}{\binom{N}{n}} = \frac{1}{\binom{7}{5}} = \frac{1}{21}$$

(*ii*) *What is the probability that the letter A will be in the sample?*

Let us now ask the question: What is the probability that the letter *A* will be in a sample of $n = 3$ which is selected from $N = 5$ letters (*A, B, C, D,* and *E*)? The probability that *A* is selected on the first draw is $1/N$.

The probability that *A* is selected on the second draw is the probability that it is not selected on the first draw times the probability it is selected on the second draw, which is

$$\frac{N-1}{N} \cdot \frac{1}{N-1}$$

The probability that *A* is selected on the third draw is

$$\frac{N-1}{N} \cdot \frac{N-2}{N-1} \cdot \frac{1}{N-2}$$

where $(N-1)/N$ is the probability that it is not selected on the first draw; $(N-2)/(N-1)$ is the probability that it is not selected on the second draw, given it was not selected on the first draw; and $1/(N-2)$ is the probability that it is selected on the third draw.

Since these 3 events are mutually exclusive, the probability that *A* is included in the sample of $n = 3$ is

$$\frac{1}{N} + \frac{N-1}{N} \cdot \frac{1}{N-1} + \frac{N-1}{N} \cdot \frac{N-2}{N-1} \cdot \frac{1}{N-2}$$

$$= \frac{1}{N} + \frac{1}{N} + \frac{1}{N} = \frac{3}{N}$$

$$= \frac{n}{N}$$

By induction, we can see that the probability of a specific letter A being in a sample of size n that is selected from a population of size N is n/N.

(*iii*) *What is the probability that the letter A will be selected on the mth draw?*

Let us first consider the case where the sampling is without replacement. The probability that A is selected on the first draw is $1/N$.

The probability that it is selected on the second draw is

$$\frac{N-1}{N} \cdot \frac{1}{N-1} = \frac{1}{N}$$

The probability that it is selected on the third draw is

$$\frac{N-1}{N} \cdot \frac{N-2}{N-1} \cdot \frac{1}{N-2} = \frac{1}{N}$$

Hence, we see by induction that the probability of selecting A on the mth draw is always $1/N$. When the sampling is with replacement, the probability is clearly $1/N$ for all drawings.

Using this result, we may derive the previous result that the probability of A being included in the sample is $n/N = 3/5$. Since the probability of selecting A on the first, second, or third draw is $1/N = 1/5$, respectively, and since A may be included in the sample at any of the $n = 3$ drawings, the probability that A is included in the sample is $n/N = 3/5$.

2.3 Expected value

Using the results of the previous two sections, we are ready to define what is meant by the mathematical expectation of a random variable X_i. Let us discuss its meaning with an example.

Suppose our experiment consists of tossing a die, and let X_i be the number that occurs. The X_i has 6 possible outcomes 1, 2, 3, ... , 6, and to each outcome we may associate a probability of $1/6$. The mean of these outcomes is

(1) $$\bar{X} = \frac{1}{6}(1 + 2 + \cdots + 6) = 3.5$$

which may be rewritten as

(2) $$\bar{X} = 1 \cdot \frac{1}{6} + 2 \cdot \frac{1}{6} + \cdots + 6 \cdot \frac{1}{6}$$

and may be interpreted as follows: The 1/6 may be considered as the relative frequency with which X_i occurs when the experiment of tossing the die is repeated a very large number of times. Hence, $\bar{X}$ may be considered as the weighted average of the X_i.

Denoting 1/6 as p_i, the right side of the (2) may be expressed as

$$(3) \qquad X_1 p_1 + X_2 p_2 + \cdots + X_6 p_6 = \sum_i^k X_i p_i$$

Here X_i is the random variable, p_i is its probability, and the Σ is over all possible values of X_i. Equation (3) is called the *expectation* of the random variable X_i. Denoting the expectation of X_i as $E(X_i)$, we finally have

$$(4) \qquad E(X_i) = \sum^k X_i p_i$$

In general, we shall define the mathematical expectation of a random variable X_i as follows: Let X_i be the random variable with possible values $X_1 \ldots, X_k$ and probabilities $p_1, \ldots, p_k$, respectively. Then the expected value of X_i is defined as

$$E(X_i) = \sum^k X_i p_i$$

where Σ is taken over all possible values of X_i.

The point to note carefully is that k is the number of all possible values of X_i. Hence, when we wish to find the expectation of the sample mean $\bar{x}$,

$$\bar{x} = \frac{1}{n} \sum^n x_i$$

where n is the sample size, we need to find all possible values of $\bar{x}$. And to find all possible values of $\bar{x}$, we need to find all possible samples of size n that can be selected from the population of size N.

Here we may use the results of the previous section and say immediately that there are N^n possible samples when sampling is with replacement, and $\binom{N}{n}$ when sampling is without replacement. Let us illustrate these points with a simple example:

Suppose there are $N = 3$ students who have $X_1 = \$1$, $X_2 = \$2$, and $X_3 = \$3$, respectively. Assuming each student has an equal chance of being selected, the expected value of X_i is

$$\begin{aligned} E(X_i) &= \sum^k X_i p_i \\ &= X_1 p_1 + X_2 p_2 + X_3 p_3 \\ &= \$1(1/3) + \$2(1/3) + \$3(1/3) = \$2 \end{aligned}$$

which is simply the population mean.

Let us now select samples of size $n = 2$ with replacement. Then there are $3^2 = 9$ possibles samples which may be shown as 9 sample points in a 2-dimen-

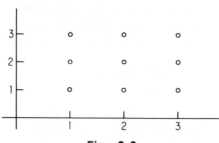

Fig. 2-2

sional sample space (Fig. 2-2). Hence, there are 9 possible sample means and we may associate a probability of 1/9 to each sample mean. The expected value of the sample mean is thus

$$E(\bar{x}) = \sum_{i}^{k=9} \bar{x}_i p_i$$

The 9-sample means are given in Table 2.1.

Table 2.1

Sample	Sum	$\bar{x}$
1, 1	2	1.0
1, 2	3	1.5
1, 3	4	2.0
2, 1	3	1.5
2, 2	4	2.0
2, 3	5	2.5
3, 1	4	2.0
3, 2	5	2.5
3, 3	6	3.0
		18.0

Hence, $E(\bar{x})$ becomes

$$E(\bar{x}) = \frac{1}{9}(1 + 1.5 + \cdots + 3.0) = \frac{18}{9} = 2$$

which is also the population mean $\bar{X}$. When sampling without replacement, there are

$$\binom{N}{n} = \binom{3}{2} = 3$$

possible samples, and hence 3 possible sample means. These are shown in Table 2.2.

Table 2.2

Samples	Sum	$\bar{x}$
1, 2	3	1.5
1, 3	4	2.0
2, 3	5	2.5
		6.0

Hence, $E(\bar{x})$ becomes

$$E(\bar{x}) = \sum_{i}^{k} \bar{x}_i p_i$$
$$= \frac{1}{3}(1.5 + 2 + 2.5) = 2$$

which is equal to $\bar{X} = \$2$.

The point to note in these examples is that we needed to know the number of all possible samples to find $E(\bar{x})$.

Suppose now that there are $N = 3$ students who have taken an exam, and the maximum grade is 5 points. Then the random variable X_i has 6 possible values 0, 1, 2, ..., 5 points. Suppose the grades of the $N = 3$ students are 1, 2, 3. What is the expected value of X_i ? By definition we have

$$E(X_i) = \sum_{i}^{k} X_i p_i = X_1 p_1 + X_2 p_2 + \cdots + X_6 p_6$$

We know that $X_1 = 0$, $X_2 = 1$, ..., $X_6 = 5$. But we do not know the p_i a priori. There is no reason to assume that $p_i = 1/6$. Instead, we shall assume that the 3 grades that actually occurred have probability 1/3 each, and the other possible grades that have not occurred have probability 0. Hence, $E(X_i)$ becomes

$$E(X_i) = \sum_{i}^{k} X_i p_i$$
$$= 0(0) + 1(1/3) + 2(1/3) + 3(1/3) + 4(0) + 5(0)$$
$$= \frac{1}{3}(1 + 2 + 3) = 2$$

$E(X_i) = 2$ points is the population mean of the grades of the $N = 3$ students.

Suppose the grades of the $N = 3$ students were 1, 5, 5, then:

$$E(X_i) = \sum_{i}^{k} X_i p_i$$
$$= 0(0) + 1(0) + 2(1/3) + 3(0) + 4(0) + 5(2/3)$$
$$= \frac{1}{3}(2 + 5 + 5) = 4$$

which is simply the mean of the 3 grades that have occurred.

The point to note in the two preceding examples is that, although theoretically $k = 6$, when the p_i are not given, we have considered the $p_i = 0$ for those values of X_i which do not occur; hence, the calculation of $E(X_i)$ involves only the N population values.

We may state our result in general form as follows. When calculating

$$E(X_i) = \sum_{i}^{k} X_i p_i$$

we take the sum Σ over all possible values of X_i. However, when given a population of N values of X_i and when the p_i are not given, we assume each of the X_i have an equal chance of occurrence, and hence $p_i = 1/N$, and for the other possible values of X_i which have not occurred, we set $p_i = 0$. The result is that the sum over all possible values of X_i becomes the sum over the N population values.

In our subsequent discussion, we shall use N to denote the possible values of X_i and the size population. The reader should, however, make a mental distinction between the size of the population and the concept of all possible values of X_i.

Problems

1. A dime is tossed. When a head (H) appears you receive the dime. When a tail (T) appears, you do not. What is your expectation of this game?

2. Suppose 2 dimes are tossed. When 2 heads appear, you get 2 dimes. When 1 head appears, you get nothing. What is the expectation of this game?

3. Suppose there is a lottery with $N = 100$ tickets. There is one first prize of $100; 10 second prizes of $10; and 20 third prizes of $5. The rest of the tickets have no prizes. What is the expectation of this lottery?

2.4 Some properties of expected values

Using the definition of expected values, let us derive several useful properties of the expected values.

(*i*) *The expected value of a constant.*

Let $X_1 = X_2 = \cdots = X_k = a$ a a constant, and let the probability be p_i. Then the expected value of $X = a$ is

$$E(a) = \sum a p_i = a \sum p_i = a$$

since $\sum p_i = 1$.

(*ii*) *The expected value of aX_i.*

Using the previous illustration where the students had $X_1 = \$2, \ldots,$ $X_5 = \$6$, the $E(X) = \$3.5$. If each of the X_i is multiplied by a constant, say, $a = 2$, then $E(aX_i) = \$3.5 \times 2 = \$7.0$. This may be shown by

$$E(aX) = \sum a X_i p_i = a \sum X_i p_i = aE(X_i)$$

(*iii*) *The expected value of $E(X_i + a)$.*

The expected value of X_i plus a constant a may be shown as follows:

$$
\begin{aligned}
E(X_i + a) &= \sum (X_i + a) p_i \\
&= \sum X_i p_i + \sum a p_i \\
&= E(X_i) + a \sum p_i \\
&= E(X_i) + a
\end{aligned}
$$

2.5 Expected value of a sample value x_i

Another important property of the expected value we shall be using frequently in subsequent discussion concerns the expected value of a sample value x_i. Suppose a sample of size n is selected from a population of size N. Let the sample be shown by $x_1, \ldots, x_n$, and let x_i be the unit drawn on the ith draw. The expected value of x_i is therefore

$$E(x_i) = \sum_{}^{N} x_i p_i$$

where N may be considered the possible values of x_i. We also know that the probability of drawing a specific item X_i on the ith draw is $1/N$. Hence, $p_i = 1/N$, and $E(x_i)$ becomes

$$E(x_i) = \sum_{}^{N} x_i \cdot \frac{1}{N} = \bar{X}$$

That is, the expectation of a sample value is equal to the population mean.

2.6 The variance

The main measure of dispersion we shall be using in our subsequent discussion is the variance. We shall find many different variances for different sampling procedures. However, as with the expected value (or mean value) of a random variable, they have a common theoretical background. It is the purpose of the subsequent several sections to discuss the basic theoretical properties of variances and provide a background for our subsequent discussions. We shall define the variance; discuss several properties of the variance; discuss the concept of a joint probability distribution; define the covariance; derive several important properties of the mean value; derive several important properties of the variance; and, finally, discuss the coefficient of variation.

The variance of a random variable X_i is defined as

(1) $$V(X_i) = E(X_i - EX_i)^2$$

From the definition of expected values, (1) becomes

(2) $$V(X_i) = \sum_{}^{N} (X_i - EX_i)^2 p_i$$

where $X_1, X_2, \ldots, X_N$ are all the possible values of X_i and $p_1, \ldots, p_N$ are the probabilities associated with the possible values.

For simple random sampling, we have seen that

$$E(X_i) = \bar{X}$$

that is, $E(X_i)$ is equal to the population mean. Furthermore, the probability of selecting any one of the N possible values X_i is, as we have already seen, $1/N$. Hence, for simple random sampling equation (2) becomes

(3)
$$\sigma^2 = \frac{\Sigma (X_i - \bar{X})^2}{N}$$

which is the usual form in which it is found in elementary texts. The numerator $\Sigma (X_i - \bar{X})^2$ is usually called the sum of the squared deviations.

2.7 Properties of the variance

Two simple properties of the variance that are used frequently are

(1)
$$V(X_i + a) = V(X_i)$$

(2)
$$V(aX_i) = a^2 V(X_i)$$

Equation (1) shows that the $V(X_i)$ is invariant to shifts of the origin and is obtained as follows.

$$V(X_i + a) = E[(X_i + a) - E(X_i + a)]^2$$
$$= E[X_i - E(X_i)]^2$$
$$= V(X_i)$$

since $E(X_i + a) = E(X_i) + a$.

Equation (2) shows that when the scale of X_i is changed by a (say $a = 2$), the variance increases by a^2 (that is, by $a^2 = 2^2 = 4$ times). This is easily derived as follows:

$$V(aX_i) = E(aX_i - EaX_i)^2$$
$$= a^2 E(X_i - EX_i)^2$$
$$= a^2 V(X_i)$$

Another important property of a variance we shall be using concerns the variance of a linear combination of random variables. To explain this, we need the concept of covariance, so let us discuss the idea of a covariance between two random variables, X_i and Y_i. But before we do, there are several preliminaries we need to discuss.

Problems

1. Find the variance of 1, 2, 3.

2. Add 5 to 1, 2, and 3, respectively, and find the variance. Note that it is the same as that found in Problem 1 above.

3. Multiply 1, 2, and 3 respectively by 5 and find the variance of these 3 variables. Note that the variance is $5^2 = 25$ times that of Problem 1.

2.8 Joint probability distribution

As mentioned in the previous section, to derive additional properties of the variance and mean value of random variables, we need the concept of the covariance between two random variables. This in turn requires the idea of a joint distribution between two random variables. In this section we shall discuss the idea of a joint distribution of two random variables X_i and Y_j, and two related concepts, statistical independence and a joint frequency function.

(i) Joint probabilility distribution.

We frequently observe in school that a person who is a good student in one subject is often good in others as well. As an illustration, let us consider economics and mathematics. A student who gets good grades in economics is in many cases also good in math. We also observe, for example, that tall brothers tend to have tall sisters.

A characteristic of the illustrations above is that we are considering two variables simultaneously. In the first illustration we have grades of economics (X_i) and grades of math (Y_j). In the second illustration we have height of brothers (X_i) and height of sisters (Y_j). The X_i and Y_j are considered jointly. Other illustrations are the grade point (X_i) and hours of study (Y_j) of a student; the expenditures (X_i) and income (Y_j) of a family; the yield of corn (X_i) and the amount of rainfall (Y_j), and so forth.

A second characteristic we note is that X_i and Y_j tend to vary together, in either the same or in opposite directions. A high grade in economics (X_i) is associated with high grades in math (Y_j), and these are cases where X_i and Y_j vary in the same direction.

Let us consider the economics and math grade illustration in a little more detail. Let the grades be A, B, C, D, and F, and let the frequency of pairs of grades of 20 students be as in Table 2.3.

Table 2.3

X_i \ Y_j	$Y_1 = A$	$Y_2 = B$	$Y_3 = C$	$Y_4 = D$	$Y_5 = F$	Frequency of X_i
$X_1 = A$	1	0	0	0	0	1
$X_2 = B$	1	3	0	0	0	4
$X_3 = C$	0	1	5	0	0	6
$X_4 = D$	0	0	1	4	1	6
$X_5 = F$	0	0	0	1	2	3
Frequency of Y_j	2	4	6	5	3	20

The table shows, for example, that there is 1 student with an A in both economics and math; 1 student with a B in economics and A in math; 3 students with a B in both economics and math, and so forth.

Observation of this table shows that a student with high grades in economics tends to have high grades in math and one with low grades in economics tends to have low grades in math. Let us assign grade points to the letter grades as follows: $A = 5$, $B = 4$, $C = 3$, $D = 2$, $F = 1$.

Let us now express Table 2.3 in terms of relative frequencies. We shall divide each number by the total, $N = 20$, and use these relative frequencies as estimates of probabilities. This is shown in Table 2.4.

Table 2.4

	Y_1	Y_2	Y_3	Y_4	Y_5	$P(X = X_i)$
X_1	0.05					0.05
X_2	0.05	0.15				0.20
X_3		0.05	0.25			0.30
X_4			0.05	0.20	0.05	0.30
X_5				0.05	0.10	0.15
$P(Y = Y_j)$	0.10	0.20	0.30	0.25	0.15	1.00

The interpretation of this table is as follows: The probability of a student having $(X_1 = A, Y_1 = A)$ is 0.05; the probability of a student having $(X_4 = D, Y_3 = C)$ is 0.05; and so forth. These probabilities may be expressed as:

$$P(X = X_1, Y = Y_1) = p(X_1, Y_1) = 0.05$$
$$P(X = X_4, Y = Y_3) = p(X_4, Y_3) = 0.05$$
$$P(X = X_1, Y = Y_2) = p(X_1, Y_2) = 0$$

and so forth. There are altogether $(5 \times 5 =)$ 25 pairs of grades, and 25 equations giving 25 corresponding probabilities. These probabilities give us a probability distribution of the pairs of grades, and this system of 25 equations showing the probability distribution of the 25 pairs of (X_i, Y_j) is called the *joint probability distribution of X_i and Y_j*. The sum of all joint probabilities is thus clearly equal to 1.

Let us now consider, for example, the 2nd row (for $X = X_2 = B$). Then

$$(1) \qquad p(X_2, Y_1) + p(X_2, Y_2) + p(X_2, Y_3) + p(X_2, Y_4) + p(X_2, Y_5)$$
$$= P(X = X_2)$$
$$= f(X_2) = 0.20$$

shows the probability of a student getting a grade of $X_2 = B$ in economics.

In similar fashion, the right hand margin shows the probabilities of getting an $X_1 = A$, $X_2 = B$, $X_3 = C$, $X_4 = D$, $X_5 = F$ in economics, and are therefore the probability distribution of the grade X_i of economics.

Likewise, the probabilities at the bottom of the table show the probability distribution of the mathematics grades Y_j.

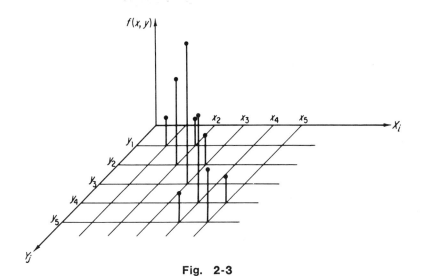

Fig. 2-3

To summarize, the probabilities in the body of the table are the joint probability distribution of X_i and Y_j. The probabilities in the right hand margin are the probability distribution of X_i and those in the lower margin are the probability distribution of Y_j. The probability distributions of X_i and Y_j are sometimes called *marginal probability distributions*. The joint distribution of X_i and Y_j is shown schematically in Fig. 2-3.

Problems

1. In the illustration above, what is the probability of a student getting either A or B in economics?

2. What is the probability of a student getting a C or D in mathematics?

3. What is the probability of a student getting an A or B in economics and B or C in mathematics?

(*ii*) *Statistical independence.*

The second concept that we shall review is statistical independence. From elementary statistics, we are acquainted with the definition that when there are two events, A and H, the probability of A, given H, is

$$P(A \mid H) = \frac{P(AH)}{P(H)}$$

where $P(H) > 0$. This is the conditional probability of A for a given H.

We are also acquainted with the definition that two events A and H are said to be statistically independent if

$$P(AH) = P(A)P(H)$$

As an illustration of two independent events, let H be the event of a head on the 1st toss, and A be the event of a head on the 2nd toss. Then, AH is the event of a head on both tosses. We know that $P(A) = 1/2$, $P(H) = 1/2$, and $P(HA) = 1/4$. Hence,

$$P(AH) = P(A)P(H) = 1/4$$

which shows that A and H are statistically independent.

When the two events are not independent, they are said to be dependent.

When extended to 3 events, A, B, and C, we shall just state that the condition for independence is

$$P(AB) = P(A)P(B)$$
$$P(AC) = P(A)P(C)$$
$$P(BC) = P(B)P(C)$$
$$P(ABC) = P(A)P(B)P(C)$$

and this may be extended to the general case.

(iii) *Joint frequency function.*

The third concept that we shall review is the joint frequency function of variables. When a coin is tossed, the probability of a head (H) or tail (T) is

$$P(\text{H}) = 1/2, \ P(\text{T}) = 1/2$$

and we know that these functions are called *probability functions.*

The two possible outcomes, H and T, may be expressed as

$$X_i = \begin{cases} 0 = X_1 & \text{head} \\ 1 = X_2 & \text{tail} \end{cases}$$

and shown as

$$P(\text{H}) = f(X_1) = 1/2$$
$$P(\text{T}) = f(X_2) = 1/2$$

These $f(X_i)$ functions are called *frequency functions* (or density functions). Quite clearly

$$f(X_i) \geq 0, \qquad \Sigma f(X_i) = 1$$

In our present case

$$f(X_1) + f(X_2) = 1/2 + 1/2 = 1$$

Let us now extend our discussion and perform an experiment consisting of tossing a coin 3 times. As we have seen, there are $2^3 = 8$ possible events:

HHH, HHT, HTH, THH, HTT, THT, TTH, TTT

and this gives us a 3-dimensional sample space with 8 sample points where each sample point is assigned a probability of 1/8. Hence, the probability of any one event is, for example,

$$P(\text{HTT}) = 1/8$$

From the discussion of statistical independence, we can see that

$$P(\text{HTT}) = P(\text{H})P(\text{T})P(\text{T})$$
$$= 1/2 \times 1/2 \times 1/2 = 1/8$$

and in terms of the frequency function, this may be written as

$$P(\text{HTT}) = f(X_1, X_2, X_3)$$
$$= f(X_1)f(X_2)f(X_3)$$
$$= 1/8$$

Furthermore,

$$\sum_i \sum_j \sum_k f(X_i, X_j, X_k)$$
$$= f(X_1, X_1, X_1) + f(X_1, X_1, X_2) + \cdots + f(X_2, X_2, X_2)$$
$$= 1/8 + 1/8 + \cdots + 1/8 = 8/8 = 1$$

The $P(\text{HTT})$ is called the *joint probability function*, and the $f(X_i, X_j, X_k)$ is called the *joint frequency function*.

When the events are dependent, the joint frequency function which corresponds to the joint probability distribution is not equal to the product of the frequency functions of the individual events. For example,

$$P(AB) \neq P(A)P(B)$$

or $$f(X_i, X_j) \neq f(X_i)f(X_j)$$

The tables in this section are examples of dependent events.

2.9 Expected value of a linear combination of random variables

In Section 2.8, we had two variables X_i (economics grades), and Y_j (math grades). Let us in this section consider the question: What is the expected value of $X_i + Y_j$?

By definition, the expected value of $X_i + Y_j$ is

(1) $$E(X_i + Y_j) = \sum_i \sum_j (X_i + Y_j)f(X_i, Y_j)$$

where $f(X_i, Y_j)$ is the joint frequency function. The right hand side of equation (1) may be expanded and rewritten as

(2)
$$\sum_i \sum_j (X_i + Y_j) f(X_i, Y_j)$$
$$= \sum_i \sum_j X_i f(X_i, Y_j) + \sum_i \sum_j Y_j f(X_i, Y_j)$$
$$= \sum_i X_i \sum_j f(X_i, Y_j) + \sum_j Y_j \sum_i f(X_i, Y_j)$$

The term $\sum_j f(X_i, Y_j)$ is the marginal probability of X_i. For the illustration of grades, we have

(3)
$$\sum_j^5 f(X_i, Y_j) = f(X_i, Y_1) + \cdots f(X_i, Y_5) = g(X_i)$$

where $g(X_i)$ is the marginal probability of X_i. The $g(X_i)$ is also used to denote the marginal probability function of X_i.

Let us reproduce Table 2.4 here as Table 2.5 to illustrate the calculations.

Table 2.5

	Y_1	Y_2	Y_3	Y_4	Y_5	$P(X = X_i)$
X_1	0.05					0.05
X_2	0.05	0.15				0.20
X_3		0.05	0.25			0.30
X_4			0.05	0.20	0.05	0.30
X_5				0.05	0.10	0.15
$P(Y = Y_j)$	0.10	0.20	0.30	0.25	0.15	1.00

For X_2, for example, (3) becomes

$$\sum_j^5 f(X_2, Y_j) = f(X_2, Y_1) + \cdots + f(X_2, Y_5)$$
$$= 0.05 + 0.15 + 0 + 0 + 0 = 0.20$$
$$= g(X_2)$$

Hence, (2) may be rewritten as

(4)
$$E(X_i + Y_j) = \sum \sum X_i f(X_i + Y_j) + \sum \sum Y_j f(X_i, Y_j)$$
$$= \sum_i X_i g(X_i) + \sum_j Y_j h(Y_j)$$

where $h(Y_j)$ is the marginal probability function of Y_j.

By definition, however,

$$\sum_i X_i g(X_i) = E(X_i)$$
$$\sum_j Y_j h(Y_j) = E(Y_j)$$

Hence, (4) becomes

(5)
$$E(X_i + Y_j) = E(X_i) + E(Y_j)$$

which is the result we seek.

Using this result, we may extend this process to 3 random variables. Suppose we have X_i (economic grades), Y_j (math grades), and Z_k (English grades). Let $W_l = X_i + Y_j$. Then

$$E(X_i + Y_j + Z_k) = E(W_l + Z_k) = E(W_l) + E(Z_k)$$

from the result above. But

$$E(W_l) = E(X_i + Y_j) = E(X_i) + E(Y_j)$$

Hence,

$$E(X_i + Y_j + Z_k) = E(X_i) + E(Y_j) + E(Z_k)$$

and as is seen, we may extend this result to N random variables by repeating this process.

Example 1. Let us find $E(X_i + Y_j)$ for the economics and math grades using Table 2.5. Since $E(X_i + Y_j) = E(X_i) + E(Y_j)$, we need only to find $E(X_i)$ and $E(Y_j)$, which is as follows:

$$
\begin{aligned}
E(X_i) &= \sum_i X_i g(X_i) \\
&= X_1 g(X_1) + \cdots + X_5 g(X_5) \\
&= 5(0.05) + 4(0.02) + 3(0.3) + 2(0.3) + 1(0.15) \\
&= 2.7 \\
E(Y_j) &= \sum_j Y_j h(Y_j) \\
&= 2.85
\end{aligned}
$$

$$\therefore \quad E(X_i + Y_j) = 2.7 + 2.85 = 5.5$$

Example 2. Find the expected value of the sample mean $\bar{x}$ of a simple random sample.

$$
\begin{aligned}
E(\bar{x}) &= E\left[\frac{1}{n}(x_1 + \cdots + x_n)\right] \\
&= \frac{1}{n}[E(x_1) + \cdots + E(x_n)] \\
&= \frac{1}{n}(n\bar{X}) \\
&= \bar{X}
\end{aligned}
$$

Problems

Let X and Y be the outcomes of die A and die B, and set $Z = X + Y$

1. Find the possible outcomes of Z and its probabilities.

2. Find $E(Z)$ using the results of 1 above.

3. Let

$$E(Z) = E(X) + E(Y)$$

Find $E(X)$ and $E(Y)$ and check that $E(X) + E(Y)$ is equal to the result obtained in 2 above.

2.10 The covariance

With our discussion of joint probability distributions and other preliminaries at an end, we may now proceed to a discussion of the covariance between two random variables X_i and Y_j. The reason for discussing the covariance is that it is necessary for the discussion of the variance of a linear combination of random variables which appears in Section 2.11.

The covariance between two variables X_i and Y_j is defined as

(1) $$\text{Cov}\,(X_i,\ Y_j) = E[(X_i - EX_i)(Y_j - EY_j)]$$

The process of substracting EX_i and EY_j from X_i and Y_j, respectively, is simply shifting the origin from $(0,0)$ to (EX_i, EY_j). We know from Section 2.3 that

$$E(X_i) = \bar{X} \qquad E(Y_j) = \bar{Y}$$

The covariance may then be written as

(2) $$\text{Cov}\,(X_i,\ Y_j) = E[(X_i - \bar{X})(Y_j - \bar{Y})]$$

From the definition of expected values and the results of Section 2.8, the right side of equation (2) becomes

(3) $$E(X_i - \bar{X})(Y_j - \bar{Y}) = \sum_i \sum_j (X_i - \bar{X})(Y_j - \bar{Y})f(X_i, Y_j)$$

where the sum $\sum_i \sum_j$ is over all possible combinations of X_i and Y_j, and where $f(X_i, Y_j)$ is the joint frequency function of X_i and Y_j.

The covariance may be considered a measure of covariability between two variables X_i and Y_j. The value of the covariance will be large and positive if X_i and Y_j vary in the same direction (for example, as in the economics and math grades of Table 2.3). The value of the covariance will be large and negative when X_i and Y_j vary in opposite directions (an example of this may be the relation between a large number of work hours and low grades).

The reason why the covariance is large and positive when X_i and Y_j vary in the same direction may be explained thus: The assumption that X_i and Y_j vary in the same direction implies that the frequency of occurrence of the joint events of a high X_i and high Y_j or a low X_i and low Y_j will be larger than the other cases. When measuring the deviations from their means, a high X_i and high Y_j will both be positive, and hence their product will be positive. Deviations of a low X_i and low Y_j from their means will both be negative, and their products also be positive.

Hence, when X_i and Y_j vary together in the same direction, the products will be positive. And since these deviations occur more frequently than the others, the covariance will be large and positive.

In graphic terms, the joint events of $(X_i,\ Y_j)$ occurring frequently are in the 1st and 3rd quadrants as shown in Fig. 2.4 (a). If the points should lie

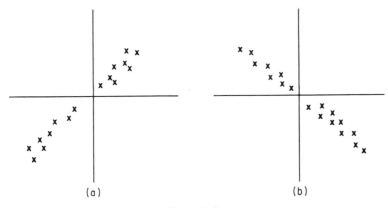

Fig. 2-4

on a straight line passing through the origin, there would be perfect covariability in the sense that any change in X_i would bring about the same change in Y_j.

When X_i and Y_j vary in opposite directions and there is covariability, the points will fall in the 2nd and 4th quadrants, as shown in Fig. 2-5(b). Similarly, if they should lie on a straight line passing through the origin, there would be perfect covariability in the sense that an increase in X_i would be accompanied by a corresponding decrease of Y_j.

Let us actually find the covariance of X_i (economic grades) and Y_j (math grades) of Table 2.3 We have seen that Table 2.4 expressed Table 2.3 in terms of relative frequencies and gave us the joint probability distribution of X_i and Y_j. Let us reproduce Table 2.3 as Table 2.6 for the sake of convenience.

Table 2.6

	Y_1	Y_2	Y_3	Y_4	Y_5	
X_1	0.05					0.05
X_2	0.05	0.15				0.20
X_3		0.05	0.25			0.30
X_4			0.05	0.20	0.05	0.30
X_5				0.05	0.10	0.15
	0.10	0.20	0.30	0.25	0.15	1.00

The summation term in equation (3) was over all possible pairs of i and j. As we can see in Table 2.6, there are $5 \times 5 = 25$ possible pairs of (i, j). These may be shown as

(4) $$\sum_i \sum_j (X_i - \bar{X})(Y_j - \bar{Y})f(X_i, Y_j)$$

$$= (X_1 - \bar{X})(Y_1 - \bar{Y})f(X_1, Y_1) + (X_1 - \bar{X})(Y_2 - \bar{Y})f(X_1, Y_2)$$
$$+ \cdots + (X_5 - \bar{X})(Y_5 - \bar{Y})f(X_5, Y_5)$$

However, we see from Table 2.6 that some of the $f(X_i, Y_j)$ are zero. For example, $f(X_1, Y_2) = 0$, $f(X_1, Y_3) = 0$, etc. Hence, the terms such as $(X_1 - \bar{X})(Y_2 - \bar{Y})f(X_1, Y_2) = 0$ and will drop out of summation (4), and only those terms with positive probabilities remain. Hence, to find the sum given by equation (4), we need only be concerned with the pairs (X_i, Y_j) with positive probabilities.

To find the sum given by equation (4), we need to find $\bar{X}$ and $\bar{Y}$ to calculate $(X_i - \bar{X})$ and $(Y_j - \bar{Y})$. Recall that we have assumed grade points of 5, 4, 3, 2, and 1 for X_1, X_2, X_3, X_4, and X_5; and similarly for $Y_1, \ldots, Y_5$. Hence, using the marginal probability distributions of X and Y in Table 2.6, we find

$$\bar{X} = E(X_i) = \sum_i X_i f(X_i)$$
$$= 5(0.05) + 4(0.2) + 3(0.3) + 2(0.3) + 1(0.15)$$
$$= 2.7$$
$$\bar{Y} = E(Y_j) = \sum_j Y_j g(Y_j)$$
$$= 5(0.1) + 4(0.2) + 3(0.3) + 2(0.25) + 1(0.15)$$
$$= 2.85$$

Using these results, we may now compute the summation of equation (4). This is shown in Table 2.7.

Table 2.7

(1) $X_i - \bar{X}$		(2) $Y_j - \bar{Y}$		(3) $(X_i - \bar{X})(Y_j - \bar{Y})$	(4) $f(X_i, Y_j)$	(3) × (4)
5 − 2.7 =	2.3	5 − 2.85 =	2.15	4.945	0.05	0.24725
4 =	1.3	5 =	2.15	2.795	0.05	0.13975
4 =	1.3	4 =	1.15	1.495	0.15	0.22425
3 =	0.3	4 =	1.15	0.345	0.05	0.01725
3 =	0.3	3 =	0.15	0.045	0.25	0.01125
2 =	−0.7	3 =	0.15	−0.105	0.05	−0.00525
2 =	−0.7	2 =	−0.85	0.595	0.20	0.11900
2 =	−0.7	1 =	−1.85	1.295	0.05	0.06475
1 =	−1.7	2 =	−0.85	1.445	0.05	0.07225
1 =	−1.7	1 =	−1.85	3.145	0.10	0.31450

1.20500

As shown in Table 2.7, the covariance is

$$\text{Cov}(X_i, Y_j) = \sum_i \sum_j (X_i - \bar{X})(Y_j - \bar{Y})f(X_i, Y_j) = 1.205$$

For theoretical purposes, the covariance is frequently expressed as

(5) $\quad \text{Cov}(X_i, Y_j) = E[(X_i - \bar{X})(Y_j - \bar{Y})]$

$\qquad\qquad\qquad = E(X_i Y_j) - \bar{X}E(Y_j) - \bar{Y}E(X_i) + \bar{X}\bar{Y}$

$\qquad\qquad\qquad = E(X_i Y_j) - \bar{X}\bar{Y}$

By definition

(6) $\qquad\qquad\qquad E(X_i Y_j) = \sum_i \sum_j X_i Y_j f(X_i, Y_j)$

This is easily calculated as shown in Table 2.8.

Table 2.8

X_i	Y_j	$X_i Y_j$	$f(X_i, Y_j)$	$X_i Y_j f(X_i, Y_j)$
5	5	25	0.05	1.25
4	5	20	0.05	1.00
4	4	16	0.15	2.40
3	4	12	0.05	0.60
3	3	9	0.25	2.25
2	3	6	0.05	0.30
2	2	4	0.20	0.80
1	1	2	0.05	0.10
1	2	2	0.05	0.10
1	1	1	0.10	0.10
				8.90

Substituting the results of Table 2.8 into equation (5), we find

$$\text{Cov}(X_i, Y_j) = E(X_i Y_j) - \bar{X}\bar{Y}$$
$$= \sum \sum X_i Y_j f(X_i, Y_j) - \bar{X}\bar{Y}$$
$$= 8.9 - (2.7)(2.85) = 1.205$$

which is what we obtained by the previous method. As shown by the calculations, equation (5) is easier to use because we do not have to find the deviations—$(X_i - \bar{X})$ and $(Y_j - \bar{Y})$—to calculate the covariance.

One additional point to note and that we shall be using in theoretical discussions is that when X_i and Y_j are independent variables, we know that

$$E(X_i Y_j) = E(X_i)E(Y_j)$$
$$= \bar{X}\bar{Y}$$

and hence,

$$\text{Cov}(X_i, Y_j) = E(X_i Y_j) - \bar{X}\bar{Y}$$
$$= \bar{X}\bar{Y} - \bar{X}\bar{Y} = 0$$

That is, if X_i and Y_j are independent, $\text{Cov}(X_i, Y_j) = 0$

Problem

Given the following frequency distribution of economic grades (X_i) and mathematics grades (Y_j), find Cov (X_i, Y_j).

	X_1 $A = 5$	X_2 $B = 4$	X_3 $C = 3$	X_4 $D = 2$	X_5 $F = 1$
$Y_1\,A = 5$	2				
$Y_2\,B = 4$	1	2			
$Y_3\,C = 3$		2	3	1	
$Y_4\,D = 2$			2	2	2
$Y_5\,F = 1$				2	1

2.11 The variance of a linear combination of random variables

Having found the expected value of $X_i + Y_j$, and defined Cov(X_i, Y_j), let us next find the variance of $X_i + Y_j$. With the background we have developed, this is a very simple problem. By the definition of a variance, we have

$$V(X_i + Y_j) = E[(X_i + Y_j) - E(X_i + Y_j)]^2$$
$$= E[(X_i - EX_i) + (Y_j - EY_j)]^2$$
$$= E(X_i - EX_i)^2 + E(Y_j - EY_j)^2$$
$$+ 2E(X_i - EX_i)(Y_j - EY_j)$$
$$= V(X_i) + V(Y_j) + 2\,\mathrm{Cov}(X_i, Y_j)$$

If X_i and Y_j are independent, then, since Cov(X_i, Y_j) = 0,

$$V(X_i + Y_j) = V(X_i) + V(Y_j)$$

These results may be generalized to the case of n random variables. For example, for 3 variables X_1, X_2, and X_3, we have

$$V(X_1 + X_2 + X_3) = V(X_1) + V(X_2) + V(X_3) + 2\,\mathrm{Cov}(X_1, X_2)$$
$$+ 2\,\mathrm{Cov}(X_2, X_3) + 2\,\mathrm{Cov}(X_3, X_1)$$

and when the variables are independent

$$V(X_1 + X_2 + X_3) = V(X_1) + V(X_2) + V(X_3)$$

Example 1. Given

$$V(X_i - Y_j) = V(X_i) + V(Y_j) - 2\,\mathrm{Cov}(X_i, Y_j)$$

then, if X_i and Y_j are independent,

$$V(X_i - Y_j) = V(X_i) + V(Y_j)$$

Example 2. Let $x_1, x_2, \ldots, x_n$ be a random sample of size n selected with replacement. Hence, the x's are independent. The sample mean is

$$\bar{x} = \frac{1}{n}(x_1 + x_2 + \cdots + x_n)$$

The variance of $\bar{x}$ is, since the $\text{Cov}(x_i, x_j) = 0$ for all i and j,

$$V(\bar{x}) = V\left[\frac{1}{n}(x_1 + x_2 + \cdots + x_n)\right]$$

$$= \frac{1}{n^2}[V(x_1) + \cdots + V(x_n)]$$

$$= \frac{1}{n^2}(n\sigma^2) = \frac{\sigma^2}{n}$$

which is the familiar formula we use in elementary statistics. The formula for $V(\bar{x})$ when sampling without replacement is discussed in Chapter 6.

Example 3. Let two independent samples be selected, each by random sampling with replacement. Then

$$V(\bar{x}_1 + \bar{x}_2) = V(\bar{x}_1) + V(\bar{x}_2)$$

$$= \frac{\sigma^2}{n_1} + \frac{\sigma^2}{n_2}$$

which is also a familiar formula from elementary statistics.

Problems

1. Show that
$$V(X - Y) = V(X) + V(Y) - 2\,\text{Cov}(X, Y)$$

2. Given a population 1, 2, 4, 5:
   (i)   find the population variance σ^2.
   (ii) find $V(\bar{x}_1)$, where $\bar{x}_1$ is the sample mean of samples of size $n_1 = 2$ selected with replacement.
   (iii) find $V(\bar{x}_2)$ where $\bar{x}_2$ is the sample mean of samples of size $n_2 = 3$ selected with replacement.
   (iv) find $V(\bar{x}_1 + \bar{x}_2)$
   (v)   find $V(\bar{x}_1 - \bar{x}_2)$
   (vi) find $V(2\bar{x}_1 + 3\bar{x}_2)$

2.12 The coefficient of variation

We have so far considered the basic concepts of expectation and variance of a random variable, the joint distribution of random variables, the covariance of two random variables, and the expectation and variance of linear combinations of random variables. Another concept we shall be using frequently in our subsequent discussion is the coefficient of variation—so let us consider this concept now.

The variance was considered as a measure of dispersion of the deviations from the population mean, that is, $X_i - \bar{X}$. These deviations were in absolute terms. In many cases, especially for purposes of comparisons, it is desirable to express the deviations in relative terms. For example, let the average grade of students in an economics class be $\bar{X} = 70$ points, and the grade of a student be $X_i = 80$ points. Then the absolute deviation is

$$X_i - \bar{X} = 80 - 70 = 10 \text{ points}$$

The variance of X_i was defined as

(1) $$\sigma^2 = \frac{\Sigma (X_i - \bar{X})^2}{N}$$

and was a measure of dispersion of these absolute deviations.

Let us now find a measure of dispersion for relative deviations. The relative deviation of X_i from $\bar{X}$ is

$$\frac{X_i - \bar{X}}{\bar{X}} = \frac{80 - 70}{70} = \frac{10}{70} = 14\%$$

for our present illustration. The measure of dispersion for such relative deviations is obtained by simply using the relative deviation instead of the absolute deviation in equation (1). We find

(2) $$C^2 = \frac{\sum\limits_{}^{N} \left(\dfrac{X_i - \bar{X}}{\bar{X}} \right)^2}{N}$$

and shall call C^2 the *relative variance* of the distribution, or simply the *rel-variance*.

Equation (2) may be rewritten as

$$C^2 = \frac{\dfrac{\Sigma (X_i - \bar{X})^2}{N}}{\bar{X}^2}$$

(3) $$= \frac{\sigma^2}{\bar{X}^2}$$

The square root of this is

(4) $$C = \frac{\sigma}{\bar{X}}$$

and is the familiar formula for the *coefficient of variation* we learn in elementary statistics.

Let us illustrate variance and rel-variance. Suppose 3 students have the following amount of money:

$$X_i : X_1 = \$1, \ X_2 = \$2, \ X_3 = \$3$$

Then the variance of X_i is

$$\sigma^2 = \frac{\Sigma (X_i - \bar{X})^2}{N}$$

$$= \frac{(1 - 2)^2 + (2 - 2)^2 + (3 - 2)^2}{3} = \frac{2}{3}$$

Hence,

$$\sigma = \sqrt{2/3} = \$0.80$$

That is, one standard deviation is about $0.80

The relative variance of X_i is

$$C^2 = \frac{\sum\limits^{N} \left(\dfrac{X - \bar{X}}{\bar{X}}\right)^2}{N}$$

$$= \frac{\left(\dfrac{1-2}{2}\right)^2 + \left(\dfrac{2-2}{2}\right)^2 + \left(\dfrac{3-2}{2}\right)^2}{3}$$

$$= \frac{1}{6} = 0.166$$

The square root of the rel-variance, that is, the *coefficient of variation* is

$$C = 0.4 = 40\%$$

This $C = 40\%$ corresponds to 1 standard deviation $\sigma = \$0.80$.

For example, for $X_1 = \$1$, we have

$$\frac{X_1 - \bar{X}}{\sigma} = \frac{1-2}{0.166} = -1.25$$

That is, $X_1 = \$1$ is 1.25 standard deviations to the left of the mean $\bar{X} = \$2$.
The deviation of X_1 from $\bar{X}$ in relative terms is

$$\frac{X_1 - \bar{X}}{\bar{X}} = \frac{1-2}{2} = -0.5$$

Since $C = 40\%$, this 50% deviation in terms of standard deviations becomes

$$\frac{-50}{40} = -1.25$$

and shows that a 50% relative deviation is equivalent to 1.25 standard deviations. Let us illustrate the meaning of C with additional examples.

Example 1. Suppose the average weight of a group of students is $\bar{X} = 100$ lb, and the standard deviation of the weights is $\sigma = 7$ lb. Find the rel-variance and coefficient of variation.

$$C = \sigma/\bar{X} = 7/100 = 0.07$$

$$\text{rel-variance} = C^2 = 0.0049$$

Hence

$$\bar{x} \pm \sigma = 100 \pm 7 = 100(1 \pm C) = 100(1 \pm 0.07)$$

Example 2. The average weight of a group of college students is $\bar{X} = 140$ lb. Suppose that from previous data we know that C is usually 7%. Estimate the standard deviation for this group of students.

$$\sigma = \bar{X} \cdot C = 140 \times (0.07) = 9.8 \text{ lb}$$

An important characteristic of C is that in certain phenomena, its value is stable. For example, the C of weights of college students may vary very little over the years; or the C of yield of wheat in the districts of a certain region may vary very little from district to district; or the C of data of a certain experiment may vary very little when the experiment is repeated many times.

A stable C provides us with an advanced estimate of the C. This characteristic may be used in two ways. One is to estimate the standard deviation, and the other is to detect irregularities in the data. We shall discuss these points again later. For the present, it will suffice if the meaning of C is understood.

We have so far considered the coefficient of variation for X_i. We may, however, state a general definition of the coefficient of variation and show how it applies to other statistics, such as the sample mean $\bar{x}$, or the estimate of the total, $\hat{X}$. Let the statistic be denoted by y. Then the coefficient of variation of y is defined as

$$C(y) = \frac{\sqrt{V(y)}}{E(y)} = \frac{\sigma(y)}{E(y)}$$

For example, when y is X_i, we get the coefficient of variation we defined in (4). When y is the sample mean, $\bar{x}$, we know that

$$\sqrt{V(\bar{x})} = \sigma_{\bar{x}} = \frac{\sigma}{\sqrt{n}}$$

and

$$E(\bar{x}) = \bar{X}$$

Hence,

$$C(\bar{x}) = \frac{\sqrt{V(\bar{x})}}{E(\bar{x})} = \frac{\sigma_{\bar{x}}}{\bar{X}}$$

$$= \frac{\sigma}{\bar{X}\sqrt{n}} = \frac{C}{\sqrt{n}}$$

When $y = \hat{X} = N\bar{x}$—which is an estimate of the total, X, as we shall see in Chapter 6,

$$C(\hat{X}) = \frac{\sqrt{V(\hat{X})}}{E(\hat{X})}$$

As we shall also see in Chapter 6,

$$V(\hat{X}) = N^2 V(\bar{x})$$

$$E(\hat{X}) = X$$

$$\therefore \quad C(\hat{X}) = \frac{N\sqrt{V(\bar{x})}}{X} = \frac{\sigma_{\bar{x}}}{X/N} = \frac{\sigma_{\bar{x}}}{\bar{X}}$$

$$= \frac{\sigma}{\bar{X}\sqrt{n}} = \frac{C}{\sqrt{n}}$$

$$(5) \qquad\qquad \therefore \quad C(\bar{x}) = C(\hat{X}) = \frac{C}{\sqrt{n}}$$

Equation (5) provides a means of estimating the sample size. From (5), we have

$$\sqrt{n} = \frac{C}{C(\bar{x})} = \frac{C}{C(\hat{X})}$$

$$n = \left[\frac{C}{C(\bar{x})}\right]^2 = \left[\frac{C}{C(\hat{X})}\right]^2$$

Example 3. Assume $C = 0.30$. That is, 1 standard deviation of X_i is equal to 30% of $\bar{X}$. Suppose we wish 1 standard deviation of $\bar{x}$ to be equal to 3% of $\bar{X}$. Then $C(\bar{x}) = 0.03$. For this we need a sample size of

$$n = \left(\frac{C}{C(\bar{x})}\right)^2 = \left(\frac{0.30}{0.03}\right)^2 = 100$$

Example 4. Suppose that in Example 3 we wished 3 standard deviations of $\bar{x}$ to be equal to 3% of $\bar{X}$. Then, $3C(\bar{x}) = 0.03$. Hence, $C(\bar{x}) = 0.01$. For this, we need a sample size of

$$n = \left[\frac{C}{C(\bar{x})}\right]^2 = \left(\frac{0.30}{0.01}\right)^2 = 900$$

Problems

1. Given 5 students with grades 60, 65, 70, 70, and 95, find the coefficient of variation of the grades.

2. Suppose samples of size $n = 2$ are selected. Find $C(\bar{x})$ and $C(\hat{X})$.

3. Suppose the coefficient of variation of weights of students is 0.75. How large a sample must we select so that $\bar{x}$ will differ from $\bar{X}$ by not more than 3% about 66% of the time? (Note that $66\% = 2/3$, which is the area of ± 1 standard deviation from $\bar{X}$).

Notes and References

2.1 For an elementary discussion of "all possible samples," see Yamane (1964), Chapter 7. For additional discussion on sample space, see Yamane (1964) Chapter 16; Feller (1958), Chapter 1.

2.2 For discussion of simple random sampling, see Feller (1958), Chapter 2; Sukhatme (1954), section 1.5; Cochran (1962), section 2.1; Hansen, Hurwitz, and Madow (1953), Chapter 4.

2.3–2.11 For discussion concerning expectation and variance, see Feller (1958), Chapter 9; Deming (1950), Chapters 3 and 4.

2.12 For discussion of rel-variance, see Hansen, Hurwitz, and Madow (1953), Chapter 4, sections 10 and 11.

About the notation used in Section 2.3: The capital X_i with a subscript is used to indicate (i) the random variable of individual population values, and (ii) the individual values of these random variables. The lower case x_i with a subscript is used to indicate (i) the random variable of individual sample values, and (ii) the individual values of these random variables. As is seen, we use capital letters to indicate population variables and their values; lower case letters to indicate sample variables and their values.

The capital $\bar{X}$ is the population mean, and the lower case $\bar{x}$ is the sample mean. In section 2.12, we have used the capital X to indicate the population total. The lower case x will indicate the sample total.

The reason for this type of notation is that there will not be enough symbols to handle the complicated sample designs (such as multistage sampling) if we use the type of notation customarily found in elementary statistics. These new symbols will be introduced gradually. The distinctions between random variables and values will usually be clear by inference of the discussion.

Yamane, T. (1964). *Statistics, An Introductory Analysis*. New York: Harper and Row, Publishers.

Feller, W. (1958) *An Introduction to Probability Theory and its Applications*. Vol. I, 2nd ed. New York: John Wiley & Sons, Inc.

CHAPTER 3

Estimation

3.1 Introduction

One more topic we shall discuss before getting into sampling theory proper is estimation. As we shall see in our subsequent discussion, the main problem of sampling surveys will be to estimate population parameters such as the mean, variance, and proportion of the population. Since most readers have probably studied the basic ideas of estimation in elementary statistics, let us review these ideas briefly (those familiar with these concepts may skip this section and proceed to Chapter 4 without loss of continuity).

The problem of estimation is finding good estimates of the population parameters. We know from elementary statistics that the sample mean, $\bar{x}$, is an estimator of the population mean $\bar{X}$. So, too, is the sample median, $\tilde{x}$. Which of these is better? To determine the answer, we need to first define what we mean by a good estimate, and then provide criteria such that when we have an estimator that satisfies these criteria, it will be a good estimator. By a good estimator, we shall mean one with its distribution concentrated near the population parameter to be estimated.

The criteria for a good estimator are: 1. unbiasedness; 2. consistency; 3. efficiency; and 4. sufficiency. In the following discussion, we shall give a nonrigorous explanation of 1, 2, and 3.

After we have explained these criteria, we shall consider the problem of how to find estimators with these desirable properties. We shall see that there are a number of ways of finding estimates, and these processes are usually discussed under the topic of *methods of estimation*. The two main methods are those of *least squares* and *maximum likelihood*. However, these methods are usually not explicitly used in sampling surveys. As we shall see, we shall mainly be concerned with finding unbiased estimates and measuring their reliability in terms of interval estimation.

Let us start with a discussion of unbiasedness.

3.2 Unbiasedness

Suppose a large group of students have taken an examination, and we wish to estimate the average grade point by taking a random sample. We are estimating an unknown $\bar{X}$, but for purposes of illustration, let us assume the following:

$$\text{population mean:} \qquad \bar{X} = 70 \text{ points}$$
$$\text{standard deviation:} \qquad \sigma = 18 \text{ points}$$
$$\text{size of population:} \qquad N = 2000$$

Recall that $E(\bar{x})$ was the expected value of $\bar{x}$ or, in other words, the mean of all possible sample means. We have seen from our previous discussion that

$$E(\bar{x}) = \bar{X}$$

The common sense of this is that the sampling distribution of $\bar{x}$ is evenly clustered around the value $\bar{X}$ and not around some other value. For example, the upper part of Fig. 3-1 shows the sampling distribution of $\bar{x}$ clustered around $\bar{X}$.

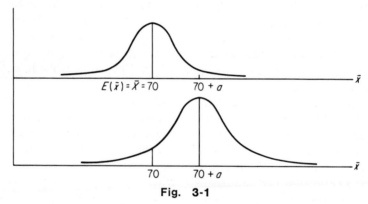

$E(\bar{x}) = \bar{X} = 70$ $70 + \sigma$

70 $70 + \sigma$

Fig. 3-1

Now let θ be some other sample characteristic that is used as an estimate. For example, let

$$\theta = \bar{x} + a$$

That is, θ is the sample mean $\bar{x}$ plus a constant a (say, $a = 5$). If the sample mean is 72 points, then $\theta = 72 + 5 = 77$ is considered an estimate of $\bar{X}$. In general, this becomes

$$E(\theta) = E(\bar{x} + a)$$
$$= E(\bar{x}) + E(a)$$
$$= \bar{X} + a$$

which implies that the sampling distribution of θ is clustered around $\bar{X} + a$, as shown in the lower part of Fig. 3-1.

It should be intuitively clear that it is desirable to use $\bar{x}$ instead of θ ($= \bar{x} + a$) as an estimator of $\bar{X}$. In general, when the expected value of the statistic used as an estimator is equal to the population parameter to be estimated, we say that the estimator is *unbiased*. In our present example, $E(\bar{x}) = \bar{X}$—and $\hat{\bar{X}} = \bar{x}$ is thus an unbiased estimator of $\bar{X}$. For $\theta = \bar{x} + a$, we had

$$E(\theta) = \bar{X} + a$$

and thus, θ is not an unbiased estimator of $\bar{X}$. We say that $\hat{\bar{X}} = \theta$ is a *biased* estimator of $\bar{X}$, and a is the bias. If $E(\theta) > \bar{X}$, θ is said to be positively biased; if $E(\theta) < \bar{X}$, it is said to be negatively biased.

Thus, the first property of a good estimator is unbiasedness, and $\hat{\bar{X}} = \bar{x}$ is an unbiased estimator of $\bar{X}$.

3.3 Consistent estimator

The second property of a good estimator is consistency. Using our illustration of the previous section, suppose a sample of size $n = 36$ is taken and $\bar{x} = 65$ points. What will happen to $\bar{x}$ if we let $n \rightarrow N$? It should be intuitively clear that as $n \rightarrow N$, the sample mean will approach $\bar{X}$. For example, suppose $N = 2000$ and $\bar{X} = 70$. If $n = 1999$ instead of 36, we can see intuitively that the $\bar{x}$ calculated from $n = 1999$ will be very close to $\bar{X} = 70$ (say, for example, 69.9 points).

Now let us assume that the median of the population is $\tilde{X} = 73$ points. Let the sample median be denoted by $\tilde{x}$ for a sample of size n. It should be clear that as $n \rightarrow N$, the sample median $\tilde{x}$ will approach the population median $\tilde{X} = 73$ points. Therefore, if $\tilde{x}$ is used as an estimator of $\bar{X}$, as $n \rightarrow N$, $\tilde{x}$ will not approach $\bar{X} = 70$ points, but rather $\tilde{X} = 73$ points.

When an estimate (such as $\bar{x}$) approaches the population parameter that is to be estimated (such as $\bar{X}$) as the sample size increases, it is said to be a *consistent estimator* of the parameter. Thus, $\hat{\bar{X}} = \bar{x}$ is a consistent estimator of $\bar{X}$, and $\hat{\bar{X}} = \tilde{x}$ is not a consistent estimator of $\bar{X}$ when we have a skewed distribution.

Thus, the second property of a good estimator is consistency, and $\hat{\bar{X}} = \bar{x}$ is a consistent estimator of $\bar{X}$.

Let us express the statements made above, more rigorously, as follows: We have seen intuitively that as n becomes larger and larger, $\bar{x}$ will approach $\bar{X}$. This may be shown symbolically as

$$\bar{x} \longrightarrow \bar{X} \quad \text{as} \quad n \longrightarrow \infty \quad \text{(or } N\text{)}$$

By using this equation, we can formally define consistency as follows; If

$$(1) \qquad P(\bar{x} \rightarrow \bar{X}) \longrightarrow 1 \quad \text{as} \quad n \rightarrow \infty$$

then $\bar{x}$ is called a consistent estimator of $\bar{X}$. Equation (1) is read as "the probability that $\bar{x}$ approaches $\bar{X}$ as n becomes larger and larger is 1".

In terms of the sampling distribution of $\bar{x}$, this means the sampling distribution of $\bar{x}$ becomes closely concentrated near $\bar{X}$ as the sample size becomes larger. Using our example of grades, we can see intuitively that the sampling distribution of $\bar{x}$ when $n = 1999$ will be more closely concentrated near $\bar{X}$ than when $n = 36$.

What we have said concerning the sample mean may now be stated in general terms; Let $\hat{\theta}$ (which is computed from a sample $x_1, \ldots, x_n$) be an estimate of the population parameter θ. If

$$P(\hat{\theta} \longrightarrow \theta) \longrightarrow 1 \quad \text{as} \quad n \longrightarrow \infty$$

then $\hat{\theta}$ is called a consistent estimator of θ.

3.4 Efficiency

Suppose we have a population that has a normal distribution, and we wish to estimate the population mean. As we have seen, we may use the sample mean $\bar{x}$, which is an unbiased and consistent estimator. We may also use the sample median $\tilde{x}$ as an estimator, which in our present case is also unbiased and consistent. Which of the two is preferable as an estimator?

We mentioned in section 3.1 that we prefer an estimate with a sampling distribution closely concentrated around the population parameter. Which of the two—the sample mean $\bar{x}$ or the sample median $\tilde{x}$—is more closely concentrated around $\bar{X}$? This may be determined by comparing the variances of both estimators: the one with the smaller variance will be preferable. The smaller the variance, the more concentrated the sampling distribution around the population parameter, assuming that we have consistent estimators. It will be shown that the variances of $\bar{x}$ and $\tilde{x}$ are for large samples,

$$V(\bar{x}) = \frac{\sigma^2}{n}$$

$$V(\tilde{x}) = \frac{\pi\sigma^2}{2n}$$

Hence, when given the same sample size,

$$\frac{V(\bar{x})}{V(\tilde{x})} = \frac{2}{\pi} = 0.64$$

That is, $V(\bar{x}) < V(\tilde{x})$, and $\bar{x}$ is thus preferable to $\tilde{x}$ as an estimator. Since, given the same sample size, the sampling distribution of $\bar{x}$ is more concentrated around $\bar{X}$ than is $\tilde{x}$, we may say that $\bar{x}$ is more efficient than $\tilde{x}$. The preceding result says

$$V(\bar{x}) = V(\tilde{x}) \times 64\%$$

That is, the variance of $\bar{x}$ is only 64% of the variance of $\tilde{x}$ when they both have sample size n.

In terms of sample size, the variance of the median from samples of size 100 is about the same as that of sample means from samples of size 64.

We summarize as follows: If we have two estimators, $\hat{\theta}_1$ and $\hat{\theta}_2$, and

$$V(\hat{\theta}_1) < V(\hat{\theta}_2)$$

then the efficiency of $\hat{\theta}_1$ relative to $\hat{\theta}_2$ is given by

$$E_f = \frac{V(\hat{\theta}_1)}{V(\hat{\theta}_2)}$$

Note that the variance of the smaller estimator is in the numerator, and thus

$$0 \leqslant E_f \leqslant 1$$

We have defined efficiency in relative terms and put the variance of the smaller estimator in the numerator. The efficiency was defined relative to this smaller variance estimator. But, if we could find an estimator with a variance that is smaller than that of any other estimator, we could use it as the basis to measure efficiency; and, in terms of efficiency, we could say that the estimator with the smallest variance is an "efficient estimator."

Then a question arises: How small can the variance of an estimator become? If we can show that the variance cannot become smaller than a certain lower bound, and if we can find an estimator with a variance that is equal to this lower bound, then that variance will be the smallest variance. We shall use the word "minimum" instead of "smallest" and call it the *minimum variance*. Furthermore, an estimator that has this minimum variance will be called a minimum variance estimator.

It turns out that there is such a lower bound, given by the Cramer-Rao inequality. A mathematical treatment of this topic is too advanced for this book, so let us omit derivations when discussing it. We can illustrate its meaning by applying it to the problem of estimating the mean $\bar{X}$.

Let $\hat{\theta}$ be an estimator of $\bar{X}$. The Cramer-Rao inequality then tells us that the variance of $\hat{\theta}$ cannot be smaller than σ^2/n. That is

$$V(\hat{\theta}) \geqq \frac{\sigma^2}{n}$$

$\hat{\theta}$ may be the sample mean $\bar{x}$, sample median $\tilde{x}$, or some other sample statistic, but no matter what it is, the variance cannot be smaller than σ^2/n. However, we know that

$$V(\bar{x}) = \frac{\sigma^2}{n}$$

This means that $\hat{\bar{X}} = \bar{x}$ has the smallest variance an estimator can have. We may thus conclude that $\bar{x}$ has the minimum variance and is hence a minimum variance estimator of $\bar{X}$.

Combining all our previous results, we may conclude that $\bar{x}$ is an unbiased, consistent, minimum variance estimator of $\bar{X}$.

3.5 Interval estimation—confidence interval

Having determined the criteria for good estimators, the problem is to find those with desirable properties. The problem of finding estimators is usually discussed under the topic of methods of estimation. Methods of estimation may be broadly classified into point estimation and interval estimation. For point estimation, there are methods such as the method of maximum likelihood, method of least squares, and method of moments. As for interval estimation, we usually rely on the concept of confidence intervals.

In sampling surveys, however, the main method of estimation we use is interval estimation. We shall therefore consider only the concept of confidence interval in this book. Let us develop our discussion by use of a simple example. Suppose we have a large population with mean $\bar{X}$ (unknown) and standard deviation σ. We wish to estimate $\bar{X}$, and for this purpose a random sample of size n is selected. We know from the central limit theorem that

$$z = \frac{\bar{x} - \bar{X}}{\sigma_{\bar{x}}}$$

is asymptotically normal with mean 0 and variance unity. From the normal area table we know that when $z = 1.96$, it corresponds to a probability of 0.95. Thus, we may write

$$P\left(-1.96 < \frac{\bar{x} - \bar{X}}{\sigma_{\bar{x}}} < 1.96\right) = 0.95$$

which is a legitimate probability statement because z is a random variable. Let us now rewrite this equation as

$$P\left(\bar{x} - 1.96\,\frac{\sigma}{\sqrt{n}} < \bar{X} < \bar{x} + 1.96\frac{\sigma}{\sqrt{n}}\right) = 0.95$$

Letting

$$\bar{x} - 1.96\frac{\sigma}{\sqrt{n}} = a$$

$$\bar{x} + 1.96\frac{\sigma}{\sqrt{n}} = b$$

we have

$$P(a < \bar{X} < b) = 0.95$$

and this may be interpreted as follows:

From the central limit theorem, we know that $\bar{x}$ is asymptotically normal, with mean $\bar{X}$ and variance σ^2/n. This is shown diagrammatically in Fig. 3-2. The random variable $\bar{x}$ takes on various values. Let us express them by

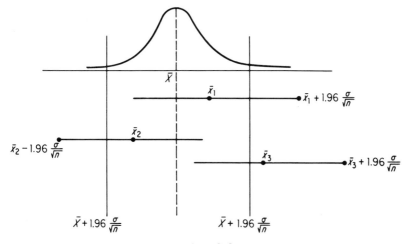

Fig. 3-2

$\bar{x}_1, \bar{x}_2, \ldots$ Now, for example, let $\bar{x}_1$ take on the value as indicated in Fig. 3-2. Then the interval will be

$$\bar{x}_1 - 1.96 \frac{\sigma}{\sqrt{n}} \quad \text{to} \quad \bar{x}_1 + 1.96 \frac{\sigma}{\sqrt{n}}$$

As the graph shows, this will include $\bar{X}$. Similarly, for another value $\bar{x}_2$, we have

$$\bar{x}_2 - 1.96 \frac{\sigma}{\sqrt{n}} \quad \text{to} \quad \bar{x}_2 + 1.96 \frac{\sigma}{\sqrt{n}}$$

which also includes $\bar{X}$. But $\bar{x}_3$, as shown in our graph, gives us the interval

$$\bar{x}_3 - 1.96 \frac{\sigma}{\sqrt{n}} \quad \text{to} \quad \bar{x}_3 + 1.95 \frac{\sigma}{\sqrt{n}}$$

which does not include $\bar{X}$. As we can see graphically, the $\bar{x}_3$ falls outside the two limiting values of $\bar{X} \pm 1.96\sigma/\sqrt{n}$.

The probability that $\bar{x}$ will be in the interval $\bar{X} \pm 1.96\sigma_{\bar{x}}$ is 0.95; that is, there are 95 chances out of 100 that the $\bar{x}$ will be between $\bar{X} - 1.96\,\sigma_{\bar{x}}$ and $\bar{X} + 1.96\sigma_{\bar{x}}$, given that the $\bar{X}$ is in fact the true value of the parameter.

Thus we can see from Fig. 3-2 that when we construct our interval

$$\bar{x} - 1.96 \frac{\sigma}{\sqrt{n}} \quad \text{to} \quad \bar{x} + 1.96 \frac{\sigma}{\sqrt{n}}$$

we can expect that 95 out of 100 such intervals will include $\bar{X}$ so long as $\bar{x}$ falls between $\bar{X} - 1.96\sigma_{\bar{x}}$ and $\bar{X} + 1.96\sigma_{\bar{x}}$. This may be shown by symbols as

$$P(\bar{X} - 1.96\sigma_{\bar{x}} < \bar{x} < \bar{X} + 1.96\sigma_{\bar{x}}) = 0.95$$

However, by using simple algebra, this may be rewritten as

$$P(\bar{x} - 1.96\sigma_{\bar{x}} < \bar{X} < \bar{x} + 1.96\sigma_{\bar{x}}) = 0.95$$

So long as $\bar{x}$ is not given a specific value and treated as a random variable, this is a legitimate probability statement.

But once we select a sample and compute $\bar{x}$, such as

$$\bar{x} = \frac{1}{4}(1 + 3 + 5 + 7) = 4$$

$\bar{x}$ becomes a fixed constant and is no longer a random variable. We then have

$$P(4 - 1.96\sigma_{\bar{x}} < \bar{X} < 4 + 1.96\sigma_{\bar{x}}) = 0.95$$

But

$$4 - 1.96\sigma_{\bar{x}} \quad \text{to} \quad 4 + 1.96\sigma_{\bar{x}}$$

is a fixed interval, so that $\bar{X}$ is either in the interval or on its outside. Thus, the probability is either 1 or 0.

Let the two limits of this fixed interval be denoted by k_1 and k_2. That is,

$$k_1 = 4 - 1.96\sigma_{\bar{x}}$$
$$k_2 = 4 + 1.96\sigma_{\bar{x}}$$

Then the probability may be expressed by

$$P(k_1 < \bar{X} < k_2) = 0.95$$

and this is not a legitimate probability. J. Neyman called the interval (k_1, k_2) a confidence interval, and 0.95 is called a *confidence coefficient* to distinguish it from a legitimate probability. The interpretation is as follows: If samples of size n are repeatedly selected 100 times, we would have 100 intervals similar to (k_1, k_2)—and we expect 95 of these intervals to contain the $\bar{X}$. The interval we computed (k_1, k_2) is one of these 100 intervals.

In general, we may write the confidence interval as

$$\bar{x} - z\sigma_{\bar{x}} < \bar{X} < \bar{x} + z\sigma_{\bar{x}}$$

and

$$P(\bar{x} - z\sigma_{\bar{x}} < \bar{X} < \bar{x} + z\sigma_{\bar{x}}) = 1 - \alpha$$

where $\bar{x}$ is the sample mean, $1 - \alpha$ is the confidence coefficient, z is the deviation corresponding to $1 - \alpha$ obtained from the normal area table, and $\sigma_{\bar{x}}$ is the standard error.

Example. Suppose we have a population of size $N = 7$ as follows:

$$X_1 = 1, X_2 = 2, X_3 = 3, X_4 = 4, X_5 = 5, X_6 = 6, X_7 = 7$$

Let us select samples of size $n = 2$. Then there are $\binom{7}{2} = 21$ possible samples, and hence 21 possible sample means. These are listed in Table 3.1.

Let us also calculate the $\bar{X}$, σ, and $\sigma_{\bar{x}}$. We find

$$\bar{X} = 4, \qquad \sigma^2 = 28/7 = 4, \qquad \sigma = 2$$

$$\sigma_{\bar{x}}^2 = \frac{\sigma^2}{n} \frac{N-n}{N-1} = \frac{4}{2} \frac{7-2}{7-1} = \frac{5}{3} = 1.666$$

$$\sigma_{\bar{x}} = \sqrt{1.666} = 1.29$$
$$z\sigma_{\bar{x}} = 1.64 \times 1.29 = 2.1$$

Table 3.1

	Sample	$\bar{x}$	$\bar{x} - 1.64\sigma_{\bar{x}} < \bar{X} < \bar{x} + 1.64\sigma_{\bar{x}}$
1.	1, 2	1.5	$-0.6 < \bar{X} < 3.6$
2.	1, 3	2.0	$-0.1 < \bar{X} < 4.1$
3.	1, 4	2.5	$.4 < \bar{X} < 4.6$
4.	1, 5	3.0	$.9 < \bar{X} < 5.1$
5.	1, 6	3.5	$1.4 < \bar{X} < 5.6$
6.	1, 7	4.0	$1.9 < \bar{X} < 6.1$
7.	2, 3	2.5	$.4 < \bar{X} < 4.6$
8.	2, 4	3.0	$.9 < \bar{X} < 5.1$
9.	2, 5	3.5	$1.4 < \bar{X} < 5.6$
10.	2, 6	4.0	$1.9 < \bar{X} < 6.1$
11.	2, 7	4.5	$2.4 < \bar{X} < 6.6$
12.	3, 4	3.5	$1.4 < \bar{X} < 5.1$
13.	3, 5	4.0	$1.9 < \bar{X} < 6.1$
14.	3, 6	4.5	$2.4 < \bar{X} < 6.6$
15.	3, 7	5.0	$2.9 < \bar{X} < 7.1$
16.	4, 5	4.5	$2.4 < \bar{X} < 6.6$
17.	4, 6	5.0	$2.9 < \bar{X} < 7.1$
18.	4, 7	5.5	$3.4 < \bar{X} < 7.6$
19.	5, 6	5.5	$3.4 < \bar{X} < 7.6$
20.	5, 7	6.0	$3.9 < \bar{X} < 8.1$
21.	6, 7	6.5	$4.4 < \bar{X} < 8.6$

Since we have set $z = 1.64$, the confidence coefficient is 90%. This means that out of 100 confidence intervals, we would expect 10 not to contain the true mean (that is, we would expect 10% not to contain the true mean).

In terms of our example, we have been able to construct 21 confidence intervals, and we would expect 10% of these confidence intervals—about 2 of them—not to contain $\bar{X}$.

We know that $\bar{X} = 4$ in our example. Hence we can easily see that the first and last confidence intervals do not contain $\bar{X} = 4$. That is,

$$-0.6 < \bar{X} < 3.6$$
$$4.4 < \bar{X} < 8.6$$

do not contain $\bar{X} = 4$.

CHAPTER 4

Basic Concepts of Sampling Theory

With our brief review of expectations, variance, and estimation finished, let us return to our discussion of sampling theory. With the development of sampling theory, a number of basic concepts used especially by sampling theorists have been developed. The two basic concepts by which the sampling theorist grasps the population (or universe) are the frame and the sampling unit. Our first task in this chapter is to define and explain these two concepts.

Using the concept of frame, we shall define the concept of a complete count and use it to define the concept of population parameters as used in sampling theory. Then, with the use of population parameters, we shall define the concept of a sampling error. By combining the concept of a sampling error with a confidence interval, we shall develop the ideas of precision and reliability from which we will be able to give a concise explanation of sampling theory.

4.1 The population

To start with, let us review the basic concepts relating to the definition of a population which we learned in elementary statistics. Suppose we wish to estimate the average grade of 5 students. Assume the grades are on a 10-point basis. That is, the grades are from 0 to 10, and only in whole numbers. Recall that three elements may be distinguished in this kind of an experiment.

(1) There are 11 *possible outcomes*, or we may say, 11 *simple events*.
(2) The entities with which we are concerned and with which measurements or attributes are associated are the 5 students. Each student is called an *elementary unit*.
(3) The *variable* X_i associated with the elementary unit (student) is the grade point. It is the characteristic that varies from elementary unit to elementary unit.

The *population* (or universe) is defined as the aggregate (totality) of the elementary units.

To summarize: When confronted with a sampling problem, we first need to determine the elementary unit, the population, the characteristics to be measured, and the variable.

4.2   The sampling unit

Once the elements mentioned above are determined, we come to the problem of selecting a sample. In elementary statistics, we merely selected n elementary units from the population of N elementary units, and the elementary unit was the unit that was selected. In sampling surveys, however, a special unit called the *sampling unit*, or the *listing unit*, is defined for the selection of a sample. Let us explain this with an example.

Suppose we are interested in the average rental value of an apartment (dwelling units) in a small city. Let $X = \$200,000$ be the total amount of rent paid for all the apartments in the city, and let there be $Y = 2000$ apartments in the city. The average rental value is then obtained by the ratio

$$R = X/Y = \$200,000/2000 = \$100 \text{ per apartment}$$

We usually know neither X nor Y, and the statistical problem is to estimate them.

Let us consider the problem of estimating X, the total value of rent. The *elementary units* in this case are the individual apartments. And the *population* is the totality of all the apartments in the city. However, to obtain a complete list of all the apartments may be a very difficult job. Is there an easier way of estimating X than to list all the individual apartments? The procedure normally used is to make a list of the apartment houses instead of the individual apartments. Each apartment house may consist of, say, 4 to 20 apartments. Hence, by listing all the apartment houses in the city, we will have covered all the apartments (elementary units).

We may think of this procedure as follows: We have a population of apartments (elementary units), and this population is divided into units of apartment houses. When a sample is to be selected from the population, these apartment houses are selected rather than the apartments. The apartment houses which are selected for the sample are called *sampling units*.

Hence, sampling units consist of none, one, or more than one elementary unit. Each elementary unit belongs to one and only one sampling unit. In our subsequent discussion, whenever we say we have a sample of size n ($= 30$, say), it means that the sample consists of $n = 30$ sampling units.

If each sampling unit contains one and only one elementary unit, the sampling unit and elementary unit coincide, but in many cases the elementary unit and sampling unit do not coincide. Using this concept of a sampling unit, let us next define a *frame*.

4.3 The frame

A frame is made up of sampling units and represents the population. It is a means by which the surveyor grasps the population. Let us explain this concept with an example.

Suppose we wish to estimate the average weight of a student in a certain college. The elementary unit is the student, which in this case will also be the sampling unit. The population is the totality of all students.

Suppose we take as the population all the students attending college on October 1, and we proceed to collect data from registration cards. Because of drop-outs and transfers, very rarely will the file of cards and the students actually attending school coincide. However, we may consider the file of registration cards a good enough approximation of the students attending school. This file of cards is the *frame* and is what we use to represent the population.

In our example of the rental value of apartments, the list of apartment houses is the frame. Each apartment house (sampling unit) has a serial number attached to it. Suppose there are 200 apartment houses. The serial numbers will then be from 001 to 200. When selecting a sample, a random number table is used, and the sample is selected from the frame.

By a *complete census* or 100% sample, we mean a sample of all the sampling units in the frame. In our example above, where the file of cards is the frame representing the students in college, we noted that there may be a difference between the students recorded in the file and those actually in college. This difference between the population and the frame is called the *gap*.

For sampling and statistical theory, it is the frame with which we work, and the results we obtain are, strictly speaking, with respect to the frame. However, the gap between the frame and population is usually small enough to allow us to claim valid results for the population as well as the frame. Since there is no statistical theory that will bridge this gap, we must rely on our subjective judgment to determine whether or not the frame adquately represents the population. This is a nonstatistical judgment.

The frame and sampling unit are also called a *list* and *listing unit*. We shall use the terms frame and sampling unit in this book. Various examples of the frame will be given as our discussion of sampling theory develops.

Example 1. Suppose we wish to estimate the average wages of sales clerks at supermarkets in a certain city. The sales clerk is the elementary unit and the totality of sales clerks is the population. Suppose, however, that there is no city-wide name list or record of sales clerks available, but there is a list of supermarkets. Then a procedure would be to use the supermarket as a sampling unit, and the list of supermarkets would become the frame.

Example 2. Suppose we wish to estimate the average amount of milk a cow produces in a certain state. The elementary unit is the cow and the totality of all cows in the state is the population. Suppose there is no list or record of the cows in the state but there is a list of dairy farms. Then a procedure would be to use the dairy farms as the sampling unit and the list of such farms as the frame.

Example 3. Suppose we wish to estimate the average amount of sugar consumption of families in a certain city. The family is the elementary unit and the totality of all families in the city is the population. Suppose there is no list of families in the city available, but there is a map of the city showing each block in detail. Then a procedure would be to partition each block in two segments and use each segment as a sampling unit. A list of these segments would be used as the frame.

Example 4. Suppose we wish to estimate the vacancy rate of hotel rooms in a certain city. The elementary unit is the hotel room and the totality of hotel rooms in the city is the population. Since there is usually no list of all the hotel rooms in a city, we may use the hotels as the sampling units. A list of the hotels would be the frame.

4.4 Complete count and population parameters

Suppose we are interested in estimating the average weight of students at a certain college. A list of names of the students for a given date are given which will be the frame from which the sample is selected. Each student is a sampling unit.

When all of the students (sampling units) are weighed or examined for the characteristic that is being observed, we have a *complete count* or *complete census* of the frame. Let the weights of the students be denoted by

$$X_1, X_2, \ldots, X_N$$

and the average by

$$\bar{X} = \frac{1}{N}(X_1 + X_2 + \cdots + X_N)$$

$\bar{X}$ is the result of the complete count of the frame and will be called the *population mean*. We shall use capital letters for population values.

Note carefully that although we have called $\bar{X}$ the population mean, it is the mean of the students in the *frame* which may be different from the universe. As mentioned in section 4.3 there may be a gap between the frame and the universe. Hence, $\bar{X}$ may not be equal to the *true value* of the population. We shall use the term *true mean* or *true value* to indicate the true parameter value of the population.

The population mean $\bar{X}$ may differ from the true mean (which we shall denote by $\bar{X}_0$) not only because of the gap between the frame and the universe, but also because of other nonsampling errors. For example, the weight scale that is used may be poorly adjusted and as a result every one may be recorded 1/2 lb heavier than he actually is. In that case, even though the frame and the universe coincide, the $\bar{X}$ will differ from $\bar{X}_0$.

In subsequent discussion, when various *population parameters* such as the population mean, population variance, or population proportion are considered, we shall always be considering such parameters to be theoretical values obtained from the frame and not the universe. When discussing a complete count or complete census, we shall mean a complete count of the frame, not the universe.

With the understanding that in all subsequent discussion, unless otherwise stated, we shall be concerned only with drawing samples from the frame, and keeping in mind that the population parameters are defined with respect to the frame, we shall—for reasons of convenience—use the terms *frame*, *population*, and *universe* interchangeably. That is, when the terms population or universe are used, they should be interpreted to mean the frame. Or, we may say that we shall assume the gap between the frame and universe to be zero for our subsequent discussion.

4.5 Sampling error

The difference between a sample estimate and the population parameter obtained by a complete count from the frame is called the *sampling error* for that sample. Let us explain this as follows.

Suppose we have a population of $N = 5$ students who have \$1, \$2, ..., \$5, respectively. These 5 students are also the frame. A sample of size $n = 2$ is selected. Assume the 2 students who have $x_1 = \$1$ and $x_2 = \$3$ have been selected. The sample mean is then

$$\bar{x} = \frac{1}{n}(x_1 + x_2) = \frac{1}{2}(1 + 3) = \$2$$

where we use lower case letters to denote sample values.

The $\bar{X}$ was defined as the population mean obtained from a complete count of the frame. In our illustration, it is

$$\bar{X} = \frac{1}{N}(X_1 + \cdots + X_5)$$

$$= \frac{1}{5}(1 + \cdots + 5) = \$3$$

Let us consider $\bar{x} = \$2$ as an estimate of $\bar{X}$. Then, the difference between $\bar{x}$ and $\bar{X}$ is called the *sampling error* of $\bar{x}$ for this sample. In our present case

$$\bar{x} - \bar{X} = \$2 - \$3 = -\$1$$

is the sampling error of $\bar{x}$.

More generally, the difference between a sample estimate and the population parameter obtained from a complete count that is to be estimated is called the sampling error of the estimate for that sample.

This concept of a sampling error is related to the ideas of expected values and unbiasedness in the following manner. When the sample estimator, say, $\bar{x}$, is an unbiased estimator of the population parameter, say $\bar{X}$, we have

$$E(\bar{x}) = \bar{X}$$

Then the sampling error becomes the difference between the estimate obtained from the sample and the expected value of the estimator:

(1)   sampling error $= \bar{x} - \bar{X} = \bar{x} - E(\bar{x})$

In general, if $\hat{\theta}$ is an unbiased estimator of the population parameter θ, then

(2)   sampling error $= \hat{\theta} - \theta = \hat{\theta} - E(\hat{\theta})$

Thus, this sampling error of $\hat{\theta}$ is to be interpreted as the difference between a *single* sample result and the population parameter.

From equation (1) we find

(3) $\bar{X} = \bar{x} -$ (sampling error)

In other words, if we know the sampling error for the given sample, then by subtracting it from the sample estimate $\bar{x}$, we can find the population parameter $\bar{X}$ we seek. This result may be shown in general form by changing equation (2) as follows.

(4) $\theta = \hat{\theta} -$ (sampling error)

Thus, if we can find the sampling error, we can find θ.

The question then becomes: How do we find the sampling error of a given sample? Noting that the sampling error is

$$\text{sampling error} = \hat{\theta} - \theta$$

we need to know θ to compute the sampling error. However, θ is the population parameter we are interested in estimating and which we do not know. Hence, we cannot compute the sampling error. Is there some way of overcoming this impasse? Is there something we can use instead of the sampling error to find θ?

Fortunately, there is something we can use as a substitute for the sampling error. It is based on the simple principle that sample statistics such as $\bar{x}$ have a sampling distribution around $E(\bar{x}) = \bar{X}$ and as a result we shall be able to find an "average" sampling error even though we do not know $\bar{X}$. This is one of the remarkable and basic results of sampling theory. Let us explain this next.

4.6 Precision

To answer the problem raised at the end of section 4.5, we first recall that the sampling error of an estimate was defined as $\hat{\theta} - \theta$ (or $\hat{\theta} - E(\hat{\theta})$

when $E(\hat{\theta}) = \theta$). And this was the sampling error for one sample. In our example, we had $\bar{x} = \$2$, $\bar{X} = \$3$, and the sampling error was

$$\bar{x} - \bar{X} = 2 - 3 = -\$1$$

However, the $\bar{X} = \$3$ is usually unknown and is what we are interested in estimating. That is, we usually have before us only $\bar{x} = \$2$ and based on this have to estimate $\bar{X}$.

In such cases, we may use the idea of a confidence interval and state our results in the following manner: The *precision* of the sample estimate is to be within \$0.30, with 95% reliability.

This statement means that when a sample of size n is selected and the estimate $\bar{x} = \$2$ (for example) is found, this $\bar{x} = \$2$ is to be within $\pm\$0.30$ of the population mean with reliability 0.95.

Or, to put it another way, the population mean $\bar{X}$ is to be within

$$\bar{x} \pm 0.30 = 2 \pm 0.30$$

with reliability 0.95.

Let us explain this statement in more detail. As a visual aid, the sampling distribution of the sample mean is shown in Fig. 4-1.

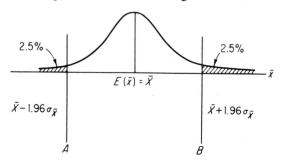

Fig. 4-1

We have shown in Chapter 3 that

$$P\left(-1.96 < \frac{\bar{x} - \bar{X}}{\sigma_{\bar{x}}} < 1.96\right) = 0.95$$

which may be transformed into

(1) $$P(-1.96\sigma_{\bar{x}} < \bar{x} - \bar{X} < 1.96\sigma_{\bar{x}}) = 0.95$$

is a legitimate probability statement so long as $\bar{x}$ is a random variable. It states that the probability that the difference $|\bar{x} - \bar{X}|$ will be less than $1.96\sigma_{\bar{x}}$ is 0.95.

In diagrammatic terms, this simply means that the probability of $\bar{x}$ falling between the two vertical lines A and B is 0.95, because so long as $\bar{x}$ is between A and B, the difference $|\bar{x} - \bar{X}|$ is less than $1.96\sigma_{\bar{x}}$.

Equation (1) may be rewritten as

(2) $$P(|\bar{x} - \bar{X}| < 1.96\sigma_{\bar{x}}) = 0.95$$

Then the maximum value $|\bar{x} - \bar{X}|$ can take is

(3) $$|\bar{x} - \bar{X}| = 1.96\sigma_{\bar{x}}$$

Note two points about this result. The first is that $|\bar{x} - \bar{X}|$ is the sampling error we defined in section 4.5. The second is that $1.96\sigma_{\bar{x}}$ is 1/2 the confidence interval.

However, the $|\bar{x} - \bar{X}|$ which is the sampling error needs to be interpreted differently in the present context of discussion. The sampling error $\bar{x} - \bar{X}$ of section 4.5 was the sampling error for a given sample. In our present case, the $\bar{x} - \bar{X}$ shows the maximum variation between the estimator and population parameter due to random sampling, and is equal to half the length of a confidence interval with a given confidence coefficient.

In other words, $\bar{x} - \bar{X}$ in this case does not show the difference between the sample estimate and the population parameter for a *given sample*. It is simply the maximum variation between the estimator and population parameter for *repeated sampling*, for a given sample size n and reliability. When $\bar{x} - \bar{X}$ is considered in this context, it is called the *precision* of the estimator, and not a sampling error.

Hence, $\bar{x} - \bar{X}$ is not for any given sample, but merely shows the maximum variation when performing random sampling. Thus, for example, we may require that the maximum variation be less than \$0.30, in which case we may simply say the *precision* is to be \$0.30.

This, then, will simply mean that 1/2 the length of the confidence interval is to be less than \$0.30.

The point to note is that the concept of a *sampling error* is for a given sample, whereas the concept of *precision* is related to the confidence interval and is defined in terms of repeated sampling.

The remarkable fact about this result is that we do not need to know the population parameter to determine the precision of the estimator. We need only know the variance. This, as we shall see later, may be estimated from the sample. Hence, by use of a single sample and statistical theory, we are able to determine the precision of the estimator.

4.7 Reliability

We stated in the previous section that, for example, the precision of the sample estimate is to be within \$0.30 with 95% reliability. Let us now explain the term reliability.

In our discussion in section 4.6, we required a reliability of 95% of the precision, and based on this we constructed a confidence interval of length

$$\bar{x} - 1.96\sigma_{\bar{x}} \qquad \text{to} \qquad \bar{x} + 1.96\sigma_{\bar{x}}$$

precision was set equal to 1/2 of the length of this confidence interval. That is,

$$|\bar{x} - \bar{X}| = 1.96\sigma_{\bar{x}}$$

If the reliability was set at 90%, the length of the confidence interval would be

$$\bar{x} - 1.64\sigma_{\bar{x}} \quad \text{to} \quad \bar{x} + 1.64\sigma_{\bar{x}}$$

and in this case

$$|\bar{x} - \bar{X}| = 1.64\sigma_{\bar{x}}$$

In other words, reliabilities of 95% or 90% correspond to confidence coefficients and with the standard error determines the length of the confidence interval.

Hence, when a reliability of, say, 95% is required of precision, we shall interpret this to mean that the precision is to be equal to or less than 1/2 the length of a confidence interval with a confidence coefficient of 95%. In symbols this is, for the sample mean, for a reliability of 95%.

$$|\bar{x} - \bar{X}| = \frac{1}{2}(\text{confidence interval})$$
$$= 1.96\sigma_{\bar{x}}$$

where $|\bar{x} - \bar{X}|$ is the precision, and 1.96 represents the 95% reliability. Let us call the 1.96 the *reliability coefficient*.

We may show this relation as

(1)   precision = (reliability) × (standard error)

or

(2) $d = z\sigma_{\bar{x}}$

where d denotes precision and z denotes the reliability coefficient. This relation expresses the very basic ideas of sampling theory, and we shall be using this basic relation over and over again in subsequent discussion.

4.8 Sample size and precision

Equation (1) of section 4.7 relating precision, reliability, and the standard error of the previous section may be used to find the relation between the precision of a sample estimator and the sample size. The relation is that as the sample size becomes larger, the precision increases, that is, d becomes smaller.

Let us explain this relation by using the sample mean $\bar{x}$ as an illustration. We have

(1) $d = z\sigma_{\bar{x}} = z\dfrac{\sigma}{\sqrt{n}}$

where $d = |\bar{x} - \bar{X}|$. Equation (1) shows that as n becomes larger, $\sigma_{\bar{x}}$ becomes smaller, and d becomes smaller. For example, suppose we wish to estimate the average weight of students at a certain college. Assume the standard deviation of the distribution of weights is known to be $\sigma = 18$ lb. Then (1) may be written as

$$(2) \qquad d = z\frac{18}{\sqrt{n}}$$

For simplicity, let $z = 2$ denote a reliability of approximately 95%. Then

$$(3) \qquad d = 2\frac{18}{\sqrt{n}}$$

If the sample size is $n = 16$, then

$$d = 2\frac{18}{\sqrt{16}} = 9 \text{ lb}$$

That is, we would expect a precision of ± 9 with a reliability of 95%.

For $n = 36$: $\qquad d = 2\frac{18}{\sqrt{36}} = 6 \text{ lb}$

For $n = 81$: $\qquad d = 2\frac{18}{\sqrt{81}} = 4 \text{ lb}$

As is seen, as n becomes larger, d becomes smaller, and the precision of the estimator increases. The common sense of this is that as the sample size increases, we would expect the sample estimator to become closer to the population parameter we are estimating.

We may also use equation (1) to find the sample size n for a given precision. Suppose we wish the precision of $\bar{x}$ to be within 4 1b with a reliability of 95%. This means

$$d = |\bar{x} - \bar{X}| \leq 4 \text{ lb}$$

Then, from (1)

$$4 = z\frac{\sigma}{\sqrt{n}} = 2\frac{18}{\sqrt{n}}$$

$$\therefore n = 81$$

We may rewrite equation (1) to show the sample size n explicitly as follows:

$$(4) \qquad n = \frac{(z\sigma)^2}{d^2}$$

Using our illustration, we find

$$n = \frac{(2 \times 18)^2}{(4)^2} = 81$$

Example 1. Suppose we wish to estimate the average weight of 1000 students, and we wish the precision to be 5 lb and the reliability to be 95%. How large a sample do we need?

We have $d = 5$ lb, and $z = 1.96$. To find n, we need to know σ, the population variance. In many cases, σ may be known from previous estimations. If not, a preliminary sample may be selected and σ may be estimated. Let us for the moment assume σ is known and is $\sigma = 15$ lb. Then

$$n = \frac{(1.96 \times 15)^2}{5^2} = 34.6 \doteq 35$$

Example 2. In many practical cases, to simplify calculations, $z = 2$ is used instead of $z = 1.96$ for the 95% level of reliability. The result will be a slightly larger sample size. Using our previous illustration, we find

$$n = \frac{(2 \times 15)^2}{5^2} = 36$$

Example 3. In many cases, the standard of $z = 3$ is used and expressed by the term *practically certain*. For a normal distribution, $z = 3$ shows a reliability of 99.7%. Using our previous example, the sample size becomes,

$$n = \frac{(3 \times 15)^2}{5^2} = 81$$

When $z = 3$, the term practically certain may be applied for most distributions, and to simplify things, it is convenient to use this standard in practical applications.

Problems

1. Suppose we wish to estimate the average weight of a large group of students and we wish the precision to be 3 lb and the reliability to be 2σ. How large a sample do we need? Assume $\sigma = 12$ lb.

2. In problem 1 above, if the precision is to be 1.5 lb, how large must the sample be? If the precision is to be 1 lb, how large must the sample be?

4.9 Sample size and precision in relative terms

In many cases, the precision of the estimators are expressed in relative (percentage) terms rather than absolute terms. For example, when estimating the weight of students at a certain school, we may require that the precision of the estimates to be with in $\pm 5\%$ of $\bar{X}$ instead of expressing the precision in absolute terms, such as (e.g.) within ± 7 lb of $\bar{X}$.

By using the coefficient of variation, the basic relation between precision, reliability, and standard error may be expressed in relative terms, and from this the relation between sample size and precision may be found in relative terms. Let us now derive the basic relation in relative terms.

First, the deviations $d = \bar{x} - \bar{X}$ may be shown in relative terms as

(1) $$d' = \frac{\bar{x} - \bar{X}}{\bar{X}} = \frac{d}{\bar{X}}$$

The basic relationship was

(2)
$$d = z\sigma_{\bar{x}}$$

Hence

(3)
$$\frac{d}{\bar{X}} = z\frac{\sigma_{\bar{x}}}{\bar{X}}$$

But from section 2.12, we found

(4)
$$C(\bar{x}) = C(\hat{X}) = \frac{C}{\sqrt{n}} \overset{\iota}{=} \frac{\sigma}{\sqrt{n}\,\bar{X}} = \frac{\sigma_{\bar{x}}}{\bar{X}}$$

Thus, from (3) and (4) we find

(5)
$$d' = zC(\bar{x}) = z\frac{C}{\sqrt{n}}$$

Solving for n, we find

(6)
$$n = \frac{(zC)^2}{(d')^2}$$

We also obtain from equations (5) and (6) that

(7)
$$n = \left(\frac{C}{C(\bar{x})}\right)^2$$

Hence there are two ways of determining n with respect to relative precision. Let us explain with examples.

Example 1. Suppose we wish to estimate the average weight of a large group of students, the relative precision of the estimator is to be within 5% of the average, and the reliability is to be $z = 3$ (that is, practically certain). How large a sample should we select? Using (6), we get

$$n = \frac{(3C)^2}{(0.05)^2}$$

If we know C, we can find n. Let us for the moment assume that $\hat{C} = 0.1$. Then

$$n = \frac{(3 \times 0.1)^2}{(0.05)^2} = 36$$

Example 2. Suppose that in Example 1, we wish the 3σ confidence interval

$$\bar{x} - 3\sigma_{\bar{x}} < X < \bar{x} + 3\sigma_{\bar{x}}$$

to be 1/2 percent. That is, we wish that half the length of the confidence interval to be 1/2 percent of $\bar{X}$. Then $C(\bar{x})$ becomes

$$3C(\bar{x}) = 0.005$$
$$\therefore \quad C(\bar{x}) = 0.0017$$

Using equation (7),

$$n = \left(\frac{C}{C(\bar{x})}\right)^2 = \left(\frac{C}{0.0017}\right)^2$$

Let us assume $\hat{C} = 0.10$. Then,

$$n = \left(\frac{0.10}{0.0017}\right)^2 = 60^2 = 3600$$

Problems

1. Suppose we wish to estimate the average amount of expenditures of students at a large college. We wish the estimate to have a relative precision of 5% or less. The coefficient of variation of weights is estimated from past studies to be $\hat{C} = 0.20$. Assuming a reliability of practically certain, how large must the sample be?

2. Suppose we wish to estimate the average amount of expenditures of students at a large college. We wish the $C(\bar{x})$ to be 0.0017 so that half the length of a 3σ confidence interval will be 0.005 ($=0.0017 \times 3$). How large a sample do we need? Assume $\hat{C} = 0.20$.

3. If (in Problem 2) we wish $C(\bar{x})$ to be 0.017 so that half the length of a 3σ confidence interval will be 0.05, how large a sample do we need?

4.10 Nonsampling errors and accuracy

We have seen that sampling errors arise when a sample is selected by simple random sampling and a sample statistic is used as an estimator of a population characteristic. However, aside from sampling errors, there are many ways in which various errors may enter.

1. Errors of reporting. The incomes a man reports to the tax collector and to his girlfriend usually differ. A child's age, as reported by his mother to a bus driver, may vary from what she tells other parents. Few people know their exact weight, height, or the number of cigarettes they smoke per day. It is often difficult to gather correct information. There are, as shown in the above examples, many sources from which errors of data may enter.

2. Nonresponse errors. A customary headache of sample surveyors is the nonresponse to questionnaires. Respondents may throw away the questionnaires, be out of town, or may even claim they are the Phanthom, or Mickey Mouse. For the "not at homes", sample surveyors usually send second and third notices requesting answers. Another problem this creates is that those answering may be one class of people whereas those not answering may be another, which results in a biased sample.

3. Errors in sample selection. The sample of bananas in a shop window may be quite different from those inside the store. The selected sample may contain the bias of the surveyors when random sampling is not strictly observed.

The precision of a sample estimate is measured by its sampling error.

When we take a complete count, the sampling error becomes zero. For example, $\bar{x}$ is the sample estimate of the population parameter $\bar{X}$. When a complete count is taken, $\bar{x}$ becomes equal to $\bar{X}$.

However, the $\bar{x} = \bar{X}$ obtained from a complete count may contain non-sampling errors, and hence differs from the true population mean. The *accuracy* of the sample estimate $\bar{x}$ refers to the difference between the sample estimate $\bar{x}$ and the true population mean. Or, we may say, the accuracy of a sample estimate is measured by its sampling error and nonsampling error.

In sampling, after obtaining a sample estimate and finding its precision and reliability, it is necsssary to consider the nonsampling error and check its accuracy. This check, however, cannot usually be made statistically.

4.11   The mean square error

One more concept that is used frequently in sampling theory to compare two estimators is the *mean square error* (MSE) of an estimator. For example, suppose we have two estimators y and z of the population mean $\bar{X}$. Let y be unbiased and z be a biased estimator of $\bar{X}$. Which estimator should we use?

We should use the one that we may expect to be closer to $\bar{X}$. Let us explain this statement with the following illustration. Suppose the distribution of y and z may be shown diagrammatically as in Fig. 4-2. As shown, the

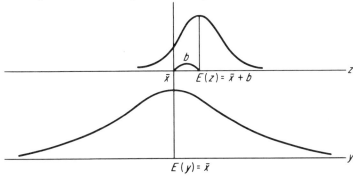

Fig. 4-2

dispersion of z is much smaller than that of y, except that z is distributed around $E(z) = \bar{X} + b$ whereas y is distributed around $E(y) = \bar{X}$. However, we can see intuitively that if the bias b is small, even though z is biased, because its disperson is much smaller than that of y, it will probably give us an estimate that is closer to $\bar{X}$.

The implication of this reasoning is that a biased estimator may be better than an unbiased one, depending on the magnitude of the variance and the bias. Let us now show these relationships by use of the MSE.

Since y and z are estimators of $\bar{X}$, the dispersion we are interested in is the dispersion around $\bar{X}$. Hence, let us define the following measure of dispersion. Let w be an estimator of the population parameter θ. Then

$$\text{(1)} \qquad \text{MSE}(w) = E(w - \theta)^2$$

is called the *mean square error* of w. In our present illustration.

$$\text{MSE}(y) = E(y - \bar{X})^2$$
$$\text{MSE}(z) = E(z - \bar{X})^2$$

The variances are

$$V(y) = E(y - Ey)^2$$
$$V(z) = E(z - Ez)^2$$

Since we have assumed that $E(y) = \bar{X}$,

$$V(y) = E(y - Ey)^2$$
$$= E(y - \bar{X})^2$$
$$= \text{MSE}(y)^2$$

That is, when y is unbiased, $V(y) = \text{MSE}(y)$.

This relation does not hold for z bacause $E(z) = \bar{X} + b$ where b is the bias. So let us now investigate MSE (z) algebraically as follows.

$$\text{MSE}(z) = E(z - \bar{X})^2$$
$$= E[(z - Ez) + (Ez - \bar{X})]^2$$
$$= E(z - Ez)^2 + (Ez - \bar{X})^2 + 2(Ez - \bar{X}) E(z - Ez)$$

Since $E(z - Ez) = 0$, we get

$$\text{(2)} \qquad \text{MSE}(z) = E(z - Ez)^2 + (Ez - \bar{X})^2$$

The 1st term on the right side is $V(z)$. As for the 2nd term, since $E(z) = \bar{X} + b$,

$$E(z) - \bar{X} = b = \text{bias}$$

Hence, (2) becomes

$$\text{(3)} \qquad \text{MSE}(z) = V(z) + (\text{bias})^2$$

And for y, we have already found

$$\text{(4)} \qquad \text{MSE}(y) = V(y)$$

Let us compare (3) and (4). Assume for the moment that $V(z)$ is much smaller than $V(y)$. Then, for MSE(z) to be much smaller than MSE(y), we need the (bias)^2 to be small. Conversely, if we have two estimators y(unbiased) and z (biased), $V(z)$ is much smaller than $V(y)$, and the bias of z is small, MSE(z) may be much smaller than MSE(y) and z may hence be a better estimator of $\bar{X}$. Then the question is: Are there such estimators as z?

The answer is yes. An illustration is the ratio estimate which we shall study in Chapter 13. Let r represent the ratio estimate. Then

$$\mathrm{MSE}(r) = V(r) + (\mathrm{bias})^2$$

The characteristic of r is that $V(r)$ is small and that the bias becomes smaller as n becomes larger. That is, r is a consistent estimator. Hence, when the sample is sufficiently large, the $(\mathrm{bias})^2$ will be small and negligible. As we shall see in Chapter 13, the ratio estimate (even though it is a biased estimator) is widely used because of the above mentioned characteristics.

This MSE is a useful measure for comparing the dispersion of different estimators which may be biased and it serves mainly as a theoretical tool. However, since most of the estimators we shall be discussing in the subsequent chapters (except the ratio estimate) will be unbiased estimators, we shall not make much use of the MSE.

Notes and References

For further reading on topics of complete count, frame, and sampling error, see Deming (1960), Chapters 3–4; Yates (1960), Chapters 1–2, pp. 20–23, and Chapter 4; Kish (1965), pp. 53–59. Yates (1960) Chapter 4 is especially recommended for illustrations of frames. For further readings on the basic relation among precision, reliability, and standard error, see Cyert and Davidson (1962), *Statistical Sampling for Accounting Information.* Englewood Cliffs, N.J.: Prentice-Hall, Inc., Chapter 4; Hansen, Hurwitz, and Madow (1953), pp. 124–129. The terms relvariance and practically certain (for 3σ) are due to Hansen, Hurwitz, and Madow. For further reading on nonsampling errors, see Deming (1960), Chapter 5; Deming (1950), Chapter 2; Hansen, Hurwitz, and Madow (1953), Chapter 2. As these readings will show, the problem of nonsampling errors is complicated and extensive. The above three references discuss the problem on a nontechnical level. For a more technical discussion see Kish (1965), Chapter 13; Cochran (1963), Chapter 13. However, it is better to postpone further study of nonsampling errors until the end of this book. An extensive bibliography concerning nonsampling errors may be found at the end of Cochran (1963), Chapter 13. For further reading on the mean square error, see Hansen, Hurwitz, and Madow (1953), pp. 35–39; Cochran (1963), pp. 15–16; Deming (1950), pp. 129–131; Deming (1960), pp. 396–402.

CHAPTER 5

Simple Random Sampling

5.1 Introduction

Our task in the subsequent chapters will be to study the various sampling techniques, such as simple random sampling, stratified random sampling, systematic sampling, cluster sampling, etc. We shall, for convenience, divide our discussion into five main steps. The first is to determine the procedure of sample selection. Suppose, for example, that we wish to estimate the average number of books per student at a certain university. Should we use simple random sampling, stratified random sampling, or some other sampling procedure. If we decide to use stratified random sampling, we first divide the population (the students) into strata (e.g., freshmen, sophomores, juniors, and seniors), and then select samples from each stratum. We need to investigate such questions as: Why did we decide to use stratified random sampling instead of some other procedure? What criteria is used for stratifying the population and selecting samples from each stratum? We shall discuss these questions by investigating the statistical theory of the various sampling techniques.

The second step is to find the estimators of the parameters we are usually interested in, namely, the population mean, the population total, the ratio, and the proportion. In our present example, we wish to estimate the average number of books—the population mean. The estimator of the population mean, as we have already seen, is the sample mean.

The third step is to find the standard errors of these estimators (sample statistics, e.g., $\bar{x}$), so that we may evaluate the precision of the estimators. It will turn out that the estimator of the standard error is based on the estimator of the population standard deviation. Hence, the problem of estimating the standard error will be reduced to estimating the population variance.

The fourth step is to construct confidence intervals for the population parameters. Once the standard errors are found, the confidence intervals are easily obtained.

The fifth step is to find the size of the sample to be selected. How many students should we select as our sample? This, of course, is not necessarily the last step. In fact, in practice, it may be the first step. However, since the standard error and confidence intervals are used to find the sample size, it will be discussed last.

Following these five steps, we shall discuss simple random sampling. We shall consider the problem of estimating the population mean in sections 5.3-5.7; the problem of estimating the population total in section 5.8; and the problem of estimating the population proportion in sections 5.9-5.10. Although the simple random sampling procedure is not used very often in practical surveys, it is nevertheless the procedure which provides the foundation of all other sampling procedures. We shall therefore discuss it in detail.

But before starting our discussion of estimating the population mean by simple random sampling, let us discuss how random samples may be selected by the use of random number tables.

5.2 Sample selection

Simple random sampling was defined in section 2.2 as a selection procedure where every possible sample has the same chance of selection. In particular, when the sample size is $n = 1$, the above definition states that every possible sampling unit has the same chance of selection.

How then can we select the sampling units so that each sampling unit has an equal chance of selection? At first glance, this may seem a simple matter which can be accomplished by selecting units at random according to ones' own subjective judgment. Such a procedure, however, usually results in including an individual's subjective bias in the selection of units. As an experiment, a student may repeatedly select 10 students at random from a class of 50 students, and thus find the average weight of the 10 students. The 10 selected students will usually tend to be either on the heavy side or on the light side. It will prove difficult to repeatedly select samples which are not biased.

To avoid subjective biases in the selection of samples, random number tables are used in practice. So let us first discuss the use of random number tables.

(*i*) *Random number tables.*

There are several random number tables, but the most convenient one to use in terms of size is the Kendall and Smith Random Number Table.* Two other well-known tables are the Interstate Commerce Commision Table,†

---

*Kendall, M. G. and B. B. Smith, *Tables of Random Sampling Numbers.* New York: Cambridge University Press, 1954.

†Interstate Commerce Commission, Bureau of Transport Economics and Statistics. *Table of* 105,000 *Random Decimal Digits* (Statement No. 4914, File No. 261-A-1). Washington, D.C., 1949.

which has 105,000 random digits, and the Rand Corporation Random Number Table*, which has 1 million digits.

Let us illustrate the use of random number tables with an example. Suppose there are 300 students and we wish to select a random sample of 8 students to estimate their average weight. A list of the students is made, and each is given a serial number from 001 up to 300.

Let us use the Kendall and Smith table to select the students. Since 300 is a 3-digit number, we use the first 3 columns. We find the following numbers from the random number table:

231	117	070	092	978
055	433	433	979	891
148	938	615	937	259
389	495	313	726	814
973	367	570	610	113

Hence, we select the following 8 numbers for our sample:

231, 55, 148, 117, 70, 92, 259, 113

We must be careful to distinguish between sampling with replacement and sampling without replacement. When sampling without replacement, the probability of the 1st selection is 1/300. That is, the probability that the 231st student is selected is 1/300. Since this student is selected and this number is removed, there are 299 numbers left. Hence, the probability of the 2nd selection (the 55th student) will be 1/299. The probability of the 3rd selection will be 1/298, and so forth. As we go down the line, we notice that the 4th number is 389, which is larger than 300. Hence, we skip it.

When sampling with replacement, the selected numbers are not removed. That is, even though 231 has appeared once, if it appears again, it is selected again. Thus, the probability of every selection will always be 1/300.

As is seen, only numbers less than 300 were selected. As a result, only 8 numbers out of 25 were selected, resulting in a loss of about 2/3 of the random numbers. Fortunately, there are several ways of avoiding such a waste of random numbers. One way is to add a constant to the number of the student we select. In our example, we add 300. Hence 001 — 300 becomes 301 — 600. By repeating this process, we also get 601 — 900.

After selecting random numbers according to the above intervals, we may revert the inflated numbers to the original numbers by subtracting the constants 300 and 600 from the inflated numbers.

Hence, for the random number 389, we may consider that we added 300 to 89, and as a result we subtract 300; that is, 389 — 300 = 89 and the 89th student is selected.

*Rand Corporation. *A Million Random Digits*. New York: The Free Press of Glencoe, Inc., 1955.

We skip 973 since the highest interval is from 601 — 900. Selecting the sample in this fashion, we obtain the following sample of 8 students:

Random numbers	Subtract constant		
231		231	1
055		55	2
148		148	3
389	−300	89	4
973	skip	—	
117		117	5
433	−300	133	6
983	skip	—	
495	−300	195	7
367	−300	67	8

As a result, the wasted random numbers are only those from 901 to 999. In the previous case, we needed 25 random numbers. We now need only 10.

Example 1. From a population of $N = 2000$ students, select a random sample of 10 students. Here, there are only 10 students, and we may therefore simply select the 10 numbers from 0001 to 2000. Or, we may construct 2 additional intervals, 2001 to 4000 and 4001 to 6000. We could also construct the interval 6001 to 8000, but for only 10 students, the numbers from 0001 to 6000 should provide efficient utilization of the tables. Let us find our sample from the random number table in the appendix. We have the following numbers.

Random numbers	Subtract constant		
2315	−2000	= 315th student	1
0554		554	2
1487		1487	3
3897	−2000	= 1897	4
9731	skip		
1174		1174	5
4336	−4000	= 336	6
9380	skip		
4954	−4000	= 954	7
3676	−2000	= 1676	8
0709		709	9
4331	−4000	= 331	10

As is seen, we were able to obtain a sample of size $n = 10$ from 12 random numbers —only 2 random numbers were discarded. Check how many random numbers would have been necessary if only the interval 0001 to 2000 were used.

A second way of avoiding wasted random numbers is to divide the random number by 300 and use the remainder as the selected random numbers. The remainder 0 corresponds to the 300th student. For our present example, we have the following results.

231	0 × 300 + 231	231	1
055	0 × 300 + 55	55	2
148	0 × 300 + 148	148	3
389	1 × 300 + 89	89	4
973	skip		
117	0 × 300 + 117	117	5
433	1 × 300 + 133	133	6
983	skip		
495	1 × 300 + 195	195	7
367	1 × 300 + 67	67	8

This is essentially the same as the method explained previously where we subtracted a constant.

Problems

1. From a population of $N = 600$ students, select a random sample of $n = 20$ students without replacement. Select the random numbers without any adjustments.

2. In Problem 1, select the random numbers by using the method of subtracting a constant.

3. In Problem 1, select the random numbers by using the method of dividing the random numbers by a constant.

5.3 Estimator of $\bar{X}$

As mentioned in section 5.1, once the sampling procedure has been decided, the next step in our sample survey will be to estimate the parameters of the population. The main parameters we are interested in are the population mean, total, and proportion. In this section, we shall consider the problem of estimating the population mean.

We already know from our discussion of estimation in Chapter 3 that the sample mean is an unbiased, consistent, and minimum variance estimator of the population mean. Hence, we shall use the sample mean as an estimator of the population mean.

To gain familiarity with the notation we shall be using, let us formally write out these well known results. Let $X_1, X_2, \ldots, X_N$ be a population of size N and $x_1, x_2, \ldots, x_n$ be a sample of size n. Then by definition

$$\bar{X} = \frac{1}{N}(X_1 + X_2 + \cdots + X_N) = \frac{1}{N}\sum_{i=1}^{N} X_i$$

$$\bar{x} = \frac{1}{n}\sum_{i=1}^{n} x_i$$

To indicate that the sample mean $\bar{x}$ is an estimator of the population mean $\bar{X}$, we write:

$$\hat{\bar{X}} = \bar{x}$$

The notation $\hat{}$ indicates an estimator. In our subsequent discussion, we shall refer to $\bar{x}$ as the sample mean or estimator of $\bar{X}$. Hence, we may write $\hat{\bar{X}}$ or $\bar{x}$ to indicate the estimator of $\bar{X}$.

As proved in section 2.9,

$$E(\bar{x}) = \bar{X}$$

and $\bar{x}$ is an unbiased estimator of $\bar{X}$.

As an example, suppose we wish to estimate the average weight of $N = 200$ students by selecting a random sample of $n = 20$ students. Using the random number table, we select 20 students and find the sample mean. Suppose it is $\bar{x} = 120$ 1b. Then $\bar{x} = 120$ 1b is the estimate of the population mean $\bar{X}$ we seek.

Problems

1. Prove that $E(\bar{x}) = \bar{X}$

2. Given a population $X_1 = 1$, $X_2 = 2$, $X_3 = 3$, select samples of size $n = 2$ and show that $E(\bar{x}) = \bar{X}$ for sampling with and without replacement.

5.4   The variance of $\bar{x}$

Having found the estimate $\bar{x} = 120$ 1b of $\bar{X}$, we ask the question: How reliable is it as an estimate of $\bar{X}$? Although we know that $\bar{x}$ is an unbiased, consistent, and minimum variance estimator of $\bar{X}$, we cannot associate with it a reliability statement indicating its reliability as an estimate of $\bar{X}$. However, we have seen in Chapter 3 that by using the confidence interval, we were able to estimate $\bar{X}$ by an interval, and also associate with this interval a reliability statement and a measure of precision. The confidence interval was given as

$$\bar{x} - z\sigma_{\bar{x}} < \bar{X} < \bar{x} + z\sigma_{\bar{x}}$$

which may be rewritten as

$$|\bar{x} - \bar{X}| = z\sigma_{\bar{x}}$$

where z showed the level of reliability and $z\sigma_{\bar{x}} = |\bar{x} - \bar{X}|$ indicated the precision.

To obtain this confidence interval, we need to know the $\sigma_{\bar{x}}$, and our problem in this section will be to find $\sigma_{\bar{x}}$. The definition of $\sigma_{\bar{x}}$ given in elementary statistics is

$$\sigma_{\bar{x}} = \frac{\sigma}{\sqrt{n}}$$

for sampling with replacement and, as is seen, it depends on σ. Hence, to find $\sigma_{\bar{x}}$, we first need to define the variance σ^2 of the population.

(i) *Variance of* x_i

In sampling theory, two alternative definitions of the variance of X_i are used. One is

(1)
$$\sigma^2 = E(X - \bar{X})^2 = \frac{1}{N} \sum_{}^{N} (X - \bar{X})^2$$

which is the basic population variance. The second definition is

(2)
$$S^2 = \frac{1}{N-1} \sum_{}^{N} (X_i - \bar{X})^2$$

where $N-1$ is used instead of N.

These population variances are used mainly to derive theoretical results, and in this case, definition (2) is found to be more useful —especially in connection with the analysis of variance techniques. In applications, we shall use sample estimates of these population variances.

Example 1. Suppose there are 5 students with the following amounts of money:
$$X_1 = \$1, \quad X_2 = \$2, \quad X_3 = \$3, \quad X_4 = \$4, \quad X_5 = \$5$$
Find the variances σ^2 and S^2. Calculations will show that $\sigma^2 = 2$, $S^2 = 2.5$.

(ii) *Variance of* $\bar{x}$

Having defined the variance of X_i, let us now define the variance of $\bar{x}$. The variance of $\bar{x}$ is defined as

(3)
$$\sigma_{\bar{x}}^2 = E(\bar{x} - E\bar{x})^2 = E(\bar{x} - \bar{X})^2$$

It may be shown that (see Reference):

(4)
$$\sigma_{\bar{x}}^2 = \frac{N-n}{N-1} \frac{\sigma^2}{n} \qquad \text{sampling without replacement}$$

(5)
$$= \frac{N-n}{N} \frac{S^2}{n} \qquad \text{sampling without replacement}$$

(6)
$$\sigma_{\bar{x}}^2 = \frac{\sigma^2}{n} \qquad \text{sampling with replacement}$$

(7)
$$= \frac{N-1}{N} \frac{S^2}{n} \qquad \text{sampling with replacement}$$

The terms
$$\frac{N-n}{N-1} \quad \text{and} \quad \frac{N-n}{N}$$

are called *finite population corrections* (fpc) *for the variances*. The square root of these terms are the fpc *for the standard errors*. The first fpc is used when σ^2 is used for the population variance, and the second fpc is used when S^2 is used for the population variance.

Using the second fpc, we find
$$\frac{N-n}{N} = 1 - \frac{n}{N}$$

where n/N is called the *sampling fraction*. As is seen, when N becomes large relative to n, that is, when n/N becomes small, the fpc approaches unity. When $n/N \leqq 0.05$ (that is, 5%), the fpc may be omitted. The implication is, after N exceeds a certain size so that n/N becomes less than 5%, the population size will have practically no effect on the standard error.

A 5% sample is a case where 1 sampling unit in 20 is selected. Hence, we may restate the above implication by saying that when the rate of sampling is 1 in 20 or less, the fpc may be omitted. For example, when the rate is 1 in 30, or 1 in 50, we may omit the fpc.

Note in passing that n/N is also the probability of a specific item being included in the sample. We shall make use of this fact and the term *sampling fraction* frequently in subsequent discussions.

Also note that

$$\frac{\sigma^2}{n} = \frac{N-1}{N}\frac{S^2}{n}$$

In almost all practical cases N is large. Hence we may set

$$\frac{N-1}{N} \doteq 1$$

where $\doteq$ means approximately equal, and obtain

$$\frac{\sigma^2}{n} \doteq \frac{S^2}{n}$$

In our subsequent discussions, we shall use this approximation, and the two formulas for $\sigma_{\bar{x}}^2$ we shall mainly use are

$$\sigma_{\bar{x}}^2 = \frac{N-n}{N}\frac{S^2}{n} \qquad \text{without replacement (exact)}$$

$$= \frac{S^2}{n} \qquad \text{with replacement (approximation)}$$

However, let us illustrate the original formulas with an example to clarify the relations. Suppose we have a population $X_1 = 1$, $X_2 = 2$, $X_3 = 3$ and samples of size $n = 2$ are selected. Then, calculations will show that

$$\sigma^2 = 2/3 \qquad S^2 = 1$$

To calculate $\sigma_{\bar{x}}^2$, let us use the original formula

$$\sigma_{\bar{x}}^2 = \frac{1}{M}\sum^{M}(\bar{x} - \bar{X})^2$$

where M is the number of sample means. Let us consider the case of sampling without replacement first. The samples are listed in Table 5.1.

Table 5.1

Sample	$\bar{x}$	$\bar{x} - \bar{X}$	$(\bar{x} - \bar{X})^2$
1, 2	1.5	−0.5	0.25
1, 3	2.0	0	0
2, 3	2.5	0.5	0.25
			0.50

Hence, the $\sigma_{\bar{x}}^2$ is

$$\sigma_{\bar{x}}^2 = \frac{1}{3}(0.5) = \frac{1}{6}$$

From our theoretical formula, we have

$$\sigma_{\bar{x}}^2 = \frac{N-n}{N}\frac{S^2}{n} = \left(\frac{3-2}{3}\right)\left(\frac{1}{2}\right) = \frac{1}{6}$$

and as can be seen we obtain the same variance $\sigma_{\bar{x}}^2 = 1/6$.

Let us now consider sampling with replacement. The samples are listed in Table 5.2.

Table 5.2

Sample	$\bar{x}$	$\bar{x} - \bar{X}$	$(\bar{x} - \bar{X})^2$
1, 1	1.0	−1.0	1.00
1, 2	1.5	−0.5	0.25
1, 3	2.0	0	0
2, 1	1.5	−0.5	0.25
2, 2	2.0	0	0
2, 3	2.5	0.5	0.25
3, 1	2.0	0	0
3, 2	2.5	0.5	0.25
3, 3	3.0	1.0	1.00
			3.00

Hence $\sigma_{\bar{x}}^2$ is

$$\sigma_{\bar{x}}^2 = \frac{1}{9}(3) = \frac{1}{3}$$

Using the theoretical formula, we have

$$\sigma_{\bar{x}}^2 = \frac{N-1}{N}\frac{S}{n} = \frac{3-1}{3}\frac{1}{2} = \frac{1}{3}$$

and as is seen we obtain the same variance $\sigma_{\bar{x}}^2 = 1/3$.

However, as mentioned above, the N is usually large in practical applications and we shall assume $\sigma_{\bar{x}}^2 = S^2/n$.

Example 2. Suppose samples of size $n = 3$ are selected from the population given in Example 1. Calculate $\sigma_{\bar{x}}$. Since $\sigma^2 = 2$, $S^2 = 2.5$ and $N = 5$.

(i) $\sigma_{\bar{x}}^2 = \dfrac{N-n}{N-1}\dfrac{\sigma^2}{n} = \dfrac{5-3}{5-1}\dfrac{2}{3} = \dfrac{1}{3}$

(ii) $\sigma_{\bar{x}}^2 = \dfrac{N-n}{N}\dfrac{S^2}{n} = \dfrac{5-3}{5}\dfrac{2.5}{3} = \dfrac{1}{3}$

(iii) $\sigma_{\bar{x}}^2 = \dfrac{\sigma^2}{n} = \dfrac{2}{3} = \dfrac{N-1}{N}\dfrac{S^2}{n} = \dfrac{5-1}{5}\dfrac{2.5}{3} = \dfrac{2}{3}$

Cases (i) and (ii) are for sampling without replacement, and (iii) is for sampling with replacement. As is seen, the variance $\sigma_{\bar{x}}^2 = 2/3$ for (iii) is much larger than for (i) and (ii). We can see the reason for this intuitively in our present problem as follows. The smallest and largest sample mean $\bar{x}$ for (i) and (ii) are

$$\bar{x} = \frac{1}{3}(1+2+3) = 2$$

$$\bar{x} = \frac{1}{3}(3+4+5) = 4$$

whereas the smallest and largest sample mean for (iii) are

$$\bar{x} = \frac{1}{3}(1+1+1) = 1$$

$$\bar{x} = \frac{1}{3}(5+5+5) = 5$$

As is seen, the variation of $\bar{x}$ for (i) and (ii) (i.e., sampling without replacement) is much smaller than that for (iii) (i.e., sampling with replacement).

Using $\sigma_{\bar{x}}^2$, we may now easily construct a confidence interval and associate with it a reliability statement. However, as we have seen, $\sigma_{\bar{x}}$ is equal to

$$\sigma_{\bar{x}} = \frac{S}{\sqrt{n}} \qquad \text{with replacement}$$

and is dependent on S which is a population parameter and is usually unknown. Hence, for practical applications, we need an estimator of S obtained from the sample. Let us consider the problem of estimating S in the next section.

References

Let us now derive equation (4). Equation (3) may be rewritten as

$$\sigma_{\bar{x}}^2 = E\left[\frac{\sum\limits_{i}^{n}(x_i - \bar{X})}{n}\right]^2$$

$$= \frac{1}{n^2}E\left[\sum\limits_{i}^{n}(x_i - \bar{X})\right]^2$$

$$= \frac{1}{n^2}E\left[\sum\limits_{i}^{n}(x_i - \bar{X})^2 + \sum\limits_{i \neq j}^{n}(x_i - \bar{X})(x_j - \bar{X})\right]$$

$$(8) \qquad = \frac{1}{n^2} \sum_{i}^{n} E(x_i - \bar{X})^2 + \frac{1}{n^2} \sum_{i \neq j}^{n} E(x_i - \bar{X})(x_j - \bar{X})$$

The probability of obtaining $(x_i - \bar{X})^2$ on the ith draw is the same as obtaining x_i on the ith draw which is, as we have already seen, $1/N$. Hence, using the definition of expected values, the first term on the right hand side of (8) becomes,

$$E(x_i - \bar{X})^2 = \sum^{N} \frac{1}{N} (x_i - \bar{X})^2 = \sigma^2$$

The second term on the right hand side becomes

$$E(x_i - \bar{X})(x_j - \bar{X}) = \frac{1}{N} \frac{1}{N-1} \sum_{i \neq j}^{N} (x_i - \bar{X})(x_j - \bar{X})$$

since the probability of selecting $(x_i - \bar{X})(x_j - \bar{X})$ on the ith and jth draw is $(1/N)[1/(N-1)]$ when sampling without replacement. The summation term may be further changed as follows.

$$\sum_{i \neq j}^{N} (x_i - \bar{X})(x_j - \bar{X}) = \left[\sum^{N} (x_i - \bar{X}) \right]^2 - \sum (x_i - \bar{X})^2$$

$$= - \sum^{N} (x_i - \bar{X})^2$$

Combining these results and substituting back into (8), we obtain

$$\sigma_{\bar{x}}^2 = \frac{1}{n^2} \sum_{i}^{n} \sigma^2 + \frac{1}{n^2} \frac{1}{N} \frac{1}{N-1} \sum_{i \neq j}^{n} \left[-\sum^{N} (x_i - \bar{X})^2 \right]$$

$$= \frac{1}{n^2} (n\sigma^2) - \frac{1}{n^2} \frac{1}{N-1} \sum_{i \neq j}^{n} \sigma^2$$

$$= \frac{\sigma^2}{n} - \frac{1}{n^2} \frac{1}{N-1} n(n-1)\sigma^2$$

$$(9) \qquad = \frac{N-n}{N-1} \frac{\sigma^2}{n}$$

Using the second definition of variance for X_i in equation (2), (9) becomes

$$(10) \qquad \sigma_{\bar{x}}^2 = \frac{N-n}{N} \frac{S^2}{n}$$

which is the form we shall be mainly using.

When sampling is with replacement, the x_i and x_j are statistically independent, and hence

$$E(x_i - \bar{X})(x_j - \bar{X}) = 0$$

and as a result (8) becomes

$$\sigma_{\bar{x}}^2 = \frac{1}{n^2} (n\sigma^2) = \frac{\sigma^2}{n}$$

which is equation (6).

Problems

1. Suppose there are $N = 5$ students with the following number of books:

$$X_1 = 3, \quad X_2 = 5, \quad X_3 = 6, \quad X_4 = 7, \quad X_5 = 9$$

(a) Find σ^2 and S^2.

(b) Suppose samples of size $n = 2$ are selected. Find $\sigma_{\bar{x}}^2$ when sampling without replacement, using formulas (4) and (5).
(c) Find $\sigma_{\bar{x}}^2$ when sampling with replacement using formulas (6) and (7).
(d) Select all possible samples of size $n = 2$ without replacement and calculate $\sigma_{\bar{x}}^2$ directly from the basic formula (3).
(e) Select all possible samples of size $n = 2$ with replacement and calculate $\sigma_{\bar{x}}^2$ directly from the basic formula (3).

2. Given $X_1 = 1$, $X_2 = 2$, $X_3 = 3$, calculate

$$\sum_{\substack{i \neq j}}^{N=3} (X_i - \bar{X})(X_j - \bar{X})$$

3. Given $X_1 = 1$, $X_2 = 2$, $X_3 = 3$, calculate

$$-\sum_{i=1}^{N=3} (X_i - \bar{X})^2$$

and verify that it is equal to the result obtained in Problem 2.

5.5 Estimator of $\sigma_{\bar{x}}^2$

As mentioned at the end of the last section, for practical applications we need to find an estimator of $\sigma_{\bar{x}}^2$. Since $\sigma_{\bar{x}}^2$ is dependent on S^2(or σ^2), the problem of finding an estimator of $\sigma_{\bar{x}}^2$ will boil down to finding an estimator of S^2(or σ^2). An unbiased estimator of S^2 will prove to be the sample variance which we shall later use to find an unbiased estimator $\sigma_{\bar{x}}^2$. So let us start by defining the sample variance.

(i) Sample variance.

There are several ways of defining the variance of a sample, which we shall call *sample variance* for short. The first type of definition is

(1) $$\frac{1}{n} \sum^{n} (x_i - \bar{x})^2$$

and is used by a number of well-known statisticians.*
The second type of definition is

(2) $$s^2 = \frac{1}{n-1} \sum (x_i - \bar{x})^2 \qquad n > 1$$
$$= 0 \qquad n = 1$$

and is recently becoming the more widely used definition.† We shall use

*For example, H. Cramer, (1951) *Mathematical Methods of Statistics*. Princeton, N.J.: Princeton University Press. E. Deming, (1950). *Some Theory of Sampling*. New York: John Wiley & Sons, Inc. R. Schlaifer, (1961). *Introduction to Statistics for Business Decisions*. New York: McGraw-Hill Book Company.

†For example: Wilks, S. *Mathematical Statistics*. (1963) New York: John Wiley & Sons, Inc., 1962. Cochran, W.G. *Sampling Techniques*. New York: John Wiley & Sons, Inc.

this definition. The main reason for using this second type is that it is, as we shall see, an unbiased estimator of the population variance, and it will be the estimator we shall be using for all of our practical applications.

(ii) Unbiased estimator of the population variance.

As shown in the reference, this s^2 is an unbiased estimator of S^2 (and σ^2). That is,

(3) $\qquad E(s^2) = \sigma^2 \qquad$ when sampling with replacement

(4) $\qquad E(s^2) = S^2 \qquad$ when sampling without replacement

Since sampling is usually without replacement in practical applications, it will be the second case that will be of main interest to us. However, when N is large, $N - 1 \doteq N$ and hence $S^2 \doteq \sigma^2$ and the S^2 and σ^2 may be considered approximately equal. Let us illustrate the meanings of equations (3) and (4) with examples.

Example 1. Suppose we have a population of $N = 3$ students who have the following amounts of money: \$2, \$3, and \$4. Then the population variance is

$$\sigma^2 = \frac{1}{N} \sum^N (X_i - \bar{X})^2 = \frac{2}{3}$$

Let us next enumerate all possible samples of $n = 2$ (when sampling is *with* replacement) and find the sample variance s^2 of each of these samples.

Sample	$\bar{x}$	$s^2 = \dfrac{1}{n-1} \sum\limits^{n} (x_i - \bar{x})^2$
\$2, 2	2.0	0.0
2, 3	2.5	0.5
2, 4	3.0	2.0
3, 2	2.5	0.5
3, 3	3.0	0.0
3, 4	3.5	0.5
4, 2	3.0	2.0
4, 3	3.5	0.5
4, 4	4.0	0.0
		6.0

$$E(s^2) = \frac{0.0 + 0.5 + \cdots + 0.5 + 0.0}{9} = \frac{6}{9} = \frac{2}{3}$$

Hence $E(s^2) = \sigma^2 = 2/3$, and s^2 is an unbiased estimator of σ^2 when sampling is with replacement.

Example 2. When sampling is *without* replacement, the population variance is defined as

$$S^2 = \frac{1}{N-1} \sum^N (X_i - \bar{X})^2 = 1$$

Let us next enumerate all possible samples and then find the s^2 for the samples.

Sample	$\bar{x}$	$s^2 = \dfrac{1}{n-1} \sum\limits^{n} (x_i - \bar{x})^2$
2, 3	2.5	0.5
2, 4	3.0	2.0
3, 4	3.5	0.5
		3.0

Hence

$$E(s^2) = \frac{0.5 + 2.0 + 0.5}{3} = \frac{3.0}{3} = 1$$

That is, when sampling is without replacement,

$$E(s^2) = S^2 = 1$$

and s^2 is an unbiased estimator of S^2.

The square root of s^2:

$$s = \sqrt{\frac{1}{n-1} \sum (x_i - \bar{x})^2}$$

is defined as the *sample standard deviation*. This is not an unbiased estimator of S. However, when n is large ($n > 30$), the bias is small, and s may be used as an estimator of S.

As mentioned above, when S^2 is unknown we shall use the sample variance s^2 as its estimator. However, when s^2 is used instead of S^2, we cannot always use the normal distribution to test hypotheses or construct confidence intervals. For example, when tests concerning the sample mean and population mean were performed in elementary statistics, we constructed the statistic

$$z = \frac{\bar{x} - \bar{X}}{\sigma_{\bar{x}}} = \frac{\bar{x} - \bar{X}}{\sigma / \sqrt{n}}$$

and found z to have a normal distribution with mean 0 and variance unity. The normal area table was used to calculate the probabilities.

However, when s^2 is used as an estimator of S^2, the statistic z becomes

$$z = \frac{\bar{x} - \bar{X}}{s / \sqrt{n}}$$

This z no longer has a normal distribution, and the normal area table cannot be used to calculate probabilities. But, as we know, this z will have a t distribution, and the t table may be used to calculate probabilities.

But it is also known that as the sample size n becomes larger, the t distribution will approach a normal distribution. Therefore, when n is large, the normal area table may be used as an approximation of the t table. In most sampling survey problems, the sample sizes are large enough so that the normal distribution may be used to calculate the probabilities even when we are using the estimator s^2 instead of S^2.

However, when the distribution of the population is extremely skewed, the normal approximation may not be good. In such cases, we may stratify the population to avoid the affects of skewness. These sampling procedures will be discussed in Chapter 6, Stratified Random Sampling.

Reference

Let us show that

$$E(s^2) = \sigma^2 \qquad \text{when sampling with replacement}$$
$$E(s^2) = S^2 \qquad \text{when sampling without replacement}$$

The definition of s^2 may be rewritten as

$$s^2 = \frac{1}{n-1} \sum_{}^{n} (x_i - \bar{x})^2$$
$$= \frac{1}{n-1} \left[\sum (x_i - \bar{X})^2 - n(\bar{x} - \bar{X})^2 \right]$$

Taking the expectation on both sides, we find,

(6) $$E(s^2) = \frac{1}{n-1} [E\{\sum (x_i - \bar{X})^2\} - E\{n(\bar{x} - \bar{X})^2\}]$$

The first term in the brackets on the right side becomes

$$E\left[\sum^{n} (x_i - \bar{X})^2 \right] = \sum^{n} [E(x_i - \bar{X})^2]$$
$$= \sum^{n} \sum^{N} \frac{1}{N} (x_i - \bar{X})^2$$
$$= \frac{1}{N} \cdot n(N-1)S^2$$

(7) $$= \frac{n(N-1)}{N} S^2$$

When sampling is *with* replacement, the second term becomes

$$E[n(\bar{x} - \bar{X})^2] = nE(\bar{x} - \bar{X})^2$$

(8) $$= n \frac{\sigma^2}{n} = \sigma^2$$

When sampling is *without* replacement, the second term becomes

$$E[n(\bar{x} - \bar{X})^2] = nE(\bar{x} - \bar{X})^2$$

(9) $$= n \cdot \frac{N-n}{N} \frac{S^2}{n} = \frac{N-n}{N} S^2$$

From (6), (7), and (8), we get

$$E(s^2) = \frac{1}{n-1} \left\{ \frac{n(N-1)}{N} S^2 - \sigma^2 \right\}$$
$$= \sigma^2 \qquad \text{(with replacement)}$$

From (6), (7), and (9), we get

$$E(s^2) = \frac{1}{n-1}\left[\frac{n(N-1)}{N}S^2 - \frac{N-n}{N}S^2\right]$$

$$= S^2 \qquad \text{(without replacement)}$$

Problems

1. Using the following data, check the result that $E(s^2) = S^2$ when sampling *without* replacement. The population is \$1, 2, 3, 4, and \$5. The sample size is $n = 3$.

2. Using the data of Example 2 above, verify that $E(s^2) = \sigma^2$ for the case where sampling is *with* replacement.

3. Using the following data, check that $E(s^2) = S^2$ when sampling without replacement. The $N = 5$ values are 3, 5, 6, 7, and 9, and the sample size is $n = 3$.

(iii) Estimation of $\sigma_{\bar{x}}^2$.

Using s^2 we may now easily find an unbiased estimator of $\sigma_{\bar{x}}^2$. Substituting the s^2 for S^2 in the formulas we find

(10) $\qquad \hat{\sigma}_{\bar{x}}^2 = \dfrac{N-n}{N}\dfrac{s^2}{n} \qquad$ without replacement

$\qquad\qquad = \dfrac{N-1}{N}\dfrac{s^2}{n} \qquad$ with replacement

$\qquad\qquad \doteq \dfrac{s^2}{n} \qquad$ with replacement

Taking the expectation of the right hand side of equation (10), we find

$$E\left(\frac{N-n}{N}\frac{s^2}{n}\right) = \frac{N-n}{N}\frac{S^2}{n}$$

and $\hat{\sigma}_{\bar{x}}^2$ is hence an unbiased estimator of $\sigma_{\bar{x}}^2$. We shall also use the notation

(11) $\qquad s_{\bar{x}}^2 = \dfrac{N-n}{N}\dfrac{s^2}{n} \qquad$ without replacement

$\qquad\qquad \doteq \dfrac{s^2}{n} \qquad$ with replacement

Problems

1. Show that

$$s^2 = \frac{1}{n-1}\left[\sum^n x_i^2 - \frac{\left(\sum^n x_i\right)^2}{n}\right]$$

(which is the computational form normally used in practice.)

2. Given the population:

$$X_1 = 1, \quad X_2 = 1, \quad X_3 = 3, \quad X_4 = 4, \quad X_5 = 6$$

Suppose the following sample has been selected:

$$x_1 = 1, \qquad x_2 = 1, \qquad x_3 = 4$$

    (i) calculate S^2
    (ii) calculate $\sigma_{\bar{x}}^2$
    (iii) calculate s^2
    (iv) calculate $s_{\bar{x}}^2$

5.6 Confidence interval

Having found the estimator $s_{\bar{x}}^2$, we may now find the confidence interval for $\bar{X}$ from the sample. This is

$$\bar{x} - zs_{\bar{x}} < \bar{X} < \bar{x} + zs_{\bar{x}}$$

As discussed in Chapter 4, we shall set $z = 2$ for the 95% level of reliability and $z = 3$ for the "practically certain" level of reliability.

Example 1. A random sample of $n = 100$ is selected to estimate the average I.Q. of a large group of students. The sample mean is found to be $\bar{x} = 110$, and the $s = 12$ points. Find the confidence interval for $\bar{X}$ where the level of reliability is to be "practically certain."

$$\bar{x} - zs_{\bar{x}} < \bar{X} < \bar{x} + zs_{\bar{x}}$$

$$\bar{x} = 110, \quad z = 3$$

$$s_{\bar{x}} = \frac{s}{\sqrt{n}} = \frac{12}{\sqrt{100}} = 1.2$$

$$106.4 < \bar{X} < 113.6$$

Problems

1. A random sample of $n = 400$ students is selected from a population of $N = 4000$ students to estimate the average weight of the students. The sample mean and sample variance are found to be $\bar{x} = 140$ lb and $s^2 = 225$. Find the 95% ($z = 2$) confidence interval.

5.7 Sample size and precision

So far we have found $\bar{x}$ as an unbiased estimator of $\bar{X}$; $s_{\bar{x}}^2$ as an unbiased estimator of $\sigma_{\bar{x}}^2$; and (using these results) we have found the confidence interval for $\bar{X}$. Our final problem is to determine the sample size n for a given reliability.

We have already discussed this problem in Chapter 4 in connection with our discussion of precision, so it will be reviewed here only briefly. Recall that the basic relationship between precision, reliability, and standard error was given by

$$d^2 = z^2 \sigma_{\bar{x}}^2$$

We have found that $s_{\bar{x}}^2$ is the estimator of $\sigma_{\bar{x}}^2$, hence this relation becomes, for sampling with replacement,

(1) $$d^2 = z s_{\bar{x}}^2 = z^2 \frac{s^2}{n}$$

from which we find

(2) $$n = \frac{(zs)^2}{d^2}$$

When sampling is without replacement, the fpc is required and the relation becomes

(3) $$d^2 = z^2 \frac{s^2}{n} \frac{N-n}{N}$$

which leads to

(4) $$n = \frac{N(zs)^2}{Nd^2 + (zs)^2}$$

As an example, suppose there is a very large number of hogs, and the variance is estimated to be $s^2 = 600$. We wish to estimate the average weight of a hog within ± 5 lb with practical certainty, that is, $z = 3$. How large a sample is needed? From (2), we find

$$n = \frac{9 \times 600}{25} = 216$$

Hence the confidence interval is

$$\bar{x} - z \frac{s}{\sqrt{n}} < \bar{X} < \bar{x} + z \frac{s}{\sqrt{n}}$$

where

$$z \frac{s}{\sqrt{n}} = (3) \frac{\sqrt{600}}{\sqrt{216}} = \sqrt{25} = 5$$

and the average weight of the hogs will be within ± 5 lb of $\bar{X}$ with practical certainty.

Suppose the total number of hogs is $N = 2000$. Then, using the fpc, the required sample size becomes

$$n = \frac{2000 \times 9 \times 600}{(2000 \times 25) + (9 \times 600)} = 195$$

If $N = 20,000$, then $n = 214$.

Summarizing our calculations, we find

$$\text{if } N = 2000 \quad \text{then} \quad n = 195$$

$$\text{if } N = 20{,}000 \quad \text{then} \quad n = 214$$

$$\text{if } N \text{ is infinity} \quad \text{then} \quad n = 216$$

Note that the size of the population has very little effect on the sample size. Or, in more concrete terms; the size of the sample that needs to be selected from a town of $N = 20{,}000$ is approximately equal to the sample that needs to be selected from the whole U.S.A. for a given precision and reliability.

This result may be stated in terms of population size and precision. The sampling variance $\sigma_{\bar{x}}^2$ is given by

$$\sigma_{\bar{x}}^2 = \frac{N - n}{N} \frac{S^2}{n}$$

This shows that when N is very large, $(N - n)/N$ is close to 1 and has very little effect on $\sigma_{\bar{x}}^2$. It is the size of the sample n that affects $\sigma_{\bar{x}}^2$ most. That is, the size of the sample has most effect on the precision of the estimator while the size of the population has very little effect when N is large.

The astute reader may have noted that the sample variance s^2 was assumed to be $s^2 = 600$, and that by using this in equation (1), we found the required sample size n. How then, the reader may ask, was s^2 found, and from what sample was s^2 calculated?

In many cases, a provisional sample is selected to calculate a provisional s^2. Suppose a provisional sample of size $n = 100$ is selected, and $s^2 = 600$ is obtained. As we have seen, the sample size we calculated using $s^2 = 600$ was 216. We may select $(216 - 100 =)116$ more hogs, and using this new sample of $(100 + 116 =) 216$ hogs, recalculate s^2 and check $s^2 = 600$. If the s^2 calculated from $n = 216$ students is significantly different from $s^2 = 600$, a new n may be calculated, and the process may be repeated until a stable value of s^2 is obtained.

Problems

1. Suppose a sample of families is to be selected without replacement to estimate their average weekly expenditures on food. The precision is to be within $\pm\$4$ with practical certainty. Assume the $s = \$12$ is known from past surveys and the total number of families is $N = 2000$. How large must the sample be?

2. Let n_0 be the sample size when sampling is *with* replacement and n be the sample size when sampling *without* replacement. Using formulas (2) and (4), show that

$$n = \frac{n_0}{1 + n_0/N}$$

3. Using the data of Problem 1, find n_0. Then calculate n, using the results of Problem 2, and verify that it is equal to the result of Problem 1.

4. Problems 2 and 3 suggest that one may calculate n_0 first, when sampling without replacement, and check n_0/N before calculating n. If n_0/N is very small, the difference between n and n_0 may be negligible. Suppose that in Problem 1, there are 10,000 families. Find n_0, then find n_0/N, and decide whether to calculate n. Actually calculate n and compare it with n_0.

5. Suppose there is a district with $N = 500$ farms, and we wish to estimate the average number of cows per farm. A preliminary random sample of $n = 30$ farms is selected with the following results.

$$
\begin{array}{ccccc}
23, 14, 38, 11, \ 7 & 31, \ 9, 16, 12, 25 \\
11, 15, 36, 24, 10 & 16, 26, 12, 25, 28 \\
34, 25, 11, \ 7, \ 9 & 33, 25, \ 9, \ 4, 19
\end{array}
$$

(a) Calculate $\bar{x}$.
(b) Calculate s and $s_{\bar{x}}$.
(c) Using s, calculate the sample size necessary for the precision to be within ± 4 cows with practical certainty ($z = 3$).

5.8 Estimator of the total X

A second parameter that is often the object of estimation is the total of a population. For example, we may wish to estimate the total amount of wheat produced in a certain region, the total number of apples in an orchard, the total amount of coffee consumed in a certain city, etc. In this chapter, we shall consider the problem of estimating the total by simple random sampling.

The basic idea is to use the relation

$$\text{total} = (\text{number of items}) \times (\text{average})$$
$$= N\bar{X}$$

and use the estimator of the average $\bar{X}$ to estimate the total.

We shall denote the population total by X and the estimator of the total by $\hat{X}$. The sample total is denoted by x.

(i) Estimator of the total.

To find the total number of books owned by a group of $N = 1000$ students we may (by using common sense) select a random sample of $n = 50$ students, find the average number of books a student has (say, 12 books per student), and multiply this by $N = 1000$. The estimated total number of books is therefore

(1) $$\hat{X} = N\bar{x} = 1000 \times 12 = 12,000 \text{ books}$$

(1) turns out to be an unbiased estimator of X. This is easily seen from

$$E(\hat{X}) = E(N\bar{x}) = NE(\bar{x}) = N\bar{X} = X$$

We shall use (1) as an estimator of the total X.

(ii) The variance of $\hat{X}$.

Having found the estimator $\hat{X}$, our next task is to find the variance of $\hat{X}$ which will be used to evaluate the precision of $\hat{X}$. The variance of $\hat{X}$ is easily found as follows. By definition

$$(2) \qquad V(\hat{X}) = E(\hat{X} - X)^2 = E(N\bar{x} - N\bar{X})^2$$
$$= N^2 E(\bar{x} - \bar{X})^2$$
$$= N^2 \frac{S^2}{n} \frac{N - n}{N} \qquad \text{without replacement}$$
$$\doteq N \frac{S^2}{n} \qquad \text{with replacement, } (N - 1)/N \doteq 1$$

We have used equations (5) and (6) of section 5.4 to evaluate $E(\bar{x} - \bar{X})^2$.

Since S^2 is usually unknown, its estimator (the sample variance s^2) is used. This gives us

$$(3) \qquad \hat{V}(\hat{X}) = N^2 \frac{s^2}{n} \frac{N - n}{N} \qquad \text{without replacement}$$
$$\doteq N^2 \frac{s^2}{n} \qquad \text{with replacement, } (N - 1)/N \doteq 1$$

which are unbiased estimators of the $V(\hat{X})$. That is,

$$E[\hat{V}(\hat{X})] = V(\hat{X})$$

This is easily obtained by taking the expectation on both sides of equations (3).

As an illustration, suppose the sample variance of the distribution of books of the $n = 50$ students in the above illustration is $s^2 = 10$. Then, since $N = 1000$, the estimate of the sampling variance of $\hat{X}$ is

$$\hat{V}(\hat{X}) = N^2 \frac{s^2}{n} \frac{N - n}{N}$$
$$= (1000)^2 \frac{10}{50} \frac{1000 - 50}{1000} = 190,000$$

Let us denote $\hat{V}(\hat{X})$ by

$$s_{\hat{x}}^2 = \hat{V}(\hat{X}) = 190,000$$

Hence, the standard error of $\hat{X}$ is $s_{\hat{x}} = 436$ books.

(iii) Confidence interval.

Having found $s_{\hat{x}}$, the confidence interval for the total X becomes

$$(4) \qquad \hat{X} - z s_{\hat{x}} < X < \hat{X} + z s_{\hat{x}}$$

where z is the reliability coefficient.

Example 1. Suppose we wish to estimate the total amount of milk consumed by students of a certain high school each day. There are $N = 2000$ students. A random sample of $n = 100$ students is selected, and the sample average of milk consumption is found to be $\bar{x} = 0.8$ quarts. Hence, the estimate we seek is

$$\hat{X} = N\bar{x} = (2000)(0.8) = 1600 \text{ quarts.}$$

Let $s = 0.3$ quarts be the sample standard deviation. The estimate of the variance of $\hat{X}$ is

$$\hat{V}(\hat{X}) = N^2 \frac{s^2}{n} \frac{N - n}{N}$$

$$= (2000)^2 \cdot \frac{(0.3)^2}{100} \cdot \frac{200 - 100}{2000} = 3420$$

and the estimated standard error of X is

$$s_{\hat{x}} = \sqrt{3420} = 58.5 \text{ quarts.}$$

Hence, the $z = 3$ confidence interval for $\hat{X}$ is

$$1600 - (3)(58.5) < X < 1600 + (3)(58.5)$$

$$1424.5 < X < 1775.5$$

(iv) *The sample size and precision of $\hat{X}$.*

The determination of the sample size for estimating X is similar to that for $\bar{X}$. The basic relationship between precision, reliability, and standard error is

(5) $$d^2 = z^2 s_{\hat{x}}^2$$

where $d = \hat{X} - X$. From equation (3), we find

(6) $$\qquad s_{\hat{x}}^2 = N^2 \frac{s^2}{n} \frac{N - n}{N} \qquad \text{without replacement}$$

(6') $$\qquad = N^2 \frac{s^2}{n} \qquad\qquad \text{with replacement}$$

Substituting equations (6) and (6') into (5) and solving for n,

(7) $$\qquad n = \frac{N^2(zs)^2}{d^2 + N(zs)^2} \qquad \text{without replacement}$$

(7') $$\qquad n_0 = \frac{N^2(zs)^2}{d^2} \qquad\qquad \text{with replacement}$$

And from (7) and (7'), we find

(7'') $$n = \frac{n_0}{1 + n_0/N}$$

Example 2. Suppose that in Example 1 above we wish the error to be within ± 100 quarts, with a reliability of $z = 3$. How large a sample must we select? Using equations (7') and (7''), we find

$$n_0 = \frac{N^2(zs)^2}{d^2} = (2000)^2 \frac{(3 \times 0.3)^2}{(100)^2} = 324$$

$$\frac{n_0}{N} = \frac{324}{2000} = 0.164$$

$$\therefore \quad n = \frac{324}{1 + 0.164} = 279$$

When the precision is stated in *relative terms*, the relationship was

(8) $$d_0^2 = z^2 C_{\hat{X}}^2$$

where

$$d_0 = \frac{\hat{X} - X}{X}$$

Recall that C and $C(\hat{X})$—which we shall also express as $C_{\hat{x}}$ in some cases—in our previous discussion were expressed in terms of σ^2. Let us now express them in terms of S^2 because we wish to use the estimator s^2. We find

$$C_{\hat{X}}^2 = \frac{V(\hat{X})}{X^2} = \frac{N^2}{X^2} \frac{S^2}{n} \frac{N-n}{N}$$

$$= \frac{1}{\bar{X}^2} \frac{S^2}{n} \frac{N-n}{N}$$

(9) $$= \frac{C^2}{n} \frac{N-n}{N} \qquad \text{without replacement}$$

(9') $$\doteq \frac{C^2}{n} \qquad \text{with replacement}$$

where we have set $C^2 = S^2/\bar{X}^2$ instead of $C^2 = \sigma^2/\bar{X}^2$. The relation between these two quantities is (since $(N-1)S^2 = N\sigma^2$):

$$C^2 = \frac{\sigma^2}{\bar{X}^2} = \frac{S^2}{\bar{X}^2} \frac{N-1}{N}$$

Hence, when N is large (as is usually the case in sample surveys) we may set $(N-1)/N \doteq 1$ and obtain

$$C^2 = \frac{\sigma^2}{\bar{X}^2} \doteq \frac{S^2}{\bar{X}^2}$$

which is what we have used in (9) and (9').

Substituting (9) and (9') into (8) and solving for n, we find

(10) $$n = \frac{N(zC)^2}{Nd_0^2 + (zC)^2} \qquad \text{without replacement}$$

(10') $$n_0 = \frac{(zC)^2}{d_0^2} \qquad \text{with replacement}$$

And from (10) and (10'), we get

(10'') $$n = \frac{n_0}{1 + n_0/N}$$

In practical applications, the estimators of C and $C(\hat{X})$ are obtained by replacing S^2 by its sample estimator, s^2.

Example 3. Suppose there are $N = 2000$ students, and a sample of $n = 100$ students is selected. Their weights are investigated and found to be $\bar{x} = 150$ lb and $s = 15$ lb. Find estimates of C, $C_{\hat{x}}$, $C_{\bar{x}}$. Let fpc $= 1$ for simplicity.

$$\hat{C}^2 = \frac{s^2}{\bar{x}^2} = \frac{15^2}{150^2} = 0.01 \qquad \hat{C} = c = 0.1$$

$$\hat{C}_{\hat{x}}^2 = \hat{C}_{\bar{x}}^2 = \frac{\hat{C}^2}{n} = \frac{0.01}{100} = 0.0001$$

$$\hat{C}_{\hat{x}} = \hat{C}_{\bar{x}} = 0.01$$

Thus, $\hat{C} = 0.1$ shows a magnitude of 1 standard deviation in relative terms. If weights are distributed normally, then $\hat{C} = 0.1$ means that approximately 68% of the weights will be within $\pm 10\%$ of the average weight, $\bar{X}$. If $\hat{C} = 0.12$, it means that approximately 68% of the weights will be within $\pm 12\%$ of the average weight, $\bar{X}$, and $\hat{C}_{\hat{x}} = 0.01$ ($\hat{C}_{\bar{x}} = 0.01$) shows that approximately 68% of the estimated totals ($\hat{X}$) (estimated means $\bar{x}$) will be within $\pm 1\%$ of the total X(mean $\bar{X}$).

Example 4. Suppose we wish to estimate the total amount of milk consumed by students at a certain high school in a day. We wish the relative error to be within $\pm 5\%$ of the total. A preliminary survey shows that $\hat{C} = 1/3$. We shall also assume there are $N = 2000$ students, and, we require a level of reliability of $z = 3$.

From equation (10), we get

$$n = \frac{N(zC)^2}{Nd_0^2 + (zC)^2}$$

$$= \frac{2000(3 \times 1/3)^2}{2000(0.05)^2 + (3 \times 1/3)^2} = 333.3$$

Hence, the sample size is $n = 333$.

After selecting a sample of $n = 333$, suppose it is found that $\bar{x} = 0.9$ quarts, and $s = 0.3$ quarts. Then

$$\hat{C} = \frac{s}{\bar{x}} = \frac{0.3}{0.9} = \frac{1}{3}$$

and is equal to the results of the preliminary survey. We shall therefore use $n = 333$ as the sample size and $\bar{x} = 0.9$ quarts as the estimate of $\bar{X}$.

Thus, the estimate for the total is

$$\hat{X} = N\bar{x} = (2000)(0.9) = 1800 \text{ quarts.}$$

To find the 3σ confidence interval for X, let us first find the estimate of the variance of X. From equation (3), we get

$$\hat{V}(\hat{X}) = N^2 \cdot \frac{s^2}{n} \cdot \frac{N-n}{N}$$

$$= (2000)^2 \frac{(0.3)^2}{333} \cdot \frac{2000 - 333}{2000} = 900$$

Hence, the standard error of $\hat{X}$ is $\sqrt{900} = 30$ quarts, and the 3σ confidence interval becomes

$$1800 - (3)(30) < X < 1800 + (3)(30)$$

$$1710 < X < 1890$$

Example 5. Suppose there are 5000 families in a certain city, and we wish to estimate the average number of eggs consumed per week by a family. We wish the precision to be 5% of the mean. A preliminary survey of $n = 200$ families show that $s = 12$ eggs and $\bar{x} = 36$ eggs. Therefore, an estimate of the coefficient of variation is $\hat{C} = 12/36 = 1/3$.

Using this preliminary estimate and assuming a reliability of $z = 3$, we find the sample size to be:

$$n = \frac{5000(3 \times 1/3)^2}{5000(0.05)^2 + (3 \times 1/3)^2} = 370.4$$

Thus, an additional $(370 - 200) = 170$ families are selected, and s and $\bar{x}$ are recalculated. Suppose we get $s = 12$ eggs and $\bar{x} = 38$ eggs. We shall then use $\bar{x} = 38$ eggs as our estimate.

The 3σ confidence interval for $\bar{X}$ is

$$38 - (3)\left(\frac{12}{\sqrt{370}}\frac{5000 - 370}{5000}\right) < \bar{X} < 38 + (3)\left(\frac{12}{\sqrt{370}}\frac{5000 - 370}{5000}\right)$$

$$36.3 < \bar{X} < 39.7$$

Problems

1. Suppose we have a hypothetical population of $N = 50$. A random sample of size $n = 10$ is selected without replacement with the following results.

$$12, \quad 10, \quad 4, \quad 8, \quad 7, \quad 11, \quad 5, \quad 9, \quad 10, \quad 7$$

(a) Calculate $\bar{x}$
(b) Estimate X
(c) Prove algebraically that $\sum_{i}^{n} (X_i - \bar{X})^2 = \sum X_i^2 - (\sum X_i)^2/n$
(d) Calculate s^2 using the result of (c)
(e) Calculate $\hat{V}(\hat{X})$
(f) Calculate the 3σ confidence interval for X.

2. Suppose we wish to estimate the total number of cigarettes students smoke at a certain college. There are $N = 1500$ students. A random sample of $n = 100$ students is selected without replacement and the sample average of cigarette consumption is found to be $\bar{x} = 8$ cigarettes a day per student and $s = 3$ cigarettes. Estimate X and also find the 3σ confidence interval.

3. Suppose we wish to estimate the total number of cigarettes that $N = 1500$ students in a certain college smoke. The precision is to be within ± 500 cigarettes with reliability $z = 2$. A preliminary survey has provided that $s = 3$ cigarettes. How large must the sample be? Assume sampling is without replacement.

4. Carry out the algebra for deriving equations (10) and (10').

5. Suppose we wish to estimate the total number of cigarettes smoked by $N = 1500$ students in a day. We wish the precision to be within $\pm 10\%$ of the total. A preliminary survey shows that $C = 1/3$. How large a sample must be selected without replacement if we require a reliability of $z = 3$?

6. Suppose there is a city with $N = 800$ blocks and we wish to estimate the total number of cars parked on the streets during the night. A random sample of $n = 30$ blocks is selected and the number of cars on the blocks were found to be as follows.

$$8, 9, 4, 2, 6 \qquad 6, 3, 0, 8, 4$$
$$3, 6, 4, 2, 3 \qquad 3, 9, 3, 0, 1$$
$$4, 2, 3, 6, 1 \qquad 7, 5, 2, 5, 2$$

(a) Estimate the total number of cars, X.
(b) Calculate s.
(c) Calculate $\hat{V}(\hat{X})$ and $s(\hat{X})$.
(d) Using s of (b), how large a sample is necessary to estimate the total with a precision of within ± 400 cars with 95% ($z = 2$) reliability?

7. Suppose apples are gathered in baskets and 4000 baskets are gathered in 4 days. A random sample of $n = 50$ baskets has shown that the average per basket is $\bar{x} = 44$ apples with $s = 5$ apples.
(a) Estimate X and $S_{\hat{X}}$
(b) Using $s = 5$, estimate the sample size necessary for the precision of the estimator $\hat{X}$ to be within ± 4000 apples with a reliability of 95% ($z = 2$).

5.9 Estimation of the population proportion P

The third population parameter for which we shall find an estimator is the population proportion P. It is a much sought after parameter in market research, public opinion surveys, and quality control. For example, a tooth paste producer, cigarette company, soap company, watch company, etc., may wish to estimate its share of the market. An opinion research company, local government, or a school board may wish to estimate the proportion of people in favor of a certain proposal. A manufacturer of electrical equipment, producer of consumer goods, or purchaser of automobile parts may wish to estimate the proportion of defective items.

As we shall see, the estimator of P will be the sample proportion p, and the various discussions concerning the estimation of p and its variance will parallel that of the sample mean. Let us start our discussion by defining the population proportion p.

(i) *Population proportion P.*

A proportion may be considered to be a special case of the mean where the variable X_i takes on only the values 0 and 1. For example, suppose we wish to find the proportion of people using brand K soap. Let there be N people, and let $X_i = 0$ when a person is not using the soap, and $X_i = 1$ when he is using the soap. Then

$$\sum_{i}^{N} X_i = X_1 + X_2 + \cdots + X_N$$

will be the number of people using soap K and

(1)
$$P = \frac{\sum\limits_{}^{N} X_i}{N}$$

will be the proportion of people using soap K. The point to note is that equation (1) is the same as that for the population mean, except that the variable X_i takes on only the values 0 and 1.

As an example, suppose $N = 5$ and that the second, third and fifth persons use soap K. Then

$$X_1 = 0,\ X_2 = 1,\ X_3 = 1,\ X_4 = 0,\ X_5 = 1$$

$$\sum\limits_{}^{N} X_i = 0 + 1 + 1 + 0 + 1 = 3$$

and

$$P = \frac{\sum\limits_{}^{N} X_i}{N} = \frac{3}{5} = 0.6$$

Because the proportion may be treated as a special case of the mean, the discussion concerning expected values, variances, and other characteristics of the proportion will be similar to discussions concerning the mean.

(ii) The sample proportion p is an unbiased estimator of P

Let $x_1, x_2, \ldots x_n$ be a random sample of size n taken from a population of size N. The sample proportion is therefore defined as

(2)
$$p = \frac{\sum\limits_{}^{n} x_i}{n}$$

where $x_i = 1$ or 0. This expression is an unbiased estimator of the population proportion P. To show that p is an unbiased estimator of P, take the expectation on both sides of equation (2).

$$E(p) = \frac{1}{n} E(\sum\limits_{}^{n} x_i)$$

$$= \frac{1}{n} \sum\limits_{}^{n} E(x_i)$$

$$= \frac{1}{n} \cdot n \cdot \sum\limits_{}^{N} \frac{1}{N} \cdot x_i = P$$

hence, p is an unbiased estimator of P, and this may be expressed as $\hat{P} = p$

Example 1. Suppose there are $N = 1000$ students, and a random sample of $n = 50$ students is selected, and 20 of these students are found to smoke. Estimate the proportion of students who smoke. We find

$$\hat{P} = p = \frac{20}{50} = 0.40$$

Example 2. Suppose there are $N = 5$ students, and 3 of them smoke. Let this be shown by $X_1 = 1$, $X_2 = 1$, $X_3 = 1$, $X_4 = 0$, $X_5 = 0$. Let us select random samples of $n = 2$ without replacement. There are $\binom{5}{2} = 10$ possible samples listed in the table below.

		$\sum x_i$	$p = \sum x_i/n$
AB	1, 1	2	1
AC	1, 1	2	1
AD	1, 0	1	0.5
AE	1, 0	1	0.5
BC	1, 1	2	1
BD	1, 0	1	0.5
BE	1, 0	1	0.5
CD	1, 0	1	0.5
CE	1, 0	1	0.5
DE	0, 0	0	0
			6

The expected value of p is

$$E(p) = \sum p \cdot Pr(p) = 6 \cdot \frac{1}{10} = \frac{3}{5}$$

The population proportion is $P = 3/5$, and $E(p) = P$. We have thus shown p to be an unbiased estimator of P.

Problem

Show that $E(p) = P$ when sampling with replacement, using the data of Example 2.

(iii) Variance of X_i for the population.

Our next task is to find the variance of p so that we may assess the precision and reliability of the estimator p. We shall use the characteristic that the variable X_i takes on only the values 1 or 0, and we shall first define the population variance of X_i and the sample variance of X_i. Then, using these variances of X_i, we shall define the variance of the sample proportion p. Note that the population proportion, P, is a parameter and not a statistic, and P therefore has no variance.

Suppose there is a group of N people, and A of them smoke. The N people may be shown by $X_1, X_2, \ldots, X_N$, where we let $X_i = 1$ for a smoker and $X_i = 0$ for a nonsmoker. Then,

$$\sum_{i}^{N} X_i = A$$

and the population proportion P is $P = A/N$. The variance of X_i is by definition

$$S^2 = \frac{1}{N-1} \sum_{i}^{N} (X_i - \bar{X})^2 = \frac{1}{N-1} [\sum_{i}^{N} X_i^2 - N\bar{X}^2]$$

But since $X_i = 1$ or 0,

$$\sum_{i}^{N} X_i^2 = A = NP$$
$$\bar{X}^2 = P^2$$

Hence the variance S^2 becomes

(3) $$S^2 = \frac{1}{N-1} (NP - NP^2) = \frac{N}{N-1} PQ$$

where $Q = 1 - P$. Note carefully that S^2 is the variance of X_i, and not P.

As an example, suppose there are $N = 100$ students, and let them be shown by $X_1, X_2, \ldots, X_{100}$ where $X_i = 1$ for a smoker and $X_i = 0$ for a non-smoker. Suppose $A = 60$ smoke. Then, $P = .6$ and the variance of X_i is

$$V(X_i) = S^2 = \frac{100}{100-1} (.6)(.4) = 0.24$$

This result shows the dispersion of the $X_i = 1$'s in the distribution.

(iv) *Variance of x_i for the sample—the sample variance.*

Given a sample of n students where a of them smoke, the sample proportion p of smokers is given by $p = a/n$. This sample may be shown by $x_1, x_2, \ldots, x_n$, where $x_i = 1$ for smokers and $x_i = 0$ for nonsmokers. Then

$$\sum_{i}^{n} x_i = a$$

The sample variance of x_i is defined as

$$s^2 = \frac{1}{n-1} \sum_{i}^{n} (x_i - \bar{x})^2 = \frac{1}{n-1} (\sum_{i}^{n} x_i^2 - n\bar{x}^2)$$

But since $x_i = 1$ or 0,

$$\sum_{i}^{n} x_i^2 = a = np$$
$$\bar{x}^2 = p^2$$

Therefore, the sample variance s^2 becomes

(4) $$s^2 = \frac{1}{n-1} (np - np^2) = \frac{n}{n-1} pq$$

where $q = 1 - p$. Once again, note that s^2 is the variance of x_i of the sample, and not the variance of p.

As an example, suppose $n = 50$ students are selected from the $N = 100$ students, and $a = 25$ are found to smoke. Then, $p = 25/50 = 0.5$. Thus, the sample variance s^2 becomes

$$s^2 = \frac{50}{50-1} (0.5)(0.5) = 0.25$$

(v) *Variance of the sample proportion p.*

Using the definition of the variance of X_i, we may now define the variance of the sample proportion p. By definition

$$V(p) = E(p - Ep)^2 = E(p - P)^2$$

We have seen that

(5) $\qquad V(\bar{x}) = E(\bar{x} - \bar{X})^2 = \dfrac{S^2}{n} \dfrac{N - n}{N}$ $\qquad$ without replacement

$$= \dfrac{S^2}{n} \qquad \text{with replacement}$$

We have also seen that by letting $X_i = 1$ or 0,

$$p = \frac{\sum\limits_{i}^{n} x_i}{n} = \bar{x}$$

$$P = \frac{\sum\limits_{i}^{N} X_i}{N} = \bar{X}$$

Hence, $V(p)$ is found by substituting $\bar{x} = p$ into (5), which becomes

(6) $\qquad V(p) = \dfrac{S^2}{n} \dfrac{N - n}{N}$ $\qquad$ without replacement

$$= \dfrac{S^2}{n} \qquad \text{with replacement}$$

where $x_i = 1$ or 0.

Substituting S^2 of equation (3) into (6), the $V(p)$ becomes

(7) $\qquad V(p) = \dfrac{N}{N - 1} PQ \dfrac{1}{n} \dfrac{N - n}{N}$

$$= \dfrac{PQ}{n} \dfrac{N - n}{N - 1} \qquad \text{without replacement}$$

$$= \dfrac{PQ}{n} \qquad \text{with replacement}$$

As an example, suppose a random sample of 50 students is selected from $N = 4000$ students. If the population proportion P of smokers is $P = 0.3$, the variance of the sample proportion (that is, the square of the standard error of p) becomes

$$V(p) = \frac{(0.3)(0.7)}{50} = 0.0042$$

That is, the variance is about 0.4%. It is the variance of the sampling distribution of the sample proportion p. We have assumed fpc $= 1$.

Therefore, in order to calculate the $V(p)$, we must know the population proportion P—which in practical applications is usually unknown. So let us next show how an unbiased estimate of $V(p)$ may be found from a sample.

(vi) Unbiased estimator of V(p).

We know from previous discussion of the sample mean $\bar{x}$ that s^2 is an unbiased estimator of S^2. In our present case, from equation (4), we have

$$s^2 = \frac{n}{n-1}pq$$

which is an unbiased estimator of

$$S^2 = \frac{N}{N-1}PQ$$

Hence, by substituting s^2 into equation (6), we get

(8) $\hat{V}(p) = \dfrac{pq}{n-1}\dfrac{N-n}{N}$ without replacement

                $= \dfrac{pq}{n-1}$ with replacement

and these are easily seen to be unbiased estimators of $V(p)$. Let us denote $\hat{V}(p)$ by s_p^2.

Example 3. Suppose there are $N = 5$ students:

$$\begin{array}{ccccc} A & B & C & D & E \\ 1 & 1 & 0 & 1 & 0 \end{array}$$

The 1 and 0 indicate whether the student is a smoker or a nonsmoker. The population proportion of smokers is

$$P = \frac{\sum\limits^{N} X}{N} = \frac{3}{5}$$

Let us select samples of size $n = 2$. The variance of the sample proportion p is

$$V(p) = \frac{PQ}{n}\frac{N-n}{N-1} = \frac{(3/5)(2/5)}{2}\frac{5-2}{5-1} = \frac{9}{100}$$

Let us next list all possible samples of $n = 2$, sampling without replacement. There are $\binom{5}{2} = 10$ possible samples.

Samples		$\sum X_i$	$p = \dfrac{\sum X}{n}$	pq
AB	1, 1	2	1	0
AC	1, 0	1	0.5	0.25
AD	1, 1	2	1	0
AE	1, 0	1	0.5	0.25
BC	1, 0	1	0.5	0.25
BD	1, 1	2	1	0
BE	1, 0	1	0.5	0.25
CD	0, 1	1	0.5	0.25
CE	0, 0	0	0	0
DE	1, 0	1	0.5	0.25

                                                                                                        1.50

The estimator of $V(p)$ was

$$\hat{V}(p) = \frac{pq}{n-1} \frac{N-n}{N}$$

The expected value of $V(p)$ is

$$E[\hat{V}(p)] = \frac{1}{n-1} \cdot \frac{N-n}{N} E(pq)$$

$$= \frac{1}{n-1} \frac{N-n}{N} (0 + 0.25 + \cdots + 0 + 0.25) \frac{1}{10}$$

$$= \frac{1}{2-1} \frac{5-2}{5} (1.5) \frac{1}{10} = \frac{9}{100}$$

Hence,

$$E[\hat{V}(p)] = V(p) = \frac{9}{100}$$

and $\hat{V}(p)$ is an unbiased estimator of $V(p)$.

Problem

Using the data of Example 3, select the samples with replacement and show that

$$E[\hat{V}(p)] = V(p)$$

where

$$V(p) = \frac{PQ}{n} \quad \text{and} \quad \hat{V}(p) = \frac{pq}{n-1}$$

(vii) *Confidence interval for p.*

Having found the standard error of p, we may easily construct a confidence interval for P. It is

$$p - zs_p < P < p + zs_p$$

When $z = 2$, we assigned a 95% level of reliability to this confidence interval. This, however, was based on the assumption that the statistic under consideration had a normal distribution. In our present case, we are assuming that the sampling distribution of p will be approximately normal. We have learned in elementary statistics that when n is large and p is neither small nor large, the sampling distribution of p will be approximately normal.

The question that naturally arises is : How large must the sample be in order that we might use the normal approximation? As we know, the sampling distribution of p becomes more skewed as p approaches 0 or 1. W.G. Cochran has presented working rules showing the necessary sample size in relation to p when the normal approximation may be used. This is shown in Table 5.1.

Table 5.1

If p equals	Use the normal approximation only if n is at least equal to
0.5	30
0.4 or 0.6	50
0.3 or 0.7	80
0.2 or 0.8	200
0.1 or 0.9	600
0.05 or 0.95	1400

Source: W.G. Cochran (1963). *Sampling Techniques*, 2nd ed. New York: John Wiley & Sons, Inc., p. 57. By permission of the author and publishers.

As an example, suppose a sample of $n = 100$ is selected from 20,000 students, and the proportion of students who chew gum is found to be $p = 0.3$. According to the table, the sample should be at least 80 to use the normal approximation. Since $n = 100$ in our present case, it satisfies the requirements. Hence, the 95% confidence interval will be

$$0.3 - 2\left(\sqrt{\frac{0.3 \times 0.7}{100 - 1}}\right) < P < 0.3 + 2\left(\sqrt{\frac{0.3 \times 0.7}{100 - 1}}\right)$$

$$0.2084 < P < 0.3916$$

In applications of market research and public opinion surveys, the sample is usually large, say, from 400 to 2000. To obtain T.V. ratings, a sample of about $n = 1500$ is selected from the U.S.A. To obtain an estimate of the market share of tooth paste, a sample of about $n = 2000$ is selected. Depending on the object of the survey and the budget, the sample sizes used vary considerably, but they usually tend to be large. Hence, in most cases, even though the sample proportion may be small (which is usually the case in estimating the proportion of market shares), we may use the normal approximation.

A simple graphic device for finding the confidence interval based on the theoretical distribution of the sampling distribution of the sample proportion has been devised by Clopper and Pearson (and is called the Clopper and Pearson chart). This is shown in Table 3 of the appendix. An explanation of the derivation of this chart may be found in the elementary texts.

Using this chart, we find for $n = 100$, $p = 0.30$, and for a confidence coefficient of 0.95, that the confidence interval is

$$0.21 < P < 0.39$$

In this case, we need not worry about the sample size (since the chart is based on the exact theoretical distribution of the sample proportion). For practical purposes, this is probably the easiest way to find the confidence interval for P.

As another example, suppose the sample size is increased to $n = 1000$. The 95% confidence interval from the graph will then be

$$0.27 < P < 0.33$$

The graph has samples up to $n = 1000$. For greater samples, we can usually use the normal approximation according to Table 5.1.

Example 4. The proportion of families owning 2 or more radios in a certain city is to be estimated. There are $N = 8,000$ families, a random sample of $n = 101$ families is selected, and we find that $p = 0.6$. Calculate the 3σ confidence interval for P.

$$s_p^2 = \frac{pq}{n-1} \frac{N-n}{N}$$

$$= \frac{(0.6)(0.4)}{101-1} \cdot \frac{8000-101}{8000} = 0.0023688$$

$$s_p = 0.0486$$

$$0.6 - (3)(0.0486) < P < 0.6 + (3)(0.0486)$$

$$0.464 < P < 0.7358$$

For $n = 400$, we get

$$0.53 < P < 0.67$$

For $n = 1000$, we get

$$0.56 < P < 0.65$$

Example 5. Suppose a sample of $n = 100$ families is selected from New York City, and $n = 60$ families are found to be in favor of a certain proposal. Find the 95% confidence interval using the Clopper and Pearson charts. We find from the charts that

$$0.50 < P < 0.70$$

Suppose $n = 400$ and $p = 0.60$. Then,

$$0.55 < P < 0.65$$

For $n = 1000$ and $p = 0.60$, we find

$$0.57 < P < 0.63$$

Example 6. Suppose $n = 2500$ and $p = 0.6$. Letting fpc $= 1$ and $n - 1 \doteq n$, we get

$$s_p = \sqrt{\frac{pq}{n}} = \sqrt{\frac{.6 \times .4}{2500}} = .0098$$

Hence, assuming the normal approximation, the 95% confidence interval will be

$$0.6 - 2(0.0098) < P < 0.6 + 2(0.0098)$$

$$0.58 < P < 0.62$$

Problems

1. Suppose we have a hypothetical population of $N = 6$ as follows:

$$X_1 = 0, \quad X_2 = 1, \quad X_3 = 1, \quad X_4 = 0, \quad X_5 = 1, \quad X_6 = 0$$

(a) Calculate S^2.

(b) Suppose the following sample $n = 4$ is selected: X_1, X_2, X_3, X_4, X_5. Calculate s^2.

(c) Calculate $\hat{V}(p)$ using the above data for sampling with and without replacement.

(d) Calculate $\hat{V}(p) = s_p^2$ using the above data, for sampling with and without replacement.

2. Calculate $E[\hat{V}(p)]$ for Problem 1 and verify that it is equal to $V(p)$.

3. Suppose a sample of $n = 900$ families is selected in a large city to estimate the proportion of families which have two or more telephones. The sample proportion is found to be $p = 0.4$. Find the 2σ confidence interval for P.

5.10 Sample size and precision concerning P

Just as we previously discussed sample size and precision concerning $\bar{X}$ and X, we shall now show how to determine sample size for a given precision when considering problems concerning P.

(*i*) *Formula for n.*

The basic relationship between the precision, reliability, and standard error was:

$$\text{precision} = (\text{reliability}) \times (\text{standard error})$$

When considering the precision of the estimator p for the population proportion P, we use

$$s_p^2 = \frac{pq}{n-1} \frac{N-n}{N}$$

as the standard error. For practical purposes, $n - 1$ may be replaced by n. The relationship is then shown as

(1) $d^2 = z^2 \dfrac{pq}{n} \dfrac{N-n}{N}$ without replacement

            $\doteq z^2 \dfrac{pq}{n}$ with replacement

The required sample size n for a given precision d and reliability z is obtained by solving (1) for n:

(2) $n = \dfrac{Nz^2 pq}{Nd^2 + z^2 pq}$ without replacement

            $= \dfrac{z^2 pq}{d^2}$ with replacement

Example 1. A preliminary random sample of $n = 50$ students is selected from $N = 4000$ students and it is found that $a = 30$ smoke. How large a sample must be selected to be practically certain ($z = 3$) that the precision of estimating P is within 5%? Using formula (2) above, we find

$$n = \frac{(4000)(3)^2(0.6)(0.4)}{4000(0.05)^2 + (3)^2(0.6)(0.4)} = 716$$

Hence, we need to select an additional $(716 - 50 =)$ 664 students. If we are satisfied with a reliability of $z = 2$, the sample size is

$$n = \frac{4000 \times 4 \times 0.24}{(4000 \times 0.0025) + (4 \times 0.24)} = 363$$

We therefore need to select an additional $(363 - 50 =)$ 313 students in this case.

Example 2. If we disregard the fpc, the sample size becomes

$$n = \frac{(3)^2(0.6)(0.4)}{(0.05)^2} = 864$$

When the reliability is $z = 2$, we get

$$n = \frac{4 \times 0.24}{0.0025} = 384$$

Example 3. An alternative and perhaps easier way of calculating n would be to use the relation

(3) $$n = \frac{n_0}{1 + n_0/N}$$

where n_0 is the sample size when fpc $= 1$. The procedure would be to first find n_0 as in Example 2, then find n using the above formula. For $z = 3$: First find $n_0 = 864$. Then

$$n = \frac{864}{1 + 864/4000} = \frac{864}{1 + 0.216} = 716$$

For $z = 2$:   First find $n_0 = 384$. Then

$$n = \frac{384}{1 + 384/4000} = \frac{384}{1 + 0.96} = 363$$

(ii) Simplification of the formula.

The reader may have noticed in Examples 1 and 2 that in order to find n, a preliminary estimate of p was calculated from a sample of size $n = 50$. Using the calculated sample size 720, a revised sample proportion p is recalculated. Let us now, instead of first finding a preliminary p, set $p = 0.5$. Then, $pq = 0.25$ is the maximum value pq can take, and it will give us the maximum value of n for a given precision and reliability. This may be shown as follows. Equation (2) was

$$n = \frac{Nz^2 pq}{Nd^2 + z^2 pq}$$

If we use $z = 2$, the n becomes

(4) $$n = \frac{N(2)^2(0.25)}{Nd^2 + (2)^2(0.25)}$$

$$= \frac{N}{Nd^2 + 1}$$

If a reliability of practically certain is required, $z = 3$, and

(5) $$n = \frac{Nz^2 pq}{Nd^2 + z^2 pq} = \frac{N(9)(0.25)}{Nd^2 + (9)(0.25)}$$

Tables based on equations (4) and (5) have been compiled (see table 4 in the appendix) and will usually be sufficient for most applications. Let us give a few examples.

Example 4. The proportion of smokers is to be estimated from a group of $N = 3000$ students. The precision is to be within 5% with a reliability of $z = 2$ (95% confidence interval). How large a sample should we select?

From the table, we see that $n = 353$. Let us check this.

$$n = \frac{N}{Nd^2 + 1} = \frac{3000}{(3000 \times 0.0025) + 1} = 352.9 = 353$$

Example 5. Suppose the reliability is to be $z = 3$ in Example 4. How large must the sample be? From the table, we find $n = 692$. Let us check this.

$$n = \frac{3000 \times 9 \times 0.25}{(3000 \times 0.0025) + (9 \times 0.25)} = 692.3 \doteq 692$$

Example 6. We may also apply equation (3) to the above cases. For $z = 2$, we have

$$n_0 = \frac{(2)^2(0.5)(0.5)}{d^2} = \frac{1}{d^2}$$

For $z = 3$ we have

$$n_0 = \frac{(3)^2(0.5)(0.5)}{d^2} = \frac{9 \times 0.25}{d^2} = \frac{9}{4d^2}$$

For Example 4:

$$n_0 = \frac{1}{(0.05)^2} = 400$$

$$n = \frac{400}{1 + 400/3000} = \frac{400}{1 + 0.133} = 353$$

For Example 5:

$$n_0 = \frac{9}{4(0.05)^2} = 900$$

$$n = \frac{9000}{1 + 900/3000} = \frac{900}{1 + 0.3} = 692$$

Problems

1. A preliminary random sample of $n = 100$ students is selected from $N = 5000$ students and it is found that $a = 40$ own cars. How large a sample must be selected to have a precision of $\pm 5\%$ with a reliability of $z = 2(95\%)$? First find n_0 for fpc $= 1$; then, find n for fpc $\neq 1$.

2. Using Table 4 in the appendix, find the sample size for $p = 0.4$, $N = 5000$ and $z = 2$ (95%) and compare it with the answer in Problem 1.

3. An aerial photo is taken of a large area to determine the proportion that is in a forest. A rectangular grid with 400 intersections is placed on the photo and 160 intersections are found to fall in the forest. Estimate the proportion P and $V(p)$ of the area that is in the forest. Note that we may assume there are an infinite number of points on the grid and that the 400 intersections may be considered as a sample of $n = 400$ points.

Notes and References

For further discussion of sample selection, see Sampford (1962), Chapter 4, which is mainly on agricultural surveys. Further study of sample selection should be postponed until the various methods of sampling are studied in the subsequent chapters. For further discussion of simple random sampling of the mean, total, and proportion, see Hansen, Hurwitz, and Madow (1953), Chapter 4, pp. 110–158; Cochran (1963), Chapters 2, 3, and 4.

Sampford, M.R. (1962). *An Introduction to Sampling Theory*. Edinburgh: Oliver and Boyd.

CHAPTER 6

Stratified Random Sampling

6.1 Introduction

Suppose we wish to estimate the average sales of supermarkets in a certain city. It is known that the majority of the supermarkets are small or middle-sized, and there are only a few very large supermarkets. It is also known that these very large supermarkets account for a substantial amount of the total sales. In other words, the sales distribution of supermarkets is highly skewed. When the simple random sampling procedure is applied to such a distribution, there is a chance that either none or too many of the very large supermarkets may be included in the sample. As a result, the sample may not adequately represent the population.

Common sense would indicate that the supermarkets should be divided into three groups, small, medium, and large, and that a certain number of supermarkets be selected from each of the three groups, and that the average sales be estimated from this combined sample. As we shall see, statistical theory will support this common sense judgment. Furthermore, if such a classification were available, separate information on the average sales of small, medium, and large supermarkets would probably be both interesting and useful.

As this illustration shows, populations may be divided into nonoverlapping subpopulations called strata. The process of breaking down the population into strata, selecting simple random samples from each stratum, and combining these into a single sample to estimate population parameters is called stratified random sampling.

There are a number of reasons for following this sampling procedure. The first and basic reason is that, given certain conditions, it may increase precision. This is based on statistical theory and will be explained later. A second reason is that information concerning individual strata may be desired. A third reason is that it may make it easier to collect information for either physical or administrative reasons. For example, instead of collecting information from randomly selected students in a large university with divisions scattered throughout a state, it may be easier to consider each division as a stratum, and apply stratified random sampling. Or, if local field offices are located in districts which may be used in the sample surveys, it may be convenient to stratify a state into counties, and use stratified random sampling.

How should the population be stratified? In our example about super-markets, should we stratify according to the location of the supermarkets or according to their size? Or should some other criteria be used?

The first thing we need to consider before we can decide on how to stratify the population is *what* we are interested in measuring. Is it the sales of the supermarket or the income of the shoppers we are interested in? If it is the sales we wish to estimate, it is probably better to stratify the supermarkets according to some measure of size— such as sales or floor space. If it is the income of the shoppers, it may be better to stratify according to the location of the supermarkets.

Suppose we wish to estimate sales and we have stratified according to floor space. The reason for stratifying according to floor space is to obtain strata that are *homogeneous* with respect to the variable (sales) under conside-ration. Hence, we may have three strata—large, medium, and small—accord-ing to floor space. We are implicitly assuming that the large supermarkets (in terms of floor space) will have large sales, and hence the supermarkets in this stratum will be homogeneous with respect to sales. When this type of homogeniety is achieved, there will be a gain precision. This point will be explained in terms of statistical theory in the subsequent sections.

However, in many practical problems, it is usually difficult to stratify with respect to the variable under consideration—especially because of physical and cost reasons. In many cases, the population is stratified accord-ing to administrative groupings, geographic grouping, and natural charac-teristics. For example, in government surveys (such as population surveys), the county or voting districts may be used as strata for reasons of cost and convenience. Geographic regions—such as the East coast, the South, etc.—may be used, or natural characteristics— such as age group or sex. How the strata should be chosen will depend mainly on the subjective judgment of the statistician.

Let us give some additional examples of stratified populations to gain familiarity with the idea of stratifying a population.

Examples   (1) The population surveys conducted by the government stratify the U.S.A. by area into 68 strata, so that each stratum has about equal population, and random samples are selected from each stratum. This process will be explained more fully in Chapter 8. It will suffice at this point to understand that strata are set up according to a combination of area and population.

(2) Manufacturing corporations may be stratified according to their size as measured by their total assets, total sales, or total number of employees.

(3) A department store wishes to estimate the average size of its 10,000 customers' accounts. It may divide the accounts into strata such as; up to $99; $100 to 199; $200 to 499; $500 to 999; over $1000.

(4) A county may be divided into 3 strata; urban, rural, and open country in order to estimate characteristics about the families in the county.

(5) Farms may be stratified according to size of crops or number of cattle.

The above examples should suffice to indicate the large number of ways in which populations may be stratified, and thus emphasize the usefulness of stratified random sampling procedures.

In our subsequent discussion, we will show how the mean and variance of the population are estimated. We shall then consider the population total and special sample designs, such as proportional allocation and optimum allocation. Finally, we shall consider the problem of determining sample size and that of stratified sampling for proportions.

6.2 Estimation of the population total and population mean

(*i*) *Definitions.*

Let us set up a hypothetical population with $L = 2$ strata to develop and illustrate our discussion of stratified random sampling and to define terms and notations. Suppose we have a population of $N = 6$ students who are classified according to whether they are freshmen or sophomores. Let $N_1 = 3$ students be freshmen, and $N_2 = 3$ students be sophomores.

Suppose we are interested in the average number of books these students have. Let the hypothetical data be represented as in Table 6.1

Table 6.1

	Freshmen N_1 X_{1i}		Sophomores N_2 X_{2i}	
	X_{11}	2 books	X_{21}	8
	X_{12}	4	X_{22}	12
	X_{13}	6	X_{23}	16
Total	X_1	12	X_2	36
Mean	$\bar{X}_1$	4	$\bar{X}_2$	12

The number of strata is shown by $L = 2$, and

$$N = \sum_h^L N_h = N_1 + N_2 = 3 + 3 = 6$$

is the total number of sampling units (students) in the frame.

The X_{hi} shows the number of books owned by the ith student in the h stratum. The X_h shows the number of books in the hth stratum. Hence, for example,

$$X_1 = X_{11} + X_{12} + X_{13} = 12$$

is the number of books in the 1st stratum (freshmen). In general, the stratum total is

(1)
$$X_h = \sum_i^{N_h} X_{hi}$$

The population total is the sum of the stratum totals, and is

$$X = X_1 + X_2 = 12 + 36 = 48$$

which is the total number of books. In general, the population total is given by

(2)
$$X = \sum_h^L X_h = \sum_h^L \sum_i^{N_h} X_{hi}$$

The stratum mean is defined as

(3)
$$\bar{X}_h = X_h/N_h$$

For the 1st and 2nd strata in our present illustration, we have

$$\bar{X}_1 = X_1/N_1 = 12/3 = 4 \text{ books per student (freshmen)}$$
$$\bar{X}_2 = X_2/N_2 = 36/3 = 12 \text{ books per student (sophomores)}$$

The population mean is defined as

(4)
$$\bar{X} = \frac{X}{N} = \frac{X_1 + X_2}{N_1 + N_2} = \frac{12 + 36}{3 + 3} = \frac{48}{6} = 8$$

and this shows the average is 8 books per student. Since $X_1 = N_1 \bar{X}_1$ and $X_2 = N_2 \bar{X}_2$, the population mean may also be written as

(5)
$$\bar{X} = \frac{N_1 \bar{X}_1 + N_2 \bar{X}_1}{N_1 + N_2} = \frac{\sum^L N_h \bar{X}_h}{N}$$

(ii) Estimation of X and $\bar{X}$.

Our problem now is to show how X and $\bar{X}$ (of equation (2) and (5)) are estimated by stratified random sampling. The basic idea is to first estimate the population total X and to divide this by N in order to estimate $\bar{X}$.

The population total is the sum of the stratum totals. Hence, an estimate of the population total is obtained by summing the estimates of the stratum totals.

An estimate of the stratum total may be obtained by

$$\hat{X}_h = N_h \bar{x}_h$$

where $\bar{x}_h$ is the sample mean of a random subsample of size n_h from the hth stratum. For example, suppose we select random subsamples of size $n_1 = 2$ and $n_2 = 2$ from the 1st and 2nd strata of our population, thus making $\bar{x}_1$ and $\bar{x}_2$ the sample means of these random subsamples, respectively. As we have already seen in our discussion of simple random sampling, $N_1\bar{x}_1$ and $N_2\bar{x}_2$ will be the unbiased estimates of the totals of the 1st and 2nd strata.

An *estimate of the population total X* is then the sum of the estimates of stratum totals and, since there are 2 strata in our illustration, it will be:

(6)
$$\hat{X}_{\text{st}} = N_1\bar{x}_1 + N_2\bar{x}_2 = \sum_{}^{L} N_h\bar{x}_h$$

Hence, an *estimate of the population mean* becomes

(7)
$$\bar{x}_{\text{st}} = \frac{\hat{X}_{\text{st}}}{N} = \frac{N_1\bar{x}_1 + N_2\bar{x}_2}{N_1 + N_2}$$

In general, this may be written as

(7′)
$$\bar{x}_{\text{st}} = \frac{\sum_{}^{L} N_h\bar{x}_h}{N}$$

and this is the estimator of the population mean we seek.

Since the stratum sample means $\bar{x}_h$ are obtained by simple random sampling, they are unbiased estimators of the stratum means $\bar{X}_h$, i.e.,

$$E(\bar{x}_h) = \bar{X}_h$$

The expected value of $\bar{x}_{\text{st}}$ thus becomes

$$E(\bar{x}_{\text{st}}) = \frac{E(N_1\bar{x}_1 + N_2\bar{x}_2)}{N}$$
$$= \frac{N_1\bar{X}_1 + N_2\bar{X}_2}{N}$$
$$= \frac{X_1 + X_2}{N} = \frac{X}{N} = \bar{X}$$

and we find that $\bar{x}_{\text{st}}$ is an unbiased estimator of $\bar{X}$.

Note how the information of N_1 and N_2 are necessary for the estimator $\bar{x}_{\text{st}}$.

Also, since $E(\bar{x}_{\text{st}}) = X/N$ we get

$$E(N\bar{x}_{\text{st}}) = X$$

But, from equation (7′),

$$N\bar{x}_{\text{st}} = \sum_{}^{L} N_h\bar{x}_h = \hat{X}_{\text{st}}$$

That is, the estimator $\hat{X}_{\text{st}}$ is also an unbiased estimator of X:

$$E(\hat{X}_{\text{st}}) = X$$

Example 1. Using our hypothetical population, let us illustrate these results. We can select $\binom{3}{2} = 3$ possible samples without replacement from each stratum.

Hence, there are altogether

$$\binom{3}{2}\binom{3}{2} = 9$$

possible samples of size

$$n = n_1 + n_2 = 2 + 2 = 4$$

These 9 possible samples are listed in Table 6.2.

Table 6.2

Strata I	II	x_1	x_2	$\bar{x}_1$	$\bar{x}_2$	$N_1\bar{x}_1$	$N_2\bar{x}_2$	$\hat{X}_{st}$
2, 4	8, 12	6	20	3	10	9	30	39
	8, 16		24		12	9	36	45
	12, 16		28		14	9	42	51
2, 6	8, 12	8	20	4	10	12	30	42
	8, 16		24		12	12	36	48
	12, 16		28		14	12	42	54
4, 6	8, 12	10	20	5	10	15	30	45
	8, 16		24		12	15	36	51
	12, 16		28		14	15	4	57
								432

The first sample consists of (2, 4, 8, 12), of which (2, 4) is from stratum I and (8, 12) is from stratum II.

The total of the subsample (2, 4) from stratum I is:

$$x_1 = 2 + 4 = 6$$

The sample mean of subsample (2, 4) from stratum I is:

$$\bar{x}_1 = x_1/n_1 = 6/2 = 3$$

Hence, an estimate of the total number of books in stratum I based on subsample (2, 4) is

$$N_1\bar{x}_1 = (3)(3) = 9$$

The values of x_2, $\bar{x}_2$ and $N_2\bar{x}_2$ are likewise calculated from subsample (8, 12).

Hence, the estimator of the total number of books in the population based on the first sample, (2, 4, 8, 12), is

$$\hat{X}_{st} = N_1\bar{x}_1 + N_2\bar{x}_2 = 9 + 30 = 39$$

and the estimator of the population mean is

$$\bar{x}_{st} = \frac{\hat{X}_{st}}{N} = \frac{39}{6} = 6.5 \text{ books}$$

Let us next show that $E(\bar{x}_{st}) = \bar{X}$. From Table 6.2, we see that

$$E(\bar{x}_{st}) = \frac{1}{9}\left[\frac{36}{6} + \frac{45}{6} + \cdots + \frac{57}{6}\right] = 8$$

But we have already found that $\bar{X} = 8$, therefore, $E(\bar{x}_{st}) = \bar{X} = 8$, and $\bar{x}_{st}$ is an unbiased estimator of $\bar{X}$.

We also note that

$$E(\hat{X}_{st}) = \frac{36 + 45 + \cdots + 57}{9} = 48 = X$$

and $\hat{X}_{st}$ is an unbiased estimator of X.

An alternate way of estimating the population mean is by finding the sample mean of the combined sample $n = n_1 + n_2$. For this, let

$$x = x_1 + x_2 = n_1\bar{x}_1 + n_2\bar{x}_2$$

where x_1 and x_2 are the sample totals of the subsamples n_1 and n_2, and hence x is the sample total. The $\bar{x}_1$ and $\bar{x}_2$ are the sample means, and the sample mean of the combined sample is thus

(8)
$$\begin{aligned} \bar{x} &= \frac{x}{n} = \frac{n_1\bar{x}_1 + n_2\bar{x}_2}{n} \\ &= \frac{\sum\limits^{L} n_h\bar{x}_h}{n} \end{aligned}$$

As may be seen, this sample mean does not require knowledge of N_1 and N_2. However, it is not generally an unbiased estimator of $\bar{X}$. In the special case where the same percentage (say, 5%) of each stratum is selected as a random subsample, equation (8) will be equal to (7) and will become an unbiased estimator of $\bar{X}$. To show this, let

$$\frac{n_1}{N_1} = \frac{n_2}{N_2} = \frac{n_1 + n_2}{N_1 + N_2} = \frac{n}{N} = f$$

This f was called the sampling fraction. Then, $n_1 = N_1 f$, $n_2 = N_2 f$, and $n = Nf$. Substituting these into (8), we find

$$\begin{aligned} \bar{x} &= \frac{N_1 f \bar{x}_1 + N_2 f \bar{x}_2}{Nf} \\ &= \frac{N_1\bar{x}_1 + N_2\bar{x}_2}{N} = \bar{x}_{st} \end{aligned}$$

This method of selecting the subsamples from each stratum in proportion to the stratum size is called proportional sampling or stratified random sampling with a uniform sampling fraction, and will be discussed in section 6.8. The characteristic of this sampling procedure is that each element in the population has the same chance of selection. This may be seen by recalling that the probability of including a specific unit in the subsample taken from the 1st stratum is n_1/N_1. Similarly, for the 2nd stratum, it is n_2/N_2. But $n_1/N_1 = n_2/N_2 = n/N$. Hence, each unit in the population has a probability n/N of being included in the sample. A sample selected so that each unit has the same probability of being selected is called a selfweighting sample.

Problems

1. Given the following hypothetical population of 2 strata, answer the following questions.

$$\text{freshmen} \quad : 2 \text{ books, 4, 6}$$
$$\text{sophomores: } 9, 12, 18, 21$$

(i) Calculate X_1, X_2, $\bar{X}_1$, $\bar{X}_2$, and X.

(ii) Select samples of size $n_1 = 2$, $n_2 = 3$ using the random number table and estimate X_1, X_2, $\bar{X}_1$, $\bar{X}_2$, and X.

(iii) Select all possible samples of size $n_1 = 2$, $n_2 = 3$ and construct a table similar to Table 6.2. Show that $E(\hat{X}_{st}) = X$.

2. Suppose a group of students have the following number of books.

$$\text{freshmen} \quad : 3, 4, 4, 2, 1 \quad \quad 1, 0, 3, 6, 3$$
$$\text{sophomores: } 4, 8, 3, 6, 4 \quad \quad 9, 9, 6$$
$$\text{juniors} \quad \quad : 12, 13, 14, 14, 10 \quad 9, 7, 13, 11$$
$$\text{seniors} \quad \quad : 11, 15, 16, 19, 13 \quad 13, 13, 18, 15, 11 \quad 19$$

(i) Assuming each grade is a stratum, calculate X_1, X_2, X_3, X_4 and X

(ii) Using a random number table, select samples of size $n_i = 4$ from each stratum, and estimate X and $\bar{X}$.

3. Suppose we wish to estimate the total floor space of supermarkets in a certain city and have obtained the following sample data.

Stratum	N_h	n_h	x_h(Square feet)
small	110	20	4000
medium	60	15	10500
large	30	10	60000

(i) Estimate $\bar{X}_1$, $\bar{X}_2$, and $\bar{X}_3$.

(ii) Estimate X_1, X_2, X_3, and X.

(iii) Estimate $\bar{X}$.

6.3 The population variances

To evaluate the precision of $\bar{x}_{st}$, we need to find its sampling variance $V(\bar{x}_{st})$. We find that $V(\bar{x}_{st})$ consists of two components; one is the variation *within* each stratum, and the second is the variation *between* strata. When $V(\bar{x}_{st})$ is expressed in terms of these two variances, it will provide us with a better understanding of the characteristics of stratified random sampling, which in turn will assist us in designing sampling plans.

To prepare for the analysis of $V(\bar{x}_{st})$, let us define various population variances which we will be using in this section. The first variance we shall define is the *stratum variance*, which shows the variation within each stratum.

Just as there were two ways of defining the population variance of simple random sampling, there are two ways of defining the stratum variance. One is

(1)
$$\sigma_h^2 = \frac{1}{N_h} \sum_i^{N_h} (X_{hi} - \bar{X}_h)^2$$

and the other is

(2)
$$S_h^2 = \frac{1}{N_h - 1} \sum_i^{N_h} (X_{hi} - \bar{X}_h)^2$$

We shall use both forms in our subsequent discussion. As is seen, when N_h is large, we may set $N_h - 1 \doteq N_h$ and, hence, $\sigma_h^2 = S_h^2$.

The second variance we shall define is the *population variance*, which is

(3)
$$\sigma^2 = \frac{1}{N} \sum_h^L \sum_i^{N_h} (X_{hi} - \bar{X})^2$$

Note carefully that $\bar{X}$ is the population mean and not a stratum mean. That is, the population variance σ^2 shows the variation of the individual values from the population mean $\bar{X}$ whereas the stratum variances S_h^2 show the variation from the respective stratum means, $\bar{X}_h$. We may of course also express σ^2 in the usual way as

$$\sigma^2 = \frac{1}{N} \sum_i^N (X_i - \bar{X})^2$$

Let us calculate these variances for our hypothetical illustration and demonstrate the use of these equations. Note, however, that in practical problems we usually calculate sample estimates, not population values. We shall find *estimators* of the variances in the next section.

For calculation purposes, the squared terms on the right hand side of equations (2) and (3) are expanded as follows:

$$\sum^{N_h} (X_{hi} - \bar{X}_h)^2 = \sum X_{hi}^2 - N_h \bar{X}_h^2 = \sum X_{hi}^2 - \frac{1}{N_h}(\sum X_{hi})^2$$

$$\sum^{N_h} (X_{hi} - \bar{X})^2 = \sum X_{hi}^2 - 2\bar{X} \sum X_{hi} + N_h \bar{X}^2$$

Using these relations let us calculate the variances.

Table 6.3

X_{1i}	X_{1i}^2	X_{2i}	X_{2i}^2
$X_{11} = 2$	4	$X_{21} = 8$	64
$X_{12} = 4$	16	$X_{22} = 12$	144
$X_{13} = 6$	36	$X_{23} = 16$	256
12	56	36	464

$$\sigma_1^2 = \frac{1}{N_1} \sum^{N_1} (X_{1i} - \bar{X}_1)^2 = \frac{1}{N_1}\left[\sum X_{1i}^2 - \frac{1}{N_h}(\sum X_{1i})^2\right]$$

$$= \frac{1}{3}[56 - \frac{1}{3}(12)^2] = \frac{8}{3}$$

$$S_1^2 = 8/2 = 4 \qquad \sigma_2^2 = 32/3 \qquad S_2^2 = 32/2 = 16$$

$$\sigma^2 = \frac{1}{N} \sum_h^L \sum_i^{N_h} (X_{hi} - \bar{X})^2$$

$$= \frac{1}{N} [\sum^{N_1} (X_{1i} - \bar{X})^2 + \sum^{N_2} (X_{2i} - \bar{X})^2]$$

$$\sum^{N_1} (X_{1i} - \bar{X})^2 = \sum^{N_1} X_{1i}^2 - 2\bar{X} \sum X_{1i} + N_1 \bar{X}^2$$
$$= 56 - 2(8)(12) + (3)(8)^2 = 56$$

$$\sum^{N_2} (X_{2i} - \bar{X})^2 = 80$$

$$\therefore \quad \sigma^2 = \frac{1}{6}(56 + 80) = \frac{136}{6}$$

Let us now derive the important relation between the stratum variances and the overall population variance by rewriting the population variance as follows:

(4)
$$\sigma^2 = \frac{1}{N} \sum_h^L \sum_i^{N_h} (X_{hi} - \bar{X})^2$$

$$= \frac{1}{N} \sum_h^L \sum_i^{N_h} [(X_{hi} - \bar{X}_h) + (\bar{X}_h - \bar{X})]^2$$

$$= \frac{1}{N} [\sum^L \sum^{N_h} (X_{hi} - \bar{X}_h)^2 + \sum^L N_h(\bar{X}_h - \bar{X})^2]$$

$$= \frac{1}{N} \sum^L N_h \sigma_h^2 + \frac{1}{N} \sum^L N_h(\bar{X}_h - \bar{X})^2$$

The first term on the right hand side shows the stratum variances and the second term shows the dispersion due to variation among stratum means. Using our illustration, these terms may be calculated as follows:

$$\frac{1}{N} \sum^L N_h \sigma_h^2 = \frac{1}{6}\left[3\left(\frac{8}{3}\right) + 3\left(\frac{32}{3}\right)\right] = \frac{40}{6}$$

$$\frac{1}{N} \sum^L N_h(\bar{X}_h - \bar{X})^2 = \frac{1}{6}[3(4 - 8)^2 + 3(12 - 8)^2] = 16$$

$$\therefore \quad \sigma^2 = \frac{40}{6} + 16 = \frac{136}{6}$$

As is seen, $\sigma^2 = 136/6$ is the same value obtained above.

Also note that σ^2 is simply the population variance, and may thus be obtained as

$$\sigma^2 = \frac{1}{N} \sum^N (X_i - \bar{X})^2$$

$$= \frac{1}{6}[(2 - 8)^2 + (4 - 8)^2 + (6 - 8)^2 + (8 - 8)^2 + (12 - 8)^2 + (16 - 8)^2]$$

$$= 136/6$$

For convenience, let us set

(5)
$$\sigma_w^2 = \frac{1}{N} \sum_{}^{L} N_h \sigma_h^2$$

(6)
$$\sigma_b^2 = \frac{1}{N} \sum_{}^{L} N_h (\bar{X}_h - \bar{X})^2$$

and call σ_w^2 the *within variance* because it shows the variation within each stratum, and σ_b^2 the *between variance* because it shows the variation between strata. The overall variance may then be shown as

(7)
$$\sigma^2 = \sigma_w^2 + \sigma_b^2$$

In our present illustration, we have

$$\sigma^2 = \sigma_w^2 + \sigma_b^2 = 40/6 + 16 = 136/6$$

The implication of this result is that when σ_w^2 is small, σ_b^2 will be large, and vice versa. That is, when the population is stratified into *homogeneous* strata, the main source of variation will be the *between* stratum variation. Conversely, if the population is stratified into *heterogeneous* strata, the main source of variation will be the *within* stratum variation.

Let us illustrate this implication with an example. Suppose we have a population

$$1, 2, 3, 4, 5, 6, 7, 8$$

where $N = 8$, $\bar{X} = 4.5$, and $\sigma^2 = 42/8$. Let us divide this population into 2 strata. We can see that if we include all the small numbers in the 1st stratum, only the large numbers will remain in the 2nd stratum and we have homogeneous strata. That is, let the 1st stratum be 1, 2, 3, 4. Then, necessarily, the 2nd stratum will be 5, 6, 7, 8.

If the units are selected so that the 1st stratum is heterogeneous, then, necessarily, the 2nd stratum will also be heterogeneous. For example, let the 1st stratum be 1, 8, 3, 6. Then, the 2nd stratum will be 2, 4, 5, 7.

As is seen, when one stratum is made homogeneous, the other stratum will automatically become homogeneous also. Conversely, if one stratum is made heterogeneous, the other stratum will automatically become heterogeneous also.

Let us check these results in terms of σ_w^2 and σ_b^2 with our example. For the homogeneous stratification:

$$1, 2, 3, 4 \qquad X_1 = 10$$
$$5, 6, 7, 8 \qquad X_2 = 26$$

We find

$$\sigma^2 = \sigma_w^2 + \sigma_b^2 = 10/8 + 4 = 42/8$$

For the heterogeneous stratification:

$$1, 8, 3, 6 \qquad X_1 = 18$$
$$2, 4, 7, 5 \qquad X_2 = 18$$

We have
$$\sigma^2 = \sigma_w^2 + \sigma_b^2 = 42/8 + 0 = 42/8$$
As is seen, $\bar{X}_1 = \bar{X}_2 = 4.5$ in this case, and hence $\sigma_b^2 = 0$. All the variation comes from σ_w^2. That is, by making the strata heterogeneous, σ_w^2 becomes large and σ_b^2 becomes small. In our case where $\bar{X}_1$ and $\bar{X}_2$ are equal, $\sigma_b^2 = 0$.

To summarize: when the population is stratified into *homogeneous* strata, the within variance σ_w^2 becomes small and the between variance σ_b^2 becomes large.

We may now ask: How does this result fit in the total picture of stratified random sampling? We shall argue in the next section that when the within variance σ_w^2 is small, the variance of the estimator $\bar{x}_{st}$ (that is, $V(\bar{x}_{st})$) will be small. And in section 6.5, we shall also show that when σ_w^2 is small, $V(\bar{x}_{st})$ will in general be smaller than $V(\bar{x})$ of simple random sampling.

Hence, putting these results together, we may argue as follows. When the population is stratified into homogeneous strata, the σ_w^2 will be small. When σ_w^2 is small, $V(\bar{x}_{st})$ will be small, and it will usually be smaller than the $V(\bar{x})$ of simple random sampling. Hence, when the population can be stratified into homogeneous strata, there is usually an increase in the precision of the estimator $\bar{x}_{st}$ over the estimator of simple random sampling, $\bar{x}$.

So let us in the next section find $V(\bar{x}_{st})$, and show that it will be small when the within variance σ_w^2 is small.

Problems

1. Work out the calculation details of the illustration on page 110.

2. Show that
$$\sigma^2 = \frac{1}{N} \sum_{}^{L} N_h \sigma_h^2 + \frac{1}{N} \sum N_h (\bar{X}_h - \bar{X})^2$$

3. Given 2, 3, 3, 4, 12, 14, 15, 15 as the population, calculate
$$\sigma^2 = \frac{1}{N} \sum (X_i - \bar{X})^2$$

4. Stratify the population in Problem 3 so that each stratum is homogeneous as follows:

stratum 1   2, 3, 3, 4
stratum 2   12, 14, 15, 15

Calculate the following quantities:

(1) $\sigma^2 = \frac{1}{N} \sum \sum (X_{hi} - \bar{X})^2$

(2) σ_1^2, σ_2^2

(3) $\sigma_w^2 = \frac{1}{N} \sum N_h \sigma_h^2$

(4) $\sigma_b^2 = \frac{1}{N} \sum N_h (\bar{X}_h - \bar{X})^2$

(5) $\sigma^2 = \sigma_w^2 + \sigma_b^2$

5. Stratify the population in Problem 3 so that the strata are heterogeneous as follows:

stratum 1   2, 12, 15, 3
stratum 2   3, 4, 14, 15

Perform the same five calculations as in Problem 4 and compare these results with those of Problem 4.

6. Explain under what conditions we may expect an increase in precision when using stratified random sampling.

7. Check the following relations algebraically.

$$\sum_{}^{N_h} (X_{hi} - \bar{X})^2 = \sum X_{hi}^2 - N_h \bar{X}_h^2 = \sum X_{hi}^2 - (\sum X_{hi})^2/N_h$$
$$\sum_{}^{N_h} (X_{hi} - \bar{X})^2 = \sum X_{hi}^2 - 2\bar{X} \sum X_{hi} + N_h \bar{X}^2$$

8. Using the data of Problem 1 on page 109, calculate σ_1^2, σ_2^2, S_1^2, S_2^2, and σ^2, using the relations in Problem 7 above. Devise a worksheet for your calculations.

9. Using the results of Problem 7, calculate σ_w^2 and σ_b^2 and check that

$$\sigma^2 = \sigma_w^2 + \sigma_b^2$$

6.4 The variance of $\bar{x}_{st}$

As mentioned at the end of the last section, we shall in this section find $V(\bar{x}_{st})$ and show it to be small when the within stratum variance is small.

But first, let us calculate $V(\bar{x}_{st})$ from the basic definition of a variance, using Table 6.1, and let us then use this result as a point of reference. Part of Table 6.2 is reproduced in Table 6.4.

Table 6.4

Strata I	II	$\hat{X}_{st}$	$\bar{x}_{st}$	$\bar{x}_{st} - \bar{X}$	$(\bar{x}_{st} - \bar{X})^2$
2, 4	8, 12	39	39/6	−9/6	81/36
	8, 16	45	45/6	−3/6	9/36
	12, 16	51	51/6	3/6	9/36
2, 6	8, 12	42	42/6	−6/6	36/36
	8, 16	48	48/6	0	0
	12, 16	54	54/6	6/6	36/36
4, 6	8, 12	45	45/6	−3/6	9/36
	8, 16	51	51/6	3/6	9/36
	12, 16	57	57/6	9/6	81/36
					270/36

As Table 6.4 shows, there are

$$M = \binom{3}{2}\binom{3}{2} = 9$$

possible samples of size $n = n_1 + n_2 = 2 + 2 = 4$ we can select. Hence, there are $M = 9$ possible samples means $\bar{x}_{st}$, and they are shown in Table 6.4. Table 6.5 is the frequency table of these 9 sample means.

Table 6.5

Class	f
39/6	1
42/6	1
45/6	2
48/6	1
51/6	2
54/6	1
57/6	1
	9

The variance of $\bar{x}_{st}$ is, by definition,

(1) $$\sigma^2_{\bar{x}_{st}} = \frac{1}{M} \sum_{}^{M} (\bar{x}_{st} - \bar{X})^2$$

where $M = 9$. Calculations of Table 6.5 will show that this is

$$\sigma^2_{\bar{x}} = \frac{1}{9}\left(\frac{270}{36}\right) = \frac{30}{36} = \frac{5}{6}$$

Equation (1) is the basic definition of $V(\bar{x}_{st})$, but let us now find the $V(\bar{x}_{st})$ in terms of the stratum variances S^2_h, which will be more useful to us in subsequent discussion and will also show us the characteristics of $V(\bar{x}_{st})$. Actually, when the population and samples are fairly large, the number of possible samples

$$M = \binom{N_1}{n_1}\binom{N_2}{n_2}$$

will be so large that calculation of $V(\bar{x}_{st})$ from equation (1) will be practically impossible.

Let us now show how $V(\bar{x}_{st})$ may be expressed in terms of S^2_h. We know that

$$\bar{x}_{st} = \frac{N_1\bar{x}_1 + N_2\bar{x}_2}{N} = w_1\bar{x}_1 + w_2\bar{x}_2$$

where $w_h = N_h/N$, and are called stratum weights. Since the samples n_h are selected by random sampling and are independent of one another, we find

$$V(\bar{x}_{st}) = w_1^2 V(\bar{x}_1) + w_2^2 V(\bar{x}_2)$$

(2) $$= w_1^2 \frac{N_1 - n_1}{N_1}\frac{S_1^2}{n_1} + w_2^2\frac{N_2 - n_2}{N_2}\frac{S_2^2}{n_2}$$

$$= \sum_{h}^{L} \left(\frac{N_h}{N}\right)^2 \frac{N_h - n_h}{N_h}\frac{S_h^2}{n_h}$$

We shall usually rewrite this equation in the following forms to facilitate comparison with the other variances we shall be deriving in subsequent discussion.

(3) $$V(\bar{x}_{st}) = \frac{1}{N^2} \Sigma \, N_h^2 \frac{N_h - n_h}{N_h} \frac{S_h^2}{n_h}$$

or

(3-1) $$V(\bar{x}_{st}) = \frac{1}{N^2} \Sigma \, \frac{N_h - n_h}{N_h} \frac{(N_h S_h)^2}{n_h}$$

or

(3-2) $$V(\bar{x}_{st}) = \frac{1}{N^2} \Sigma \, \frac{(N_h S_h)^2}{n_h} - \frac{1}{N^2} \Sigma \, N_h S_h^2$$

When the fpc $= 1$, equation (3) becomes

(3-3) $$V(\bar{x}_{st}) = \frac{1}{N^2} \Sigma \, \frac{(N_h S_h)^2}{n_h}$$

Hence, equation (3-2) may be considered as showing the two parts of $V(\bar{x}_{st})$: the term

$$\frac{1}{N^2} \Sigma \, \frac{(N_h S_h)^2}{n_h}$$

shows the variance of $\bar{x}_{st}$ when sampling with replacement (*i.e.*, fpc $= 1$), and the term

$$-\frac{1}{N^2} \Sigma \, N_h S_h^2$$

shows the adjustment that is necessary when sampling without replacement. We shall use all these forms in our subsequent discussion. Equations (3-1) and (3-2) are usually more convenient for calculation purposes.

In our present illustration, we have $S_1^2 = 4$, $S_2^2 = 16$. Hence, (3-1) becomes

$$V(\bar{x}_{st}) = \frac{1}{N^2} \left(\frac{N_1 - n_1}{N_1} \frac{(N_1 S_1)^2}{n_1} + \frac{N_2 - n_2}{N_2} \frac{(N_2 S_2)^2}{n_2} \right)$$
$$= \frac{1}{36} \left(\frac{3 - 2}{3} \frac{9 \cdot 4}{2} + \frac{3 - 2}{3} \frac{9 \cdot 16}{2} \right)$$
$$= \frac{30}{36} = \frac{5}{6}$$

and this is equal to the $V(\bar{x}_{st})$ calculated from the basic formula (1).

Example 1. Given the following data where samples of $n_1 = 2$ and $n_2 = 2$ are selected from each stratum, calculate $V(\bar{x}_{st})$ using equation (3).

X_{1t}	X_{1t}^2	X_{2t}	X_{2t}^2
$X_{11} = 1$	1	$X_{21} = 10$	100
$X_{12} = 3$	9	$X_{22} = 16$	256
$X_{13} = 5$	25	$X_{23} = 22$	484
9	35	48	840

$$S_1^2 = 4, \qquad S_2^2 = 36$$
$$\therefore \quad V(\bar{x}_{st}) = 5/3$$

The equation

(4)
$$V(\bar{x}_{st}) = \frac{1}{N^2} \sum \frac{N_h - n_h}{N_h} \frac{(N_h S_h)^2}{n_h}$$

shows that $V(\bar{x}_{st})$ is dependent on S_h^2 when N, N_h, and n_h are given. The S_h^2 shows the variance within each stratum. Hence, we obtain the very important conclusion that when the variance within each stratum is small, $V(\bar{x}_{st})$ will be small, and the precision of $\bar{x}_{st}$ will be high.

This may be seen intuitively as follows: If a group of students is divided into 2 groups, 1 group has 7 boys of the same weight (100 1b), and the 2nd group has 5 boys of the same weight (150 1b), then

$$\bar{x}_{st} = \frac{(7 \times 100) + (5 \times 150)}{7 + 5} = \frac{1450}{12} = \bar{X}$$

That is, $\bar{x}_{st}$ is exactly equal to $\bar{X}$. Hence, the variance of $\bar{x}_{st}$ is zero.

In terms of equation (4), we can see that $S_h^2 = 0$ for both strata, and hence, according to equation (4), $V(\bar{x}_{st}) = 0$. That is, $\bar{x}_{st}$ is absolutely precise.

For practical applications, this means that the more homogeneous the strata, with respect to the characteristics under consideration, the smaller $V(\bar{x}_{st})$ will be, and hence, the more precise the estimator will be when compared to random sampling. This is one of the important results of stratified sampling, and it should be firmly understood.

Let us illustrate this conclusion by comparing $V(\bar{x})$ obtained from a random sample of size $n = 4$. Since we have already found $\sigma^2 = 136/6$ on page 111, $V(\bar{x})$ is as follows:

$$\sigma_{\bar{x}}^2 = \frac{\sigma^2}{n} \frac{N - n}{N - 1} = \frac{136/6}{4} \frac{6 - 4}{6 - 1} = \frac{34}{15} = 2.3$$

Previous calculations show that

$$V(\bar{x}_{st}) = 5/6 = 0.833$$

As shown, $V(\bar{x}_{st})$ is much smaller than $\sigma_{\bar{x}}^2$. That is, the dispersion of the $\bar{x}_{st}$ is smaller than that of x obtained from random sampling.

This may be seen intuitively as follows. The smallest and largest $\bar{x}$ obtained from random sampling are:

minimum: $(1/4)(2 + 4 + 6 + 8) = 5$
maximum: $(1/4)(6 + 8 + 12 + 16) = 10.5$

The smallest and largest $\bar{x}_{st}$ from stratified sampling are:

minimum: $(1/4)(2 + 4 + 8 + 12) = 6.5$
maximum: $(1/4)(4 + 6 + 12 + 16) = 9.5$

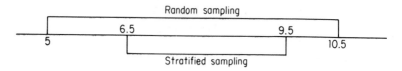

Fig. 6-1

Thus, we see that the range of $\bar{x}$ for random sampling is from 5 to 10.5, whereas that obtained for stratified sampling is from 6.5 to 9.5. (See Fig. 6-1.) The reason for this is because the small values (2, 4, 6) were in the 1st stratum, whereas the large values (8, 12, 16) were in the 2nd stratum. When selecting samples, we therefore had to select some units from the small values (1st stratum), and some from the large values (2nd stratum): whereas in random sampling there is the possibility that all may have come from either the small or large values. That is, we obtained this result because the strata were made homogeneous.

If the strata were not homogeneous, stratification may not have produced a reduction in the variance of the sample mean. We shall discuss these points again in section 6.12.

Let us now recall the result we obtained in section 6.3. From equations (1) and (2) of section 6.3, we can see that when N_h is large, we may set $N_h - 1 \doteq N_h$. Then, $S_h^2 \doteq \sigma_h^2$.

Recall also that

$$\sigma^2 = \sigma_w^2 + \sigma_b^2$$

$$\sigma_w^2 = \frac{1}{N} \Sigma N_h \sigma_h^2$$

Hence, we may set

$$\sigma_w^2 \doteq \frac{1}{N} \Sigma N_h S_h^2$$

That is, the within variance σ_w^2 is the weighted average of S_h^2.

We may now link our present conclusion with those reached previously, and state as follows: By stratifying the population into homogeneous strata, S_h^2 will be small, its weighted average σ_w^2 will also be small, and as we have just seen, this leads to a small $V(\bar{x}_{st})$. As a result, when the population is stratified into homogeneous strata, there will be an increase in the precision of $\bar{x}_{st}$. We may also state that when the variation between strata is made large, this leads to a small σ_w^2, and hence to a small $V(\bar{x}_{st})$.

This is therefore an important guide to sample design, indicating under what situations it is advantageous to use stratified sampling.

The astute reader may have noticed that $V(\bar{x}_{st})$ depends only on the within variance σ_w^2 and does not depend on the between variance σ_b^2. The reason for this will become clear when we consider cluster sampling. For the present we shall simply state that $V(\bar{x}_{st})$ is not affected by σ_b^2 because the random samples are taken from all the strata.

Also note that when $N_h = n_h$, the contribution to $V(\bar{x}_{st})$ of the variance from stratum h becomes zero because $(N_h - n_h)/N_h = 0$. For example, if supermarkets are stratified into small, medium, and large, and because there are only $N_3 = 10$ large supermarkets, they are all selected, we get $N_3 = n_3 = 10$ (i.e., $(N_3 - n_3)/N_3 = 0$), and the contribution to $V(\bar{x}_{st})$ from this third stratum will be zero.

Problems

1. Given the following population of 2 strata, answer the following questions.

> freshmen   : 2 books, 4, 6
> sophomores: 9, 12, 18, 21

(i) Select all possible samples of size $n_1 = 2$, $n_2 = 3$ and construct a table similar to Table 6.4 which shows all possible $\bar{x}_{st}$.

(ii) Calculate $V(\bar{x}_{st})$ using the basic definition given by equation (1) on page 115.

(iii) Using the S_1^2 and S_2^2 calculated in problem 8 on page 114, calculate $V(\bar{x}_{st})$ using equation (3-1).

2. Given 2, 4, 6, 9, 12, 18, 21 as a population of size $N = 7$, calculate $V(\bar{x})$ for a random sample of size $n = 5$. Compare $V(\bar{x})$ with $V(\bar{x}_{st})$ obtained above and explain the reasons for the difference.

6.5 Estimator of $V(\bar{x}_{st})$

Since the formula for $V(\bar{x}_{st})$ includes S_h^2, it cannot be used in most practical problems where S_h^2 is usually unknown. Hence, we have to use an estimator for S_h^2 and derive the estimator for $V(\bar{x}_{st})$.

The procedure of estimating $V(\bar{x}_{st})$ is similar to that of simple random sampling. A subsample n_h is randomly selected from stratum N_h, and the sample variance

$$(1) \qquad s_h^2 = \frac{1}{n_h - 1} \sum_i^{n_h} (x_{hi} - \bar{x}_h)^2$$

is calculated. We know from simple random sampling theory that s_h^2 is an unbiased estimator of S_h^2. Substituting s_h^2 into equation (3) of section 6.7, we find

$$(2) \qquad \hat{V}(\bar{x}_{st}) = \frac{1}{N^2} \sum^L N_h^2 \frac{N_h - n_h}{N_h} \frac{s_h^2}{n_h}$$

The expected value of (2) is simply the expected value of s_h^2 on the right hand side which will become S_h^2. Hence, $\hat{V}(\bar{x}_{st})$ is an unbiased estimator of $V(\bar{x}_{st})$.

Let us illustrate the calculation procedure of equation (2) with our example. Suppose the random sample that has been selected is

x_{1i}	x_{2i}
$x_{11} = 2$	$x_{21} = 8$
$x_{12} = 4$	$x_{22} = 16$

Then from equation (1), $s_1^2 = 2$, $s_2^2 = 32$. Hence, from equation (2),

$$\hat{V}(\bar{x}_{st}) = \frac{1}{N^2} \sum N_h^2 \frac{N_h - n_h}{N_h} \frac{s_h^2}{n_h}$$

$$= \frac{1}{36}\left[9 \cdot \left(\frac{3-2}{3}\right) \cdot \left(\frac{2}{2}\right) + 9 \cdot \left(\frac{3-2}{3}\right) \cdot \left(\frac{32}{2}\right)\right] = \frac{51}{36}$$

Example 1. Find all $M = 9$ possible estimates of $\hat{V}(\bar{x}_{st})$ and show that

$$E[\hat{V}(\bar{x}_{st})] = V(\bar{x}_{st})$$

Let us reproduce Table 6.4 here for convenience.

Table 6.6

Strata I	II	s_1^2	s_2^2	$\hat{V}(\bar{x}_{st})$
2, 4	8, 12	2	8	15/36
	8, 16		32	51/36
	12, 16		8	15/36
2, 6	8, 12	4	8	24/36
	8, 16		32	60/36
	12, 16		8	24/36
4, 6	8, 12	5	8	15/36
	8, 16		32	51/36
	12, 16		8	15/36

Using the results of this table, we can calculate the 9 possible estimates of $V(\bar{x}_{st})$. For example, for sample (2, 4, 8, 12), we get

$$\hat{V}(\bar{x}_{st}) = \frac{1}{36}\left[9\left(\frac{3-2}{3}\right)\left(\frac{2}{2}\right) + 9\left(\frac{3-2}{3}\right)\left(\frac{8}{2}\right)\right] = \frac{15}{36}$$

In similar fashion, we get the rest of the $\hat{V}(\bar{x}_{st})$ as shown in the last column of Table 6.6.

Hence, the expected value of $\hat{V}(\bar{x}_{st})$ is

$$E[\hat{V}(\bar{x}_{st})] = \frac{1}{9}\left(\frac{15}{36} + \frac{51}{36} + \cdots + \frac{15}{36}\right) = \frac{30}{36}$$

Recall from section 6.4 that $V(\bar{x}_{st}) = 30/36$. Thus,

$$E[\hat{V}(\bar{x}_{st})] = V(\bar{x}_{st}) = 30/36$$

So far we have found estimators of the population mean and variance for stratified random sampling. However, note that unless we know how n and n_h are determined, we cannot use these results in practical applications. The results we have derived so far are the basic theoretical results of stratified random sampling and, using these results, we shall find the procedures for determining n and n_h. However, before considering this problem, let us extend our basic theoretical discussion to the problem of estimating the population total and its variance.

Problems

1. Using the data of Problem 1 on page 119, construct a table similar to Table 6.6 and calculate all possible estimates of $V(\bar{x}_{st})$ and show that $E[\hat{V}(\bar{x}_{st})] = V(\bar{x}_{st})$.

2. Using the data of Problem 2 on page 109, select samples of size $n_h = 4$ using a random number table and estimate S_h^2.

3. Continuing Problem 2, estimate $V(\bar{x}_{st})$.

4. Suppose we are interested in estimating the average size of farms in a certain county. The farms are divided into four strata, and the following sample is obtained.

Strata	N_h	n_h	x_{hi} (Acres)
0–100 acres	100	6	40, 50, 90, 70, 20, 60
101–200	80	5	140, 150, 140, 130, 180
201–300	60	5	240, 280, 260, 250, 220
301 and over	40	4	350, 330, 310, 380

(i) Find $\bar{x}_{st}$.
(ii) Find $\hat{V}(\bar{x}_{st})$ and $s(\bar{x}_{st})$.

6.6 The variance of the population total and its estimator

The variance of $\hat{X}_{st}$ is easily found by using the results of the discussion concerning the variance of $\bar{x}_{st}$. The variance of $\hat{X}_{st}$ is

$$V(\hat{X}_{st}) = V(N\bar{x}_{st})$$
$$= N^2 V(\bar{x}_{st})$$

(1)
$$= N^2 \left(\frac{1}{N^2} \sum N_h^2 \frac{N_h - n_h}{N_h} \frac{S_h^2}{n_h} \right)$$

$$= \sum_{h}^{L} N_h^2 \frac{N_h - n_h}{N_h} \frac{S_h^2}{n_h}$$

That is, it is equal to $V(\bar{x}_{st})$ with the $1/N^2$ removed.

The estimate of $V(\hat{X}_{st})$ is obtained as it was for $V(\bar{x}_{st})$, namely, by replacing S_h^2 by s_h^2. Hence, the estimate is

(2)
$$\hat{V}(\hat{X}_{st}) = \sum_{h}^{L} N_h^2 \frac{N_h - n_h}{N_h} \frac{s_h^2}{n_h}$$

where

$$s_h^2 = \frac{1}{n_h - 1} \sum_{}^{n_h} (x_{hi} - \bar{x}_h)^2$$

By using the result that $\hat{V}(\bar{x}_{st})$ is an unbiased estimator of $V(\bar{x}_{st})$, we may easily show that $\hat{V}(\hat{X}_{st})$ is an unbiased estimator of $V(\hat{X}_{st})$. We know that

$$E[\hat{V}(\bar{x}_{st})] = V(\bar{x}_{st})$$

But $\bar{x}_{st} = \hat{X}_{st}/N$. Substituting this into both sides of the above equation gives us

$$E\left[\frac{1}{N^2}\hat{V}(\hat{X}_{st})\right] = \frac{1}{N^2}V(\hat{X}_{st})$$

Hence

$$E[\hat{V}(\hat{X}_{st})] = V(\hat{X}_{st})$$

Example 1. Using the data of Table 6.4, we have:

X_{1t}	X_{2t}
$X_{11} = 2$	$X_{21} = 8$
$X_{12} = 4$	$X_{22} = 12$
$X_{13} = 6$	$X_{23} = 16$

$S_1^2 = 4,\ S_2^2 = 16$

$$\therefore \quad V(\hat{X}_{st}) = \sum \frac{N_h - n_h}{N_h} \frac{(N_h S_h)^2}{n_h}$$

$$= \left[\frac{(3-2)}{3} \cdot \frac{(9 \times 4)}{2}\right] + \left[\frac{(3-2)}{3} \cdot \frac{(9 \times 16)}{2}\right] = 30$$

Example 2. Using the results of Example 1 of section 6.5, we find the following results (see Table 6.4):

$$E[\hat{V}(\hat{X}_{st})] = (1/9)(15 + 51 + \cdots + 15) = 270/9 = 30$$

Hence, from the result of Example 1 above, we get

$$E[\hat{V}(\hat{X}_{st})] = V(\hat{X}_{st}) = 30$$

and $\hat{V}(\hat{X}_{st})$ is an unbiased estimator of $V(\hat{X}_{st})$.

Problems

1. Using the data of Problem 1 of page 119, calculate $V(\hat{X}_{st})$.

2. Using the results of Problem 1 on page 121, find all possible values of $\hat{V}(\hat{X}_{st})$ and verify that $E[\hat{V}(\hat{X}_{st})] = V(\hat{X}_{st})$.

3. Using the results of Problem 4 of page 121, find $\hat{X}_{st}$ and $s(\hat{X}_{st})$.

6.7 Allocation of the sample

As mentioned at the end of section 6.5, unless the sample size n and subsample sizes n_h are known, the estimators for the population mean $\bar{x}_{st}$ and the variance $V(\bar{x}_{st})$ cannot be calculated. In the next several sections, let us show how n and n_h are found.

There are thus two problems that need to be considered: determining the sample size n and allocating this sample among the h strata in order to determine n_h.

We shall in the next several sections consider the second problem—allocating the sample n among the strata and determining n_h. What is a desirable allocation? By a good allocation, we shall mean one where maximum precision is obtained with minimum cost. Since the precision of the estimator is measured by its variance, we may restate the criterion as follows: minimize the cost for a given variance or minimize the variance for a given cost. We shall, depending on the problem, use either of these criteria.

Now, to use these criteria, we need to define what is meant by costs of sampling. Costs of sampling include the cost of designing the sample, constructing the frame, training interviewers, collecting, compiling, and calculating the data, office expenses, other overhead expenses, etc. However, for analytical purposes, we shall divide the cost into two parts: a cost that is a function of the size of the sample, and a cost that is fixed. This may be shown as

(1)
$$c = c_0 + \sum_{}^{L} c_h n_h$$

where c_0 is the fixed cost and c_h is the cost per unit in stratum h. Equation (1) is called a *cost function*. Other, more complicated cost functions can be constructed, but it is usually difficult to construct an accurate and usable one. We shall use the cost function given by equation (1) for our subsequent discussion.

Having established the criterion for allocating the sample among strata and determining a cost function, let us now proceed and find the various ways of allocating the sample. The simplest method of allocation is to select equal numbers of sampling units from each stratum:

$$\bar{n} = \frac{n}{L}$$

The next simplest method of allocation is to allocate the sample in proportion to the stratum sizes. This method is the most frequently used method in practice and, quite clearly, does not depend on cost considerations. As we shall see, we merely need to know the stratum sizes. The other methods we shall consider such as the optimum allocation and the Neyman allocation will require specific consideration of costs to determine n_h. We start our discussion with proportional allocation in section 6.8, consider optimum allocation in section 6.9 and, finally, study the Neyman allocation in section 6.10.

6.8 Proportional allocation

(*i*) *Introduction.*

The simplest and most frequently used way of allocating a sample among strata is to allocate it proportionally to the size of the strata. For example, if a sample of size $n = 50$ is to be selected from a population of $N = 500$, it means that the sampling fraction is to be $n/N = 50/500 = 0.1$, and that 10% of each stratum is to be selected for the sample. Then

$$\frac{n_1}{N_1} = \frac{n_2}{N_2} = \cdots = \frac{n_L}{N_L} = \frac{n}{N} = 10\%$$

Although more refined methods are available, as our subsequent discussion will show, this method compares favorably in terms of precision, and is both simpler and more convenient than the other methods. The reason why its precision does not differ greatly from that of the more refined methods is because $V(\bar{x}_{\text{st}})$ is a quantity which fluctuates only slightly (even though there may be moderate changes in the sample size, especially when the sample size is rather large).

Let us first illustrate the sample selection procedure by proportional allocation with an example. Our hypothetical population was:

Strata I		Strata II	
X_{11}	2	X_{21}	8
X_{12}	4	X_{22}	12
X_{13}	6	X_{23}	16

We wish to select a sample of $n = 4$ from the population. We shall discuss how $n = 4$ is determined later, so for the moment let us assume we know that $n = 4$. According to proportionate allocation, the sample is allocated according to $f = n/N$. This implies that

(1) $$\frac{n_1}{N_1} = \frac{n_2}{N_2} = \frac{n}{N} = f$$

For our problem, $f = n/N = 4/6$. Hence, the samples n_h from the strata are:

$$n_1 = N_1 \times f = 3 \times \frac{4}{6} = 2$$

$$n_2 = N_2 \times f = 3 \times \frac{4}{6} = 2$$

$$\overline{4}$$

Since we are using simple random sampling in each stratum, the probability of any sampling unit in stratum h being included in the subsample n_h is $n_h/N_h = f$. Hence, since $n_h/N_h = f$ for all strata, any unit in the population has the same probability $f = 4/6$ of being included in the sample.

The idea of proportional allocation may also be shown by rewriting equation (1) as follows.

(2)
$$n_h = \frac{N_h}{N} \times n$$

This simply shows that n should be allocated according to N_h/N. For our present example,

$$n_1 = \frac{N_1}{N} \times n = \frac{4}{6} \times 3 = 2$$

$$n_2 = \frac{N_2}{N} \times n = \frac{4}{6} \times 3 = 2$$

Let us now find the estimator $\bar{x}_{st}$ of the population mean and $V(\bar{x}_{st})$ when proportional allocation is used.

(*ii*) *Estimator of* $\bar{X}$.

The unbiased estimator of $\bar{X}$ for stratified random sampling was

(3)
$$\bar{x}_{st} = \frac{\sum\limits^{L} N_h \bar{x}_h}{\sum N_h}$$

Substituting the condition that $N_h = n_h/f$ into (3), we find

$$\bar{x}_{st} = \frac{\sum \frac{n_h}{f} \cdot \frac{x_h}{n_h}}{\sum \frac{n_h}{f}}$$

(4)
$$= \frac{\sum\limits^{L} n_h \bar{x}_h}{n}$$

$$= \frac{\sum\limits^{L} \sum\limits^{n_h} x_{hi}}{n}$$

This shows that the estimator $\bar{x}_{st}$ is merely the sample mean of the sample n, and is an unbiased estimator of $\bar{X}$.

Suppose we select the following sample in our illustration:

$$N_1 \times f = 3 \times \frac{4}{6} = 2: \quad x_{11} = 2,\ x_{12} = 6$$

$$N_2 \times f = 3 \times \frac{4}{6} = 2: \quad x_{21} = 8,\ x_{22} = 12$$

Then, an estimate of $\bar{X}$ is

$$\bar{x}_{st} = \frac{2 + 6 + 8 + 12}{4} = 7$$

Example 1. Given the following hypothetical population, estimate the average number of cigarettes a person smokes by selecting a stratified random sample of size $n = 5$ by proportional allocation. The sampling fraction is $f = 5/10 = 1/2$. Hence, we select

Stratum I (men)		Stratum II (women)	
X_{11}	20	X_{21}	10
X_{12}	25	X_{22}	12
X_{13}	35	X_{23}	8
X_{14}	30	X_{24}	6
X_{15}	24		
X_{16}	26		
	180		36

$$N_1 \times f = 6 \times (1/2) = 3$$
$$N_2 \times f = 4 \times (1/2) = \frac{2}{5}$$

from each stratum. Using the random number table, we select

$$x_{11} = 25, x_{12} = 20, x_{13} = 35 \qquad \text{from stratum I}$$
$$x_{21} = 10, x_{22} = 6 \qquad \text{from stratum II}$$

Hence, the estimator $\bar{x}_{st}$ is

$$\bar{x}_{st} = \frac{1}{5}(25 + 20 + 35 + 10 + 6) = 19.2 \text{ cigarettes}$$

The true average is

$$\bar{X} = \frac{1}{10}(180 + 36) = 21.6 \text{ cigarettes}$$

Note that the probability of any person being included in the sample is $f = 1/2$.

(iii) $V(\bar{x}_{st})$ with proportional allocation.

The $V(\bar{x}_{st})$ obtained in our basic theoretical discussion was

(5)
$$V(\bar{x}_{st}) = \frac{1}{N^2} \sum N_h^2 \frac{N_h - n_h}{N_h} \frac{S_h^2}{n_h}$$

To obtain $V(\bar{x}_{st})$ for porportional allocation, substitute $n_h = (N_h/N) \cdot n$ into equation (5). Then

(6)
$$V(\bar{x}_{prop}) = \frac{N - n}{N} \sum^{L} \frac{N_h}{N} \frac{S_h^2}{n} \qquad \text{fpc} \neq 1$$
$$= \sum^{L} \frac{N_h}{N} \frac{S_h^2}{n} \qquad \text{fpc} = 1$$

An unbiased estimator of (6) is obtained by replacing S_h^2 by its unbiased sample estimator s_h^2. That is,

(7)
$$\hat{V}(\bar{x}_{prop}) = \frac{N - n}{N} \sum \frac{N_h}{N} \frac{s_h^2}{n} \qquad \text{fpc} \neq 1$$
$$= \sum \frac{N_h}{N} \frac{s_h^2}{n} \qquad \text{fpc} = 1$$

where

$$s_h^2 = \frac{1}{n_h - 1} \sum_i^{n_h} (x_{hi} - \bar{x}_h)^2$$

Since $V(\bar{x}_{prop})$ is obtained merely by substituting $n_h = (N_h/N) \cdot n$ into (5), we may also calculate $V(\bar{x}_{prop})$ from equation (5) by substituting in the values of n_h instead of using (6). In our calculations, we shall use both equations (5) and (6). Equation (6) will also be used later when comparing the various stratified sampling procedures.

Example 2. In our illustration, we selected a sample of (2, 6) from stratum I and

(8, 12) from stratum II. Then, $s_1^2 = 8$, $s_2^2 = 8$. Hence, the estimated variance becomes,

$$\hat{V}(\bar{x}_{\text{prop}}) = \frac{N-n}{N} \sum_{h}^{L} \frac{N_h}{N} \frac{s_h^2}{n}$$

$$= \frac{6-4}{6}\left[\left(\frac{3}{6} \cdot \frac{8}{4}\right) + \left(\frac{3}{6} \cdot \frac{8}{4}\right)\right] = \frac{4}{6}$$

Example 3. Using the data from Example 1 above, estimate $V(\bar{x}_{\text{prop}})$. Let the selected samples be:

$$\text{Stratum I :}\quad 25,\ 24,\ 26$$
$$\text{Stratum II:}\quad 10,\ 8$$
$$s_1^2 = 1 \qquad s_2^2 = 2$$

$$\hat{V}(\bar{x}_{\text{prop}}) = \frac{10-5}{10}\left[\left(\frac{6}{10} \cdot \frac{1}{5}\right) + \left(\frac{4}{10} \cdot \frac{2}{5}\right)\right] = \frac{7}{50}$$

Example 4. Suppose 500 supermarkets are stratified according to floorspace as follows: Estimate the average amount of sales and the sampling variance by proportionate stratified sampling. Let the sample size be $n = 40$.

Strata	N_h	n_h	s_h^2	$\bar{x}_h$	$n_h \bar{x}_h$	$N_h s_h^2$
Small	300	24	1	$4	96	300
Medium	150	12	4	$12	144	600
Large	50	4	16	$24	96	800
	500	40			336	1700

We shall select from each stratum the following number of stores.

$$n \times (N_1/N) = 40 \times (300/500) = 24$$
$$n \times (N_2/N) = 40 \times (150/500) = 12$$
$$n \times (N_3/N) = 40 \times (50/500) = 4$$

The next step in the sample survey is to select the subsamples $n_1 = 24$, $n_2 = 12$, and $n_3 = 4$ by simple random sampling from the small, medium, and large strata, respectively, and calculate the sample means $\bar{x}_h$ and sample variances s_h^2.

Assume the sample means $\bar{x}_h$ and sample variances s_h^2 of the strata are as shown in the table, in units of $1000. The estimator of the population mean is then

$$\bar{x}_{\text{st}} = \frac{1}{n} \sum_{h}^{L} \sum_{i}^{n_h} x_{hi}$$

$$= \frac{1}{n} \sum_{h}^{L} n_h \bar{x}_h$$

$$= \frac{1}{40}(336) = 8.4$$

Thus the average amount of sales is estimated to be $8400 per supermarket. The estimator of $V(\bar{x}_{\text{st}})$ is

$$\hat{V}(\bar{x}_{st}) = \frac{N-n}{N} \sum^{L} \frac{N_h}{N} \frac{s_h^2}{n}$$

$$= \frac{500-40}{500} \cdot \frac{1}{500} \cdot \frac{1}{40} \cdot 1700$$

$$= \frac{782}{10,000} = 0.0782$$

$$s(\bar{x}_{st}) = \sqrt{0.0782} = 0.28$$

Thus, the standard error of $\bar{x}_{st}$ is estimated to be $280.

Summarizing our discussion, we may state the advantages of proportional allocation as follows:

(1) The allocation does not require knowledge of the stratum variances, as required by the other methods.
(2) The allocation does not require knowledge of the costs of sampling units in the different strata, as required by the other methods.
(3) The increase in precision obtained from other, more complicated methods is not very large.
(4) The sample mean $\bar{x}$ can be obtained from the sample as shown in equation (4)

As will be shown, when there is a very large variation in stratum variances, the gain in precision obtained by other methods—such as the optimum allocation methods—may outweigh the simplicity of the procedure of proportional allocation. This method, however, is the one most frequently used in practice.

Problems

1. Given the following population of 2 strata, select a random sample of size $n = 8$ by proportional allocation.
   stratum I :   5, 9, 4, 5, 2   8, 4, 5, 2
   stratum II: 13, 16, 18, 16, 18,   17, 19, 17, 16, 11,   18, 14, 13, 15, 12

2. Using the sample selected in Problem 1, estimate $\bar{X}$ and X.

3. Continuing Problem 2, find $\hat{V}(\bar{x}_{prop})$ and $s(\bar{x}_{prop})$.

4. Also calculate $\hat{V}(\hat{X}_{prop})$ and $s(\hat{X}_{prop})$.

5. Suppose 1000 retail outlets of a certain commodity are stratified according to the number of employees as follows.

Strata	N_h	s_h^2	$\bar{x}_h$
small	600	2	$ 5
medium	300	8	$15
large	100	32	$30

Estimate the total sales and sampling variance of the commodity by proportional stratified sampling. Let the sample size be $n = 80$ and carry out the calculations in the following order.

  (i) Determine n_h.
  (ii) Assume s_h and $\bar{x}_h$ (in units of $1000) have been found from the subsamples as shown in the table. Estimate X.
  (iii) Find $\hat{V}(\hat{X}_{prop})$ and $s(\hat{X}_{prop})$.
  (iv) Find the $z = 2$ (95 %) confidence interval for X.

  6. Suppose 500 farms are stratified according to size (acres) as in the following table. We wish to estimate the total number of hogs.

Strata	N_h	s_h	$\bar{x}_h$
large	80	12	50 hogs
medium	160	8	30
small	260	4	10

  (i) Select a sample of size $n = 100$ by proportional allocation.
  (ii) Assuming the average number of hogs $\bar{x}_h$ and s_h are as given in the table. Estimate X.
  (iii) Find $\hat{V}(\hat{X}_{prop})$ and $s(\hat{X}_{prop})$.
  (iv) Find the $z = 2$ confidence interval.

  7. Work out the details of the derivation of equation (6) from equation (5).

6.9 Optimum allocation

   In some cases it may be necessary to conduct a sample survey with a fixed budget, but with varying costs of selecting sampling units from different strata. For example, when families are stratified into urban and rural classifications in order to survey their average income, the cost of selecting sampling units from urban and rural families will usually differ.
   As we have already discussed in section 6.7, the costs were divided into fixed and variable categories, and the cost function was shown by

(1)
$$c = c_0 + \sum_{}^{L} c_h n_h$$

The c_0 was the fixed cost, and included office rent, fixed administrative costs, equipment costs, etc., and did not depend on the size of the sample survey. The c_h was the variable cost, and showed the cost per sampling unit in the hth stratum. Hence, $c_h n_h$ is the cost of selecting n_h families from the hth stratum.
   It will, however, be convenient for our subsequent analysis to simplify this cost function as follows:

(2)
$$c - c_0 = \sum_{}^{L} c_h n_h$$

and further simplify this by letting the single letter c represent $c - c_0$. Then, (2) becomes

(3)
$$c = \sum_{h}^{L} c_h n_h$$

The reason for this simplification is that in the subsequent discussion of finding conditions for minimizing variances, the fixed cost (c_0) has no effect. In our present problem, where the budget for the survey is given, c is given.

Using cost function (3), we may state our problem as follows: Given a fixed budget c, select a sample of size n, and allocate this sample into n_1 and n_2 so that the sampling variance of the average income—$V(\bar{x}_{\text{st}})$—is minimized. This method of allocating the sample n among strata so as to minimize $V(\bar{x}_{\text{st}})$ is called *optimum allocation*.

The variance of $\bar{x}_{\text{st}}$ was found to be

(4)
$$V(\bar{x}_{\text{st}}) = \frac{1}{N^2} \sum_{h}^{L} N_h^2 \frac{N_h - n_h}{N_h} \frac{S_h^2}{n_h}$$

Hence, we may state our problem in mathematical terminology as follows: Find values of n_h that will minimize $V(\bar{x}_{\text{st}})$ subject to the linear budget constraint (3). This is a simple calculus problem, and its solution is given in the reference. The result is

(5)
$$n_h = \frac{N_h S_h / \sqrt{c_h}}{\sum^{L} (N_h S_h) / \sqrt{c_h}} \cdot n$$

This equation shows that n_h is proportional to $N_h S_h$, which means that when N_h or S_h are large, a large n_h must be taken. For example, if there are a large number of urban families relative to rural families, select more urban families. And if the variation within the urban stratum is large, select more units from that stratum. This is intuitively obvious. The more heterogeneous the stratum, the larger the sample necessary to represent that stratum. The cost factor $\sqrt{c_h}$ shows that we should take more units from the stratum where the cost c_h is smaller.

The variance for optimum allocation is obtained by substituting (5) into (4). To prepare for this, let us first rewrite (4) as follows:

(6)
$$V(\bar{x}_{\text{st}}) = \sum \left(\frac{N_h}{N}\right)^2 \frac{S_h^2}{n_h} - \frac{1}{N^2} \sum N_h S_h^2$$

Substituting (5) into the right hand side gives us:

(7)
$$V(\bar{x}_{\text{opt}}) = \frac{1}{N^2} \frac{1}{n} (\sum N_h S_h \sqrt{c_h})\left(\sum \frac{N_h S_h}{\sqrt{c_h}}\right) - \frac{1}{N^2} \sum N_h S_h^2$$

which is the variance for the optimum allocation.

The estimator of $V(\bar{x}_{\text{opt}})$ is obtained by substituting

(8)
$$s_h^2 = \frac{1}{n_h - 1} \sum^{n_h} (x_{hi} - \bar{x}_h)^2$$

for S_h^2 in equation (7)

Example 1. Given the following population, allocate the sample of size $n = 4$ by the optimum allocation procedure and find estimators for the population mean and its sampling variance. Assume $c_1 = \$1$, $c_2 = \$4$.

Stratum I	Stratum II
2	8
2	8
4	12
6	16
6	16

(i) Find n_h.

We find $S_1^2 = 4$, $S_1 = 2$, $S_2^2 = 16$, $S_2 = 4$. Hence we set up the following worksheet.

	N_h	S_h	S_h^2	c_h	$\sqrt{c_h}$	$N_h S_h$	$(N_h S_h)/\sqrt{c_h}$
I	5	2	4	1	1	10	10
II	5	4	16	4	2	20	10
							20

$$n_1 = \frac{N_1 S_1/\sqrt{c_1}}{\sum (N_h S_h)/\sqrt{c_h}} \cdot n = \frac{10}{20}(4) = 2$$

$$n_2 = \frac{N_2 S_2/\sqrt{c_2}}{\sum (N_h S_h)/\sqrt{c_h}} \cdot n = \frac{10}{20}(4) = 2$$

As is seen, the n_h have been obtained by first calculating the population variances S_1^2 and S_2^2. In practical problems, S_1^2 and S_2^2 are usually unknown and need to be estimated. However, in the present example, the main object is to illustrate the computational procedure of the formulas, and the population parameters S_1^2 and S_2^2 have been calculated.

(ii) Find $\bar{x}_{st}$.

Using a random number table, select $n_1 = 2$ and $n_2 = 2$ sampling units from strata I and II. Suppose we select:

$$\bar{x}_{st} = \frac{N_1 \bar{x}_1 + N_2 \bar{x}_2}{N}$$

$$= \frac{5 \times 5 + 5 \times 12}{10} = 8.5$$

I	II
$x_{11} = 4$	$x_{21} = 8$
$x_{12} = 6$	$x_{22} = 16$
$x_1 = 10$	$x_2 = 24$
$\bar{x}_1 = 5$	$\bar{x}_2 = 12$

(iii) Find $V(\bar{x}_{opt})$.

	$N_h S_h \sqrt{c_h}$	$N_h S_h^2$	$(N_h S_h)^2$	$(N_h S_h)^2/n_h$
I	10	20	100	50
II	40	80	400	200
	50	100		250

$$V(\bar{x}_{opt}) = \frac{1}{N^2}\frac{1}{n}(\sum N_h S_h \sqrt{c_h})\left(\sum \frac{N_h S_h}{\sqrt{c_h}}\right) - \frac{1}{N^2}\sum N_h S_h^2$$

$$= (1/10)^2(1/4)\,(50)(20) - (1/10)^2(100) = 2.5 - 1 = 1.5$$

We may obtain $V(\bar{x}_{opt})$ by substituting the values of n_h found in (i) directly into equation (4). Since $n_1 = 2$ and $n_2 = 2$, we get

$$V(\bar{x}_{st}) = \frac{1}{N^2} \sum N_h^2 \frac{S_h^2}{n_h} - \frac{1}{N^2} \sum N_h S_h^2$$
$$= (1/10)^2(250) - (1/10)^2(100) = 2.5 - 1 = 1.5$$

which is the same result as we have already found.

(iv) Find $\hat{V}(\bar{x}_{opt})$.

The estimator $\hat{V}(\bar{x}_{opt})$ is found by substituting s_h^2 for S_h^2. The values of s_1^2 and s_2^2 are obtained from the samples that have been selected in (iii) above. We find $s_1^2 = 2$ and $s_2^2 = 32$. Hence, the worksheet becomes:

	N_h	N_h^2	s_h^2	$(N_h s_h)^2$	$(N_h s_h)^2/n_h$	$N_h s_h^2$
I	5	25	2	50	25	10
II	5	25	32	800	400	160
					425	170

$$\hat{V}(\bar{x}_{opt}) = (1/10)^2(425) - (1/10)^2(170)$$
$$= 4.25 - 1.7 = 2.55$$
$$s(\bar{x}_{opt}) = \sqrt{2.55} = 1.59$$

Note that in practical problems, s_h^2 must be estimated, and these results are used to determine n_h.

Example 2. Using the data in the table given below, let us find $\bar{x}_{st}$ and its sampling variance by the optimum stratified sampling procedure. Let the sample size be $n = 100$, $c_1 = \$9$, $c_2 = \$4$, and $c_3 = \$1$.

(i) Find n_h.

As mentioned in Example 1, in order to find n_h we need to know s_h, and to calculate s_h, we need to know n_h. To overcome this impasse, we may select preliminary samples (or *subordinate samples*) of size n_h', and obtain preliminary estimates of s_h which we shall call s_h'. After n_h are found by using the s_h', we can relaculate s_h to check the preliminary estimates of s_h'. Let us assume for simplicity that $s_h' = s_h$, and that the values of s_h are as given in the table.

Strata	N_h	s_h	$N_h s_h$	c_h	$\sqrt{c_h}$	$(N_h s_h)/\sqrt{c_h}$
I	80	12	960	9	3	320
II	160	8	1280	4	2	640
III	260	4	1040	1	1	1040
						2000

$$n_1 = (320/2000) \times 100 = 16$$
$$n_2 = (640/2000) \times 100 = 32$$
$$n_3 = (1040/2000) \times 100 = 52$$
$$\overline{\hspace{3em}100}$$

(ii) Find $\bar{x}_{st}$.

Using the results of $n_1 = 16$, $n_2 = 32$, and $n_3 = 52$, the sample means $\bar{x}_h$ are obtained. Assume they are as in the table below. Then, $\bar{x}_{st}$ is obtained as follows:

N_h	$\bar{x}_h$	$N_h \bar{x}_h$
80	50	4000
160	30	4800
260	10	2600
500		11400

$$\bar{x}_{st} = \sum N_h \bar{x}_h / N$$
$$= 11{,}400/500 = 22.8$$

(iii) Find $\hat{V}(\bar{x}_{opt})$.

$(N_h s_h)^2$	(A) $(N_h s_h)^2/n_h$	(B) $(N_h - n_h)/N_h$	(A) × (B)
960^2	$960^2/16$	$64/80$	46,080
1280^2	$1280^2/32$	$128/160$	40,960
1040^2	$1040^2/52$	$208/260$	16,640
			103,680

$$\hat{V}(\bar{x}_{opt}) = \frac{1}{N^2} \sum \frac{N_h - n_h}{N_h} \frac{(N_h s_h)^2}{n_h}$$
$$= (1/500)^2(103{,}680) = 0.41472$$
$$s(\bar{x}_{opt}) = 0.643$$

(iv) Find the 3σ confidence interval.
$$22.8 - 3(0.643) < \bar{X} < 22.8 + 3(0.643)$$
$$20.9 < \bar{X} < 24.7$$

As is seen from

$$n_h = \frac{N_h s_h/\sqrt{c_h}}{\sum (N_h s_h/\sqrt{c_h})} \cdot n$$

the characteristics of this method are that we need to know s_h and c_h. However, accurate knowledge of c_h is usually unknown. In some cases, such as using the mail questionnaire procedure or hiring interviewers on a daily basis and assigning quotas, c_h may be known. However, as can be seen from the equation, it is not necessary to know the absolute values of c_h— only the ratio of costs for the different strata are necessary. For example, suppose the ratio is $1 : 3$ for $L = 2$ strata. Then, for stratum 1, we have, since $c_2 = 3c_1$,

$$n_1 = \frac{N_1 s_1/\sqrt{c_1}}{(N_1 s_1/\sqrt{c_1}) + (N_2 s_2/\sqrt{c_2})} \cdot n$$
$$= \frac{N_1 s_1}{N_1 s_1 + (N_2 s_2/\sqrt{3})} \cdot n$$

and the absolute value of c_h does not need to be known. When accurate knowledge of cost ratios are not available, which is usually the case, they may be estimated in an indirect way. For example, when the first stratum is urban and the second stratum is rural, it may be known that it takes three times as much time to interview a person in the rural area, and hence the cost for stratum 2 may be estimated to be three times that of stratum 1.

Variances are also usually unknown, and hence need to be estimated in advance. For this purpose, it may be necessary to conduct a pilot survey or to use previous information. Also note that to calculate n_h, it is necessary to know only the ratio of the s_h for the various strata. Hence, if the s_h for the urban and rural population are known to be $1:2$, knowing the absolute value of s_h is not necessary.

Another point to note is that when the differences of s_h for the various strata are not large and the differences of c_h are not large, we may set $s_1 = s_2$ and $c_1 = c_2$, and equation (3) becomes

$$n_h = \frac{N_h}{N} \cdot n$$

which is the proportional allocation. That is, when the s_h and c_h do not differ greatly, the optimum allocation method becomes similar to the proportional allocation method.

Conversely, we may say that for the characteristic of the optimum allocation method to be fully realized, the s_h and c_h should vary from stratum to stratum. The practical implication of this is that when strata are similar, the optimum allocation method may not produce a large improvement in precision over proportional allocation. For example, when stratifying according to geographical districts, the variation of s_h may not be very large. Suppose we wish to estimate the average sales of supermarkets. We may stratify according to districts and select random samples of supermarkets—in this case, the variation between strata may not be large. We may also stratify the supermarkets according to floor space. Floor space is a continuous variable, and when stratifying with respect to a continuous variable, large variations in s_h may be obtained.

However, in many surveys the object may be to estimate a number of different characteristics. We may wish to estimate the average sales of supermarkets, the average number of customers per day, the average number of hours they are open, etc. As a result, stratification that brings about a large variation of s_h for one characteristic may produce only a small variation for another. Thus, the overall result may not differ greatly from proportional allocation.

Reference

Equation (5) may be found by using the Lagrange multiplier method. We have

(3)
$$c = \sum_{h}^{L} c_h n_h$$

(4)
$$V(\bar{x}_{st}) = \frac{1}{N^2} \sum_{h}^{L} N_h^2 \frac{N_h - n_h}{N_h} \frac{S_h^2}{n_h}$$

Minimize (4) subject to the linear constraint (3). Using the Lagrange multiplier method, we get

$$\phi = \frac{1}{N^2} \sum N_h^2 \frac{N_h - n_h}{N_h} \frac{S_h^2}{n_h} + \lambda (\sum_{}^{L} c_h n_h - c)$$

$$\frac{\partial \phi}{\partial n_h} = 0: \qquad -\frac{N_h^2}{N^2} \frac{S_h^2}{n_h^2} + \lambda c_h = 0$$

(9)
$$\therefore \quad n_h = \frac{1}{\sqrt{\lambda}} \frac{N_h S_h}{N \sqrt{c_h}}$$

Sum both sides over L:

$$\sum n_h = n = \frac{1}{\sqrt{\lambda}} \sum \frac{N_h S_h}{N \sqrt{c_h}}$$

$$\therefore \quad \sqrt{\lambda} = \frac{1}{n} \cdot \frac{1}{N} \cdot \sum \frac{N_h S_h}{\sqrt{c_h}}$$

Substitute this into (9). Then

$$n_h = \frac{N_h S_h / \sqrt{c_h}}{\sum (N_h S_h / \sqrt{c_h})} \cdot n$$

Problems

1. Substitute equation (5) into (4) and derive (7).

2. Find $V(\hat{X}_{\text{opt}})$ from $V(\bar{x}_{\text{opt}})$.

3. Given the following population, allocate a sample of size $n = 10$ by optimum allocation.

  stratum I   :   2, 4, 4, 6, 6, 8
  stratum II :   8, 8, 12, 16, 16, 18
  stratum III :   16, 16, 18, 22, 22, 26

Assume $c_1 = \$1$, $c_2 = \$4$, $c_3 = \$9$.

4. Using the data of Problem 3, calculate $V(\bar{x}_{\text{opt}})$.

5. Using the n_h found in Problem 3, select random subsamples and estimate $\bar{X}$.

6. Continuing Problem 5, find $\hat{V}(\bar{x}_{\text{opt}})$ and the 2σ confidence interval for $\bar{X}$.

7. Using the data of Problem 1 on page 128, select a sample of size $n = 8$ by optimum allocation. Let $c_1 = \$1$, $c_2 = \$4$.

8. Using the sample selected in Problem 7,
   (i) Estimate $\bar{X}$ and X.
   (ii) Find $\hat{V}(\bar{x}_{\text{opt}})$ and $s(\bar{x}_{\text{opt}})$.
   (iii) Find $\hat{V}(\hat{X}_{\text{opt}})$ and $s(\hat{X}_{\text{opt}})$.

9. Using the data of Problem 5 on page 128,
   (i) Allocate a sample of size $n = 80$ by optimum allocation. Let $c_1 = \$1$, $c_2 = \$4$, $c_3 = \$9$.
   (ii) Estimate X. Use the $\bar{x}_h$ of the table.
   (iii) Find $\hat{V}(\hat{X}_{\text{opt}})$ and $s(\hat{X}_{\text{opt}})$. Use the s_h of the table.
   (iv) Find the $z = 2$ confidence interval for X.

10. Using the data of Problem 6 on page 129,
   (i) Allocate a sample of size $n = 100$ by optimum allocation. Let $c_1 = \$9$, $c_2 = \$4$, $c_3 = \$1$.
   (ii) Estimate X(the total number of hogs). Use the $\bar{x}_h$ of the table.
   (iii) Find $s(\hat{X}_{\text{opt}})$. Use the $\bar{x}_h$ of the table.
   (iv) Find the $z = 2$ confidence interval for X.

6.10 Neyman allocation

In some cases, the costs c_h for different strata may not differ greatly, and may thus allow us to assume c_h are equal for all strata. Let us set $c_h = c_f$. The cost function of the previous section then becomes

$$c = c_0 + c_f \sum_{}^{L} n_h = c_0 + c_f n$$

which may be rewritten as

$$n = \frac{c - c_0}{c_f}$$

Hence, the sample size n becomes fixed.

Using this result, the problem of optimum allocation may be restated as follows. Given a fixed sample size n, find n_h which minimize $V(\bar{x}_{\text{st}})$. In terms of symbols, we have

(1) $$V(\bar{x}_{\text{st}}) = \sum_{}^{L} \left(\frac{N_h}{N}\right)^2 \frac{N_h - n_h}{N_h} \frac{S_h^2}{n_h}$$

(2) $$n_1 + n_2 + \cdots + n_L = n = \text{fixed}$$

By using calculus, we can find the n_h that minimizes (1). However, we may simply use our result of section 6.9. By letting $c_h = c_f = $ constant in equation (3) of section 6.9, it becomes

(3) $$n_h = \frac{N_h S_h}{\sum N_h S_h} \cdot n$$

This shows that the sample n is allocated in proportion to $N_h S_h$. That is, take more from the large strata, and from strata that are more heterogeneous. For example, if a city is stratified into two districts, and in one district there is very little difference among family incomes whereas in the second district there is a large variation, equation (3) tells us to take more from the second district (which has the larger S_h.) This is clearly in accord with common sense. The greater the variation in a district, the larger the sample must be to avoid an unrepresentative sample.

This method of allocation was proposed by J. Neyman in 1934 and is sometimes called Neyman's allocation. We shall use this term to distinguish it from the optimum allocation of section 6.9.

The population mean is estimated by substituting the $\bar{x}_h$ obtained from the subsamples n_h calculated from equation (3) into

(4)
$$\bar{x}_{st} = \frac{\sum N_h \bar{x}_h}{N}$$

Since $\bar{x}_h$ is an unbiased estimator of $\bar{X}_h$, $\bar{x}_{st}$ is an unbiased estimator of $\bar{X}$. The variance of $\bar{x}_{st}$ obtained by the Neyman allocation becomes, by substituting (3) into (1):

(5)
$$V(\bar{x}_{Ney}) = \frac{1}{N^2} \frac{(\sum N_h S_h)^2}{n} - \frac{1}{N^2} \sum N_h S_h^2$$

The characteristic of equation (5) is that it does not involve the n_h. It is, however, not necessary to use the form of equation (5) to calculate $V(\bar{x}_{Ney})$. We may simply substitute the values of n_h into (1) and find the value of $V(\bar{x}_{st})$.

When the variances S_h^2 are unknown, the sample estimates s_h^2 are used. It is necessary to know the n_h to calculate the s_h^2. On the other hand, it is necessary to know the s_h^2 to calculate the n_h. Hence, to overcome this impasse, it is usually necessary to draw subordinate samples n_h' or use past data or some other means, and make preliminary estimates of s_h which we shall denote as s_h'.

Using these s_h', the n_h are calculated and the s_h are recalculated and checked against the preliminary estimates s_h'. If the discrepancy between s_h and s_h' may be ignored, we shall use this allocation of n_h. Otherwise, this process may be repeated until the values of s_h become stable.

Example 1. Using the data of Example 2, section 6.9, find $\bar{x}_{st}$ and $\hat{V}(\bar{x}_{st})$ by Neyman's sampling procedure. Assume that the s_h have been estimated from past data and that $n = 100$.

Strata	N_h	n_h	s_h	$N_h s_h$	$\bar{x}_h$	$N_h \bar{x}_h$
1	80	29	12	960	80	4000
2	160	39	8	1280	30	4800
3	260	32	4	1040	10	2600
	500	100		3280		11400

(i) Find n_h.

$$n_h = \frac{N_h s_h}{\sum N_h s_h} \cdot n$$

$$n_1 = \left(\frac{960}{3280}\right) \times 100 \doteq 29$$

$$n_2 = \left(\frac{1280}{3280}\right) \times 100 \doteq 39$$

$$n_3 = \left(\frac{1040}{3280}\right) \times 100 \doteq 32$$

(ii) Find $\bar{x}_{st}$.

Drawing samples of n_h, we calculate the subsample means $\bar{x}_h$ and the results are assumed to be as shown in the above table. Then $\bar{x}_{st}$ is:

$$\bar{x}_{st} = \frac{\sum N_h \bar{x}_h}{N} = \frac{11,400}{500} = 22.8$$

(iii) Find $\hat{V}(\bar{x}_{Ney})$.

$(N_h s_h)^2$	(A) $(N_h s_h)^2/n_h$	(B) $(N_h - n_h)/N_h$	(A) × (B)
960^2	$960^2/29$	$51/80$	20,000
1280^2	$1280^2/39$	$121/160$	31,000
1040^2	$1040^2/32$	$228/260$	30,000
			81,000

$$\hat{V}(\bar{x}_{Ney}) = \frac{1}{N^2} \sum \frac{N_h - n_h}{N_h} \frac{(N_h s_h)^2}{n_h}$$
$$= (1/500)^2(81,000) = 0.32$$
$$s(\bar{x}_{Ney}) = 0.566$$

(iv) Find the $z = 2$ (95%) confidence interval for $\bar{X}$.

$$22.8 - 2(0.57) < \bar{X} < 22.8 + 2(0.57)$$
$$21.66 < \bar{X} < 23.94$$

One additional point to note about the Neyman allocation is that when all the S_h^2 are assumed to be equal, equation (3) becomes

$$n_h = \frac{N_h}{\sum N_h} \cdot n = \frac{N_h}{N} \cdot n$$

which is the formula for proportional allocation.

Problems

1. Substitute equation (3) into (1) and show how (5) is derived.

2. Find $V(\hat{X}_{Ney})$ from $V(\bar{x}_{Ney})$.

3. Using the data of Problem 1 on page 128,
   (i) Calculate S_1 and S_2.
   (ii) Select a sample of size $n = 8$ by Neyman's procedure using the S_1 and S_2 obtained in (i). Assume the c_h are all equal.
   (iii) Calculate $V(\bar{x}_{Ney})$.
   (iv) Using the sample that has been selected in (ii), estimate $\bar{X}$ and X.
   (v) Find s_1 and s_2 from the sample.
   (vi) Allocate the sample $n = 8$ using s_1 and s_2.
   (vii) Calculate $\hat{V}(\bar{x}_{Ney})$ and $s(\bar{x}_{Ney})$.

4. Using the data of Problem 3 of page 135, (assume the c_h are equal)
   (i) Calculate S_1, S_2, S_3.

(ii) Select a sample of size $n = 10$ by Neyman's allocation using the results of (i).

(iii) Estimate X and $\bar{X}$ using the results of (ii)

(iv) Find s_1, s_2 and s_3.

(v) Allocate the sample $n = 10$ using the s_1, s_2 and s_3.

(vi) Estimate X and $\bar{X}$ using the results of (v).

(vii) Calculate $\hat{V}(\hat{X}_{\mathrm{Ney}})$ and $s(\hat{X}_{\mathrm{Ney}})$.

5. Using the data of Problem 5 of page 128

(i) Select a sample of size $n = 80$ by Neyman's allocation.

(ii) Estimate X (total sales).

(iii) Find $\hat{V}(\hat{X}_{\mathrm{Ney}})$ and $s(\hat{X}_{\mathrm{Ney}})$.

(iv) Calculate the $z = 2$ confidence interval for X.

6.11 Determination of the sample size n.

In section 6.7 we proposed two problems: the first was the allocation of the sample n, and the second was the determination of n. In sections 6.8, 6.9, and 6.10 we assumed a given sample size n and considered how this was allocated among the different strata. We found methods such as proportional allocation, optimum allocation, and Neyman allocation. Let us now consider the second problem—how the sample size n is determined.

We found in simple random sampling that the determination of n depends on the sampling variance of the estimator. Similarly, for stratified sampling, we need to know the sampling variances of the various methods of allocation to determine n for each of these methods. So let us first summarize the methods of allocation as follows:

1. Equal samples from each stratum.
2. Proportional allocation.
3. Optimum allocation—fixed budget, varying sampling costs among strata.
4. Neyman allocation—fixed sample size, equal sampling costs among strata.

The stratum sample sizes n_h for these methods of allocation are:

(1) $$n_h = \frac{n}{L}$$ (equal samples)

(2) $$n_h = \frac{N_h}{N} \cdot n$$ (proportional)

(3) $$n_h = \frac{N_h S_h / \sqrt{c_h}}{\sum (N_h S_h / \sqrt{c_h})} \cdot n$$ (optimum)

(4) $$n_h = \frac{N_h S_h}{\sum N_h S_h} \cdot n$$ (Neyman)

As mentioned above, we need to know the variances of these methods to determine the sample size n. So let us next find the variances for these various methods of allocation. Since the basic form of the variance of $\bar{x}_{\text{st}}$ is

$$(5) \qquad V(\bar{x}_{\text{st}}) = \Sigma \left(\frac{N_h}{N}\right)^2 \frac{N_h - n_h}{N_h} \frac{S_h^2}{n_h}$$

the variance for the various methods of allocation are obtained by substituting the formulas for the n_h of (1)—(4) into (5). The results are

$$(6) \qquad V(\bar{x}_{\text{eq}}) = \frac{L}{N^2} \Sigma \frac{N_h^2 S_h^2}{n} - \frac{1}{N^2} \Sigma N_h S_h^2$$

$$(7) \qquad V(\bar{x}_{\text{prop}}) = \frac{1}{N} \Sigma \frac{N_h S_h^2}{n} - \frac{1}{N^2} \Sigma N_h S_h^2$$

$$(8) \qquad V(\bar{x}_{\text{opt}}) = \frac{1}{N^2} \frac{1}{n} (\Sigma N_h S_h \sqrt{c_h}) \left(\Sigma \frac{N_h S_h}{\sqrt{c_h}}\right) - \frac{1}{N^2} \Sigma N_h S_h^2$$

$$(9) \qquad V(\bar{x}_{\text{Ney}}) = \frac{1}{N^2} \frac{(\Sigma N_h S_h)^2}{n} - \frac{1}{N^2} \Sigma N_h S_h^2$$

With this much preparation, let us now consider how n is determined. As in the previous sections, we start with the basic formula

$$(10) \qquad d^2 = z^2 V(\bar{x}_{\text{st}})$$

where d is the required precision, z is the level of reliability, and $V(\bar{x}_{\text{st}})$ is the variance of the estimator $\bar{x}_{\text{st}}$.

Suppose we are given a precision d_0 to attain, and a level of reliability z_0. Then, from (10),

$$(11) \qquad V(\bar{x}_{\text{st}}) = \frac{d_0^2}{z_0^2}$$

gives us the variance necessary to achieve the desired d_0 and z_0. Hence, we shall call (11) the *desired variance*. Let us indicate the desired variance by D^2. That is,

$$(12) \qquad V(\bar{x}_{\text{st}}) = \frac{d_0^2}{z_0^2} = D^2$$

We know that as the sample size n becomes larger, the $V(\bar{x}_{\text{st}})$ becomes smaller. Thus, our problem of finding the sample size n may be stated a follows: We wish to find a sample size n such that the variance of $\bar{x}_{\text{st}}$ is equal to D^2.

For the first method of allocating the sample equally among strata, we find from (11) and (6)

$$(13) \qquad D^2 = \frac{L}{N^2} \Sigma \frac{N_h^2 S_h^2}{n} - \frac{1}{N^2} \Sigma N_h S_h^2$$

which becomes

$$N^2 D^2 + \Sigma N_h S_h^2 = \frac{1}{n} L \Sigma N_h^2 S_h^2$$

Solving for n, we find

(14)
$$n = \frac{L \sum N_h^2 S_h^2}{N^2 D^2 + \sum N_h S_h^2}$$

When the sampling fraction n_h/N_h is very small or negligible, the fpc $= 1$, and the variance in equation (5) becomes

(15)
$$V(\bar{x}_{st}) = \sum \left(\frac{N_h}{N}\right)^2 \frac{S_h^2}{n_h}$$

Substituting equation (1) into this gives us

(16)
$$V(\bar{x}_{eq}) = \frac{L}{N^2} \sum \frac{N_h^2 S_h^2}{n}$$

Setting this equal to the desired variance D^2 and solving for n gives us

(17)
$$n = \frac{L \sum N_h^2 S_h^2}{N^2 D^2}$$

In other words, when the sampling fraction n_h/N_h is very small, and fpc $= 1$, we may omit the second term $\sum N_h S_h^2$ in the denominator of (14).

Applying similar procedures to find n in the other three cases, we find:

(18) $n = \dfrac{N \sum N_h S_h^2}{N^2 D^2 + \sum N_h S_h^2}$ (proportional)

(19) $n = \dfrac{(\sum N_h S_h \sqrt{c_h})(\sum N_h S_h / \sqrt{c_h})}{N^2 D^2 + \sum N_h S_h^2}$ (optimum)

(20) $n = \dfrac{(\sum N_h S_h)^2}{N^2 D^2 + \sum N_h S_h^2}$ (Neyman)

When n_h/N_h is small and fpc $= 1$, the second term in the denominator on the right side of the equation may be omitted, leaving only $N^2 D^2$.

The formulas for n have been stated in terms of the population variances S_h^2; but in practical applications, its unbiased estimator s_h^2 is used. And as explained in the previous sections, a preliminary sample may be selected or past data may be used, or some other method devised to obtain a preliminary estimator, $s_h'^2$.

Let us illustrate the use of the formulas for n with a hypothetical example. Suppose restaurants in a city have been divided into 3 strata: 600 small, 300 medium, and 100 large, We are interested in the average number of customers per day. Let the standard deviation be 20, 30, and 50 customers for the restaurants in each stratum, respectively.

Strata	N_h	s_h	s_h^2	$N_h s_h$	$N_h s_h^2$	$N_h^2 s_h^2$
1	600	20	400	12,000	240,000	144,000,000
2	300	30	900	9,000	270,000	81,000,000
3	100	50	2500	5,000	250,000	25,000,000
	1000			26,000	760,000	250,000,000

Case 1. Equal size samples ($n_h = n/L$).

To determine the sample size n when equal size subsamples $n_h = n/L$ are selected from each stratum, we first need to determine the magnitude of D, the desired standard error. As in our previous examples, we shall assume that the level of reliability is to be "practically certain", that is, $z = 3$. Suppose we wish the precision to be within ± 3 customers. Then

$$D = d/z = 3/3 = 1 \text{ customer}$$

This simply means we are setting 1 standard error equal to 1 customer. Hence, a confidence interval of $\pm 3\sigma_{\bar{x}}$ becomes equal to an interval of ± 3 customers. With $D = 1$, we can find n as follows. From equation (14)

$$n = \frac{L \sum N_h^2 s_h^2}{N^2 D^2 + \sum N_h s_h^2}$$

$$= \frac{3(250,000,000)}{(1000)^2(1)^2 + 760,000} = 426$$

Thus, every n_h is

$$n_h = \frac{n}{L} = \frac{426}{3} = 142$$

However, note that stratum 3 has only 100 restaurants. In a case such as this, where the number of sampling units allocated to the stratum exceeds the number of units in the stratum, all of the units in the stratum are used and the difference ($142 - 100 = 42$) is allocated evenly to the other strata. In our present case, it will be ($142 + 42/2$) for each of the remaining two strata.

However, if proportional allocation or optimum allocation are used, all of the sampling units in the third stratum would be used, and the sample size (n_h) for the other strata would be recomputed. This procedure will be shown later.

Let us calculate the variance as an exercise and check. Since we have determined the sample size $n = 426$ so that the desired variance $D^2 = 1$, the variance obtained from equation (6) should also equal 1. To find this, substitute $n = 426$ into (6). Then

$$\hat{V}(\bar{x}_{eq}) = \frac{L}{N^2} \sum \frac{N_h^2 s_h^2}{n} - \frac{1}{N^2} \sum N_h s_h^2$$

$$= \frac{1}{(1000)^2} \left[\frac{3(250,000,000)}{426} - 760,000 \right]$$

$$= 1.76 - 0.76 = 1$$

Case 2. Proportional allocation.

For proportional allocation the sample size is, from equation (18)

$$n = \frac{N \sum N_h s_h^2}{N^2 D^2 + \sum N_h s_h^2}$$

$$= \frac{1000(760,000)}{(1000)^2(1) + 760,000} = 432$$

Then, the n_h for the strata are

$$n_h = (N_h/N) \times n$$
$$n_1 = (600/1000) \times 432 = 259$$
$$n_2 = (300/1000) \times 432 = 130$$
$$n_3 = (100/1000) \times 432 = \underline{43}$$
$$432$$

The variance is

$$\hat{V}(\bar{x}_{\text{prop}}) = \frac{1}{N} \sum \frac{N_h s_h^2}{n} - \frac{1}{N^2} \sum N_h s_h^2$$
$$= \frac{1}{1000}\left(\frac{760,000}{432} - \frac{760,000}{1000}\right)$$
$$= 1.76 - 0.76 = 1$$

and checks with our requirement that $D^2 = 1$.

Case 3. Optimum allocation.

For optimum allocation, we need to know the cost c_h of selecting sampling units. Let it be $c_1 = \$1$, $c_2 = \$2$, and $c_3 = \$3$. Then, the various parts of equation (19) are as follows:

$N_h s_h$	$\sqrt{c_h}$	$N_h s_h \sqrt{c_h}$	$N_h s_h / \sqrt{c_h}$
12,000	1	12,000	12,000
9,000	1.414	12,730	6,360
5,000	1.732	8,660	2,890
26,000		35,390	21,250

$$n = \frac{(\sum N_h s_h \sqrt{c_h})(\sum N_h s_h / \sqrt{c_h})}{N^2 D^2 + \sum N_h s_h^2} = \frac{(33,390)(21,250)}{1,000,000 + 760,000} = 403$$

$$n_h = \frac{N_h s_h / \sqrt{c_h}}{\sum N_h s_h / \sqrt{c_h}} \cdot n$$
$$n_1 = (12,000/21,250) \times 403 = 228$$
$$n_2 = (6,360/21,250) \times 403 = 120$$
$$n_3 = (2,890/21,250) \times 403 = \underline{55}$$
$$403$$

$$\hat{V}(\bar{x}_{\text{opt}}) = \frac{1}{N^2} \frac{1}{n}(\sum N_h s_h \sqrt{c_h})\left(\frac{\sum N_h s_h}{\sqrt{c_h}}\right) - \frac{1}{N^2} \sum N_h s_h^2$$
$$= \left[\left(\frac{1}{1000}\right)^2 \left(\frac{1}{403}\right)(33,390)(21,250)\right] - \left[\left(\frac{1}{1000}\right)^2 (760,000)\right]$$
$$= 1.76 - 0.76 = 1$$

Case 4. Neyman allocation

For the Neyman allocation, n is (assuming the c_h are all equal)

$$n = \frac{(\sum N_h s_h)^2}{N^2 D^2 + \sum N_h s_h^2} = \frac{(26,000)^2}{(1000)^2(1)^2 + 760,000} = 384$$

$$n_h = \frac{N_h s_h}{\sum N_h s_h} \cdot n$$

$$n_1 = (12,000/26,000) \times 384 = 177$$
$$n_2 = (9,000/26,000) \ \times 384 = 133$$
$$n_3 = (5,000/26,000) \ \times 384 = \underline{\ 73}$$
$$384$$

A check will show that $\hat{V}(\bar{x}_{\text{Ney}}) = 1$. This check is left as an exercise.

Problems

1. Work out the details of the derivations of equations (18), (19), and (20).

2. Note that the formulas (14), (17), (18), (19), and (20) were obtained when we were estimating the population mean $\bar{X}$, and the precision and desired variance were in terms of $\bar{x}_{\text{st}}$. The desired variance was $(d/z)^2 = D^2(\bar{x}_{\text{st}})$. Show that when estimating the population total X, and the precision and desired variance are expressed in terms of $\hat{X}_{\text{st}}$, the desired variance becomes $(Nd/z)^2$.

3. Continuing Problem 2, show that when we are estimating the population total and the desired variance is in terms of $\hat{X}_{\text{st}}$, equation (17) becomes

(17′)
$$n = \frac{L \sum N_h^2 S_h^2}{D^2}$$

That is, it does not have the N^2 in the denominator. In similar fashion, show that equation (14) becomes

(14′)
$$n = \frac{L \sum N_h^2 S_h^2}{D^2 + \sum N_h S_h^2}$$

4. Continuing Problem 2, derive the equations corresponding to (18), (19), and (20) for the case where the desired variance is in terms of $\hat{X}_{\text{st}}$.

5. Suppose 1000 retail outlets of a certain commodity are stratified according to the number of employees as follows:

Strata	N_h	s_h	$\bar{x}_h$
small	600	$10	$40
medium	300	20	60
large	100	30	80

We wish to estimate the average amount of sales per store with the precision to be within $\pm\$3$ with a reliability of $z = 3$.

  (i) Calculate the desired variance and explain its meaning.

  (ii) Estimate the sample size n for the equal size samples case ($n_h = n/L$), assuming fpc = 1.

  (iii) Estimate the sample size n, assuming fpc $\neq 1$.

(iv) Allocate the sample.

(v) Substitute the n obtained in (ii) in the equation for $V(\bar{x}_{st})$ and check that it becomes equal to the desired variance obtained in (i).

6. Using the data of Problem 4,

(i) Find n for proportional allocation, assuming fpc $= 1$.

(ii) Find n for the case where fpc $\neq 1$.

(iii) Allocate the sample.

(iv) Substitute the n obtained in (ii) in the equation for $V(\bar{x}_{prop})$ and check that it becomes equal to the desired variance.

7. Perform the operations in Problem 5 for the optimum allocation case. Assume $c_1 = \$1$, $c_2 = \$2$, and $c_3 = \$3$.

8. Perform the operations of Problem 5 for the Neyman allocation case.

9. Suppose Problem 4 is stated in terms of estimating total sales and we wish the precision to be within $\pm\$3000$ with $z = 3$. Estimate the sample size. Assume fpc $= 1$.

10. Using the data of Problem 6 on page 129, find the sample size so that the precision of the estimator of the total number of hogs will be within ± 900 hogs with $z = 3$. Assume the equal size sample case of allocation is to be used.

6.12 Comparison of stratified random sampling with simple random sampling

Is stratified random sampling more efficient than simple random sampling? For example, suppose we wish to estimate the total amount of sales of supermarkets in a certain city, and a sample of 100 supermarkets is to be selected for estimation purposes. Should a simple random sample of 100 supermarkets be selected or should a stratified random sample be selected? Which sampling procedure will give a more precise estimate of the total amount of sales?

As we shall see, with adequate stratification and appropriate allocation of the sample, stratified random sampling will be more efficient than simple random sampling. Let us first compare proportional stratified random sampling with simple random sampling and illustrate this point.

(*i*) *Comparison of proportional stratified sampling with simple random sampling.*

To compare the efficiencies of these procedures, we need to compare the variances of the estimators obtained by the two different methods. We know that the variance of the estimators for proportional stratified sampling consists of two parts, the within and between variances of strata. Hence, we shall partition the variance of the estimator obtained from simple random sampling into two parts, the within and between variances. This will enable us to compare the variance of the two sampling procedures. Let us start by partitioning the variance of the estimator obtained by simple random sampling. The variance for simple random sampling is

(1) $$V(\bar{x}) = \frac{N-n}{N} \frac{S^2}{n}$$

For simplicity, assume $N \gg n^*$ and let fpc $= 1$. Then (1) becomes

(2) $$V(\bar{x}) = \frac{S^2}{n}$$

To partition this into two parts, the within and between variances of strata, we use the result of section 6.3, namely,

(3) $$\sigma^2 = \sigma_w^2 + \sigma_b^2$$

When $N \gg 1$, we may set $N - 1 \doteq N$, and then $\sigma^2 \doteq S^2$. Hence (3) becomes

(4) $$S^2 = \sigma_w^2 + \sigma_b^2$$

Substituting this into (2) gives us

(5) $$V(\bar{x}_{\text{ran}}) = \frac{1}{n}(\sigma_w^2 + \sigma_b^2)$$

and we have partitioned the $V(\bar{x}_{\text{ran}})$ into two parts, the within and between variances for strata.

The variance of the estimator for proportional stratified sampling may also be expressed in terms of within and between variances. We know from section 6.8 that

(6) $$V(\bar{x}_{\text{prop}}) = \frac{N-n}{N} \Sigma \frac{N_h S_h^2}{Nn}$$

We also know from Section 6.3 that

(7) $$\sigma_w^2 = \frac{1}{N} \overset{L}{\Sigma} N_h \sigma_h^2$$

When $N_h \gg 1$, we may set $N_h - 1 \doteq N_h$. Then $\sigma_h^2 = S_h^2$, and (7) becomes

(8) $$\sigma_w^2 = \frac{1}{N} \Sigma N_h S_h^2$$

Substituting this into (6) gives us

$$V(\bar{x}_{\text{prop}}) = \frac{N-n}{N} \frac{1}{n} \sigma_w^2$$

(9)

$$\doteq \frac{1}{n} \sigma_w^2$$

where we have set fpc $= 1$.

Hence, substituting (9) into (5), we find

(10) $$V(\bar{x}_{\text{ran}}) = V(\bar{x}_{\text{prop}}) + \frac{1}{n} \sigma_b^2$$

*The symbol $\gg$ means n is very small relative to N

This shows that the variance of proportional stratified random sampling is smaller than $V(\bar{x}_{\text{ran}})$ by $(1/n)\sigma_b^2$.

Since $\sigma_b^2 = 1/N \sum\limits^{L} N_h(\bar{x}_h - \bar{x})^2$ is the variance between the stratum means and the population mean, the precision of proportional stratified random sampling is greater when the variation between strata is large. For example, when estimating the average sales of supermarkets, the large supermarkets are considerably larger than the middle-sized and small ones. In this case, it is more efficient to use stratified sampling. Estimating the average number of acres per farm is another illustration where proportional allocation will be better than simple random sampling because of the great variation in the size of farms.

(*ii*) *Comparison of proportional with Neyman stratified random sampling.*

Let the variance for the Neyman stratified random sampling be shown as

$$(11) \qquad V(\bar{x}_{\text{Ney}}) = \frac{1}{N^2} \frac{(\sum N_h S_h)^2}{n} - \frac{1}{N^2} \sum N_h S_h^2$$

By definition

$$V(\bar{x}_{\text{prop}}) > V(\bar{x}_{\text{Ney}})$$

Let us derive the difference between $V(\bar{x}_{\text{prop}})$ and $V(\bar{x}_{\text{Ney}})$ explicitly and investigate what factors cause this difference. This result will give us criteria as to when to use the Neyman allocation instead of proportional allocation.

The variance for proportional allocation was

$$
\begin{aligned}
V(\bar{x}_{\text{prop}}) &= \frac{N-n}{N} \sum \frac{N_h S_h^2}{Nn} \qquad (\text{fpc} \neq 1) \\
&= \sum \frac{N_h S_h^2}{Nn} \qquad (\text{fpc} = 1)
\end{aligned}
$$
(12)

Using the formula where fpc = 1, we may rewrite this as

$$
\begin{aligned}
V(\bar{x}_{\text{prop}}) &= \sum \frac{N_h S_h^2}{Nn} + \frac{(\sum N_h S_h)^2}{nN^2} - \frac{(\sum N_h S_h)^2}{nN^2} \\
&= V(\bar{x}_{\text{opt}}) + \left[\sum \frac{N_h S_h^2}{Nn} - \frac{(\sum N_h S_h)^2}{nN^2} \right]
\end{aligned}
$$
(13)

The term in brackets may be changed algebraically as follows:

$$
\begin{aligned}
&\frac{1}{nN} \left[\sum N_h S_h^2 - \frac{1}{N} (\sum N_h S_h)^2 \right] \\
&= \frac{1}{nN} \left[\sum N_h S_h^2 - \frac{2}{N} (\sum N_h S_h)^2 + \frac{\sum N_h}{N^2} (\sum N_h S_h)^2 \right] \\
&= \frac{1}{nN} \sum N_h \left[S_h^2 - \frac{2}{N} S_h (\sum N_h S_h) + \frac{1}{N^2} (\sum N_h S_h)^2 \right] \\
&= \frac{1}{nN} \sum N_h \left(S_h - \frac{1}{N} \sum N_h S_h \right)^2 \\
&= \frac{1}{nN} \sum N_h (S_h - \bar{S}_h)^2
\end{aligned}
$$

where

$$\bar{S}_h = \frac{1}{N} \sum N_h S_h$$

Hence, equation (13) becomes

(14) $$V(\bar{x}_{\text{prop}}) = V(\bar{x}_{\text{opt}}) + \frac{1}{nN} \sum N_h(S_h - \bar{S}_h)^2$$

The term $\bar{S}_h$ may be considered a weighted average of S_h (the stratum standard deviation). Hence, the term $\sum N_h(S_h - \bar{S}_h)^2$ may be considered as showing the dispersion of S_h around its mean $\bar{S}_h$. The greater the scatter of S_h around $\bar{S}_h$, the larger the term $(S_h - \bar{S}_h)^2$, and the greater the difference between $V(\bar{x}_{\text{prop}})$ and $V(\bar{x}_{\text{opt}})$.

In practical terms, this means that when there is a great difference between stratum sizes and also a large variation between stratum variances, there will be an increase in efficiency when the Neyman allocation is used instead of proportional allocation. Sampling supermarkets, farms, chemical corporations, etc., where there are large differences in size, would be illustrations where the Neyman allocation would be more efficient.

However, in many cases where stratification is in terms of geographic location, the difference of strata may not be large, and the gain due to the more complicated Neyman allocation over the simple proportional allocation may not be large.

6.13 Stratified random sampling for proportions

Stratified random sampling may be used advantageously when population proportions are to be estimated. For example, suppose we wish to find the proportions of students who wear glasses in college. We may know from previous studies that the proportion increases rapidly as the students advance to higher grades. Let P be the overall population proportion; P_1, P_2, P_3, and P_4 be the proportions of the first- second- third- and fourth-year students who wear glasses. We wish to estimate these population parameters.

By stratifying the students according to grade, we get a stratified population to which we may apply the stratified random sampling procedure. Since a proportion P is simply a special case of the mean $\bar{X}$ (as we have discussed in Chapter 5), we may use the results of the previous sections on stratified random sampling for the mean to estimate P. Let us in this section show how P is estimated; find its sampling variance; show how the sample is allocated; and finally, show how the sample size is determined.

(*i*) *Estimator of P.*

The population mean $\bar{X}$ in a stratified population was obtained as follows:

(1) $$\bar{X} = \frac{\sum N_h \bar{X}_h}{N}$$

where $\bar{X}_h$ were the stratum means. In terms of proportions, $\bar{X}_h$ is,

(2) $$P_h = \bar{X}_h = \frac{1}{N_h} \sum_i^{N_h} X_{hi}$$

where $X_{hi} = 0$ or 1. Hence, the population proportion P is

(3) $$P = \frac{\sum^L N_h P_h}{N}$$

$$= \frac{\sum^L \sum^{N_h} X_{hi}}{N}$$

We found that

(4) $$\hat{\bar{X}} = \bar{x}_{st} = \frac{\sum^L N_h \bar{x}_h}{N}$$

was an unbiased estimator of $\bar{X}$ for stratified random sampling. In terms of proportions, this becomes

(5) $$\hat{P} = p_{st} = \frac{\sum^L N_h p_h}{N}$$

where

(6) $$p_h = \frac{1}{n_h} \sum_i^{n_h} x_{hi}$$

It is easily seen that p_{st} is an unbiased estimator of P as follows. From (6), we have

$$E(p_h) = \frac{1}{n_h} \sum^{n_h} E(x_{hi})$$

$$= \frac{1}{n_h} \cdot n_h \cdot \sum^{N_h} \frac{1}{N_h} x_{hi}$$

$$= \frac{1}{N_h} \sum_i^{N_h} x_{hi} = P_h$$

Hence, taking the expectation of p_{st} of (5), we have

$$E(p_{st}) = \frac{\sum N_h E(p_h)}{N}$$

$$= \frac{\sum N_h P_h}{N} = P$$

Example 1. Suppose we have the following data concerning students wearing glasses. (i) Find P, P_h. (ii) Draw samples of size $n_1 = 3$, $n_2 = 2$, from strata I and II, and estimate P_1 and P_2. (iii) Estimate P.

(i) Find P, P_h.

$$P_1 = \frac{\sum^5 X_{1i}}{N_1} = \frac{2}{5}$$

$$P_2 = \frac{\sum^5 X_{2i}}{N_2} = \frac{4}{5}$$

	Strata		
	I		II
X_{11}	1	X_{21}	1
X_{12}	0	X_{22}	0
X_{13}	1	X_{23}	1
X_{14}	0	X_{24}	1
X_{15}	0	X_{25}	1
	$\frac{2}{5}$		$\frac{4}{5}$

The population proportion P is

$$P = \frac{\sum\limits^{N} X_i}{N} = \frac{6}{10}$$

which may also be obtained as

$$P = \frac{\sum\limits^{L} N_h P_h}{N} = \frac{N_1 P_1 + N_2 P_2}{N}$$

$$= \frac{5(2/5) + 5(4/5)}{10} = \frac{6}{10}$$

(ii) Let samples $n_1 = 2$ and $n_2 = 3$ be as in the table at right:

n_1	n_2
$x_{11} = 1$	$x_{21} = 1$
$x_{12} = 0$	$x_{22} = 1$
	$x_{23} = 0$

Hence, the subsample proportions are

$$p_1 = \frac{\sum\limits^{n_1} x_{1i}}{n_1} = \frac{1}{2}, \qquad p_2 = \frac{\sum\limits^{n_2} x_{2i}}{n_2} = \frac{2}{3}$$

Hence

$$\hat{P}_1 = p_1 = 1/2, \qquad \hat{P}_2 = p_2 = 2/3$$

(iii) Estimate P.

$$p_{st} = \frac{\sum N_h p_h}{N}$$

$$= \frac{(5)(1/2) + (5)(2/3)}{10} = \frac{7}{12}$$

$$\therefore \quad \hat{P} = p_{st} = 7/12$$

Example 2. Given the following population with two strata, select samples of $n_1 = 2$ and $n_2 = 2$ from each stratum and show that $E(p_{st}) = P$.

I	II
1	1
0	0
1	0

We may select $\binom{3}{2}\binom{3}{2} = 9$ possible samples of size $n = n_1 + n_2 = 2 + 2 = 4$ from the population. These are listed in the following table.

I	II	p_1	p_2	p_{st}
1, 0	1, 0	.5	.5	.50
	1, 0		.5	.50
	0, 0		0.0	.25
1, 1	1, 0	1.0	.5	.75
	1, 0		.5	.75
	0, 0		.0	.50
0, 1	1, 0	.5	.5	.50
	1, 0		.5	.50
	0, 0		0.0	.25
				4.50

$$E(p_{st}) = \frac{1}{9}(4.5) = 0.5$$

$$P = \frac{2+1}{6} = \frac{1}{2} = 0.5$$

$$\therefore \quad E(p_{st}) = P = 0.5$$

Example 3. Given the following hypothetical population of students in the first, second, third, and fourth grades, estimate the population proportion. Assume the p_h are known from a preliminary survey.

Year	N_h	n_h	p_h	$N_h p_h$
1	200	50	.1	20
2	160	40	.3	48
3	120	30	.4	48
4	120	30	.7	84
	600			200

$$p_{st} = \frac{1}{N} \sum_{}^{L} N_h p_h$$

$$= \frac{1}{600}(200) = \frac{1}{3}$$

(*ii*) *Variance of p_{st}.*

We have seen in section 5.10 that, given a population of size N where $X_i = 1$ or 0, the variance of X_i is

$$(7) \qquad\qquad S^2 = \frac{N}{N-1} PQ$$

In stratified random sampling, each stratum is of size N_h, and in our present case, $X_{hi} = 1$ or 0. Hence, the stratum variances S_h^2 will be

$$(8) \qquad\qquad S_h^2 = \frac{N_h}{N_h - 1} P_h Q_h$$

where P_h was defined in equation (2), and $Q_h = 1 - P_h$.

We have already shown that $\bar{x}_{st}$ corresponds to p_{st} of equation (5). Hence, the variance of p_{st} will correspond to the variance of $\bar{x}_{st}$—except that the X_i are either 0 or 1. We know that

$$(9) \qquad\qquad V(\bar{x}_{st}) = \frac{1}{N^2} \sum_{}^{L} N_h^2 \frac{N_h - n_h}{N_h} \frac{S_h^2}{n_h}$$

and when $X_i = 0$ or 1, this becomes

$$(10) \qquad V(p_{st}) = \frac{1}{N^2} \sum N_h^2 \frac{N_h - n_h}{N_h} \frac{1}{n_h} \frac{N_h}{N_h - 1} P_h Q_h$$

where we have substituted (8) into S_h^2. This is the variance of p_{st} we seek.

If $N_h \gg n_h$, and we let fpc $= 1$, equation (10) becomes

$$(11) \qquad\qquad V(p_{st}) = \frac{1}{N^2} \sum N_h^2 \frac{P_h Q_h}{n_h}$$

Example 4. Using the data of Example 1, let us calculate S_h^2 and $V(p_{st})$

$$S_1^2 = \frac{N_1}{N_1 - 1} P_1 Q_1 = \left(\frac{5}{5-1}\right)\left(\frac{2}{5}\right)\left(\frac{3}{5}\right) = \frac{3}{10}$$

$$S_2^2 = \frac{N_2}{N_2 - 1} P_2 Q_2 = \left(\frac{5}{5-1}\right)\left(\frac{4}{5}\right)\left(\frac{1}{5}\right) = \frac{1}{5}$$

Let the subsamples that are selected be $n_1 = 2$, $n_2 = 3$ as follows:

n_1	n_2
$x_{11} = 1$	$x_{21} = 1$
$x_{12} = 0$	$x_{22} = 1$
	$x_{23} = 0$

Then

$$V(p_{st}) = \frac{1}{N^2} \sum N_h^2 \frac{N_h - n_h}{N_h} \frac{1}{n_h} \frac{N_h}{N_h - 1} P_h Q_h$$

$$= \frac{1}{10^2}\left\{\left[(5^2)\left(\frac{5-2}{5}\right)\left(\frac{1}{2}\right)\left(\frac{5}{5-1}\right)\left(\frac{2}{5}\right)\left(\frac{3}{5}\right)\right] \right.$$

$$\left. + \left[(5^2)\left(\frac{5-3}{5}\right)\left(\frac{1}{3}\right)\left(\frac{5}{5-1}\right)\left(\frac{4}{5}\right)\left(\frac{1}{5}\right)\right]\right\}$$

$$= 0.029$$

(*iii*) *An estimator of* $V(p_{st})$.

The population proportions P, P_h are usually unknown, and $V(p_{st})$ needs to be estimated. It turns out that we may obtain an unbiased estimator of $V(p_{st})$ by substituting p_h for P_h. That is,

(12) $$\hat{V}(p_{st}) = \frac{1}{N^2} \sum_{h}^{L} N_h^2 \frac{N_h - n_h}{N_h} \frac{1}{n_h} \frac{N_h}{N_h - 1} p_h q_h$$

is an unbiased estimator of $V(p_{st})$.

When $N_h \gg n_h$, (12) may be written as

(13) $$\hat{V}(p_{st}) = \frac{1}{N^2} \sum_{h}^{L} N_h^2 \frac{p_h q_h}{n_h}$$

Example 5. From the two samples—$n_1 = 2$ and $n_2 = 3$—of Example 4, we find $p_1 = 1/2$, $p_2 = 2/3$. Hence,

$$\hat{V}(p_{st}) = \frac{1}{N^2} \sum N_h^2 \frac{N_h - n_h}{N_h} \frac{1}{n_h} \frac{N_h}{N_h - 1} p_h q_h$$

$$= \frac{1}{100}\left\{\left[(25)\left(\frac{5-2}{5}\right)\left(\frac{1}{2}\right)\left(\frac{5}{5-1}\right)\left(\frac{1}{2}\right)\left(\frac{1}{2}\right)\right] \right.$$

$$\left. + \left[(25)\left(\frac{5-3}{5}\right)\left(\frac{1}{3}\right)\left(\frac{5}{5-1}\right)\left(\frac{2}{3}\right)\left(\frac{1}{3}\right)\right]\right\}$$

$$= 0.0327$$

Example 6. Using the data of Example 3, find $\hat{V}(p_{st})$. The equation for finding $\hat{V}(p_{st})$ may be rewritten as follows for calculation purposes:

$$\hat{V}(p_{st}) = \frac{1}{N^2} \sum N_h(N_h - n_h) \cdot \frac{1}{n_h} p_h q_h$$

N_h	n_h	$N_h - n_h$	$p_h q_h$	$N_h(N_h - n_h)(1/n_h)p_h q_h$
200	50	150	(0.1)(0.9)	54.0
160	40	120	(0.3)(0.7)	100.8
120	30	90	(0.4)(0.6)	86.4
120	30	90	(0.7)(0.3)	75.6
				316.8

Substituting the calculations of the table into the above formula, we find that $\hat{V}(p_{st})$ is:

$$\hat{V}(p_{st}) = \left(\frac{1}{600}\right)^2 (54 + 100.8 + 86.4 + 75.6) = 0.00088$$

$$s(p_{st}) = 0.0297$$

(*iv*) *Allocation of the sample.*

Let us now consider the allocation of the sample. Following our previous procedure, let us first work out the various allocation procedures—such as proportional allocation, optimum allocation, and Neyman allocation. The procedure for determining the size of the sample will be considered in the next section.

(a) Proportional allocation.

The procedure for proportional allocation is

$$n_h = \frac{N_1}{N} \cdot n$$

and is accomplished when we know N_h and N. It does not require knowledge of S_h.

(b) Optimum allocation.

The characteristic of this allocation procedure was that $V(p_{st})$ is to be minimized if the cost (c_h) varies and the total cost is fixed. When considering the population mean, the result was

(14)
$$n_h = \frac{N_h S_h/\sqrt{c_h}}{\Sigma (N_h S_h/\sqrt{c_h})} \cdot n$$

When considering the population proportion, we note that

(15)
$$S_h^2 = \frac{N_h}{N_h - 1}P_h Q_h$$

(16)
$$\doteq P_h Q_h$$

Substituting equation (16) into (14) gives us

(17)
$$n_h = \frac{N_h\sqrt{P_h Q_h}/\sqrt{c_h}}{\Sigma (N_h\sqrt{P_h Q_h}/\sqrt{c_h})} \cdot n$$

Usually P_h and Q_h are unknown, and it is necessary to estimate them from a preliminary survey. Let these estimators be represented by p_h and q_h. We may then find n_h by using these estimators.

(c) Neyman allocation.

The assumption of the Neyman allocation was that $c_h =$ constant and, as a result, n becomes fixed. Since $c_h =$ constant, equation (17) becomes

$$(18) \qquad n_h = \frac{N_h \sqrt{P_h Q_h}}{\sum N_h \sqrt{P_h Q_h}} \cdot n$$

When P_h and Q_h are unknown, preliminary estimators are used to find n_h.

(v) Determination of sample size n.

Following our previous procedure for determining the sample size, let us first discuss the desired variance and then show how n is determined.

(a) Desired variance.

The desired variance was defined as $D^2 = (d/z)^2$ where d showed the error (precision), and z showed the level of reliability. In our present case, since we wish to estimate the population proportion P,

$$(19) \qquad d = |\hat{P} - P| = |p_{\text{st}} - P|$$

For example, we may wish to estimate P with a precision of within ± 3 percentage points. Then,

$$d = |p_{\text{st}} - P| \leq 0.03$$

If $z = 3$, then

$$D = \frac{d}{z} = \frac{0.03}{3} = 0.01$$

which means we wish the sample size to be such that 1 standard error is to be $0.01(1\%)$. In other words, the width of the 3σ confidence interval will be $\pm 3\%$.

(b) Determination of n for proportional allocation.

For section 6.11, we know that for proportional allocation, the sample size is determined by

$$n = \frac{N \sum N_h S_h^2}{N^2 D^2 + \sum N_h S_h^2} \qquad \text{fpc} \neq 1$$

$$= \frac{N \sum N_h S_h^2}{N^2 D^2} \qquad \text{fpc} = 1$$

For proportions, we therefore have:

$$(20) \qquad n = \frac{N \sum N_h P_h Q_h}{N^2 D^2 + \sum N_h P_h Q_h} \qquad \text{fpc} \neq 1$$

$$(21) \qquad = \frac{N \sum N_h P_h Q_h}{N^2 D^2} \qquad \text{fpc} = 1$$

When P and P_h are unknown, their estimators—p_{st} and p_h— are used.

Example 7. A preliminary survey is made of 3 cities, and the proportion of families with 2 or more TV sets is estimated. (i) Using this preliminary data, determine n if the precision is to be within ± 3 percentage points of P, with $z = 3$. (ii) Allocate n by proportional allocation.

Cities	Families	p_h	$N_h p_h$	$N_h p_h q_h$
A	2000	0.10	200	180
B	3000	0.15	450	382.5
C	5000	0.20	1000	800.0
	10000		1650	1362.5

(i) Find n.

$$n = \frac{10000 \times 1362.5}{\left(10000 \times \dfrac{0.03}{3}\right)^2 + 1362.5} \doteq 1220$$

(ii) Allocate n

$$n_1 = \frac{2000}{10000} \times 1220 = 260$$

$$n_2 = \frac{3000}{10000} \times 1220 = 390$$

$$n_3 = \frac{5000}{10000} \times 1220 = 650$$

(c) Determination of n for optimum allocation.

For optimum allocation, the formula was (see p. 141)

(22) $$n = \frac{\left(\sum N_h S_h \sqrt{c_h}\right)\left(\sum N_h S_h/\sqrt{c_h}\right)}{N^2 D^2 + \sum N_h S_h^2}$$

when considering the population mean. When considering the population proportion, we merely substitute

$$S_h^2 = P_h Q_h$$

into equation (22). Hence,

(23) $$n = \frac{\left(\sum N_h \sqrt{c_h P_h Q_h}\right)\left(\sum N_h \sqrt{P_h Q_h/c_h}\right)}{N^2 D^2 + \sum N_h P_h Q_h} \qquad \text{fpc} \neq 1$$

(24) $$= \frac{\left(\sum N_h \sqrt{c_h P_h Q_h}\right)\left(\sum N_h \sqrt{P_h Q_h/c_h}\right)}{N^2 D^2} \qquad \text{fpc} = 1$$

When P_h is unknown (which is usually the case), we use its estimator, p_h, which is obtained from a preliminary survey.

(d) Determination of n for Neyman allocation.

For the Neyman allocation, c_h is considered constant. Hence, the c_h in the numerator of equation (23) cancels out and we get

$$(25) \qquad n = \frac{(\sum N_h \sqrt{P_h Q_h})^2}{N^2 D^2 + \sum N_h P_h Q_h}$$

and when P_h is unknown, we use its estimate p_h.

Sampling for proportions is widely used in opinion surveys. market research, and quality control. Let us give some examples.

Example 8. Suppose a large company wishes to investigate the proportion of employees in favor of a certain pension plan. It has 7 plants throughout the country and it has classified its employees into white collar and blue collar workers. There are then $(7 \times 2 =)14$ strata from which samples are to be taken. The simplest procedure would be to select the samples by proportional allocation. Since the cost is probably not very great and does not vary much between strata, and the stratum variances also do not differ too much, there is probably little to be gained by using the optimum or Neyman allocation.

Example 9. In Example 8, strata may be further classified by age groups. For example, they may be classified into 3 age groups: up to 29, 30–39, 40 and up. There would then be $7 \times 2 \times 3 = 42$ strata.

This stratification is therefore based on geographic, administrative, and physical characteristics, and not on the characteristic of the variable under consideration.

Example 10. A department store chain wishes to estimate the proportion of customers accounts which are 4 weeks or more overdue. It has 5 department stores. Each department store may be considered a stratum, and stratified random sampling may be applied to find the proportion.

Problems

1. Suppose there are two groups of consumers and their opinions concerning a certain commodity are as follows:

$$\text{Group I} \ : \ 1, 1, 0, 1, 0 \qquad 1, 1, 1$$
$$\text{Group II} \ : \ 1, 0, 0, 0, 1 \qquad 0, 1, 0$$

where 1 indicates in favor and 0 indicates not in favor.

   (i) Find P and P_h.

   (ii) Select samples of size $n_h = 3$ and calculate p_1 and p_2.

   (iii) Using the results of (ii), estimate P.

2. Given the following hypothetical population:

$$\text{Stratum I} \ : \ 1, 0, 1$$
$$\text{Stratum II} \ : \ 1, 0, 0, 0, 1$$

Select all possible samples of size $n_1 = 2$, $n_2 = 3$ and verify that $E(p_{st}) = P$.

3. Using the data of Problem 1, calculate S_1^2 and S_2^2.

4. Continuing Problem 3, suppose the following 2 subsamples are selected:

$$n_1 = 3 \ : \ x_{11} = 1, \ x_{12} = 0, \ x_{13} = 0$$
$$n_2 = 4 \ : \ x_{21} = 1, \ x_{22} = 0, \ x_{23} = 1, \ x_{24} = 1$$

   (i) Calculate $V(p_{st})$

   (ii) Calculate $\hat{V}(p_{st})$

5. Given the following hypothetical population of students at 4 schools, estimate the proportion of students who have visited a doctor at least once during the past year. Assume the p_h are found from a preliminary survey. Also find $\hat{V}(p_{st})$ and $s(p_{st})$.

School	N_h	n_h	p_h
1	2000	100	0.2
2	1600	80	0.3
3	1200	60	0.4
4	1200	60	0.3
	6000		

6. Using the data of Problem 5,
  (i) Determine the sample size n such that the precision is within ±4 percentage points with $z = 2$. Assume the case for proportional allocation.
  (ii) Also allocate the sample by proportional allocation.

7. Assume the costs are $c_1 = \$1$, $c_2 = \$2$, $c_3 = \$3$, $c_4 = \$4$ in Problem 5 and determine n for optimum allocation. Also allocate the sample.

8. Using the data of Problem 5, determine n for the Neyman allocation and allocate the sample.

9. Suppose a large manufacturing company wishes to investigate the proportion of employees who have been absent because of illness during a certain month. It has 4 plants and a preliminary survey has given the following data.

Plant	N_h	p_h
A	1000	0.10
B	2000	0.15
C	3000	0.20
D	4000	0.15

  (i) Find the sample size n such that the precision is to be within ±3 percentage points with $z = 3$. Assume proportional allocation.
  (ii) Allocate the sample.
  (iii) Using the p_h in the table, estimate P.
  (iv) Calculate $\hat{V}(p_{st})$, using the n_h found in (ii) and the p_h in the table.

10. Suppose a department store chain has 3 stores and wishes to estimate the proportion of accounts which are 2 weeks or more overdue. A preliminary survey has produced the following data:

Store	N_h	p_h
A	2000	0.4
B	3000	0.3
C	5000	0.6

(i) Determine n such that the precision is within ± 3 percentage points with $z = 3$. Assume the Neyman allocation procedure is used.

(ii) Allocate the sample.

(iii) Estimate P using the p_h in the table.

(iv) Calculate $\hat{V}(p_{\mathrm{st}})$ using the results of (ii).

Notes and References

For a clear and nontechnical discussion of the principles of stratified sampling, see Stuart (1962), pp. 44–66. The following references are recommended after Chapter 6 of the text has been read. They are: Hansen, Hurwitz, and Madow (1953), Chapter 5 (excluding section 4); Deming (1950), Chapter 6; Yates(1960), sections 3.3–3.5, 6.5–6.7; Kish(1965), Chapter 3. For discussion on a more advanced level, see Cochran(1963), Chapter 5. All of the necessary proofs of formulas may be found here. Additional references may be found at the end of Cochran's Chapter 5, but they are on an advanced level. However, for purposes of acquiring familiarity with journal articles, Neyman's (1934) article is recommended. Also see Chapter 5A of Cochran(1963) for further study of special aspects of stratified sampling.

One of the problems in sample design is to estimate the variance prior to selecting a sample. There is no pat answer to this problem and various procedures are used. For discussion and illustrations of this point, see Hansen, Hurwitz, and Madow (1953), p. 425, pp. 450–455, pp. 213–219; Kish(1965), pp. 49–53, pp. 277–278; Samford(1963), pp. 81–82. An illustration of how advanced estimates of variances are obtained may be found in *A Chapter on Population Sampling*(1947), Bureau of Census, pp. 31–41. For discussion of subordinate samples to reduce the burden of calculation of variances, see Deming(1950), pp. 329–342.

For a discussion of cost functions, see Hansen, Hurwitz, and Madow(1953), pp. 220–224, 270–284.

Stuart, A. (1962). *Basic Ideas of Scientific Sampling*. London: Charles Griffen and Company, Limited.

Neyman, J.(1934). On the two different aspects of the representative method; the method of stratified sampling and the method of purposive selection. *J. Roy. Stat. Soc.*, **97**, 558–606.

Bureau of Census (1947). *A Chapter on Population Census*. Bureau of Census, U.S. Department of Commerce Washington, D.C.: U.S. Govt. Printing Office.

CHAPTER 7

Systematic Sampling

7.1 Introduction

Suppose a magazine publisher wants to know whether subscribers prefer a green cover or a pink cover for his magazine. There are 50,000 subscribers, and we wish to select a random sample of 1000 subscribers to investigate this problem.

As we can see, if the sample is to be selected by simple random sampling, the subscribers must be numbered serially from 1 to 50,000 and 1000 names would then be selected by using a random number table. This would obviously involve quite a bit of work.

An alternative way of selecting the sample may be to select 1 name from every 50 names. Suppose that all subscription cards are kept in a number of files. The procedure would then be to select 1 card at random from the first 50 cards—the 20th, for example, and select every 50th card from this 20th card; that is,

$$20, 70 \ 120, 170, \ldots, 49{,}970$$

This method of selecting the sample saves much time and effort, and is more efficient than simple random sampling in certain situations. Selecting the sample in this manner according to a predetermined pattern is called systematic sampling. It is widely used in practice— often with other sampling procedures, such as stratified random sampling, cluster sampling, etc.

Systematic sampling is also used in many cases in lieu of simple random sampling. For example, in our previous example about the selection of subscribers, we may use systematic sampling instead of simple random sampling. As we shall explain in the subsequent discussion, systematic sampling will give us a precision approximately equivalent to that obtainable by simple random sampling when the population is randomly ordered.

As another example, suppose we wish to estimate the total sales of supermarkets in a very large city. The supermarkets are stratified as being either large, medium, or small. Using proportional stratified sampling, subsamples of size n_1, n_2, and n_3 are to be selected. The usual procedure would be to select these subsamples by simple random sampling. However, since the sampling units in each stratum are randomly ordered, we may use systematic sampling and achieve a precision comparable to that obtained by random sampling. One of the main points of our investigation of systematic sampling will be to find the conditions under which we may use systematic sampling in lieu of simple random sampling.

As can be seen from the previous examples, there are a number of advantages to be gained from the use of systematic sampling. One is the ease of drawing a sample. In practical surveys, drawing a sample becomes an important problem, especially if the interviewers are not professional statisticians. An example of this is found in population census where a small subsample is selected along with the census to obtain a more detailed and quick estimate of various results. If a 5% sample is to be selected, it means that 1 in 20 persons is to be selected for special interview. Every 20th person is given a special questionnaire and interviewed thoroughly. This 20th person is selected by giving the interviewer a printed schedule that has, say, 40 lines, and 2 of these 40 lines are designated for the special interview. A selection procedure such as this is simple to understand and easy to execute, even by a nonprofessional interviewer.

Some other examples include forest sampling, where a grid is placed on a map and the squares in the grid may then be selected by a predetermined pattern. Or sampling every other block in a small city, or selecting every kth customer, or selecting apples from every kth tree, etc.

Another advantage is that the sample is usually spread out more evenly over the population, and is thus often more representative of the population. However, this will depend on the characteristics of the population, and may not apply in some cases. We shall discuss the characteristics of the population under which it will be advantageous to use systematic sampling in section 7.5.

A third advantage is that we may use systematic sampling in lieu of simple random sampling under certain conditions. This quite clearly is a very useful approximation, and will be explained in section 7.6.

Because of these advantages, systematic sampling is widely used. We shall, as the occasion arises, show how it is used with other sampling procedures. In this chapter, however, we shall concentrate on the basic theory of systematic sampling. Our order of discussion will be as follows: In the next section we shall discuss two different procedures of selecting the sampling units. Then, in the subsequent sections, we shall investigate how the population mean is estimated, analyze the variance of systematic samples to understand the characteristics of systematic sampling, and, in particular, discuss the concept of intraclass correlation. Using the concept of intraclass correlation, we shall explain under what conditions systematic sampling may be used instead of simple random sampling.

7.2 Sample selection procedure

We shall distinguish two methods of selection which we shall call Method A and Method B. When selecting a sample by systematic sampling, the sample is expressed by saying "a 1 in 10 sample," or, "a 1 in 20 sample." In general, this may be expressed by saying "a 1 in k sample." This simply means the sampling fraction is $1/k$.

(*i*) *Method A.*

Suppose we have a population

$$X_1 \ X_2 \ X_3 \ X_4 \ X_5 \ X_6 \ X_7 \ X_8 \ X_9 \ X_{10} \ X_{11} \ X_{12}$$

and we wish to select a 1 in $k = 3$ systematic sample. One method of selection is to randomly select a sampling unit from the first 3 sampling units (say, the $j = 2$nd unit), and then select every 3rd unit from this unit. Hence, we get

$$X_1 \ X_2 \ X_3| \ X_4 \ X_5 \ X_6| \ X_7 \ X_8 \ X_9| \ X_{10} \ X_{11} \ X_{12}$$
$$X_2 \ X_5 \ X_8 \ X_{11}$$

We shall call this selection procedure Method A.

As is seen, the population has been divided into

$$n = \frac{N}{k} = \frac{12}{3} = 4$$

groups, and from each group we have selected 1 sampling unit. We shall call these groups *zones* or *strata*. The characteristic of this illustration is that $N = nk$, and population is an exact multiple of k.

In this case, $k = 3$ shows the size of the strata and $n = 4$ shows the number of strata. Since we select 1 sampling unit from each stratum, $k = 3$ shows the number of possible systematic samples that can be selected, and $n = 4$ shows the size of the samples.

The $k = 3$ possible systematic samples we can select from the above population by this procedure are listed in the table below.

#1	#2	#3
X_1	X_2	X_3
X_4	X_5	X_6
X_7	X_8	X_9
X_{10}	X_{11}	X_{12}

These samples may be shown by

$$j \qquad j+k \qquad j+2k \qquad j+3k$$

where $j = 1$, 2, or 3, and $k = 3$.

Since the starting sampling unit is randomly selected from the first $k = 3$ units, the probability of selecting any one of these $k = 3$ sampling units is $1/k = 1/3$, and the probability of selecting any one of these systematic samples is therefore also $1/k = 1/3$.

In general, we may write for a sample of size n,

$$j, j + k, j + 2k, \ldots, j + (n - 1)k$$

and the probability of selecting any one of these k systematic samples is $1/k$.

Let us now consider the case where $N \neq nk$. For example, suppose we wish to select a 1 in $k = 5$ sample. Then,

$$\frac{N}{k} = \frac{12}{5} = 2\frac{2}{5}$$

Hence, the sample size will be either 2 or 3. That is,

$$2 < \frac{12}{5} = 2\frac{2}{5} < 3$$

The procedure for selecting the sample will be to select a random start from the first $k = 5$ sampling units, and then select every 5th sampling unit from this start. We get the $k = 5$ systematic samples below. The sample size is therefore either 2 or 3, and there is a difference of 1 sampling

#1	#2	#3	#4	#5
X_1	X_2	X_3	X_4	X_5
X_6	X_7	X_8	X_9	X_{10}
X_{11}	X_{12}			

unit. We also note that the probability of selecting any one of these samples is $1/5$ regardless of whether the sample size is 2 or 3. Let us give several additional examples.

Example 1. Suppose $N = 37$ and a 1 in 8 systematic sample is to be selected. To find the sample size, we set

$$\frac{N}{k} = \frac{37}{8} = 4\frac{5}{8}$$

Hence the sample size will be

$$4 < 4\frac{5}{8} < 5$$

That is, the sample size is 4 or 5. The $k = 8$ samples are listed below.

1	2	3	4	5	6	7	8
X_1	X_2	X_3	X_4	X_5	X_6	X_7	X_8
X_9	X_{10}	X_{11}	X_{12}	X_{13}	X_{14}	X_{15}	X_{16}
X_{17}	X_{18}	X_{19}	X_{20}	X_{21}	X_{22}	X_{23}	X_{24}
X_{25}	X_{26}	X_{27}	X_{28}	X_{29}	X_{30}	X_{31}	X_{32}
X_{33}	X_{34}	X_{35}	X_{36}	X_{37}			

The procedure for selecting the sample will be to select a random start from the first 8 sampling units, and to then select every 8 th sampling unit from this start. As is seen, the 8 systematic samples are either of size 4 or 5, and the difference is 1 unit. The probability of selecting any one of these samples is $1/k = 1/8$.

Example 2. Suppose $N = 666$ and a 1 in 20 sample is to be selected. Then

$$\frac{N}{k} = \frac{666}{20} = 33\frac{6}{20}$$

Hence, the sample size will be either 33 or 34. The procedure is to select a sampling unit from the first 20 units (say, the jth), and to then select every 20th unit from j. The probability of selecting any sample is $1/20$.

(*ii*) *Method B.*

Let us now illustrate Method B with an example. Assume that $N = nk = 12$, and suppose we wish to select a 1 in $k = 3$ sample. A sampling unit (say, the jth unit) is randomly selected from the population. Let j be the 8th unit. Then

$$\frac{j}{k} = \frac{8}{3} = 2 \quad \text{with remainder} \quad r = 2$$

We note that $r = 2 < k = 3$ and that the values r can take will be 0, 1, and 2. When $r = 1$, select X_1; when $r = 2$, select X_2; and when $r = 0$, select X_3 as the starting point. Then select every $k = 3$rd sampling unit from the starting point. The systematic samples we obtain will be (since $N = nk = 12$) as follows.

#1	#2	#3
X_1	X_2	X_3
X_4	X_5	X_6
X_7	X_8	X_9
X_{10}	X_{11}	X_{12}

We shall designate this sampling procedure as Method B. As is seen, the samples are the same as those of Method A.

Let us now apply Method B to the case where $N \neq nk$. Assume $N = 11$. Then we find

$$\frac{j}{k} = \frac{8}{3} = 2 \quad \text{with remainder} \quad r = 2$$

and perform the same selection procedure as in the above case. For $r = 2$, we select X_2 as the starting point and select every $k = 3$rd sampling unit. The result will be

#1	#2	#3
X_1	X_2	X_3
X_4	X_5	X_6
X_7	X_8	X_9
X_{10}	X_{11}	

In this case the systematic samples are not of the same size. The 3rd systematic sample has only 3 sampling units, whereas the others have 4.

The characteristic of this selection procedure is that the probability of selecting the systematic sample will be n/N, and not $1/k$. This can be easily shown as follows: The probability of selecting, say, X_2, X_5, X_8, or X_{11} is $1/11$, respectively. When any of these are selected we get the $\#2$ systematic sample. Hence, the probability of selecting this sample is

$$\frac{1}{11} + \frac{1}{11} + \frac{1}{11} + \frac{1}{11} = \frac{4}{11}$$

Similarly, the probability of selecting (X_3, X_6, X_9) will be $3/11$.

Hence, the main difference between Methods A and B is that although the same systematic samples are obtained, there is a difference in the probability of selection. This result will be used in the next section.

Another difference between Methods A and B may be illustrated by an example. Suppose we wish to select a 1-in-20 sample of customers from 7 to 10 a.m. at a certain restaurant to estimate their average expenditures at this restaurant. In this case, since N is unknown, we cannot use Method B. Using Method A, we select a random number between 1 and 20. Suppose it is 7. We then select every 20th sampling unit (customer) from the 7th customer. The sample will be

$$7, 7 + 20, 7 + (2 \times 20), \ldots$$

and we shall continue this until 10 a.m. A sample of 1 in 20 may be expressed by saying a $1/20 = 5\%$ sample. That is, we have selected a 5% sample.

Problems

1. Given the following hypothetical population,

        2, 9, 5, 4, 8   6, 6, 4, 7, 2   4, 9, 4, 8, 3
        3, 6, 9, 9, 2   2, 4, 9, 1, 5   1, 3, 5

(i) Select all possible 1 in 6 systematic samples using Method A.

(ii) Select all possible 1 in 6 systematic samples using Method B.

(iii) What are the probabilities associated with the samples selected in (i) and (ii)?

2. Suppose there is a 555 page book and we wish to estimate the number of times the word "that" is used in the book. A 1 in 20 systematic sample is to be selected.

(i) What will be the sample size, according to Method A? According to Method B?

(ii) How many possible samples can be selected, according to Method A, according to Method B?

(iii) What will be the probabilities associated with the samples selected by Method A and Method B?

(iv) Select a 1 in 20 sample by Method A and show what the first 3 pages and last 2 pages in the sample will be.

(v) Do the same as in (iv) using Method B.

3. Suppose a department store wishes to estimate the average amount of time customers spend in the store. A 1 in 20 systematic sample is to be selected during 10–11 a.m. Which method should be used, A or B, and why?

4. Suppose there is a university of $N = 12,000$ students and you wish to select a sample of size $n = 200$. Explain how the sample may be selected by systematic sampling.

5. Assume New York City has 60,000 blocks and you wish to select a sample of 2000 blocks to determine the degree of cleanliness. Assuming maps of blocks are available, explain how the sample may be selected by systematic sampling.

7.3   Estimator of the population mean

Having discussed the procedure of selecting a sample by systematic sampling, let us next consider the problem of estimating the mean of the population and estimating the variance of this estimator. It turns out that when the sampling procedure of Method A is used and when $N = nk$, the sample mean of a systematic sample is an unbiased estimator of the population mean.

When $N \neq nk$, the sample mean is a biased estimator of the population mean. However, when the sampling procedure of Method B is used, the sample mean will always be an unbiased estimator regardless of whether $N = nk$ or $N \neq nk$.

To show that the sample mean of a systematic sample is an unbiased estimator of the population mean when using Method A with $N = nk$, let

$$(1) \qquad\qquad \bar{x}_i = \frac{1}{n} \sum_{}^{n} x_{ij}$$

be the sample mean for the ith systematic sample. Then

$$E(\bar{x}_{sy}) = \frac{1}{k}(\bar{x}_1 + \bar{x}_2 + \cdots + \bar{x}_k)$$

since there are only k possible samples we can select, and the probability of selecting a certain systematic sample is $1/k$. Using our example of the previous section, we have $N = 12$, $k = 3$, and $n = 4$. Then

$$E(\bar{x}_{sy}) = \frac{1}{k}(\bar{x}_1 + \bar{x}_2 + \bar{x}_3)$$

$$= \frac{1}{k}\frac{1}{n}(x_1 + x_2 + \cdots + x_N)$$

$$= \frac{1}{12}(x_1 + \cdots + x_{12}) = \bar{X}$$

Hence,

(2) $E(\bar{x}_{sy}) = \bar{X}$

Example 1. Given the number of books $N = 9$ children have, select a 1 in 3 sample by systematic sampling and estimate the population mean.

$$1, 2, 3, 4, 5, 6, 7, 8, 9$$
$$N = 9 = 3 \times 3 = nk$$

There are 3 systematic samples we can select:

Sample #1	Sample #2	Sample #3
1	2	3
4	5	6
7	8	9
12	15	18

Hence, the sample means are $\bar{x}_1 = 12/3 = 4$, $\bar{x}_2 = 5$, and $\bar{x}_3 = 6$. These are also the estimates of the population mean.

Example 2. Using the data of Example 1, show that $E(\bar{x}_{sy}) = \bar{X}$.

$$E(\bar{x}_{sy}) = \frac{1}{3}(4 + 5 + 6) = 5$$

$$\bar{X} = \frac{1}{9}(1 + 2 + \cdots 9) = \frac{45}{9} = 5$$

$$\therefore \quad E(\bar{x}_{sy}) = \bar{X}$$

Example 3. In Example 1, the numbers were arrayed. Let us rearrange the numbers randomly. Suppose we get:

$$6, 3, 4, | \, 9, 2, 5 \, | \, 1, 7, 8$$

Then, the 3 systematic samples are:

Sample #1	Sample #2	Sample #3
6	3	4
9	2	5
1	7	8
16	12	17

The 3 sample means are $\bar{x}_1 = 16/3$, $\bar{x}_2 = 12/3$, and $\bar{x}_3 = 17/3$. We find that

$$E(\bar{x}_{sy}) = \frac{1}{3}\left(\frac{16}{3} + \frac{12}{3} + \frac{17}{3}\right) = \frac{45}{9} = 5 = \bar{X}$$

and $\bar{x}_{sy}$ is an unbiased estimator of $\bar{X}$.

Example 4. Given the population

$$X_1 \quad X_2 \quad X_3 \quad X_4 \quad X_5 \quad X_6 \quad X_7 \quad X_8 \quad X_9 \quad X_{10}$$

select a 1 in 3 systematic sample by Method A and show that the systematic sample mean is a biased estimator of $\bar{X}$. We have

$$\frac{N}{k} = \frac{10}{3} = 3\frac{1}{3}$$

Hence, the sample size is 3 or 4. These samples are as follows:

#1	#2	#3
X_1	X_2	X_3
X_4	X_5	X_6
X_7	X_8	X_9
X_{10}		

Hence

$$E(\bar{x}_{sy}) = \frac{1}{3}\left[\frac{1}{4}(X_1 + X_4 + X_7 + X_{10}) + \frac{1}{3}(X_2 + X_5 + X_8)\right.$$
$$\left. + \frac{1}{3}(X_3 + X_6 + X_9)\right]$$
$$\neq \frac{1}{10}(X_1 + X_2 + X_3 + \cdots + X_{10}) = \bar{X}$$

and $\bar{x}_{sy}$ is a biased estimator of $\bar{X}$.

Let us now use the following population where $N \neq nk$ and show that Method B will give us an unbiased estimator of $\bar{X}$.

$$X_1\ X_2\ X_3\ |\ X_4\ X_5\ X_6\ |\ X_7\ X_8\ X_9\ |\ X_{10}\ X_{11}$$

Let $k = 3$, then $n = 3$ or 4. The samples we obtain by Method B are as follows:

#1	#2	#3
X_1	X_2	X_3
X_4	X_5	X_6
X_7	X_8	X_9
X_{10}	X_{11}	

As we have seen, the probability of samples #1, #2, and #3 are 4/11, 4/11, 3/11, respectively. Hence

$$E(\bar{x}_{sy}) = \frac{4}{11}(\bar{x}_1) + \frac{4}{11}(\bar{x}_2) + \frac{3}{11}(\bar{x}_3)$$
$$= \frac{4}{11}\left[\frac{1}{4}(X_1 + X_4 + X_7 + X_{10})\right]$$
$$+ \frac{4}{11}\left[\frac{1}{4}(X_2 + X_5 + X_8 + X_{11})\right]$$
$$+ \frac{3}{11}\left[\frac{1}{3}(X_3 + X_6 + X_9)\right]$$
$$= \frac{1}{11}(X_1 + X_2 + \cdots + X_{11}) = \bar{X}$$

and the sample mean of a systematic sample will be an unbiased estimator of $\bar{X}$. It is clear that this also holds when $N = nk$.

Example 5. Given the number of books $N = 8$ children have, select 1 in 3 samples by systematic sampling and estimate the population mean by using Method B. Assume we select $j = $ 7th unit. Then:

$$\frac{j}{k} = \frac{7}{3} = 2 \quad \text{with remainder} \quad r = 1$$
$$1, 2, 3\ |\ 4, 5, 6\ |\ 7, 8$$

When using Method B, there will be 3 systematic samples:

Sample #1	Sample #2	Sample #3
1	2	3
4	5	6
7	8	
12	15	9

and the probabilities associated with these samples will be 3/8, 3/8, and 2/8. Hence, the expected value of $\bar{x}_{sy}$ is

$$E(\bar{x}_{sy}) = \frac{3}{8}\left(\frac{12}{3}\right) + \frac{3}{8}\left(\frac{15}{8}\right) + \frac{2}{8}\left(\frac{9}{2}\right) = 4.5$$

The population mean is $\bar{X} = 36/8 = 4.5$ and clearly $E(\bar{x}_{sy}) = \bar{X}$. That is, $\bar{x}_{sy}$ is an unbiased estimator of $\bar{X}$. This result was obtained because the probabilities associated with the samples are proportional to the size of the samples.

As mentioned in the previous section, when $n > 50$, we may consider Methods A and B equivalent. For our subsequent discussion, we shall assume that $N = nk$ and that Method A is used for the sample selection. This will simplify our discussion considerably.

Problems

1. Given the following hypothetical population:
$$3, 2, 5, 4, 3 \quad 6, 4, 6, 9, 1 \quad 4, 7, 5, 6, 1$$
(i) Find X and $\bar{X}$.
(ii) Select a 1 in 5 systematic sample by Method A and estimate $\bar{X}$.
(iii) Select all possible 1 in 5 systematic samples by Method A and verify that $E(\bar{x}_{sy}) = \bar{X}$.

2. Using the data of Problem 1, select all possible 1 in 4 systematic samples by Method A and show that $E(\bar{x}_{sy}) \neq \bar{X}$.

3. Using the data of Problem 1, select all possible 1 in 4 systematic samples by Method B and show that $E(\bar{x}_{sy}) = \bar{X}$.

7.4 The variance of $\bar{x}_{sy}$

Having found the estimator $\bar{x}_{sy}$ of $\bar{X}$, let us now find $V(\bar{x}_{sy})$. We shall find that calculating $V(\bar{x}_{sy})$ requires knowledge of all k systematic samples, and hence cannot be used for practical applications. However, an analysis of $V(\bar{x}_{sy})$ will show us under what situations the use of systematic sampling will increase the precision of the estimator $\bar{x}_{sy}$, and will in particular show when systematic sampling may be used in lieu of simple random sampling.

This result is therefore very useful in practical applications. For example, when using stratified random sampling, we may use systematic sampling to select the subsamples from the strata when the necessary conditions (to be explained later) are fulfilled.

Our plan of discussion will be to first define $V(\bar{x}_{sy})$, show how it may be expressed in terms of the intraclass correlation coefficient ρ, and then give an explanation of ρ which will prepare us for a discussion of the types of population under which it will be advantageous to use systematic sampling. So let us start by defining $V(\bar{x}_{sy})$.

From the basic definition of a variance, we have

$$(1) \qquad V(\bar{x}_{sy}) = \frac{1}{k} \sum_i^k (\bar{x}_i - \bar{X})^2$$

since there are k possible samples and each has a probability of $1/k$ of being selected.

By algebraic transformation (see reference) the right side of (1) may be rewritten as

$$(2) \qquad V(\bar{x}_{sy}) = \frac{N-1}{N} S^2 - \frac{1}{N} \sum_i^k \sum_j^n (X_{ij} - \bar{X}_i)^2$$

where

$$(3) \qquad S^2 = \frac{1}{N-1} \sum_i^k \sum_j^n (X_{ij} - \bar{X})^2$$

As is seen, $V(\bar{x}_{sy})$ has been divided into two parts. The first term, which includes S^2, shows the variance for the population as a whole. The second term

$$-\frac{1}{N} \sum \sum (X_{ij} - \bar{X}_i)^2$$

shows the pooled within variation of the k systematic samples. The greater the variation within the systematic samples, the smaller $V(\bar{x}_{sy})$ becomes. A large variation within a systematic sample indicates that the sample is heterogeneous. Hence, when the sampling units within a systematic sample are heterogeneous, the precision of systematic sampling will increase. Before explaining this point, let us first illustrate the calculation procedure of (1).

Example 1. Using the data of Example 1 of section 7.3, let us calculate $V(\bar{x}_{sy})$. The population was

$$1, 2, 3 \,|\, 4, 5, 6 \,|\, 7, 8, 9$$

and the $k = 3$ samples of size $n = 3$ were

Sample #1		Sample #2		Sample #3	
X_{1j}	X_{1j}^2	X_{2j}	X_{2j}^2	X_{3j}	X_{3j}^2
1	1	2	4	3	9
4	16	5	25	6	36
7	49	8	64	9	81
12	66	15	93	18	126

First calculate S^2.

$$S^2 = \frac{1}{N-1} \sum_i^k \sum_j^n (X_{ij} - \bar{X})^2$$

$$= \frac{1}{9-1} \left[\sum^n (X_{1j} - \bar{X})^2 + \sum^n (X_{2j} - \bar{X})^2 + \sum^n (X_{3j} - \bar{X})^2 \right]$$

$$= \frac{1}{8}(21 + 18 + 21) = \frac{60}{8}$$

This is simply the variance of the population as a whole. Next calculate the second term on the right hand side.

$$\frac{1}{N} \sum_i^k \sum_j^n (X_{ij} - \bar{X}_i)^2$$

$$= \frac{1}{9} \left[\sum (X_{1j} - \bar{X}_1)^2 + \sum (X_{2j} - \bar{X}_2)^2 + \sum (X_{3j} - \bar{X}_3)^2 \right]$$

$$= \frac{1}{9}(18 + 18 + 18) = \frac{54}{9}$$

This is the pooled within variance. Hence, substituting these two results into equation (2), we find

$$V(\bar{x}_{sy}) = \frac{N-1}{N} S^2 - \frac{1}{N} \sum \sum (X_{ij} - \bar{X}_i)^2$$

$$= \frac{9-1}{9} \left(\frac{60}{8}\right) - \frac{54}{9} = \frac{2}{3}$$

Let us calculate $V(\bar{x}_{sy})$ from the basic definition of equation (1) and check this result. We find

$$V(\bar{x}_{sy}) = \frac{1}{k} \sum (\bar{x}_i - \bar{X})^2$$

$$= \frac{1}{3}[(4-5)^2 + (5-5)^2 + (6-5)^2] = \frac{2}{3}$$

and we see that both calculations give a variance of 2/3.

Note the following points. First—when referring to the homogeneity or heterogeneity of sampling units within the k systematic samples, we do not mean that the zones are homogeneous or heterogeneous.

Second—knowledge of all k systematic samples is necessary to calculate $V(\bar{x}_{sy})$. Hence, in practical application where only a single sample is selected, it is of no use for finding the variance of $\bar{x}_{sy}$.

Let us now illustrate how the within variation $\sum \sum (X_{ij} - \bar{X}_i)^2$ affects $V(\bar{x}_{sy})$. To take an extreme example, suppose the population is as follows:

$$1\ 2\ 3\ 4\ 5 \mid 1\ 2\ 3\ 4\ 5 \mid 1\ 2\ 3\ 4\ 5$$

That is, the units in the population show periodicity. If, say, 2 from the first zone is selected, and then every subsequent $k = 5$th sampling unit is selected, we get as a systematic sample

$$2\ 2\ 2$$

which is homogeneous and not representative of the population. The within variation is zero in this case, and $V(\bar{x}_{sy})$ will be large.

A question that naturally arises is: How do we measure this homogeneity or heterogeneity?

A measure which expresses the degree of homogeneity in a systematic sample is the intraclass correlation coefficient ρ between pairs of units in the same systematic sample. This coefficient is defined as

$$(4) \qquad \rho = \frac{E(X_{ij} - \bar{X})(X_{ij'} - \bar{X})}{E(X_{ij} - \bar{X})^2}$$

Using ρ, we may express $V(\bar{x}_{sy})$ as (see reference for derivation)

$$(5) \qquad V(\bar{x}_{sy}) = \frac{S^2}{n} \frac{N-1}{N}[1 + (n-1)\rho]$$

where

$$(6) \qquad \rho = \frac{2}{n-2} \sum_{i}^{k} \sum_{j<j'}^{n} (X_{ij} - \bar{X})(X_{ij'} - \bar{X})\frac{1}{N-1}\frac{1}{S^2}$$

for calculation purposes.

Equation (5) shows that when ρ is large and positive, $V(\bar{x}_{sy})$ is large; and when ρ is small and positive or negative, $V(\bar{x}_{sy})$ will be small; and when $\rho = 0$, $V(\bar{x}_{sy})$ will become equal to the variance of $\bar{x}$ for simple random sampling.

A large and positive ρ is obtained when the units are homogeneous in the systematic sample, and a small and positive or negative ρ is obtained when the units are heterogeneous in the systematic sample. Let us explain this relation next—but before that, let us illustrate the calculation procedure of ρ.

Example 2. Using the data of Example 1, let us calculate $V(\bar{x}_{sy})$ by equation (5) and show that the result is the same as that obtained in Example 1. We first find

$$\rho = \frac{2}{n-1} \sum_{i}^{k} \sum_{j<j'}^{n} (X_{ij} - \bar{X})(X_{ij'} - \bar{X})\frac{1}{N-1}\frac{1}{S^2}$$

Let us calculate the cross products for the $k = 3$ systematic samples. For $i = 1$, we find:

$$\sum_{j<j'}^{n} (X_{1j} - \bar{X})(X_{1j'} - \bar{X})$$
$$= (X_{11} - \bar{X})(X_{12} - \bar{X}) + (X_{11} - \bar{X})(X_{13} - \bar{X}) + (X_{12} - \bar{X})(X_{13} - \bar{X})$$
$$= (1 - 5)(4 - 5) + (1 - 5)(7 - 5) + (4 - 5)(7 - 5) = -6$$

Similarly, for $i = 2$ we get -9; for $i = 3$ we get -6. Since $S^2 = 60/8$ from Example 1, ρ becomes:

$$\rho = \frac{2}{3-1}(-6 - 9 - 6)\frac{1}{9-1}\frac{1}{60/8} = -\frac{21}{60}$$

We have a negative intraclass correlation coefficient, and the sampling units are heterogeneous. Substituting this into equation (5), we get,

$$V(\bar{x}_{sy}) = \frac{S^2}{n} \frac{N-1}{N} [1 + (n-1)\rho]$$

$$= \frac{60/8}{3} \frac{9-1}{9} \left[1 + (3-1)\left(-\frac{21}{60} \right) \right] = \frac{2}{3}$$

which is what we found in Example 1.

Let us now investigate ρ a little further to gain insight of its meaning. Suppose there are 2 groups of 3 children each. One (A) coming from a high income group and the other (B) from a low income group. Let the number of books they have be as follows:

Group A: 7, 8, 9

Group B: 1, 2, 3

The average number of books for the $N = 6$ children is $\bar{X} = 30/6 = 5$ books. We wish to calculate the intraclass correlation coefficient ρ for the $N = 6$ children by using equation (6), which is reproduced for convenience.

$$(6) \qquad \rho = \frac{2}{n-1} \Sigma \Sigma (X_{ij} - \bar{X})(X_{ij'} - \bar{X}) \frac{1}{N-1} \frac{1}{S^2}$$

The characteristic of equations (4) and (6) is that the deviations of the sampling units in a sample are measured from the overall population mean $\bar{X}$, and *not* the respective systematic sample means. Let us show the $(X_{ij} - \bar{X})$ $\cdot (X_{ij'} - \bar{X})$ in terms of a graph to obtain an intuitive understanding of the meaning of ρ.

Since we have j and j', we have a 2-dimensional sample space as shown in Fig. 7-1. Since the deviations are measured from the population mean $\bar{X}$, the origin of the graph is $\bar{X} = 5$, and each combination which may be considered as a sample point is plotted relative to this origin. For groups A and B, we have the following combinations:

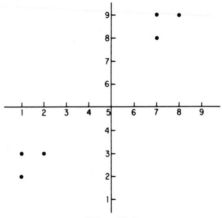

Fig. 7-1

A	B
7, 8	1, 2
7, 9	1, 3
8, 9	2, 3

As Fig. 7-1 shows, the points which represent the combinations for group A are all in the northeast quadrant, and those for group B are all in the southwest quadrant. In terms of this graph, the points in the northeast quadrant represent positive deviations from $\bar{X} = 5$ and the cross products $(X_{ij} - \bar{X})(X_{ij'} - \bar{X})$ will therefore be positive. For example, consider point (7, 8). The cross product corresponding to this sample point is

$$(7 - 5)(8 - 5) = (2)(3) = 6 > 0$$

and is positive. This applies also for the other two points, (7, 9) and (8, 9)

The characteristic of this scatter of points is that all the individual elements X_{ij} are greater than $\bar{X}$. That is, $X_{ij} > \bar{X}$ when the sample points are in the northeast quadrant. And in this case

(7) $$(X_{ij} - \bar{X})(X_{ij'} - \bar{X}) > 0$$

In terms of our example, the sampling units X_{ij} of group A(7, 8, 9) are all greater than $\bar{X} = 5$, and the cross products $(X_{ij} - \bar{X})(X_{ij'} - \bar{X})$ are all positive in terms of these sample points.

$$(7 - 5)(8 - 5) = 6 \;\; > 0$$
$$(7 - 5)(9 - 5) = 8 \;\; > 0$$
$$(8 - 5)(9 - 5) = 12 > 0$$

We may say that these sampling units X_{ij} are homogeneous with respect to $\bar{X}$.

As for group B, all the X_{ij} (1, 2, 3) are smaller than $\bar{X} = 5$ and the deviations $(X_{ij} - X)$ are negative. However, the cross products are all positive.

$$(1 - 5)(2 - 5) = (-4)(-3) = 12 > 0$$
$$(1 - 5)(3 - 5) = (-4)(-2) = \;\; 8 > 0$$
$$(2 - 5)(3 - 5) = (-3)(-2) = \;\; 6 > 0$$

We may say that these sampling units are homogeneous with respect to $\bar{X}$.

As we have just seen, the common sense meaning of the expression that "the sampling units of group A are homogeneous" is that they are similar to one another with respect to some criterion. And in our present case, the criterion is $\bar{X}$.

Likewise, the sampling units in B are similar to one another with respect to $\bar{X}$. As another example, A may represent college graduates and B high school graduates, and the criterion may be the number of school years finished.

To express this common sense idea in terms of a mathematical quantity, we use the sum of the cross products

$$\sum_i \sum_{j<j'} (X_{ij} - \bar{X})(X_{ij'} - \bar{X})$$

We can see from the graph that when the sampling units of a group are homogeneous, the sample points $(X_{ij}, X_{ij'})$ will fall in either the northeast or southwest quadrants.

The greater the difference between groups A and B, the greater will be the distance of the sampling points from the origin $(\bar{X}, \bar{X})$.

When the difference between group A and B are small, the sample points will be close to the origin.

When the sampling units are heterogeneous, the sampling units of group A, for example, will be scattered around the origin. Suppose we have (1, 2, 7) as group A. (See Fig. 7–2.) Then the combinations are

1, 2   1, 7   2, 7

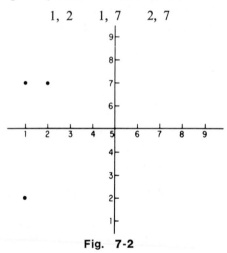

Fig. 7-2

And in this case

$$(1 - 5)(2 - 5) = (-4)(-3) = 12$$
$$(1 - 5)(7 - 5) = (-4)(2) = -8$$
$$(2 - 5)(7 - 5) = (-3)(2) = -6$$

Hence, when the sampling units are heterogeneous,

$$\sum_i \sum_{j<j'} (X_{ij} - \bar{X})(X_{ij'} - \bar{X})$$

will tend to be small or perhaps even negative.

Let us illustrate our discussion with the hypothetical data we have been using. We have as our population

1, 2, 3 | 4, 5, 6 | 7, 8, 9

and the systematic samples that can be selected are

$$
\begin{array}{ll}
i = 1: & 1, 4, 7 \\
i = 2: & 2, 5, 8 \\
i = 3: & 3, 6, 9
\end{array}
$$

We can see by observation that the systematic samples are heterogeneous with respect to the population mean $\bar{X} = 5$. And from Example 2, we found that

$$
\rho = -\frac{21}{60} \quad \text{and} \quad V(\bar{x}_{sy}) = \frac{2}{3}
$$

Let us now make the population be

$$
1, \ 4, \ 7, \ 2, \ 5, \ 8, \ 3, \ 6, \ 9
$$

and select the following systematic samples:

$$
\begin{array}{ll}
i = 1: & 1, 2, 3 \\
i = 2: & 4, 5, 6 \\
i = 3: & 7, 8, 9
\end{array}
$$

We can see that these samples are homogeneous with respect to the population mean, $\bar{X} = 5$. The intraclass correlation coefficient is

$$
\begin{aligned}
\rho &= \frac{2}{n-1} \Sigma \Sigma (X_{ij} - \bar{X})(X_{ij'} - \bar{X}) \frac{1}{N-1} \frac{1}{S^2} \\
&= \frac{2}{3-1}(26 - 1 + 26) \frac{1}{9-1} \frac{1}{60/8} = \frac{51}{60}
\end{aligned}
$$

As is seen, ρ has changed from $-21/60$ to $51/60$ and shows that the data have become homogeneous. Thus, $V(\bar{x}_{sy})$ becomes

$$
\begin{aligned}
V(\bar{x}_{sy}) &= \frac{S^2}{n} \frac{N-1}{N}[1 + (n-1)\rho] \\
&= \frac{60/8}{3} \frac{9-1}{9}\left[1 + (3-1)\left(\frac{51}{60}\right)\right] = 6
\end{aligned}
$$

In Example 1, $\rho = -21/60$ and $V(\bar{x}_{sy}) = 2/3$. In our present case, $\rho = 51/60$ and $V(\bar{x}_{sy}) = 6$. There has been a very large increase in the magnitude of $V(\bar{x}_{sy})$.

The variance for simple random sampling is

$$
V(\bar{X}_{ran}) = \frac{S^2}{n} \frac{N-1}{N} = 2
$$

and is much smaller than $V(\bar{x}_{sy}) = 6$ when the sample units in the sample are homogeneous.

With this background, let us now show how the intraclass correlation coefficient ρ may be applied to our systematic sampling procedure.

As is seen, the question boils down to: are the sampling units in a systematic sample homogeneous or not? Which in turn leads to the question: Under what circumstances do we get homogeneous and heterogeneous sampling units in systematic samples? This question leads to an investigation of the characteristics of the population which we shall consider in the next section.

Reference

Show how equation (2) is obtained from equation (1).

$$(1) \qquad V(\bar{x}_{sy}) = \frac{1}{k} \sum_{i}^{k} (\bar{x}_i - \bar{X})^2$$

We know that

$$\sum_{i}^{k} \sum_{j}^{n} (X_{ij} - \bar{X})^2 = \sum \sum [(X_{ij} - \bar{X}_i) + (\bar{X}_i - \bar{X})]^2$$
$$= \sum \sum [(X_{ij} - \bar{X}_i)^2 + (\bar{X}_i - \bar{X})^2 + 2(X_{ij} - \bar{X}_i)(\bar{X}_i - \bar{X})]$$
$$= \sum \sum (X_{ij} - \bar{X}_i)^2 + \sum \sum (\bar{X}_i - \bar{X})^2$$
$$+ 2 \sum \sum (X_{ij} - \bar{X}_i)(\bar{X}_i - \bar{X})$$

The second and third terms may be rewritten as follows:

$$\sum_{i}^{k} \sum_{j}^{n} (\bar{X}_i - \bar{X})^2 = n \sum_{i}^{k} (\bar{X}_i - \bar{X})^2$$

$$2 \sum \sum (X_{ij} - \bar{X}_i)(\bar{X}_i - \bar{X}) = 2 \sum_{i}^{k} [(\bar{X}_i - \bar{X}) \sum_{j}^{n} (X_{ij} - \bar{X}_i)]$$

$$= 2 \sum_{i}^{k} (\bar{X}_i - \bar{X}) \cdot 0 = 0$$

Hence,

$$(8) \qquad \sum \sum (X_{ij} - \bar{X})^2 = n \sum (\bar{X}_i - \bar{X})^2 + \sum \sum (X_{ij} - \bar{X}_i)^2$$

From (1) and (8) we find

$$kn V(\bar{x}_{sy}) = \sum \sum (X_{ij} - \bar{X})^2 - \sum \sum (X_{ij} - \bar{X}_i)^2$$

which becomes

$$(9) \qquad V(\bar{x}_{sy}) = \frac{1}{kn} \sum \sum (X_{ij} - \bar{X})^2 - \frac{1}{kn} \sum \sum (X_{ij} - \bar{X}_i)^2$$

We know that the variance for X_{ij} obtained from simple random sampling is

$$S^2 = \frac{1}{N-1} \sum \sum (X_{ij} - \bar{X})^2$$

and also that $N = kn$. Hence, (9) becomes

$$(10) \qquad V(\bar{x}_{sy}) = \frac{N-1}{N} S^2 - \frac{1}{N} \sum_{i}^{k} \sum_{j}^{n} (X_{ij} - \bar{X}_i)^2$$

By definition the variance of $\bar{x}_{sy}$ is

$$V(\bar{x}_{sy}) = E(\bar{x}_i - E\bar{x}_i)^2$$
$$= E(\bar{x}_{sy} - \bar{X})^2$$
$$= \frac{1}{k} \sum_{i}^{k} (\bar{x}_i - \bar{X})^2$$
$$= \frac{1}{k} \sum_{i}^{k} \left(\frac{1}{n} \sum_{i}^{n} X_{ij} - \bar{X} \right)^2$$
$$= \frac{1}{k} \frac{1}{n^2} \sum_{i}^{k} \left[\sum_{i}^{n} (X_{ij} - \bar{X}) \right]^2$$

$$(11) \qquad = \frac{1}{k} \frac{1}{n^2} \left[\sum_{i}^{k} \sum_{i}^{n} (X_{ij} - \bar{X})^2 + 2 \sum_{i}^{k} \sum_{j<j'}^{n} (X_{ij} - \bar{X})(X_{ij'} - \bar{X}) \right]$$

To evaluate the second term on the right hand side, we define

$$(12) \qquad \rho = \frac{E(X_{ij} - \bar{X})(X_{ij'} - \bar{X})}{E(X_{ij} - \bar{X})^2}$$

where ρ is the intraclass correlation coefficient between pairs of units in the same systematic samples.

When there are n sampling units in a systematic sample, there are

$$\binom{n}{2} = \frac{n(n-1)}{2}$$

different pairs of sampling units we can select. Since there are k systematic samples, there are $kn(n-1)/2$ different pairs. Hence, the numerator becomes

$$E(X_{ij} - \bar{X})(X_{ij'} - \bar{X})$$
$$= \frac{2}{kn(n-1)} \sum_{i}^{k} \sum_{j<j'}^{n} (X_{ij} - \bar{X})(X_{ij'} - \bar{X})$$

And for the denominator, we get

$$E(X_{ij} - \bar{X})^2 = \frac{1}{N} \sum_{i}^{k} \sum_{j}^{n} (X_{ij} - \bar{X})^2$$
$$= \frac{N-1}{N} \frac{1}{N-1} \sum \sum (X_{ij} - \bar{X})^2$$
$$= \frac{N-1}{N} S^2$$

Hence, the intraclass correlation coefficient ρ becomes

$$\rho = \frac{2}{kn(n-1)} \sum_{i}^{k} \sum_{j<j'}^{n} (X_{ij} - \bar{X})(X_{ij'} - \bar{X}) \cdot \frac{N}{(N-1)S^2}$$
$$= \frac{2}{n-1} \sum_{i}^{k} \sum_{j<j'}^{n} (X_{ij} - \bar{X})(X_{ij'} - \bar{X}) \cdot \frac{1}{(N-1)S^2}$$

$$(13) \qquad \therefore \ \sum_{i}^{k} \sum_{i}^{n} (X_{ij} - \bar{X})(X_{ij'} - \bar{X}) = \frac{n-1}{2} \frac{S^2(N-1)}{1} \rho$$

Substituting (13) into (11) gives us

$$V(\bar{x}_{sy}) = \frac{1}{k} \frac{1}{n^2} \left[\sum \sum (X_{ij} - \bar{X})^2 + 2 \left(\frac{n-1}{2} \frac{(N-1)S^2}{1} \rho \right) \right]$$

$$= \frac{1}{k}\frac{1}{n^2}[\sum\sum(X_{ij} - \bar{X})^2 + (N - 1)S^2(n - 1)\rho]$$

$$= \frac{1}{k}\frac{1}{n^2}[(N - 1)S^2 + (N - 1)S^2(n - 1)\rho]$$

$$= \frac{1}{nN}(N - 1)S^2[1 + (n - 1)\rho]$$

(14)
$$= \frac{S^2}{n}\frac{N - 1}{N}[1 + (n - 1)\rho]$$

This result shows that when ρ is large, $V(\bar{x}_{sy})$ will be large.

Problems

1. Given the following hypothetical population:
$$1, 2, 3, 4, 5, 6, 7, 8, 9, 10, 11, 12$$
(i) Select all possible 1 in 4 systematic samples.
(ii) Calculate $V(\bar{x}_{sy})$ using equation (2).
(iii) Calculate $V(\bar{x}_{sy})$ using equation (1).

2. Using the population in Problem 1, repeat the three operations in Problem 1 but select all possible 1 in 3 systematic samples.

3. Using the data of Problem 1,
(i) Calculate ρ assuming 1 in 4 systematic samples have been selected.
(ii) Using ρ and equation (5), calculate $V(\bar{x}_{sy})$ and verify that it is equal to the $V(\bar{x}_{sy})$ found in Problem 1.

4. Repeat the operations of Problem 3 assuming 1 in 3 systematic samples have been selected.

5. Given 2 groups of children with the following numbers of books:
$$\text{Group A: } 10, 11, 12, 13$$
$$\text{Group B: } 3, 4, 5, 6$$
(i) Select all possible pairs of numbers from each group respectively and plot on a 2-dimensional sample space as in Fig. 7-1.
(ii) Calculate
$$\sum_i\sum_{j<j'}(X_{ij} - \bar{X})(X_{ij'} - \bar{X})$$
for the northeast quadrant and southwest quadrant, respectively.

6. Suppose the two groups in Problem 5 were as follows.
$$\text{Group A: } 3, 11, 5, 3$$
$$\text{Group B: } 10, 4, 12, 6$$
Perform the two operations in Problem 5, and compare the results with those of Problem 5.

7. Suppose the data in Problem 1 is arranged as follows:
$$1, 4, 7, 10, 2, 5, 8, 11, 3, 6, 9, 12$$
(i) Select all possible 1 in 4 systematic samples and calculate ρ.

(ii) Using ρ, calculate $V(\bar{x}_{sy})$.

(iii) Calculate $V(\bar{x}_{ran})$, and compare ρ, $V(\bar{x}_{sy})$, and $V(\bar{x}_{ran})$ obtained in Problem 1 and here.

7.5   Types of population

In section 7.4 we showed that

$$V(\bar{x}_{sy}) = \frac{S^2}{n}\frac{N-1}{N}[1 + (n-1)\rho]$$

and that when the sampling units in a sample were heterogeneous, ρ will be small and $V(\bar{x}_{sy})$ will become small. The practical implication of this result is that we should try to make the sampling units in the sample heterogeneous and keep ρ small. The practical question is: what kind of populations tend to generate systematic samples with heterogeneous sampling units? Let us classify the population into the following three types and consider this problem.

(*i*) *Sampling units in a population are in random order.*

Many populations are in random order. For example, suppose we wish to estimate the average weight of $N = 2000$ freshmen students at a certain university and a list of their names is available. We may assume that the weights of students and their names are unrelated and the weights may be considered to be in random order. Let us give several other examples.

Examples. 1. Suppose a magazine publisher wishes to investigate the type of articles the subscribers prefer. We may assume the names of the subscribers are not related to their preference, and their preferences are in random order.

2. A soap manufacturer wishes to estimate the soap preference of consumers in a certain city. The city is stratified according to its 20 voting districts and the voting register is used as the frame. The names listed in the voting directory may be assumed to be unrelated to the preference of soap of the voters and their preferences may then be considered randomly ordered.

3. It is desired to estimate the amount of milk produced in a certain state. The state is stratified into counties, and a list of farms in each county is available. The names of the farms and the amount of milk they produce may be considered unrelated, and the amount of milk per farm may be considered randomly ordered.

In cases where the sampling units in the population are randomly ordered, the sampling units in the systematic samples will also be randomly ordered. Hence, the systematic sample may be treated as if it were a random sample. This random ordered sample will be heterogeneous and will have a small ρ, and as we shall see in the next section, when ρ is small $V(\bar{x}_{sy})$ and $V(\bar{x}_{ran})$ will be approximately equal.

(ii) An ordered population.

When a population is ordered, it is clear that the selection of a systematic sample will provide a heterogeneous sample, and $V(\bar{x}_{sy})$ will generally be smaller than $V(\bar{x}_{ran})$. For example, suppose we wish to estimate the yield of corn and have a population of farms. We may order the farms according to area and select a systematic sample. The result will generally be a heterogeneous systematic sample, and $V(\bar{x}_{sy})$ will be smaller than that found by random sampling.

The reason for this is intuitively clear. A systematic sample will cover the whole population and will avoid chances of selecting samples containing too many large or small farms. That is to say, a systematic sample will tend to be more representative of the population than a random sample.

In general, we may say that the sampling units in a systematic sample from an ordered population will generally be more heterogeneous than those in a random sample. Hence ρ will be small and, as will be explained in the next section, $V(\bar{x}_{sy})$ will be smaller than $V(\bar{x}_{ran})$.

Our data in Example 1 of section 7.4 was an ordered population, and $V(\bar{x}_{sy}) = 2/3$. In the illustration in section 7.4, this same population was rearranged into 3 samples that were homogeneous, and we found that $V(\bar{x}_{sy}) = 6$. The very large reduction in magnitude of the variance when the population is ordered is apparent.

(iii) Populations with periodic variations.

A hypothetical illustration of a periodic variation was given in section 7.4. We had

$$1,\ 2,\ 3,\ 4,\ 5 \qquad 1,\ 2,\ 3,\ 4,\ 5 \qquad 1,\ 2,\ 3,\ 4,\ 5$$

and when every fifth sampling unit was selected, the systematic sample was $(2, 2, 2)$. In this case, the sampling units in the sample are clearly homogeneous and ρ will be large. Calculations show that

$$\rho = \frac{2}{n-1} \Sigma \Sigma (X_{ij} - \bar{X})(X_{ij'} - \bar{X}) \cdot \frac{1}{N-1} \cdot \frac{1}{S^2}$$

$$= \left(\frac{2}{3-1}\right)(12 + 3 + 0 + 3 + 12)\left(\frac{1}{14-1}\right)\left(\frac{1}{30/14}\right) = 1$$

This, of course, is an extreme case of homogeneity, but there are many practical situations where there is periodicity in the population. For example, the sales of a supermarket are high on Fridays and Saturdays, and low on Mondays and Tuesdays, and will have a weekly periodicity. In a factory making a certain product on an assembly line, the product may be affected by the degree of fatigue of the employees, and there may hence be a variation in workmanship between the morning and afternoon production.

In cases where there is periodicity, samples may be selected by shifting the position of the sampling unit each time. For example, take the kth sampling unit first; then take the $(k + 1)$th unit from the first selected unit; etc. However, if a preliminary investigation of the population shows there is definite periodicity, it is better to use a different type of sampling procedure, depending on the nature of the population and the object of investigation.

7.6 Estimator of $V(\bar{x}_{sy})$

The $V(\bar{x}_{sy})$ found in section 7.4 required a knowledge of all k systematic samples. For practical applications we obviously need to find an estimator of $V(\bar{x}_{sy})$ based on a single sample.

Unfortunately, an unbiased estimator of $V(\bar{x}_{sy})$ based on a single systematic sample cannot be found. Under certain conditions, however, we may consider a systematic sample to be approximately equal to simple random sampling and we are thus able to use the sample variance to estimate $V(\bar{x}_{sy})$. As can easily be seen, this is an extremely useful result for practical applications.

Let us first start with a review of $V(\bar{x}_{ran})$ for random sampling and analyze its characteristics. We found in section 5.5 that

$$\text{(1)} \qquad \sigma_{\bar{x}}^2 = \frac{S^2}{n} \frac{N - n}{N} \qquad \text{without replacement}$$

$$\text{(2)} \qquad S^2 = \frac{1}{N - 1} \Sigma (X_i - \bar{X})^2$$

and its estimator was

$$\text{(3)} \qquad \hat{\sigma}_{\bar{x}}^2 = s_{\bar{x}}^2 = \frac{s^2}{n} \frac{N - n}{N}$$

$$\text{(4)} \qquad s^2 = \frac{1}{n - 1} \sum^{n} (x_i - \bar{x})^2$$

We also know that the basic definition of $\sigma_{\bar{x}}^2$ is

$$\text{(5)} \qquad \sigma_{\bar{x}}^2 = \frac{1}{M} \sum^{M} (\bar{x}_i - \bar{X})^2$$

where M is the number of all possible samples.

From equation (5) it is quite clear that $\sigma_{\bar{x}}^2$ shows the variation of the sample means $\bar{x}_i$ from $\bar{X}$, and this of course is the basic meaning of $V(\bar{x}_{ran}) = \sigma_{\bar{x}}^2$. However, in equations (1) and (2), we note that S^2 shows the variation of the individual values X_i from $\bar{X}$, and $\sigma_{\bar{x}}^2$ (which represents the variation of $\bar{x}_i$) is expressed in terms of the variation of X_{ij}.

In the estimator, (3), s^2 shows the variation of x_i from the sample mean, and s^2 therefore shows the variation of x_i within the sample. That is to say, to estimate $\sigma_{\bar{x}}^2$ (which shows the variation of $\bar{x}_i$ from $\bar{X}$ for all possible samples) we use s^2—which shows the variation of x_i within a single sample.

We may also express this characteristic as follows: $\sigma_{\bar{x}}^2$ shows the variation between sample means for all possible samples. However, $\sigma_{\bar{x}}^2$ is estimated by the within variation of a single sample. Furthermore, from section 5.5 and its reference, we know that (3) is an unbiased estimator of (1) no matter what the population. Hence, for simple random sampling, we obtain the remarkable result that the variation between sample means is estimated by the variation within a single sample.

For systematic sampling, $V(\bar{x}_{sy})$ shows the variation between sample means $\bar{x}_{sy}$ for all possible systematic samples. Now the question is : can we find an unbiased estimator of $V(\bar{x}_{sy})$ from the variation within a single systematic sample? The answer is no. However, under certain conditions we can consider the systematic sample to be equivalent to a random sample, and hence use the sample variance to estimate $V(\bar{x}_{sy})$. Quite clearly, it will be very useful in practical applications if we can consider the systematic sample as approximately equivalent to a simple random sample.

Let us first show why we cannot find an unbiased estimator of $V(\bar{x}_{sy})$ from a single systematic sample, and then show under what condisions we may consider the systematic sample as equivalent to a random sample.

Consider the following population

$$1 \ 2 \ 3 \ | \ 1 \ 2 \ 3 \ | \ 1 \ 2 \ 3$$

A 1 in 3 systematic sample will be

Sample 1	Sample 2	Sample 3
1	2	3
1	2	3
1	2	3

The sample means are therefore:

$$\bar{x}_1 = 1 \qquad \bar{x}_2 = 2 \qquad \bar{x}_3 = 3$$

and the sample variances are all zero. However,

$$V(\bar{x}_{sy}) = \frac{1}{3} \Sigma \ (\bar{x}_i - \bar{X})^2$$

$$= \frac{1}{3} [(1-2)^2 + (2-2)^2 + (3-2)^2] = \frac{2}{3}$$

From this example, we note that the variation between sample means is 2/3, but we also see that the variation within any single sample is zero, and hence we cannot use the variation within any single sample to estimate $V(\bar{x}_{sy})$.

The example we have used is an extreme case of periodicity in the population. However, this has no effect on the simple random sampling procedure. That is, we have

$$M = \binom{9}{3} = 84$$

possible samples and

$$V(\bar{x}_{ran}) = \frac{S^2}{n} \frac{N-n}{N}$$

$$= \frac{1}{M} \overset{M}{\Sigma} (\bar{x}_i - \bar{X})^2 = \frac{4}{27}$$

And the estimator of $V(\bar{x}_{ran})$ is obtained from

$$\hat{V}(\bar{x}_{ran}) = \frac{s^2}{n} \frac{N-n}{N}$$

where s^2 is the sample variance which may be obtained from any one of the $M = 84$ possible samples.

We may thus conclude that we cannot in general find an unbiased estimator of $V(\bar{x}_{sy})$ from a single systematic sample. However, all is not lost. As mentioned near the beginning of this section, we may under certain conditions consider the systematic sample as equivalent to the simple random sample, and therefore use the estimator for $V(\bar{x}_{ran})$ as an estimator for $V(\bar{x}_{sy})$.

Let us show that when $\rho = 0$, $V(\bar{x}_{sy})$ will be approximately equal to $V(\bar{x}_{ran})$, thus enabling us to use the estimator of $V(\bar{x}_{ran})$ as an estimator of $V(\bar{x}_{sy})$.

From equation (8) of section 7.4, we have

(6) $$V(\bar{x}_{sy}) = \frac{S^2}{n} \frac{N-1}{N}[1 + (n-1)\rho]$$

The efficiency of systematic sampling relative to random sampling is

(7) $$\frac{V(\bar{x}_{sy})}{V(\bar{x}_{ran})} = \frac{(N-1)[1 + (n-1)\rho]}{n(k-1)}$$

For both methods to have equal precision, we set

$$\frac{(N-1)[1 + (n-1)\rho]}{n(k-1)} = 1$$

Solving for ρ, we find

(8) $$\rho = \frac{-1}{nk-1} = \frac{-1}{N-1}$$

Hence, when $\rho = -1/(N-1)$, both sampling procedures give equal precision.

Since N is usually large, ρ must be small to satisfy equation (8). In other words, when the intraclass correlation coefficient is small (when the sampling units in the systematic samples are heterogeneous) the precision of systematic and random sampling will be approximately equal. We have argued in the previous section that ρ will be small if the sampling units in the population are randomly distributed.

Now that we have found that we may use $V(\bar{x}_{ran})$ of simple random sampling for systematic sampling when ρ is small, let us next find the estimator of this variance. We know that the estimator of $V(\bar{x}_{\text{ran}})$ is

(9)
$$\hat{V}(\bar{x}_{\text{ran}}) = \frac{N-n}{N} \frac{s^2}{n}$$

(10)
$$s^2 = \frac{1}{n-1} \sum_{i}^{n} (x_i - \bar{x})^2$$

Hence, for practical applications we simply calculate the sample variance s^2 and use (9) to estimate the variance of $\bar{x}_{\text{sy}}$.

Reference

As an exercise, let us find the expected value of $\hat{V}(\bar{x})$. According to our previous discussion, we shall find that the expected value of $\hat{V}(\bar{x})$ becomes equal to $V(\bar{x}_{\text{sy}})$ when $\rho = -1/(N-1)$.

(11)
$$E\left(\frac{N-n}{N} \frac{s^2}{n}\right) = \frac{N-n}{N} \frac{1}{n} E(s^2)$$

(12)
$$E(s^2) = \frac{1}{n-1} E\left[\sum_{i}^{n} (x_{ij} - \bar{x})^2\right]$$
$$= \frac{1}{n-1} E\left(\sum_{i}^{n} x_{ij}^2 - n\bar{x}^2\right)$$
$$= \frac{1}{n-1} E\left(\sum_{i}^{n} x_{ij}^2\right) - nE(\bar{x}^2)$$

(13)
$$E\left(\sum_{i}^{n} x_{ij}^2\right) = \frac{1}{k} \sum_{i}^{k} \sum_{j}^{n} x_{ij}^2$$

(14)
$$E(\bar{x}^2) = \bar{X}^2 + V(\bar{x}_{\text{sy}})$$

(15)
$$\therefore \quad E(s^2) = \frac{1}{n-1}\left[\frac{1}{k} \sum \sum x_{ij}^2\right] - n[\bar{X}^2 + V(\bar{x}_{\text{sy}})]$$
$$= \frac{1}{n-1} \frac{1}{k}[\sum \sum x_{ij}^2 - kn\bar{X}^2] - nV(\bar{x}_{\text{sy}})$$
$$= \frac{N-1}{N} S^2(1 - \rho)$$

(16)
$$\therefore \quad E\left(\frac{N-n}{N} \frac{s^2}{n}\right) = \frac{N-n}{N} \frac{1}{n} \frac{(N-1)S^2}{N}(1 - \rho)$$
$$= \frac{N-1}{N} \frac{S^2}{n}\left[\frac{N-n}{N}(1 - \rho)\right]$$

We have the relation $\rho = -1/(N-1)$ and $N = 1 - 1/\rho$. Thus the term in the brackets becomes

$$\frac{N-n}{N}(1 - \rho) = (1 - \rho)\left(1 - \frac{n}{N}\right)$$
$$= 1 - \rho + n\rho$$
$$= 1 + (n-1)\rho$$

Substituting this into (16) gives us

$$E\left(\frac{N-n}{N}\frac{s^2}{n}\right) = \frac{N-1}{N}\frac{S^2}{n}[1 + (n-1)\rho]$$
$$= V(\bar{x}_{sy})$$

Problems

1. Using the results of Problem 7 of page 178, calculate the efficiency of systematic sampling relative to random sampling, using equation 7 on page 183.

2. Repeat the operations of Problem 1, using the results of Problem 3 on page 178.

3. Select a random sample of size $n = 3$ from the population of Problem 1 of page 178 and find $\hat{V}(\bar{x}_{ran})$. Then compare this with $V(\bar{x}_{sy})$ obtained from Problem 3 and 7 on page 178. Explain the results.

Notes and References

For illustrations of systematic sampling, see Hansen, Hurwitz, and Madow (1953), pp. 507–512. Also see the article by Stephan et.al. (1940). Other illustrations related to estimating timber may be found in Yates(1960), pp. 83–85; U.S. Department of Agriculture(1962), pp. 60–61. For a good discussion of systematic sampling on an intermediate level, see Sampford(1962), Chapter 5. For an advanced discussion, containing the proofs of the various formulas, see Cochran(1963), Chapter 8; Kish(1965), Chapter 4. For advanced references, see the bibliography in Cochran (1963), p. 233.

Stephan, F.F., Deming, E.W., and Hansen, M.H. (1940). The sampling procedure of the 1940 population census. *J. Amer. Stat. Assoc.*, **35**, pp. 615–630.

Madow, L.H. (1946). Systematic sampling and its relation to other sampling designs. *J. Amer. Stat. Assoc.* **41**, pp. 204–217.

Buckland, W.R. (1951). A review of the literature of systematic sampling. *J. Roy. Stat. Soc.* **B13**, pp. 208–215.

U.S. Department of Agriculture(1962). *Elementary forest sampling*. Agriculture Handbook No. 232. Washington, D.C.: U.S. Govt. Printing Office.

CHAPTER 8

Simple Cluster Sampling

8.1 Introduction

Suppose there are 10 classes in the eighth grade of a school, and each class has about 40 students as shown in Fig. 8.1. We wish to estimate the average number of books a student has.

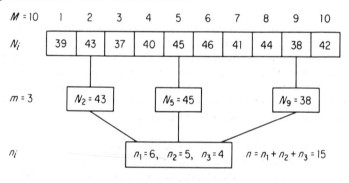

Fig. 8-1

We have so far studied a number of sampling procedures that could be used. If we use simple random sampling, a list of the students will have to be made. The list becomes the frame from which a random sample is selected. We may also use systematic sampling or stratified random sampling, considering each class as a stratum.

When the total size of the population is not very large, as in our illustration, any one of the above sampling procedures may be used without difficulty. However, when the population size becomes large, such procedures lead to several difficulties. One is the difficulty of preparing a frame. The second is the high cost of surveying scattered sampling units. And a third is the difficulty of administering a sampling plan where the sampling units are widely scattered.

As an example, suppose we wish to estimate the weekly expenditure on food of families in New York City. To use simple random sampling, we need a list of the families, and for all practical purposes, this is impossible to get. We face a similar problem in systematic sampling.

To apply stratified random sampling, New York City must be stratified—so that similar income groups are in the same stratum, if possible. Since similar income groups tend to live in the same neighborhood, this may be achieved to some extent by stratifying New York City by area. However, even if this were possible, we are left with the task of making a list of families in each area, and this, for all practical purposes, is impossible. An alternative would be to use the voting districts, where there would be voter registration records, and utilizing this, it may be possible to work out some kind of list, although a little reflection should easily show that this will also be an enormous task.

However, suppose there is a list of families in New York City that may be used, and we are able to hurdle this first difficulty. We may select a random sample from this list, but there is now the problem of visiting these families which are widely scattered throughout the city. If the population were New York State or the U.S. as a whole, visiting widely scattered families would involve prohibitive costs. The administrative problem of managing a sampling plan where sampling units and investigators are widely scattered would also be cumbersome.

We can see intuitively that it would make the sampling survey easier in terms of preparation, cost, and administration if the sampling units that are to be selected were in clusters. For example, suppose New York City is divided into M voting districts. Each voting district may be considered as a cluster of families. Then, a random sample of m voting districts is selected. In other words, instead of selecting families one at a time we have selected m groups of families and, in our present case, each group of families lives in the same voting district. Then, random samples of $n_1, n_2, \ldots, n_m$ families are selected from each of the m districts, and the combined sample we seek is $n = n_1 + n_2 + \ldots + n_m$.

When sampling units are selected in this fashion, we therefore only need a list of the M voting districts and a list of the families in the m voting districts that were selected. Furthermore, since the families that have been selected are clustered in voting districts, they will be easier to visit than if scattered throughout the population, and the overall administration of the sampling plan will also be easier.

In many cases, this reduction in cost and ease of administration allows a selection of a larger sample than would be the case if simple random sampling were used, and this larger sample may more than compensate in terms of precision for the use of cluster sampling rather than the use of simple random sampling.

Going back to our original illustration of estimating the total number of books the students have, we shall first select several classes, say $m = 3$ classes (clusters) from the $M = 10$ classes. These $M = 10$ clusters will be called *primary sampling units* (psu).

Then, from the $m = 3$ classes, we shall select $n_1 = 6$, $n_2 = 5$, and $n_3 = 4$ students from the $N_2 = 43$, $N_5 = 45$, and $N_9 = 38$ students, respectively. These students (elementary units) are called *secondary sampling units* (ssu). Note that the subscript 1 of n_1 shows $n_1 = 6$ is the group of students selected from $N_2 = 43$, which is the first cluster to be selected. Similarly, $n_2 = 5$ is the group of students selected from $N_5 = 45$, which is the second cluster to be selected, and so forth. These $n_1 = 6$, $n_2 = 5$, and $n_3 = 4$ are called *ultimate clusters*.

Our sample is then

$$n = n_1 + n_2 + n_3 = 6 + 5 + 4 = 15$$

students. Using this sample of $n = 15$ students, we wish to estimate the average number of books a student has in the population.

This process of selecting a sample of size n and estimating the population parameters is called cluster sampling.

What we propose to do now is to show how the population total, mean, and variance may be estimated from a cluster sample of size n. We shall start with a discussion of the estimator for the population total.

8.2 Estimation of the population total

The characteristics of cluster sampling is that the sampling units are selected in two stages. The first is the selection of the m primary sampling units (psu) from the M psu; the second is the selection of n_i (where $i = 1$, $2, \ldots, m$) secondary sampling units (ssu) from the ith psu.

Hence, the process of estimating the total proceeds in two steps. The first step is to estimate the m cluster totals, and the second step is to use these estimated m cluster totals to estimate the total of the M clusters.

The rationale of estimating the total is very simple. For example, suppose there are $M = 10$ classes and we wish to estimate the total number of books the students have. Suppose we select $m = 2$ classes where each class has $N_i = N_j = 40$ students, and random samples of $n_1 = n_2 = 10$ students are selected from each class. Suppose we find that the $n_1 = 10$ students have an average of 5 books and that the $n_2 = 10$ students have an average of 7 books.

The natural thing to do then in order to estimate the total number of books the $N_i = 40$ students have is to multiply the average of 5 books by $N_i = 40$, that is, 5 books $\times$ 40 = 200 books. For $N_j = 40$, we have 7 $\times$ 40 = 280 books. We know, however, from simple random sampling theory, that this common sense procedure of estimation gives us unbiased estimators.

The average of these 2 classes is

$$(200 + 280)/2 = 240 \text{ books}$$

Hence, an estimate of the total number of books for the $M = 10$ classes will be

$$240 \text{ books} \times 10 = 2400 \text{ books}$$

What we propose to do now is to organize this common sense procedure into a systematic sampling procedure. As we shall see, this procedure will give us an unbiased estimator of the total.

Using our illustration of students where the total number of books are to be estimated, we have selected $m = 3$ clusters, and from these we have selected $n_1 = 6$, $n_2 = 5$, $n_3 = 4$ students.

Focusing our attention on the first cluster that was selected, let us estimate the total number of books the students in that cluster (class) have. Suppose the $n_1 = 6$ students have the following number of books.

$$x_{11} = 3 \qquad x_{12} = 5 \qquad x_{13} = 4$$
$$x_{14} = 5 \qquad x_{15} = 4 \qquad x_{16} = 3$$

Thus, the total number of books for the 1st ultimate cluster is

$$x_1 = x_{11} + x_{12} + \ldots + x_{16}$$
$$= 3 + 5 + \ldots + 3 = 24$$

This may be written as

$$x_1 = \sum_{j}^{n_1=6} x_{1j} = 24 \text{ books}$$

and the average number of books per student in the 1st ultimate cluster is

$$\bar{x}_1 = x_1/n_1 = 24/6 = 4 \text{ books per student}$$

Using the results of simple random sampling, we know that an unbiased estimate of the total number of books in the 1st cluster (psu) is

$$\hat{X}_1 = N_1\bar{x}_1 = 43 \times 4 = 172 \text{ books}$$

In symbols this is

$$\hat{X}_1 = N_1\bar{x}_1 = N_1\frac{x_1}{n_1} = \frac{N_1}{n_1}\sum_{j}^{n_1} x_{1j}$$

For the 2nd and 3rd clusters that were selected, let us assume the totals have been estimated as

$$\hat{X}_2 = N_2\bar{x}_2 = 45 \times 3.4 = 153 \text{ books}$$
$$\hat{X}_3 = N_3\bar{x}_3 = 38 \times 4.5 = 171 \text{ books}$$

Thus, the estimate of the total number of books for the sample of the $m = 3$ clusters is

$$\hat{x} = \hat{X}_1 + \hat{X}_2 + \hat{X}_3 = 172 + 153 + 171 = 496$$

where the symbol $\hat{x}$ is used to indicate the estimated total for the $m = 3$ clusters. Note that x has been used to denote a sample total. We have added the $\wedge$ to denote it is the estimated total for the sample of $m = 3$ clusters.

In symbols, the estimated total for the sample of $m = 3$ clusters is written as

$$\hat{x} = \sum_i^m \hat{X}_i = \sum_i^m \frac{N_i}{n_i} \sum_j^{n_i} x_{ij}$$

Finally, we note that $m = 3$ is from the $M = 10$ clusters. The estimated total for $m = 3$ clusters is $\hat{x} = \sum \hat{X}_i = 496$. Hence, the estimate of the total for the $M = 10$ clusters becomes

$$\hat{X} = \frac{10}{3} \times 496 = 1653 \text{ books}$$

Note that we use $\hat{X}$ to indicate the estimator of the total for the population. In symbols, this is

(1) $$\hat{X} = \frac{M}{m} \sum_i^m \hat{X}_i = \frac{M}{m} \sum_i^m \frac{N_i}{n_i} \sum_j^{n_i} x_{ij}$$

which is the estimator of X we seek. It turns out that

$$E(\hat{X}) = X$$

and $\hat{X}$ of equation (1) is an unbiased estimator of X.

We may summarize the rationale of equation (1) as follows.

(1') $$\hat{X} = M \left[\frac{1}{m} \sum_i^m N_i \left(\frac{1}{n_i} \sum_j^{n_i} x_{ij} \right) \right]$$

$$= M \left[\frac{1}{m} \sum_i^m N_i(\bar{x}_i) \right] \qquad \text{Step 1}$$

$$= M \left[\frac{1}{m} \sum_i^m \hat{X}_i \right]$$

$$= M(\hat{\bar{X}}) \qquad \text{Step 2}$$

Step 1: (a) Find an estimate of the average of the ith ultimate cluster, $\bar{x}_i$.

(b) Multiply $\bar{x}_i$ by N_i, that is, $N_i \bar{x}_i$, to estimate the total X_i.

Step 2: (a) Find an estimate of the average of the primary clusters, $\hat{\bar{X}}$.

(b) Multiply $\hat{\bar{X}}$ by M, that is, $M\hat{\bar{X}}$, to estimate X.

Hence, we are merely using the simple random sampling procedure of estimating a total—that is, $\hat{X} = N\bar{x}$—two times, once at the ssu stage, and then at the psu stage.

It is easy to see that this rationale may easily be extended to 3 or more stages. We shall do this in Chapter 11 when we discuss three-stage cluster sampling.

Example 1. Using the following hypothetical data, let us illustrate the process of estimating the population total by cluster sampling, and let us show that the estimator is unbiased. Supposing we have $M = 3$ groups (A, B, and C) of children, let X_{ij} show the number of books the jth child in the ith cluster has. Select $m = 2$ groups, select from these $n_1 = 2$ and $n_2 = 2$ children, and from these $n = n_1 + n_2 = 4$ children, estimate the total number of books of the $N = 9$ children.

Cluster	X_{ij}	X_i	$\bar{\bar{X}}_i$
A	1, 3, 5	9	3
B	3, 5, 7	15	5
C	5, 7, 9	21	7
		45	

(i) The number of possible samples.

The number of possible samples we can select are as follows: The number of possible combinations of psu are

$$\binom{M}{m} = \binom{3}{2} = 3$$

The number of possible samples of size $n_1 = 2$ and $n_2 = 2$ from the $m = 2$ psu are

$$\binom{3}{2}\binom{3}{2} = 3 \times 3 = 9$$

The total number of possible samples are

$$\binom{M}{m}\binom{3}{2}\binom{3}{2} = 3 \times 3 \times 3 = 27$$

These 27 samples are listed in the following table.

Table 8.1

A	B	$\hat{X}$	A	C	$\hat{X}$	B	C	$\hat{X}$
1, 3	3, 5	27	1, 3	5, 7	36	3, 5	5, 7	45
	3, 7	31.5		5, 9	40.5		5, 9	49.5
	5, 7	36		7, 9	45		7, 9	54
1, 5	3, 5	31.5	1, 5	5, 7	40.5	3, 7	5, 7	49.5
	3, 7	36		5, 9	45		5, 9	54
	5, 7	40.5		7, 9	49.5		7, 9	58.5
3, 5	3, 5	36	3, 5	5, 7	45	5, 7	5, 7	54
	3, 7	40.5		5, 9	49.5		5, 9	58.5
	5, 7	45		7, 9	54		7, 9	63
		324			405			486

(ii) Estimate X.

Using the first sample in the table as an illustration, namely, (1, 3, 3, 5), let us estimate the population total. From equation (1), we have

$$\hat{X} = \frac{M}{m} \sum_i^m \frac{N_i}{n_i} \sum_j^{n_i} x_{ij}$$

$$= \frac{3}{2}\left[\frac{N_1}{n_1} \sum^{n_1} x_{1j} + \frac{N_2}{n_2} \sum^{n_2} x_{2j}\right]$$

$$= \frac{3}{2}\left[\frac{3}{2}(x_{11} + x_{12}) + \frac{3}{2}(x_{21} + x_{22})\right]$$

$$= \frac{3}{2}\left[\frac{3}{2}(1 + 3) + \frac{3}{2}(3 + 5)\right]$$

$$= \frac{3}{2}(6 + 12) = 27$$

As is seen

$$\frac{N_1}{n_1}\sum^{n_1} x_{1j} = \frac{3}{2}(1 + 3) = 3 \times 2 = N_1\bar{x}_1 = 6$$

is the estimated total of cluster A obtained by using the basic relation $\hat{X} = N\bar{x}$. In similar manner we have found the estimated total of cluster B as 12. Hence, $(6 + 12)/2 = 9 = \hat{\bar{X}}$ is the average number of books per cluster based on the $m = 2$ clusters A and B. Therefore, using the basic relation $\hat{X} = N\bar{x}$ again, an estimate of the total number of books is (since there are $M = 3$ clusters):

$$\hat{X} = \frac{3}{2}(6 + 12) = 3 \times 9 = M\hat{\bar{X}} = 27$$

Column $\hat{X}$ in the table has been computed in this fashion for the 27 possible samples.

(iii) Find $E(\hat{X})$.

As previously mentioned, the sampling procedure is performed in two stages. For example, we first select $m = 2$ clusters from the $M = 3$ clusters. From these $m = 2$ clusters, we then select random samples of n_1 and n_2. We have thus performed random sampling twice: once when selecting the $m = 2$ clusters, and again when selecting the n_1 and n_2 samples.

As a result of this two-stage sampling procedure, the process of evaluating $E(\hat{X})$ will also be divided into two stages. One is to find the expectation for the first random sampling stage and the other is to find the expectation for the second random sampling stage.

Random sampling of the 2nd stage therefore depends on the 1st stage. Samples n_1 and n_2 are selected from $m = 2$ clusters which must be selected first, and hence may be considered given when considering the 2nd stage.

These relationships may be shown as follows:

$$\hat{X} = \frac{M}{m}\sum_i^m \frac{N_i}{n_i}\sum^{n_i} x_{ij}$$

$$E(\hat{X}) = E_i\left[E_j\frac{M}{m}\sum_i^m \frac{N_i}{n_i}\sum^{n_i} x_{ij}\right]$$

The E_j indicates that the expectation is to be taken over j, holding i constant (that is, holding the 1 st stage psu's constant). The first E_i on the right indicates the expectation is to be taken over all i, that is, over all psu.

In terms of our example, suppose the $m = 2$ are A and B. Then, for the case where A and B are assumed to be given,

$$E_j\frac{M}{m}\sum_i^m \frac{N_i}{n_i}\sum_j^{n_i} x_{ij}$$

shows that the expectation is to be taken over the 9 possible samples corresponding to A and B in the table. We know that

$$\frac{M}{m} \Sigma \frac{N_i}{n_i} \Sigma x_{ij}$$

is the estimator of the total $\hat{X}$ and we have calculated these estimators in the table.

Since the 9 possible samples from A and B have equal chances of being selected, we have, for the given A and B

$$E_i \frac{M}{m} \overset{m}{\Sigma} \frac{N_i}{n_i} \overset{n_i}{\Sigma} x_{ij}$$

$$= \Sigma \frac{1}{9} \left(\frac{M}{m} \overset{m}{\Sigma} \frac{N_i}{n_i} \overset{n_i}{\Sigma} x_{ij} \right) \text{ [Where } \Sigma \text{ is over all 9 possible samples—(see table).]}$$

$$= \frac{1}{9} (27 + 31.5 + 36 + \cdots + 40.5 + 45)$$

$$= \frac{1}{9} (324) = 36$$

The second step is to perform this operation for all $\binom{M}{m} = \binom{3}{2} = 3$ possible combinations, namely, the (A, B), (A, C), and (B, C) possible samples of $m = 2$ psu's. Since each of these 3 possible samples of psu have the same chance of being selected, we have

$$E(X) = E_i \left[E_j \frac{M}{m} \overset{m}{\Sigma} \frac{N_i}{n_i} \overset{n_i}{\Sigma} x_{ij} \right]$$

$$= \frac{1}{3} \left[\frac{1}{9} (27 + 31.5 + \cdots + 45) \right] \qquad \text{for } A \text{ and } B$$

$$+ \frac{1}{3} \left[\frac{1}{9} (36 + 40.5 + \cdots + 54) \right] \qquad \text{for } A \text{ and } C$$

$$+ \frac{1}{3} \left[\frac{1}{9} (45 + 49.5 + \cdots + 63) \right] \qquad \text{for } B \text{ and } C$$

$$= \frac{1}{3} \cdot \frac{1}{9} (324 + 405 + 486) = 45$$

The total number of books calculated from the original data is

$$X = 1 + 3 + \cdots + 7 + 9 = 45$$
$$\therefore \quad E(\hat{X}) = X = 45$$

Example 2. Given the following data, show that $E(\hat{X}) = X$.

psu	X_{ij}	X_i
A	1, 2, 3	6
B	2, 2, 3, 5	12
C	4, 5, 6	15
		33

(i) $X = \overset{M}{\underset{i}{\Sigma}} X_i = 33$

(ii) $m = 2$; suppose A and C have been selected.

A: $n_1 = 2$,   Suppose 1 and 2 have been selected.

C: $n_2 = 2$,   Suppose 4 and 5 have been selected.

$$\therefore \quad \hat{X} = \frac{M}{m} \sum \frac{N_i}{n_i} \sum x_{ij}$$

$$= \frac{3}{2} \left[\frac{3}{2}(1 + 2) + \frac{3}{2}(4 + 5) \right] = \frac{3}{2}\left(\frac{36}{2}\right) = 27$$

(iii) All possible samples

$$A \text{ and } B: \qquad \binom{3}{2}\binom{4}{2} = 3 \times 6 = 18$$

$$A \text{ and } C: \qquad \binom{3}{2}\binom{3}{2} = 3 \times 3 = 9$$

$$B \text{ and } C: \qquad \binom{4}{2}\binom{3}{2} = 6 \times 3 = 18$$

$$\overline{45}$$

The following table gives the 9 possible samples from (A, C).

Table 8.2

A	C	$\hat{X}$	
1, 2	4, 5	(3/2)(36/2)	27
	4, 6	(3/2)(39/2)	29.25
	5, 6	(3/2)(42/2)	31.5
1, 3	4, 5	(3/2)(39/2)	29.25
	4, 6	(3/2)(42/2)	31.5
	5, 6	(3/2)(45/2)	33.75
2, 3	4, 5	(3/2)(42/2)	31.5
	4, 6	(3/2)(45/2)	33.75
	5, 6	(3/2)(48/2)	36
		(3/2)(378/2)	283.5

The other 36 possible samples may be obtained in the same fashion.

(iv) $E_j \dfrac{M}{m} \sum \dfrac{N_i}{n_i} \sum x_{ij}$

For A and B: (1/18)(486)
For A and C: (1/9)(283.5)
For B and C: (1/18)(729)

(v) $E(\hat{X})$

$$E(\hat{X}) = E_i \left[E_j \frac{M}{m} \sum_i^m \frac{N_i}{n_i} \sum_j^{n_i} x_{ij} \right]$$

$$= \frac{1}{3}\left[\frac{1}{18}(486) + \frac{1}{9}(283.5) + \frac{1}{18}(729) \right] = 33$$

$$\therefore \quad E(\hat{X}) = X = 33$$

Example 3. Show that $E(\hat{X}) = X$ algebraically. Since the sampling is performed in two stages, the expected value of $\hat{X}$ is

$$E(\hat{X}) = E_i E_j(\hat{X})$$

where E_i is the process of taking the expected value over the 1 st stage, that is, over the M psu's; and E_j is the process of taking the expected value over the 2nd stage, that is, over the N_i sampling units, for a given ith psu. Hence, to calculate $E(\hat{X})$, we shall first hold i constant (that is, assume the ith psu is given), find E_j, then find E_i.

$$E(\hat{X}) = E_i E_j(\hat{X})$$

$$= E_i E_j \left[\frac{M}{m} \overset{m}{\Sigma} \frac{N_i}{n_i} \overset{n_i}{\Sigma} x_{ij} \right]$$

$$= E_i \left[\frac{M}{m} \overset{m}{\Sigma} \frac{N_i}{n_i} \overset{n_i}{\Sigma} E_j(x_{ij}) \right]$$

Given the ith psu, a random sample of n_i is selected. Hence,

$$E_j(x_{ij}) = \bar{\bar{X}}_i$$

which is the mean of the ith psu. Substituting this into the above equation and continuing, we have

$$= E_i \left[\frac{M}{m} \overset{m}{\Sigma} \frac{N_i}{n_i} \overset{n_i}{\Sigma} \bar{\bar{X}}_i \right]$$

$$= E_i \left[\frac{M}{m} \overset{m}{\Sigma} \frac{N_i}{n_i} (n_i \bar{\bar{X}}_i) \right]$$

$$= E_i \left[\frac{M}{m} \overset{m}{\Sigma} N_i \bar{\bar{X}}_i \right]$$

$$= E_i \left[\frac{M}{m} \overset{m}{\Sigma} X_i \right]$$

where X_i is the total of the ith psu. Note carefully, however, that X_i was obtained under the assumption that the ith psu was given. Now we wish to take the expectation over the M psu, and thus X_i becomes a random variable where $i = 1$, $2, \ldots, M$. Furthermore, since the psu are selected by simple random sampling, the probability of selecting any one of the M psu is $1/M$. Hence we get (continuing from above):

$$= E_i \left[\frac{M}{m} \overset{m}{\Sigma} X_i \right]$$

$$= \frac{M}{m} \overset{m}{\Sigma} E_i(X_i)$$

$$= \frac{M}{m} \overset{m}{\Sigma} \overset{M}{\Sigma} \frac{1}{M} X_i$$

$$= \frac{M}{m} \cdot m \cdot \frac{1}{M} \overset{M}{\Sigma} X_i = X$$

That is, $E(\hat{X}) = X$, and $\hat{X}$ is an unbiased estimator of X.

Problems

1. Given the following hypothetical population, $m = 2$ clusters are selected, and from each cluster subsamples of size $n_1 = 2$, $n_2 = 2$ are selected.

Cluster	X_{ij}
A	2, 2, 5
B	3, 5, 7
C	5, 7, 12

(i) How many possible samples of size $n_1 + n_2$ can be selected? List all the samples in a table.

(ii) Estimate the total X, using the samples found in (i) and list them in the table.

(iii) Verify that $E(\hat{X}) = X$.

2. In Example 2, work out the details of the calculations for clusters A, B and B, C.

3. Suppose we wish to estimate the total number of hogs in a certain state. There are $M = 20$ counties and a sample of $m = 4$ counties is selected, then subsamples of n_i farms are selected and the following data is obtained:

Counties	N_i	x_{ij}
1	20	12, 15, 18, 19, 11
2	35	13, 10, 17, 16, 14
3	30	16, 17, 15, 12
4	25	14, 19, 13, 11, 12, 15

N_i is the number of farms in the ith county and x_{ij} is the number of hogs in the jth farm of the ith county. Estimate the total number of hogs.

4. A certain government agency wishes to estimate the total number of visitors it has during a given week. It has $M = 50$ departments and has selected $m = 5$ departments. Each department has N_i employees. The employees of the $m = 5$ departments are asked to keep a record of the number of visitors they receive during a week. Subsamples of employees are selected and the results are as follows. Estimate the total number of visitors.

Department	N_i	x_{ij} (number of visitors)
1	10	5, 3, 0, 8
2	15	11, 6, 5, 9, 4
3	10	4, 3, 5
4	20	6, 8, 2, 4
5	15	2, 0, 9, 9

5. A department store wishes to estimate the total amount of accounts due of credit customers during a month. It has a ledger of $M = 500$ pages and each page has $N_i = 40$ entries. A random sample of $m = 20$ pages is selected, and from each page, samples of size $\bar{n} = 10$ entries (customers) are selected. The results of the investigation were as follows:

Pages	$\sum x_{ij}$	Pages	$\sum x_{ij}$	Pages	$\sum x_{ij}$	Pages	$\sum x_{ij}$
1	$1	6	$9	11	$7	16	$6
2	4	7	5	12	9	17	9
3	4	8	1	13	2	18	0
4	0	9	3	14	0	19	7
5	2	10	7	15	5	20	5

The $\sum x_{ij}$ are in units of $100. Hence, for example, $\sum x_{ij} = \$100$ for the 1st sample page, and it shows the $\bar{n} = 10$ entries had a total of \$100 due. Estimate the total amount of accounts due.

6. The Air Force wishes to estimate the total number of miles flown by a certain type of airplane during a given month. There are $M = 120$ airfields and each has N_i airplanes. A sample of $m = 10$ airfields is selected and n_i airplanes are selected at each airfield. The $\sum x_{ij}$ gives the total number of miles flown in units of 1,000 miles. Estimate the total number of miles flown.

Airfield	N_i	n_i	$\sum x_{ij}$	Airfield	N_i	n_i	$\sum x_{ij}$
1	10	5	20	6	15	5	30
2	15	6	30	7	15	5	25
3	15	5	25	8	10	4	28
4	15	4	16	9	10	4	16
5	10	4	24	10	15	6	36

8.3   The variance of $\hat{X}$ and its estimator

(i) The variance of $\hat{X}$

Now that the estimator $\hat{X}$ has been found, we need the variance of $\hat{X}$ to assess its precision. As with the estimator $\hat{X}$, we need to consider the two stages of sampling when deriving $V(\hat{X})$. We can see intuitively that there are two sources of variation: one is the variation due to the sampling of psu and is called the variation *between* the psu; the other is the variation due to the selection of random samples from the psu and is called the variation *within* the psu.

For example, suppose we wish to estimate the total number of books students in $M = 10$ classes have. First, a random sample of $m = 3$ classes (psu) is selected, and random samples of size n_1, n_2, and n_3 are then selected from the $m = 3$ psu. The first source of variation is due to the selection of $m = 3$ psu, and may be referred to as the variation *between* the psu (classes). The second source of variation is due to the selection of sample n_i from the ith sampled psu, and may be referred to as the variation *within* the psu.

Thus, the variance of $\hat{X}$ may be shown schematically as

$$V(\hat{X}) = (\text{variation between psu}) + (\text{variation within psu})$$

As we shall derive later (reference 1), $V(\hat{X})$ is

(1)
$$V(\hat{X}) = M^2 \frac{M - m}{M} \frac{S_b^2}{m} + \frac{M}{m} \sum^M N_i^2 \frac{(N_i - n_i)}{N_i} \frac{S_i^2}{n_i}$$

where

(2)
$$S_b^2 = \frac{1}{M-1} \sum_i^M (X_i - \bar{X})^2$$

(3)
$$S_i^2 = \frac{1}{N_i - 1} \sum_j^{N_i} (X_{ij} - \bar{\bar{X}}_i)^2$$

In terms of our illustration using books, note that

X_i total number of books in ith class (psu)

$\bar{X} = X/M$ average number of books per class (psu)

$\bar{\bar{X}}_i = X_i/N_i$ average number of books per student (ssu) in the ith class

The S_b^2 shows the variance between cluster totals. That is, it shows the dispersion of the X_i around $\bar{X}$.

The S_i^2 shows the variance of X_{ij} around $\bar{\bar{X}}_i$ within the ith class. We know from simple random sampling that S_i^2/n_i shows the sampling variance of $\bar{x}_i$ around $\bar{\bar{X}}_i$, where $\bar{x}_i$ is the sample mean (average number of books per student in the sample) of a sample of size n_i taken from N_i. We also know that $N_i^2(S_i^2/n_i)$ is the sampling variance of $\hat{X}_i = N_i\bar{x}_i$ around $X_i = N_i\bar{\bar{X}}_i$. Therefore, we can see that when $N_i = n_i$, the $\bar{x}_i = \bar{\bar{X}}_i$, $\hat{X}_i$ becomes equal to X_i, and the sampling variance of $\hat{X}_i$ around X_i becomes zero.

In terms of equation (1), when all of the sampling units in the psu are selected (that is, $N_i = n_i$), $V(\hat{X})$ becomes

$$V(\hat{X}) = M^2 \frac{M - m}{M} \frac{S_b^2}{m} + 0$$

and $V(\hat{X})$ is affected only by S_b^2. The variation within the psu (classes) becomes equal to zero. Only the variation between psu remains.

Conversely, if the ssu (students) are taken from all the M psu (classes), that is, $M = m$, $V(\hat{X})$ becomes

$$V(\hat{X}) = 0 + \frac{M}{m} \sum_i^M N_i^2 \frac{N_i - n_i}{N_i} \frac{S_i^2}{n_i}$$

$$= \sum_i N_i^2 \frac{N_i - n_i}{N_i} \frac{S_i^2}{n_i}$$

The variance between clusters becomes zero, and only the within variation remains. Note that the result is equal to the $V(\hat{X}_{st})$ equation for stratified random sampling, which was the sampling procedure where subsamples were taken from all strata.

Let us now illustrate the meaning of $V(\hat{X})$ by examples.

Example 1. Using the data of Example 1 of section 8. 2, find $V(\hat{X})$.

Cluster	X_{ij}	X_i	$\bar{\bar{X}}_i$
A	1, 3, 5	9	3
B	3, 5, 7	15	5
C	5, 7, 9	21	7
		45	

$$V(\hat{X}) = M^2 \frac{M - m}{M} \frac{S_b^2}{m} + \frac{M}{m} \sum_i N_i^2 \frac{N_i - n_i}{N_i} \frac{S_i^2}{n_i}$$

$$S_b^2 = \frac{1}{M - 1} \sum^M (X_i - \bar{X})^2$$

$$= \frac{1}{3-1}[(9-15)^2 + (15-15)^2 + (21-15)^2] = 36$$

$$S_1^2 = \frac{1}{N_1 - 1} \sum_j^{N_1} (X_{1j} - \bar{X}_1)^2$$

$$= \frac{1}{3-1}[(1-3)^2 + (3-3)^2 + (5-3)^2] = 4$$

$$S_2^2 = 4 \qquad S_3^2 = 4$$

$$\therefore \quad V(\hat{X}) = \left[(3)^2 \left(\frac{3-2}{3}\right)\left(\frac{36}{2}\right) \right] + \frac{3}{2}\left[(3)^2 \left(\frac{3-2}{3}\right)\left(\frac{1}{2}\right)(4+4+4) \right] = 81$$

Example 2. Using the data of Example 3, of section 8.2, calculate $V(\hat{X})$.

Cluster	X_{ij}	X_i	$\bar{X}_i$
A	1, 2, 3	6	2
B	2, 2, 3, 5	12	3
C	4, 5, 6	15	5
		33	

$$S_b^2 = \frac{1}{M-1} \sum (x_i - \bar{X})^2$$

$$= \frac{1}{3-1}[(6-11)^2 + (12-11)^2 + (15-11)^2] = 21$$

$$S_i^2 = \frac{1}{N_i - 1} \sum (X_{ij} - \bar{X}_i)^2$$

$$S_1^2 = \frac{1}{3-1}[(1-2)^2 + (2-2)^2 + (3-2)^2] = 1$$

$$S_2^2 = 2, \quad S_3^2 = 1$$

$$\therefore \quad V(\hat{X}) = M^2 \frac{M-m}{M} \frac{S_b^2}{m} + \frac{M}{m} \sum N_i^2 \frac{N_i - n_i}{N_i} \frac{S_i^2}{n_i}$$

$$= (3)^2 \left(\frac{3-2}{3}\right)\left(\frac{21}{2}\right) + \frac{3}{2}\left[(3)^2 \left(\frac{3-2}{3}\right)\left(\frac{1}{2}\right) + (4)^2 \left(\frac{4-2}{4}\right)\left(\frac{2}{2}\right) \right.$$

$$\left. + (3)^2 \left(\frac{3-2}{3}\right)\left(\frac{1}{2}\right) \right] = 48$$

The characteristic of $V(\hat{X})$ is that the effect of S_b^2 tends to dominate the magnitude of $V(\hat{X})$. In Example 1, we had

$$S_b^2 = 36$$

$$S_1^2 = S_2^2 = S_3^2 = 4$$

The practical implication of this observation is that it may be desirable to keep the variation between clusters small at the expense of a certain degree of heterogeneity in the clusters. For example, when sampling the consumption of electricity of families in a certain city, the city may be divided into clusters of similar income groups which usually live in similar neighborhoods. In this case, S_b^2 (which shows the variation between the groups) will tend to be large, and S_i^2 (which shows the variation within the groups) will tend to be small.

In contrast to this grouping of clusters, the clusters may be made larger to include different income groups. The effect will be to reduce the difference between clusters, and hence reduce S_b^2—but increase the heterogeneity within the clusters, and hence increase the magnitude of S_i^2. The overall effect will probably be to reduce $V(\hat{X})$.

When the clusters are made large, the cost may be reduced by selecting a few clusters and many sampling units from each cluster. As discussed above, this may also reduce $V(\hat{X})$.

The data in Example 1 were grouped into homogeneous clusters. Let us mix it so the data within the clusters become heterogeneous and calculate $V(\hat{X})$.

Cluster	X_{ij}	X_i	$\bar{X}_i$
A	1, 5, 9	15	5
B	3, 7, 3	13	13/3
C	7, 5, 5	17	17/3

As is seen, the sampling units within the clusters have become heterogeneous, but the variations between clusters have been reduced. Let us calculate S_b^2 and S_i^2.

$$S_b^2 = \frac{1}{M-1} \sum_{}^{M} (X_i - \bar{X})^2$$

$$= \frac{1}{3-1}[(15-15)^2 + (13-15)^2 + (17-15)^2] = 4$$

$$S_i^2 = \frac{1}{N_1 - 1} \sum_{}^{N_1} (X_{1j} - x)^2$$

$$= \frac{1}{3-1}[(1-5)^2 + (5-5)^2 + (9-5)^2] = 16$$

$$S_2^2 = 5\frac{1}{3} \qquad S_3^2 = 1\frac{1}{3}$$

Let us compare the results with Example 1.

	Example 1	Example 2
S_b^2	36	4
S_1^2	4	16
S_2^2	4	$5\frac{1}{3}$
S_3^2	4	$1\frac{1}{3}$

The reduction in S_b^2 and increase in S_i^2 due to the mixing of the data is clear, and $V(\hat{X})$ is

$$V(\hat{X}) = \left[(3)^2 \left(\frac{3-2}{3} \right) \left(\frac{4}{2} \right) \right] + \frac{3}{2} \left[(3)^2 \left(\frac{3-2}{3} \right) \left(\frac{1}{2} \right) \left(16 + 5\frac{1}{3} + 1\frac{1}{3} \right) \right]$$

$$= 6 + 51 = 57$$

In our previous case $V(\hat{X}) = 81$, and as is seen, there has been a reduction in $V(\hat{x})$.

(ii) *Estimator of* $V(\hat{X})$.

In practical applications the population is large and a direct calculation of $V(\hat{X})$ is, for all practical purposes, impossible. We shall, instead, use an estimator. To find an estimator of $V(\hat{X})$, we first note it is made up of two components; the between variance, S_b^2, and the within variance, S_i^2. Following this line of thought, we shall find that an estimator of $V(\hat{X})$ will be obtained by using estimators of S_b^2 and S_i^2. These estimators turn out to be

(4)
$$\hat{V}(\hat{X}) = M^2 \frac{M-m}{M} \frac{s_b^2}{m} + \frac{M}{m} \sum^m N_i^2 \frac{N_i - n_i}{N_i} \frac{s_i^2}{n_i}$$

where

(5)
$$s_b^2 = \frac{1}{m-1} \sum^m (\hat{X}_i - \hat{\bar{X}})^2$$

(6)
$$s_i^2 = \frac{1}{n_i - 1} \sum^{n_i} (x_{ij} - \bar{x}_i)^2$$

As is seen, there are three differences between $V(\hat{X})$ and its estimator, $\hat{V}(\hat{X})$. One is that s_b^2 is used instead of S_b^2, the second is that s_i^2 is used instead of S_i^2, and the third is that the sum $\sum$ is over m psu instead of over M psu in the second term.

The s_b^2 shows the variation of $\hat{X}_i$ between the m psu. The $\hat{X}_i$:

$$\hat{X}_i = N_i \bar{x}_i; \qquad \bar{x}_i = \frac{x_i}{n_i}$$

is an estimator of the ith cluster total, where $\bar{x}_i$ is the sample mean of the subsample n_i. The

$$\hat{\bar{X}} = \frac{1}{m} \sum^m \hat{X}_i$$

is the average of the $\hat{X}_i$, $i = 1, 2, \ldots, m$.

The s_i^2 shows the variation of x_{ij} within the ultimate cluster from the ith psu. Since n_i is a random sample from N_i, and $\bar{x}_i$ is simply the sample mean of n_i, we know from simple random sampling theory that s_i^2 is an unbiased estimator of S_i^2. That is,

$$E(s_i^2) = S_i^2$$

However, s_b^2 is not an unbiased estimator of S_b^2. As is shown in the reference

$$E(s_b^2) = S_b^2 + \frac{1}{M} \sum^M N_i^2 \frac{N_i - n_i}{N_i} \frac{S_i^2}{n_i}$$

Finally, it is shown in the reference that

$$E[\hat{V}(\hat{X})] = V(\hat{X})$$

and equation (4) is an unbiased estimator of $V(\hat{X})$.

Let us now give several examples of $\hat{V}(\hat{X})$ and verify these relations.

Example 3. Using the data of Example 1, let us calculate $\hat{V}(\hat{X})$.

Cluster	X_{ij}	X_i	$\bar{\bar{X}}_i$
A	1, 3, 5	9	3
B	3, 5, 7	15	5
C	5, 7, 9	21	7

Assuming that $m = 2$ psu are selected and that $n_1 = 2$, $n_2 = 2$ ssu are selected from the psu, there are then

$$\binom{M}{m}\binom{N_1}{n_1}\binom{N_2}{n_2} = \binom{3}{2}\binom{3}{2}\binom{3}{2} = 27$$

possible samples which are listed in Table 8.1.
Let us consider the first sample.

$$A: 1, 3; \qquad B: 3, 5$$

Then $\hat{X}$, s_b^2, and s_i^2 are as follows:

(i) $\displaystyle \hat{X} = \frac{M}{m} \sum^m \frac{N_i}{n_i} \sum^{n_i} x_{ij}$

$\displaystyle \quad = \frac{3}{2}\left[\frac{3}{2}(1+3) + \frac{3}{2}(3+5)\right] = 27$

(ii) $\displaystyle s_b^2 = \frac{1}{m-1} \sum^m (\hat{X}_i - \hat{\bar{X}})^2$

$\displaystyle \hat{X}_1 = N_1\bar{x}_1 = 3\left(\frac{1+3}{2}\right) = 6$

$\displaystyle \hat{X}_2 = N_1\bar{x}_2 = 3\left(\frac{3+5}{2}\right) = 12$

$\displaystyle \hat{\bar{X}} = \frac{1}{m} \sum^m \hat{X}_i = \frac{1}{2}(\hat{X}_1 + \hat{X}_2) = \frac{1}{2}(6 + 12) = 9$

$\displaystyle \therefore \quad s_b^2 = \frac{1}{2-1}[(6-9)^2 + (12-9)^2] = 18$

In a similar manner, 26 other values for s_b^2 are computed and shown in Table 8.3.

(iii) The second term on the right side of $\hat{V}(\hat{X})$ is

$$\frac{M}{m} \sum^m N_i^2 \frac{N_i - n_i}{N_i} \frac{s_i^2}{n_i}$$

Hence, in our example, where $m = 2$, we need s_1^2 and s_2^2. From the table above, $m = 2$ psu, and n_1 and n_2 for the first sample n are:

$$A: \quad n_1 \quad 1, 3 \quad \text{and} \quad B: \quad n_2 \quad 3, 5$$

Let us calculate s_1^2. We have

$$\bar{x}_1 = \frac{1}{n_1} \sum^{n_1} x_{1j} = \frac{1}{2}(1+3) = 2$$

Table 8.3

	A	B	s_1^2	s_2^2	s_b^2
1	1, 3	3, 5	2	2	18
2		3, 7		8	40.5
3		5, 7		2	72
4	1, 5	3, 5	8	2	4.5
5		3, 7		8	18
6		5, 7		2	40.5
7	3, 5	3, 5	2	2	0
8		3, 7		8	4.5
9		5, 7		2	18

	A	C	s_1^2	s_2^2	s_b^2
10	1, 3	5, 7	2	2	72
11		5, 9		8	112.5
12		7, 9		2	162
13	1, 5	5, 7	8	2	40.5
14		5, 9		8	72
15		7, 9		2	112.5
16	3, 5	5, 7	2	2	18
17		5, 9		8	40.5
18		7, 9		2	72

	B	C	s_1^2	s_2^2	s_b^2
19	3, 5	5, 7	2	2	18
20		5, 9		8	40.5
21		7, 9		2	72
22	3, 7	5, 7	8	2	4.5
23		5, 9		8	18
24		7, 9		2	40.5
25	5, 7	5, 7	2	2	0
26		5, 9		8	4.5
27		7, 9		2	18

Hence

$$s_1^2 = \frac{1}{n_1 - 1} \sum_{}^{n_1} (x_{1j} - \bar{x}_1)^2 = \frac{1}{2 - 1}[(1 - 2)^2 + (3 - 2)^2] = 2$$

In a similar manner, $\bar{x}_2 = (3 + 5)/2 = 4$ and

$$s_2^2 = \frac{1}{2 - 1}[(3 - 4)^2 + (5 - 4)^2] = 2$$

In Table 8.3, we have the s_i^2 for the 27 possible samples.

(iv) We may now find the 27 possible values of $\hat{V}(\hat{X})$ and show that $E[\hat{V}(\hat{X})] = V(\hat{X})$. Since $M = 3$, $m = 2$, $N_i = 3$, $n_i = 2$, we get

$$\hat{V}(\hat{X}) = (3)^2 \frac{3-2}{3} \frac{s_b^2}{2} + \frac{3}{2} \sum^m (3)^2 \frac{3-2}{3} \frac{s_i^2}{2}$$

$$= \frac{3}{2} s_b^2 + \frac{9}{4}(s_1^2 + s_2^2)$$

Let us now calculate the 27 possible values of $\hat{V}(\hat{X})$.

Table 8.4

A, B			A, C			B, C		
s_b^2	$s_1^2 + s_2^2$	$\hat{V}(\hat{X})$	s_b^2	$s_1^2 + s_2^2$	$\hat{V}(\hat{X})$	s_b^2	$s_1^2 + s_2^2$	$\hat{V}(\hat{X})$
18.0	4	36	72.0	4	117	18.0	4	36
40.5	10	83.25	112.5	10	191.25	40.5	10	83.25
72.0	4	117	162.0	4	252	72.0	4	117
4.5	10	29.25	40.5	10	83.25	4.5	10	29.25
18.0	16	63	72.0	16	144	18.0	16	63
40.5	10	83.25	112.0	10	191.25	40.5	10	83.25
0.0	4	9	18.0	4	36	0.0	4	9
4.5	10	29.25	40.5	10	29.25	4.5	10	29.25
18.0	4	36	72.0	4	117	18.0	4	36
						1134.0	216	2187

$$E[\hat{V}(\hat{X})] = \frac{1}{27}(2187) = 81$$

We have found in Example 1 that $V(\hat{X}) = 81$ and hence

$$E[\hat{V}(\hat{X})] = V(\hat{X}) = 81$$

(v) $E(s_1^2) = S_1^2$

$E(s_1^2)$ shows the expectation of s_1^2, and s_1^2 is the sample variance of a sample taken from the 1st psu (A). From Table 8.3 we see that there are 3 possible samples [(1, 3), (1,5), and (3,5)] and we find

$$E(s_1^2) = \frac{1}{3} [(s_1^2 | 1,3) + (s_1^2 | 1,5) + (s_1^2 | 3,5)]$$

$$= \frac{1}{3} (2 + 8 + 2) = 4$$

We have found earlier that $S_1^2 = 4$. Hence $E(s_1^2) = S_1^2 = 4$, and the other two cases for s_2^2 and s_3^2 may be verified in a similar manner.

(vi) $E(s_b^2)$

We wish to verify that

$$E(s_b^2) = S_b^2 + \frac{1}{M} \sum^M N_i^2 \frac{N_i - n_i}{N_i} \frac{S_i^2}{n_i}$$

From Table 8.4, we find for the left side,

$$E(s_b^2) = (1/27)(1134) = 42$$

For the right side, using the results of Example 1, we find

$$36 + \frac{1}{3}\left[(3)^2 \frac{3-2}{3}\frac{1}{2}(4+4+4)\right] = 42$$

Hence the left side is equal to the right side, and we have verified that the above relation holds.

Example 4. Using the data of Example 2 on page 199 (which is reproduced for

cluster	X_{ij}	X_i	$\bar{x}_i$
A	1, 2, 3,	6	2
B	2, 2, 3, 5	12	3
C	4, 5, 6	15	5
		33	

convenience), perform the following operations. Select $m = 2$ psu, and from each psu select $n_1 = n_2 = 2$ sampling units.
  (i) Calculate $E(s_b^2)$ from all possible samples.
  (ii) Calculate S_b^2.
  (iii) Calculate

$$E(s_b^2) = S_b^2 + \frac{1}{M}\sum_{i}^{M} N_i^2 \frac{N_i - n_i}{N_i}\frac{S_i^2}{n_i}$$

and show that it is equal to $E(s_b^2)$ as calculated in (i).
  (iv) Show that $E[\hat{V}(\hat{X})] = V(\hat{X})$.

The s_i^2 and s_b^2 are calculated for all possible samples in the following table. Note, the s_i^2 and s_b^2 are multiplied by 2 and 8, respectively, to avoid fractions. The results are readjusted by multiplying by 1/2 and 1/8, respectively.

Table 8.5

A	B	$2s_1^2$	$2s_2^2$	$8s_b^2$
1, 2	2, 2	1	0	49
	2, 3	1	1	121
	2, 3	1	1	121
	2, 5	1	9	361
	2, 5	1	9	361
	3, 5	1	4	529
1, 3	2, 2	4	0	16
	2, 3	4	1	64
	2, 3	4	1	64
	2, 5	4	9	256
	2, 5	4	9	256
	3, 5	4	4	400
2, 3	2, 2	1	0	1
	2, 3	1	1	25
	2, 3	1	1	25
	2, 5	1	9	169
	2, 5	1	9	169
	3, 5	1	4	289
		36	72	3276

From this table we find

$$E(s_b^2 | A, B) = (1/8)(1/18)(3276) = 22\tfrac{3}{4}$$

In similar manner, calculations will show that

$$E(s_b^2 | A, C) = (1/8)(1/9)(3024) = 42$$

$$E(s_b^2 | B, C) = (1/8)(1/18)(1332) = 9\tfrac{1}{4}$$

(i) Calculate $E(s_b^2)$ from all possible samples.

$$E(s_b^2) = E_i(E_j s_b^2)$$

$$= \frac{1}{3}[E(s_b^2) | A, B) + E(s_b^2 | A, C) + E(s_b^2 | B, C)]$$

$$= \frac{1}{3}(22\tfrac{3}{4} + 42 + 9\tfrac{1}{4}) = \frac{74}{3}$$

(ii) Calculate S_b^2.

$$S_b^2 = \frac{1}{M-1} \sum_{i}^{M} (X_i - \bar{X})^2 = \frac{1}{M-1}(\sum X_i^2 - M\bar{X}^2)$$

$$= \frac{1}{2}[405 - 3(11)^2] = 21$$

(iii) Calculate $E(s_b^2)$ using the theoretical formula.

$$E(s_b^2) = S_b^2 + \frac{1}{M} \sum_{i}^{M} N_i \frac{N_i - n_i}{N_i} \frac{S_i^2}{n_i}$$

$$= 21 + \frac{1}{3}\left[(3)^2\left(\frac{3-2}{3}\right)\left(\frac{1}{2}\right) + (4)^2\left(\frac{4-2}{4}\right)\left(\frac{2}{2}\right) + (3)^2\left(\frac{3-2}{3}\right)\left(\frac{1}{2}\right)\right] = \frac{74}{3}$$

which is the same result we obtained in (i).

(iv) Show that $E[\hat{V}(\hat{X})] = V(\hat{X})$

$$\hat{V}(\hat{X}) = M^2 \frac{M-m}{M} \frac{s_b^2}{m} + \frac{M}{m} \sum_{i}^{m} N_i \frac{N_i - n_i}{N_i} \frac{s_i^2}{n_i}$$

$$E[\hat{V}(\hat{X})] = M^2 \frac{M-m}{M} \frac{E(s_b^2)}{m} + \frac{M}{m} E_i \sum_{i}^{m} N_i^2 \frac{N_i - n_i}{N_i} \frac{E_j(s_i^2)}{n_i} = M^2 \frac{M-m}{M} \frac{E(s_b^2)}{m}$$

$$+ \frac{M}{m} \frac{1}{3}\left\{\left[N_1^2 \frac{N_1 - n_1}{N_1} \frac{E(s_1^2)}{n_2} + N_2^2 \frac{N_2 - n_2}{N_2} \frac{E(s_2^2)}{n_2}\right]\right. \qquad \text{for A and B}$$

$$+ \left[N_1^2 \frac{N_1 - n_1}{N_1} \frac{E(s_1^2)}{n_1} + N_3^2 \frac{N_3 - n_3}{N_3} \frac{E(s_3^2)}{n_3}\right] \qquad \text{for A and C}$$

$$+ \left[N_2^2 \frac{N_2 - n_2}{N_2} \frac{E(s_2^2)}{n_2} + N_3^2 \frac{N_3 - n_3}{N_3} \frac{E(s_3^2)}{n_3}\right]\right\} \qquad \text{for B and C}$$

$$= \frac{3}{2}(3-2)\frac{74}{3} + \frac{3}{2} \cdot \frac{1}{3}\left\{\left[(3)^2\left(\frac{3-2}{3}\right)\left(\frac{1}{2}\right) + (4)^2\left(\frac{4-2}{4}\right)\left(\frac{2}{2}\right)\right]\right.$$

$$+ \left[(3)^2\left(\frac{3-2}{3}\right)\left(\frac{1}{2}\right) + (3)^2\left(\frac{3-2}{3}\right)\left(\frac{1}{2}\right)\right]$$

$$+ \left[(4)^2\left(\frac{4-2}{4}\right)\left(\frac{2}{2}\right) + (3)^2\left(\frac{3-2}{3}\right)\left(\frac{1}{2}\right)\right]\right\}$$

$$= 37 + \frac{1}{2}\left(\frac{3}{2} + 8 + \frac{3}{2} + \frac{3}{2} + 8\frac{3}{2}\right) = 48$$

But in Example 2 on page 199, we found that $V(\hat{X}) = 48$. Hence,

$$E[\hat{V}(\hat{X})] = V(\hat{X}) = 48$$

Problems

1. Given the following hypothetical population, $m = 2$ clusters are selected. Calculate $V(\hat{X})$.

Cluster	X_{ij}
A	1, 3, 5
B	3, 6, 6
C	7, 9, 14

2. Suppose the data in Problem 1 are mixed as follows.

Cluster	X_{ij}
A	1, 6, 14
B	3, 3, 9
C	5, 6, 7

(i) Calculate $V(\hat{X})$.

(ii) Compare this result with that of Problem 1 and explain the reasons for the difference.

3. Using the data of Problem 2, suppose $m = 2$ clusters are selected and $\bar{n} = 2$ ssu are selected from each cluster.

   (i) How many possible samples may be selected? Construct a table similar to Table 8.3 and show all the samples.

   (ii) Calculate the s_1^2 and s_2^2 corresponding to the samples in (i) and list in the table.

   (iii) Calculate the s_b^2 for all the samples and list in the table.

   (iv) Calculate all possible values for $\hat{V}(\hat{X})$ and verify that $E[\hat{V}(\hat{X})]$ is equal to the $V(\hat{X})$ found in Problem 2.

   (v) Show that $E(s_1^2) = S_1^2$.

   (vi) Verify that

   $$E(s_b^2) = S_b^2 + \frac{1}{M} \sum_{i}^{M} N_i^2 \frac{N_i - n_i}{N_i} \frac{S_i^2}{n_i}$$

   by using the above data.

4. Using the data of Problem 3 on page 196,

   (i) Calculate s_i^2.

   (ii) Calculate s_b^2.

   (iii) Calculate $\hat{V}(\hat{X})$ and $s(\hat{X})$.

   (iv) Find the 2σ confidence interval for X using the $\hat{X}$ found in Problem 3 on page 196.

5. Using the data of Problem 4 on page 196,

   (i) Calculate $\hat{V}(\hat{X})$ and $s(\hat{X})$.

   (ii) Find the 2σ confidence interval for X, using the $\hat{X}$ of Problem 4 of page 196.

6. The Air Force wishes to estimate the total number of miles flown by a certain type of airplane during a given month. There are $M = 120$ airfields and each has N_i airplanes. A sample of $m = 10$ airfields is selected and at each airfield $N_i = n_i$ airplanes are selected. The $\sum x_{ij}$ gives the total number of miles flown in units of 1,000 miles. Calculate $\hat{X}$ and $s(\hat{X})$.

Airfield	$N_i = n_i$	$\sum x_{ij}$	Airfield	$N_i = n_i$	$\sum x_{ij}$
1	5	20	6	5	30
2	6	30	7	5	25
3	5	25	8	4	28
4	4	16	9	4	16
5	4	24	10	6	36

Reference

Let us give a nonrigorous derivation of the variance formula (1).

By definition, the variance of $\hat{X} = (M/m) \sum\limits^{m} \hat{X}_i$ is

(7) $$V(\hat{X}) = E(\hat{X} - X)^2$$

and our problem is to evaluate $(\hat{X} - X)^2$. We note that there are two stages of sampling, and that we need to consider both stages; the first stage is selecting the psu, and the second stage is selecting the ssu. We shall start with the second stage, assuming the first stage is given or fixed. For instance, we had in our example 5 classes (psu) from which 2 were selected by random sampling.

Then, from these 2 classes, random subsamples of students (ssu) were selected. To evaluate the variance of $\hat{X}$, we shall first assume the 2 classes to be fixed, and consider the contribution to the variance due to the random sampling of sub-samples (students) from these 2 classes (psu). If, for example, all of the students in the 2 classes were selected, there would be no variation due to subsampling. In this case $N_i = n_i$, and as can be seen from equation (1), the second term on the right hand side becomes zero because $N_i - n_i = 0$:

$$\frac{M}{m} \sum\limits^{m} N_i^2 \frac{N_i - n_i}{N_i} \frac{S_i^2}{n_i} = 0$$

This shows there is no contribution to the variance from S_i^2, which shows the within psu variation.

After considering the variation due to the second stage sampling, we shall consider the contribution to the variance due to sampling first stage units (psu). Here we note that only $m = 2$ psu (classes) are selected from the $M = 5$ psu (classes), and we wish to consider the sampling variation due to this random sampling. If, for example, all of the classes are selected ($M = m$), then there will be no sampling variation from this first stage sampling procedure. This may also be seen from equation (1). Noting that $M - m = 0$ in this case, the first term on the right becomes

$$M^2 \frac{M - m}{M} \frac{S_b^2}{m} = 0$$

and shows there is no contribution from S_b^2 which shows the between variation of the psu.

With this general procedure in mind, let us now evaluate (7). We first note that $(\hat{X} - X)^2$ may be changed algebraically as follows:

$$(\hat{X} - X)^2 = \left[\frac{M}{m} \sum^m \hat{X}_i - X\right]^2$$

$$= \left[\left(\frac{M}{m} \sum^m \hat{X}_i - \frac{M}{m} \sum^M X_i\right) + \left(\frac{M}{m} \sum^m X_i - X\right)\right]^2$$

$$= \left(\frac{M}{m} \sum^m X_i - X\right)^2 + 2\left(\frac{M}{m} \sum^m X_i - X\right)\left(\frac{M}{m} \sum^m \hat{X}_i - \frac{M}{m} \sum^m X_i\right)$$

$$+ \left(\frac{M}{m} \sum^m \hat{X}_i - \frac{M}{m} \sum^m X_i\right)^2$$

$$= \left(\frac{M}{m} \sum^m X_i - X\right)^2 + 2\left(\frac{M}{m}\right)\left(\frac{M}{m} \sum^m X_i - X\right) \sum (\hat{X}_i - X_i)$$

$$+ \left(\frac{M}{m}\right)^2 [\sum^m (\hat{X}_i - X_i)]^2$$

$$= \left(\frac{M}{m} \sum^m X_i - X\right)^2 + 2\left(\frac{M}{m}\right)\left(\frac{M}{m} \sum^m X_i - X\right) \sum (\hat{X}_i - X_i)$$

$$+ \left(\frac{M}{m}\right)^2 \sum^m (\hat{X}_i - X_i)^2 + \left(\frac{M}{m}\right)^2 \sum_{i \neq i'}^m (\hat{X}_i - X_i)(\hat{X}_{i'} - X_i)$$

$$= A + B + C + D$$

Let us now take the expectation of $(\hat{X} - X)^2$ holding i (psu) constant. That is, the expectation is taken over the ssu which is denoted by the subscript j. Thus, this will be expressed by

(8) $$E_j(\hat{X} - X)^2 = E_j(A) + E_j(B) + E_j(C) + E_j(D)$$

Starting with $E_j(A)$, we find

$$E_j\left(\frac{M}{m} \sum^m X_i - X\right)^2 = \left(\frac{M}{m} \sum^m X_i - X\right)^2$$

because it does not involve sampling of second stage units (ssu)—only first stage units.

The second term, $E_j(B)$, becomes

$$E_j(B) = E_j\left[2\left(\frac{M}{m}\right)\left(\frac{M}{m} \sum^m X_i - X\right) \sum^m (\hat{X}_i - X_i)\right]$$

$$= 2\left(\frac{M}{m}\right)\left(\frac{M}{m} \sum^m X_i - X\right) E_j \sum^m (\hat{X}_i - X_i)$$

because $\hat{X}_i$ is a statistic obtained from random sampling of ssu. It is the *estimate* of the total number of books of the ith class based on a random sample of n_i students. However, we already know from our discussion of simple random sampling that $E(\hat{X}_i) = X_i$. We also know from statistical theory that

$$E \sum X = \sum EX$$

Hence,

$$E_j \sum^m (\hat{X}_i - X_i) = \sum^m E_j(\hat{X}_i - X_i) = 0$$

and thus $E_j(B) = 0$.

The fourth term, $E_j(D)$, is treated as was the third term. We find

$$E_j\left(\frac{M}{m}\right)^2 \sum_{i\neq i'}^{m} (\hat{X}_i - X_i)(\hat{X}_{i'} - X_i) = 0$$

because the ssu (students) are obtained by simple random sampling, and $\hat{X}_i$ and $\hat{X}_{i'}$ are therefore independent of each other.

The third term, $E_j(C)$, is

$$E_j\left[\left(\frac{M}{m}\right)^2 \sum_{i}^{m} (\hat{X}_i - X_i)^2\right]$$

$$= \left(\frac{M}{m}\right)^2 E_j \sum (\hat{X}_i - X_i)^2$$

$$= \left(\frac{M}{m}\right)^2 \sum_{i}^{m} E_j(\hat{X}_i - X_i)^2$$

When i is held constant, the subsampling of ssu (students) from the psu (classes) that are held constant may be considered as simple random sampling. In our present illustration, the 2 classes (psu) that were selected may be considered as the 2 strata, and the subsamples of ssu (students) are selected from these strata by simple random sampling. Hence, using the results of simple random sampling, we have

$$E_j(\hat{X}_i - X_i)^2 = N_i^2 \frac{N_i - n_i}{N_i} \frac{S_i^2}{n_i}$$

$$S_i^2 = \frac{1}{N_i - 1} \sum_{j}^{N_i} (X_{ij} - \bar{X}_i)^2$$

which is the variance for X_{ij} when simple random sampling is used.

Substituting the results of the first and third terms in (8), we find

(9) $$E_j(\hat{X} - X)^2 = \left(\frac{M}{m}\sum_{i}^{m} X_i - X\right)^2 + \left(\frac{M}{m}\right)^2 \sum_{i}^{m} N_i^2 \frac{N_i - n_i}{N_i} \frac{S_i^2}{n_i}$$

Our next step is to consider the expectation taken over all possible samples of psu taken from the M psu. In our illustration, $m = 2$ psu were selected from $M = 5$ psu by simple random sampling. The expectation is then to be taken over the $\binom{M}{m} = \binom{5}{2} = 10$ possible ways of selecting the $m = 2$ psu. The i of $E_j(\hat{X} - X)^2$ is not held constant and $E_j(\hat{X} - X)^2 = y_i$ becomes a random variable. Our problem now is to find the expectation of the random variable y_i, which becomes

(10) $$E_i[E_j(\hat{X} - X)^2] = E_i\left[\frac{M}{m}\sum_{i}^{M} X_i - X\right]^2 + E_i\left(\frac{M}{m}\right)^2 \sum_{i}^{m} N_i^2 \frac{N_i - n_i}{N_i} \frac{S_i^2}{n_i}$$

Let us first consider the second term on the right and rewrite this as

$$E_i\left(\frac{M}{m}\right)^2 \sum_{i}^{m} U_i$$

where

$$U_i = N_i^2 \frac{N_i - n_i}{N_i} \frac{S_i^2}{n_i}$$

As shown, U_i $(i = 1, 2, 3, \ldots, M)$ is a random variable with M possible values each having probability of $1/M$, since each psu is selected by simple random sampling. Then

(11)
$$E_i\left(\frac{M}{m}\right)^2 \sum_i^m U_i = \left(\frac{M}{m}\right)^2 \sum_i^m E_i U_i$$

$$= \left(\frac{M}{m}\right)^2 \sum_i^m \left[\sum_i^M \frac{1}{M} U_i\right]$$

$$= \left(\frac{M}{m}\right)^2 m \frac{1}{M} \sum_i^M N_i^2 \frac{N_i - n_i}{N_i} \frac{S_i^2}{n_i}$$

As shown, this is the variation due to S_i^2 (the within variation of the ith psu).
    For the first term, we find

$$E_i\left[\frac{M}{m} \sum_i^m X_i - X\right]^2$$

where

$$\frac{M}{m} \sum_i^m X_i$$

may be considered as the estimate of X due to a random sample of m psu. We may therefore use the results of simple random sampling concerning estimates of totals. Then, using equation (2) of section 6.8, we find

(12)
$$E_i\left[\frac{M}{m} \sum_i^m X_i - X\right]^2 = M^2 E_i\left[\frac{1}{m} \sum_i^m X_i - \bar{X}\right]^2$$

$$= M^2 \frac{M - m}{M} \frac{1}{m} \frac{\sum (X_i - \bar{X})^2}{M - 1}$$

Hence from (10), (11), and (12), the variance of $\hat{X}$ we seek is:

(13)
$$V(\hat{X}) = \frac{M^2}{m} \frac{M - m}{M} S_b^2 + \frac{M}{m} \sum_i^M N_i^2 \frac{N_i - n_i}{N_i} \frac{S_i^2}{n_i}$$

$$S_b^2 = \frac{1}{M - 1} \sum_i^M (X_i - \bar{X})^2$$

$$S_i^2 = \frac{1}{N_i - 1} \sum_i^{N_i} (X_{ij} - \bar{X})^2$$

which completes the proof.

Reference 2

The estimator of (13) was given as

(14)
$$\hat{V}(\hat{X}) = M^2 \frac{M - m}{M} \frac{s_b^2}{m} + \frac{M}{m} \sum_i^m N_i^2 \frac{N_i - n_i}{N_i} \frac{s_i^2}{n_i}$$

where

(15)
$$s_b^2 = \frac{1}{m - 1} \sum^m (\hat{X}_i - \hat{\bar{X}}_i)^2$$

$$= \frac{1}{m - 1} \sum^m \left(\hat{X}_i - \frac{\sum^m \hat{X}_i}{m}\right)^2$$

(16)
$$s_i^2 = \frac{1}{n_i - 1} \sum_j^{n_i} (x_{ij} - \bar{x}_i)^2$$

$$= \frac{1}{n_i - 1} \sum^{n_i} \left(x_{ij} - \frac{x_i}{n_i}\right)^2$$

Note carefully that in equation (14), the summation in the second term on the right is over m—not over M. As we shall see, s_i^2 is an unbiased estimator of S_i^2, but s_b^2 is not an unbiased estimator of S_b^2. Hence, the estimator given in (14) is not obtained by automatically replacing S_b^2 and S_i^2 by s_b^2 and s_i^2. However, the estimate $\hat{V}(\hat{X})$ is an unbiased estimator of $V(\hat{X})$, that is,

$$E[\hat{V}(\hat{X})] = V(\hat{X})$$

which is what we shall now prove.

The expectation of $V(\hat{X})$ must be considered in two steps—the expectation with respect to the first stage of sampling and the conditional expectation with respect to the second stage of sampling, holding the first stage psu constant. Taking the expectation of (14), we find

(17) $\qquad E[\hat{V}(\hat{X})] = M(M - m)\dfrac{E s_b^2}{m} + \dfrac{M}{m} E_i \left[E_j \overset{m}{\sum} N_i(N_i - n_i) \dfrac{s_i^2}{n_i} \right]$

where E_j is the conditional expectation over j holding the ith psu constant.

For the first term on the right we derive $E_i s_b^2$ first and find (see reference 3 for derivation)

(18) $\qquad\qquad\qquad E s_b^2 = S_b^2 + \dfrac{1}{M} \overset{M}{\sum} N_i(N_i - n_i) \dfrac{S_i^2}{n_i}$

Hence, the first term on the right side of equation (17) becomes

(19) $\quad M(M - m)\dfrac{1}{m} E s_b^2 = M(M - m)\dfrac{1}{m}S_b^2 + (M - m)\dfrac{1}{m} \overset{M}{\sum} N_i(N_i - n_i) \dfrac{S_i^2}{n_i}$

As shown in (18), $E s_b^2 \neq S_b^2$. Also note how S_i^2 has entered the equation and contributes to the bias.

For the second term on the right of equation (17), we first find the conditional expectation over j holding i constant, and then take the expectation over all i. Since the ssu are selected by simple random sampling, holding i constant, $E_j s_i^2$ is equivalent to taking the expectation for the simple random sample case. Hence, we know that $E_j s_i^2 = S_i^2$. Thus, the second term becomes

(20) $\qquad\qquad\quad \dfrac{M}{m} E_i \left[E_j \overset{m}{\sum} N_i(N_i - n_i) \dfrac{s_i^2}{n_i} \right]$

$$= \dfrac{M}{m} \cdot m \cdot \dfrac{1}{M} \overset{M}{\sum} N_i(N_i - n_i) \dfrac{S_i^2}{n_i}$$

$$= \overset{M}{\sum} N_i(N_i - n_i) \dfrac{S_i^2}{n_i}$$

Substituting equations (19) and (20) into (18) gives us

$$E[\hat{V}(\hat{X})] = M(M - m)\dfrac{S_b^2}{m} + (M - m)\dfrac{1}{m} \overset{M}{\sum} N_i(N_i - n_i)\dfrac{S_i^2}{n_i} + \overset{M}{\sum} N_i(N_i - n_i)\dfrac{S_i^2}{n_i}$$

$$= M(M - m)\dfrac{S_b^2}{m} + \dfrac{M}{m} \overset{M}{\sum} N_i(N_i - n_i)\dfrac{S_i^2}{n_i} = V(\hat{X})$$

That is, $\hat{V}(\hat{X})$ is an unbiased estimator of $V(\hat{X})$.

Reference 3

As mentioned above, $E_j(s_i^2) = S_i^2$, but $E_i(s_b^2) \neq S_b^2$, and we have not merely replaced S_b^2 by its sample estimate s_b^2. We shall show in this reference how equation (18) was obtained.

We define s_b^2 as

(21)
$$s_b^2 = \frac{1}{m-1} \sum_{}^{m} \left(\hat{X}_i - \frac{\sum \hat{X}_i}{m} \right)^2$$

$$= \frac{1}{m-1} \frac{m}{m} \sum_{}^{m} \left(\hat{X}_i - \frac{1}{M} \frac{M}{m} \sum_{}^{m} \hat{X}_i \right)^2$$

$$= \frac{m}{m-1} \frac{1}{m} \sum_{}^{m} \left(\hat{X}_i - \frac{\hat{X}}{M} \right)^2$$

Hence, (21) may be rewritten as

(22)
$$\frac{m-1}{m} s_b^2 = \frac{1}{m} \sum_{}^{m} \left(\hat{X}_i - \frac{\hat{X}}{M} \right)^2$$

$$= \frac{1}{m} \sum_{}^{m} \left[\hat{X}_i^2 - 2\hat{X}_i \frac{\hat{X}}{M} + \left(\frac{\hat{X}}{M} \right)^2 \right]$$

$$= \frac{1}{m} \left[\sum_{}^{m} \hat{X}_i^2 - 2m \left(\frac{\hat{X}}{M} \right)^2 + m \left(\frac{\hat{X}}{M} \right)^2 \right]$$

$$= \frac{1}{m} \sum_{}^{m} \hat{X}_i^2 - \left(\frac{\hat{X}}{M} \right)^2$$

Since two stages are involved, the expected value of (22) becomes:

(23)
$$E\left(\frac{m-1}{m} s_b^2 \right) = E_i \left(E_j \frac{1}{m} \sum_{}^{m} \hat{X}_i^2 \right) - E\left(\frac{\hat{X}}{M} \right)^2$$

$$= E_i \left(\frac{1}{m} \sum_{}^{m} E_j \hat{X}_i^2 \right) - \frac{E\hat{X}^2}{M^2}$$

$$= \frac{1}{m} \cdot m \cdot \sum_{}^{M} \frac{1}{M} E_j \hat{X}_i^2 - \frac{E\hat{X}^2}{M^2}$$

$$= \frac{1}{M} \sum_{}^{M} E_j \hat{X}_i^2 - \frac{E\hat{X}^2}{M^2}$$

To evaluate this, we must find $E_j\hat{X}_i^2$ and $E\hat{X}^2$, and we shall use the following general relation:

$$E(\bar{x} - \bar{X})^2 = E\bar{x}^2 - \bar{X}^2$$

(24)
$$E\bar{x}^2 = E(\bar{x} - \bar{X})^2 + \bar{X}^2$$

To apply this to $E_j\hat{X}_i^2$ we set

$$\hat{X}_i = \hat{X}_i - X_i + X_i$$

$$\hat{X}_i^2 = (\hat{X}_i - X_i)^2 + X_i^2 + 2(\hat{X}_i - X_i)X_i$$

Taking the conditional expectation E_j over j and holding i constant, we get

$$E_j\hat{X}_i^2 = E_j(\hat{X}_i - X_i)^2 + E_jX_i^2 + 0$$

$$= V_j(\hat{X}_i) + X_i^2$$

But $V_j(\hat{X}_i)$ is the variance for $\hat{X}_i$ under conditions of simple random sampling when i is assumed fixed, and X_i is constant when i is assumed fixed. Hence

(25)
$$E_j \hat{X}_i^2 = N_i^2 \frac{N_i - n_i}{N_i} \frac{S_i^2}{n_i} + X_i^2$$

Applying the same technique to $E\hat{X}^2$, let

$$\hat{X} = \hat{X} - X + X$$
$$\hat{X}^2 = (\hat{X} - X)^2 + X^2 + 2(\hat{X} - X)X$$

Taking the expectation on both sides, we get

$$E\hat{X}^2 = E(\hat{X} - X)^2 + EX^2 + 0$$
$$= V(\hat{X}) + X^2$$

But $V(\hat{X})$ is obtained in (13). Hence

(26)
$$E\hat{X}^2 = V(\hat{X}) + X^2$$
$$= M(M - m) \frac{S_b^2}{m} + \frac{M}{m} \sum_{}^{M} N_i(N_i - n_i) \frac{S_i^2}{n_i} + X^2$$

Substituting (25) and (26) into (23), we get

$$E\left(\frac{m-1}{m} s_b^2\right) = \frac{1}{M} \sum_{}^{M} \left(N_i^2 \frac{N_i - n_i}{N_i} \frac{S_i^2}{n_i} + X_i^2\right)$$
$$- \left(\frac{1}{M}\right)^2 \left[M(M - m) \frac{S_b^2}{m} + \frac{M}{m} \sum_{}^{M} (N_i - n_i) \frac{S_i^2}{n_i} + X^2\right]$$
$$= \frac{1}{M} A + \frac{1}{M} \sum_{}^{M} X_i^2 - \left(\frac{1}{M}\right)^2 \left[M(M - m) \frac{S_b^2}{m} + \frac{M}{m} A + X^2\right]$$
$$= \frac{1}{M}\left(1 - \frac{1}{m}\right) A + \left(\frac{1}{M} \sum_{}^{M} X_i^2 - \frac{X^2}{M^2}\right) - \frac{M - m}{M} \frac{S_b^2}{m}$$
$$= \frac{1}{M}\left(\frac{m-1}{m}\right) A + \frac{M - 1}{M} S_b^2 - \frac{M - m}{M} \frac{S_b^2}{m}$$
$$= \frac{1}{M}\left(\frac{m-1}{m}\right) A + \frac{m - 1}{m} S_b^2$$

where we have set

$$A = \sum N_i^2 \frac{N_i - n_i}{N_i} \frac{S_i^2}{n_i}$$

Canceling out $(m - 1)/m$ from both sides, we get

$$E(s_b^2) = \frac{1}{M} A + S_b^2$$
$$= S_b^2 + \frac{1}{M} \sum_{}^{M} N_i^2 \frac{N_i - n_i}{N_i} \frac{S_i^2}{n_i}$$

which is the desired result.

8.4 Computational forms for $\hat{V}(\hat{X})$

As the discussion of section 8.3 shows, $\hat{V}(\hat{X})$ is quite formidable, and any simplification of the equation will be of great help. If we can assume $M \gg m$ and $N_i \gg n_i$, we may also assume that

$$\frac{m}{M} \doteq 0$$

$$\frac{M - m}{M} = 1 - \frac{m}{M} \doteq 1$$

$$\frac{N_i - n_i}{N_i} = 1 - \frac{n_i}{N_i} \doteq 1$$

as approximations. For example, when $m/M < 1\%$, then

$$\frac{M - m}{M} = 1 - 0.01 \doteq 1$$

may be used as an approximation.

With this in mind, let us show how the $\hat{V}(\hat{X})$ equation may be simplified. We shall devise four cases.

Case 1.

First recall that:

(1) $$\hat{V}(\hat{X}) = M^2 \frac{M - m}{M} \frac{s_b^2}{m} + \frac{M}{m} \sum_i^m N_i^2 \frac{N_i - n_i}{N_i} \frac{s_i^2}{n_i}$$

(2) $$s_b^2 = \frac{1}{m - 1} \sum_i^m \left(\hat{X}_i - \frac{\sum^m \hat{X}_i}{m} \right)^2$$

(3) $$s_i^2 = \frac{1}{n_i - 1} \sum_j^{n_i} (x_{ij} - \bar{x}_i)^2$$

In Case 1, we shall consider formula (1) as is, and merely set up a calculation procedure. As is seen, the main problem is to devise simple calculation procedures for s_b^2 and s_i^2. The square terms of s_b^2 and s_i^2 may be rewritten as follows:

(4) $$\sum_i^m \left(\hat{X}_i - \frac{\sum \hat{X}_i}{m} \right)^2 = \sum_i^m \hat{X}_i^2 - m \left(\frac{\sum \hat{X}_i}{m} \right)^2$$

(5) $$\sum_j^{n_i} (x_{ij} - \bar{x}_i)^2 = \sum_j^{n_i} x_{ij}^2 - n_i(\bar{x}_i)^2$$

(6) $$\bar{x}_i = \frac{x_i}{n_i} = \frac{1}{n_i} \sum x_{ij}$$

Hence, by calculating $\sum^m \hat{X}_i$, $\sum^m \hat{X}_i^2$, and $\sum^m x_{ij}^2$, we can easily calculate s_b^2 and s_i^2. Let us illustrate this procedure with the following examples:

Example 1. Using the following hypothetical data, let us illustrate the calculation of $\hat{V}(X)$.

psu	X_{ij}	X_i
A	1, 2, 3	6
B	2, 2, 3, 5	12
C	4, 5, 6	15

| | | 33 |

Let $m = 2$ psu be A and B. Suppose $n_1 = 2$ and $n_2 = 3$ are (1, 3) and (2, 2, 5) as follows:

x_{1j}	x_{1j}^2	x_{2j}	x_{2j}^2
1	1	2	4
3	9	2	4
		5	25
4	10	9	33
$\sum x_{ij}$	N_i/n_i	$\hat{X}_i = (N_i/n_i) \sum x_{ij}$	$\hat{X}_i^2$

	$\sum x_{ij}$	N_i/n_i	$\hat{X}_i = (N_i/n_i) \sum x_{ij}$	$\hat{X}_i^2$
$i = 1$	4	3/2	6	36
$i = 2$	9	4/3	12	144
			18	180

$$\bar{x}_1 = 4/2 = 2 \qquad \bar{x}_2 = 9/3 = 3$$

$$s_b^2 = \frac{1}{m-1}\left[\sum^m \hat{X}_i^2 - m\left(\frac{\sum^m \hat{X}_i}{m}\right)^2\right]$$

$$= \frac{1}{2-1}\left[180 - 2\left(\frac{18}{2}\right)^2\right] = 18$$

$$s_1^2 = \frac{1}{n_1-1}\left[\sum x_{1j}^2 - n_1(\bar{x}_1)^2\right]$$

$$= \frac{1}{2-1}\left[10 - 2(2)^2\right] = 2$$

$$s_2^2 = \frac{1}{3-1}\left[33 - 3(3)^2\right] = 3$$

$N_i^2(N_i - n_i)/N_i$ $= N_i(N_i - n_i)$	$\dfrac{s_i^2}{n_i}$	$N_i(N_i - n_i)\dfrac{s_i^2}{n_i}$
$3(3 - 2) = 3$	$2/2 = 1$	3
$4(4 - 3) = 4$	$3/3 = 1$	4
		7

$$\therefore \quad \hat{V}(\hat{X}) = 3(3 - 2)(18/2) + (3/2)(7) = 37.5$$

Recall that $V(\hat{X}) = 48$. Note carefully that this is a hypothetical example—in practice, populations are never that small.

Case 2.

When $M \gg m$ and $N_i \gg n_i$, equation (1) may be simplified by letting the fpc $= 1$. We find

(7)
$$\hat{V}(\hat{X}) = M^2 \frac{s_b^2}{m} + \frac{M}{m}\sum^m N_i^2 \frac{s_i^2}{n_i}$$

The worksheet used in Case 1 may be used for this case also.

Case 3.

Using $M \gg m$, we may simplify (7) further as follows:

$$(8) \qquad \hat{V}(\hat{X}) = \left(\frac{M}{m}\right)^2 \left(ms_b^2 + \frac{m}{M} \sum_{i}^{m} N_i^2 \frac{s_i^2}{n_i}\right) \doteq \left(\frac{M}{m}\right)^2 (ms_b^2 + 0) = M^2 \frac{s_b^2}{m}$$

This may be used when $m/M < 1\%$.

Case 4.

In addition to $M \gg m$ and $N_i \gg n_i$, let us assume that $N_i = \bar{N} = N/M$, that is, (for example) each psu (class) has about the same number of ssu (students). Equation (8) may then be simplified as follows:

$$(9) \qquad \hat{V}(\hat{X}) = M^2 \frac{s_b^2}{m}$$

$$= M^2 \frac{1}{m} \frac{1}{m-1} \sum_{i}^{m} \left(\hat{X}_i - \frac{\sum \hat{X}_i}{m}\right)^2$$

$$= (M\bar{N})^2 \frac{1}{m} \frac{1}{m-1} \sum_{i}^{m} \left(\frac{\hat{X}_i}{\bar{N}} - \frac{\sum \hat{X}_i}{\bar{N} m}\right)^2$$

$$= (M\bar{N})^2 \frac{1}{m} \frac{1}{m-1} \sum_{i}^{m} (\hat{\bar{X}}_i - \hat{\bar{X}})^2$$

which may also be written as

$$(10) \qquad \hat{V}\left(\frac{\hat{X}}{M\bar{N}}\right) = \hat{V}(\hat{\bar{X}}) = \frac{1}{m} \frac{1}{m-1} \sum_{i}^{m} (\hat{\bar{X}}_i - \hat{\bar{X}})^2$$

For example, $\hat{\bar{X}}$ is an estimate of the average number of books per student in the population, and $\hat{\bar{X}}_i$ is the average number of books per student in the ith class. We shall find the general form of $V(\hat{\bar{X}})$ in the next two sections We have considered case 4 in this section for convenience.

Problems

1. Work out the algebraic details of equations (4) and (5).

2. Using the data of Problem 3 of page 196, devise a worksheet for the calculation of $\hat{V}(\hat{X})$ and calculate $\hat{X}$, $\hat{V}(\hat{X})$, and $s(\hat{X})$.

3. Using the data of Problem 4 of page 196, devise a worksheet for the calculation of $\hat{V}(\hat{X})$ and calculate $\hat{X}$, $\hat{V}(\hat{X})$, and $s(\hat{X})$.

4. Suppose we wish to estimate the number of dwelling units in the city. It has $M = 8000$ blocks and a sample of $m = 80$ blocks is selected. Each block is divided into $N_i = 4$ approximately equal segments, $n_i = 2$ segments are selected from each block and the number of dwelling units are counted.
   (i) Show that we may obtain $(M - m)/M \doteq 1$ as an approximation, and that
   $$\hat{V}(\hat{X}) = (M/m)^2(80\ s_b^2 + 0.08 \sum s_i^2/n_i)$$

Explain what s_b^2 and s_i^2 express in terms of our problem about dwelling units.

(ii) Explain under what situations we may simplify $\hat{V}(\hat{X})$ to

$$\hat{V}(\hat{X}) = (M/m)^2(80\ s_b^2)$$

In this case, note that $N_i = 4$ and $n_i = 2$.

8.5 Estimation of the population mean

Let us now consider the problem of estimating the population mean $\bar{\bar{X}}$ per unit by cluster sampling. We may (using our previous example) wish to estimate the average number of books a student has, or the average sales per supermarket, or the average number of cigarettes a college student smokes in a certain state.

The process of finding the estimator of $\bar{\bar{X}}$ is very simple. Simply divide the estimator of the total by N. That is,

$$(1) \qquad \hat{\bar{\bar{X}}} = \frac{\hat{X}}{N} = \frac{1}{N}\frac{M}{m}\sum^{m}\frac{N_i}{n_i}\sum^{n_i} x_{ij}$$

Note carefully that $\hat{\bar{\bar{X}}}$ is not the sample average. It is the estimator of the population mean $\bar{\bar{X}}$ obtained by dividing the estimate of the total X by the total population, N. In contrast, the sample mean is

$$(2) \qquad \bar{x} = \frac{x}{n}$$

where x is the total number of books in the sample and n is the number of students in the sample.

We have already shown that $\hat{X}$ is an unbiased estimator of X. Hence, the expected value of (1) will be

$$E(\hat{\bar{\bar{X}}}) = \frac{E(\hat{X})}{N} = \frac{X}{N} = \bar{\bar{X}}$$

and $\hat{\bar{\bar{X}}}$ is an unbiased estimator of the population mean $\bar{\bar{X}}$.

The variance of $\hat{\bar{\bar{X}}}$ is

$$V(\hat{\bar{\bar{X}}}) = V\left(\frac{\hat{X}}{N}\right) = \frac{1}{N^2}V(\hat{X})$$

Hence, using the formula for $V(\hat{X})$ of the previous section, we find

$$(3) \qquad V(\hat{\bar{\bar{X}}}) = \frac{1}{N^2}\left(M^2\frac{M-m}{M}\frac{S_b^2}{m} + \frac{M}{m}\sum^{M} N_i^2\frac{N_i-n_i}{N_i}\frac{S_i^2}{n_i}\right)$$

The estimate of $V(\hat{\bar{\bar{X}}})$ is also obtained by using the results of the previous sections. That is,

$$(4) \qquad \hat{V}(\hat{\bar{\bar{X}}}) = \frac{1}{N^2}\left(M^2\frac{M-m}{M}\frac{s_b^2}{m} + \frac{M}{m}\sum^{m} N_i^2\frac{N_i-n_i}{N_i}\frac{s_i^2}{n_i}\right)$$

One of the difficulties of using formulas (1) and (4) is that N is in some cases unknown. There are, however, several ways of overcoming this impasse. One is to assume that all psu are of equal size and to select the same number of ssu from the sampled psu, a second method is to use an approximation, and a third is to select psu with probability proportional to size. We shall consider the first two problems in the following sections, and consider the third procedure in the next chapter because of its importance.

8.6   When cluster sizes and subsample sizes are equal

In some problems, we may assume that the cluster sizes N_i are equal and the size of the subsamples selected from the clusters n_i are also equal. These subsamples were called ultimate clusters. In symbols, we have

$$(1) \qquad\qquad N_i = \bar{N} = \frac{N}{M}$$

$$(2) \qquad\qquad n_i = \bar{n} = \frac{n}{m}$$

As an example, in estimating volumes of timber or yields of wheat, the area may be divided into uniform blocks of, say, 10 acres. Each block is a psu and there are a total of M blocks. Each 10 acre block is subdivided into $\bar{N} = 40$ plots which are each 1/4 of an acre. A random sample of m blocks (psu) is selected, and from each block a certain number (say, $\bar{n} = 10$) of uniform plots (1/4 of an acre plots) are selected. These plots are the ssu, and each $\bar{n} = 10$ of the 1/4 acre plots are the ultimate clusters. There will be m ultimate clusters.

As another example, there may be $M = 60$ classes of 6th graders in a certain city school system, and each class may have $\bar{N} = 40$ students. A random sample of $m = 6$ classes may be selected and, from each of these classes, $\bar{n} = 10$ students may be selected. There are $m = 6$ ultimate clusters, each having $\bar{n} = 10$ students. If we are interested in estimating the total number of books the student have, X_{ij} shows the number of books the jth student (ssu) in the ith class (psu) has. For example, $X_{34} = 7$ books shows that the 4th student in the 3rd class has 7 books. The capital, X_{ij}, is for population values and the lower case, x_{ij}, is for sample values.

When conditions such as (1) and (2) may be used, the estimator $\hat{\bar{X}}$ becomes

$$(3) \qquad\qquad \hat{\bar{X}} = \frac{M}{Nm} \sum_i^m \frac{\bar{N}}{\bar{n}} \sum_j^{\bar{n}} x_{ij} = \frac{1}{m\bar{n}} \sum_{}^{m} \sum_{}^{\bar{n}} x_{ij}$$

which is simply the sample mean. That is, $m\bar{n} = n$ and is the sample size; for example $m\bar{n} = 6 \times 10 = 60$ students is the sample size. Thus, $\sum \sum x_{ij}$ is the total number of books the $n = 60$ students of the sample have. It is also easily seen that $\hat{\bar{X}}$ is an unbiased estimator of $\bar{\bar{X}}$.

The point to note in equation (3) is that we do not need to know N to estimate the population mean $\bar{X}$.

The variance of $\hat{\bar{X}}$ which was

$$(4) \qquad V(\hat{\bar{X}}) = \frac{1}{N^2}\left[M^2 \frac{M-m}{M} \frac{S_b^2}{m} + \frac{M}{m} \sum^{M} N_i^2 \frac{N_i - n_i}{N_i} \frac{S_i^2}{n_i}\right]$$

may be rewritten, using (1) and (2) as follows. For the first term on the right, we have

$$\frac{1}{N^2} M^2 \frac{M-m}{M} \frac{S_b^2}{m} = \frac{M-m}{M}\frac{1}{m} \frac{S_b^2}{\bar{N}^2}$$

Recall that

$$S_b^2 = \frac{1}{M-1} \sum^{M} (X_i - \bar{X})^2$$

Hence

$$\frac{S_b^2}{\bar{N}^2} = \frac{1}{M-1}\sum^{M}\left(\frac{X_i}{\bar{N}} - \frac{\bar{X}}{\bar{N}}\right)^2 = \frac{1}{M-1}\sum^{M}(\bar{X}_i - \bar{\bar{X}})^2$$

which shows the variance among the psu means. It is the "between variance," $\bar{X}_i$ shows the average number of books owned by a student in the ith class (psu), and $\bar{\bar{X}}$ is the population average number of books a student has. Let us denote this variance by

$$(5) \qquad S_{1b}^2 = \frac{S_b^2}{\bar{N}^2} = \frac{1}{M-1}\sum(\bar{X}_i - \bar{\bar{X}})^2$$

For the second term on the right-hand side, we have

$$\frac{1}{N^2}\frac{M}{m}\sum \bar{N}^2 \frac{\bar{N} - \bar{n}}{\bar{N}} \frac{S_i^2}{\bar{n}}$$

$$= \frac{1}{N^2}\frac{M}{m}\frac{N^2}{M^2}\frac{\bar{N} - \bar{n}}{\bar{N}}\sum \frac{S_i^2}{\bar{n}}$$

$$(6) \qquad = \frac{\bar{N} - \bar{n}}{\bar{N}}\frac{1}{M}\sum^{M} \frac{S_i^2}{m\bar{n}}$$

We know that

$$\frac{1}{M}\sum^{M} S_i^2 = \frac{1}{M}\frac{1}{\bar{N}-1}\sum^{M}\sum^{\bar{N}}(X_{ij} - \bar{X}_i)^2$$

is the pooled variance among elements within the psu, and we denote it by

$$(7) \qquad S_{2i}^2 = \frac{1}{M}\sum^{M} S_i^2 = \frac{1}{M(\bar{N}-1)}\sum^{M}\sum^{\bar{N}}(X_{ij} - \bar{X}_i)^2$$

Then, by substituting (5) and (7) into (4), we find

$$(8) \qquad V(\hat{\bar{X}}) = \frac{M-m}{M}\frac{S_{1b}^2}{m} + \frac{\bar{N} - \bar{n}}{\bar{N}}\frac{S_{2i}^2}{m\bar{n}}$$

The reason why we have rewritten (4) as (8) is because of its simplicity and similarity to the equation for the variance of simple random sampling. The estimate of (8) may also be shown in a similar form. Let us now find this estimate.

The variance $V(\overset{\triangle}{\bar{X}})$ given by (4) may be rewritten by substituting in (5) and (6) as

$$(9) \qquad V(\overset{\triangle}{\bar{X}}) = \frac{M-m}{M}\frac{S_{1b}^2}{m} + \frac{\bar{N}-\bar{n}}{\bar{N}}\frac{1}{M}\sum_{}^{M}\frac{S_i^2}{m\bar{n}}$$

An unbiased estimate of this $V(\overset{\triangle}{\bar{X}})$ is

$$(10) \qquad \hat{V}(\overset{\triangle}{\bar{X}}) = \frac{M-m}{M}\frac{s_{1b}^2}{m} + \frac{\bar{N}-\bar{n}}{\bar{N}}\frac{1}{M}\sum_{}^{m}\frac{s_i^2}{m\bar{n}}$$

where

$$s_{1b}^2 = \frac{1}{m-1}\sum_{}^{m}(\bar{x}_i - \bar{x})^2$$

$$\bar{x}_i = \frac{x_i}{\bar{n}}, \qquad \bar{x} = \frac{x}{n}$$

$$s_i^2 = \frac{1}{\bar{n}-1}\sum_{}^{\bar{n}}(x_{ij} - \bar{x}_i)^2$$

The meaning of equation (10) may be explained as follows. The $\bar{x}_i$ is the average number of books a student in the ith ultimate cluster has, and $\bar{x}$ is the average number of books a student in the sample has. Hence, s_{1b}^2 is the variance between sample means $\bar{x}_i$ of the ultimate clusters and s_i^2 is the variance among the sampling units (students) within the ith ultimate cluster.

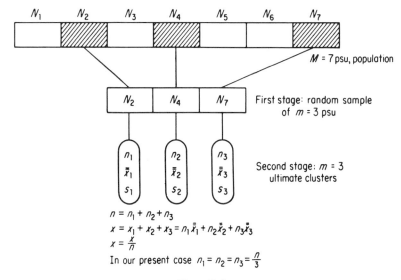

$n = n_1 + n_2 + n_3$

$x = x_1 + x_2 + x_3 = n_1\bar{x}_1 + n_2\bar{x}_2 + n_3\bar{x}_3$

$\bar{x} = \frac{x}{n}$

In our present case $n_1 = n_2 = n_3 = \frac{n}{3}$

Fig. 8-2

As equations (9) and (10) show, the total population size N does not appear explicitly in both equations. However, since $N = M\bar{N}$, it does appear implicitly in both equations, and hence the formulas do require knowledge of N.

Equation (10) may be rewritten to conform to the format given in equation (8) as follows:

$$\hat{V}(\hat{\bar{X}}) = \frac{M-m}{M}\frac{s_{1b}^2}{m} + \frac{\bar{N}-\bar{n}}{\bar{N}}\frac{1}{M}\sum^m \frac{s_i^2}{m\bar{n}}$$

$$= \frac{M-m}{M}\frac{s_{1b}^2}{m} + \frac{\bar{N}-\bar{n}}{\bar{N}}\frac{m}{M}\frac{1}{m\bar{n}}\frac{1}{m}\sum^m s_i^2$$

(11)
$$= \frac{M-m}{M}\frac{s_{1b}^2}{m} + \frac{\bar{N}-\bar{n}}{\bar{N}}\frac{m}{M}\frac{s_{2i}^2}{m\bar{n}}$$

where

$$s_{2i}^2 = \frac{1}{m}\sum^m s_i^2$$

$$= \frac{1}{m(\bar{n}-1)}\sum_i^m \sum_j^{\bar{n}} (x_{ij} - \bar{x}_i)^2$$

which shows the pooled variance of the within variances.

To summarize; the estimator of the mean and its variance when $\bar{N} = N/m$ and $\bar{n} = n/m$ are

(2)
$$\hat{\bar{X}} = \frac{1}{m\bar{n}}\sum^m \sum^{\bar{n}} x_{ij}$$

(8)
$$V(\hat{\bar{X}}) = \frac{M-m}{M}\frac{S_{1b}^2}{m} + \frac{\bar{N}-\bar{n}}{\bar{N}}\frac{S_{2i}^2}{m\bar{n}}$$

The estimator of (8) is

(11)
$$\hat{V}(\hat{\bar{X}}) = \frac{M-m}{M}\frac{s_{1b}^2}{m} + \frac{\bar{N}-\bar{n}}{\bar{N}}\frac{m}{M}\frac{s_{2i}^2}{m\bar{n}}$$

Computational procedure

We usually expand s_{1b}^2 and s_{2i}^2 to facilitate computations. The procedure is to express these variances in terms of $\sum x^2$ and $(\sum x)^2$. Let us start with s_{1b}^2:

$$s_{1b}^2 = \frac{1}{m-1}\sum^m (\bar{x}_i - \bar{x})^2 = \frac{1}{m-1}(\sum \bar{x}_i^2 - m\bar{x}^2)$$

$$\sum \bar{x}_i^2 = \left(\frac{1}{\bar{n}}\right)^2 \sum^m (\sum^{\bar{n}} x_{ij})^2$$

$$\bar{x}^2 = \left(\frac{1}{m\bar{n}}\right)^2 (\sum^m \sum^{\bar{n}} x_{ij})^2$$

We may expand s_{2i}^2 in similar fashion as follows:

$$s_{2i}^2 = \frac{1}{m(\bar{n}-1)} \sum^m \sum^{\bar{n}} (x_{ij} - \bar{x}_i)^2$$

$$= \frac{1}{m(\bar{n}-1)} \sum^m [\sum^{\bar{n}} x_{ij}^2 - \bar{n}\bar{x}_i^2]$$

$$= \frac{1}{m(\bar{n}-1)} [\sum^m \sum^{\bar{n}} x_{ij}^2 - \bar{n} \sum^m \bar{x}_i^2]$$

$$= \frac{1}{m(\bar{n}-1)} \left[\sum^m \sum^{\bar{n}} x_{ij}^2 - \frac{1}{\bar{n}} \sum^m (\sum^{\bar{n}} x_{ij})^2 \right]$$

Example 1. Let us illustrate the use of these computational formulas with a hypothetical example.

psu	X_{ij}	X_i	$\bar{X}_i$
A	1, 3, 5	9	3
B	3, 5, 7	15	5
C	5, 7, 9	21	7
		45	

Let us select $m = 2$ psu and $n_1 = n_2 = 2$ ssu. Suppose we get

$$A: \ 3, 5; \quad B: \ 5, 7$$

x_{1j}	x_{1j}^2	x_{2j}	x_{2j}^2
3	9	5	25
5	25	7	49
8	34	12	74

$$\sum_i^m \bar{x}_i^2 = \left(\frac{1}{\bar{n}}\right)^2 \sum^m \left(\sum^n x_{ij}\right)^2$$

$$= \left(\frac{1}{\bar{n}}\right)^2 \left[\left(\sum_j^{\bar{n}} x_{1j}\right)^2 + \left(\sum^{\bar{n}} x_{2j}\right)^2\right] = \left(\frac{1}{2}\right)^2 [(8)^2 + (12)^2] = 52$$

$$\bar{\bar{x}}^2 = \left(\frac{1}{m\bar{n}}\right)^2 \left(\sum^m \sum^{\bar{n}} x_{ij}\right)^2$$

$$= \left(\frac{1}{2 \times 2}\right)^2 (\sum x_{1j} + \sum x_{2j})^2 = \frac{1}{16}(8 + 12)^2 = 25$$

$$s_{1b}^2 = \frac{1}{m-1} (\sum \bar{x}_i^2 - m\bar{\bar{x}}^2) = \frac{1}{2-1} [52 - (2)(25)] = 2$$

$$s_{2i}^2 = \frac{1}{m(\bar{n}-1)} \sum^m \sum^{\bar{n}} (x_{ij} - \bar{x}_i)^2$$

$$= \frac{1}{m(\bar{n}-1)} \left[\sum^m \sum^{\bar{n}} x_{ij}^2 - \frac{1}{\bar{n}} \sum^m (\sum^{\bar{n}} x_{ij})^2 \right]$$

$$= \frac{1}{2(2-1)} \left\{ (34 + 74) - \frac{1}{2}[(8)^2 + (12)^2] \right\} = 2$$

$$\therefore \quad \hat{V}(\hat{\bar{X}}) = \frac{M-m}{M} \frac{s_{1b}^2}{m} + \frac{\bar{N}-\bar{n}}{\bar{N}} \frac{m}{M} \frac{s_{2i}^2}{m\bar{n}}$$

$$= \frac{3-2}{3} \frac{2}{2} + \frac{3-2}{3} \frac{2}{3} \frac{2}{2 \times 2} = \frac{4}{9}$$

Simplification

If $M \gg m$ and $\bar{N} \gg \bar{n}$, equation (11) simplifies to

$$(12) \qquad \hat{V}(\hat{\bar{X}}) = \frac{s_{1b}^2}{m} = \frac{1}{m(m-1)} \sum^m (\bar{x}_i - \bar{x})^2$$

In other words, variations within the ultimate clusters are ignored.

Problems

1. Using the data of Problem 1 of page 207, select a sample of $m = 3$ psu and $\bar{n} = 2$ ssu from each psu.

(i) Calculate $\hat{\bar{X}}$ from the sample you have selected.

(ii) Calculate S_{1b}^2 and S_{2i}^2.

(iii) Calculate s_{1b}^2 and s_{2i}^2 from the sample you have selected.

(iv) Calculate $V(\hat{\bar{X}})$.

(v) Calculate $\hat{V}(\hat{\bar{X}})$ from the sample you ave have selected.

2. Using the data of Problem 2 of page 207, repeat the 5 operations of Problem 1 above.

3. Suppose we wish to estimate the average amount of money 6th graders spend on lunch during a week. There are $M = 400$ classes of 6th graders in the city and each class has approximately $\bar{N} = 40$ students. A sample of $m = 10$ classes is selected and $\bar{n} = 10$ students are selected from each class. The following data is obtained:

Class	$\sum_j x_{ij}$	Class	$\sum_j x_{ij}$
1	$25	6	$18
2	30	7	24
3	20	8	27
4	19	9	20
5	23	10	21

(i) Find $\hat{\bar{X}}$.

(ii) Assume for simplicity that we may use equation (12). Find $\hat{V}(\hat{\bar{X}})$ and $s(\hat{\bar{X}})$.

4. Continuing Problem 3, suppose the data for $m = 5$ classes is as follows.

Class	x_{ij} (weekly expenditures)	
1	$2.5, 2.4, 2.7, 2.0, 1.8	3.0, 2.8, 2.1, 2.2, 4.0
2	1.6, 2.0, 2.0, 2.0, 2.5	2.4, 2.0, 1.5, 1.7, 2.3
3	2.1, 2.5, 2.3, 2.4, 2.2	1.8, 2.0, 1.9, 2.2, 2.6
4	2.7, 2.0, 2.1, 2.3, 1.7	2.8, 2.2, 2.4, 1.9, 2.9
5	1.8, 1.5, 1.7, 2.3, 1.9	1.4, 1.8, 1.5, 2.0, 2.2

(i) Using this data, calculate $\hat{\bar{X}}$, $\hat{V}(\hat{\bar{X}})$, and $s(\hat{\bar{x}})$.

(ii) Using the s_{2i}^2 obtained from this data as an estimate for the s_{2i}^2 for the data of Problem 3 above, calculate $\hat{V}(\hat{\bar{X}})$ for Problem 3 and compare it with the result of (ii) of Problem 3.

8.7 Comparison of cluster sampling with simple random sampling

Up to now we have selected m psu and then subsampled n_i ssu without consideration of how many m or n_i should be selected to give the most efficient sample design. By an efficient sample design, we shall mean a sample that will give us an estimator with a smaller sampling variance. To be more specific, we shall consider the following problem: should we take a large number of psu (classes) and a small number of ssu (students) from each psu (class); or should we select a few psu (classes) and a large number of ssu (students) from each psu (class)?

We may argue intuitively that when the elementary units within the psu are homogeneous, only a small number of elementary units are necessary to represent the psu. Suppose, for example, that we are testing the strength of cloth that is being made at a certain factory. We may assume the cloth produced on a given machine is approximately uniform, although it may differ from machine to machine. Then, the intuitively sensible thing to do would be to select a large number of machines (psu), and a small amount of cloth (ssu) from each machine.

This illustration shows that a criteria for deciding whether or not only a small number of ssu is necessary will depend on the degree of homogeneity within clusters. Hansen, Hurwitz, and Madow (1953) have developed a criterion that uses the intraclass (cluster) correlation coefficient to investigate the degree of homogeneity and efficiency of cluster sampling relative to simple random sampling. We shall in this section discuss their method of comparing cluster sampling with simple random sampling and show how it is used as a criterion for sample design.

Our problem thus is to compare the variance of $\hat{\bar{X}}$ for cluster sampling with that of simple random sampling. To accomplish this, we shall first define the variance of $\hat{\bar{X}}$ for simple random sampling. We shall then relate the variance of $\hat{\bar{X}}$ for cluster sampling with $V(\hat{\bar{X}})$, which we obtained from simple random sampling by use of the intraclass correlation coefficient. Let us start our discussion by defining $V(\hat{\bar{X}})$ when the sample is selected by simple random sampling.

To simplify our discussion, we shall assume as we did in section 8.6, that

$$N_i = \bar{N} = \frac{N}{M} \quad \text{and} \quad n_i = \bar{n} = \frac{n}{m}$$

That is, the cluster sizes are equal $(\bar{N})$ and the same number $(\bar{n})$ of ssu are selected from the m psu. Then from equation (3) in section 8.6,

(1)
$$\hat{\bar{X}} = \frac{1}{m\bar{n}} \sum^{m} \sum^{\bar{n}} x_{ij}$$

which is the sample mean of the $n = m\bar{n}$ sampling units. We have also seen that this is an unbiased estimator of

(2)
$$\bar{\bar{X}} = \frac{X}{N}$$

From the results of simple random sampling the variance of $\hat{\bar{X}}$, becomes

(3)
$$V(\hat{\bar{X}}) = \frac{M\bar{N} - m\bar{n}}{M\bar{N}} \frac{S^2}{m\bar{n}}$$

where

(4)
$$S^2 = \frac{1}{M\bar{N} - 1} \sum^{M} \sum^{\bar{N}} (X_{ij} - \bar{\bar{X}})^2$$

$$\bar{\bar{X}} = \frac{X}{M\bar{N}}$$

As is seen, $M\bar{N}$ is the population size; $m\bar{n}$ is the sample size, and (3) above corresponds to the variance formula

$$\frac{N - n}{N} \frac{S^2}{n}$$

for simple random sampling.

The variance of $\hat{\bar{X}}$ for cluster sampling is, from equation (11) of section 8.6,

(5)
$$V(\hat{\bar{X}}) = \frac{M - m}{M} \frac{S_{1b}^2}{m} + \frac{\bar{N} - \bar{n}}{\bar{N}} \frac{S_{2i}^2}{m}$$

To compare the variance of (3) with that of (5), we need to express S_{1b}^2 and S_{2i}^2 of equation (5) in terms of S^2.

It turns out that (see reference for derivation)

(6)
$$S_{1b}^2 = \frac{M\bar{N} - 1}{\bar{N}^2(M - 1)} S^2 [1 + (\bar{N} - 1)\rho]$$

where

(7)
$$\rho = \frac{E(X_{ij} - \bar{\bar{X}})(X_{ik} - \bar{\bar{X}})}{E(X_{ij} - \bar{\bar{X}})^2}$$

(8)
$$= \frac{2 \sum_{i}^{M} \sum_{j<k}^{\bar{N}} (X_{ij} - \bar{\bar{X}})(X_{ik} - \bar{\bar{X}})}{(\bar{N} - 1)(M\bar{N} - 1)S^2}$$

As for S_{2i}^2, we get

(9)
$$S_{2i}^2 = \frac{M\bar{N} - 1}{M\bar{N}} S^2 (1 - \rho)$$

Now that S_{1b}^2 and S_{2i}^2 have been expressed in terms of S^2 and ρ, let us substitute expressions (6) and (9) into equation (5) so that $V(\hat{\bar{X}})$ may be expressed in terms of S^2 and ρ. We find

$$(10) \qquad V(\hat{\bar{X}}_{cl}) = \frac{M\bar{N}-1}{M\bar{N}} \frac{S^2}{m\bar{n}} \left[\frac{\bar{N}-\bar{n}}{\bar{N}} + \frac{M-m}{M-1} \frac{\bar{n}}{\bar{N}} \right.$$
$$\left. + \left\{ \frac{M-m}{M-1} \frac{\bar{n}}{\bar{N}} (\bar{N}-1) - \frac{\bar{N}-\bar{n}}{\bar{N}} \right\} \rho \right]$$

As is seen, the term

$$(11) \qquad \frac{M\bar{N}-1}{M\bar{N}} \frac{S^2}{m\bar{n}}$$

in (10) is approximately the same as

$$(12) \qquad V(\hat{\bar{X}}_{ran}) = \frac{M\bar{N}-m\bar{n}}{M\bar{N}} \frac{S^2}{m\bar{n}}$$

If $m\bar{n} \ll M\bar{N}$, we may consider (11) to be approximately equal to (12), which is the variance of $\hat{\bar{X}}$ for simple random sampling.

When this approximation holds, equation (10) shows that the variance due to cluster sampling $V(\hat{\bar{X}}_{cl})$ is equal to $V(\hat{\bar{X}}_{ran})$ with the adjustment factor in the brackets on the right side.

To bring out the implications of this adjustment factor more clearly, let us assume that $\bar{N} \gg \bar{n}$ and $M \gg m$. Then

$$\frac{\bar{N}-\bar{n}}{\bar{N}} = 1 - \frac{\bar{n}}{\bar{N}} \doteq 1$$

$$\frac{M-m}{M-1} \frac{\bar{n}}{\bar{N}} = 1 \cdot \frac{\bar{n}}{\bar{N}} \doteq 0$$

$$\frac{M-m}{M-1} \frac{\bar{n}}{\bar{N}} (\bar{N}-1) = \frac{M-m}{M-1} \frac{\bar{N}-1}{\bar{N}} \bar{n} \doteq \bar{n}$$

$$\frac{\bar{N}-\bar{n}}{\bar{N}} = 1 - \frac{\bar{n}}{\bar{N}} \doteq 1$$

Hence (10) becomes

$$V(\hat{\bar{X}}_{cl}) = \frac{M\bar{N}-1}{M\bar{N}} \frac{S^2}{m\bar{n}} [1 + 0 + (\bar{n}-1)\rho]$$

$$(13) \qquad\qquad \doteq \frac{S^2}{m\bar{n}} [1 + (\bar{n}-1)\rho]$$

$$(13') \qquad\qquad = V(\hat{\bar{X}}_{ran})[1 + (\bar{n}-1)\rho]$$

where $S^2/m\bar{n}$ may be considered the variance of $\hat{\bar{X}}$ due to simple random sampling.

If $m\bar{n} = n = $ constant, that is, the sample size is constant, and if $\rho > 0$, then the larger $\bar{n}$, the greater $V(\hat{\bar{X}}_{cl})$ will be compared to $S^2/m\bar{n} = V(\hat{\bar{X}}_{ran})$. For example, if $\bar{n} = 6$ and $\rho = 0.8$,

$$1 + (\bar{n} - 1)\rho = 1 + (5 \times 0.8) = 5$$

and there will be a 400% increase in the variance when cluster sampling is used. Or we may say we need a sample four times larger than simple random sampling to obtain the same precision.

Equation (13) gives us insight into the effects of m and $\bar{n}$. Noting that S^2 remains constant regardless of how the population is divided into clusters, the $V(\hat{\bar{X}}_{cl})$ will depend on the values of m, $\bar{n}$, and ρ.

To investigate the effects of m and $\bar{n}$, we may set $m\bar{n} = n = $ constant and see the effects of m and $\bar{n}$. Suppose $m\bar{n} = 200$. Then, when $\bar{n} = 2$, $m = 100$; when $\bar{n} = 4$, $m = 50$; when $\bar{n} = 10$, $m = 20$; and so forth. In any of these cases, $S^2/m\bar{n}$ remains constant. The change will occur in $[1 + (\bar{n} - 1)\rho]$.

When $\rho > 0$, as $\bar{n}$ becomes large, $[1 + (\bar{n} - 1)\rho]$ will become large, and hence $V(\hat{\bar{X}}_{cl})$ will become large. That is, for a given sample size n, $V(\hat{\bar{X}}_{cl})$ will be larger when $\bar{n}$ is larger. Hence, when $\rho > 0$, it would be desirable to keep $\bar{n}$ small and m large.

When $\rho < 0$, $V(\hat{\bar{X}}_{cl})$ will be smaller when $\bar{n}$ is larger. Hence, when $\rho < 0$, it would be desirable to make $\bar{n}$ large and m small.

Let us now investigate the effect of ρ by holding both m and $\bar{n}$ constant. Equation (13) tells us that $V(\hat{\bar{X}}_{cl})$ becomes large as ρ approaches 1.

When $\rho > 0$, and approaches 1, it means that the sampling units in the clusters become homogeneous. This implies that the difference between clusters will tend to be large. In terms of our cloth illustration, the cloth from each machine is of uniform quality, but there is a difference in quality between machines. We can see intuitively that since cluster sampling selects only a sample of the machines, when the machines produce different quality cloth, $V(\hat{\bar{X}}_{cl})$ will tend to be large—even though the quality per machine may be uniform. The natural thing to do in this case is to select a small amount of cloth from many machines. This common sense conclusion is supported by our theoretical conclusion above. Namely, that when $\rho > 0$, reduce $\bar{n}$(cloth—ssu) and increase m(machines—psu).

When $\rho = 0$ or close to it, it means the sampling units are heterogeneous within the clusters. In this case, the clusters will tend to be similar and the variation between clusters will tend to be small. Hence, common sense would indicate that we take few clusters and more ssu. Equation (13) shows that when $\rho = 0$, $\bar{n}$ and m will have no effect on $V(\hat{\bar{X}}_{cl})$. However, for clarification, let $\rho < 0$. That is, when we have heterogeneity, we may get a negative ρ. For example, let $\rho = -0.1$. Then, from $[1 + (\bar{n} - 1)\rho]$, we can see that

$$\bar{n} = 2: 1 + (\bar{n} - 1)\rho = 1 + (2 - 1)(-0.1) = 0.9$$
$$\bar{n} = 10: 1 + (\bar{n} - 1)\rho = 1 + (10 - 1)(-0.1) = 0.1$$

and $[1 + (\bar{n} - 1)\rho]$ becomes smaller as $\bar{n}$ becomes larger.

Let us now compare $V(\hat{\bar{X}}_{cl})$ with $V(\hat{\bar{X}}_{ran})$ by using equation (13′). As shown, when $\rho = 0$ or close to it, the difference in precision is small. $\rho = 0$ implied heterogeneity, and we can see intuitively that selecting a sample by cluster sampling in this case will be similar to selecting a sample by random sampling. This also leads us to observe that when the sampling units are heterogeneous within clusters, $M \gg m$, and $\bar{N} \gg \bar{n}$, we may use $S^2/m\bar{n}$ (or its estimate, $s^2/m\bar{n}$) as an estimate of $V(\hat{\bar{X}}_{cl})$. This considerably simplifies calculations of the variance because we need only calculate s^2 from the sample of $m\bar{n}$ units (which is considered as a random sample).

The above discussion suggests that it is desirable to have ρ small, and—if possible—to design the sample so as to have heterogeneity within the clusters. This may often be accomplished by letting the psu become large. For example, when we wish to estimate the average food expenditures of urban families in large cities, the psu may be large cities. In this case, the food expenditures of families in a city may be heterogeneous and ρ may thus be small. In this case, we should increase the size of $\bar{n}$ (families) and decrease the size of m (cities).

On the other hand, when the psu are small, ρ tends to be large. In this case, we may let $\bar{n}$ be small and m be large. For example, suppose we wish to estimate the average amount of wheat produced per acre in a certain state. The psu may be counties and the average amount of wheat per acre in a county may be similar whereas there may be considerable variation between counties. In this case, ρ will tend to be large, and our formula suggests that we let m(sample of counties) be large and $\bar{n}$ (sample of acres) be small.

Reference 1

Let us show how S_{1b}^2 may be expressed in terms of S^2. The S_{1b}^2 is defined in equation (5) of section 8.6 as

$$S_{1b}^2 = \frac{1}{M-1} \sum^{M} (\bar{\bar{X}}_i - \bar{\bar{X}})^2$$

$$= \frac{1}{M-1} \sum^{M} \left(\frac{X_i}{\bar{N}} - \frac{\bar{X}}{\bar{N}}\right)^2$$

(14)
$$= \frac{1}{\bar{N}^2(M-1)} \sum^{M} (X_i - \bar{X})^2$$

The squared term on the right may be changed algebraically as follows. Let

$$(X_i - \bar{X}) = (X_{i1} - \bar{\bar{X}}) + (X_{i2} - \bar{\bar{X}}) + \cdots + (X_{i\bar{N}} - \bar{\bar{X}})$$

Now square and sum over all M clusters. Then

$$(15) \qquad \sum_i^M (X_i - \bar{X})^2 = \sum_i^M \sum_j^{\bar{N}} (X_{ij} - \bar{X})^2 + 2 \sum_i^M \sum_{j<k}^{\bar{N}} (X_{ij} - \bar{X})(X_{ik} - \bar{X})$$

We note that the first term on the right is related to S^2 and that the second is related to the covariance between pairs of X_{ij}.

To evaluate the second term on the right, let us define the intraclass correlation coefficient ρ. This was discussed in Chapter 6, Systematic Sampling, but will be repeated here to adjust the notation to cluster sampling. We define ρ as

$$(16) \qquad \rho = \frac{E(X_{ij} - \bar{X})(X_{ik} - \bar{X})}{E(X_{ij} - \bar{X})^2}$$

and ρ should therefore be called the intracluster correlation coefficient, because it shows the correlation between pairs of X_{ij} and X_{ik} within the ith cluster.

The numerator of (16) is defined as

$$(17) \qquad E(X_{ij} - \bar{X})(X_{ik} - \bar{X}) = \sum_i^M \sum_{j<k}^{\bar{N}} \frac{1}{[M\bar{N}(\bar{N} - 1)/2]} (X_{ij} - \bar{X})(X_{ik} - \bar{X})$$

since there are $\bar{N}(\bar{N} - 1)/2$ possible ways of selecting pairs of X_{ij} and X_{ik} out of the ith cluster of size $\bar{N}$, and there are altogether M clusters.

The denominator of (16) becomes

$$(18) \qquad E(X_{ij} - \bar{X})^2 = \sum_i^M \sum_j^{\bar{N}} \frac{1}{M\bar{N}} (X_{ij} - \bar{X})^2 = \frac{1}{M\bar{N}} (M\bar{N} - 1)S^2$$

Hence, from (16), (17), and (18), ρ becomes

$$(19) \qquad \rho = \frac{2/[M\bar{N}(\bar{N} - 1)] \sum \sum (X_{ij} - \bar{X})(X_{ik} - \bar{X})}{(1/M\bar{N})(M\bar{N} - 1)S^2}$$
$$= \frac{2 \sum \sum (X_{ij} - \bar{X})(X_{ik} - \bar{X})}{(\bar{N} - 1)(M\bar{N} - 1)S^2}$$

From this we find

$$(20) \qquad 2 \sum_i^M \sum_{j<k}^{\bar{N}} (X_{ij} - \bar{X})(X_{ik} - \bar{X}) = \rho(\bar{N} - 1)(M\bar{N} - 1)S^2$$

which we note is the second term on the right side of equation (15).

Hence, using (4) and (20), we may express (15) in terms of S^2 and ρ as follows:

$$(21) \qquad \sum_i^M (X_i - \bar{X})^2 = \sum_i^M \sum_j^{\bar{N}} (X_{ij} - \bar{X})^2 + 2 \sum_i^M \sum_{j<k}^{\bar{N}} (X_{ij} - \bar{X})(X_{ik} - \bar{X})$$
$$= (M\bar{N} - 1)S^2 + \rho(\bar{N} - 1)(M\bar{N} - 1)S^2$$
$$= (M\bar{N} - 1)S^2[1 + (\bar{N} - 1)\rho]$$

Using (21), we may now express S_{1b}^2 given by equation (14) in terms of S^2 and ρ as follows:

$$(22) \qquad S_{1b}^2 = \frac{1}{\bar{N}^2(M - 1)} \sum_i^M (X_i - \bar{X})^2$$
$$= \frac{M\bar{N} - 1}{\bar{N}^2(M - 1)} S^2[1 + (\bar{N} - 1)\rho]$$

Having obtained S_{1b}^2 in terms of S^2 and ρ, our next task is to express S_{2i}^2 in terms of S^2 and ρ.

Reference 2

To find the relation between S_{2i}^2, S^2, and ρ, we start with the fundamental identity

$$\sum_{i}^{M} \sum_{j}^{\bar{N}} (X_{ij} - \bar{\bar{X}})^2 = \bar{N} \sum_{i}^{M} (\bar{X}_i - \bar{\bar{X}})^2 + \sum_{i}^{M} \sum_{j}^{\bar{N}} (X_{ij} - \bar{X}_i)^2$$

which may be rewritten as

$$(M\bar{N} - 1)S^2 = (M - 1)\bar{N}S_{1b}^2 + M(\bar{N} - 1)S_{2i}^2$$

and transferring terms we get

(23) $$M(\bar{N} - 1)S_{2i}^2 = (M\bar{N} - 1)S^2 - (M - 1)\bar{N}S_{1b}^2$$

Then by substituting (22) which expresses S_{1b}^2 in terms of S^2 and ρ into (23), we will be able to express S_{2i}^2 in terms of S^2 and ρ. We find

$$M(\bar{N} - 1)S_{2i}^2 = (M\bar{N} - 1)S^2 - (M - 1)\bar{N}\frac{M\bar{N} - 1}{\bar{N}(M - 1)}\frac{S^2}{\bar{N}}[1 + (\bar{N} - 1)\rho]$$

$$= (M\bar{N} - 1)S^2 - (M\bar{N} - 1)\frac{S^2}{\bar{N}^2}[1 + (\bar{N} - 1)\rho]$$

$$= \frac{S^2}{\bar{N}}(M\bar{N} - 1)[(\bar{N} - 1) - (\bar{N} - 1)\rho]$$

$$= (\bar{N} - 1)\frac{S^2}{\bar{N}}(M\bar{N} - 1)(1 - \rho)$$

Hence, S_{2i}^2 is found to be

(24) $$S_{2i}^2 = \frac{M\bar{N} - 1}{M\bar{N}} S^2(1 - \rho)$$

when expressed in terms of S^2 and ρ.

Problems

1. Using the following hypothetical data, answer the questions.

Cluster	X_{ij}
A	1, 3, 5
B	3, 5, 7
C	5, 7, 9

(i) Calculate

$$\sum_{i}^{M} \sum_{j<k}^{\bar{N}} (X_{ij} - \bar{\bar{X}})(X_{ik} - \bar{\bar{X}})$$

and show it is equal to 12.

(ii) Using equation (4), calculate S^2 and show it is equal to 6.

(iii) Using equation (8), calculate ρ and show that it is equal to 3/12.

(iv) Using the result of (iii), calculate $V(\hat{\bar{X}}_{cl})$ and show it is equal to 1.

2. Continuing Problem 1, note that $V(\hat{X}) = 81$, $S_b^2 = 36$, $S_1^2 = S_2^2 = S_3^2 = 4$ from Example 1 on page 198.

   (i) Using equation (4) of section 8.6 (p. 220), show that $V(\hat{\bar{X}}) = 1$.

   (ii) Find S_{1b}^2 from equation (5) on page 220, using the result that $S_b^2 = 36$ and show it is equal to 4.

   (iii) Find S_{1b}^2 from equation (6) on page 226 using the result that $\rho = 3/12$ and $S^2 = 6$ from Problem 1 above and verify it is equal to the result in (ii) above.

3. Continuing Problem 1 and 2,

   (i) Calculate S_{2t}^2 from equation (7) on page 220 using the result that $S_1^2 = S_2^2 = S_3^2 = 4$, and show it is equal to 4.

   (ii) Calculate S_{2t}^2 from equation (9) on page 226, noting that $S^2 = 6$ and $\rho = 3/12$, and verify it is equal to the result in (i) above.

4. Substitute equations (6) and (9) into (5) and work out the algebraic details of equation (10).

5. Given the following hypothetical data:

Cluster	I	II	III
A	1, 3, 3	1, 3, 5	1, 5, 9
B	5, 5, 5	3, 5, 7	3, 7, 3
C	7, 7, 9	7, 5, 9	7, 5, 5

Population I has been grouped into homogeneous clusters, population II is less homogeneous, and population III is the least homogeneous.

   (i) Calculate ρ for each group and compare.

   (ii) Calculate $V(\hat{\bar{X}}_{cl})$ using equation (10) for each group and compare.

6. Given the following hypothetical data:

Cluster	X_{ij}
A	1, 1, 1
B	2, 2, 2
C	3, 3, 3

   (i) Calculate ρ and show it is equal to 1.

   (ii) Calculate $V(\hat{\bar{X}})$ and show it is equal to 1/6.

   (iii) Calculate S_{1b}^2 and S_{2t}^2 and show they are equal to 1 and 0, respectively.

   (iv) Calculate $V(\hat{\bar{X}})$ from equation (5) and show it is equal to 1/6.

7. Discuss the implications of the relation

$$V(\hat{\bar{X}}_{cl}) = V(\hat{\bar{X}}_{ran})[1 + (\bar{n} - 1)\rho]$$

on designing a sample.

8.8 Allocation of the sample

In section 8.7, we compared cluster sampling with simple random sampling and found criteria of how to allocate m and $\bar{n}$. In this discussion, however, no mention was made of cost. What we shall do in this section is to consider the optimum allocation of m and $\bar{n}$ given a fixed budget. By optimum allocation, we shall mean an allocation that has minimum variance given a fixed budget. Hence, our first problem is to define a cost function.

(i) Cost function.

The simplest cost function is obtained when we assume c_1 and c_2 to be the cost of selecting a psu and ssu, respectively, and that the relation is linear. That is,

(1) $$c = c_1 m + c_2 m\bar{n}$$

where c is total cost. If the fixed cost is denoted by c_0, we may include this and write

$$c = c_0 + c_1 m + c_2 m\bar{n}$$

but since it will have no effect on the problem of allocating the sample, we shall omit c_0 from our subsequent discussion.

(ii) Optimum allocation.

The variance for cluster sampling was

(2) $$V(\hat{\bar{X}}) = \frac{M - m}{M} \frac{S_{1b}^2}{m} + \frac{\bar{N} - \bar{n}}{\bar{N}} \frac{S_{2i}^2}{m\bar{n}}$$

and the cost function above was

(1) $$c = c_1 m + c_2 m\bar{n}$$

The problem of finding the optimum allocation therefore becomes a problem of finding the values of m and $\bar{n}$ that minimize $V(\hat{\bar{X}})$ given the budget constraint (1). We may easily find m and $\bar{n}$ by the Lagrange multiplier technique. As derived in Reference 1, $\bar{n}$ is:

(3) $$\bar{n} = \sqrt{\frac{c_1}{c_2} \frac{S_{2i}^2}{S_{1b}^2 - (S_{2i}^2/\bar{N})}}$$

and m may be obtained by substituting this value into the cost function and solving for m.

When $\bar{n} \ll \bar{N}$, the variance becomes

(4) $$V(\hat{\bar{X}}) = \frac{M - m}{M} \frac{S_{1b}^2}{m} + \frac{S_{2i}^2}{m\bar{n}}$$

and when the Lagrange multiplier technique is applied, we find

(5) $$\bar{n} = \sqrt{\frac{c_1}{c_2} \frac{S_{2i}^2}{S_{1b}^2}}$$

Equation (5) shows that when $c_1 > c_2$ (when it costs more to sample the psu), we should take more of the ssu. When $S_{2i}^2 < S_{1b}^2$ (when it is more homogeneous within the clusters), we should take less of the ssu. This result is in accordance with our previous results concerning the intraclass correlation coefficient.

We can, in fact express (3) in terms of the intraclass correlation coefficient as follows (see Reference 2 for the derivation):

$$(6) \qquad \bar{n} = \sqrt{\frac{c_1}{c_2} \frac{1 - \rho}{\rho}}$$

Hence, as ρ becomes large, $\bar{n}$ becomes small, which is what we stated previously.

Reference 1

Derivation of equation (3). Letting λ be the Lagrange multiplier, we set

$$F = V(\hat{\bar{X}}) + \lambda(c_1 m + c_2 m\bar{n} - c)$$

$$(7) \qquad \frac{\partial F}{\partial m} = -\frac{S_{1b}^2}{m^2} - \frac{S_{2i}^2}{m^2 \bar{n}} + \frac{S_{2i}^2}{\bar{N}m^2} + \lambda(c_1 + c_2\bar{n}) = 0$$

$$(8) \qquad \frac{\partial F}{\partial \bar{n}} = -\frac{S_{2i}^2}{m\bar{n}^2} + \lambda c_2 m = 0$$

Multiply (7) by m and (8) by $\bar{n}$ and substract (8) $\times$ $\bar{n}$ from (7) $\times$ m. We get

$$(9) \qquad \lambda m^2 = \frac{S_{1b}^2 - (S_{2i}^2/\bar{N})}{c_1}$$

From (8) we get

$$(10) \qquad \lambda m^2 = \frac{S_{2i}^2}{c_1 \bar{n}^2}$$

Hence, from (9) and (10), we can find $\bar{n}$:

$$\bar{n}^2 = \frac{c_1}{c_2} \frac{S_{2i}^2}{S_{1b}^2 - (S_{2i}^2/\bar{N})}$$

$$(11) \qquad \bar{n} = \sqrt{\frac{c_1}{c_2} \frac{S_{2i}^2}{S_{1b}^2 - (S_{2i}^2/\bar{N})}}$$

After finding $\bar{n}$, we substitute this value into the cost function and solve for m.

Reference 2

Derivation of equation (6). We can, in fact, express (3) in terms of the intraclass correlation coefficient as follows. We know from equation (6) and (9) of section 8.7

$$(12) \qquad S_{1b}^2 = \frac{M\bar{N} - 1}{\bar{N}^2(M - 1)} S^2 [1 + (\bar{N} - 1)\rho]$$

$$(13) \qquad S_{2i}^2 = \frac{M\bar{N} - 1}{M\bar{N}} S^2 (1 - \rho)$$

These may be approximated by

(12')
$$S_{1b}^2 = \frac{M\bar{N}}{\bar{N}^2 M} S^2[1 + (\bar{N} - 1)\rho]$$

$$= \frac{1}{\bar{N}} S^2[1 + (\bar{N} - 1)\rho]$$

(13')
$$S_{2i}^2 = S^2(1 - \rho)$$

The term $S_{1b}^2 - S_{2i}^2/\bar{N}$ in (3) becomes

$$S_{1b}^2 - \frac{S_{2i}^2}{\bar{N}} = \frac{1}{\bar{N}} S^2[1 + (\bar{N} - 1)\rho] - \frac{1}{\bar{N}} S^2(1 - \rho)$$

$$= \frac{1}{\bar{N}} S^2[1 + (\bar{N} - 1)\rho - 1 + \rho]$$

$$= \frac{1}{\bar{N}} S^2(\bar{N}\rho) = S^2\rho$$

Substituting this into (3) gives us

(14)
$$\bar{n} = \sqrt{\frac{c_1}{c_2} \frac{S^2(1 - \rho)}{S^2\rho}}$$

$$= \sqrt{\frac{c_1}{c_2} \frac{1 - \rho}{\rho}}$$

Hence, as ρ becomes larger, $\bar{n}$ becomes smaller—which is as stated previously.

Problems

1. Suppose the cost of traveling to a cluster is $45, and that of interviewing the ssu in a cluster is $5. Assume that the fixed cost is $200 and a budget of $1200 has been provided. Assume also that from previous data we have an estimate for ρ of 0.1. How large should m and $\bar{n}$ be?

Notes and References

For further discussion of simple cluster sampling, see Hansen, Hurwitz and Madow(1953), Chapter 6. A detailed discussion of selecting an area sample is given on pp. 247–252, with an illustration of a Sanborn map. Also see Sampford (1962), Chapter 8; Deming(1950), Chapter 5; Kish(1965), Chapter 5. For discussion on an advanced level with proofs of formulas, see Cochran(1963), Chapters 9 and 10.

For an excellent discussion of the intraclass correlation coefficient, see Hansen, Hurwitz and Madow(1953), pp. 259–270. See their tables on pp. 264–265 for illustrative values of the intraclass correlation coefficient obtained from past surveys.

For further discussion of cost functions and their use in allocating the sample, see Hansen, Hurwitz and Madow(1953), pp. 270–302; Sampford(1962), pp. 175–182; Deming(1950), pp. 150–154; Cochran(1963), pp. 245–247; Kish(1965), pp. 263–272.

Chapters 5(Simple Random Sampling), 6(Stratified Sampling), 7(Systematic Sampling), and 8(Simple Cluster Sampling) are the basic chapters. The subsequent chapters are mainly extensions of these chapters and give the sampling techniques that are used most often in practice.

CHAPTER 9

Cluster Sampling (II):

Probability Proportional to Size

9.1 Introduction

In the previous sections, the probability of selecting a psu (cluster) was assumed to be $1/M$. For example, when $m = 2$ clusters (classes) where to be selected from $M = 4$ clusters (classes), the probability of selecting any cluster (class) was $1/M = 1/4$; that is, each class had the same probability of being selected.

Suppose, however, that there are 10, 20, 40, and 80 students, respectively, in the $M = 4$ classes. Assuming each student is of equal importance, it is intuitively obvious that a sample representative of the population cannot be selected by giving each cluster (class) equal importance, that is, a probability of $1/M = 1/4$. The problem we shall consider in this chapter is this: How should the sample be selected so that it is representative of the population and so that each element in the population is given equal importance when the cluster sizes vary?

Common sense indicates that when some classes are very large and others very small, the larger classes should be assigned larger probabilities of selection and given a greater chance of being selected. By using such a procedure, the probability of selecting sampling units (students) from the larger classes can be made equivalent to that of selecting those in the smaller classes.

As another example, suppose the food expenditures of families are to be estimated, and M cities (say, $M = 200$) are designated as the psu. From this, we shall select m(say, $m = 10$) cities as the sample, and from each of these cities, a certain number of families (n_i) are selected as the ultimate cluster. Some cities—such as New York City—have millions of people, whereas others—such as Madison, Wisconsin—will have only 100,000. In a case such as this, it would seem reasonable to assign larger probabilities to the larger cities so that the selected sample will be representative of the population and so that the chances of selecting families in New York City will be equivalent to that of selecting those in Madison.

In this chapter we shall consider the problem of selecting a sample representative of the population by assigning probabilities to the psu according to their size. The reason for designing such a sampling procedure is, of course, to obtain a method of selection that will provide unbiased estimators of the population mean and that will also have higher precision than the previous cluster sampling methods we have considered. We shall discover that this method of selection has these properties and has the further advantage of providing very simple estimators of the population mean and variance.

Let us now show what is meant by sampling with probability proportional to size (pps) with a simple illustration. Suppose there are five classes of students as shown in the following table.

Class (psu)	Size N_i	$\sum N_i$	Assigned range
A	5	5	1 − 5
B	7	12	6 − 12
C	4	16	13 − 16
D	15	31	17 − 31
E	6	37	32 − 37

A number between 1 and 37 is selected at random. The probability that a 1, 2, 3, 4, or 5 will be selected is 5/36. And when 1, 2, 3, 4, or 5 is selected, the first psu (class A) is selected. Hence the probability of selecting class A is 5/37. Likewise, the probability of selecting the ith class will be $N_i/\sum N_i$. Let us denote this by

$$(1) \qquad\qquad p_i = \frac{N_i}{\sum N_i}$$

Now suppose that $m = 2$ classes are to be selected and the number 14 is selected from the random number table. The third psu (class C) is then selected. To draw the second psu, another random number is drawn. Suppose the second random number drawn is 16. The third psu (class C) will then be selected again. That is, we are sampling *with replacement*. The reason for sampling with replacement is that the formulas for the mean and variance are simpler when this procedure is used.

Furthermore, when $m \ll M$, as is often the case, the probability of selecting the same psu repeatedly is small, and sampling with replacement is approximately the same as sampling without replacement.

After the psu (cities) are selected by pps and with replacement, the ssu (families) may be selected from the psu in several different ways. One way is to select the ssu with replacement, and another is to select the ssu without replacement.

When sampling the ssu without replacement from a psu, however, we must consider the case where the same psu may be selected two or more times since they are selected with replacement. When the same psu (class) is selected, a new subsample of ssu (students) is selected without replacement after replacing the ssu (students) that were selected when this psu (class) was selected the first time. Hence, some of the ssu (students) of the second subsample may be the same as those of the first subsample. But, as can be seen, these subsamples are statistically independent.

There are other ways of selecting ssu. For example, when the same psu is selected twice, the ssu that are selected the second time may be selected so that they are not the same that were selected the first time. The two subsamples will therefore not be statistically independent.

We shall in the subsequent discussion consider the case where the ssu are selected without replacement, and in a manner such that when the same psu is selected two or more times, the subsamples are selected anew each time so as to remain statistically independent.

9.2 Estimator of the population mean and total

In section 8.5, the estimator of the population mean was

$$(1) \qquad \hat{\bar{X}} = \frac{1}{N} \frac{M}{m} \sum_i^m \frac{N_i}{n_i} \sum_j^{n_i} x_{ij}$$

which was an unbiased estimator. In section 8.6, where we assumed

$$N_i = \bar{N} = \frac{N}{M} \quad \text{and} \quad n_i = \bar{n} = \frac{n}{m}$$

the estimator (1) became

$$(2) \qquad \hat{\bar{X}} = \frac{1}{m\bar{n}} \sum^m \sum^{\bar{n}} x_{ij}$$

The characteristic of (2) is that $\hat{\bar{X}}$ is simply the sample mean of a sample of size $m\bar{n}$ and that no weighting of any kind has been used to obtain $\hat{\bar{X}}$. An estimator of this type is said to be self-weighting.

A close investigation reveals that in a self-weighting sample, the probability of including a ssu of the population in the sample $m\bar{n} = n$ is equal for all members of the population. That is, the probability of a ssu being included in the sample $m\bar{n} = n$ is n/N. This may be shown as follows: Since m psu are selected from M psu by simple random sampling, the probability of any psu being included in the sample is m/M.

The probability of a ssu being included in the subsample $n_i = \bar{n}$ will be $\bar{n}/\bar{N}$. The probability of a ssu being included in the total sample $m\bar{n} = n$ is therefore

$$\frac{m}{M} \times \frac{\bar{n}}{\bar{N}} = \frac{m}{M} \times \frac{n/m}{N/M} = \frac{n}{N}$$

The two characteristics—(i) the probability of any ssu being included in the sample is equal to n/N, and (ii) the estimator of the population mean is simply the sample mean, needs no weighting, and is therefore easy to calculate—makes self-weighting estimators desirable.

Estimator (2) is desirable but, unfortunately, it is based on the restrictive assumptions that the cluster sizes are $\bar{N}$, and subsample sizes are $\bar{n}$.

Is there another way of estimating the population mean $\hat{\bar{X}}$ so that the above mentioned characteristics are retained while avoiding restrictive assumptions such as those of equation (2)?

The answer is yes. When cluster sampling with pps is used, the unweighted sample mean becomes an unbiased estimator of the population mean and will also be found to be more precise than the previous cluster sampling results.

This is clearly, a very useful and convenient result, because although the size of the cluster may vary, we merely need the sample mean as an estimator of the population mean. The cluster size enters only as a criteria when selecting the psu.

The first thing we notice when selecting the psu with pps is that we have here for the first time a selection procedure where the probability of selection of the psu vary. That is to say, in all our previous sampling procedures, the psu were sampled with equal probability $(1/M)$. In our present case, the psu are sampled with probability N_i/N. Let us first consider this new problem (the general problem of sampling with unequal probabilities), and then show how this is developed into sampling with pps.

Let us start with the following simple observation: Suppose $p = 1/4$ of a pie weighs $X = 10$ ounces. The whole pie will then weigh

$$\frac{X}{\hat{p}} = \frac{10}{1/4} = 40 \text{ ounces}$$

Suppose there are now $M = 3$ clusters, and each has X_1, X_2, and X_3 books. Then

$$X = X_1 + X_2 + X_3$$

is the total number of books. We wish to estimate X by selecting $m = 1$ cluster. Suppose we have selected X_1. If we know what proportion of the total X_1 is, as is seen in the pie illustration, we can easily estimate the total. Suppose $\hat{p}_1$ represents this proportion. Then

$$\hat{X} = \frac{X_1}{\hat{p}_1}$$

is the estimate. Since we have assumed $\hat{p}_1$ to give the proportion of the total, it may be written as

$$\hat{p}_1 = \frac{X_1}{X}$$

so that

$$\hat{X} = \frac{X_1}{\hat{p}_1} = \frac{X_1}{X_1/X} = X$$

and $X_1/\hat{p}_1$ estimates X exactly.

In general, we have

(3) $$\hat{X} = \frac{X_i}{\hat{p}_i}$$

and because $\hat{p}_i = X_i/X$, $\hat{X}$ is exactly equal to X.

However, it is obvious that the $\hat{p}_i$ are not known in sampling problems. We may know the *probabilities* of X_i instead. Let us denote these probabilities by p_i. Assuming that the p_i are good approximations of $\hat{p}_i$, we may then find the estimator as

(4) $$\hat{X} = \frac{X_i}{p_i}$$

Only when $p_i = \hat{p}_i = X_i/X$ will $\hat{X}$ be exactly equal to X.

The more p_i differs from $\hat{p}_i = X_i/X$, the greater the discrepancy between $\hat{X}$ and X. For example, suppose we have

$$X_i = 1, \qquad X_2 = 3, \qquad X_3 = 6$$

The proportion of X_1 is then $\hat{p}_1 = 1/10$, and the estimator based on X_1 becomes

$$\hat{X} = \frac{X_1}{\hat{p}_1} = \frac{1}{1/10} = 10 = X$$

But if the probability is $\hat{p}_1 = 3/10$, for example, and $\hat{p}_1$ is used instead of $\hat{p}_1$, then

$$\hat{X} = \frac{X_1}{\hat{p}_1} = \frac{1}{3/10} = \frac{10}{3}$$

and if $\hat{p}_1 = 6/10$ then

$$\hat{X} = \frac{X_1}{p_1} = \frac{1}{6/10} = \frac{10}{6}$$

and as is seen, $\hat{X}$ deviates further from $X = 10$. That is, the more p_i deviates from $\hat{p}_i$, the greater the deviation of $\hat{X}$ from X.

However, when using the probability p_i instead of the proportion p_i, an important sampling property is obtained. That is, the estimator $\hat{X}$ becomes an unbiased estimator of X. This is easily seen as follows.

$$\hat{X} = \frac{X_i}{p_i}$$

$$\therefore \quad E(\hat{X}) = \sum_{i}^{M} p_i \frac{X_i}{p_i} = \sum_{i}^{M} X_i = X$$

and $\hat{X}$ is thus an unbiased estimator of X.

Let us now explain the estimation process for a sample of $m = 2$ clusters and generalize our discussion one step further. Suppose X_1 and X_2 have been selected to estimate the total. Then X_1/p_1, X_2/p_2 are respective estimates of the total X. An estimate of the total may thus be obtained as an average of these estimates. That is,

$$\hat{X} = \frac{1}{2}\left(\frac{X_1}{p_1} + \frac{X_2}{p_2}\right)$$

(5)

$$= \frac{1}{m}\sum^{m}\frac{X_i}{p_i}$$

Formula (5) may be considered as a general formula for estimating X and is also an unbiased estimator of X. This may be shown as

$$E(\hat{X}) = \frac{1}{m}\sum^{m} E\frac{X_i}{p_i}$$

$$= \frac{1}{m}\sum^{m}\sum^{M} p_i \frac{X_i}{p_i} = \sum^{M} X_i = X$$

To obtain a graphic interpretation of this process, let us construct a sample space for the $m = 2$ cluster case. The sample space may be shown as in Fig. 9-1 It is a 2-dimensional sample space with $3^2 = 9$ sample points (since we are sampling with replacement).

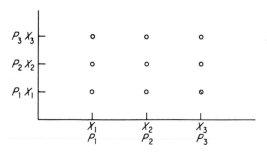

Fig. 9-1

Let us consider the sample point (X_1, X_2). The estimate $\hat{X}$ using this sample point is therefore

$$\hat{X} = \frac{1}{2}\left(\frac{X_1}{p_1} + \frac{X_2}{p_2}\right)$$

and the probability of selecting this point is $p_1 p_2$—and likewise for the remaining sample points.

Using these 9 sample points, the expected value of $\hat{X}$ may be calculated as follows:

$$E(\hat{X}) = \frac{1}{2}\left(\frac{X_1}{p_1} + \frac{X_1}{p_1}\right)p_1 p_1 + \frac{1}{2}\left(\frac{X_1}{p_1} + \frac{X_2}{p_2}\right)p_1 p_2 + \cdots$$

$$+ \frac{1}{2}\left(\frac{X_3}{p_3} + \frac{X_2}{p_2}\right)p_3 p_2 + \frac{1}{2}\left(\frac{X_3}{p_3} + \frac{X_3}{p_3}\right)p_3 p_3$$
$$= X_1 + X_2 + X_3 = X$$

and it shows again that $\hat{X}$ is an unbiased estimator of X.

The problem that remains is the reconciliation between the probability p_i and the proportion $\hat{p}_i$. The closer p_i is to $\hat{p}_i = X_i/X$, the greater the precision of the estimator. When $p_i = \hat{p}_i$, then $\hat{X} = X$ and the variance is zero. For example, suppose we select (X_1, X_2) as our sample, Then

$$\hat{X} = \frac{1}{2}\left(\frac{X_1}{p_1} + \frac{X_2}{p_2}\right)$$
$$= \frac{1}{2}\left(\frac{X_1}{X_1/X} + \frac{X_2}{X_2/X}\right) = X$$

and there is no discrepancy between $\hat{X}$ and X. This applies for all the other possible samples, and $V(\hat{X})$ will therefore be zero.

Thus the practical problem that remains is to determine p_i that will be close to $\hat{p}_i = X_i/X$. Since X is the unknown parameter which we want to estimate, $\hat{p}_i$ is also unknown. How then, shall we determine p_i?

One answer is to select psu with probability proportional to size, and "hope" that the probabilities will be close to $\hat{p}_i$. Let us explain why we may consider our "hope" to be reasonable. In our illustration in section 9.1, we had the following table:

Class psu	Size N_i	$\sum N_i$	Assigned range
1	5	5	1 – 5
2	7	12	6 – 12
3	4	16	13 – 16
4	15	31	17 – 31
5	6	37	32 – 37

The first class has $N_1 = 5$ students, the second class has $N_2 = 7$ students, and so forth. Suppose we are interested in estimating the total number of books these $N = 37$ students have. Let $X_1, X_2, \ldots, X_5$ be the number of books in the first, second, $\ldots$, fifth class, and let

$$X = X_1 + X_2 + \cdots + X_5$$

In our previous cluster sampling procedures, the psu (classes) were selected by simple random sampling, that is, each psu was assigned a probability of $1/M = 1/5$. We now wish to assign probabilities p_i that will be close to the proportions $\hat{p}_i$ in order to reduce the discrepancy between $\hat{X}$ and X as much as possible. Or, we may say we wish to reduce the variance of $\hat{X}$.

The psu are therefore selected with probability proportional to size, (pps), where the term "size" indicates the size of the psu in terms of N_i and *not* in terms of X_i. The next question thus arises: Is N_i/N a good approximation of X_i/X?

Let us analyze this question using the concepts of homogeneity and heterogeneity. We have discussed in the previous chapters that when the sampling units within a cluster are heterogeneous, the variation between clusters will become small, and we have seen that in this case the cluster means do not vary greatly. For example, suppose there are $M = 3$ clusters with the following sampling units:

	X_{ij}	X_i	$\bar{X}_i$
$N_1 = 2$	2, 8	10	5
$N_2 = 5$	1, 2, 3, 10, 10	25	5
$N_3 = 3$	1, 6, 8	15	5

As is seen, the variation within each cluster is large, but the cluster means are $\bar{X}_1 = \bar{X}_2 = \bar{X}_3 = 5$—there is no variation between cluster means. In this case, the cluster proportions are

$$\frac{X_1}{X} = \frac{10}{50}, \qquad \frac{X_2}{X} = \frac{25}{50}, \qquad \frac{X_3}{X} = \frac{15}{50}$$

The probability proportional to size N_i/N becomes

$$\frac{N_1}{N} = \frac{2}{10} = \frac{10}{50}, \qquad \frac{N_2}{N} = \frac{5}{10} = \frac{25}{50}, \qquad \frac{N_3}{N} = \frac{3}{10} = \frac{15}{50}$$

As is seen, $X_i/X = N_i/N$. We may express this result as follows: When the variation between cluster means is small, N_i/N is a good approximation of X_i/X.

The result that $N_i/N = X_i/X$ for the above example may also be shown as follows. Since $\bar{X}_1 = \bar{X}_2 = \bar{X}_3 = 5$, we also get $\bar{\bar{X}} = 5$. Hence,

$$\frac{X_1}{X} = \frac{N_1 \bar{X}_1}{N \bar{\bar{X}}} = \frac{N_1}{N}$$

and likewise for the other $X_i/X = N_i/N$.

Hence, when the variation between cluster means is small, sampling with pps will provide unbiased estimators with small variances.

Up to this point we have considered the sampling process of the psu. Let us now extend our result to the ssu. In terms of our example of estimating the total number of books, we first select the psu (classes), say $m = 2$ classes, and then from these $m = 2$ classes we select subsamples of n_1 and n_2 students. Using these subsamples of students, we estimate X_1 and X_2, which we shall denote by $\hat{X}_1$ and $\hat{X}_2$.

The subsamples n_1 and n_2 are selected by simple random sampling without replacement. Let the subsample total of books be

$$x_1 = \sum^{n_1} x_{1j} \qquad \text{and} \qquad x_2 = \sum^{n_2} x_{2j}$$

Then, from the simple random sampling theory the estimates of X_1 and X_2 become

$$\hat{X}_1 = \frac{N_1}{n_1}x_1 \quad \text{and} \quad \hat{X}_2 = \frac{N_2}{n_2}x_2$$

In general, we may express this result as

(6)
$$\hat{X}_i = \frac{N_i}{n_i}x_i$$

and we also know from simple random sampling theory that

$$E(\hat{X}_i) = N_i\bar{\bar{X}}_i = X_i$$

Let us now combine the results of the first stage psu process and the second stage ssu process by substituting (6) into (5). We find

(7)
$$\hat{X} = \frac{1}{m}\sum_{}^{m}\frac{\hat{X}_i}{p_i}$$
$$= \frac{1}{m}\sum_{}^{m}\frac{1}{p_i}\left(\frac{N_i}{n_i}x_i\right)$$
$$= \frac{1}{m}\sum_{}^{m}\frac{1}{p_i}\left(\frac{N_i}{n_i}\sum_{}^{n_i}x_{ij}\right)$$

which is the general result we seek where p_i is the probability of selecting X_i, and (7) is thus an unbiased estimator of X. This is easily seen by

$$E(\hat{X}) = E_i\left(E_j\frac{1}{m}\sum_{}^{m}\frac{1}{p_i}\hat{X}_i\right)$$
$$= E_i\left(\frac{1}{m}\sum_{}^{m}\frac{1}{p_i}X_i\right)$$
$$= \frac{1}{m}\sum_{}^{m}\sum_{}^{M}p_i\left(\frac{1}{p_i}X_i\right)$$
$$= \sum_{}^{M}X_i = X$$

Using (7), we may now very easily derive the estimators of simple cluster sampling and cluster sampling with pps as special cases. Let us start with the simple cluster sampling case. In our previous case of simple cluster sampling, $p_i = 1/M$. Substituting this into (7) gives us

(8)
$$\hat{X} = \frac{M}{m}\sum_{}^{m}\frac{N_i}{n_i}x_i$$
$$= \frac{M}{m}\sum_{}^{m}\frac{N_i}{n_i}\sum_{}^{n_i}x_{ij}$$

which is what was obtained for simple cluster sampling.

For cluster sampling with pps, we have $p_i = N_i/N$. Hence, (7) becomes

$$\hat{X} = \frac{1}{m} \sum^m \frac{N}{N_i} \frac{N_i}{n_i} x_i$$

(9)
$$= \frac{N}{m} \sum^m \frac{1}{n_i} x_i$$

$$= \frac{N}{m} \sum^m \frac{1}{n_i} \sum^{n_i} x_{ij}$$

which is the general formula for cluster sampling with pps. If $n_i = \bar{n} = n/m$, (9) simplifies to

(10)
$$\hat{X} = \frac{N}{m\bar{n}} \sum^m \sum^{\bar{n}} x_{ij}$$

For the estimator of the population mean, we get

(11)
$$\hat{\bar{X}} = \frac{1}{m\bar{n}} \sum^m \sum^{\bar{n}} x_{ij}$$

As is seen, (11) is simply the sample mean of the sample $n = m\bar{n}$ and is self-weighting. It is also an unbiased estimator of $\bar{X}$.

Since the $\hat{\bar{X}}$ is the sample mean of $n = m\bar{n}$, we shall denote it as

$$\hat{\bar{X}} = \bar{x}_{pps} = \frac{1}{m\bar{n}} \sum^m \sum^{\bar{n}} x_{ij}$$

Example 1. Given the following hypothetical population, estimate the population mean by cluster sampling with pps.

psu	X_{ij}	N_i	X_i	$\bar{X}_i$
A	1, 2, 3	3	6	2
B	5, 6, 6, 7	4	24	6
C	9, 9, 10, 11, 11	5	50	10
		12	80	

(i) Select psu with pps.

psu	N_i	$\sum N_i$	Assigned range
A	3	3	1 — 3
B	4	7	4 — 7
C	5	12	8 — 12

Select a sample of $m = 2$ psu. From the random number table, we get 2 and 11. Hence we select A and C. The probability of selecting A is $N_1/N = 3/12$ and the probability of selecting C is $N_3/N = 5/12$.

(ii) Select samples of $\bar{n} = 2$ from A and C by random sampling. Suppose we get the following:

A	C
x_{1j}	x_{2j}
$x_{11} = 1$	$x_{21} = 10$
$x_{12} = 2$	$x_{22} = 11$
$x_1 = 3$	$x_2 = 21$

(iii) Calculate $\bar{\bar{x}}_{pps}$.

$$\bar{\bar{x}}_{pps} = \frac{1}{m\bar{n}} \sum^{m} \sum^{\bar{n}} x_{ij}$$

$$= \frac{1}{2 \times 2}(3 + 21) = 6$$

The population mean is

$$\bar{\bar{X}} = \frac{\sum \sum X_{ij}}{N} = \frac{80}{12} = 6\frac{2}{3}$$

Example 2. Given the following hypothetical population, show that $E(\bar{\bar{x}}_{pps}) = \bar{\bar{X}}$.

psu	X_{ij}	N_i	X_i	$\bar{X}_i$
A	1, 2, 3	3	6	2
B	2, 2, 3, 5	4	12	3
C	4, 5, 6	3	15	5
		10	33	

To show that $E(\bar{\bar{x}}_{pps}) = \bar{\bar{X}}$, we need to select all possible samples and find the values of $\bar{\bar{x}}_{pps}$ and the associated probabilities. Let us first find all possible samples of $m = 2$ psu, and then find all possible samples of n_i taken from $m = 2$ psu.

(i) All possible samples of $m = 2$ psu.

Recall that we assumed that selection of the psu was with replacement. Hence, the number of all possible samples of $m = 2$ psu from A, B, C is $3 \times 3 = 9$.

$$\begin{array}{ccc} AA & AB & AC \\ BA & BB & BC \\ CA & CB & CC \end{array}$$

(ii) Assuming $\bar{n} = 2$, let us find all possible samples of $\bar{n} = 2$ taken from $m = 2$ psu respectively.

The following table gives $\bar{n} = 2$ for (A, A) and (A, B).

A	A	$\sum\limits^{m} \sum\limits^{\bar{n}} x_{ij}$
1, 2	1, 2	$3 + 3 = 6$
	1, 3	$4 = 7$
	2, 3	$5 = 8$
1, 3	1, 2	$4 + 3 = 7$
	1, 3	$4 = 8$
	2, 3	$5 = 9$
2, 3	1, 2	$5 + 3 = 8$
	1, 3	$4 = 9$
	2, 3	$5 = 10$

72

A	B	$\sum\limits^{m}\sum\limits^{\bar{n}} x_{ij}$
1, 2	2, 2	$3 + 4 = 7$
	2, 3	$5 = 8$
	2, 5	$7 = 10$
	2, 3	$5 = 8$
	2, 5	$7 = 10$
	3, 5	$8 = 11$
1, 3	2, 2	$4 + 4 = 8$
	2, 3	$5 = 9$
	2, 5	$7 = 11$
	2, 3	$5 = 9$
	2, 5	$7 = 11$
	3, 5	$8 = 12$
2, 3	2, 2	$5 + 4 = 9$
	2, 3	$5 = 10$
	2, 5	$7 = 12$
	2, 3	$5 = 10$
	2, 5	$7 = 12$
	3, 5	$8 = 13$

$$180$$

Using only (A, A) and (A, B) as an illustration, let us show the procedure for evaluating $E(\bar{\bar{x}}_{\text{pps}})$. For (A, A) we calculate

$$\frac{3}{10} \times \frac{3}{10} \times \left[\frac{1}{9}\left(\frac{6}{4} + \frac{7}{4} + \cdots + \frac{9}{4} + \frac{10}{4} \right) \right] = \frac{3}{10} \times \frac{3}{10} \times \frac{1}{9} \times \frac{72}{4}$$

That is, the probability of selecting A is $N_A/N = 3/10$ since we are sampling with pps. Furthermore, since sampling is with replacement, the probability of selecting (A, A) is $(3/10)(3/10)$.

The number of possible samples of $\bar{n} = 2$ for (A, A) is

$$\binom{3}{2}\binom{3}{2} = 3 \times 3 = 9$$

since sampling is without replacement. However, note carefully, after $\bar{n} = 2$ is selected from A, $\bar{n} = 2$ is replaced, and the next $\bar{n} = 2$ is again selected from A. Hence, the probability of selecting any one of these samples is 1/9. Thus, the portion of $E(\bar{\bar{x}}_{\text{pps}})$ with respect to (A, A) is as we have written above.

For (A, B), we get

$$\frac{3}{10} \times \frac{4}{10} \times \left[\frac{1}{18}\left(\frac{7}{4} + \frac{8}{4} + \cdots + \frac{12}{4} + \frac{13}{4} \right) \right] = \frac{3}{10} \times \frac{4}{10} \times \frac{1}{18} \times \frac{180}{4}$$

In this case, the probability of selecting B is 4/10, and the number of possible samples selected from A and B are

$$\binom{3}{2}\binom{4}{2} = 3 \times 6 = 18$$

Applying this procedure to the 9 possible samples AA, AB, AC, . . . , CB, CC we get,

$$E(\bar{x}_{pps}) = \left(\frac{3}{10}\right)\left(\frac{3}{10}\right)\left(\frac{1}{9} \times \frac{72}{4}\right) \qquad \text{for} \quad AA$$

$$+ \left(\frac{3}{10}\right)\left(\frac{4}{10}\right)\left(\frac{1}{18} \times \frac{180}{4}\right) \qquad \text{for} \quad AB$$

$$+ \left(\frac{3}{10}\right)\left(\frac{3}{10}\right)\left(\frac{1}{9} \times \frac{126}{4}\right) \qquad \text{for} \quad AC$$

$$+ \left(\frac{3}{10}\right)\left(\frac{4}{10}\right)\left(\frac{1}{18} \times \frac{180}{4}\right) \qquad \text{for} \quad BA$$

$$+ \left(\frac{4}{10}\right)\left(\frac{4}{10}\right)\left(\frac{1}{36} \times \frac{432}{4}\right) \qquad \text{for} \quad BB$$

$$+ \left(\frac{4}{10}\right)\left(\frac{3}{10}\right)\left(\frac{1}{18} \times \frac{288}{4}\right) \qquad \text{for} \quad BC$$

$$+ \left(\frac{3}{10}\right)\left(\frac{3}{10}\right)\left(\frac{1}{9} \times \frac{126}{4}\right) \qquad \text{for} \quad CA$$

$$+ \left(\frac{3}{10}\right)\left(\frac{4}{10}\right)\left(\frac{1}{18} \times \frac{288}{4}\right) \qquad \text{for} \quad CB$$

$$+ \left(\frac{3}{10}\right)\left(\frac{3}{10}\right)\left(\frac{1}{18} \times \frac{180}{4}\right) \qquad \text{for} \quad CC$$

$$= \frac{660}{200} = 3\frac{3}{10}$$

The population mean is

$$\bar{X} = \frac{33}{10} = 3\frac{3}{10}$$

Hence

$$E(\bar{x}_{pps}) = \bar{X} = \frac{33}{10}$$

Example 3. Suppose there is a small town with $M = 3$ schools, A, B, C with 20, 15, and 25 children, respectively. We wish to estimate the average pieces of chewing gum a child chews per day. Select $m = 2$ schools and $\bar{n} = 5$ children and estimate the average by cluster sampling with pps.

(i) Select $m = 2$ psu.

psu	N_i	$\sum N_i$
A	20	1 − 20
B	15	21 − 35
C	25	36 − 60

From the random number table, we find 25 and 39. Hence, we select B and C.

(ii) Select $\bar{n} = 5$ from B and C.

Using random sampling without replacement, suppose we get the following samples.

B x_{1j}		C x_{2j}	
x_{11}	3	x_{21}	4
x_{12}	5	x_{22}	6
x_{13}	4	x_{23}	4
x_{14}	5	x_{24}	4
x_{15}	3	x_{25}	3
x_1	20	x_2	21

(iii) Calculate $\bar{x}_{pps}$.

$$\bar{x}_{pps} = \frac{1}{m\bar{n}} \sum^m \sum^{\bar{n}} x_{ij}$$

$$= \frac{1}{2 \times 5}(20 + 21)$$

$$= 4.1 \text{ pieces per day}$$

Example 4. Suppose a city is divided into $M = 15$ districts and there are N_i supermarkets in each district. We wish to make a quick estimate of the total amount of a certain product in stock at these supermarkets. Let the N_i supermarkets be as in the following table:

District	N_i	$\sum N_i$
1	8	8
2	12	20
3	4	24
4	20	44
5	14	58
6	6	64
7	5	69
8	12	81
9	5	86
10	24	110
11	6	116
12	8	124
13	4	128
14	9	137
15	13	150
	150	

(i) Select $m = 6$ psu (districts) with pps.

We select 6 numbers from the random number table between $001 - 150$. We find 55, 148, 117, 70, 92, 113. Hence, from the $\sum N_i$ column, we select districts 5, 15, 12, 8, 10, and 11. Putting these in order, we have 5, 8, 10, 11, 12, 15.

(ii) Select $\bar{n} = 4$ ssu from each of these $m = 6$ psu.

District	x_{ij}	x_i	$\bar{x}_i$
5	2, 3, 2, 5	12	3
8	2, 5, 5, 4	16	4
10	1, 4, 8, 7	20	5
11	4, 8, 9, 7	28	7
12	1, 1, 6, 4	12	3
15	4, 3, 3, 6	16	4

$$104$$

Here we shall assume that x_{ij} show the amount of stock in units of 100.

(iii) Estimate $\bar{\bar{X}}$.

$$\bar{x}_{\text{pps}} = \frac{1}{m\bar{n}} \sum_i^m \sum_j^{\bar{n}} x_{ij}$$

$$= \frac{1}{6 \times 4} (12 + 16 + 20 + 28 + 12 + 16)$$

$$= \frac{104}{24} = \frac{13}{3} = 4\frac{1}{3}$$

(iv) Estimate X.

$$\hat{X} = N\bar{x}_{\text{pps}} = (150)\frac{13}{3} = 650$$

Example 5. Suppose we wish to estimate the average weight of a student at a certain school. Records of the weights are kept in $M = 200$ files, each containing $\bar{N} = 100$ records. Suppose we wish to select $m = 20$ files, and from each file we select $\bar{n} = 5$ records.

(i) Select $m = 20$ psu (files).

Since $\bar{N} = 100$, selecting the psu by random sampling is the same as selecting with pps. Hence, using the random number table, we shall select $m = 20$ psu.

If we can assume the order of the files and records are randomly ordered with respect to weights, an alternative and simpler way of selecting the $m = 20$ files would be to find the sampling interval $200/20 = 10$ and select a file at random from the first 10 files (say, for example, the 3rd file), and then to select every 10th file from that file on. That is,

3rd, $3 + 10 = 13$th, $3 + 10 \times 2 = 23$rd, $\ldots$, $3 + 10(20 - 1) = 193$rd

(ii) Select the $\bar{n} = 5$ records (ssu).

Use systematic sampling again. Find the sampling interval $100/5 = 20$ and select a record at random from the first 10 files (say, for example, the 7th record), and then select every 20th record from this 7th record on. That is,

7th, $7 + 20 = 27$th, $7 + (20 \times 2) = 47$th, $\ldots$, $7 + 20(5 - 1) = 87$th

(iii) Calculate $\bar{x}_{\text{pps}}$.

Suppose we get $\sum \sum x_{ij} = 15{,}000$ lb from $m\bar{n} = 20 \times 5 = 100$ records. Then

$$\bar{x}_{pps} = \frac{1}{m\bar{n}} \Sigma \Sigma x_{ij} = \frac{1}{100} \times (15,000) = 150 \text{ lb}$$

is the estimate of the average weight of a student.

Problems

1. In Example 2, the calculations for (A, A) and (A, B) have been worked out. Complete the calculations for the other 7 possible samples and verify the results of p. 249.

2. Given the following hypothetical population:

Cluster	X_{ij}
1	1, 2, 3
2	5, 5
3	9, 9, 10

   (i) Find that $\bar{\bar{X}}$ is equal to $44/8 = 362/64$
   (ii) Select $m = 2$ psu and $\bar{n} = 2$ ssu and find all possible samples.
   (iii) Find all possible values of $\bar{x}_{pps}$.
   (iv) Show that $E(\bar{x}_{pps}) = 352/64 = 44/8$ and verify that $E(\bar{x}_{pps}) = \bar{\bar{X}}$.

3. Suppose there is a small town with $M = 5$ schools. We wish to estimate the average amount of money a child spends for lunch. Select $m = 3$ schools and $\bar{n} = 5$ children and estimate the average expenditure by cluster sampling with pps, given the following data:

psu	N_i
1	70
2	50
3	80
4	40
5	60

   (i) Select $m = 3$ psu.

   (ii) Suppose the result is as in the table. Estimate the average.

x_{1j}	x_{2j}	x_{3j}
25¢	20¢	40¢
20	25	25
20	25	35
20	30	20
25	30	30

4. Suppose a state is divided into $M = 15$ districts and there are N_i farms in each district. We wish to make a quick estimate of the average number of hogs on each farm and of the total number of hogs in the state. Select $m = 5$ psu with pps and $\bar{n} = 4$ farms. Let the data be as follows:

District	N_i
1	9
2	13
3	11
4	16
5	7
6	14
7	13
8	6
9	18
10	9
11	12
12	10
13	8
14	16
15	14

x_{1j}	22	21	23	18
x_{2j}	15	18	28	13
x_{3j}	11	15	21	27
x_{4j}	18	20	16	16
x_{5j}	22	22	24	12

(i) Select $m = 5$ psu.

(ii) Calculate $\bar{x}_{\text{pps}}$ and $\hat{X}$.

5. Suppose there are $M = 20$ colleges in a certain state with N_i students in each college. We wish to estimate the average weight of a student. $m = 5$ colleges are selected according to pps, and $\bar{n} = 20$ students are selected from each college. Supposing we get the following data, find $\bar{x}_{\text{pps}}$.

College	N_i	$\sum\limits^{\bar{n}} x_{ij}$
1	600	3000 lb
2	800	3200
3	500	2900
4	900	3100
5	700	3300

6. Suppose we wish to estimate the average food expenditures per family per week in $M = 200$ cities. Select $m = 10$ cities according to pps and $\bar{n} = 30$ families in each city. Suppose the results are as follows. Estimate the average expenditures. The N_i is in units of 1000.

Cities	N_i	$\sum\limits^{\bar{n}} x_{ij}$
1	41	$1200
2	64	1050
3	34	1260
4	35	1140
5	121	1440
6	51	990
7	25	1110
8	115	1230
9	14	1320
10	287	1080

9.3 The variance of $\bar{x}_{pps}$

In this section we shall first present the variance of $\bar{x}_{pps}$, $V(\bar{x}_{pps})$, and then the estimator of $V(\bar{x}_{pps})$. The derivations of these equations are given in the reference.

(i) *The variance of* $\bar{x}_{pps}$.

The variance of $\bar{x}_{pps}$ is, by definition,

(1) $$V(\bar{x}_{pps}) = E(\bar{x}_{pps} - \bar{\bar{X}})^2$$

since $E(\bar{x}_{pps}) = \bar{\bar{X}}$. To evaluate equation (1) we need to find the expectation $E(\bar{x}_{pps} - \bar{\bar{X}})^2$. It turns out that this becomes (see reference)

(2) $$V(\bar{x}_{pps}) = \frac{1}{mN} \sum_{}^{M} N_i(\bar{X}_i - \bar{\bar{X}})^2 + \frac{1}{mN} \sum_{}^{M} (N_i - \bar{n}) \frac{S_i^2}{\bar{n}}$$

$$S_i^2 = \frac{1}{N_i - 1} \sum_{}^{N_i} (X_{ij} - \bar{X}_i)^2$$

As is seen, the first term on the right-hand side shows the variation between cluster means. The second term on the right hand side shows the variation of the ssu within the clusters. That is, S_i^2 shows the variance of X_{ij} within the ith cluster.

In our previous discussion of sampling with varying probabilities, we first considered the psu stage only. That is, we selected the whole cluster and discussed the estimation process. In terms of equation (2) above, this means $N_i = \bar{n}$.   Hence, the variance when the whole cluster is sampled and when only the psu stage is considered will be

(3) $$V(\bar{x}_{pps}) = \frac{1}{mN} \sum_{}^{M} N_i(\bar{X}_i - \bar{\bar{X}})^2$$

Recall that in our previous discussion where $m = 2$ classes were selected to estimate the total number of books, we found that when the average number of books per student in the $M = 3$ classes varied by only a small amount, the discrepancy between $\hat{X}$ and X was very small. In terms of equation (3) above, this means that when the variation between $\hat{X}$ and X is small, the variance of $\bar{x}_{pps}$ will be small. As is easily seen, this theoretical equation (3) also shows that when the variation between $\hat{X}$ and X is small—the $V(\bar{x}_{pps})$ will tend to be small.

Another theoretical result we notice is that in the second term we have $m\bar{n}$ in the denominator. Hence, the allocation of m and $\bar{n}$ will have no effect on the second term. However, the first term has only m in its denominator. Therefore, by making m large and $\bar{n}$ small, we can further reduce $V(\bar{x}_{pps})$.

This observation raises the question: when should m be large and $\bar{n}$ be small? Or we may say; how should m and $\bar{n}$ be allocated? We shall consider this question in section 9.4.

The characteristic of equation (2) from a practical point of view is that the knowledge of X_{ij} for N_i and all M is required and this makes its computations impractical. So let us next find the sample estimator of $V(\bar{x}_{pps})$.

(*ii*) *Unbiased estimator of* $V(\bar{x}_{pps})$.

One of the attractive characteristics of sampling with pps is that the unbiased estimator of $V(\bar{x}_{pps})$ is very simple and easy to calculate. It is (see reference 1 for derivation):

$$ (4) \qquad \hat{V}(\bar{x}_{pps}) = \frac{1}{m(m-1)} \sum_{}^{m} (\bar{x}_i - \bar{x}_{pps})^2 $$

$$ (5) \qquad \bar{x}_i = \frac{x_i}{\bar{n}} $$

$$ (6) \qquad \bar{x}_{pps} = \frac{1}{m\bar{n}} \sum_{}^{m} \sum_{}^{\bar{n}} x_{ij} = \frac{1}{m} \sum_{}^{m} \bar{x}_i $$

For example, $\bar{x}_i$ is the average number of books a student has in the ith ultimate cluster, and $\bar{x}_{pps}$ is then the average number of books a student has in the total sample. The estimate (4) shows the variance between ultimate clusters. That is, the estimator depends only on the variation between ultimate clusters and not on the variation within an ultimate cluster.

This is indeed a very useful result for sample design. It shows that by making the sampling units within clusters heterogeneous and the variation between cluster means small, we may reduce $\hat{V}(\bar{x}_{pps})$. This would indicate that it would be advisable to select more of $\bar{n}$ and less of m.

For example, when cities are used as clusters (psu), select fewer of these cities and more of the sampling units (for example, families) from the selected cities. This is also generally less expensive. We shall consider these points again in section 9.4.

Let us give several hypothetical examples to illustrate the use of the equations and calculation procedures.

Example 1. Using the data in Example 1, section 9.2, calculate $V(\bar{x}_{pps})$

psu	X_{ij}	N_i	X_i	$\bar{X}_i$
A	1, 2, 3	3	6	2
B	5, 6, 6, 7	4	24	6
C	9, 9, 10, 11, 11	5	50	10
		12	80	

The first term on the right side of equation (2) of $V(\bar{x}_{pps})$ becomes

$$ \frac{1}{mN} \sum_{}^{M} N_i(\bar{X}_i - \bar{X})^2 = \frac{1}{2 \times 12} \times \frac{368}{3} = \frac{46}{9} $$

The second term becomes

$$ \frac{1}{mN} \sum_{}^{M} (N_i - \bar{n}) \frac{S_i^2}{\bar{n}} = \frac{1}{2 \times 12}\left(\frac{8}{3}\right) = \frac{1}{9} $$

Thus, $V(\bar{x}_{pps})$ becomes

$$V(\bar{x}_{pps}) = \frac{46}{9} + \frac{1}{9} = \frac{47}{9} = 5\frac{2}{9}$$

Example 2. Using the data in Example 1, select a sample by pps and calculate $\hat{V}(\bar{x}_{pps})$.

(i) Select $m = 2$ psu and $\bar{n} = 2$.

Suppose we select

A		C	
x_{1j}		x_{2j}	
x_{11}	1	x_{21}	10
x_{12}	2	x_{22}	11
x_1	3	x_2	21

$$\bar{x}_{pps} = \frac{1}{m\bar{n}} \sum^m \sum^{\bar{n}} x_{ij} = \frac{1}{2 \times 2}(3 + 21) = 6$$

We also find that $\bar{x}_1 = 3/2$, $\bar{x}_2 = 21/2$. Hence

$$\hat{V}(\bar{x}_{pps}) = \frac{1}{2}\left[\left(\frac{3}{2} - 6\right)^2 + \left(\frac{21}{2} - 6\right)^2\right]$$

$$= \frac{1}{2} \times \frac{81}{2} = 20\frac{1}{4}$$

$$\therefore \quad s(\bar{x}_{pps}) = 4.5$$

Example 3. Using the data in Example 3, section 9.1, estimate $V(\bar{x}_{pps})$. First find $\bar{x}_{pps}$.

$$\bar{x}_{pps} = \frac{x}{n} = \frac{41}{10} = 4.1$$

Since $\bar{x}_1 = 20/5 = 4$ and $\bar{x}_2 = 21/5 = 4.2$, we find

	B	C
	x_{1j}	x_{2j}
	3	4
	5	6
	4	4
	5	4
	3	3
	20	21

$$\hat{V}(\bar{x}_{pps}) = \frac{1}{2(2 - 1)}[(4 - 4.1)^2 + (4.2 - 4.1)^2] = 0.01$$

$$\therefore \quad s(\bar{x}_{pps}) = \sqrt{0.01} = 0.1$$

Example 4. For calculation purposes, $\hat{V}(\bar{x}_{pps})$ may be rewritten as follows:

$$\hat{V}(\bar{x}_{pps}) = \frac{1}{m(m - 1)} \sum^m (\bar{x}_i - \bar{x}_{pps})^2$$

$$= \frac{1}{m(m - 1)}\left[\sum^m \bar{x}_i^2 - m\bar{x}_{pps}^2\right]$$

The terms $\sum^m \bar{x}^2$ and $m\bar{x}_{pps}^2$ may either be rewritten or used as is. Since $\bar{x}_{pps}$ is usually calculated first, a single worksheet may be set up to calculate $\bar{x}_{pps}$ and $\hat{V}(\bar{x}_{pps})$. For this purpose, we may rewrite $\sum\limits^m \bar{x}_i^2$ as follows.

$$\sum^m \bar{x}_i^2 = \sum^m \left(\frac{x_i}{\bar{n}}\right)^2 = \frac{1}{\bar{n}^2}\sum^m x_i^2$$

Since

$$\bar{x}_{pps} = \frac{1}{m\bar{n}}\sum^m \sum^{\bar{n}} x_{ij} = \frac{1}{m\bar{n}}\sum^m x_i$$

the term $m\bar{x}_{pps}^2$ becomes

$$m\bar{x}_{pps}^2 = \frac{1}{m\bar{n}^2}\left(\sum^m x_i\right)^2$$

Hence, we may set up the following worksheet.

A	B		
x_{1j}	x_{2j}		
x_{11}	x_{21}		
x_{12}	x_{22}		
.	.		
.	.		
.	.		
$x_{1\bar{n}}$	$x_{2\bar{n}}$		
x_1	x_2	$\sum x_i$	$(\sum x_i)^2$
x_1^2	x_2^2	$\sum x_i^2$	

$$\bar{x}_{pps} = \frac{1}{m\bar{n}}\sum x_i$$

$$\hat{V}(\bar{x}_{pps}) = \frac{1}{m(m-1)}\left[\frac{1}{\bar{n}^2}\sum^m x_i^2 - \frac{1}{m\bar{n}^2}(\sum x_i)^2\right]$$

$$= \frac{1}{m(m-1)}\frac{1}{\bar{n}^2}\left[\sum x_i^2 - \frac{1}{m}(\sum x_i)^2\right]$$

Using the data of Example 2, let us illustrate.

A	C		
x_{1j}	x_{2j}		
1	10		
2	11		
3	21	$\sum x_i = 24$	$(\sum x_i)^2 = 576$
9	441	$\sum x_i^2 = 450$	

$$\bar{x}_{pps} = \frac{1}{m\bar{n}}\sum x_i = \frac{1}{2\times 2}(24) = 6$$

$$\hat{V}(\bar{x}_{pps}) = \frac{1}{2(2-1)}\frac{1}{4}\left[450 - \frac{1}{2}(576)\right] = \frac{81}{4}$$

Problems

1. Using the hypothetical population of Problem 2 on page 252, answer the following questions.

Cluster	X_{ij}
1	1, 2, 3
2	5, 5
3	9, 9, 10

(i) Select samples of size $m = 2$ psu and $\bar{n} = 2$ ssu and calculate $V(\bar{\bar{x}}_{pps})$ from equation (2) and show it is equal to $V(\bar{\bar{x}}_{pps}) = 61/12 + 1/24 = 41/8$.

(ii) Select all possible samples and calculate all possible values of $\hat{V}(\bar{\bar{x}}_{pps})$ using equation (4).

(iii) Calculate $E[\hat{V}(\bar{\bar{x}}_{pps})]$ and show it is equal to $328/64 = 41/8$ and verify that $E[\hat{V}(\bar{\bar{x}}_{pps})] = V(\bar{\bar{x}}_{pps})$.

2. Using the data of Example 4 of p. 250, calculate $\hat{V}(\bar{\bar{x}}_{pps})$ and $s(\bar{\bar{x}}_{pps})$ and find the 2σ confidence interval for $\bar{\bar{X}}$.

3. Using the data of Problem 3 on page 252, calculate $\hat{V}(\bar{\bar{x}}_{pps})$ and $s(\bar{\bar{x}}_{pps})$ and find the 2σ confidence interval for $\bar{\bar{X}}$.

4. Using the data of Problem 4 on page 252, calculate $\hat{V}(\bar{\bar{x}}_{pps})$ and $s(\bar{\bar{x}}_{pps})$ and find the 2σ confidence interval for $\bar{\bar{X}}$.

5. Suppose we wish to estimate the average wages of sales clerks in the department stores of a certain city. There are $M = 15$ department stores, and a sample of $m = 4$ has been selected by pps. From each department store, $\bar{n} = 10$ sales clerks have been selected, and the following data has been obtained:

x_{1j}	\$61 64 64 69 75	72 70 60 60 60
x_{2j}	66 76 76 63 66	73 60 61 65 68
x_{3j}	64 61 63 68 72	63 63 57 69 73
x_{4j}	84 78 58 71 66	75 69 62 77 61

(i) Find $\bar{\bar{x}}_{pps}$.

(ii) Find $\hat{V}(\bar{\bar{x}}_{pps})$.

Reference 1

The variance of $\bar{\bar{x}}_{pps}$.

The variance of $\bar{\bar{x}}_{pps}$ is, by definition,

$$V(\bar{\bar{x}}_{pps}) = E(\bar{\bar{x}}_{pps} - \bar{\bar{X}})^2$$

since $E(\bar{\bar{x}}_{pps}) = \bar{\bar{X}}$. To evaluate this, we need to find the expectation of $(\bar{\bar{x}}_{pps} - \bar{\bar{X}})^2$. Our problem thus becomes one of transforming this squared term into factors for which we can find expectations. With this in mind, let

(7) $$\bar{\bar{x}}_{pps} - \bar{\bar{X}} = \left(\bar{\bar{x}}_{pps} - \frac{1}{m}\sum_{}^{m}\bar{\bar{X}}_i\right) + \left(\frac{1}{m}\sum_{}^{m}\bar{\bar{X}}_i - \bar{\bar{X}}\right)$$

$$= A + B$$

Squaring both sides, we find

(8) $$(\bar{x}_{\text{pps}} - \bar{\bar{X}})^2 = A^2 + B^2 + 2AB$$

Hence the variance of $\bar{x}_{\text{pps}}$ becomes

(9) $$V(\bar{x}_{\text{pps}}) = E(\bar{x}_{\text{pps}} - \bar{\bar{X}})^2$$
$$= E(A^2) + E(B^2) + E(2AB)$$

The expectation on the right side of (2) needs to be taken in two steps: the first step assumes the ith psu as given and the expectation is taken over j, while the second step is taken over all possible values of i. Let us start with the term 2AB. We first find

$$2AB = 2\left(\frac{1}{m}\sum_{}^{m}\bar{x}_i - \frac{1}{m}\sum_{}^{m}\bar{X}_i\right)\left(\frac{1}{m}\sum_{}^{m}\bar{X}_i - \bar{\bar{X}}\right)$$
$$= 2\frac{1}{m}\sum_{}^{m}(\bar{x}_i - \bar{X}_i)\left(\frac{1}{m}\sum_{}^{m}\bar{X}_i - \bar{\bar{X}}\right)$$

Let E_j denote the expectation taken over j with the ith psu as given. Then

$$E_i[E_j(2AB)] = E_i\left[E_j 2\frac{1}{m}\sum_{}^{m}(\bar{x}_i - \bar{X}_i)\left(\frac{1}{m}\sum_{}^{m}\bar{X}_i - \bar{\bar{X}}\right)\right]$$

Since A and B are independent (because the ultimate clusters are independent) and $E(\bar{x}_i) = \bar{X}_i$, we find

(10) $$E_j(2AB) = 0$$

as our first result.

For A^2, we find

$$A^2 = \left(\bar{x}_{\text{pps}} - \frac{1}{m}\sum_{}^{m}\bar{X}_i\right)^2$$
$$= \left(\frac{1}{m}\sum_{}^{m}\bar{x}_i - \frac{1}{m}\sum_{}^{m}\bar{X}_i\right)^2$$
$$= \frac{1}{m^2}\left[\sum_{}^{m}(\bar{x}_i - \bar{X}_i)\right]^2$$
$$= \frac{1}{m^2}\left[\sum_{i}^{m}(\bar{x}_i - \bar{X}_i)^2 + 2\sum_{i}^{m}\sum_{i \neq i'}^{m}(\bar{x}_i - \bar{X}_i)(\bar{x}_{i'} - \bar{X}_i)\right]$$

When the expectation of A^2 is taken, we therefore find

$$E_i(E_j A^2) = E_i\left[E_j \frac{1}{m^2}\sum_{}^{m}(\bar{x}_i - \bar{X}_i)^2 + E_j 2\sum_{i}\sum_{i \neq i'}(\bar{x}_i - \bar{X}_i)(\bar{x}_{i'} - \bar{X}_i)\right]$$

Since the ultimate clusters are independent, the second term on the right-hand side is 0. For the first term on the right-hand side, we get

$$E_i\left(E_j \frac{1}{m^2}\sum_{}^{m}(\bar{x}_i - \bar{X}_i)^2\right) = E_i\left(\frac{1}{m^2}\sum_{}^{m}\frac{N_i - \bar{n}}{N_i}\frac{S_i^2}{\bar{n}}\right)$$

where

$$S_i^2 = \frac{1}{N_i - 1}\sum_{}^{N_i}(X_{ij} - \bar{X}_i)^2$$

which is merely the standard error of the sample mean, $\bar{x}_i$, for simple random sampling. This then becomes (continuing from above):

$$= \frac{1}{m^2} \cdot m \cdot \sum^{M} \frac{N_i}{N} \frac{N_i - \bar{n}}{N_i} \frac{S_i^2}{\bar{n}}$$

$$= \frac{1}{mN} \sum^{M} (N_i - \bar{n}) \frac{S_i^2}{\bar{n}}$$

because there are M possible values of i and, according to our assumption, the probability of selecting the ith psu is N_i/N. Hence

(11) $$E_i(A^2) = \frac{1}{mN} \sum^{M} (N_i - \bar{n}) \frac{S_i^2}{\bar{n}}$$

The final result we seek is the evaluation of B^2. We first find

$$B^2 = \left(\frac{1}{m} \sum^{m} \bar{X}_i - \bar{X} \right)^2$$

$$= \left[\frac{1}{m} \sum^{m} (\bar{X}_i - \bar{X}) \right]^2$$

$$= \frac{1}{m^2} \left[\sum^{m} (\bar{X}_i - \bar{X})^2 + 2 \sum_i \sum_{i \neq i'} (\bar{X}_i - \bar{X})(\bar{X}_{i'} - \bar{X}) \right]$$

Since the psu are sampled with replacement, and

$$E_i(\bar{X}_i) = \sum^{M} \frac{N_i}{N} \bar{X}_i = \bar{X}$$

the second term on the right-hand side becomes zero. The first term becomes

$$\frac{1}{m^2} E_i \left[\sum^{m} (\bar{X}_i - \bar{X})^2 \right]$$

$$= \frac{1}{m^2} \cdot m \cdot \sum^{M} \frac{N_i}{N} (\bar{X}_i - \bar{X})^2$$

$$= \frac{1}{mN} \sum^{M} N_i (\bar{X}_i - \bar{X})^2$$

Hence the expectation of B^2 becomes

(12) $$E_i(B^2) = \frac{1}{mN} \sum^{M} N_i (\bar{X}_i - \bar{X})^2$$

Substituting (10), (11), and (12) back into (9) gives us

(13) $$V(\bar{x}_{pps}) = \frac{1}{mN} \sum^{M} N_i (\bar{X}_i - \bar{X})^2 + \frac{1}{mN} \sum^{M} (N_i - \bar{n}) \frac{S_i^2}{\bar{n}}$$

where

$$S_i^2 = \frac{1}{N_i - 1} \sum^{N_i} (X_{ij} - \bar{X}_i)^2$$

which is the variance of $\bar{x}_{pps}$ we seek. As is seen, the first term on the right side is the variance between the cluster means and the second term is the variance of the elements within the clusters.

Reference 2

Proof of $E[\hat{V}(\bar{x}_{\text{pps}})] = V(\bar{x}_{\text{pps}})$

Let us now show that (4) is an unbiased estimator of (2). For this, let us first make the following algebraic change.

$$\bar{x}_i - \bar{x}_{\text{pps}} = \bar{x}_i - \frac{1}{m} \sum \bar{x}_i$$

$$= \bar{x}_i - \frac{1}{m}\bar{x}_i - \frac{1}{m} \sum_{i' \neq i}^{m} \bar{x}_{i'}$$

$$= \frac{m-1}{m}\bar{x}_i - \frac{1}{m} \sum_{i' \neq i}^{m} \bar{x}_{i'}$$

Substituting this into (4) gives us

(14) $$\hat{V}(\bar{x}_{\text{pps}}) = \frac{1}{m}\frac{1}{m-1} \sum^{m} \left(\frac{m-1}{m}\bar{x}_i - \frac{1}{m}\sum_{i'\neq i}\bar{x}_{i'}\right)^2$$

$$= \frac{1}{m}\left[\frac{1}{m-1} \sum^{m} \left\{\left(\frac{m-1}{m}\bar{x}_i\right)^2 + \left(\frac{1}{m}\sum_{i'\neq i}^{m}\bar{x}_{i'}\right)^2 \right.\right.$$

$$\left.\left. - 2\left(\frac{m-1}{m}\bar{x}_i\right)\left(\frac{1}{m}\sum_{i'\neq i}^{m}\bar{x}_{i'}\right)\right\}\right]$$

(14′) $$= \frac{1}{m}(A + B - C)$$

What we shall do now is to reduce A, B, and C algebraically to a simpler form to which we can apply the process of taking expectations. Let us start with A.

(15) $$A = \frac{1}{m-1} \sum^{m} \left(\frac{m-1}{m}\bar{x}_i\right)^2 = \frac{m-1}{m^2} \sum_i^{m} \bar{x}_i^2$$

For B, we find:

(16) $$B = \frac{1}{m-1} \sum_i^{m} \left(\frac{1}{m}\sum_{i'\neq i}^{m}\bar{x}_{i'}\right)^2$$

$$= \frac{1}{m^2(m-1)} \sum_i^{m} \left(\sum_{i'\neq i}^{m}\bar{x}_{i'}\right)^2$$

$$= \frac{1}{m^2(m-1)} \sum_i^{m} \left(\sum_i^{m}\bar{x}_i - \bar{x}_i\right)^2$$

$$= \frac{1}{m^2(m-1)} \sum^{m} \left[\left(\sum\bar{x}_i\right)^2 - 2\bar{x}_i\sum^{m}\bar{x}_i + \bar{x}_i^2\right]$$

$$= \frac{1}{m^2(m-1)} \left[m\left(\sum^{m}\bar{x}_i\right)^2 - 2(\sum\bar{x}_i)^2 + \sum^{m}\bar{x}_i^2\right]$$

$$= \frac{1}{m^2(m-1)} \left[(m-2)\left(\sum^{m}\bar{x}_i\right)^2 + \sum^{m}\bar{x}_i^2\right]$$

$$= \frac{1}{m^2(m-1)} \left[(m-2)\left(\sum^{m}\bar{x}_i^2 + \sum_{i\neq i'}^{m}\bar{x}_i\bar{x}_{i'}\right) + \sum^{m}\bar{x}_i^2\right]$$

$$= \frac{1}{m^2(m-1)} \left[(m-1)\sum^{m}\bar{x}_i^2 + (m-2)\sum_{i\neq i'}^{m}\bar{x}_i\bar{x}_{i'}\right]$$

(16′) $$= \frac{1}{m^2} \sum^{m}\bar{x}_i^2 + \frac{m-2}{m^2(m-1)} \sum_{i\neq i'}^{m}\bar{x}_i\bar{x}_{i'}$$

For C, we get

(17)
$$C = \frac{1}{m-1} \sum_i^m \left[2\left(\frac{m-1}{m} \bar{x}_i\right)\left(\frac{1}{m} \sum_{i' \neq i}^m \bar{x}_{i'}\right) \right]$$

$$= \frac{2}{m^2} \sum_i^m \bar{x}_i \sum_{i' \neq i}^m \bar{x}_{i'}$$

(17′)
$$= \frac{2}{m^2} \sum_{i \neq i'}^m \bar{x}_i \bar{x}_{i'}$$

Substituting (15), (16′), and (17′) into (14′), we get

(18)
$$\hat{V}(\bar{x}_{pps}) = \frac{1}{m}\left[\frac{m-1}{m^2} \sum_i^m \bar{x}_i^2 + \frac{1}{m^2} \sum_i^m \bar{x}_i^2 + \frac{(m-2)}{m^2(m-1)} \sum_{i \neq i'}^m \bar{x}_i \bar{x}_{i'} - \frac{2}{m^2} \sum_{i \neq i'}^m \bar{x}_i \bar{x}_{i'} \right]$$

$$= \frac{1}{m}\left[\frac{1}{m} \sum_i^m \bar{x}_i^2 - \frac{1}{m(m-1)} \sum_{i \neq i'} \bar{x}_i \bar{x}_{i'} \right]$$

(18′)
$$= \frac{1}{m} D$$

We are now ready to take the expectation of $\hat{V}(\bar{x}_{pps})$. The expectation is taken in two steps: first for the case where the ith psu is given (that is, we are taking conditional expectations) and second, for the case where i varies over all possible M psu. We find

(19)
$$E[\hat{V}(\bar{x}_{pps})] = E_i\left(E_j \frac{1}{m} D\right)$$

$$= \frac{1}{m} E_i(E_j D)$$

so let us first consider $E_j D$. This becomes

(20)
$$E_j D = E_j\left[\frac{1}{m} \sum_i^m \bar{x}_i^2 - \frac{1}{m(m-1)} \sum_{i \neq i'} \bar{x}_i \bar{x}_{i'} \right]$$

$$= E_j(F - G)$$

The first term on the right-hand side becomes

(21)
$$E_j F = E_j\left(\frac{1}{m} \sum_i^m \bar{x}_i^2\right) = \frac{1}{m} \sum_i^m E_j \bar{x}_i^2$$

We know that for simple random sampling the following relation holds:

$$E(\bar{x} - \bar{X})^2 = E\bar{x}^2 - \bar{X}^2$$

which may be shown as

$$E\bar{x}^2 = \bar{X}^2 + E(\bar{x} - \bar{X})^2$$

$$= \bar{X}^2 + \frac{N-n}{N} \frac{S^2}{n}$$

Applying this relation to (21), we get

(22)
$$E_j F = \frac{1}{m} \sum_i^m \left(\bar{X}_i^2 + \frac{N_i - \bar{n}}{N_i} \frac{S_i^2}{\bar{n}} \right)$$

$$S_i^2 = \frac{1}{N_i - 1} \sum^{N_i} (X_{ij} - \bar{X})^2$$

The second term, G, becomes,

(23)
$$E_j G = \frac{1}{m(m-1)} E_j \sum_{i \neq i'}^{m} \bar{x}_i \bar{x}_{i'}$$
$$= \frac{1}{m(m-1)} \sum_{i \neq i'}^{m} \bar{X}_i \bar{X}_{i'}$$

This is so because the ssu are selected by simple random sampling, and we have assumed that in the event the same ith psu is selected repeatedly, the sample is replaced and drawn again independently from the ith sampled psu—$\bar{x}_i$ and $\bar{x}_{i'}$ are therefore independent.

Substituting this into (20) and (19), we find

(24)
$$E_i(E_j D) = E_i(E_j F - E_j G)$$
$$= E_i \left[\frac{1}{m} \sum^{m} \bar{X}_i^2 + \frac{1}{m} \sum^{m} \frac{N_i - \bar{n}}{N_i} \frac{S_i^2}{\bar{n}} - \frac{1}{m(m-1)} \sum_{i \neq i'}^{m} \bar{X}_i \bar{X}_{i'} \right]$$
$$= E_i(\mathrm{H} + \mathrm{J} - \mathrm{K})$$

Starting from H, we find

(25)
$$E_i(\mathrm{H}) = \frac{1}{m} E_i \sum^{m} \bar{x}_i^2$$
$$= E_i \bar{X}_i^2$$
$$= \bar{\bar{X}}^2 + \frac{1}{N} \sum^{M} N_i (\bar{X}_i - \bar{\bar{X}})^2$$

For J, we find

(26)
$$E_i(\mathrm{J}) = E_i \left(\frac{1}{m} \sum^{m} \frac{N_i - \bar{n}}{N_i} \frac{S_i^2}{\bar{n}} \right)$$
$$= E_i \frac{N_i - \bar{n}}{N_i} \frac{S_i^2}{\bar{n}}$$
$$= \sum^{M} \frac{N_i}{N} \frac{N_i - \bar{n}}{N_i} \frac{S_i^2}{\bar{n}}$$

Finally, for K, we find

(27)
$$E_i(\mathrm{K}) = \frac{1}{m(m-1)} E_i \left(\sum_{i \neq i'}^{m} \bar{X}_i \bar{X}_{i'} \right)$$
$$= \frac{1}{m(m-1)} m(m-1) \bar{\bar{X}}^2 = \bar{\bar{X}}^2$$

Thus, from (24), (25), (26), and (27), we find

(28)
$$E_i(E_j D) = \bar{\bar{X}}^2 + \frac{1}{N} \sum^{M} N_i (\bar{X}_i - \bar{\bar{X}})^2 + \sum^{M} \frac{N_i}{N} \frac{N_i - \bar{n}}{N_i} \frac{S_i^2}{\bar{n}} - \bar{\bar{X}}^2$$
$$= \frac{1}{N} \sum^{M} N_i (\bar{X}_i - \bar{\bar{X}})^2 + \frac{1}{N} \sum^{M} (N_i - \bar{n}) \frac{S_i^2}{\bar{n}}$$

Finally, substituting (28) back into (19) gives us

$$E[\hat{V}(\bar{\bar{x}}_{pps})] = \frac{1}{m} E_i(E_j D)$$
$$= \frac{1}{mN} \sum^{M} N_i (\bar{X}_i - \bar{\bar{X}})^2 + \frac{1}{mN} \sum^{M} (N_i - \bar{n}) \frac{S_i^2}{\bar{n}}$$
$$= V(\bar{\bar{x}}_{pps})$$

That is, (4) is an unbiased estimator of $V(\bar{\bar{x}}_{pps})$.

9.4 Allocation of the sample

We have left a problem unanswered up to this point: How to decide how many m psu are to be selected from M psu and how many $\bar{n}$ ssu are to be selected from each of the m psu. We wish to determine m and $\bar{n}$ such that $V(\bar{x}_{\mathrm{pps}})$, the variance, will be at a minimum.

As an example, consider estimating the average food expenditure of families in cities. There are M cities, and we need to determine how many cities (m) to select and how many families $(\bar{n})$ to select from each of these cities.

We saw in section 9.2 that when $n_i = \bar{n} = n/m$, the estimator $\bar{x}_{\mathrm{pps}}$ is simply the sample mean and, in section 9.3, $\hat{V}(\bar{x}_{\mathrm{pps}})$ was found to be very simple. Hence, for most practical problems, a uniform $\bar{n}$ is used instead of n_i.

Let us also assume for our discussion that m psu are selected with pps and that the ultimate clusters are all of the same size $\bar{n}$, and are selected by simple random sampling without replacement. The variance of $\bar{x}_{\mathrm{pps}}$ (from equation (2), section 9.3) is therefore

$$(1) \qquad V(\bar{x}_{\mathrm{pps}}) = \frac{1}{mN} \sum_i^M N_i(\bar{\bar{X}}_i - \bar{\bar{X}})^2 + \frac{1}{mN} \sum_i^M (N_i - \bar{n})\frac{S_i^2}{\bar{n}}$$

Assume we are given the following cost function:

$$(2) \qquad c = c_1 m + c_2 m\bar{n}$$

Our problem now becomes one of finding the values of m and $\bar{n}$ that will minimize the variance of (1) subject to the linear constraint (2). Using the Lagrange multiplier method (see reference 1), we find

$$(3) \qquad \bar{n}^2 = \frac{c_1}{c_2} \frac{S_{\mathrm{wt}i}^2}{S_{\mathrm{wtb}}^2 - (\bar{S}_i^2/\bar{N})}$$

or

$$(4) \qquad \bar{n} = \sqrt{\frac{c_1}{c_2} \frac{S_{\mathrm{wt}i}^2}{S_{\mathrm{wtb}}^2 - (\bar{S}_i^2/\bar{N})}}$$

where

$$(5) \qquad S_{\mathrm{wtb}}^2 = \frac{1}{N} \sum_i^M N_i(\bar{\bar{X}}_i - \bar{\bar{X}})^2$$

$$(6) \qquad S_{\mathrm{wt}i}^2 = \frac{1}{N} \sum_i^M N_i S_i^2$$

$$(7) \qquad \bar{S}_i^2 = \frac{1}{M} \sum_i^M S_i^2$$

$$(8) \qquad S_i^2 = \frac{1}{N_i - 1} \sum_i^{N_i} (X_{ij} - \bar{\bar{X}}_i)^2$$

The variation between clusters is shown by S_{wtb}^2 and, as is seen, it is weighted by the cluster sizes N_i. Hence, equation (4) shows that when the variation between clusters is large, we should decrease $\bar{n}$, and increase m. For example, suppose the variation of average expenditures of families between cities is large. Then (4) tells us to select more cities (m) and fewer families ($\bar{n}$) from each of the m cities.

We may consider $S^2_{\text{wt}i}$ as the weighted average of S^2_i. Since S^2_i shows the variation within clusters, we see from equation (4) that when the variation within clusters is small, we should keep $\bar{n}$ small. For example, when expenditures of families in a city are similar, S^2_i will be small and $\bar{n}$ will therefore also be small. In other words, when sampling units in the clusters are homogeneous, we should keep $\bar{n}$ small and increase m.

As shown by equation (4), $\bar{S}^2_i$ is also an average of S^2_i and may be interpreted in the same manner as $S^2_{\text{wt}i}$.

We know from c_1 and c_2 that when the cost of selecting a psu (c_1)(city) is large, we should take more of the ssu ($\bar{n}$)(families) and less of the psu (m) (cities). When the cost of selecting an ssu (c_2)(family) is large, take less of the ssu ($\bar{n}$) (families) and more of the psu (m)(cities). This clearly agrees with common sense.

The preceding formal analysis gives us an answer as to what $\bar{n}$ should be, but let us now reconsider equations (1) and (2) from a common sense viewpoint to see if we can obtain a better understanding and feeling of how to allocate m and $\bar{n}$, and let us compare it with the results of equation (4). The first point to note is as follows: from equation (1), we see that when the total sample size $m\bar{n} = n$ is given, the size of $\bar{n}$ has no effect on $V(\bar{x}_{\text{pps}})$. The second point to note is that, from equation (2), we see that when $m\bar{n} = n$ is given, $\bar{n}$ has no effect on the total cost. We can see that of the two elements (m and $\bar{n}$), it is thus the size of m that affects $V(\bar{x}_{\text{pps}})$ and the cost, c. Furthermore, from (1) and (2), we can see that the larger m is, the smaller $V(\bar{x}_{\text{pps}})$ becomes, but the greater the cost, c. Hence, the allocation of m and $\bar{n}$ becomes a problem of obtaining a balance between an increase in cost and a decrease in precision.

The equation (4) we derived mathematically gives us the value of $\bar{n}$ (and hence m) that will achieve this balance.

Another point that must be considered in equation (1) is that $V(\bar{x}_{\text{pps}})$ will be small when S^2_{wtb} and S^2_i are small. It would be desirable if both variances could be made small simultaneously. However, as discussed in Chapter 8, when the sampling units within a cluster are made homogeneous, the variation between clusters tend to become large and vice versa. In our present case, this means that when the between cluster variation (S^2_{wtb}) is small, the within cluster variation (S^2_i) will tend to become large. Should we try to make S^2_{wtb} small and S^2_i large? And, if so, why?

We already discussed in section 9.3 that when the between cluster variation is small, $\hat{X}$ will tend to be close to X and, as a result, the overall $V(\hat{X}_{\text{pps}})$ will tend to be small. This is equivalent to saying that when S^2_{wtb} is small, $\bar{x}_{\text{pps}}$ will be close to $\bar{X}$ and $V(\bar{x}_{\text{pps}})$ will tend to be small. Hence it will be desirable to have S^2_{wtb} small and S^2_i large rather than vice versa.

An example of sample design where heterogeneous sampling units are combined to construct heterogeneous psu may be found in the population surveys of the Bureau of Census. The procedure of the Bureau of Census is to first define psu which are made up of several counties and then combine them into strata. A single psu is then selected from each stratum.

In defining the psu, the Bureau of Census tries to increase the heterogeneity within the psu by making the psu large and by including counties with different characteristics (such as industrial or agricultural, urban or rural, etc). The characteristics which the Bureau of Census considers important to gain heterogeneity are the farm and nonfarm characteristics. On the other hand, the sizes of the psu are limited by cost of survey, and the psu are therefore kept between 1500 and 2000 square miles.

There are about 3000 counties in the U.S.A. grouped into about 2000 psu, which are in turn grouped into 68 strata. As mentioned before, 1 psu is selected from each stratum.

When $\bar{n} \ll N_i$, the variance of (1) becomes

$$V(\bar{x}_{\mathrm{pps}}) = \frac{1}{mN} \sum_{}^{M} N_i(\bar{\bar{X}}_i - \bar{\bar{X}})^2 + \frac{1}{mN} \sum_{}^{M} N_i \frac{N_i - \bar{n}}{N_i} \frac{S_i^2}{\bar{n}}$$

$$= \frac{1}{mN} \sum_{}^{M} N_i(\bar{\bar{X}}_i - \bar{\bar{X}})^2 + \frac{1}{mN} \sum_{}^{M} \frac{N_i S_i^2}{\bar{n}}$$

Using this, $\bar{n}$ will be found to be

(9)
$$\bar{n} = \sqrt{\frac{c_1}{c_2} \frac{S_{\mathrm{wt}i}^2}{S_{\mathrm{wtb}}^2}}$$

As shown, the term $- \bar{S}_i^2/\bar{N}$ in the right-hand denominator has been eliminated.

In practice, however, S_i^2, $S_{\mathrm{wt}i}^2$, S_{wtb}^2, and $\bar{S}_i^2$ are usually unknown, and we must use sample estimates of these parameters to find $\bar{n}$. We know the following estimators from previous discussion. For (8), we have

(10)
$$s_i^2 = \frac{1}{n_i - 1} \sum_{}^{n_i} (x_{ij} - \bar{x}_i)^2$$

For (5), we shall use

(11)
$$s_{\mathrm{wtb}}^2 = \frac{1}{m - 1} \sum_{}^{m} (\bar{x}_i - \bar{x}_{\mathrm{pps}})^2$$

This is obtained from equation (4) of section 9.3.

The estimator of $S_{\mathrm{wt}i}^2$ in (6), which may be considered as a weighted average of S_i^2, becomes

(12)
$$s_{\mathrm{wt}i}^2 = \frac{1}{n} \sum_{}^{m} n_i s_i^2$$

and $s_{\mathrm{wt}i}^2$ may be considered as the weighted average of s_i^2, which was defined in (10). The s_i^2, s_{wtb}^2, and $s_{\mathrm{wt}i}^2$ are usually obtained from a pilot survey.

The estimator of $\bar{S}_i^2$ in (7)—which may be considered as a simple average of S_i^2—becomes

$$(13) \qquad \bar{s}_i^2 = \frac{1}{m} \sum_{}^{m} s_i^2$$

Using estimates (11), (12), and (13), the sample size ($\bar{n}$) becomes

$$(14) \qquad \bar{n} = \sqrt{\frac{c_1}{c_2} \frac{s_{\text{wt}i}^2}{s_{\text{wtb}}^2 - (\bar{s}_i^2/\bar{N})}}$$

To find m, we substitute the $\bar{n}$ of equation (14) into the cost function

$$c = c_1 m + c_2 m \bar{n}$$

and solve for m, which may be expressed as

$$(15) \qquad m = \frac{c}{c_1 + c_2 \bar{n}}$$

Problems

1. Using the data of Example 4 on p. 250, suppose the cost of going to a district is $c_1 = \$10$ and that of visiting a supermarket and checking the stocks of a certain product is $c_2 = \$2$. Suppose also that the total budget is $130 and the fixed cost is $22. If we decide to select $\bar{n} = 4$ supermarkets from each district, how many districts m should we select? What is the total sample size?

2. Continuing Problem 1 above, suppose the sample is as given in Example 4, p. 250, and consider this a pilot survey.
(i) Calculate s_{wtb}^2 using equation (11).
(ii) Calculate $s_{\text{wt}i}^2$ using equation (12).
(iii) Calculate $\bar{s}_i^2$ using equation (13).
(iv) Calculate $\bar{n}$ using equation (14).
(v) Calculate m using the cost function.

3. Using the data of Problem 4 of p. 252, repeat the operations of Problem 2 above. Let the budget be $150, the fixed cost $30, $c_1 = \$10$, and $c_2 = \$2$.

Reference 1

Equation (4) of $\bar{n}$ is obtained in the following manner: We have

$$(16) \qquad V(\bar{x}_{\text{pps}}) = \frac{1}{mN} \sum^{M} N_i(\bar{X}_i - \bar{X})^2 + \frac{1}{mN} \sum^{M} (N_i - \bar{n}) \frac{S_i^2}{\bar{n}}$$

For brevity, let us set

$$(17) \qquad S_{\text{wtb}}^2 = \frac{1}{N} \sum^{M} N_i(\bar{X}_i - \bar{X})^2 = A$$

$$(18) \qquad S^2_{\text{w}ti} = \frac{1}{N} \sum_{i}^{M} N_i S^2_i = B$$

$$(19) \qquad \bar{S}^2_i = \frac{1}{M} \sum_{i}^{M} S^2_i = D$$

Substituting these into (1), we find

$$(20) \qquad V(\bar{x}_{\text{pps}}) = \frac{A}{m} + \frac{B}{m\bar{n}} - \frac{D}{m\bar{N}}$$

The cost function is

$$(21) \qquad c = c_1 m + c_2 m\bar{n}$$

Hence our problem becomes one of minimizing the variance of (20) subject to the linear constraint (21). Using the Lagrange multiplier method, we find

$$Z = \frac{A}{m} + \frac{B}{m\bar{n}} - \frac{D}{m\bar{N}} + \lambda(c_1 m + c_2 m\bar{n} - c)$$

$$(22) \qquad \frac{\partial Z}{\partial m} = -\frac{A}{m^2} - \frac{B}{m^2 \bar{n}} + \frac{D}{m^2 \bar{N}} + \lambda c_1 + \lambda c_2 \bar{n} = 0$$

$$(23) \qquad \frac{\partial Z}{\partial \bar{n}} = -\frac{B}{m\bar{n}^2} + \lambda c_2 m = 0$$

From (22) and (23), we find

$$(24) \qquad \lambda = \frac{1}{c_1}\left(A - \frac{D}{\bar{N}}\right)$$

From (23), we find

$$(25) \qquad \lambda = \frac{1}{c_2} \times \frac{B}{\bar{n}^2}$$

Hence, from (24) and (25), we can solve for $\bar{n}$:

$$\bar{n}^2 = \frac{c_1}{c_2} \frac{B}{A - (D/\bar{N})} = \frac{c_1}{c_2} \frac{S^2_{\text{w}ti}}{S^2_{\text{wtb}} - \bar{S}^2_i/\bar{N}}$$

And thus,

$$(26) \qquad \bar{n} = \sqrt{\frac{c_1}{c_2} \frac{S^2_{\text{w}ti}}{S^2_{\text{wtb}} - (\bar{S}^2_i/\bar{N})}}$$

We may find m by substituting (26) into (21):

$$(27) \qquad m = \frac{c}{c_1 + c_2 \bar{n}}$$

9.5 Comparison of $V(\bar{x}_{\text{pps}})$ with $V(\hat{\bar{X}}_{\text{cl}})$

The main reason for selecting the psu with pps is to obtain a more representative sample of the population and hence increase the precision of the estimators as compared to simple cluster sampling.

We have seen that the main difference between simple cluster sampling and cluster sampling with pps is that in the former, the psu are selected by simple random sampling whereas in the latter, it is selected by pps. The ssu are selected by simple random sampling in both cases.

Hence, if there is a difference in precision, we may expect it to be caused by the different selection procedures of the psu. Therefore, we shall compare $V(\hat{\bar{X}}_{cl})$ and $V(\bar{x}_{pps})$ by considering only the psu.

With these points in mind, let us compare $V(\bar{x}_{pps})$ with $V(\hat{\bar{X}}_{cl})$. The variance of $\bar{x}_{pps}$ was

$$(1) \qquad V(\bar{x}_{pps}) = \frac{1}{mN} \sum_{}^{M} N_i(\bar{\bar{X}}_i - \bar{\bar{X}})^2 + \frac{1}{mN} \sum_{}^{M} (N_i - \bar{n}) \frac{S_i^2}{\bar{n}}$$

and the variance of $\hat{\bar{X}}_{cl}$ was

$$(2) \qquad V(\hat{\bar{X}}_{cl}) = \frac{1}{N^2}\left(M^2 \frac{M - m}{M} \frac{S_b^2}{m} + \frac{M}{m} \sum_{}^{M} N_i^2 \frac{N_i - n_i}{N_i} \frac{S_i^2}{n_i}\right)$$

We shall set $N_i = n_i$ and eliminate the influence of the ssu on the variance. Then (1) and (2) become

$$(3) \qquad V(\bar{x}_{pps}) = \frac{1}{mN} \sum_{}^{M} N_i(\bar{\bar{X}}_i - \bar{\bar{X}})^2$$

$$(4) \qquad V(\hat{\bar{X}}_{cl}) = \frac{M^2}{N^2} \frac{M - m}{M} \frac{S_b^2}{m}$$

$$= \frac{1}{\bar{N}^2} \frac{M - m}{M} \frac{1}{m} \frac{1}{M - 1} \sum_{}^{M} (X_i - \bar{X})^2$$

Let us set $(M - m)/M = 1$ and $M - 1 \doteq M$. Then (4) becomes

$$(5) \qquad V(\hat{\bar{X}}_{cl}) = \frac{1}{m} \frac{1}{M} \sum_{}^{M} \left(\frac{X_i}{\bar{N}} - \bar{X}\right)^2$$

$$= \frac{1}{mM} \sum_{}^{M} \frac{(N_i\bar{\bar{X}}_i - \bar{N}\bar{X})^2}{\bar{N}^2}$$

Equation (3) may be rewritten as

$$(6) \qquad V(\bar{x}_{pps}) = \frac{1}{m} \sum_{}^{M} \frac{N_i}{N}(\bar{\bar{X}}_i - \bar{\bar{X}})^2$$

We may now compare $V(\bar{x}_{pps})$ with $V(\hat{\bar{X}}_{cl})$ using equations (5) and (6). As mentioned earlier, the pps procedure is mainly used when there are large variations in the cluster sizes N_i. We also argued that when the magnitude of the clusters X_i varies proportionally with N_i, the estimator $\bar{x}_{pps}$ can be expected to be close to $\bar{X}$. This pps sampling procedure is therefore most useful when this condition is satisfied.

With these points in mind, let us compare $V(\bar{x}_{pps})$ with $V(\hat{\bar{X}}_{cl})$ by subtracting one from the other. We have

$$(7) \qquad V(\hat{\bar{X}}_{cl}) - V(\bar{x}_{pps}) = \frac{1}{mM} \frac{\sum (N_i\bar{\bar{X}}_i - \bar{N}\bar{X})^2}{\bar{N}^2} - \frac{1}{m} \sum_{}^{M} \frac{N_i}{N}(\bar{\bar{X}}_i - \bar{\bar{X}})^2$$

$$= \frac{1}{m} \frac{\sum (N_i - \bar{N})}{N\bar{N}} \bar{\bar{X}}_i^2 + \frac{1}{m} \frac{1}{N} \sum (N_i - \bar{N})(\bar{\bar{X}}_i^2 - \bar{\bar{X}}^2)$$

The first thing we note in the above result is that when $N_i = \bar{N} = N/M$,

$$V(\hat{\bar{X}}_{\text{cl}}) - V(\bar{\bar{x}}_{\text{pps}}) = 0$$

and both procedures have the same precision. This is easily understood by noting that

$$\frac{N_i}{N} = \frac{\bar{N}}{N} = \frac{N/M}{N} = \frac{1}{M}$$

and the probability of selecting any one of the psu by pps is $1/M$— the same as selecting the psu by simple random sampling. Hence, we should expect that $V(\hat{\bar{X}}_{\text{cl}}) = V(\bar{\bar{x}}_{\text{pps}})$.

When N_i vary considerably, and when $V(\hat{\bar{X}}_{\text{cl}}) - V(\bar{\bar{x}}_{\text{pps}}) > 0$, the precision of sampling with pps is better than simple cluster sampling. To check this, we note that the first term on the right is

$$\frac{1}{m} \frac{\sum (N_i - \bar{N})^2}{N\bar{N}} \bar{\bar{X}}_i^2 > 0$$

As for the second term

$$\frac{1}{m} \frac{1}{N} \sum (N_i - \bar{N})(\bar{\bar{X}}_i^2 - \bar{\bar{X}}^2)$$

there are several points to consider. The first is that in cluster sampling, we usually wish to keep the variation between cluster means small, so as to reduce $V(\hat{\bar{X}}_{\text{cl}})$ or $V(\bar{\bar{x}}_{\text{pps}})$—as already explained on several occasions. Under the usual conditions, when pps is used, we may therefore expect that the absolute value of $(\bar{\bar{X}}_i^2 - \bar{\bar{X}}^2)$ will be relatively small compared to $\bar{\bar{X}}^2$ or $\bar{\bar{X}}_i^2$ alone.

The second point to note is that $N_i - \bar{N} < 0$ only when the cluster size N_i is small (which will be the case for about half the clusters). The second term will thus be the sum of terms alternating in sign, and each term will be small.

Therefore, we may expect that $V(\hat{\bar{X}}_{\text{cl}}) - V(\bar{\bar{x}}_{\text{pps}}) > 0$ under the usual conditions when sampling with pps is used. That is, the precision of sampling with pps will be better than that of simple cluster sampling.

Problems

1. Work out the algebraic details of equation (7).

Notes and References

As shown in this chapter, cluster sampling with pps is a very useful technique. In many cases, however, it is used with stratified sampling or extended to three stages. For example, the Census Bureau uses stratified cluster sampling with pps to estimate populations. These illustrations will be pointed out in subsequent chapters after additional sampling techniques are introduced. For the moment, the following references are recommended for further study. For a nontechnical basic discussion of the principles of cluster sampling, see Stuart (1962), pp. 67–98. For discussion on an advanced level see Kish(1965), Chapter 7. For a mathematical treatment see Cochran(1963), sections 9.9, 11.2, 11.3, 11.8, 11.9, and Chapters 9, 10, and 11 in general. Other comments may be found in Hansen, Hurwitz and Madow(1953), pp. 341–348; Yates(1960), pp. 167–169, 224–225; Deming(1950), pp. 393–396; Sampford(1962), pp. 170–175. The Deming reference is an illustration of cluster sampling as applied to a population survey of Greece and will be recommended again after Chapter 12, Stratified Cluster Sampling.

CHAPTER 10

Cluster Sampling (III):
Estimation of Proportion

10.1 Introduction

In many cases we wish to estimate proportions by cluster sampling. As an illustration, suppose we wish to estimate the proportion of students who smoke. We may have $M = 1000$ colleges from which $m = 10$ are selected by random sampling. And from these $m = 10$ colleges, subsamples of size $\bar{n} = 100$ may be selected. Using the data from these subsamples we wish to estimate the population proportion of students who smoke.

Many other examples of surveys seeking proportions may be cited. In market research, for example, the market share of a certain product may be sought. In opinion surveys, a candidate or newspaper may wish to estimate the proportion of voters in favor of a certain proposal. In industrial surveys, the proportion of defective products in a certain shipment may be sought. In population surveys, we may wish to know the proportion of unemployed, or that of families with two cars, etc.

In these various cases of finding the proportion, the simple cluster sampling for proportions we are going to discuss in this chapter is quite often used with other techniques, such as cluster sampling with pps, 3-stage cluster sampling, or stratified cluster sampling. Our object in this chapter, however, will be to obtain a basic knowledge of cluster sampling for proportions.

To prepare for our subsequent discussion, let us first establish some new notation with an illustration. Suppose we wish to find the proportion of students who smoke and set $X_{ij} = 1$ for smoker and $X_{ij} = 0$ for a non-smoker. Let there be M classes. Then

$$X_1 = \sum_{j}^{N_1} X_{1j} = A_1$$

will be the number of smokers in class 1. The proportion of smokers in class (psu) 1 will therefore be

$$P_1 = \frac{A_1}{N_1} = \frac{\sum\limits_{j}^{N_1} X_{1j}}{N_1} = \frac{X_1}{N_1}$$

Or, in general, the proportion of smokers in class (psu) i is

(1) $$P_i = \frac{X_i}{N_i}$$

We also define

(2) $$Q_i = 1 - P_i$$

which is the proportion of nonsmokers in class (psu) i.

The population proportions P and Q are defined as

(3) $$P = \frac{X}{N} = \frac{\sum\limits_{i}^{M} X_i}{N} = \frac{\sum\limits_{i}^{M} N_i P_i}{N}$$

$$Q = 1 - P$$

Suppose a subsample n_i is drawn from N_i. The subsample proportion P_i is then

(4) $$p_i = \frac{a_i}{n_i} = \frac{\sum\limits_{j}^{n_i} x_{ij}}{n_i} = \frac{x_i}{n_i}$$

With this background, let us now show how the population proportion is estimated. We shall find that the various estimators for proportions we seek will be very easily obtained by letting $X_{ij} = 1$ or 0 in the formulas we have already derived for the mean and variance in cluster sampling, where $X_{ij} = 1$ when the element has the characteristic, and $X_{ij} = 0$ when it does not. This procedure is the same as that used for proportions in Chapter 5, Simple Random Sampling.

10.2 Estimation of the population proportion

Our problem is to estimate the population proportion P with subsample proportions p_i. For example, suppose we wish to estimate the proportion of smokers in M classes. A sample of m (e.g., $m = 3$) classes (psu) is selected, and from these $m = 3$ classes, subsamples of $n_1, n_2,$ and n_3 $(n = n_1 + n_2 + n_3)$ students are selected. From each subsample, we can calculate the p_i. Using this, we wish to estimate P.

Noting that a proportion is a special case of the mean where the variable $X_{ij} = 1$ or 0, let us start with the cluster sampling estimator of the population mean we have already found. That was

(1) $$\hat{\bar{X}} = \frac{M}{Nm} \sum\limits_{i}^{m} \frac{N_i}{n_i} \sum\limits_{j}^{n_i} x_{ij}$$

Substituting the result of (4), section 10.1 into (1), we find

$$\hat{\bar{X}} = \frac{M}{Nm} \sum_{}^{m} N_i p_i$$

which is the estimator of P we seek. We shall denote $\hat{P}$ as the estimator of P. Hence we have

(2) $$\hat{P} = \frac{M}{Nm} \sum_i^m N_i p_i$$

Let us interpret equation (2) to obtain a better understanding of it. The term $N_i p_i$ is an estimate of the number of smokers in class i. Hence, $\sum N_i p_i$ is an estimate of the total number of smokers in the $m = 3$ classes.

The term $(1/m) \sum N_i p_i$ is therefore an estimate of the average number of smokers per cluster. Since there are M classes, $(M/m) \sum N_i p_i$ is an estimate of the total number of smokers for the M classes. Since there are a total of N students, an estimate of the proportion of students who also are smokers is obtained by dividing $(M/m) \sum N_i p_i$ by N, which is equation (2) above.

Equation (2) is an unbiased estimator of P. This may be shown by taking its expectation in two steps as follows:

$$E(\hat{P}) = E_i\left(E_j \frac{M}{Nm} \sum^m N_i p_i\right)$$

$$= E_i\left(\frac{M}{Nm} \sum^m N_i P_i\right)$$

$$= \frac{M}{Nm} \cdot m \sum^M \frac{1}{M} N_i P_i$$

$$= \frac{\sum^M N_i P_i}{N} = P$$

In some cases we may assume that $\bar{N} = N_i = N/M$. For example, suppose the M classes are about equal in size so that we may assume there are $\bar{N} = N_i = 50$ (for example) students in each of the $M = 10$ (for example) classes. Or, as another example, we may wish to estimate the proportion of customers who have unpaid accounts in excess of \$100 at a department store. Suppose the entry for each customer consists of a line in a record book which has 400 pages with 30 lines per page. Then $M = 400$ and $\bar{N} = N_i = 30$.

In these cases, the estimator $\hat{P}$ in (2) becomes

(3) $$\hat{P} = \frac{M}{Nm} \sum^m N_i p_i = \frac{1}{\bar{N}m} \sum^m \bar{N} p_i = \frac{1}{m} \sum^m p_i$$

Hence, the estimation procedure of $\hat{P}$ and $\hat{\bar{X}}$ become the same. That is, to estimate P, we merely need to find the average of the p_i.

In some cases, we may further assume that $\bar{n} = n_i = n/m$. For example, subsamples of $\bar{n} = 10$ students may be selected from each of the m classes. In this case, p_i becomes

$$p_i = \frac{a_i}{\bar{n}} = \frac{x_i}{\bar{n}}$$

Hence, $\hat{P}$ of (3) becomes

(4) $$\hat{P} = \frac{1}{m}\sum_{i}^{m} p_i = \frac{1}{m\bar{n}}\sum_{i}^{m} x_i$$

Example 1. Using the data in Example 4, section 9.2, suppose we wish to estimate the proportion of supermarkets that stay open after 7 PM. Then $X_{ij} = 1$ or 0, and when $X_{ij} = 1$, it means that the jth supermarket of the ith cluster stays open after 7 PM. Suppose the data in Example 4 gives us:

District	N_i	x_{ij}	x_i	p_i	$N_i p_i$
#5	14	1, 1, 0, 1	3	3/4	42/4
8	12	0, 1, 0, 1	2	2/4	24/4
10	24	0, 0, 1, 0	1	1/4	24/4
11	6	1, 1, 0, 1	3	3/4	18/4
12	8	1, 1, 1, 1	4	4/4	32/4
15	13	0, 0, 1, 1	2	2/4	26/4
			15		166/4

(i) Calculate the p_i (the results are given in the table).

(ii) Calculate $\hat{P}$ from equation (2).

$$\hat{P} = \frac{M}{Nm}\sum_{i}^{m} N_i p_i$$

$$= \frac{15}{150 \times 6}\left[\left(14 \times \frac{3}{4}\right) + \left(12 \times \frac{2}{4}\right) + \left(24 \times \frac{1}{4}\right)\right.$$

$$\left. + \left(6 \times \frac{3}{4}\right) + \left(8 \times \frac{4}{4}\right) + \left(13 \times \frac{2}{4}\right)\right]$$

$$= \frac{83}{120}$$

Example 2. Suppose we wish to estimate the proportion of families owning T.V. sets in cities of a certain state. Suppose there are $M = 50$ cities with a total of $N = 160{,}000$ families, and a random sample of $m = 4$ cities (psu) is selected.

Cities	N_i	$\bar{n}$	p_i	$N_i p_i$
A	1000	100	0.70	700
B	2000	100	0.75	1500
C	3000	100	0.80	2400
D	4000	100	0.85	3400
				8000

Samples of size $\bar{n} = 100$ are selected from the $m = 4$ cities and the sample proportions p_i are calculated as shown in the table. Then $\hat{P}$ becomes

$$\hat{P} = \frac{M}{Nm}\sum_{i}^{m} N_i p_i = \frac{50}{160{,}000 \times 4}(8000) = \frac{5}{8} = 0.625$$

The reader may have noticed that this estimate of $\hat{P} = 0.625$ is smaller than any p_i in the table. Why?

To answer this question, let us analyze our estimating equation by dividing it into four steps. The first is $\sum N_i p_i$, where $N_i p_i$ is the estimated number of families with T.V. for cluster N_i, and $\sum N_i p_i$ is therefore an estimate of the total number of families owning T.V. sets for the $m = 4$ cities.

The second step is $(1/m) \sum N_i p_i$, which gives an estimate of the average number of families with T.V. sets per cluster.

The third step is $(M/m) \sum N_i p_i$, which gives the estimated number of families with T.V. sets for the $M = 50$ clusters.

Since there are $N = 160,000$ families, the estimate of the proportion is found by $(M/Nm) \sum N_i p_i$—which is the fourth step.

In the above, the second step $(1/m) \sum N_i p_i$ is the villain in our story. It gave the average number of families with T.V. sets *per cluster*. The assumption is that this "per cluster" is a reasonable estimate of the average size of a cluster. Based on this assumption, in the next step, we multiplied $(1/m) \sum N_i p_i$ by $M = 50$.

We can easily see that if the sampled N_i are smaller than $N/M = \bar{N}$, $(1/m) \sum N_i p_i$ will underestimate the true average number of set-owning families per cluster. In our present case, the average number of families per cluster is $N/M = 160,000/50 = 3200$.

However, in our hypothetical example only D is larger than 3200. In fact, the average of A, B, C, and D is only 2500. As a result, $(1/m) \sum N_i p_i$ assumes an average cluster size of 2500 which is much smaller than the average of $N/M = 3200$ families per cluster, and hence underestimates the average number of families with T.V. sets per cluster. Thus, when this is multiplied by $M = 50$, it underestimates the total number of families with T.V. sets. As a result, the proportion $\hat{P}$ obtained by dividing $(M/m) \sum N_i p_i$ by N will also be underestimated.

Let us next change the figures of N_i in Example 2 so that the average of the A, B, C, and D will be close to N/M and let us estimate the proportion P.

Example 3. Given the following new set of N_i for the data in Example 2, estimate the proportion P.

Cities	N_i	$\bar{n}$	p_i	$N_i p_i$
A	2000	100	0.70	1400
B	3000	100	0.75	2250
C	4000	100	0.80	3200
D	5000	100	0.85	4150
	14,000			11,000

$$\hat{P} = \frac{M}{Nm} \sum N_i p_i$$

$$= \frac{50}{160,000 \times 4}(11,000) = 0.86$$

As shown, the estimate is now $\hat{P} = 0.86$ and is larger than any of the sample proportions. The average size of the four cities is $14000/5 = 3500$—larger than $N/M = 3200$—and the estimator, $\hat{P} = 0.86$, will now be biased on the high side.

Another factor pulling the estimate up is that along with the increase in the sizes of A, B, C, and D, the sampling proportion (p_i) is also increasing. This means that the larger p_i are more heavily weighted than the smaller ones and, as a result, the estimate $\hat{P}$ is biased on the high side.

Problems

1. Show that when $n_i = \bar{n}$, we get

$$\hat{P} = \frac{M}{Nm\bar{n}} \sum^m N_i x_i$$

2. Using the data of Example 1, recalculate $\hat{P}$ using the equation given in Problem 1 above. Devise a work sheet.

3. Suppose in Example 1, the data were as follows; $M = 15$, $m = 6$, $N = 150$, $\bar{n} = 4$. Find $\hat{P}$.

District	N_i	x_i
5	14	2
8	12	3
10	24	3
11	6	1
12	8	4
15	13	1

4. Suppose we wish to estimate the proportion of voters in favor of new tax program in a certain city. The city has $M = 40$ voting districts, each with a voter registration file. There are a total of $N = 80,000$ voters. A random sample of $m = 8$ districts is selected, and $\bar{n} = 50$ voters are selected from the registration files with the following results. Find $\hat{P}$.

District	N_i	x_i
#2	1600	15
8	2500	20
11	2100	19
17	1900	17
22	2400	21
27	1800	18
32	1800	16
35	2100	17

10.3   The variance of $\hat{P}$

The main reasons for finding $V(\hat{P})$ will be to acquaint the student with the process of transforming variance formulas for sample means into variance formulas for proportions, and also to use it as a preliminary for the estimator of $V(\hat{P})$. We shall use the result of Chapter 5, Simple Random Sampling, where we saw how the sample mean and the proportion were selected. In the next section, we shall see how $V(\hat{P})$ and its estimator are related.

The procedure for finding $V(\hat{P})$ will be to start with the variance of $\hat{\bar{X}}$ obtained from cluster sampling and to express it in terms of P and Q. The variance of $\hat{\bar{X}}$ for cluster sampling was

$$(1) \qquad V(\hat{\bar{X}}) = \frac{1}{N^2}\left(M^2\frac{M-m}{M}\frac{S_b^2}{m} + \frac{M}{m}\sum_{}^{M} N_i^2\frac{N_i - n_i}{N_i}\frac{S_i^2}{n_i}\right)$$

$$= \frac{1}{\bar{N}^2}\frac{M-m}{M}\frac{S_b^2}{m} + \frac{M}{m}\frac{1}{N^2}\sum_{}^{M} N_i^2\frac{N_i - n_i}{N_i}\frac{S_i^2}{n_i}$$

What we wish to do now is to express S_b^2 and S_i^2 in terms of P and Q. We showed the variation between clusters as,

$$(2) \qquad S_b^2 = \frac{1}{M-1}\sum_{}^{M} (X_i - \bar{X})^2$$

From equation (1), section 10.1, we see that

$$(3) \qquad X_i = N_i P_i$$

As for $\bar{X}$, using equation (3), section 10.1, we find

$$(4) \qquad \bar{X} = \frac{X}{M} = \frac{\sum_{}^{M} X_i}{M} = \frac{N}{M}\frac{\sum_{}^{M} X_i}{N} = \bar{N}P$$

Hence, by substituting (3) and (4) into (2), S_b^2 becomes

$$(5) \qquad S_b^2 = \frac{1}{M-1}\sum_{}^{M} (N_i P_i - \bar{N}P)^2$$

Let us next express S_i^2 in terms of P and Q. The S_i^2 which shows the variation within the ith cluster is defined as

$$(6) \qquad S_i^2 = \frac{1}{N_i - 1}\sum_{j=1}^{N_i} (X_{ij} - \bar{\bar{X}}_i)^2$$

From our discussion of simple random sampling, we know that

$$\sum_{}^{N_i} (X_{ij} - \bar{\bar{X}}_i)^2 = N_i P_i Q_i$$

Hence, (6) becomes

$$(7) \qquad S_i^2 = \frac{1}{N_i - 1}(N_i P_i Q_i)$$

Substituting (5) and (7) into (1), we find

$$(8) \quad V(\hat{P}) = \frac{M-m}{M(M-1)\bar{N}^2}\frac{\sum_{}^{M} (N_i P_i - \bar{N}P)^2}{m} + \frac{M}{mN^2}\sum_{}^{M} \frac{N_i^2(N_i - n_i)}{N_i - 1}\frac{P_i Q_i}{n_i}$$

which is the variance of $\hat{P}$ we seek.

The first term on the right shows the variation due to selecting m psu from M psu by random sampling. If subsamples are selected from all of the M psu, then $M = m$, and there will be no sampling variation at this stage. As shown, when $M = m$, the first term vanishes.

When a subsample of size n_i is selected from the ith psu which is of size N_i, there will be a sampling variation caused by this process. It may be considered as the sampling variation within the ith psu. The second term on the right may be thought of as the sum of these sampling variations. Quite clearly, when $N_i = n_i$(that is, when the whole psu is selected as the subsample), there will be no sampling variation between the subsample and the psu.

In terms of our formulas, when $M = m$, $V(\hat{P})$ becomes

$$V(\hat{P}) = \frac{1}{N^2} \sum^{M} \frac{N_i^2(N_i - n_i)}{N_i - 1} \frac{P_i Q_i}{n_i}$$

which is equal to the variance for stratified sampling as given by equation (11), section 6.13.

The standard error will be expressed as

$$\sigma(\hat{P}) = \sqrt{V(\hat{P})}$$

Example 1. Suppose there are $M = 3$ groups of children, and they are asked whether or not they watch a certain T.V. program. The result of the survey is as follows:

Group	N_i	X_{ij}	X_i	P_i	Q_i
1	3	1, 0, 1	2	2/3	1/3
2	4	1, 0, 1, 0	2	2/4	2/4
3	5	1, 0, 1, 1, 0	3	3/5	2/5
	12		7		

Calculate $V(\hat{P})$. Assume $n_i = \bar{n} = 2$.

$\bar{N} = N/M = 12/3 = 4$

$P = X/N = 7/12$

$\bar{N}P = 4(7/12) = 7/3$

$$\sum^{M} (N_i P_i - \bar{N}P) = (3(2/3) - 7/3)^2 + (4(2/4) - 7/3)^2 + (5(3/5) - 7/3)^2 = 6/9$$

$$\sum^{M} N_i^2 \frac{N_i - n_i}{N_i - 1} \frac{P_i Q_i}{n_i} = (3)^2 \frac{3 - 2}{3 - 1} \frac{(2/3)(1/3)}{2} + (4)^2 \frac{4 - 2}{4 - 1} \frac{(2/4)(2/4)}{2}$$

$$+ (5)^2 \frac{5 - 2}{5 - 1} \frac{(3/5)(2/5)}{2} = \frac{49}{12}$$

$$V(\hat{P}) = \left(\frac{3 - 2}{3(3 - 1)(4)^2}\right)\left(\frac{1}{2}\right)\left(\frac{6}{9}\right) + \left(\frac{3}{2(12)^2}\right)\left(\frac{49}{12}\right) = 0.046$$

$$\sigma(\hat{P}) = \sqrt{0.046} = 0.21$$

When we may assume that $\bar{N} = N_i = N/M$ and $\bar{n} = n_i = n/m$, the variance of (8) simplifies to

$$(9) \qquad V(\hat{P}) = \frac{M - m}{M(M - 1)} \frac{\sum\limits^{M}(P_i - P)^2}{m} + \frac{\bar{N} - \bar{n}}{M(\bar{N} - 1)} \frac{\sum\limits^{M}P_iQ_i}{m\bar{n}}$$

This formula also shows clearly that $V(\hat{P})$ is made up of the variation between clusters (shown by the first term on the right) and the variation within clusters (shown by the second term).

For practical applications, the population parameters P_i and P are usually unknown, and hence an estimator of $V(\hat{P})$ is used. Let us next discuss the estimator of $V(\hat{P})$.

Problems

1. Suppose there are $M = 4$ groups of students and we wish to estimate the proportions of students who plan to enter graduate school. The result is as follows:

Group	N_i	X_i	x_i
1	5	3	3
2	4	3	0
3	7	4	2
4	12	6	3

(i) Calculate P.

(ii) Assume groups 1, 3, and 4 have been selected and from each group $\bar{n} = 4$ students have been selected. The number of students planning to enter graduate school in these subsamples is given by x_i. Find $\hat{P}$.

(iii) Calculate $V(\hat{P})$.

10.4 Estimation of $V(\hat{P})$

As mentioned in the previous section, we need to know the population values P_i and P to calculate $V(\hat{P})$. Hence, it is almost never used in practice. Our problem in this section is to derive an estimator of $V(\hat{P})$ which may be easily obtained from the sample.

The derivation of the estimator of $V(\hat{P})$ may be approached by recalling that $V(\hat{P})$ was obtained from $V(\hat{X})$ by setting $X_{ij} = 1$ or 0. The estimator of $V(\hat{P})$ will be obtained in a similar manner by using the estimator of $V(\hat{X})$ and setting $X_{ij} = 1$ or 0.

We shall present three estimators of $V(\hat{P})$. The first one is an estimator of the variance given in equation (8), section 10.3. The second is obtained from the first by assuming $N_i = \bar{N}$ and $n_i = \bar{n}$. The third estimator is obtained from the second by further assuming that $M \gg m$.

Case 1.

We know from section 8.5 that the unbiased estimator of $V(\hat{\bar{X}})$ is given by

(1)
$$\hat{V}(\hat{\bar{X}}) = \frac{1}{N^2}\left(M^2\frac{M-m}{M}\frac{s_b^2}{m} + \frac{M}{m}\sum^m N_i^2\frac{N_i-n_i}{N_i}\frac{s_i^2}{n_i}\right)$$

$$s_b^2 = \frac{1}{m-1}\sum^m(\hat{X}_i - \hat{\bar{X}})^2$$

$$s_i^2 = \frac{1}{n_i-1}\sum^{n_i}_j(x_{ij}-\bar{x}_i)^2$$

We also know that $\hat{X}_i$ and $\hat{\bar{X}}$ may be expressed in terms of p_i as follows:

$$\hat{X}_i = N_i\bar{x}_i = N_ip_i$$

$$\hat{\bar{X}} = \frac{1}{m}\sum^m\hat{X}_i = \frac{1}{m}\sum^m N_i\bar{x}_i = \frac{1}{m}\sum^m N_ip_i$$

Substituting these relations into s_b^2, we find

(2)
$$s_b^2 = \frac{1}{m-1}\sum^m\left(N_ip_i - \frac{1}{m}\sum^m N_ip_i\right)^2$$

We also know from simple random sampling that

$$\sum^{n_i}_j(x_{ij}-\bar{x}_i)^2 = n_ip_iq_i$$

Using this result, s_i^2 may be shown as

(3)
$$s_i^2 = \frac{1}{n_i-1}\sum^{n_i}_j(x_{ij}-\bar{x}_i)^2 = \frac{1}{n_i-1}(n_ip_iq_i)$$

And substituting these results into (1), we find $\hat{V}(\hat{P})$:

(4)
$$\hat{V}(\hat{P}) = \frac{1}{N^2}\left[M^2\frac{M-m}{M}\frac{1}{m}\frac{1}{m-1}\sum^m\left(N_ip_i - \frac{1}{m}\sum^m N_ip_i\right)^2\right.$$
$$\left. + \frac{M}{m}\sum^m N_i^2\frac{N_i-n_i}{N_i}\frac{1}{n_i}\frac{1}{n_i-1}(n_ip_iq_i)\right]$$

The standard error will be denoted by

$$s(\hat{P}) = \sqrt{\hat{V}(\hat{P})}$$

Example 1. Using the data in Example 1 section 10.2, let us illustrate the use of equation (4).

Group	N_i	X_{ij}	X_i	P_i	Q_i
1	3	1, 0, 1	2	2/3	1/3
2	4	1, 0, 1, 0	2	2/4	2/4
3	5	1, 0, 1, 1, 0	3	3/5	2/5
	12		7		

Select a sample of $m = 2$ psu. Let these be groups 1 and 3. Select samples of size $\bar{n} = 2$. Suppose we have:

x_{1j}	x_{2j}
1	1
0	1
1	2
p_i 1/2	2/2

$$\frac{1}{m} \sum^m N_i P_i = \frac{1}{2}\left[3\left(\frac{1}{2}\right) + 5\left(\frac{2}{2}\right)\right] = \frac{13}{4}$$

$$\sum^m \left(N_i P_i - \frac{1}{m}\sum^m N_i P_i\right)^2 = \frac{49}{8}$$

$$\sum^m \frac{N_i - n_i}{N_i}\frac{1}{n_i}\frac{1}{n_i - 1}(n_i p_i q_i) = \frac{3}{4}$$

$$\therefore \quad \hat{V}(\hat{P}) = \frac{1}{(12)^2}\left[\frac{3}{2}\left(\frac{49}{8}\right) + \frac{3}{2}\left(\frac{3}{4}\right)\right] = \frac{1}{144} \times \frac{165}{16} = 0.072$$

$$s(\hat{P}) = 0.268$$

Case 2.

In some cases we may assume $\bar{N} = N_i = N/M$ and $\bar{n} = n_i = n/m$. For example, we may have an $M = 200$-page student directory where each page has $\bar{N} = N_i = 40$ names. Suppose we wish to estimate the proportion of students commuting to school in their own car. We may take a sample of $m = 20$ pages, and from each page select $\bar{n} = n_i = 10$ names to estimate this proportion.

To find the estimator of $V(\hat{P})$ in this case, we need only substitute $\bar{N} = N_i$ and $\bar{n} = n_i$ into equation (4). We find

$$(5) \quad \hat{V}(\hat{P}) = \frac{M - m}{M}\frac{1}{m}\frac{1}{m - 1}\sum^m (p_i - \bar{p})^2 + \frac{\bar{N} - \bar{n}}{\bar{N}}\frac{1}{M}\frac{1}{m(\bar{n} - 1)}\sum^m p_i q_i$$

The estimator, $\hat{P}$, becomes

$$(6) \quad \hat{P} = \frac{M}{Nm}\sum^m N_i p_i = \frac{1}{m}\sum^m p_i = \bar{p}$$

Hence, $\bar{p}$ is simply the mean of the p_i.

Furthermore, since $p_i = x_i/n_i = x_i/\bar{n}$, equation (6) becomes

$$(7) \quad \bar{p} = \frac{1}{m}\sum^m p_i = \frac{1}{m\bar{n}}\sum^m x_i$$

which is a convenient form to use for calculation purposes.

Let us illustrate the use of these formulas.

Example 2. Suppose there are $M = 5$ classes of students and we are interested in estimating the proportion of students who wear glasses. We shall select $m = 2$

classes. Let these be the second and fourth classes. The results are given in the following table.

	N_i	n_i	x_i	p_i
1	49			
2	52	10	5	.5
3	51			
4	48	10	3	.3
5	50			
		20	8	

$\bar{n} = 10$ students are selected from each of the $m = 2$ classes, and the number of students wearing glasses are found to be 5 and 3, respectively. Then, letting $\bar{N} = N_i = 50$, the proportion is estimated as:

$$\hat{P} = \frac{1}{m\bar{n}} \Sigma x_i = \frac{8}{20} = 0.4$$

The estimated variance of $\hat{P}$ is

$$\hat{V}(\hat{P}) = \frac{M-m}{M} \frac{1}{m} \frac{1}{m-1} \sum^m (p_i - \bar{p})^2 + \frac{\bar{N}-\bar{n}}{\bar{N}} \frac{1}{M} \frac{1}{m(\bar{n}-1)} \sum^m p_i q_i$$

$$= \frac{5-2}{5} \frac{1}{2} \frac{1}{2-1}[(.5 - .4)^2 + (.5 - .3)^2]$$

$$+ \frac{50-10}{50} \frac{1}{5} \frac{1}{2(10-1)}[(.5)(.5) + (.3)(.7)] = 0.01$$

There are cases where $\bar{N} = \bar{n}$ will lead to further simplifications. For example, suppose there is a 400-page record book with 30 lines per page. On each line is an entry showing the number of days a customer needs to pay up his account. The firm wishes to estimate the proportion of customers who require more than 4 weeks.

To estimate this proportion, we may select, say, $m = 10$ pages from the $M = 400$ pages. On each page there are $\bar{N} = 30$ lines, and we shall check *all* 30 lines. Hence, $\bar{n} = \bar{N} = 30$. In this case, the estimator $\hat{P}$ becomes

$$\hat{P} = \frac{1}{m} \sum^m p_i = \frac{1}{m\bar{n}} \sum^m x_i$$

and, the variance for $\hat{P}$ becomes, since $\bar{N} = \bar{n}$,

$$\hat{V}(\hat{P}) = \frac{M-m}{M} \frac{1}{m} \frac{1}{m-1} \sum^m (p_i - \bar{p})^2 + \frac{\bar{N}-\bar{n}}{\bar{N}} \frac{1}{M} \frac{1}{m(m-1)} \sum^m p_i q_i$$

$$= \frac{M-m}{M} \frac{1}{m(m-1)} \sum^m (p_i - \bar{p})^2$$

As is seen, $\hat{V}(\hat{P})$ is calculated by treating p_i as if it were x_i and p as if it were $\bar{x}$. We are in fact considering each psu as a sampling unit and drawing a random sample of size m from M. Hence, $\hat{V}(\hat{P})$ has the same form as the variance for a sample mean $\bar{x}$.

We conclude that when $\bar{N} = \bar{n}$, $\hat{P}$ and $\hat{V}(\hat{P})$ are calculated as if p_i were the individual values and $\bar{p}$ were the sample mean of a sample size m taken from a population of size M.

Example 3. Suppose the results of the sample survey mentioned above are as follows: Since there are $M = 400$ pages and we wish to select $m = 10$ pages, we shall calculate the sampling interval $400/10 = 40$. Let 10 be the random number selected between 1 and 40. Then our sample of $m = 10$ psu is as follows:

	Page (psu)	$\bar{N} = \bar{n}$	Number of accounts over 4 weeks	p_i
1	10	25	5	.20
2	50	25	6	.24
3	90	25	5	.20
4	130	25	4	.16
5	170	25	8	.32
6	210	25	7	.28
7	250	25	3	.12
8	290	25	5	.20
9	330	25	6	.24
10	370	25	6	.24
		250	55	2.20

Since $\bar{N} = \bar{n}$, we may treat p_i as if it were x_i and find $\hat{P}$ and $\hat{V}(\hat{P})$. Solving for $\hat{P}$:

$$\hat{P} = \frac{1}{m\bar{n}} \sum^{m} x_i = \frac{1}{250}(55) = 0.22$$

or

$$\hat{P} = \frac{1}{m} \sum^{m} p_i = \frac{1}{10}(2.2) = 0.22$$

For $\hat{V}(\hat{P})$:

	p_i	$p_i - \bar{p}$	$(p_i - \bar{p})^2$
1	.20	−0.02	.0004
2	.24	0.02	.0004
3	.20	−0.02	.0004
4	.16	−0.06	.0036
5	.32	0.10	.0100
6	.28	0.06	.0036
7	.12	−0.10	.0100
8	.20	−0.02	.0004
9	.24	0.02	.0004
10	.24	0.02	.0004
		0.00	.0296

$$\hat{V}(\hat{p}) = \frac{M - m}{M} \frac{1}{m(m - 1)} \sum^{m} (p_i - \bar{p})^2$$

$$= \frac{400 - 10}{400} \frac{1}{10(10 - 1)} (0.0296) = 0.000329$$

$$s(\hat{P}) = 0.018$$

Case 3.

In addition to $\bar{N} = N_i$ and $\bar{n} = n_i$, if we can assume $m \ll M$, the estimator $\hat{V}(\hat{p})$ becomes

$$\hat{V}(\hat{P}) = \frac{M-m}{M}\frac{1}{m}\frac{1}{m-1}\sum_{}^{m}(p_i - \bar{p})^2$$

$$+ \frac{\bar{N}-\bar{n}}{\bar{N}}\frac{1}{M}\frac{1}{m(\bar{n}-1)}\sum_{}^{m}p_iq_i$$

$$\doteq \frac{1}{m}\frac{1}{m-1}\sum_{}^{m}(p_i-\bar{p})^2$$

because $1/M \doteq 0$ and $(M-m)/M \doteq 1$. This is a very useful approximation because of its simplicity.

Example 4. Suppose there are $M = 600$ elementary schools in a large city, and we wish to estimate the proportion of sixth graders who watch a certain T.V. program. Let us select $m = 10$ schools and $\bar{n} = 20$ students from the each of the $m = 10$ schools. To select the $m = 10$ schools, let us use systematic sampling. Since $M/m = 600/10 = 60$, we select a random number between 1 and 60. Assuming we get 30, the sample will be:

$$30, 90, 150, 210, 270, 330, 390, 450, 510, 570$$

That is, the 30th school; the 90th school; etc.
   Upon selecting $\bar{n} = 20$ students from each of the $m = 10$ schools, we find:

m	$\bar{n}$	x_i	p_i	$p_i - \bar{p}$	$(p_i - \bar{p})^2$
1	20	5	.25	−.01	.0001
2	20	7	.35	.09	.0081
3	20	4	.20	−.06	.0036
4	20	4	.20	−.06	.0036
5	20	6	.30	.04	.0016
6	20	5	.25	−.01	.0001
7	20	3	.15	−.11	.0121
8	20	7	.35	.09	.0081
9	20	5	.25	−.01	.0001
10	20	6	.30	.04	.0016
	200	52	2.60	0.00	0.0390

Let us assume that we may set $\bar{N} = N_i = 200$. Then the estimators $\hat{P}$ and $\hat{V}(\hat{P})$ will be:

$$\hat{P} = \frac{1}{m\bar{n}}\sum_{}^{m}x_i = \frac{52}{200} = 0.26$$

$$\hat{V}(\hat{P}) = \frac{1}{m(m-1)}\sum_{}^{m}(p_i - \bar{p})^2$$

$$= \frac{1}{10(10-1)}(0.039) = 0.0004$$

$$s(\hat{P}) = \sqrt{0.0004} = 0.02$$

Problems

1. Show that when $n_t = \bar{n}$,

(i)
$$s_b^2 = \frac{1}{m-1}\left(\frac{1}{\bar{n}}\right)^2 \sum^m \left(N_i x_i - \frac{1}{m}\sum^m N_i x_i\right)^2$$

(ii)
$$s_i^2 = \frac{x_i(\bar{n}-x_i)}{\bar{n}(\bar{n}-1)}$$

(iii)
$$\hat{V}(\hat{P}) = \frac{1}{N^2}\left[M^2\frac{M-m}{M}\frac{1}{m}\frac{1}{m-1}\left(\frac{1}{\bar{n}}\right)^2 \sum^m\left(N_i x_i - \frac{1}{m}\sum^m N_i x_i\right)^2\right.$$
$$\left.+ \frac{M}{m}\sum^m N_i^2\frac{N_i-\bar{n}}{N_i}\frac{1}{\bar{n}}\frac{1}{\bar{n}-1}\frac{x_i(\bar{n}-x_i)}{\bar{n}}\right]$$

(iv)
$$\sum\left(N_i x_i - \frac{1}{m}\sum^m N_i x_i\right)^2 = \sum(N_i x_i)^2 - \frac{1}{m}\left(\sum N_i x_i\right)^2$$

2. Using the data of Example 1 and the relations derived in Problem 1 above, calculate $\hat{V}(\hat{P})$. Devise a worksheet.

3. Assuming $\bar{N} = N_i$ and $\bar{n} = n_i$, show that equation (5) may be rewritten as

(i)
$$\hat{V}(\hat{P}) = \frac{M-m}{M}\frac{1}{m}\frac{1}{m-1}\left(\frac{1}{\bar{n}}\right)^2 \sum^m\left(x_i - \frac{1}{m}\sum^m x_i\right)^2$$
$$+ \frac{\bar{N}-\bar{n}}{\bar{N}}\frac{1}{M}\frac{1}{m(\bar{n}-1)}\left(\frac{1}{\bar{n}}\right)^2 \sum^m x_i(\bar{n}-x_i)$$

(ii)
$$\sum^m\left(x_i - \frac{1}{m}\sum^m x_i\right)^2 = \sum x_i^2 - \frac{1}{m}\left(\sum x_i\right)^2$$

4. Let $\bar{N} = \bar{n}$. Then show that the equation in Problem 3 becomes

$$\hat{V}(\hat{P}) = \frac{M-m}{M}\frac{1}{m}\frac{1}{m-1}\left(\frac{1}{\bar{n}}\right)^2 \sum\left(x_i - \frac{1}{m}\sum x_i\right)^2$$

5. Using the data of Example 2, calculate $\hat{V}(\hat{P})$ using the equations found in Problem 3. Devise a worksheet.

6. Using the data of Example 3, calculate $\hat{V}(\hat{P})$ using the equation found in Problem 4.

7. Using the data of Problem 4 of page 277, calculate $\hat{V}(\hat{P})$.

8. In Problem 7 above, assume $N_i = \bar{N} = 2000$ and calculate $\hat{V}(\hat{P})$ and compare with the result found in Problem 7.

9. A large mail order company wishes to estimate the proportion of orders that are over \$40. It receives about $M = 200$ bags of mail every morning. A sample of $m = 10$ bags is selected, and from each bag $\bar{n} = 50$ mail orders are selected. The result is as follows.

Bags	N_i	x_i
1	220	5
2	210	6
3	230	4
4	180	5
5	190	6
6	200	3
7	240	5
8	170	5
9	190	4
10	190	4

It is estimated that there are about $N = 40{,}000$ mail orders.

(i) Find $\hat{P}$.
(ii) Find $\hat{V}(\hat{P})$ and $s(\hat{P})$.
(iii) Find the 2σ confidence interval for P.

10. Use the data of Problem 9, but assume $N_i = \bar{N} = 200$, and find $\hat{P}$ and $\hat{V}(\hat{P})$. Also find the 2σ confidence interval for P.

10.5   Cluster sampling with pps for proportions

We may easily extend the results of simple cluster sampling for proportions to cluster sampling with pps. Recall that this procedure was used when the cluster sizes varied, and the estimators obtained by this procedure were found to be easier to compute and more precise than those obtained from simple cluster sampling. It is therefore widely used in opinion surveys, market research, and other fields to estimate proportions.

As an example, suppose we wish to estimate the market share of brand A soap in a certain state. We may divide the state into counties (psu) and from a sample of m counties (psu), select $\bar{n}$ families (ssu). These $m\bar{n}$ families will be the sample $n = m\bar{n}$ from which we shall estimate the proportion of families using soap A (which we shall consider as an estimate of the market share of soap A).

Let us now find the estimator of the population proportion for cluster sampling with pps and its variance. We know that the estimator for the population mean for cluster sampling with pps is

$$(1) \qquad \bar{x}_{\text{pps}} = \frac{1}{m\bar{n}} \sum^m \sum^{\bar{n}} x_{ij} = \frac{1}{m} \sum^m \bar{x}_i$$

By considering the following point we may easily show that $\bar{x}_{\text{pps}}$ is the estimator for the population proportion P. That is, $\bar{x}_{\text{pps}}$ is simply the sample mean of the sample $m\bar{n} = n$. The term $\sum \sum x_{ij}$ is simply the number of families in the sample that are using soap A, because $x_{ij} = 1$ for families using soap A, and $x_{ij} = 0$ for families not using soap A. Hence, $\bar{x}_{pps}$ is the sample proportion—which we shall denote as $\hat{P}_{pps}$

Furthermore, the term

$$\frac{1}{\bar{n}} \sum_{}^{\bar{n}} x_{ij}$$

is the sample proportion of the subsample i drawn from the ith cluster. Hence, we shall denote this as

$$p_i = \frac{1}{\bar{n}} \sum_{j}^{\bar{n}} x_{ij} = \frac{x_i}{\bar{n}}$$

Using these results, equation (1) may be rewritten as

(2) $$\hat{P}_{pps} = \frac{1}{m\bar{n}} \sum_{}^{m} \sum_{}^{\bar{n}} x_{ij} = \frac{1}{m} \sum_{}^{m} p_i$$

and, furthermore, $E(\hat{P}_{pps}) = P$— (2) is an unbiased estimator of P.

The variance of $\hat{P}_{pps}$ may easily be worked out by using the results of sections 10.1-10.4. The main purpose of finding $V(\hat{P}_{pps})$ is to understand the characteristics of sampling with pps and to learn how to design a sample representative of the population. The characteristics of sampling with pps have been already discussed in Chapter 9. For practical applications, it is also the estimator of the $V(\hat{P}_{pps})$ that is used. We shall therefore skip discussion of $V(\hat{P}_{pps})$ and proceed directly to a discussion of the estimator of $V(\hat{P}_{pps})$.

The estimator of $V(\bar{x}_{pps})$ was:

(3) $$\hat{V}(\bar{x}_{pps}) = \frac{1}{m} \frac{1}{m-1} \sum (\bar{x}_i - \bar{x}_{pps})^2$$

Substituting the results we obtained above into equation (3), we find

(4)
$$\hat{V}(\hat{P}_{pps}) = \frac{1}{m} \frac{1}{m-1} \sum \left(p_i - \frac{1}{m} \sum p_i \right)^2$$

$$= \frac{1}{m} \frac{1}{m-1} \sum (p_i - \hat{P}_{pps})^2$$

which is very easy to calculate.

Example 1. Using the data of Example 3, section 10.2, find $\hat{P}_{pps}$ and $\hat{V}(\hat{P}_{pps})$, where the psu are assumed to have been selected by sampling with pps.

Cities	N_i	$\bar{n}$	p_i	$p_i - \hat{P}_{pps}$	$(p_i - \hat{P}_{pps})^2$
A	2000	100	.70	−0.075	.005625
B	3000	100	.75	0.0	.000000
C	4000	100	.80	0.025	.000625
D	5000	100	.85	0.075	.005625
			3.10	0.025	.011875

$$\hat{P}_{pps} = \frac{1}{m} \sum_{}^{m} p_i = \frac{1}{4}(3.10) = 0.775$$

$$\hat{V}(\hat{P}_{pps}) = \frac{1}{m}\frac{1}{m-1}\Sigma(p_i - \hat{P}_{pps})^2 = \frac{1}{4}\frac{1}{4-1}(0.011875) = 0.00098958$$

$$s(\hat{P}_{pps}) = 0.0314$$

Problems

1. Show that equation (2) may be rewritten as

$$\hat{P}_{pps} = \frac{1}{m\bar{n}}\overset{m}{\Sigma}x_i = \frac{x}{m\bar{n}}$$

where $\qquad x = \overset{m}{\Sigma}x_i, \qquad$ and $\qquad x_i = \overset{\bar{n}}{\Sigma}x_{ij}$

2. Show that equation (4) may be rewritten as

$$\hat{V}(\hat{P}_{pps}) = \frac{1}{m}\frac{1}{m-1}\left(\frac{1}{\bar{n}}\right)^2 \Sigma\left(x_i - \frac{1}{m}\Sigma x_i\right)^2$$

$$\Sigma\left(x_i - \frac{1}{m}\overset{m}{\Sigma}x_i\right)^2 = \Sigma x_i^2 - \frac{1}{m}(\Sigma x_i)^2$$

3. A state government wishes to estimate the proportion of factory workers with wages under \$1.75 in a certain industry. There are $M = 200$ plants in the state, a sample of $m = 10$ plants is selected with pps, and from each plant $\bar{n} = 20$ workers are selected. The results are as follows:

Plants	N_i	x_i
1	80	4
2	120	3
3	30	10
4	50	5
5	40	5
6	200	0
7	60	5
8	110	4
9	90	2
10	150	2

It is estimated that a there are $N = 18,000$ workers. The x_i is the number of workers with wages under \$1.75. Using the formulas found in Problems 1 and 2 above
   (i) Find $\hat{P}_{pps}$.
   (ii) Find $\hat{V}(\hat{P}_{pps})$.

Notes and References

For further discussion of estimation of proportions, see Sampford(1962), Chapter 12. It is a general discussion of estimation of proportions and not specifically on estimation of proportions by cluster sampling. For a mathematical discussion see Cochran(1963), pp. 247–248, 278–279.

At this point, it is recommended that the student start reading the excellent and very interesting book by Stephan and McCarthy(1958), Sampling Opinions. Although the book is written for the nonspecialist, a knowledge of what is covered in Chapters 10, 11, and 12 of this book should be helpful in understanding their book. Conversely, the simultaneous reading of their book along with chapters 10, 11, and 12 of this book should greatly enhance the understanding and appreciation of the techniques covered in this book. It is suggested that the student read the whole book. It is available in paperback. It also has many nontechnical references at the end of each chapter.

Stephan, F.F. and McCarthy, P.J. (1958). *Sampling Opinions. An Analysis of Survey Procedures.* New York: John Wiley & Sons, Inc.

CHAPTER 11

Three-Stage Cluster Sampling

11.1 Introduction

The 2-stage cluster sampling we discussed in the previous chapters may easily be extended to three stages. As an example of the type of problem to which 3-stage cluster sampling may be used, let us assume we wish to estimate the total number of books owned by sixth-graders in the New York City public school system. There are, say, $L = 580$ elementary public schools (psu), and let us assume $l = 10$ are selected as a random sample of psu. The ith sampled school (psu) has M_i classes (ssu) in the sixth grade, and suppose $\bar{m} = 2$ classes (ssu) are selected from each sampled school. Finally, we may assume there are N_{ij} students (tertiary, or third-stage sampling units, which we abbreviate as tsu) in the jth sampled class of the ith sampled school, and a subsample of n_{ij} students are selected from the jth class. Suppose $n_{ij} = 3$ students. That is, 3 students are selected from the $N_{ij} = 50$ students (say) of the jth class in the ith school. The number of books owned by each of these students in the jth class may be shown by

$$x_{ij1} = 4 \text{ books}, \qquad x_{ij2} = 3 \text{ books}, \qquad x_{ij3} = 5 \text{ books}$$

In general, the number of books owned by the kth student in the subsample may be shown by x_{ijk}. A capital X_{ijk} is used when population values are being considered.

It should be recalled that the same subscripts are used in two different manners. One is for the population and the other for the sample. For example, $X_{ij} = X_{35}$ is the $j = 5$th class in the $i = 3$rd school *in the population*. However, $x_{ij} = x_{35}$ is the $j = 5$th sampled class in the $i = 3$rd sampled school. The student should distinguish these two different uses from the context of the discussion.

Let us consider another illustration. Suppose we wish to estimate the yield of wheat in a certain region. Let there be $L = 500$ villages (psu), of which $l = 10$ villages are selected as a sample of psu. There are M_i fields (ssu) in the ith sampled village, and a sample of $\bar{m} = 3$ fields (say)are selected as a random sample. Finally, the jth field of the ith sampled village is considered to be made up of N_{ij} plots (say, 1/4 acre plots), and a random sample of n_{ij} plots is selected. Let x_{ijk} be the yield of the kth plot in the jth field of the ith village.

As a third example, suppose we wish to estimate the average amount of coffee consumed by an adult in a certain city. Let there be $L = 2000$ blocks (psu), and suppose a sample of $l = 40$ blocks is selected. There are M_i households (ssu) on the ith sampled block, and a sample of $\bar{m} = 10$ households (ssu) is selected. There are N_{ij} persons (tsu) in the jth household of the ith sampled block. Suppose n_{ij} persons are selected from among N_{ij} persons. For convenience, we may select $n_{ij} = 1$ person per household. Then, x_{ijk} is simply x_{ij1} or x_{ij}.

To summarize, we have

L	l	psu	schools,	villages,	blocks
M_i	$\bar{m}$	ssu	classes,	fields,	households
N_{ij}	n_{ij}	tsu	students,	plots,	persons

The value of the sample tsu was shown by x_{ijk}, and the value of the population tsu was shown by X_{ijk}.

The advantages of 3-stage sampling are similar to those of 2-stage sampling. First, we need to prepare the frame only for the psu, ssu, and tsu that have been selected as the sample. Second, compared to random sampling, this procedure reduces traveling and administration cost.

However, various difficulties common to those of the 2-stage case may be encountered in the use of the 3-stage sampling procedure. One is that when selecting the psu, ssu, and tsu by simple random sampling, these units should be roughly equal in size. It may in some cases be difficult to achieve this—especially for psu. For example, in the above illustration estimating the amount of coffee consumed (using blocks), it may be difficult to have blocks of uniform size, and it may be necessary to combine or split blocks for this reason. When selecting a sample of cities to investigate some characteristic about urban consumers, this tacit assumption of roughly equal size psu will be hard to fulfill. Fortunately, there are other sampling procedures which may be used when there is considerable variation in size between psu, such as selecting the psu with probability proportional to size, or using stratified cluster sampling (as will be explained in the next chapter).

A second difficulty is that there may be considerable heterogeneity among psu, but homogeneity among ssu and tsu. In this case, it can be seen intuitively that a large number of ssu or tsu will not add much more information than a small number of ssu and tsu. It will be necessary to increase the number of psu to obtain more information about the population—but this may increase the cost of traveling and administration if the psu are scattered over a wide area, and thus defeat the original purpose of trying to reduce the cost of sampling.

However, although such difficulties exist, it is quite clear that there are numerous situations where 3-stage cluster sampling may be effectively used.

With this background, let us now show how the total, mean, and variance are estimated by 3-stage cluster sampling.

11.2 Estimator of the population total and population mean

The idea used to find the estimator of the population total X or population mean $\bar{\bar{X}}$ is similar to that used to find the 2-stage case. Let us use a hypothetical example and illustrate the process.

Suppose there are L schools (psu), and we wish to estimate the total number of books the sixth graders have. A sample of l schools is selected, from each school we take a sample of $\bar{m}$ classes, and from each of the $\bar{m}$ classes we select a subsample of n_{ij} students. Let x_{ijk} be the number of books owned by the kth student in the jth class of the ith school. An estimate of the total number of books is given by

(1)
$$\hat{X} = \frac{L}{l} \sum_i^l \frac{M_i}{\bar{m}} \sum_j^{\bar{m}} \frac{N_{ij}}{n_{ij}} \sum_k^{n_{ij}} x_{ijk}$$

The basic idea behind this estimate is as follows: First estimate the total number of books in a class, then estimate the total number of books in a school, and finally add these estimates to find the total number of books.

Let us now show how this idea is expressed by equation (1): The $(1/n_{ij}) \sum x_{ijk}$ shows the average number of books the n_{ij} students selected from the jth class have. Hence, $(N_{ij}/n_{ij}) \sum x_{ijk}$ is an estimate of the total number of books in the jth class.

The sum $A = \sum (N_{ij}/n_{ij}) \sum x_{ijk}$ is an estimate of the total number of books for the $\bar{m}$ classes selected from the ith school. Hence, $(1/\bar{m})(A)$ gives an estimate of the average number of books per class in the ith school, and $(M_i/\bar{m})(A)$ gives the estimate of the total number of books in the ith school.

The sum $B = \sum (M_i/\bar{m})(A)$ is the total number of books for the l sampled schools. Hence, $(1/l)(B)$ is an estimate of the average number of books per school. Thus, $(L/l)(B)$ will be an estimate of the total number of books for the L schools.

Let us use simple hypothetical data and illustrate this process numerically.

Suppose there are $L = 3$ schools (psu,) and we wish to estimate the total number of books owned by the sixth graders. For simplicity, let us assume each school (psu) has $M_i = 3$ classes (ssu), and each class has $N_{ij} = 3$ students (tsu). The complete population is given in Table 11.1.

Table 11.1

Population

School L	Class M_i	Students N_{1j}	Books X_{ijk}	N_{2j}		N_{3j}	
1	$M_1 = 3$	$N_{11} = 3$	$X_{111} = 2$ $X_{112} = 4$ $X_{113} = 6$	$N_{12} = 3$	$X_{121} = 4$ $X_{122} = 6$ $X_{123} = 8$	$N_{13} = 3$	$X_{131} = 6$ $X_{132} = 8$ $X_{133} = 10$
2	$M_2 = 3$	$N_{21} = 3$	$X_{211} = 4$ $X_{212} = 6$ $X_{213} = 8$	$N_{22} = 3$	$X_{221} = 6$ $X_{222} = 8$ $X_{223} = 10$	$N_{23} = 3$	$X_{231} = 8$ $X_{232} = 10$ $X_{233} = 12$
3	$M_3 = 3$	$N_{31} = 3$	$X_{311} = 6$ $X_{312} = 8$ $X_{313} = 10$	$N_{32} = 3$	$X_{321} = 2$ $X_{322} = 4$ $X_{323} = 6$	$N_{33} = 3$	$X_{331} = 4$ $X_{332} = 6$ $X_{333} = 8$

Table 11.2

Sample

$l = 2$	$\bar{m} = 2$	$n_{ij} = 2$	$X_{ijk},\ x_{ijk}$	
$M_1 = 3$	$N_{12} = 3$ $N_{13} = 3$	$n_{11} = 2$ $n_{12} = 2$	$X_{122} = x_{111} = 6$ $X_{131} = x_{121} = 6$	$X_{121} = x_{112} = 4$ $X_{133} = x_{122} = 10$
$M_3 = 3$	$N_{31} = 3$ $N_{33} = 3$	$n_{21} = 2$ $n_{22} = 2$	$X_{313} = x_{211} = 10$ $X_{331} = x_{221} = 4$	$X_{312} = x_{212} = 8$ $X_{333} = x_{222} = 8$

As shown in Table 11.1, there are a total of $N = 27$ students and $X = 180$ books.

What we wish to do is to select a sample of $l = 2$ schools (psu), from each school select $\bar{m} = 2$ classes (ssu), from each class select $n_{ij} = \bar{n} = 2$ students (tsu), and construct a sample. We will thus have a sample of size $l\bar{m}\bar{n} = n = 8$ students from which we want to estimate the total number of books.

Suppose, as shown in Fig. 11-1, that the 1st and 3rd schools (psu) are selected as the sample of psu.

From the 1st sampled school (psu), we select the 2nd and 3rd classes (ssu), which we shall call A and B; and from the 2nd sampled school (psu), we select the 1st and 3rd classes (ssu), which we shall call C and D.

From the 1st sampled class—(class A)—of the 1st sampled school, we select $n_{11} = 2$ students. The number of books of the 1st student is shown by $x_{111} = 6$ books. The subscript 111 shows that it is the 1st sampled student (tsu) of the 1st sampled class (ssu) of the 1st sampled school (psu).

The number of books of the 2nd student is shown by $x_{112} = 6$ books.

We have similarly selected 2 students from every other sampled class. These are shown in Table 11.2.

Let us now estimate the total number of books. We start by estimating

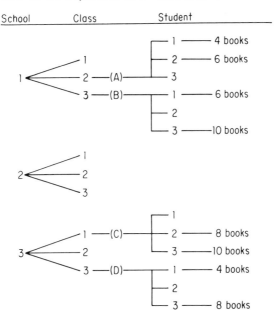

Fig. 11-1

the total number of books in the classes (ssu) which were selected as samples. Since the students (tsu) are selected from each class by simple random sampling, estimating the total for the class is merely using the general formula

$$\hat{X} = N\bar{x}$$

where $\bar{x}$ is the sample mean and N is the population size. Our problem is thus to specify $\bar{x}$ and N in our present situation.

Since a subsample of $n_{ij} = \bar{n} = 2$ students is selected from the jth class in the ith school, the total number of books these $\bar{n} = 2$ students have is shown by

(2)
$$X_{ij} = \sum_{k=1}^{n_{ij}} x_{ijk}$$

Hence, the average number of books for the $n_{ij} = \bar{n} = 2$ students is

(3)
$$\bar{x}_{ij} = \frac{1}{n_{ij}} \sum_{k=1}^{n_{ij}} x_{ijk}$$

This corresponds to $\bar{x}$ in the $\hat{X} = N\bar{x}$ formula, and (3) is therefore an unbiased estimator of the average number of books per student in class j of school i. Hence,

(4)
$$\frac{N_{ij}}{n_{ij}} \sum_{k=1}^{n_{ij}} x_{ijk}$$

is an unbiased estimator of the total number of books of the N_{ij} students in the jth sampled class.

In terms of our example, the total number of books for the sampled students of the 4 sampled classes (ssu) are as follows:

$$\text{class A} \quad \sum_{k}^{n_{11}} x_{11k} = x_{111} + x_{112} = 6 + 6 = 12$$

$$\text{B} \quad \sum_{k}^{n_{12}} x_{12k} = x_{121} + x_{122} = 4 + 10 = 14$$

$$\text{C} \quad \sum_{k}^{n_{21}} x_{21k} = x_{211} + x_{212} = 10 + 4 = 14$$

$$\text{D} \quad \sum_{k}^{n_{22}} x_{22k} = x_{221} + x_{222} = 8 + 8 = 16$$

Hence, the unbiased estimates of the averages and totals for the 4 sampled classes become as shown in Table 11.3.

Table 11.3

	$\bar{x}_{ij} = \dfrac{1}{n_{ij}} \sum^{n_{ij}} x_{ijk}$	$\hat{X}_{ij} = N_{ij}\bar{x}_{ij} = \dfrac{N_{ij}}{n_{ij}} \sum^{n_{ij}} x_{ijk}$
A	$(1/\bar{n})(12) = (1/2)(12) = 6$	$(3/2)(12) = 18$
B	$(1/\bar{n})(14) = (1/2)(14) = 7$	$(3/2)(14) = 21$
C	$(1/\bar{n})(14) = 7$	$(3/2)(14) = 21$
D	$(1/\bar{n})(16) = 8$	$(3/2)(16) = 24$

The next step is to estimate the totals for the schools (psu) from the estimated totals of the classes (ssu). Since the classes (ssu) that were selected from a school (psu) are a random sample, we may again use the $\hat{X} = N\bar{x}$ formula. These calculation procedures are carried out in Tables 11.3 and 11.4.

Table 11.4

	$\displaystyle\sum_{j}^{\bar{m}} \dfrac{N_{ij}}{n_{ij}} \sum_{k}^{n_{ij}} x_{ijk}$	$\hat{\bar{X}}_i = \dfrac{1}{\bar{m}} \sum_{j}^{\bar{m}} \dfrac{N_{ij}}{n_{ij}} \sum_{k}^{n_{ij}} x_{ij}$
A + B	$(3/2)(12) + (3/2)(14) = 39$	$(1/2)(39) = 39/2$
C + D	$(3/2)(14) + (3/2)(16) = 45$	$(1/2)(45) = 45/2$

The $(1/2)(39)$ and $(1/2)(45)$ books are the unbiased estimates of the average number of books per class (ssu) in the $i = $ 1st and $i = $ 2nd sampled schools (psu). Hence, the unbiased estimated total number of books in these two schools are obtained by multiplying these averages by the total number of classes in each school.

There are $M_i = 3$ classes in each of the two schools. Hence, the estimated totals for the $l = 2$ sampled schools are as shown in Table 11.5.

Table 11.5

$$\hat{X}_i = \frac{M_i}{\bar{m}} \sum_j^{\bar{m}} \frac{N_{ij}}{n_{ij}} \sum_k^{n_{ij}} x_{ijk}$$

$i = 1$	$\hat{X}_1 = (3/2)(39)$
$i = 2$	$\hat{X}_2 = (3/2)(45)$

Having found the unbiased estimated totals for $l = 2$ schools, we may easily estimate the unbiased total for the $L = 3$ schools. Using the $\hat{X} = N\bar{x}$ formula again, we first find the average number of books per sampled school and then multiply this average by the total number of schools, $L = 3$. The average number of books per sampled school (since $l = 2$ schools were selected as the sample), is as follows:

$$\hat{\bar{X}} = \frac{1}{l} \sum_i^l \frac{M_i}{\bar{m}} \sum_j^{\bar{m}} \frac{N_{ij}}{n_{ij}} \sum^{n_{ij}} x_{ijk}$$

$$= \frac{1}{2} \left[\frac{3}{2}(39) + \frac{3}{2}(45) \right] = 63$$

Hence, an unbiased estimator of the total number of books is

$$\hat{X} = L\hat{\bar{X}} = \frac{L}{l} \sum^l \frac{M_i}{\bar{m}} \sum_j^{\bar{m}} \frac{N_{ij}}{n_{ij}} \sum^{n_{ij}} x_{ijk} = 3(63) = 189 \text{ books}$$

To summarize: the unbiased estimator of the total number of books is given by

(5)
$$\hat{X} = L\hat{\bar{X}}$$

$$= \frac{L}{l} \sum_j^l \hat{X}_i$$

$$= \frac{L}{l} \sum_i^l M_i \hat{\bar{X}}_i$$

$$= \frac{L}{l} \sum_i^l \frac{M_i}{\bar{m}} \sum_j^{\bar{m}} \hat{X}_{ij}$$

$$= \frac{L}{l} \sum_i^l \frac{M_i}{\bar{m}} \sum_j^{\bar{m}} N_{ij}\bar{x}_{ij}$$

$$= \frac{L}{l} \sum_i^l \frac{M_i}{\bar{m}} \sum_j^{\bar{m}} \frac{N_{ij}}{n_{ij}} \sum_k^{n_{ij}} x_{ijk}$$

(6)
$$\hat{\bar{X}} = \frac{\hat{X}}{N}$$

Problems

1. Following the illustration of the population in Table 11.1, let the number of books the students have be as follows:

School	Class 1	Class 2	Class 3
1	2	4	7
	3	7	1
	7	3	6
2	6	2	3
	5	2	7
	3	6	1
3	7	1	4
	2	8	2
	4	6	9

(i) Select a sample following Table 11.2.

(ii) Following the steps in Tables 11.3, 11.4, and 11.5, calculate $\hat{X}$ and $\overset{\triangleq}{X}$.

2. Suppose we wish to estimate the average amount of sugar consumed by families in a city. There are $L = 1000$ blocks and a sample of $l = 5$ blocks is selected. From each block $\bar{m} = 2$ dwelling units are selected, and from each dwelling unit $\bar{n} = 5$ families are selected. The result is as follows. Estimate $\hat{X}$ and $\overset{\triangleq}{X}$. It is known from past data that $N = 140,000$.

Blocks	Dwelling units	Families	Sugar
l	M_i	N_{ij}	$\overset{n_{ij}}{\underset{}{\sum}} x_{ijk}$
1	13	12	6 lb
		23	5
2	8	15	4
		13	6
3	10	14	7
		11	6
4	14	19	5
		10	4
5	9	12	4
		15	7

3. On page 245, for cluster sampling with pps, we found

$$\hat{X} = \frac{1}{m} \overset{m}{\sum} \frac{1}{p_i} \left(\frac{N_i}{n_i} \overset{n_i}{\sum} x_{ij} \right)$$

For simple cluster sampling, $p_i = 1/M$, and for pps, $p_i = N_i/N$. For 3-stage sampling, we found $\hat{X} = (L/l) \overset{l}{\sum} \hat{X}_i$ which may be rewritten as

$$\hat{X} = \frac{1}{l} \overset{l}{\sum} \frac{1}{1/L} \hat{X}_i = \frac{1}{l} \overset{l}{\sum} \frac{1}{p_i} \hat{X}_i$$

where $p_i = 1/L$ is the probability of selecting a psu. Using the reasoning of pps, derive a formula for $\hat{X}$ for the 3-stage sampling case where the psu are selected with pps, where the size is measured in terms of the number of ssu in the psu. Let $M = \sum\limits_{i}^{L} M_i$.

4. Continuing Problem 3, derive a formula where the size is measured in terms of the number of tsu in the psu. Let $N = \sum\limits_{i}^{L} \sum\limits_{j}^{M_i} N_{ij} = \sum\limits_{i}^{L} N_i$.

5. Suppose we wish to estimate the average weight of 6th graders in a certain state. There are $L = 200$ elementary schools of varying size with respect to enrollment. Let M_i be the number of 6th grade classes in the ith school and N_{ij} be the number of students in the jth class in the ith school. Using the result obtained in Problem 4, explain how a sample may be drawn.

6. Suppose we wish to estimate the average number of times a college student goes to the movies during a month in a certain state. There are $L = 70$ colleges. Let M_i be the number of pages of the student directory of the ith college, and N_{ij} be the number of names on the jth page. Using the result obtained in Problem 4, explain how a sample may be selected.

11.3 Variance of $\hat{X}$

The variance of the unbiased estimator of the total, $\hat{X}$, for 3-stage cluster sampling is obtained by combining two 2-stage cluster sampling variances. This may be presented schematically as follows. For the 2-stage case we had

$$\text{psu} \text{———} \text{ssu}$$

and, corresponding to this, $V(\hat{X})$ was

$$V(\hat{X}) = (\text{psu variance } S_b^2) + (\text{ssu variance } S_i^2)$$

For the 3-stage case, we have

$$\text{psu} \text{—} \text{ssu} \text{—} \text{tsu}$$

This may be considered as combining two 2-stage cases:

$$\text{psu} \text{————} \text{ssu}$$
$$(\text{1st case}) \quad \text{ssu} \text{————} \text{tsu}$$
$$(\text{2nd case})$$

that is, there is a 2-stage case between psu and ssu, and another 2-stage case between ssu and tsu.

The variance of $\hat{X}$ for the 2-stage case was

(1)
$$V(\hat{X}) = M^2 \frac{M - m}{M} \frac{S_b^2}{m} + \frac{M}{m} \sum_{i}^{M} N_i^2 \frac{N_i - n_i}{N_i} \frac{S_i^2}{n_i}$$

where

$$S_b^2 = \frac{1}{M - 1} \sum_{i}^{M} (X_i - \bar{X})^2$$

$$S_i^2 = \frac{1}{N_i - 1} \sum_{j}^{N_i} (X_{ij} - \bar{\bar{X}}_i)^2$$

When applying this variance to the psu and ssu of the 3-stage case, we get

(2)
$$L^2 \frac{L-l}{L} \frac{S_b^2}{l} + \frac{L}{l} \sum_i^L M_i^2 \frac{M_i - \bar{m}}{M_i} \frac{S_i^2}{\bar{m}}$$

where

$$S_b^2 = \frac{1}{L-1} \sum^L (X_i - \bar{X})^2$$

$$S_i^2 = \frac{1}{M_i - 1} \sum^{M_i} (X_{ij} - \bar{\bar{X}}_i)^2$$

Let us now apply the 2-stage variance to the ssu and tsu of the 3-stage case. Then

(3)
$$M_i^2 \frac{M_i - \bar{m}}{M_i} \frac{S_i^2}{\bar{m}} + \frac{M_i}{\bar{m}} \sum_j^{M_i} N_{ij}^2 \frac{N_{ij} - n_{ij}}{N_{ij}} \frac{S_{ij}^2}{n_{ij}}$$

where

$$S_{ij}^2 = \frac{1}{N_{ij} - 1} \sum_k^{N_{ij}} (X_{ijk} - \bar{\bar{X}}_{ij})^2$$

Hence, $V(\hat{X})$ for the 3-stage case may be obtained by combining (2) and (3):

(4)
$$V(\hat{X}) = L^2 \frac{L-l}{L} \frac{S_b^2}{l} + \frac{L}{l} \sum^L \left(M_i^2 \frac{M_i - \bar{m}}{M_i} \frac{S_i^2}{\bar{m}} \right.$$
$$\left. + \frac{M_i}{\bar{m}} \sum^{M_i} N_{ij}^2 \frac{N_{ij} - n_{ij}}{N_{ij}} \frac{S_{ij}^2}{n_{ij}} \right)$$
$$= L^2 \frac{L-l}{L} \frac{S_b^2}{l} + \frac{L}{l} \sum^L M_i^2 \frac{M_i - \bar{m}}{M_i} \frac{S_i^2}{\bar{m}}$$
$$+ \frac{L}{l} \sum^L \frac{M_i}{\bar{m}} \sum^{M_i} N_{ij}^2 \frac{N_{ij} - n_{ij}}{N_{ij}} \frac{S_{ij}^2}{n_{ij}}$$

Let us analyze (4) in the following manner—We may divide it into three components:

$$V(\hat{X}): \qquad \frac{S_b^2}{l} \qquad \frac{S_i^2}{l\bar{m}} \qquad \frac{S_{ij}^2}{l\bar{m}\bar{n}}$$

where, for simplicity, we have set $n_{ij} = \bar{n}$, thus making $l\bar{m}\bar{n} = n$ the total sample size.

Hence, if n is fixed, l and $\bar{m}$ will increase as $\bar{n}$ becomes smaller. As l and $\bar{m}$ become larger, S_b^2/l and $S_{ij}^2/l\bar{m}$ will become smaller.

Furthermore, if n is given and $\bar{n}$ is small and given, the size of $l\bar{m}$ is fixed. Hence, as $\bar{m}$ is made smaller, l will become larger. Thus, S_b^2/l will become smaller.

This would indicate that if the costs of selecting psu, ssu, and tsu are similar, we will be able to decrease the size of $V(\hat{X})$ by selecting more psu and less of ssu and tsu.

We may also argue intuitively as follows: When the differences between schools (psu) are large while those between classes within a school and students within a class are small, we may decrease $V(\hat{X})$ by selecting more of the psu (schools) and fewer of the ssu (classes) and tsu (students).

As an example, suppose we wish to test the salt content of butter at $L = 100$ different factories (psu). Suppose each factory has $M_i = 10$ vats (ssu). We select a small sample of butter (tsu) from $\bar{m} = 3$ vats. If we assume that the butter is fairly homogeneous in each vat as well as in the $M_i = 10$ vats in a factory, but that there is a variation between factories, we should select more factories (psu), and fewer vats (ssu) and samples of butter (tsu).

Example 1. Using the example in section 11.2, let us calculate the variance for $\hat{X}$.

(i) Find X_{ij} (total number of books of jth class in ith school).

For X_{11}, we have

$$X_{11} = \sum_{k}^{N_{11}=3} X_{11k} = X_{111} + X_{112} + X_{113} = 2 + 4 + 6 = 12$$

Calculating the other X_{ij} in similar fashion, we find:

$$\begin{array}{lll} X_{11} = 12, & X_{12} = 18, & X_{13} = 24 \\ X_{21} = 18, & X_{22} = 24, & X_{23} = 30 \\ X_{31} = 24, & X_{32} = 12, & X_{33} = 18 \end{array}$$

(ii) Find X_i (total number of books of ith school).

For X_1 we find

$$X_1 = \sum_{j}^{M_1} X_{1j} = X_{11} + X_{12} + X_{13} = 12 + 18 + 24 = 54$$

Similarly, we find

$$X_1 = 54, \qquad X_2 = 72, \qquad X_3 = 54$$

(iii) Find $\bar{X}$ (average number of books per school).

$$\bar{X} = \frac{1}{L} \sum^{L} X_i = \frac{1}{3}(54 + 72 + 54) = 60$$

(iv) Find S_b^2.

$$S_b^2 = \frac{1}{L-1} \sum^{L} (X_i - \bar{X})^2 = \frac{1}{3-1}[(54 - 60)^2 + (72 - 60)^2 + (54 - 60)^2] = 108$$

(v) Find $\bar{\bar{X}}_i$ (average number of books per class in ith school).

For $i = 1$, we have

$$\bar{\bar{X}}_1 = \frac{1}{M_1} \sum^{M_1} X_{1j} = \frac{1}{3}(12 + 18 + 24) = 18$$

Similarly, we find

$$\bar{\bar{X}}_1 = 18, \qquad \bar{\bar{X}}_2 = 24, \qquad \bar{\bar{X}}_3 = 18$$

(vi) Find S_i^2.

$$S_1^2 = \frac{1}{M_1 - 1} \sum^{M_1} (X_{1j} - \bar{\bar{X}}_1)^2 = \frac{1}{3-1}[(12 - 18)^2 + (18 - 18)^2 + (24 - 18)^2] = 36$$

Similarly, $S_2^2 = 36$ and $S_3^2 = 36$

(vii) Find $\bar{\bar{X}}_{ij}$ (average number of books per student in jth class of ith school).

$$\bar{\bar{X}}_{11} = \frac{1}{N_{11}} \Sigma X_{11k} = \frac{1}{3}(12) = 4$$

Similarly, we find

$$\begin{array}{lll} \bar{\bar{X}}_{11} = 4, & \bar{\bar{X}}_{12} = 6, & \bar{\bar{X}}_{13} = 8 \\ \bar{\bar{X}}_{21} = 6, & \bar{\bar{X}}_{22} = 8, & \bar{\bar{X}}_{23} = 10 \\ \bar{\bar{X}}_{31} = 8, & \bar{\bar{X}}_{32} = 4, & \bar{\bar{X}}_{33} = 6 \end{array}$$

(viii) Find S_{ij}^2.

$$S_{11}^2 = \frac{1}{N_{11} - 1} \overset{N_{11}}{\Sigma} (X_{11k} - \bar{\bar{X}}_{111})^2 = \frac{1}{3 - 1}[(2 - 4)^2 + (4 - 4)^2 + (6 - 4)^2] = 4$$

Similarly, we find

$$\begin{array}{llll} S_{12}^2 = 4, & S_{13}^2 = 4, & S_{21}^2 = 4, & S_{22}^2 = 4 \\ S_{23}^2 = 4, & S_{31}^2 = 4, & S_{32}^2 = 4, & S_{33}^2 = 4 \end{array}$$

(ix) Calculate the 1st term on the right side of the variance.

$$L^2 \frac{L - l}{L} \frac{S_b^2}{l} = (3^2)\left(\frac{3 - 2}{3}\right)\left(\frac{108}{2}\right) = 162$$

(x) Calculate the 2nd term on the right side of the variance.

$$\frac{L}{l} \overset{L}{\Sigma} M_i^2 \frac{M_i - \bar{m}}{M_i} \frac{S_i^2}{\bar{m}} = \frac{3}{2}\left\{\left[(3^2)\left(\frac{3 - 2}{3}\right)\left(\frac{36}{2}\right)\right] + \left[(3^2)\left(\frac{3 - 2}{3}\right)\left(\frac{36}{2}\right)\right]\right.$$
$$\left. + \left[(3^2)\left(\frac{3 - 2}{3}\right)\left(\frac{36}{2}\right)\right]\right\} = 243$$

(xi) Calculate the 3rd term

$$\frac{L}{l} \overset{M}{\underset{m}{\Sigma}} \Sigma N_{ij}^2 \frac{N_{ij} - n_{ij}}{N_{ij}} \frac{S_{ij}^2}{n_{ij}}$$
$$= \frac{L}{l}\left[\frac{M_1}{\bar{m}}\left(N_{11}^2 \frac{N_{11} - n_{11}}{N_{11}} \frac{S_{11}^2}{n_{11}} + \cdots + N_{13}^2 \frac{N_{13} - n_{13}}{N_{13}} \frac{S_{13}^2}{n_{13}}\right) + \cdots \right.$$
$$\left. + \frac{M_3}{\bar{m}}\left(N_{31}^2 \frac{N_{31} - n_{31}}{N_{31}} \frac{S_{31}^2}{n_{31}} + \cdots + N_{33}^2 \frac{N_{33} - n_{33}}{N_{33}} \frac{S_{33}^2}{n_{33}}\right)\right]$$
$$= \frac{3}{2}\left[\frac{3}{2}(12) + \frac{3}{2}(12) + \frac{3}{2}(12)\right] = 81$$

(xii) Combine the three terms and calculate $V(\hat{X})$

$$V(\hat{X}) = L^2 \frac{L - l}{L} \frac{S_b^2}{l} + \frac{L}{l} \overset{L}{\Sigma} M_i^2 \frac{M_i - \bar{m}}{M_i} \frac{S_i^2}{\bar{m}} + \frac{L}{l} \overset{M}{\underset{m}{\Sigma}} M_i \overset{M_i}{\Sigma} N_{ij}^2 \frac{N_{ij} - n_{ij}}{N_{ij}} \frac{S_{ij}^2}{n_{ij}}$$
$$= 162 + 243 + 81 = 486$$
$$\therefore \quad \sigma(\hat{X}) = 22$$

Problem

1. Using the data of Problem 1 of page 297 calculate $V(\hat{X})$.

11.4 Estimator of $V(\hat{X})$

The form of the estimator of $V(\hat{X})$ for 3-stage cluster sampling is similar to that of the 2-stage case, which was as follows:

$$(1) \qquad \hat{V}(\hat{X}) = M^2 \frac{M-m}{M} \frac{s_b^2}{m} + \frac{M}{m} \sum^m N_i^2 \frac{N_i - n_i}{N_i} \frac{s_i^2}{n_i}$$

$$s_b^2 = \frac{1}{m-1} \sum^m (\hat{X}_i - \hat{\bar{X}})^2$$

$$s_i^2 = \frac{1}{n_i - 1} \sum^{n_i}_j (x_{ij} - \bar{x}_i)^2$$

$$\hat{X}_i = \frac{N_i}{n_i} \sum^{n_i} x_{ij}$$

$$\hat{\bar{X}} = \frac{1}{m} \sum^m \hat{X}_i$$

$$\bar{x}_i = \frac{x_i}{n_i}$$

$$x_i = \sum^{n_i}_j x_{ij}$$

For the 3-stage case, the estimator of the variance becomes

$$(2) \qquad \hat{V}(\hat{X}) = L^2 \frac{L-1}{L} \frac{s_b^2}{l} + \frac{L}{l} \sum^l M_i^2 \frac{M_i - \bar{m}}{M_i} \frac{s_i^2}{\bar{m}}$$

$$+ \frac{L}{l} \sum^l \frac{M_i}{\bar{m}} \sum^{\bar{m}} N_{ij}^2 \frac{N_{ij} - n_{ij}}{N_{ij}} \frac{s_{ij}^2}{n_{ij}}$$

$$s_b^2 = \frac{1}{l-1} \sum^l (\hat{X}_i - \hat{\bar{X}})^2$$

$$s_i^2 = \frac{1}{m_i - 1} \sum^{m_i}_j (\hat{X}_{ij} - \hat{\bar{X}}_i)^2$$

$$s_{ij}^2 = \frac{1}{n_{ij} - 1} \sum^{n_{ij}}_k (x_{ijk} - \overset{\equiv}{x}_{ij})^2$$

$x_{ijk} =$ the number of books owned by the kth student in the sample taken from the jth sampled class of the ith sampled school.

$\overset{\equiv}{x}_{ij} = \dfrac{1}{n_{ij}} \sum^{n_{ij}}_k x_{ijk}$ is the average number of books per student in the sample n_{ij} taken from the jth sampled class of the ith sampled school.

$\hat{X}_{ij} = \dfrac{N_{ij}}{n_{ij}} \sum^{n_{ij}} x_{ijk} = N_{ij}\overset{\equiv}{x}_{ij}$ is the unbiased estimator of the total number of books in the jth class of the ith school.

$\hat{X}_i = \dfrac{M_i}{\bar{m}} \sum_j^{\bar{m}} \hat{X}_{ij} = M_i \hat{\bar{X}}_i$ is the unbiased estimator of the total number of books in the ith sampled school.

$\hat{\bar{X}}_i = \dfrac{1}{l} \sum_i^l \hat{X}_i$ is the average number of books per school of the l sampled schools and also an unbiased estimator of the average number of books per school.

$\hat{\bar{X}}_i = \dfrac{1}{\bar{m}} \sum_j^{\bar{m}} \hat{X}_{ij}$ is the average number of books per class of the $\bar{m}$ classes taken from the ith school and also an unbiased estimator of the average number of books per class in the ith school.

Example 1. Using the data of Example 1, section 11.2, let us find $\hat{V}(\hat{X})$. We shall compute the various components of equation (2), and then combine these to find $\hat{V}(\hat{X})$.

(i) Calculate $\hat{X}_i$, which is an unbiased estimate of the total number of books of the ith sampled school (psu).

$$\hat{X}_1 = \frac{M_1}{\bar{m}} \sum_j^{\bar{m}=2} \hat{X}_{1j} = \frac{M_1}{\bar{m}}(\hat{X}_{11} + \hat{X}_{12})$$
$$= (3/2)(15 + 24) = (3/2)(39)$$
$$\hat{X}_2 = (3/2)(45)$$

(ii) Calculate $\hat{\bar{X}}$ (which is an unbiased estimate of the average number of books per school).

$$\hat{\bar{X}} = (1/l) \sum_i^l X_i = (1/2)(\hat{X}_1 + \hat{X}_2)$$
$$= (1/2)[(3/2)(39) + (3/2)(45)] = (3/2)(42)$$

(iii) Calculate s_b^2 (using the results of (i) and (ii)).

$$s_b^2 = \frac{1}{l-1} \sum_i^l (\hat{X}_i - \hat{\bar{X}})^2$$
$$= \frac{1}{2-1}\{[(3/2)(39) - (3/2)(42)]^2 + [(3/2)(45) - (3/2)(42)]^2\} = 81/2$$

(iv) Calculate $s_i^2 = \dfrac{1}{\bar{m}-1} \sum^{\bar{m}} (\hat{X}_{ij} - \hat{\bar{X}}_i)^2$.

$$\hat{\bar{X}}_1 = \frac{1}{\bar{m}} \sum^{\bar{m}} \hat{X}_{1j} = \frac{1}{\bar{m}}(\hat{X}_{11} + \hat{X}_{12})$$
$$= (1/2)(15 + 24) = (1/2)(39)$$
$$\hat{\bar{X}}_2 = (1/2)(27 + 18) = (1/2)(45)$$
$$\therefore \quad s_1^2 = \frac{1}{2-1}[(\hat{X}_{11} - \hat{\bar{X}}_1)^2 + (\hat{X}_{12} - \hat{\bar{X}}_1)^2]$$
$$= [15 - (1/2)(39)]^2 + [24 - (1/2)(39)]^2 = 81/2$$
$$s_2^2 = 81/2$$

(v) Calculate s_{ij}^2.

$$s_{ij}^2 = \frac{1}{n_{ij} - 1} \sum_k^{n_{ij}} (x_{ijk} - \overline{\overline{x}}_{ij})^2$$

$$\overline{\overline{x}}_{11} = \frac{1}{n_{11}}(x_{111} + x_{112}) = \frac{1}{2}(6 + 4) = 5$$

$$\overline{\overline{x}}_{12} = 8, \qquad \overline{\overline{x}}_{21} = 9, \qquad \overline{\overline{x}}_{22} = 12$$

$$s_{11}^2 = \frac{1}{2-1}[(6-5)^2 + (4-5)^2] = 2$$

$$s_{12}^2 = 8, \qquad s_{21}^2 = 2, \qquad s_{22}^2 = 8$$

(vi) $\dfrac{L}{l} \sum^l M_i^2 \dfrac{M_i - \bar{m}}{M_i} \dfrac{s_i^2}{\bar{m}}$

$$= \frac{3}{2}\left\{\left[(3^2)\left(\frac{3-2}{3}\right)\left(\frac{1}{2}\right)\left(\frac{81}{2}\right)\right] + \left[(3^2)\left(\frac{3-2}{3}\right)\left(\frac{1}{2}\right)\left(\frac{81}{2}\right)\right]\right\} = \frac{81 \times 9}{4}$$

(vii) $\dfrac{L}{l} \sum^l \dfrac{M_i}{\bar{m}} \sum^{\bar{m}} N_{ij}^2 \dfrac{N_{ij} - n_{ij}}{N_{ij}} \dfrac{s_{ij}^2}{n_{ij}} = \dfrac{3}{2}(45)$

(viii) Calculate $\hat{V}(\hat{X})$.

$$\hat{V}(\hat{X}) = \left[(3^2)\left(\frac{3-2}{3}\right)\left(\frac{1}{2}\right)\left(\frac{81}{2}\right)\right] + \left[\frac{81 \times 9}{4}\right] + \left[\frac{3}{2}(45)\right] = 310.5$$

$$s(\hat{X}) = \sqrt{310.5} \doteq 17.6$$

Recall that the variance $V(\hat{X})$ based on the population was $V(\hat{X}) = 486$.

When $l \ll L$, we may simplify the estimator of the variance (2) as follows:

$$(3) \qquad \hat{V}(\hat{X}) = \left(\frac{L}{l}\right)^2 \left[\frac{L-l}{L} l s_b^2 + \frac{l}{L} \sum^l M_i^2 \frac{M_i - m_i}{M_i} \frac{s_i}{m_i}\right.$$

$$\left. + \frac{l}{L} \sum^l \frac{M_i}{m_i} \sum^{m_i} N_{ij}^2 \frac{N_{ij} - n_{ij}}{N_{ij}} \frac{s_{ij}^2}{n_{ij}}\right]$$

$$\doteq L^2 \frac{s_b^2}{l}$$

Example 2. Suppose there are $L = 580$ schools. A sample of $l = 5$ schools is selected. We select $\bar{m} = 2$ classes from each school and $\bar{n} = 4$ students from each class. Estimate the total number of books.

Since $L = 580$ and $l = 5$, $l/L = 5/580 = 1/116$. Hence we may expect S_b^2 to be the dominant element affecting $\hat{V}(\hat{X})$. From (3), we then set

$$\hat{V}(\hat{X}) \doteq L^2 \frac{s_b^2}{l}$$

and the problem is to find s_b^2. Assume that $M_i = \bar{M} = 6$ classes per school, and $N_{ij} = \bar{N} = 40$ students per class.

School	Student	Class $j = 1$	Class $j = 2$
1	$k = 1$	$x_{111} = 5$	$x_{121} = 4$
	2	$x_{112} = 4$	$x_{122} = 6$
	3	$x_{113} = 7$	$x_{123} = 1$
	4	$x_{114} = 7$	$x_{124} = 5$
		$\sum^{n_{11}} x_{11k} = 23$	$\sum^{n_{12}} x_{12k} = 16$
2	$k = 1$	$x_{211} = 4$	$x_{221} = 2$
	2	$x_{212} = 4$	$x_{222} = 3$
	3	$x_{213} = 5$	$x_{223} = 6$
	4	$x_{214} = 3$	$x_{224} = 6$
		$\sum^{n_{21}} x_{21k} = 16$	$\sum^{n_{22}} x_{22k} = 17$
3	$k = 1$	$x_{311} = 4$	$x_{321} = 1$
	2	$x_{312} = 2$	$x_{322} = 3$
	3	$x_{313} = 5$	$x_{323} = 8$
	4	$x_{314} = 1$	$x_{324} = 3$
		$\sum^{n_{31}} x_{31k} = 12$	$\sum^{n_{32}} x_{32k} = 15$
4	$k = 1$	$x_{411} = 2$	$x_{421} = 1$
	2	$x_{412} = 4$	$x_{422} = 5$
	3	$x_{413} = 1$	$x_{423} = 6$
	4	$x_{414} = 3$	$x_{424} = 9$
		$\sum^{n_{41}} x_{41k} = 10$	$\sum^{n_{42}} x_{42k} = 21$
5	$k = 1$	$x_{511} = 7$	$x_{521} = 9$
	2	$x_{512} = 3$	$x_{522} = 3$
	3	$x_{513} = 4$	$x_{523} = 2$
	4	$x_{514} = 7$	$x_{524} = 3$
		$\sum^{n_{51}} x_{51k} = 21$	$\sum^{n_{52}} x_{52k} = 17$

To find s_b^2, we need $\hat{X}_i$ and $\hat{X}$.

(i) Calculate $\hat{X}_i$.

$$\hat{X}_i = \frac{M_i}{\bar{m}} \sum^{\bar{m}} \hat{X}_{ij} \qquad \hat{X}_{ij} = \frac{N_{ij}}{n_{ij}} \sum^{n_{ij}} x_{ijk}$$

School	Class 1	Class 2
1	$\hat{X}_{11} = (40/4)(23) = 230$	$\hat{X}_{12} = (40/4)(16) = 160$
2	$\hat{X}_{21} = 160$	$\hat{X}_{22} = 170$
3	$\hat{X}_{31} = 120$	$\hat{X}_{32} = 150$
4	$\hat{X}_{41} = 100$	$\hat{X}_{42} = 210$
5	$\hat{X}_{51} = 210$	$\hat{X}_{52} = 170$

$$\hat{X}_i$$

$$\hat{X}_1 = (6/2)(230 + 160) = 3(390)$$
$$\hat{X}_2 = 3(330)$$
$$\hat{X}_3 = 3(270)$$
$$\hat{X}_4 = 3(310)$$
$$\hat{X}_5 = 3(380)$$

$$3(1680)$$

$$\hat{\bar{X}} = \frac{1}{l} \sum_{i}^{l=5} \hat{X}_i = \frac{1}{5}(3 \times 1680) = 3(336)$$

(ii) Calculate s_b^2

$$s_b^2 = \frac{1}{l-1} \sum^{l} (\hat{X}_i - \hat{\bar{X}})^2$$

$$= \frac{1}{5-1}(9 \times 9920) = \frac{9 \times 9920}{4}$$

(iii) Calculate $\hat{V}(\hat{X})$.

$$\hat{V}(\hat{X}) = L^2 \frac{s_b^2}{l} = (580)^2 \cdot \left(\frac{1}{5}\right)\left(\frac{9 \times 9920}{4}\right)$$

$$s(\hat{X}) = \sqrt{\hat{V}(\hat{X})} = 38{,}750 \text{ books}$$

(iv) Calculate $\hat{X}$.

$$\hat{X} = \frac{L}{l} \sum^{l} \frac{M_i}{\bar{m}} \sum^{\bar{m}} \frac{N_{ij}}{n_{ij}} \sum_{k}^{n_{ij}} x_{ijk}$$

$$= \frac{580}{5} \cdot \frac{6}{2} \cdot \frac{40}{4}(23 + 16 + \cdots + 21 + 17)$$

$$= 584{,}640 \text{ books}$$

Problems

1. Using the data of Problem 1 of page 297,
   (i) Calculate $\hat{V}(\hat{X})$ and $s(\hat{X})$.
   (ii) Find the 2σ confidence interval for X.

2. Suppose there are $L = 2500$ colleges in the country, and a sample of $l = 5$ colleges are selected. Let M_i be the number of pages of the student directory of the ith school, and N_{ij} be the number of names on the ith page. A sample of $\bar{m} = 2$ pages and $\bar{n} = 10$ students were selected and interviewed. The data on the number of times they go to movies during a month are as follows:

College	Pages	Names	$\sum^{\bar{n}} x_{ijk}$
l	M_i	N_{ij}	
1	40	30	20
		30	25
2	20	40	20
		40	30
3	120	40	25
		40	18
4	300	50	15
		50	25
5	220	40	20
		40	22

(i) Find $\hat{X}$.

(ii) Find $\hat{V}(\hat{X})$ using equation (3).

(iii) Find the 2σ confidence interval for X.

3. Suppose that in Problem 2 above you wish to select the colleges by pps. Explain the steps you would take and the formula for $\hat{X}$ you would use.

4. Suppose that in Problems 2 and 3 you wish to estimate the proportion of college students who smoke. Extend the results of Chapter 10 and explain how $\hat{P}$ may be estimated using 3-stage cluster sampling.

11.5 Allocation of the sample

In the previous section, we gave a heuristic argument that when the costs of selecting the psu, ssu, and tsu are similar, the variance may become smaller by keeping $\bar{n}$ small and increasing l. Let us now investigate this problem more carefully by considering explicitly the cost of selecting the sample.

Let the costs of selecting psu, ssu, and tsu be c_1, c_2, and c_3, and let the total cost be set as c. Then

$$(1) \qquad\qquad c = c_1 l + c_2 l\bar{m} + c_3 l\bar{m}\bar{n}$$

Our problem is to determine l, $\bar{m}$, and $\bar{n}$ that will minimize $\hat{V}(\hat{X})$ where

$$(2) \qquad \hat{V}(\hat{X}) = L^2 \frac{L-1}{L} \frac{s_b^2}{l} + \frac{L}{l} \sum_i^l M_i^2 \frac{M_i - \bar{m}}{M_i} \frac{s_i^2}{\bar{m}}$$

$$+ \frac{L}{l} \sum_i^l \frac{M_i}{\bar{m}} \sum_j^{\bar{m}} N_{ij}^2 \frac{N_{ij} - \bar{n}}{N_{ij}} \frac{s_{ij}^2}{\bar{n}}$$

As shown, this is quite a formidable formula, and we shall simplify it by assuming that the finite multipliers are close to unity, and may thus be omitted. Furthermore, for simplicity, we are assuming that $n_{ij} = \bar{n}$. Hence, (2) becomes

$$(3) \qquad \hat{V}(\hat{X}) = L^2 \frac{s_b^2}{l} + L \sum_i^l M_i^2 \frac{s_i^2}{l\bar{m}} + L \sum_i^l M_i \sum_j^{\bar{m}} N_{ij}^2 \frac{s_{ij}^2}{l\bar{m}\bar{n}}$$

$$= L^2 \left(\frac{s_b^2}{l} + \frac{s_{2i}^2}{l\bar{m}} + \frac{s_{3j}^2}{l\bar{m}\bar{n}} \right)$$

where

$$s_{2i}^2 = \frac{1}{L} \sum_i^l M_i^2 s_i^2$$

$$s_{3j}^2 = \frac{1}{L} \sum_i^l M_i \sum_j^{\bar{m}} N_{ij}^2 s_{ij}^2$$

Hence our problem is to minimize (3) subject to the linear constraint (1). Using the Lagrange multiplier method, we find

(4)
$$Z = \hat{V}(\hat{X}) + \lambda(c - c_1 l - c_2 l\bar{m} - c_3 l\bar{m}\bar{n})$$

$$\frac{\partial Z}{\partial l} = \frac{-L^2}{l^2}\left(s_b^2 + \frac{s_{2i}^2}{\bar{m}} + \frac{s_{3i}^2}{l\bar{m}\bar{n}}\right) + \lambda(-c_1 - c_2\bar{m} - c_3\bar{m}\bar{n}) = 0$$

$$\frac{\partial Z}{\partial \bar{m}} = \frac{-L^2}{\bar{m}^2}\left(-\frac{s_{2i}^2}{l} - \frac{s_{3j}^2}{l\bar{n}}\right) + \lambda(-c_2 l - c_3 l\bar{n}) = 0$$

$$\frac{\partial Z}{\partial \bar{n}} = \frac{-L^2}{\bar{n}^2}\left(-\frac{s_{3j}^2}{l\bar{m}}\right) + \lambda(-c_3 l\bar{m}) = 0$$

From the above equations we get
$$L^2 s_b^2 + \lambda c_1 l^2 = 0$$
$$L^2 s_{2i}^2 + \lambda c_2 (l\bar{m})^2 = 0$$
$$L^2 s_{3j}^2 + \lambda c_3 (l\bar{m}\bar{n})^2 = 0$$

Hence, from these equations, we find
$$\bar{m}^2 = \frac{c_1}{c_2} \cdot \frac{s_{2i}^2}{s_b^2}$$

$$\bar{n}^2 = \frac{c_2}{c_3} \cdot \frac{s_{3j}^2}{s_b^2}$$

which leads to

(5)
$$\bar{m} = \sqrt{\frac{c_1}{c_2}} \cdot \frac{s_{2i}}{s_b}$$

(6)
$$\bar{n} = \sqrt{\frac{c_2}{c_3}} \cdot \frac{s_{3j}}{s_b}$$

The l is found from (1) by substituting these values for $\bar{m}$ and $\bar{n}$.

As shown, when s_b is large relative to s_{2i} and s_{3j}, select less of $\bar{m}$ and $\bar{n}$. That is, when the variation among psu is large relative to the variation among ssu and tsu, select more psu and less of ssu and tsu.

The ratio of the costs in (5) indicate that when c_1 is large relative to c_2 (that is, when the cost of selecting psu is large relative to that of selecting ssu), increase $\bar{m}$ by selecting more of ssu.

A similar interpretation holds for $\bar{n}$ with respect to $\bar{m}$ in (6).

Notes and References

For further discussion and proofs of the results of 3-stage sampling, see Cochran (1963), pp. 285–288; Hansen, Hurwitz and Madow(1953) pp. 332–335; Deming (1950), pp. 135–165. Also see Kish(1965), Chapter 10, which provides a number of illustrations of multistage sampling applied to various surveys.

As mentioned in the previous notes and references, Stephan and McCarthy's *Sampling Opinions* (1958) is recommended.

Since 3-stage sampling is in many cases discussed with stratified cluster sampling, the student may postpone reading the above references until he has finished the next chapter of this book.

CHAPTER 12

Stratified Cluster Sampling

12.1 Introduction

In stratified sampling, precision was obtained by stratifying homogeneous sampling units together and selecting subsamples by random sampling from each stratum. In some cases, however, we may consider each stratum as a population made up of clusters and apply cluster sampling to each stratum. For example, suppose each of $L = 580$ elementary schools is considered as a stratum. The M_i classes in each school are therefore the clusters (psu) from which a random sample of m_i psu's (classes) are selected. And subsamples of n_{ij} students are selected from each of the m_i classes.

Thus, the difference between stratified cluster sampling and 3-stage cluster sampling is that $L = l$ for stratified cluster sampling. That is, instead of selecting l schools from the $L = 580$ schools, and then selecting m_i classes from each of the l schools, the procedure is to select m_i classes from *each* of the $L = 580$ schools.

Hence, the formulas for the estimators of the population total, mean, and variances may be easily obtained from the 3-stage sampling formulas by letting $L = l$.

The stratified cluster sampling procedure, like all the previous sampling procedures, starts from a basic relation and then utilizes the two basic principles involved in stratification and clustering. The basic relation which we have already mentioned is that when sampling units are grouped into, say, two groups so that the units within each group are similar, then both groups will tend to be heterogeneous with respect to each other. That is, when homogeneous sampling units are grouped together, the groups will be heterogeneous. For example, if there are 10 persons (5 boys and 5 girls) and the boys are placed in one group, the second will necessarily be made up of girls.

Conversely, when the sampling units are grouped into two groups so that each group contains dissimilar units, then both groups will tend to be homogeneous. That is, when heterogeneous sampling units are grouped together, the groups will be homogeneous. For example, if the first group is a mixture of boys and girls, the second group will also be a mixture of boys and girls, and the groups will be similar.

The implication is that when groups are heterogeneous with respect to one another (boys in one group and girls in the other), a sample more representative of the population will be obtained by selecting samples from more groups. Conversely, when groups are homogeneous with respect to one another (that is, each group is a mixture of boys and girls), it will suffice to select samples from a few groups to obtain a sample representative of the population.

Stratified random sampling utilizes these relations by grouping similar sampling units into homogeneous strata (boys in one group, girls in the other), and as a result the strata are heterogeneous with respect to one another Random samples are therefore taken from *each* stratum to obtain a sample representative of the population.

Cluster sampling utilizes these relations by grouping dissimilar sampling units into heterogeneous clusters (each group a mixture of boys and girls), and as a result the clusters are homogeneous with respect to one another. Hence, *several* clusters are selected, and random samples are selected from these clusters to obtain a sample representative of the population.

Stratified cluster sampling combines the characteristics of stratified sampling and cluster sampling. It breaks down the population into strata which are internally homogeneous, and therefore heterogeneous among one another, and clusters are selected from *each* stratum. Clusters are made internally heterogeneous within each stratum—hence, homogeneous among one another. As a result, only a few clusters need to be selected from a stratum in order to represent it.

The advantages of this type of stratified cluster sampling are easy to recognize and are similar to those of 3-stage cluster sampling. The first is that we need to prepare the frame for only the psu and ssu that are to be selected as the sample. Second (compared to simple random or stratified random sampling), it reduces traveling and administrative costs. Third, the more stages there are, the more flexibility is obtained in sample design.

Because of these and other advantages, stratified cluster sampling is used widely in practice. For opinion surveys, a country may be divided into say, $L = 300$ strata, where each stratum may correspond to an area (such as a county). Each stratum may be divided into $\bar{M} = 12$ clusters, where (for example) each cluster may correspond to a voting district. Then the sampling process may be to select $\bar{m} = 1$ cluster (voting district) by simple random sampling from each stratum (county), and then to select $\bar{n} = 10$ persons from the voting register of that voting district. We will thus obtain a sample of $n = L\bar{m}\bar{n} = 300 \times 1 \times 12 = 3600$ voters.

In this example, the $\bar{M} = 12$ clusters (voting districts) should be made as heterogeneous as possible within themselves. This implies that the clusters will be homogeneous among themselves, and it is therefore necessary to select only a few clusters in order to represent the stratum. In our example, we have selected only $\bar{m} = 1$ cluster.

If the survey is to be made in a city such as New York we may first stratify it into voting districts or some other areal unit, then divide these into blocks. The sampling process will be to select a sample of, say, $\bar{m} = 2$ blocks, and to then select a sample of $\bar{n} = 3$ families from each block. We may go one step further and select $k = 1$ person from each family.

The population survey procedure used by the Bureau of Census is another example. In 1950, the U.S. was divided into $L = 68$ strata, so that each stratum had a population of about 1.95 million. The strata were designed to be homogeneous within themselves with respect to the degree of urbanization, type of industry, and other criteria. The implication was that the strata were heterogeneous among themselves.

The $L = 68$ strata included about 2000 psu. The psu were in turn made up of several counties, and the counties in a psu were combined to maximize heterogeneity. This was achieved by including farm and nonfarm segments in the psu. By making the psu heterogeneous within themselves, they become more homogeneous among themselves. The implication was that it would be necessary to select only a few psu to represent a stratum. The psu were divided into segments, the segments were selected by simple random sampling, and dwelling units were selected from these. The sample segments were selected by the staff in Washington, but the list of dwelling units was made by field personnel.

With this background, let us proceed to a discussion of the statistical theory of stratified cluster sampling to support these common sense arguments.

12.2 Estimator of the population total X

The estimator of the population total for stratified cluster sampling is obtained by setting $L = l$ in the estimator of the population total X for 3-stage cluster sampling.

For 3-stage sampling, we had

(1)
$$\hat{X} = \frac{L}{l} \sum^{l} \frac{M_h}{m_h} \sum^{m_h} \frac{N_{hi}}{n_{hi}} \sum^{n_{hi}} x_{hij}$$

where L was used to indicate clusters. By setting $L = l$, and letting L indicate strata instead of clusters, we obtain

(2)
$$\hat{X} = \sum^{L} \frac{M_h}{m_h} \sum^{m_h} \frac{N_{hi}}{n_{hi}} \sum^{n_{hi}} x_{hij}$$

which is an unbiased estimator of the total for stratified cluster sampling.

The interpretation of equation (2) is similar to that in the 3-stage case. The term $(N_{hi}/n_{hi}) \sum x_{hij}$ is an estimate of the total for the ith cluster in the hth stratum. Hence, $A = \sum (N_{hi}/n_{hi}) \sum x_{hij}$ is an estimate of the total for the sampled m_h clusters in stratum h.

The term $B = (M_h/m_h)A$ is an estimate of the total of the hth stratum.

Hence $\overset{L}{\sum} B$ is an estimate of the total for all L strata.

Example 1. Let us illustrate the use of this formula. Suppose there are $L = 3$ schools (strata), each of which has $M_h = 2$ classes (psu), and where each class has $N_{hi} = 3$ students (ssu). The term X_{hij} shows the number of books owned by these students.

Strata	Class		X_{hij}		
I	1	$X_{111} = 4$	$X_{112} = 3$	$X_{113} = 2$	9
	2	$X_{121} = 2$	$X_{122} = 4$	$X_{123} = 6$	12
II	1	$X_{211} = 6$	$X_{212} = 2$	$X_{213} = 1$	9
	2	$X_{221} = 6$	$X_{222} = 3$	$X_{223} = 3$	12
III	1	$X_{311} = 3$	$X_{312} = 9$	$X_{313} = 3$	15
	2	$X_{321} = 8$	$X_{322} = 1$	$X_{323} = 3$	12
					69

Suppose we select $m_h = 1$ class (psu) from each stratum and $n_{hi} = 2$ students (ssu) from each selected class (psu). We wish to estimate the total number of books owned by the $N = 18$ students. Suppose the following sample is selected:

Strata	Class (psu)	X_{hij}(Books)	
I	#2	$X_{121} = 2$	$X_{123} = 6$
II	#1	$X_{211} = 6$	$X_{212} = 2$
III	#1	$X_{311} = 3$	$X_{313} = 3$

In sample notation, this becomes

x_{hij}(Books)		$\sum x_{hij}$
$x_{111} = 2$	$x_{112} = 6$	8
$x_{211} = 6$	$x_{212} = 2$	8
$x_{311} = 3$	$x_{312} = 3$	6

$$\therefore \quad \hat{X} = \sum^{L} \frac{M_h}{m_h} \sum^{m_h} \frac{N_{hi}}{n_{hi}} \sum^{n_{hi}} x_{hij}$$

$$= \frac{M_1}{m_1} \sum^{m_1} \frac{N_{1j}}{n_{1j}} \sum^{n_{1i}} x_{1ij} + \frac{M_2}{m_2} \sum^{m_2} \frac{N_{2i}}{n_{2i}} \sum^{n_{2i}} x_{2ij} + \frac{M_3}{m_3} \sum^{m_3} \frac{N_{3i}}{n_{3i}} \sum^{n_{1i}} x_{3ij}$$

$$= \frac{M_1}{m_1}\left[\frac{N_{11}}{n_{11}}(x_{111} + x_{112})\right] + \frac{M_2}{m_2}\left[\frac{N_{21}}{n_{21}}(x_{211} + x_{212})\right] + \frac{M_3}{m_3}\left[\frac{N_{31}}{n_{31}}(x_{311} + x_{312})\right]$$

$$= \frac{2}{1}\left[\frac{3}{2}(2 + 6)\right] + \frac{2}{1}\left[\frac{3}{2}(6 + 2)\right] + \frac{2}{1}\left[\frac{3}{2}(3 + 3)\right] = 66$$

Hence the estimate is $\hat{X} = 66$ books. The actual population total is $X = 69$ books.

Example 2. As shown in Example 1, the calculation of estimates for stratified cluster sampling becomes cumbersome. It would be helpful if an easy-to-follow routine could be set up. Many such routines can be set up—depending on the ingenuity of the researcher. Let us use a hypothetical example and set up a calculation table as an illustration. Suppose there are $L = 2$ strata (schools), each stratum has $M_h = 3$ clusters (classes), and each cluster has $N_{hi} = 5$ elements (students). A sample of $m_h = 2$ clusters (classes) is selected and $n_{hi} = 3$ elements (students) are selected from each cluster (class). A simple calculation routine may be set up as follows:

$m_h = 2$	Stratum I 1	Stratum I 2	Stratum II 1	Stratum II 2
(1)	$\sum x_{11j}$	$\sum x_{12j}$	$\sum x_{21j}$	$\sum x_{22j}$
(2)	N_{11}/n_{11}	N_{12}/n_{12}	N_{21}/n_{21}	N_{22}/n_{22}
(3) = (1) × (2)	A	B	C	D
(4)	$E = A + B$		$F = C + D$	
(5)	M_1/m_1		M_2/m_2	
(6) = (4) × (5)	G		H	

$$\therefore \quad \hat{X} = G + H$$

In equation (2), $\hat{X}$ was found by stratifying the psu, and the ssu were sampled from the psu. In this case, the strata were schools, the classes were the psu, and the students were the ssu. However, equation (2) may be easily extended to cases including additional stages of sampling. For example, suppose we wished to estimate the total number of books owned by 6th graders in a particular state. The state may be stratified into counties (L strata); in each stratum (county), there are schools (M_h psu); in each school (psu), there are classes (N_{hi} ssu); and in each class (ssu), there are students (W_{hij} tsu). Then X_{hijk} will show the number of books owned by the kth student (tsu) in the jth class (ssu) in the ith school (psu) in the hth county (stratum).

We may obtain an estimate for this process by extending equation (2) as follows:

$$(3) \qquad \hat{X} = \sum^{L} \frac{M_i}{m_h} \sum^{m_h} \frac{N_{hi}}{n_{hi}} \sum^{n_{hi}} \frac{W_{hij}}{w_{hij}} \sum^{w_{hij}} x_{hijk}$$

which is an unbiased estimate of the population total. As shown, this estimation procedure may be similarly extended to include additional stages.

Three-stage stratified cluster sampling is widely used in government statistics, opinion surveys, market research, agricultural research, and other fields because of its flexibility in sample design, ease of administration, and low cost. Let us study several examples.

Example 3. We have already discussed the population surveys conducted by the Bureau of Census, but let us reconsider them now because they use 3-stage stratified cluster sampling. The Bureau of Census conducts a survey of employment and other characteristics of the labor force by using 3-stage stratified cluster sampling procedure. There are about 3000 counties in the U.S. which are grouped into about 2000 psu. The counties are grouped according to geographical proximity and also in order to achieve heterogeneity within the psu.

The psu are divided into 68 strata and so as to try to obtain homogeneity within the strata.

The sampling process is to select l psu from each strata by pps, then to select areal segments (ssu) from the psu, and finally to select families (tsu) from the segments. The areal segments are defined so that there are about 50 households per segment from which about 6 households are selected as the ultimate clusters.

Example 4. Suppose we wish to estimate the average amount of soap used each month by an adult in a certain state. The state may be stratified into counties (strata). The counties may be divided into voting districts (psu) represented by the voting registers. The pages of the voting registers may be the ssu and the names may be considered as the tsu. Then, X_{hijk} is the amount of soap used by the kth person (tsu) on the jth page (ssu) of the ith voting register (psu) in the hth county (stratum).

In example 3, we mentioned that the psu were selected by pps. Use of the pps procedure leads to a uniform sampling fraction, and—as shown in Chapter 9—leads to self-weighting estimators that are of a simple form. Let us explain how the pps sampling procedure in 3-stage stratified cluster sampling leads to a uniform sampling fraction.

By selecting the psu and ssu by pps and the tsu by simple random sampling, a uniform sampling fraction is obtained. This may be shown easily: Suppose the county is the stratum and there are $M_h = 3$ schools (psu) in the county. Assume each school (psu) has $N_{hi} = 3$ classes (ssu) and each class has W_{hij} students (tsu). The data for one county are given in Table 12.1.

Table 12.1

County I (Stratum I)

School(psu)	ssu		Class size (Students)			
1	$N_{11} = 3$ classes	$A_1 = 20$	$B_1 = 30$	$C_1 = 50$	100
2	$N_{12} = 3$ "	$A_2 = 50$	$B_2 = 70$	$C_2 = 80$	200
3	$N_{13} = 3$ "	$A_3 = 80$	$B_3 = 100$	$C_3 = 120$	300
						600

Select the psu by pps. Hence, for cluster 1 of stratum I, the probability of selection is $100/600$.

Of the $N_{11} = 3$ classes (ssu), one class is selected by probability proportional to size. Suppose B_1 has been selected. Its probability of selection is $30/100$.

Finally, we select, say, one student by simple random sampling from class (ssu) B_1. The probability of selection is then $1/30$.

Thus, the probability of selecting a sampling unit of class B_1 is

$$\frac{100}{600} \times \frac{30}{100} \times \frac{1}{30} = \frac{1}{600}$$

A check will show that the probability of selecting any sampling unit in stratum I (that is, county I) will be 1/600. We have therefore obtained a uniform sampling fraction for this process.

Problems

1. Given the following data of books owned by students, estimate the total number of books by selecting $m_h = 1$ class from each stratum and $n_{hi} = 2$ students from each class. Devise a calculation routine. Also find the average number of books per student.

School	Class	X_{hij}(Books)
I	1	3, 4, 2
	2	8, 2, 4
II	1	5, 3, 1
	2	6, 4, 2
II	1	4 2 8
	2	5 2 3

2. Given the following data of books owned by students, estimate the total number of books by selecting $m_h = 1$ school, $n_{hi} = 1$ class, and $w_{hij} = 2$ students. Devise a calculation routine. Also find the average number of books per student.

County	School	Class	X_{hijk}(Books)
I	1	1	5, 3, 9, 4
		2	8, 2, 2
	2	1	9, 6, 2
		2	1, 4, 6, 7
II	1	1	3, 6, 9
		2	2, 3, 5, 5
	2	1	4, 3, 1, 9
		2	6, 3, 9
III	1	1	5, 4, 9, 3
		2	7, 5, 2, 1
		3	8, 5, 3
	2	1	7, 1, 4, 6, 8
		2	2, 6, 1, 9

3. Suppose we wish to estimate the average amount of soap used each month by an adult in a certain state. There are $L = 10$ counties; each county has $M_h = \bar{M}$

$= 10$ voting districts; each voting register of a district has about $N_{hi} = \bar{N} = 50$ pages; and each page has about $W_{hij} = \bar{W} = 30$ names. Suppose we select $m_h = \bar{m} = 2$ voting registers; $n_{hi} = \bar{n} = 5$ pages; and $w_{hij} = \bar{w} = 5$ names.

(i) What is the total sample size?

(ii) Suppose the result of the survey is as follows. Estimate the total amount of soap used by the adults.

Counties	$\sum x_{h1jk}$	$\sum x_{h2jk}$
1	22.5	32.5
2	42.5	35.0
3	42.5	22.5
4	25.0	42.5
5	22.5	25.0
6	25.0	40.0
7	40.0	30.0
8	27.5	20.0
9	50.0	37.5
10	37.5	37.5

4. Suppose in Problem 3, the data is as follows. Estimate the average amount of soap used by adults.

Counties	M_h	N_{hi}	W_{hij}	$\sum x_{h1jk}$	$\sum x_{h2jk}$
1	8	48	30	45	22.5
2	12	55	30	42.5	32.5
3	10	50	30	32.5	47.5
4	9	42	30	35.0	50.0
5	7	40	30	27.5	42.5
6	11	45	30	40.0	40.0
7	10	56	30	30.0	35.0
8	9	50	30	25.0	20.0
9	6	46	30	47.5	50.0
10	8	48	30	20.0	30.0

5. Suppose the data in Table 12.1 is as follows. The psu (schools) and ssu (classes) are selected by pps. The tsu(students) are selected by simple random sampling. What is the probability of selecting a sampling unit (tsu) from class A_1? What is the probability when selecting from B_2? From C_3?

School	Class	Students			
1	$N_{11} = 4$	$A_1 = 20$	$B_1 = 30$	$C_1 = 50$	$D_1 = 60$
2	$N_{12} = 2$	$A_2 = 50$	$B_2 = 70$		
3	$N_{13} = 3$	$A_3 = 80$	$B_3 = 100$	$C_3 = 120$	

12.3 The variance of $\hat{X}$

From our discussion of 3-stage cluster sampling and the discussions of sections 12.1 and 12.2, we can see that the variance of $\hat{X}$ for stratified cluster sampling may be obtained from the variance of $\hat{X}$ for 3-stage sampling by letting $L = l$. Let us show how this is done.

The variance of $\hat{X}$ for 3-stage cluster sampling was (from equation (8), section 11.3):

(1)
$$V(\hat{X}) = L^2 \frac{L-l}{L} \frac{S_b^2}{l} + \frac{L}{l} \sum^L M_i^2 \frac{M_i - \bar{m}}{M_i} \frac{S_i^2}{\bar{m}}$$
$$+ \frac{L}{l} \sum^L \frac{M_i}{\bar{m}} \sum^{M_i} N_{ij}^2 \frac{N_{ij} - n_{ij}}{N_{ij}} \frac{S_{ij}^2}{n_{ij}}$$

When we let $L = l$ and use h instead of i for the subscripts, to indicate strata instead of clusters, equation (1) becomes:

(2)
$$V(\hat{X}) = \sum^L M_h^2 \frac{M_h - m_h}{M_h} \frac{S_h^2}{m_h} + \sum^L \frac{M_h}{m_h} \sum^{M_h} N_{hi}^2 \frac{N_{hi} - n_{hi}}{N_{hi}} \frac{S_{hi}^2}{n_{hi}}$$

(3)
$$S_h^2 = \frac{1}{M_h - 1} \sum_i^{M_h} (X_{hi} - \bar{X}_h)^2$$

(4)
$$S_{hi}^2 = \frac{1}{N_{hi} - 1} \sum^{N_{hi}} (X_{hij} - \bar{X}_{hi})^2$$

X_{hij} is the number of books owned by the jth student in the hith psu (class). The capital letters indicate population values.

$\bar{X}_{hi} = \frac{1}{N_{hi}} \sum^{N_{hi}} X_{hij}$ is the average number of books per student in the hith psu (class).

$X_{hi} = \sum^{N_{hi}} X_{hij}$ is the total number of books in the hith psu.

$\bar{X}_h = \frac{1}{M_h} \sum^{M_h} X_{hi}$ is the average number of books per psu (class) in the hth stratum (school).

S_h^2 represents the variation between psu's (classes) within stratum h.

S_{hi}^2 represents the variation within the ith psu (class) of stratum h.

As shown, S_b^2, the variation between clusters (which become strata in this case) drops out of the equation.

If we set $m_h = \bar{m}$ and $n_{hi} = \bar{n}$, equation (2) shows that when $L\bar{m}\bar{n} = n$ is given, $V(\hat{X})$ may be reduced by decreasing $\bar{n}$ and increasing $\bar{m}$. In terms of our example, this means that in order to reduce $V(\hat{X})$, take more classes (psu), and fewer students (ssu).

The magnitude of $\bar{n}$ is usually around $5 - 15$, whereas $\bar{m}$ may be very small or very large, depending on the problem. For example, suppose a sample of n families is to be selected from the 5 boroughs of New York City. Then $L = 5$ strata. From each stratum, select $m_h = \bar{m} = 50$ blocks (psu), and select $\bar{n} = 10$ families (ssu) from each block. The sample will then be $n = L\bar{m}\bar{n} = 5 \times 50 \times 10 = 2500$ families.

Since $V(\hat{X})$ involves population parameters such as S_h^2 and S_{hi}^2, it is obviously not used in practice. Instead, as with the other cases, the estimator is obtained by letting $L = l$ in the estimator of the variance for 3-stage cluster sampling. From equation (3), section 11.4, we find the estimator of the variance for 3-stage cluster sampling to be

$$\hat{V}(\hat{X}) = L^2 \frac{L-l}{L} \frac{s_i^2}{l} + \frac{L}{l} \sum_i^l M_i^2 \frac{M_i - \bar{m}}{M_i} \frac{s_i^2}{\bar{m}}$$

(5)

$$+ \frac{L}{l} \sum_i^l M_i \sum_{ij}^{\bar{m}} N_{ij}^2 \frac{N_{ij} - n_{ij}}{N_{ij}} \frac{s_{ij}^2}{n_{ij}}$$

For the stratified cluster sampling case, we set $L = l$ and let i become h in the subscripts. Then (5) becomes

(6) $$\hat{V}(\hat{X}) = \sum^L M_h^2 \frac{M_h - m_h}{M_h} \frac{s_h^2}{m_h} + \sum^L \frac{M_h}{m_h} \sum^{m_h} N_{hi}^2 \frac{N_{hi} - n_{hi}}{N_{hi}} \frac{s_{hi}^2}{n_{hi}}$$

$$s_h^2 = \frac{1}{m_h - 1} \sum^{m_h} (\hat{X}_{hi} - \hat{\bar{X}}_h)^2$$

$$s_{hi}^2 = \frac{1}{n_{hi} - 1} \sum_j^{n_{hi}} (x_{hij} - \bar{x}_{hi})^2$$

$$\hat{X}_{hi} = \frac{N_{hi}}{n_{hi}} \sum^{n_{hi}} x_{hij} = \frac{N_{hi}}{n_{hi}} x_{hi} = N_{hi} \bar{x}_{hi}$$

$$\hat{\bar{X}}_h = \frac{1}{m_h} \sum^{m_h} \hat{X}_{hi}$$

$$\bar{x}_{hi} = \frac{1}{n_{hi}} \sum^{n_{hi}} x_{hij}$$

As shown in (6), $\hat{V}(\hat{X})$ depends on s_h^2 and s_{hi}^2. When we set $m_h = \bar{m}$ and $n_{hi} = \bar{n}$ as we did above, we can see that $\hat{V}(\hat{X})$ is affected mainly by the term which includes s_h^2. This point becomes more salient when $m_h \ll M_h$, and (6) may be simplified to

(7) $$\hat{V}(\hat{X}) = \sum^L \left\{ \left(\frac{M_h}{m_h}\right)^2 \left[\frac{M_h - m_h}{M_h} m_h s_h^2 + \left(\frac{m_h}{M_h}\right) \sum^{m_h} N_{hi}^2 \frac{N_{hi} - n_{hi}}{N_{hi}} \frac{s_{hi}^2}{n_{hi}}\right] \right\}$$

$$\doteq \sum^L M_h^2 \frac{s_h^2}{m_h}$$

For example, if a borough has $M_h = 2000$ blocks and $\bar{m} = 50$ blocks are selected, $\bar{m}/M_h = 50/2000 = 2.5\%$. Thus, we may expect that the effect of the term including s_{hi}^2 will be very small in relation to the term including s_h^2. That is, the $\hat{V}(\hat{X})$ will be affected mainly by the variation between the psu.

Problems

1. Using the data of Problem 1 of page 297 calculate $V(\hat{X})$ using equation (2).

2. Using the sample that has been selected for Problem 1 of page 297, calculate $\hat{V}(\hat{X})$.

3. In Problem 2 of page 298, we have 3-stage stratified cluster sampling. Find the $V(\hat{X})$ for this case by first finding the $V(\hat{X})$ for 4-stage cluster sampling, and then noting that the psu are selected from each stratum.

4. Using the result of Problem 3, find an estimator $\hat{V}(\hat{X})$ following the procedure of equations (5) and (6).

5. Using the sample selected in Problem 2 of page 298, calculate $\hat{V}(\hat{X})$ using the equation derived in Problem 4 above.

12.4 Allocation of the sample

In our illustration of $L = 580$ schools, we selected m_h classes (psu) from the hth school (stratum) and n_{hi} students (ssu) from the hith class. Since classes (psu) are selected from every school (stratum), the cost of going to and surveying the schools (strata) is fixed. Hence, consideration of the strata does not enter into the problem of allocating the sample. We need only consider how m_h and n_{hi} should be determined so that $V(\hat{X})$ will be at a minimum, given a fixed budget. Hence, our problem is: How many classes m_h, and how many students n_{hi} from the hith class should be selected? Should we select fewer classes m_h and more students n_{hi}, or vice versa?

The procedure for investigating this problem is similar to our previous cases. We first find the variance, then a cost function which serves as a linear constraint, and then find m_h and n_{hi} in order to minimize the variance subject to this given cost function. Our first step is therefore to find the variance. We have already found the variance in section 12.3, but we shall make several assumptions and simplify it in order to facilitate our analysis.

To simplify the variance, we note subsamples of the same proportion are often taken from the psu's. Hence, we shall assume that

$$(1) \qquad\qquad \frac{N_{hi}}{n_{hi}} = f_{2h}$$

For example, if $f_{2h} = 0.05$, it means 5% of N_{hi} students are taken as a random sample. If there are, for example, $M_h = 10$ classes in the hth school, then

$$(2) \qquad\qquad \frac{n_{h1}}{N_{h1}} = \frac{n_{h2}}{N_{h2}} = \cdots = \frac{n_{h10}}{N_{h10}} = f_{2h}$$

which may be rewritten algebraically as

$$\frac{\frac{1}{10}(n_{hi} + \cdots + n_{h10})}{\frac{1}{10}(N_{h1} + \cdots + N_{h10})} = f_{2h}$$

which we shall express as

$$(3) \qquad\qquad \frac{\bar{n}_h}{\bar{N}_h} = f_{2h}$$

where $\bar{N}_h$ is the average number of students per class in the hth school and may also be considered as the expected value of N_{hi}. It may be written as

$$\bar{N}_h = \frac{N_h}{M_h} = \frac{\sum\limits^{M_h} N_{hi}}{M}$$

Similarly, $\bar{n}_h$ may also be considered as the expected value of n_{hi}. It may be shown as

$$\bar{n}_h = f_{2h}\bar{N}_h$$

Note that this interpretation is different from that which sets

$$\bar{n}_h = \frac{1}{m_h} \sum\limits_i^{m_h} n_{hi}$$

which is simply a sample average of $m_h = 2$ (say) classes.

Using $\bar{n}_h$ and $\bar{N}_h$ as defined in (3), we shall rewrite the equation for the variance given in equation (2), section 12.3 as

$$(4) \qquad V(\hat{X}) = \sum\limits^L M_h \frac{M_h - m_h}{M_h} \frac{S_h^2}{m_h} + \sum\limits^L \frac{M_h}{m_h} \sum\limits^{M_h} \bar{N}_h^2 \frac{\bar{N}_h - \bar{n}_h}{\bar{N}_h} \frac{S_{hi}^2}{\bar{n}_h}$$

The second term on the right of equation (4) is further simplified as follows:

$$\sum\limits^L \frac{M_h}{m_h} \sum\limits^{M_h} \bar{N}_h^2 \frac{\bar{N}_h - \bar{n}_h}{\bar{N}_h} \frac{S_{hi}^2}{\bar{n}_h} = \sum\limits^L \frac{N_h^2}{m_h \bar{n}_h} \frac{\bar{N}_h - \bar{n}_h}{\bar{N}_h} \frac{\sum\limits^{M_h} N_{hi} S_{hi}^2}{M_h \bar{N}_h}$$

$$= \sum\limits^L \frac{N_h^2}{m_h \bar{n}_h} \frac{\bar{N}_h - \bar{n}_h}{\bar{N}_h} S_{2h}^2$$

where we have let $\bar{N}_h = N_{hi}$ and $\bar{N}_h = N_h/M_h$. In the term:

$$S_{2h}^2 = \frac{1}{M_h \bar{N}_h} \sum\limits_i^{M_h} N_{hi} S_{hi}^2$$

$M_h \bar{N}_h$ shows the total number of students of the hth school, while $\sum\limits^{M_h} N_{hi} S_{hi}^2$ may be interpreted as showing the pooled sums of squares of the variation within a class in the hth school for all M_h classes. Hence, S_{2h}^2 may be considered as representing the within variation of classes pooled for the hth school.

Using S_{2h}^2, equation (4) becomes

$$(5) \qquad V(\hat{X}) = \sum\limits^L M_h^2 \frac{M_h - m_h}{M_h} \frac{S_h^2}{m_h} + \sum\limits^L \frac{N_h^2}{m_h \bar{n}_h} \frac{\bar{N}_h - \bar{n}_h}{\bar{N}_h} S_{2h}^2$$

and we have finally obtained the simplified variance that we shall use to facilitate our analysis.

Our problem thus becomes one of finding m_h and $\bar{n}_h$ so that (5) will be minimized subject to a given budget.

The budget or cost of the survey involves the cost of going to the schools (strata), selecting the classes (psu), and interviewing the students (ssu). As mentioned, all the schools (strata) are surveyed, and this is a fixed cost. The variable costs are those of selecting classes (psu)—which we shall denote as c_{1h}—and those of interviewing students (ssu)—which we shall denote as c_{2h}. The cost of the survey may then be shown by the simple cost function

$$(6) \qquad\qquad c = \sum_{}^{L} c_{1h}m_h + \sum_{}^{L} c_{2h}m_h\bar{n}_h$$

where the fixed cost is excluded because it has no effect on the determination of m_h and $\bar{n}_h$.

Our problem may now be stated formally as follows: Minimize $V(\hat{X})$ of equation (5) subject to the budget constraint (6). Using the Lagrange multiplier technique, we find (see reference for derivation),

$$(7) \qquad\qquad \bar{n}_h = \bar{N}_h\sqrt{\frac{c_{1h}}{c_{2h}}\frac{S_{2h}^2}{S_h^2 - \bar{N}_hS_{2h}^2}}$$

$$(8) \qquad\qquad m_h = \frac{cN_hS_{2h}/\bar{n}_h\sqrt{c_{2h}}}{\sum_{}^{L}(c_{1h} + c_{2h}\bar{n}_h)(N_hS_{2h}/\bar{n}_h\sqrt{c_{2h}})}$$

Equation (7) shows that $\bar{n}_h$ will be large when $\bar{N}_h$, c_{1h}/c_{2h}, and $S_{2h}^2/(S_h^2 - \bar{N}_hS_{2h}^2)$ are large. For example, a large $\bar{N}_h$ means, that the average number of students (ssu) per class in the hth school (strata) is large.

A large c_{1h}/c_{2h} may be interpreted to mean the cost of selecting classes (psu) is larger than that of selecting students (ssu). In that event, (7) shows that more students (ssu) should be selected.

A large $S_{2h}^2/(S_h^2 - \bar{N}_hS_{2h}^2)$ implies that when S_{2h}^2 is large, $\bar{n}_h$ will tend to be large. In our example, when the variation within the psu (class) is large, select more ssu (students).

For m_h of equation (8), we may accept the denominator as given and consider only the numerator. It shows that when c, N_h, and S_{2h} are large, m_h will be larger. A large c means there is a larger budget to work with and, in this case, the formula suggests that greater precision will be obtained when a larger m_h (more classes) is taken. Note the very interesting result that c has no effect on $\bar{n}_h$—$\bar{n}_h$ is determined independently of the total budget.

A large N_h means that there is a large number of students (ssu) in the hth school and, in this case, the formula suggests that more classes (psu) m_h should be taken from the hth school. If one school has twice as many students as another, the formula suggests taking twice as many classes (psu) from the larger school.

A large S_{2h} indicates that the ssu (students) within the psu (classes) of stratum h are heterogeneous. Hence, (8) indicates that more psu (classes) should be selected from the strata where the ssu (students) are more heterogeneous within the psu (classes). This is a rather unexpected result.

However, note that (8) also tells us how m_h is allocated among strata.

It tells us to take more psu from strata where the within variations of the psu are larger.

On the other hand, a large $\bar{n}_h$ and c_{2h} indicate m_h should be smaller, that is, a smaller number of classes should be selected from the hth school. Since the total cost c is given, a large $\bar{n}_h$ will reduce the size of m_h. A large c_{2h} means that when the cost of selecting students (ssu) is large, a smaller number of classes m_h should be taken. This may also be interpreted to be caused by the fact that the total cost c is given. That is, when c_{2h} is large, the amount left for c_{1h} will be reduced, and as a result will cause a decrease in m_h (psu).

Reference

Let us show how equations (7) and (8) are derived.

$$(9) \qquad F = V + \lambda \left(\sum_{}^{L} c_{1h} m_h + \sum_{}^{L} c_{2h} m_h \bar{n}_h - c \right)$$

where we have set $V = V(\hat{X})$ for brevity. Differentiating F with respect to m_h and $\bar{n}_h$, we find,

$$(10) \qquad -\frac{M_h^2 S_h^2}{m_h^2} - \frac{N_h^2 S_{2h}^2}{m_h^2 \bar{n}_h} + \frac{N_h^2 S_{2h}^2}{m_h^2 \, \bar{N}_h} + \lambda(c_{1h} + c_{2h}\bar{n}_h) = 0$$

$$(11) \qquad -\frac{N_h^2 S_{2h}^2}{m_h \bar{n}_h^2} + \lambda c_{2h} m_h = 0$$

From (11), we find

$$(12) \qquad \lambda m_h^2 = \frac{N_h^2 S_{2h}^2}{c_{2h} \bar{n}_h^2}$$

We substract (11) $\times \bar{n}_h$ from (10) $\times m_h$, and find

$$(13) \qquad \lambda m_h^2 = \frac{M_h^2 S_h^2 - N_h^2 S_{2h}^2 / \bar{N}_h}{c_{1h}}$$

Using (12) and (13), we may solve for $\bar{n}_h$:

$$(14) \qquad \bar{n}_h = \bar{N}_h \sqrt{\frac{c_{1h}}{c_{2h}} \frac{S_{2h}^2}{S_h^2 - \bar{N}_h S_{2h}^2}}$$

We next wish to find m_h. From (12)

$$(15) \qquad m_h = \frac{1}{\sqrt{\lambda}} \frac{N_h S_{2h}}{\bar{n}_h \sqrt{c_{2h}}}$$

Substituting (15) into the cost function, we find

$$(16) \qquad \sqrt{\lambda} = \frac{\sum_{}^{L} (c_{1h} + c_{2h}\bar{n}_h)(N_h S_{2h} / \bar{n}_h \sqrt{c_{2h}})}{c}$$

Substituting (16) into (15) gives us

$$(17) \qquad m_h = \frac{c N_h S_{2h} / \bar{n}_h \sqrt{c_{2h}}}{\sum_{}^{L} (c_{1h} + c_{2h}\bar{n}_h)(N_h S_{2h} / \bar{n}_h \sqrt{c_{2h}})}$$

as the optimum value for m_h.

12.5 Gains due to stratification

After having developed this elaborate procedure for stratified cluster sampling, the question that naturally arises is when to use it. The general principle is that it should be used when there is a reduction in the variance of the estimators and when we wish to lower the cost of the survey. In this section, we shall consider the first problem—under what conditions will there be a reduction of the variance of the estimator when stratified cluster sampling is used?

To consider the reduction in variance, we need to compare the variance of the estimator of stratified cluster sampling with that of simple cluster sampling or simple random sampling. Let us start our discussion with a comparison of the variance of stratified cluster sampling with that of simple cluster sampling and use as an illustration the problem of estimating the average number of books owned by a 6-th grader in a city public school system.

For simplicity, let us assume there are $L = 3$ schools and each school has $M_h = 10$ classes. A random sample of $m_h = 2$ classes is selected from each school, hence we have $2 \times 3 = 6$ classes as our sample of psu's. From these sampled psu's, we select subsamples of students (ssu). As shown, we have used stratified cluster sampling to select the sample.

However, if simple cluster sampling were to be used, we would select the sample as follows: There is no stratification, and we therefore have 30 classes (psu). From these 30 classes, we shall select a random sample of 6 classes (psu). And from these 6 classes, we select subsamples (ultimate clusters) of students.

The question we are interested in is: assuming the same number of students are selected, which of the two sampling procedures gives us a smaller variance of the estimated total or mean?

The process thus consists of comparing the variance between psu's when stratified cluster sampling is used with that obtained by simple cluster sampling. Note that we are confining our attention to the psu's (classes) and do not need to consider the secondary sampling units (students).

The variance of the average number of books owned by a student in the stratified cluster sampling case is as follows: For simplicity, we shall assume —as we have done above—that all the M_h are equal and that all the N_{hi} are also equal. That is, each school has the same number of classes and each class has the same number of students. Let us denote this by

(1) $$M_h = \bar{M} = \frac{\sum\limits^{L} M_h}{L} = \frac{M}{L}$$

(2) $$m_h = \bar{m} = \frac{\sum\limits^{L} m_h}{L} = \frac{m}{L}$$

(3)
$$N_{hi} = \bar{N} = \frac{1}{\bar{M}L} \sum_{}^{L} \sum_{}^{M} N_{hi}$$

We shall furthermore assume the same number of students is subsampled from the sampled psu's. That is, the n_{hi} are equal for all sampled psu's.

The sampling procedure for the stratified case consisted of selecting a random sample of $\bar{m} = 2$ classes from each school which each had $M_h = 10$ classes. Hence, in this simplified case, we have (so far as selecting classes is concerned) proportional stratified sampling of the psu's where the sampling fraction is $\bar{m}/M_h = 2/10 = .2$ for each stratum. From section 6.8, the variance of a mean for a proportional stratified sample was

(4)
$$V(\bar{x}_{\text{prop}}) = \frac{N - n}{N} \sum_{}^{L} \frac{N_h}{N} \frac{S_h^2}{n}$$

Applying this to our present case, the sampling units are the psu's and N and n are therefore replaced by M (total number of classes) and m (total number of sampled classes), so that (4) becomes

(5)
$$V(\bar{x}_{st}) = \frac{M - m}{M} \sum_{}^{L} \frac{M_h}{M} \frac{S_h^2}{m}$$
$$= \frac{M - m}{M} \sum_{}^{L} \frac{M/L}{M} \frac{S_h^2}{m}$$
$$= \frac{M - m}{M} \sum_{}^{L} \frac{1}{L} \frac{S_h^2}{m}$$

(6)
$$S_h^2 = \frac{1}{\bar{M} - 1} \sum_{i}^{\bar{M}} (\bar{\bar{X}}_{hi} - \bar{\bar{X}}_h)^2$$

(7)
$$\bar{\bar{X}}_{hi} = \frac{X_{hi}}{N_{hi}}$$
$$\bar{\bar{X}}_h = \frac{1}{\bar{M}} \sum_{i}^{\bar{M}} \bar{\bar{X}}_{hi}$$

In (6) and (7), $\bar{\bar{X}}_{hi}$ shows the average number of books per student in the ith class of the hth school; $\bar{\bar{X}}_h$ shows the average number of books per student in the hth school; and S_h^2 shows the variation between classes (psu) of the hth school.

Let us now consider the variance of the mean for a simple random sample of m clusters. We first make a list of the $L \times \bar{M} = 3 \times 10 = 30$ classes (psu) and select a random sample of $m = L \times \bar{m} = 3 \times 2 = 6$ classes from this list. We know from our discussion in Chapter 5, Simple Random Sampling, that the variance of the mean for a simple random sample of m clusters is

(8)
$$\sigma_{\text{ran}}^2 = \frac{M - m}{M} \frac{(1/M) \sum_{}^{L} \sum_{}^{\bar{M}} (\bar{\bar{X}}_{hi} - \bar{\bar{X}})^2}{m}$$
$$\bar{\bar{X}} = \frac{1}{M} \sum_{}^{L} \sum_{}^{\bar{M}} \bar{\bar{X}}_{hi} = \frac{1}{\bar{M}L} \sum_{}^{L} \sum_{}^{\bar{M}} \bar{\bar{X}}_{hi}$$

Note that $\bar{X}$ is the average number of books a student has for all M classes. The double sum in the numerator on the right shows that the sum is over all $M = L \times \bar{M} = 30$ classes, and σ_{ran}^2 therefore shows the variation between the psu's (classes).

To evaluate the gains of stratification, we wish to compare the two variances—(5) and (8). Let us restate these variances for convenience. We have

$$(9) \qquad \sigma_{st}^2 = \frac{M-m}{M} \sum^{L} \frac{1}{L} \frac{S_h^2}{m}$$

$$= \frac{M-m}{Mm} \frac{1}{L} \frac{1}{\bar{M}-1} \sum^{L} \sum^{\bar{M}} (\bar{X}_{hi} - \bar{\bar{X}}_h)^2$$

$$(10) \qquad \sigma_{ran}^2 = \frac{M-m}{Mm} \frac{1}{M} \sum^{L} \sum^{\bar{M}} (\bar{X}_{hi} - \bar{\bar{X}})^2$$

$$= \frac{M-m}{Mm} \frac{1}{L} \frac{1}{\bar{M}} \sum^{L} \sum^{\bar{M}} (\bar{X}_{hi} - \bar{\bar{X}})^2$$

When $1 \ll \bar{M}$, we may let $\bar{M} \doteq \bar{M} - 1$ so that (9) and (10) may be simplified to

$$(9') \qquad \sigma_{st}^2 = W \sum^{L} \sum^{\bar{M}} (\bar{X}_{hi} - \bar{\bar{X}}_h)^2$$

$$(10') \qquad \sigma_{ran}^2 = W \sum^{L} \sum^{\bar{M}} (\bar{X}_{hi} - \bar{\bar{X}})^2$$

where

$$W = \frac{M-m}{Mm} \frac{1}{L} \frac{1}{\bar{M}}$$

The absolute gain due to stratification is found by

$$(11) \qquad \sigma_{ran}^2 - \sigma_{st}^2 = W \left[\sum^{L} \sum^{\bar{M}} (\bar{X}_{hi} - \bar{\bar{X}})^2 - \sum^{L} \sum^{\bar{M}} (\bar{X}_{hi} - \bar{\bar{X}}_h)^2 \right]$$

The bracketed terms may be changed algebraically as follows:

$$\sum^{L} \sum^{\bar{M}} (\bar{X}_{hi} - \bar{\bar{X}})^2 - \sum^{L} \sum^{\bar{M}} (\bar{X}_{hi} - \bar{\bar{X}}_h)^2 = \sum^{L} \sum^{\bar{M}} [(\bar{X}_{hi} - \bar{\bar{X}})^2 - (\bar{X}_{hi} - \bar{\bar{X}}_h)^2]$$

$$= \sum_{h}^{L} \sum_{i}^{M} (\bar{\bar{X}}_h - \bar{\bar{X}})(2\bar{X}_{hi} - \bar{\bar{X}} - \bar{\bar{X}}_h)$$

$$= \sum^{L} (\bar{\bar{X}}_h - \bar{\bar{X}})(2\bar{M}\bar{\bar{X}}_h - \bar{M}\bar{\bar{X}} - \bar{M}\bar{\bar{X}}_h)$$

$$= \sum^{L} (\bar{\bar{X}}_h - \bar{\bar{X}})^2 \bar{M}$$

Hence (11) becomes

$$(12) \qquad \sigma_{ran}^2 - \sigma_{st}^2 = W \sum^{L} (\bar{\bar{X}}_h - \bar{\bar{X}})^2 \bar{M}$$

$$= \frac{M-m}{Mm} \frac{1}{L} \sum^{L} (\bar{\bar{X}}_h - \bar{\bar{X}})^2$$

which may be expressed as

$$(13) \qquad \sigma^2_{\text{ran}} = \sigma^2_{st} + \frac{M-m}{Mm} \frac{1}{L} \overset{L}{\Sigma} (\bar{\bar{X}}_h - \bar{\bar{X}})^2$$

This shows that stratified cluster sampling has a smaller variance than simple cluster sampling and is more efficient when the variation of $\bar{\bar{X}}_h$ is large. For example, $\bar{\bar{X}}_h$ was the average number of books per student in the hth school (strata), and $\bar{\bar{X}}$ was the average number of books per student in the whole population. Hence, the larger the variation between schools (strata), the more efficient stratified cluster sampling becomes. When there is no difference between strata, the difference between stratified cluster sampling and simple cluster sampling will be negligible or zero. This result suggests use of stratified cluster sampling when the variance between strata is large.

Notes and References

For further discussion of stratified cluster sampling, see Hansen, Hurwitz and Madow(1957), Chapter 7. Also see pp. 559–568 of their book which gives an explanation of the procedure used for the population survey of 1950 by the Bureau of Census. They also explain the estimation procedure, but this requires a knowledge of ratio estimates which we shall cover in Chapter 13.

Additional references for illustrations of stratified cluster sampling will be given at the end of Chapter 13 because, in many cases, knowledge of ratio estimate is necessary to understand the illustrations.

CHAPTER 13

The Ratio Estimate

13.1 Introduction

In this chapter we shall consider the ratio estimate procedure. To understand this chapter, it is important to first understand that this is a method of estimation, and not a method of selecting samples.

The methods of selecting samples we have studied are:

> simple random sampling
> stratified random sampling
> systematic sampling
> cluster sampling

After a sample was selected by these methods, we calculated the sample mean $\bar{x}$ and used it as an estimator of the population mean $\bar{X}$.

What we wish to do in this chapter is to select samples by these various methods, and from these samples calculate a sample ratio r, and use this r to estimate the population ratio R and $\bar{X}$. This procedure is called the ratio estimation procedure.

We shall consider only the cases of estimating R from simple random samples, stratified random samples, and cluster samples, and omit estimating R from a systematic sample because it may in most practical cases be considered to be approximately the same as a simple random sample.

The reason for using a sample ratio r to estimate $\bar{X}$ instead of simply using the sample mean $\bar{x}$ is because, under certain conditions, the ratio estimation procedure may improve the precision of estimation. Our problem thus is to explain under what conditions the use of r will give a better precision than simply using the sample mean $\bar{x}$ as an estimator of $\bar{X}$.

In addition to estimating $\bar{X}$, r will also be an estimator of the population ratio, R, which is an important measure. We shall illustrate the uses of R in the next section.

Our order of discussion will be to first define and explain the concept of a ratio R, and then to consider the methods of estimating R and $\bar{X}$ vis-a-vis the various sample selection methods.

13.2 The sample ratio r

Suppose we have a total population of $N = 3$ families, as shown in Table 13.1.

Table 13.1

Family	X_i (Males)	Y_i (Total persons)
1	2	4
2	5	6
3	1	3
	8	13

We have

$$X = \Sigma X_i = 8 \qquad \text{total number of males}$$
$$Y = \Sigma Y_i = 13 \qquad \text{total number of persons}$$

We define

(1) $$R = \frac{X}{Y} = \frac{8}{13} = 0.62$$

as the population ratio of males ($R = 0.62$ simply means that 62% of the persons are males).

Let us now select random samples of $n = 2$ families and estimate R. We can select $\binom{N}{n} = \binom{3}{2} = 3$ different samples from which we can calculate the sample ratios r.

Sample	Sample ratio r
1, 2	$r_1 = \dfrac{x_1 + x_2}{y_1 + y_2} = \dfrac{2 + 5}{4 + 6} = \dfrac{7}{10} = 0.70$
1, 3	$r_2 = \dfrac{x_1 + x_3}{y_1 + y_3} = \dfrac{2 + 1}{4 + 3} = \dfrac{3}{7} = 0.43$
2, 3	$r_3 = \dfrac{x_2 + x_3}{y_2 + y_3} = \dfrac{5 + 1}{6 + 3} = \dfrac{6}{9} = 0.66$

The sample ratio, r, may be expressed as

(2) $$r = \frac{\Sigma x_i}{\Sigma y_i} = \frac{x}{y}$$

which is the definition of a sample ratio. In our present case, it gives the sample proportion of males—but is it a proportion? Let us investigate the nature of r a little further.

To start with, let us recall that the definition of a proportion was

$$p = \frac{\sum x_i}{n}$$

where $x_i = 1$ when the sampling unit had the characteristic under consideration, and $x_i = 0$ when it did not. The point to note here is that the denominator is the sample size n and not a random variable, whereas the numerator ($\sum x_i$) is a random variable that varies from sample to sample.

However, the common sense meaning of the word proportion is the relation of one part to the whole, and is not as narrow as in our definition. As a result, we shall use the term proportion in two ways: one way is as we have defined it in the above equation, which is related to a definite statistical procedure; the other way will be the nonstatistical common-sense meaning. These two meanings will usually be made clear from the context of the discussion.

Returning now to our illustration above, we note that for $r = x/y$, the elementary unit is a person and the characteristic associated with the elementary unit is its sex (male). Thus, $x = \sum x_i$ is the number of elementary units with the characteristic (that is, the number of males in the sample), and $y = \sum y_i$ is the total number of elementary units in the sample.

Hence, using the term proportion in the general meaning, $r = x/y$ is the proportion of males in the sample.

Note, however, that the sampling unit is a family. We selected $n = 2$ families from $N = 3$ families, and as a result found x males and y persons in the sample. Hence, x and y will vary from sample to sample, as shown in the above calculations of r_1, r_2, and r_3.

This means that x and y are both random variables, and $r = x/y$ is a ratio of 2 random variables. Therefore r is not a proportion in the narrow statistical sense. The implication of this result is that we cannot apply our previous statistical theory of proportions to r.

Let us give several examples to illustrate the meaning of the ratio, r.

Example 1. A sample of $n = 50$ families is selected from $N = 5000$ families. Let

$x = \sum x_i$ be the total amount of rent

$y = \sum y_i$ be the total amount of income

Then $r = x/y$ is the proportion of income that is paid as rent. For example, if $r = 0.25$, it means that 25% of the income is paid for rent in this sample. In this case, the families are the sampling units and also the elementary units, and x and y are random variables dependent on the $n = 50$ families that have been selected. Hence, $r = x/y$ is a ratio of 2 random variables.

Example 2. A sample of n families is selected from N families. Let

$x = \sum x_i$ be the total number of individuals under 10 years of age

$y = \sum y_i$ be the total number of people in the sample

Then $r = x/y$ is the proportion of children in the sample. That is, if $r = 0.4$, it means that 40% of the people in the population are under 10 years of age. Note that the families are the sampling units, the children and the people are the elementary units, and x and y are random variables.

Example 3. A sample of n families is selected. Let

$x = \Sigma\, x_i$ be the total number of AM-FM radios in 1965

$y = \Sigma\, y_i$ be the total number of AM-FM radios in 1960

where the same sample is used for both years. Then $r = x/y$ shows the relative increase in the number of AM-FM radios. For example, if $r = 3$, it means that there has been a 300% increase in the number of AM-FM radios. The sampling unit is the family, the elementary units are the AM-FM radios, and x and y are random variables dependent on the sample.

Example 4. A sample of n hogs is selected from a shipment of N hogs. Let

x_i be the weight recorded by the meat packing company

y_i be the weight stamped on the ith hog

Then $r = x/y$ shows the ratio of the accurate versus the claimed weight. For example, if $r = 0.95$, it means the true weight is only 95% of the claimed weight for the sample. The hog is the sampling unit and also the elementary unit, and x and y are random variables dependent on the sample that is selected.

Example 5. A sample of n apartment houses is selected. Let

$x = \Sigma\, x_i$ be the total number of people

$y = \Sigma\, y_i$ be the total number of apartments

in the sample. Then, $r = x/y$ is the number of people per apartment. If, $r = 3.5$, it means there are 3.5 persons per apartment in the sample.

Example 6. A sample of n area segments is selected in a state. Let

$x = \Sigma\, x_i$ be the total number of unemployed males between 20 and
          40 years of age

$y = \Sigma\, y_i$ be the total number of males between 20 and 40 years of age

Then $r = x/y$ gives the proportion of unemployed males.

Example 7. A sample of n villages is selected in a region. Let

$x = \Sigma\, x_i$ be the number of bushels of wheat

$y = \Sigma\, y_i$ be the total acreage planted

in the sample. Then $r = x/y$ gives the yield of wheat per acre in the sample.

Example 8. A sample of n companies is selected. Let

$x = \Sigma\, x_i$ be the total labor cost

$y = \Sigma\, y_i$ be the total expenditure

in the sample. Then $r = x/y$ gives the proportion of labor cost.

Example 9. A sample of n companies is selected. Let

$$x = \Sigma\, x_i \qquad \text{be the total sales for December}$$
$$y = \Sigma\, y_i \qquad \text{be the total sales for November}$$

in the sample. Then $r = x/y$ gives the percentage change in sales.

Example 10. A sample of n companies is selected. Let

$$x = \Sigma\, x_i \qquad \text{be the liquid assets}$$
$$y = \Sigma\, y_i \qquad \text{be the total assets}$$

in the sample. Then $r = x/y$ gives the proportion of liquid assets.

Example 11. A sample of n families is selected. Let

$$x = \Sigma\, x_i \qquad \text{be the expenditures on food}$$
$$y = \Sigma\, y_i \qquad \text{be the total income}$$

in the sample. Then $r = x/y$ gives the proportion of food expenditures.

There are many reasons for considering the ratio estimate, r. One—as we have seen—is when the denominator of the ratio is not the sample size n, but a random variable, we cannot apply the theory of proportions discussed in Chapter 5. In many cases (as in examples 2 and 3 above), the sampling units differ from the elementary units, necessitating the use of the ratio estimate.

Another reason is that when there is a correlation between the random variables, x and y, the ratio estimate may give a better estimate of $\bar{X}$ or X than the sample mean. This may best be shown by an example:

Suppose we wish to estimate the total amount of wheat produced in a certain county. There are $N = 300$ farms, and a sample of $n = 20$ farms is selected. Let $x = \Sigma\, x_i = 600$ bushels be the total amount of wheat produced by the $n = 20$ farms. Then

$$\bar{x} = \frac{1}{n} \Sigma\, x_i = \frac{600}{20} = 30 \text{ bushels}$$

is the average amount of wheat per farm in the sample. Since there are $N = 300$ farms, the total amount of wheat is estimated as

$$\hat{X} = N\bar{x} = 300 \times 30 = 9000 \text{ bushels}$$

However, a check on the size of the farms shows that there is a large variation in the size of farms. Some may be as small as 200 acres, whereas others may be as large as 3000 acres. If, by chance, the sample of $n = 20$ farms that was selected consisted mostly of small farms, the average of $\bar{x} = 30$ bushels *per farm* may be underestimating the population average $\bar{X}$ and, as a result, the estimate $\hat{X} = 9000$ bushels may be much smaller than the population total X.

Further investigation may reveal that the amount of wheat *per acre* on any farm is about the same, a small farm producing a small total amount of wheat and a large farm producing a large amount. Furthermore, let us assume that the total amount of acreage in the county is known. Let this be Y. The natural thing to do then is to estimate the wheat output *per acre* from the sample and multiply it by Y.

To find the wheat output per acre, let $y_1, y_2, \ldots, y_n$ be the acreage of the farms in the sample, and let $y = \sum y_i = 200$ acres be the total acreage of the farms. Then, the ratio

$$r = \frac{x}{y} = \frac{600}{200} = 3 \text{ bushels per acre}$$

is an estimate of R. The total amount of wheat is thus estimated as

$$\hat{X} = rY = \left(\frac{x}{y}\right)Y = 3 \times 4000 = 12{,}000 \text{ bushels}$$

Let us now start our discussion of the properties of r when the sample is selected by simple random sampling.

13.3 Simple random sampling case

We shall first find r and check its bias for the simple random sampling case. We will then find the variance of r, its sample estimate, and also investigate its properties. Finally, we shall show how the ratio estimate is used to estimate totals.

(*i*) *Sample ratio r.*

The population and sample ratios have already been defined as

$$R = \frac{\sum\limits^{N} X_i}{\sum Y_i} = \frac{X}{Y}$$

$$r = \frac{\sum\limits^{n} x_i}{\sum y_i} = \frac{x}{y}$$

and illustrated by a hypothetical example. Let us in this subsection give one more illustration before we investigate the properties of r. In particular, we shall find that r is a biased but consistent estimator of R, but that the bias may be ignored for moderately large samples.

Example 1. Suppose we wish to estimate the vacancy rate of apartments in a certain district. A list of apartment houses for the district is available, from which a sample of $n = 10$ apartment houses are selected with the following results:

Table 13.2

Apartment houses	Apartments y_i	Vacancies x_i
1	20	4
2	10	2
3	30	6
4	40	8
5	20	5
6	15	3
7	25	5
8	30	6
9	20	4
10	20	4
	230	46

$$r = \frac{\sum^n x_i}{\sum y_i} = \frac{x}{y} = \frac{46}{230} = 0.20$$

(ii) Bias of r

Let us now consider the bias of r. The purpose of investigating the bias of r in detail is to obtain a better understanding of why we may ignore the bias for moderately large samples. We shall first set

$$\bar{x} = \bar{X} + (\bar{x} - \bar{X}) = \bar{X}\left(1 + \frac{\bar{x} - \bar{X}}{\bar{X}}\right)$$

$$\bar{y} = \bar{Y} + (\bar{y} - \bar{Y}) = \bar{Y}\left(1 + \frac{\bar{y} - \bar{Y}}{\bar{Y}}\right)$$

Then,

$$r = \frac{\bar{x}}{\bar{y}} = \frac{\bar{X}}{\bar{Y}}\left(1 + \frac{\bar{x} - \bar{X}}{\bar{X}}\right)\left(1 + \frac{\bar{y} - \bar{Y}}{\bar{Y}}\right)^{-1}$$

$$= \frac{\bar{X}}{\bar{Y}}\left(1 + \frac{\bar{x} - \bar{X}}{\bar{X}}\right)\left(1 - \frac{\bar{y} - \bar{Y}}{\bar{Y}} + \frac{(\bar{y} - \bar{Y})^2}{\bar{Y}^2} - \cdots\right)$$

$$= R\left(1 + \frac{\bar{x} - \bar{X}}{\bar{X}} - \frac{\bar{y} - \bar{Y}}{\bar{Y}} + \frac{(\bar{y} - \bar{Y})^2}{\bar{Y}^2} - \frac{(\bar{x} - \bar{X})(\bar{y} - \bar{Y})}{\bar{X}\bar{Y}} \cdots\right)$$

where we have used Taylor's formula to expand $[1 + (\bar{y} - \bar{Y})/\bar{Y}]^{-1}$.

At this point we introduce the assumption of a moderately large sample. By this, we mean that we shall assume that the difference of $\bar{y} - \bar{Y}$ is small. How small? We shall assume three cases. One is that the difference is small enough so that we may assume $\bar{y} \approx \bar{Y}$. The second is where the difference is small enough so that the terms beyond $(\bar{y} - \bar{Y})^2/\bar{Y}^2$ (including this term) may be ignored. And the third case is where the difference is small enough so that the term $(\bar{x} - \bar{X})(\bar{y} - \bar{Y})/\bar{X}\bar{Y}$ (excluding this term) may be ignored.

Case 1.

$$r \doteq R\left(1 + \frac{\bar{x} - \bar{X}}{\bar{X}} - 0 + 0 \cdots\right) = R + \frac{\bar{x} - \bar{X}}{\bar{X}} \cdot R$$

$$\therefore \quad E(r) = R + E\left(\frac{\bar{x} - \bar{X}}{\bar{X}}\right) \cdot R = R + 0$$

and r is an unbiased estimator of R.

Case 2.

$$r \doteq R\left(1 + \frac{\bar{x} - \bar{X}}{\bar{X}} - \frac{\bar{y} - \bar{Y}}{\bar{Y}}\right)$$

$$\therefore \quad E(r) \doteq R + E\left(\frac{\bar{x} - \bar{X}}{\bar{X}}\right) \cdot R - E\left(\frac{\bar{y} - \bar{Y}}{\bar{Y}}\right) \cdot R = R + 0 - 0$$

and r is an unbiased estimator of R.

Case 3.

$$r = R\left[1 + \frac{\bar{x} - \bar{X}}{\bar{X}} - \frac{\bar{y} - \bar{Y}}{\bar{Y}} + \frac{(\bar{y} - \bar{Y})^2}{\bar{Y}^2} - \frac{(\bar{x} - \bar{X})(\bar{y} - \bar{Y})}{\bar{X}\bar{Y}}\right]$$

$$E(r) = R + 0 - 0 + E\frac{(\bar{y} - \bar{Y})^2}{\bar{Y}^2}R - E(\bar{x} - \bar{X})(\bar{y} - \bar{Y})\frac{1}{\bar{X}\bar{Y}}R$$

$$E(\bar{y} - \bar{Y})^2 = \frac{N - n}{N}\frac{S_y^2}{n}$$

$$E(\bar{x} - \bar{X})(\bar{y} - \bar{Y}) = \frac{N - n}{N}\rho\frac{S_x S_y}{n}$$

$$\therefore \quad E(r) = R + \frac{N - n}{N}\frac{S_y^2}{n}\frac{1}{\bar{Y}^2}R - \frac{N - n}{N}\rho\frac{S_x S_y}{n}\frac{1}{\bar{X}\bar{Y}}R$$

$$\text{Bias} = E(r - R) = \frac{N - n}{N}\frac{S_y^2}{n}\frac{1}{\bar{Y}^2}R - \frac{N - n}{N}\rho\frac{S_x S_y}{n}\frac{1}{\bar{X}\bar{Y}}\frac{\bar{X}}{\bar{Y}}$$

$$= \frac{N - n}{Nn}\frac{1}{\bar{Y}^2}[RS_y^2 - \rho S_x S_y]$$

and the bias will be zero if

$$RS_y^2 - \rho S_x S_y = 0$$

which leads to

$$RS_y = \rho S_x$$

Let us show that this result holds when the regression of x on y is a straight line through the origin. That is, we get $E(r) = R$, and r is unbiased.

To show this, assume the regression line goes through the origin. Then

$$X_i = \beta Y_i$$

Hence, $\bar{X}/\bar{Y} = \beta$. But $\bar{X}/\bar{Y} = R$. Thus, when the regression line goes through the origin, $R = \beta$, and the left side of the equation becomes

$$RS_y = \beta S_y = \frac{\sum\limits^{N} (x - \bar{X})(y - \bar{Y})}{\sum (y - \bar{Y})^2} S_y$$

$$= \frac{\text{Cov}(x, y)}{S_y^2} S_y = \frac{\text{Cov}(x, y)}{S_y}$$

The right side is

$$\rho S_x = \frac{\text{Cov}(x, y)}{S_x S_y} S_x = \frac{\text{Cov}(x, y)}{S_y}$$

Thus

$$RS_y = \rho S_x$$

Hence, when the regression of x on y is a straight line and goes through the origin, we have

$$E(r - R) = \frac{N - n}{Nn} \frac{1}{\bar{Y}^2} (RS_y^2 - \rho S_x S_y) = 0$$

and r is an unbiased estimator of R.

In solving actual problems, we may easily check whether the data approximately satisfy this condition by plotting the data on a graph.

When the regression of x on y does not go through the origin, we have

$$\text{Bias} = E(r - R) = \frac{N - n}{Nn} \frac{1}{\bar{Y}^2} (RS_y^2 - \rho S_x S_y)$$

$$= \frac{N - n}{Nn} \frac{1}{\bar{Y}^2} \left(\frac{\bar{X}}{\bar{Y}} S_y^2 - \rho S_x S_y \right)$$

$$= \frac{N - n}{Nn} R \left(\frac{S_y^2}{\bar{Y}^2} - \rho \frac{\bar{Y}}{\bar{X}} \cdot \frac{1}{\bar{Y}^2} S_x S_y \right)$$

$$= \frac{N - n}{Nn} R[C_y^2 - \rho C_x C_y]$$

where C_x and C_y are coefficients of variation. Unless the distributions are very skewed, we may expect that the values of C_x and C_y will not be very large and $|\rho| \leq 1$. Hence, if n is moderately large, we may expect the bias to be small. Small compared to what? Small compared to the standard error of r. This point will be explained again after we discuss the variance of r.

(iii) *Geometric interpretation of r.*

Let us interpret R and r geometrically to get a better understanding of them. We defined R as

(1)
$$R = \frac{\sum\limits^{N} X_i}{\sum Y_i} = \frac{X}{Y} = \frac{\bar{X}}{\bar{Y}}$$

If we assume the individual ratios to be

(2)
$$R_i = \frac{X_i}{Y_i} = R$$

then we may write

(3) $$X_i = RY_i$$

and this becomes a straight line through the origin as shown in Fig. 13-1.

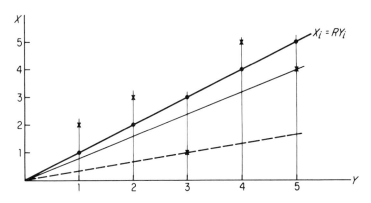

Fig. 13-1

Let us call this the population regression line. Quite clearly, if we sum both sides over N, we get

$$X = RY$$

and if we divide this by N, we get

$$\bar{X} = R\bar{Y}$$

The R_i are, of course, not usually equal to R, and will therefore be scattered around the population regression line.

To illustrate this, consider the following example where $N = 5$:

Sampling unit	X_i	Y_i	$RY_i = X'_i$	$X_i - X'_i$
1	1	3	3	$1 - 3 = -2$
2	2	1	1	$2 - 1 = 1$
3	3	2	2	$3 - 2 = 1$
4	4	5	5	$4 - 5 = -1$
5	5	4	4	$5 - 4 = 1$
	15	15		$15 - 15 = 0$

$$\therefore \quad R = 15/15 = 1$$

The population regression line therefore goes through the origin at a 45 degree angle and may be expressed by

$$X'_i = RY_i$$

where we have written X'_i to distinguish it from the actual value X_i. As shown, when $Y_i = 1$, then $X'_i = 1$; when $Y_i = 2$, then $X'_i = 2$; etc, and the X'_i will fall on the population regression line.

However, the actual X_i (which are shown by $\times$ in Fig. 13-1) are scattered around the population regression line. The 5 lines that go through the origin and each of the points express the individual ratios R_i and are scattered around the population regression line. We have drawn in only one of these lines to keep the diagram simple.

The statistical problem is to estimate R by selecting a sample of points from these $N = 5$ points. Let the sample size be $n = 3$. Then there will be $\binom{5}{3} = 10$ possible samples:

Sample		x_i	y_i	$r = \sum x_i / \sum y_i$
#1	1,2,3	1,2,3	3,1,2	6/6 = 1.00
2	1,2,4	1,2,4	3,1,5	7/9 = 0.78
3	1,2,5	1,2,5	3,1,4	8/8 = 1.00
4	1,3,4	1,3,4	3,2,5	8/10 = 0.80
5	1,3,5	1,3,5	3,2,4	9/9 = 1.00
6	1,4,5	1,4,5	3,5,4	10/12 = 0.847
7	2,3,4	2,3,4	1,2,5	9/8 = 1.12
8	2,3,5	2,3,5	1,2,4	10/7 = 1.43
9	2,4,5	2,4,5	2,4,4	11/10 = 1.10
10	3,4,5	3,4,5	2,5,4	12/11 = 1.09

There are 10 sample ratios calculated in the table. We may draw 10 sample regression lines based on these r's, and express them by

$$x'_i = ry_i$$

For example: for the 2nd sample, which consists of the 1st, 2nd, and 4th sampling units, we have

$$x'_i = 0.78y_i$$

This sample regression line is shown in Fig. 13-2.

Y_i	$RY_i = X'_i$	$ry_i = x'_i$	X_i
3	3	$0.78 \times 3 = 2.34$	1
1	1	$0.78 \times 1 = 0.78$	2
2	2	$0.78 \times 2 = 1.56$	3
5	5	$0.78 \times 5 = 3.90$	4
4	4	$0.78 \times 4 = 3.12$	5

The x'_i which are estimates of X_i are given in the table above. They are the

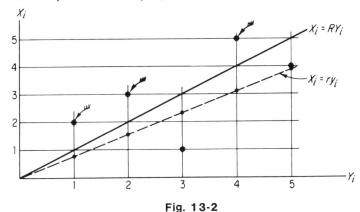

Fig. 13-2

points lying on the sample regression line. The actual values of X_i are shown by the $\bigcirc$, and the sample which consists of $n = 3$ sample points we have selected is shown by the arrows. These $n = 3$ sample points were used to find $r = 0.78$ and gave us the sample regression line.

We can draw $\binom{5}{3} = 10$ such sample lines, and the one we have drawn is merely one of these.

Note carefully that there are two problems of estimation involved. One is to estimate R and the other is to estimate the individual values of X_i. We are concerned with estimating R, not the individual values of X_i. However, we shall consider how X_i may be estimated to obtain a better understanding of how R is estimated.

To see how X_i is estimated, let us consider the case where $Y_i = 3$. Then

$$X_i = 1 \qquad \text{actual } X_i \text{ value}$$

$$X_i' = RY_i = (1)(3) = 3 \qquad \text{value on population regression line}$$

$$x_i' = rY_i = 0.78(3) = 2.34 \qquad \text{value on sample regression line}$$

where $x_i' = 2.34$ may be considered as an estimate of $X_i = 1$ when estimating the individual values of X_i. But it is an estimate of $X_i' = 3$ when the problem is to estimate R.

In our present discussion, it is the estimate of R that we are interested in. The sample regression line we have drawn is an estimate of the population regression line.

(*iv*) *Variance of r—V(r).*

Let us now find the variance of r. That is, we wish to find

$$(4) \qquad\qquad V(r) = E(r - R)^2$$

Geometrically, it is a measure of the scatter of the sample regression lines around the population regression line. Using our previous example, we may calculate $V(r)$ as follows:

Samples	r	$r - R = r - 1$	$(r - R)^2$
#1	$6/6 = 1$	0	$0 = 0.0000$
2	$7/9 = 0.78$	$-2/9$	$4/81 = 0.0495$
3	$8/8 = 1$	0	$0 = 0.0000$
4	$8/10 = 0.8$	$-2/10$	$1/25 = 0.0400$
5	$9/9 = 1$	0	$0 = 0.0000$
6	$10/12 = 0.83$	$-2/12$	$1/36 = 0.0278$
7	$9/8 = 0.75$	$1/8$	$1/64 = 0.0156$
8	$10/7 = 1.43$	$3/7$	$9/49 = 0.1840$
9	$11/10 = 1.1$	$1/10$	$1/100 = 0.0100$
10	$12/11 = 1.1$	$1/11$	$1/121 = 0.0080$

$$0.3349$$

$$V(r) = E(r - R)^2 = \frac{0.3349}{10} = 0.03349$$

Such a direct calculation of $V(r)$ was only possible because of the artificially small population ($N = 5$). In practice, the population is large and $V(r)$ has to be estimated from a sample. To find the estimate of $V(r)$, let us next derive $V(r)$ theoretically, and then find the sample estimate of $V(r)$.

Let us first explain our approach geometrically. As mentioned above, we wish to measure the dispersion of the sample regression lines around the population regression line. We have drawn one sample regression line in Fig. 13-3. Our problem now is: How are we going to show the deviation $r - R$?

As shown in Fig. 13-3, we may show the deviation of the sample regres-

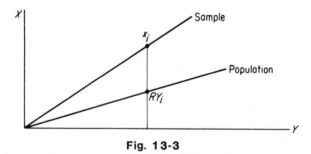

Fig. 13-3

sion line and the population regression line by $x_i - RY_i$. Then the question is: Does the deviation $x_i - RY_i$ correspond to $r - R$? As we shall show, it does. Hence, the deviation $r - R$ may be considered in terms of $x_i - RY_i$. With this geometrical interpretation in mind, let us now find $V(r)$.

We first express $r - R$ in terms of $X_i - RY_i$. From the discussion concerning bias, we found that if $\bar{y} \doteq \bar{Y}$, then

$$r \doteq R\left(1 + \frac{\bar{x} - \bar{X}}{\bar{X}}\right)$$

$$r - R = \frac{\bar{x} - \bar{X}}{\bar{X}} R = \frac{\bar{x} - \bar{X}}{\bar{X}} \frac{\bar{X}}{\bar{Y}} = \frac{\bar{x} - \bar{X}}{\bar{Y}} = \frac{\bar{x} - R\bar{Y}}{\bar{Y}}$$

But since we assumed that $\bar{y} = \bar{Y}$, we may write

$$r - R = \frac{\bar{x} - R\bar{y}}{\bar{Y}}$$

and by doing this, the numerator has $\bar{x}$ and $\bar{y}$ which are both sample values. Continuing this derivation, we find

$$r - R \doteq \frac{1}{\bar{Y}}\left[\frac{1}{n}\sum_{}^{n}(x_i - Ry_i)\right] = \frac{1}{\bar{Y}}\left[\frac{1}{n}\sum_{}^{n}d_i\right]$$

where we have set

$$d_i = x_i - Ry_i$$

Let us also set

$$\bar{d} = \frac{1}{n}\sum_{}^{n}(x_i - Ry_i) = \frac{1}{n}\sum d_i$$

$$\therefore \quad r - R = \frac{1}{\bar{Y}}\bar{d}$$

We may also write

$$\frac{\sum_{}^{N}d_i}{N} = \frac{1}{N}\sum_{}^{N}(x_i - Ry_i) = \bar{X} - R\bar{Y} = 0$$

$$\therefore \quad \bar{D} = \frac{\sum_{}^{N}d_i}{N} = 0$$

which may be considered the population mean of the d_i. Then $\bar{d}$ is the sample mean of a sample size n. Substituting these results into $r - R$ gives us

$$r - R = \frac{1}{\bar{Y}}(\bar{d} - \bar{D})$$

Substituting these into $E(r - R)^2$ gives us

$$E(r - R)^2 = E\left[\frac{1}{\bar{Y}}(\bar{d} - \bar{D})\right]^2 = \frac{1}{\bar{Y}^2}E(\bar{d} - \bar{D})^2$$

But $E(\bar{d} - \bar{D})^2$ is simply the variance of the sample mean $\bar{d}$. Thus

$$V(r) = E(r - R)^2 = \frac{1}{\bar{Y}^2}\left(\frac{N - n}{N}\frac{\sum_{}^{N}(d_i - \bar{D})^2}{n(N - 1)}\right)$$

$$= \frac{1}{\bar{Y}^2}\frac{N - n}{nN}\frac{\sum_{}^{N}d_i^2}{N - 1}$$

(4')
$$= \frac{1}{\bar{Y}^2}\frac{N - n}{nN}\frac{\sum_{}^{N}(x_i - Ry_i)^2}{N - 1}$$

which is the result we seek.

The relationship between this formula and that for $V(\bar{x})$ is that, in the latter case, the deviations of x_i are from $\bar{x}$, whereas in $V(r)$, the deviations of x_i are from Ry_i, (that is, from the sample regression line).

Let us find $V(r)$ from our illustration using this result.

x_i	$Ry_i = y_i$ $(R = 1)$	$x_i - Ry_i$	$(x_i - Ry_i)^2$
1	3	-2	4
2	1	1	1
3	2	1	1
4	5	-1	1
5	4	1	1
			8

$$V(r) = \frac{1}{3^2}\frac{5-3}{3\cdot5}\frac{8}{5-1} = \frac{4}{135} = 0.0295$$

The value of $V(r)$ we found earlier was $V(r) = 0.0335$. This discrepancy is mainly due to the fact that the population and sample were very small.

Our next task is to start from the basic formula

(4') $$V(r) = \frac{1}{\bar{Y}^2}\frac{N-n}{nN}\frac{\sum\limits^{N}(x_i - Ry_i)^2}{N-1}$$

and develop an alternate form which will be more convenient for investigating the conditions under which the ratio method will be more efficient than simple random sampling.

(v) *Alternate form of $V(r)$.*

To find the alternate form of equation (4'), let us rewrite the squared deviations of the numerator as follows:

$$\sum\limits^{N}(x_i - Ry_i)^2 = \sum\limits^{N}[(x_i - \bar{X}) - R(y_i - \bar{Y})]^2$$
$$= \sum\limits^{N}(x_i - \bar{X})^2 + R^2 \sum(y_i - \bar{Y})^2 - 2R\sum(x_i - \bar{X})(y_i - \bar{Y})$$

We know that

$$\sum\limits^{N}(x_i - \bar{X})^2 = (N-1)S_x^2$$
$$\sum\limits^{N}(y_i - \bar{Y})^2 = (N-1)S_y^2$$
$$\rho = \frac{\sum\limits^{N}(x_i - \bar{X})(y_i - \bar{Y})}{(N-1)S_x S_y}$$
$$\therefore \quad \sum\limits^{N}(x_i - Ry_i)^2 = (N-1)(S_x^2 + R^2S_y^2 - 2R\rho S_x S_y)$$

Substituting this into (4') gives us

$$V(r) = \frac{1}{\bar{Y}^2} \frac{N-n}{nN} \frac{1}{N-1}[(N-1)(S_x^2 + R^2 S_y^2 - 2R\rho S_x S_y)]$$

(5)
$$= \frac{1}{\bar{Y}^2} \frac{N-n}{nN}(S_x^2 + R^2 S_y^2 - 2\rho R S_x S_y)$$

which is the alternate form we seek.

Let us investigate the implications of this result. One of the objects of a sample design is the increase in precision. That is, we wish $V(r)$ to be as small as possible. In (5), we note that S_x, S_y, and R are positive and $-1 \leq \rho \leq 1$. Hence, $V(r)$ will be at a minimum when $\rho = 1$. That is, the ratio method will have a minimum variance when there is perfect positive correlation between x and y. Graphically, when the sample points (x_i, y_i) fall on a straight line, $V(r)$ will be at a minimum. If, in addition, the straight line goes through the origin, r will be unbiased.

We are now in a position to explain the statement made at the end of subsection (ii), which was that we may expect the bias to be small compared to the standard error of r, and that when n is moderately large the bias may therefore be neglected. To explain this, let us compare the bias and $V(r)$. We have

$$\text{bias} = E(r - R) = \frac{N-1}{N} \frac{1}{n} \frac{1}{\bar{Y}^2}(RS_y^2 - \rho S_x S_y)$$

and

$$V(r) = \frac{N-n}{N} \frac{1}{n} \frac{1}{\bar{Y}^2}(S_x^2 + R^2 S_y^2 - 2\rho R S_x S_y)$$

The effect of an increase of n on the bias and the standard error, $\sqrt{V(r)}$, may now be seen. When the sample size increases, say, 400%, that is, it becomes $4n$, the bias will decrease by approximately $1/4$, whereas, for $\sqrt{V(r)}$, it will decrease by $1/\sqrt{4}$. Hence, as n increases k times, whereas the bias will decrease by $1/k$, the standard error will decrease by $1/\sqrt{k}$. Therefore, for moderately large samples, the bias may be small relative to the standard error, and may even be negligible.

(*vi*) *Estimate of* $V(r)$.

The $V(r)$ we obtained was a theoretical result based on population values. What we need to do now is to obtain a sample estimate. The formula for $V(r)$ was

(6)
$$V(r) = \frac{1}{\bar{Y}^2} \frac{N-n}{nN} \frac{\sum\limits^{N} (x_i - Ry_i)^2}{N-1}$$

For an estimate of (6) we use

(7)
$$\hat{V}(r) = \frac{1}{\bar{y}^2} \frac{N-n}{nN} \frac{\sum\limits^{n} (x_i - ry_i)^2}{n-1}$$

For calculation purposes, we set

$$\sum_{}^{n} (x_i - ry_i)^2 = \sum_{}^{n} x_i^2 + r^2 \sum y_i^2 - 2r \sum x_i y_i$$

Example 2. Given sample #2 of the table on p. 338, find $\hat{V}(r)$.

x_i	y_i	x_i^2	y_i^2	$x_i y_i$
1	3	1	9	3
2	1	4	1	2
4	5	16	25	20
7	9	21	35	25

$$r = 7/9 = 0.785$$

$$\sum_{}^{n} (x_i - ry_i)^2 = 21 + (7/9)^2 \, 35 - 2(7/9)25 = 266/81 = 3.3$$

$$\therefore \quad \hat{V}(r) = \frac{1}{(9/3)^2} \frac{5-3}{3 \cdot 5} \cdot \frac{3 \cdot 3}{3-1} = 0.0245$$

$$s(r) = 0.155$$

Example 3. Using the data of Example 1 (p. 333), find $\hat{V}(r)$ and $s(r)$. We find $\sum x_i = 46$, $\sum y_i = 230$, $\sum x_i^2 = 247$, $\sum y_i^2 = 5950$, $\sum x_i y_i = 1210$, and $n = 10$. Also, for simplicity, set $(N - n)/N = 1$. Then, $r = 46/230 = 0.20$:

$$\sum (x_i - ry_i)^2 = 247 + (0.20)^2(5950) - 2(0.20)(1210) = 1$$

$$\therefore \quad \hat{V}(r) = \frac{1}{(230/10)^2} \left(\frac{1}{10}\right)\left(1\right)\left(\frac{1}{10-1}\right) = \frac{1}{47610}$$

$$\therefore \quad s(r) = 0.067$$

(vii) *Determination of the sample size.*

We have derived formulas for r and $V(r)$ based on a sample of size n. Our problem in this subsection is to see how n is determined.

To determine the sample size, let us start with

(8)
$$\hat{V}(r) = \frac{1}{\bar{y}^2} \frac{N-n}{nN} \frac{\sum_{}^{n} (x_i - ry_i)^2}{n-1}$$

$$= \frac{1}{\bar{y}^2} \frac{N-n}{nN} s_d^2$$

Take a preliminary sample of size n' and find

$$s_d^2 = \frac{\sum_{}^{n'} (x_i - ry_i)^2}{n' - 1}$$

and consider it as an estimate of s_d^2. Then (1) becomes

(9)
$$\hat{V}(r) = \frac{1}{\bar{y}^2} \frac{N-n}{nN} s_d^2$$

Suppose we wish the precision to be within d with a reliability of, say, z. Then (note that d indicates precision and is different from d_i)

(10)
$$d^2 = z^2 \hat{V}(r) = z^2 \frac{1}{\bar{y}^2} \frac{N - n}{Nn} s_d^2$$

Let us first set $(N - n)/N = 1$ and find n, which we shall denote as n_0. Then, using n_0, let us find n.

$$d^2 = z^2 \frac{1}{\bar{y}^2} \frac{s_d^2}{n_0}$$

(11)
$$n_0 = \frac{z^2 s_d^2}{d^2 \bar{y}^2}$$

Equation (10) may be rewritten as

$$\frac{d^2 \bar{y}^2}{z^2 s_d^2} = \frac{N - n}{nN}$$

$$\therefore \quad n_0 = \frac{nN}{N - n}$$

Solving for n gives us

(12)
$$n = \frac{n_0}{1 + n_0/N}$$

As shown in this result, when N is large relative to n_0 and n_0/N may be ignored, we have $n = n_0$.

Example 4. In Example 1 (p. 333), we found $r = 0.2$. Suppose we wish the precision of r to be within ± 0.005. If R is around 0.2, this means an error of about $0.005/0.2 = 2.5\%$. Let $z = 2$. Also assume the sample in Example 1 is a pilot sample. We have found that

$$s_d^2 = \frac{\sum(x_i - ry_i)^2}{n' - 1} = \frac{1}{10 - 1} = \frac{1}{9}$$

Hence,

$$n_0 = \frac{z^2 s_d^2}{d^2 \bar{y}^2} = \frac{(2)^2(1/9)}{(0.005)^2(23)^2} = 33.6$$

Note that our hypothetical example has only 10 observations, which is too small to obtain a reliable result.

After finding n, we may calculate s_d^2 and compare it with $\hat{s}_d^2$. If there is a large discrepancy, recalculate n_0 and n until it becomes small.

Assuming that n, s_d^2, and $\hat{V}(r)$ are determined, let us next find a confidence interval for R. For this, we need to know the distribution of r. Following Cochran's suggestion, we shall assume the distribution of r approximates a normal distribution when $n > 30$ and the coefficients of variation of $\bar{x}$ and $\bar{y}$ are both less than 0.1. Then the confidence interval for R is

$$r - z\sqrt{\hat{V}(r)} < R < r + z\sqrt{\hat{V}(r)}$$

(viii) *Estimation of the total.*

We have illustrated in section 13.1 how the ratio estimation procedure may be used to estimate a total. That was

(13)
$$\hat{X} = rY$$

where

$$r = \frac{\sum\limits^{n} x_i}{\sum y_i} = \frac{x}{y}$$

As shown, it is necessary to know the total Y, which we shall call *supplementary information* or *supplementary data*. The reason for using this form of estimation for totals was also explained in section 13.1. In this section, let us compare the $\hat{X}$ of (13) with

(14)
$$\hat{X} = N\bar{y}$$

which is the usual simple random sampling procedure of estimating the total.

To compare which of the two estimates is better, we need to compare their variances. For the ratio estimate case, we have

$$V(r) = \frac{1}{\bar{Y}^2}\frac{N-n}{nN}(S_x^2 + R^2 S_y^2 - 2\rho R S_x S_y)$$

$$= \frac{N^2}{Y^2}\frac{N-n}{nN}(S_x^2 + R^2 S_y^2 - 2\rho R S_x S_y)$$

This may be rewritten as

(15)
$$V(rY) = V(\hat{X}) = N^2\frac{N-n}{nN}(S_x^2 + R^2 S_y^2 - 2\rho R S_x S_y)$$

The $V(\hat{X})$ of simple random sampling is

(16)
$$V(\hat{X}_{\text{simp}}) = N^2\frac{N-n}{nN}S_x^2$$

Hence, let us compare (15) and (16).

$$V(\hat{X}_{\text{simp}}) - V(\hat{X}_R) = N^2\frac{N-n}{Nn}(2\rho R S_x S_y - R^2 S_y^2)$$

and $V(\hat{X}_{\text{simp}}) > V(\hat{X}_R)$ when

$$2\rho R S_x S_y > R^2 S_y^2$$

$$\rho > \frac{1}{2}\frac{S_y}{S_x}R$$

$$= \frac{1}{2}\frac{S_y}{S_x}\frac{\bar{X}}{\bar{Y}} = \frac{1}{2}\frac{C_y}{C_x}$$

When this relation holds, $V(\hat{X}_R)$ will be more efficient than $V(\hat{X}_{\text{simp}})$. When

$C_y \leqq C_x$, then $C_y/C_x \leqq 1$. Thus, when the coefficient of variation of X is greater than that of Y, the ratio method will be more efficient when ρ is greater than $1/2$.

A measure of the relative efficiency is found by

$$E_f = \frac{V(\hat{X}_{\text{simp}})}{V(\hat{X}_R)} = \frac{S_x^2}{S_x^2 + R^2 S_y^2 - 2\rho R S_x S_y}$$

$$= \frac{C_x^2}{C_x^2 + C_y^2 - 2\rho C_x C_y}$$

$$= \frac{1}{1 + (C_y/C_x)^2 - 2\rho(C_y/C_x)}$$

As shown, when $\rho > C_y/2C_y$, then $E_f > 1$. This condition implies that when C_y/C_x is small and ρ is large, it will be advantageous to use the ratio method, and C_y/C_x will be small when C_x is larger than C_y.

Example 5. Suppose $C_y/C_x = 1$, and $\rho = 0.9$. Then

$$E_f = \frac{1}{1 + (1)^2 - 2(0.9)(1)} = 5$$

This shows that only $1/5$ of a sample size is necessary for the ratio estimate as compared to simple random sampling.

Example 6. Suppose $C_y/C_x = 1$ and $\rho = 0.7$. Then

$$E_f = \frac{1}{1 + (1)^2 - 2(0.7)(1)} = 1.66$$

and there is still a considerable improvement in the efficiency when the ratio method is used.

As shown, there may be considerable improvement in the estimation of X when the ratio method is used. This method, however, requires that supplementary information be available.

Illustrations of cases where supplementary information is available include the case of population census. For example, a population census may be taken every 5 years, and may be used as the Y for the intervening years with the ratio method to estimate the population total. Or, in crop surveys, information about the total area of agricultural land under consideration may be available from prior surveys and considered to be unchanged, and may thus be used as the Y to estimate crops by the ratio method. Or, in order to estimate the number of pieces of mail order, the total weight of the mail Y may be known, and with a sample estimate of

$$r = x/y = \text{pieces of mail} / \text{weight of mail}$$

we may estimate $\hat{X} = rY$. As shown, there are many cases where the supplementary information (Y) is available.

Problems

1. Given the following hypothetical population:

Sampling units	X_i	Y_i
1	1	2
2	2	1
3	3	4
4	4	3
5	5	5

(i) Find R.
(ii) Select all possible samples of size $n = 3$ without replacement and find the sample ratios r.
(iii) Calculate the bias $E(r - R)$.
(iv) Show the population ratio R diagramatically. Also select 3 sample ratios r and show them on the same diagram as in (iii).

2. Using the data of Problem 1 above, calculate $V(r)$ from equation (4).

3. Continuing Problem 2, calculate $V(r)$ from equation (4') and explain why there is a discrepancy.

4. Using one of the samples selected in Problem 1 above, calculate $\hat{V}(r)$ and $s(r)$.

5. Suppose we wish to estimate the vacancy rate of apartment houses. A sample of size $n = 20$ has been selected and we have the following data:

Apartment houses	Apartments y_i	Vacancies x_i	Apartment houses	Apartments y_i	Vacancies x_i
1	20	4	11	60	15
2	10	2	12	50	8
3	30	6	13	30	5
4	40	8	14	80	15
5	20	5	15	50	12
6	15	3	16	30	7
7	25	5	17	40	8
8	30	6	18	90	20
9	20	3	19	60	12
10	20	5	20	70	8

(i) Calculate r.
(ii) Calculate $\hat{V}(r)$, assuming $(N - n)/N = 1$.
(iii) Using the data above, find the sample size n so that the precision is within ± 0.005 with a reliability of $z = 2$.

6. Suppose we wish to estimate the total number of cows in 1966 in a certain state. The total number of cows for 1964 was $Y = 5000$. The sampling unit was the farm and it is assumed that there has been no change in the number of farms which we shall assume to be $N = 500$. A sample of $n = 20$ farms is selected and the data is as follows. Estimate the total number of cows for 1966.

Farm	1964 y_i	1966 x_i	Farm	1964 y_i	1966 x_i
1	12	14	11	11	14
2	22	25	12	17	19
3	38	37	13	12	12
4	15	18	14	22	23
5	18	20	15	14	16
6	31	30	16	26	28
7	15	15	17	8	9
8	20	21	18	16	15
9	10	12	19	13	15
10	25	28	20	19	20

13.4   Stratified random sampling case

Let us now consider the ratio estimate procedure as used with stratified random sampling with the following illustration: Suppose we wish to estimate the rate of vacancies of hotels in a particular city. For simplicity, let the hotels be classified as follows:

		N_h	n_h	X_{hi} (Vacancies)	X_h	Y_{hi} (Rooms)	Y_h
I	Small, 1–10 rooms	3	2	1, 2, 3	6	4, 5, 6	15
II	Medium, 11–20 rooms	3	2	3, 4, 5	12	14, 16, 18	48
III	Large, over 21 rooms	3	2	4, 5, 6	15	22, 24, 26	72
		9	6		33		135

That is, the hotels are classified into 3 strata: small (I), medium (II), and large (III), and there are 3 hotels in each stratum.

Our problem is to estimate the rate of vacancies, R, by selecting a stratified random sample. But before getting into the procedures of estimation, let us first consider a general question of estimating R. We know that the estimator of the ratio, R, is

(1)
$$r = \frac{x}{y} = \frac{\bar{x}}{\bar{y}} = \frac{\bar{x}N}{\bar{y}N} = \frac{\hat{X}}{\hat{Y}}$$

Hence, to estimate R, we may use

(2)
$$r = \frac{\hat{X}}{\hat{Y}}$$

The question then becomes: How do we find $\hat{X}$ and $\hat{Y}$?

In (2), we are using simple random sampling and, as we know, $\hat{X}$ and $\hat{Y}$ are found by

$$\hat{X} = \bar{x}N \quad \text{and} \quad \hat{Y} = \bar{y}N$$

This procedure suggests that by estimating $\hat{X}$ and $\hat{Y}$ by other methods of sampling, we may develop various ways of estimating R. In this section, we shall use stratified random sampling to estimate $\hat{X}$ and $\hat{Y}$ and find an estimate of R. We will show that there are two ways of estimating R using stratified random sampling. One is called the combined ratio estimate (or compound ratio estimate), and the second is called the separate ratio estimate. Let us start with the combined ratio estimate.

(*i*) *Combined ratio estimate.*

(a) Estimation of R.

In this case, we merely estimate X and Y by stratified random sampling and find r. We know that

(3)
$$\hat{X}_{st} = \sum_{}^{L} \frac{N_h}{n_h} \sum_{}^{n_h} x_{hi} = \sum N_h \bar{x}_h$$

(4)
$$\hat{Y}_{st} = \sum_{}^{L} \frac{N_h}{n_h} \sum_{}^{n_h} y_{hi} = \sum N_h \bar{y}_h$$

Hence, r is

(5)
$$r_c = \frac{\hat{X}_{st}}{\hat{Y}_{st}} = \frac{\sum^{L} N_h/n_h \sum^{n_h} x_{hi}}{\sum N_h/n_h \sum y_{hi}}$$

where the subscript c is added to denote that r_c is the combined ratio estimate. Let us illustrate this with the example of hotel vacancies.

Suppose we select random samples of size $n = 2$ from each stratum as follows:

	n_h	x_{hi}	x_h	$\bar{x}_h$	y_{hi}	y_h	$\bar{y}_h$
I	2	1, 3	4	2	4, 6	10	5
II	2	3, 4	7	3.5	14, 16	30	15
III	2	5, 6	11	5.5	24, 26	50	25
	6		22			90	

Hence, we obtain the following results:

$$\hat{X} = \sum N_h \bar{x}_h = (3 \times 2) + [3 \times (7/2)] + [3 \times (11/2)] = 33$$
$$\hat{Y} = \sum N_h \bar{y}_h = 135$$
$$\therefore \quad r_c = \hat{X}_{st}/\hat{Y}_{st} = 33/135 = 0.25$$

If, say, a 10% sample is selected from each stratum, then $n_h/N_h = 0.10$ is fixed. Then,

$$r_c = \frac{\sum\limits^{L}\sum\limits^{n_h} x_{hi}}{\sum\sum y_{hi}} = \frac{\sum\limits^{L} x_h}{\sum y_h} = \frac{x}{y}$$

where r_c is simply the ratio of sample totals and becomes equal to the simple random sampling case. In terms of our illustration, we have $n_h/N_h = 2/3$. Hence, r_c becomes

$$r_c = x/y = 22/90 = 33/135 = 0.25$$

and the result is the same as that found above.

(b) $V(r_c)$.

The variance of r_c is:

(6) $\quad V(r_c) = \dfrac{1}{N^2}\dfrac{1}{\bar{Y}^2}\sum\limits^{L} N_h^2 \dfrac{N_h - n_h}{N_h}\dfrac{1}{n_h}(S_{xh}^2 + R^2 S_{yh}^2 - 2R\rho_h S_{xh}S_{yh})$

$\qquad\qquad = \dfrac{1}{Y^2}\sum\limits^{L} N_h^2 \dfrac{N_h - n_h}{N_h}\dfrac{1}{n_h}S_{ch}^2$

where

(7) $\quad S_{xh}^2 = \dfrac{1}{N_h - 1}\sum\limits^{N_h} (X_{hi} - \bar{X}_h)^2$

(8) $\quad \rho_h = \dfrac{S_{xyh}}{S_{xh}S_{yh}}$

$\qquad\qquad = \dfrac{[1/(N_h - 1)]\sum\limits^{N_h} (X_{hi} - \bar{X}_h)(Y_{hi} - \bar{Y}_h)}{\sqrt{\sum (X_{hi} - \bar{X}_h)^2/(N_h - 1)}\sqrt{\sum (Y_{hi} - \bar{Y}_h)^2/(N_h - 1)}}$

which is an approximation. Characteristics of this formula are that it includes only the population ratio R, does not require the stratum ratios R_h, but does require the stratum correlation coefficients, ρ_h.

Since R is usually positive, the formula shows that when ρ_h is large (that is, when there is a high positive correlation in each stratum), $V(r_c)$ will tend to be small. We shall discuss the characteristics of $V(r_c)$ again after we have considered the separate ratio estimate.

Let us calculate $V(r_c)$ using our illustration. Note that, in practice, we use the estimate of $V(r_c)$ which we give in the next subsection, and it is only calculated here to provide a better understanding of the formula. We find as follows:

Strata	S_{xh}^2	R^2	S_{yh}^2	$R^2S_{yh}^2$	ρ_h	$2R\rho_h S_{xh}S_{yh}$	S_{ch}^2
I	1	0.06	1	0.06	1	0.5	0.56
II	1	0.06	4	0.24	1	1.0	0.24
III	1	0.06	4	0.24	1	1.0	0.24

$$1.04$$

$$S_{x1}^2 = \frac{1}{3-1}[(1-2)^2 + (2-2)^2 + (3-2)^2] = 1$$

and S_{x2} and S_{x3} are found in a similar manner.

$$S_{xy1} = \frac{1}{3-1}[(1-2)(4-5) + (2-2)(5-5) + (3-2)(6-5)] = 1$$

The other S_{xyh} are found in a similar manner.

$$\therefore \quad \rho_1 = \frac{S_{xy1}}{\sqrt{S_{x1}^2}\sqrt{S_{y1}^2}} = \frac{1}{\sqrt{1}\sqrt{1}} = 1$$

and ρ_2, and ρ_3 are found in a similar manner. Thus, S_{ch}^2 is found as shown in the table.

Since $N_h = 3$ and $n_h = 2$, $V(r_c)$ becomes

$$V(r_c) = \left(\frac{1}{135}\right)^2 (3)^2 \left(\frac{3-2}{3}\right)\left(\frac{1}{2}\right)(1.04) = 0.00008$$

$$\sigma(r_c) = 0.0089$$

We have already found that $r_c = 0.25$.

(c) $\hat{V}(r_c)$

For practical applications, we obtain the sample estimates of S_{hx}, S_{hy}, R, and ρ_h and substitute them into $V(r_c)$. That is,

$$(9) \qquad \hat{V}(r_c) = \frac{1}{N^2}\frac{1}{\hat{\bar{Y}}^2} \sum_{h}^{L} N_h^2 \frac{N_h - n_h}{N_h} \frac{1}{n_h}(s_{hx}^2 + r_c^2 s_{yh}^2 - 2r_c \rho_h s_{xh} s_{yh})$$

$$= \frac{1}{\hat{\bar{Y}}^2} \sum_{h}^{L} N_h^2 \frac{N_h - n_h}{N_h} \frac{1}{n_h} s_{ch}^2$$

where, for example,

$$(10) \qquad s_{xh}^2 = \frac{1}{n_h - 1} \sum^{n_h} (x_{hi} - \bar{x}_h)^2$$

Example 1. Suppose we wish to estimate the weekly change in sales of supermarkets in New York City from April to May. The supermarkets are stratified into small, medium, and large categories with the following data:

Strata	Floor space (square feet)	N_h	n_h	$\bar{x}_h$ (May)	$\bar{y}_h$ (April)
Small (I)	under 500	1000	50	10	10
Medium (II)	500–999	500	50	33	30
Large (III)	over 1000	200	50	60	50

where $\bar{x}_h$ is the sample average sales per week in $1000 units during May, $\bar{y}_h$ is the sample average for April, and $n_h = 50$ for each stratum.

(a) Find r_c

$$\hat{X}_{st} = \sum^L \frac{N_h}{n_h} \sum x_{hi} = 1000(10) + 500(33) + 200(60) = 38500$$

$$\hat{Y}_{st} = 35000$$

$$\therefore \quad r_c = 38500/35000 = 1.1$$

(b) Find $\hat{V}(r_c)$. Suppose the data is as follows:

	s_{xh}^2	r_c^2	s_{yh}^2	$r_c^2 s_{yh}^2$	ρ_h	$2r_c \rho_h s_{xh} s_{yh}$	s_{ch}^2
I	1	1.21	1	1.21	1	2.2	0.01
II	2	1.21	2	2.42	1	4.4	0.02
III	3	1.21	3	3.63	1	6.6	0.03

Note that the units are in terms of $1000.

$$\hat{V}(r_c) = \frac{1}{\hat{Y}^2} \sum^L N_h^2 \frac{N_h - n_h}{N_h} \frac{1}{n_h} s_{ch}^2 = 0.0025$$

$$s(r_c) = 0.05$$

Thus, $r_c = 1.1$ and $s(r_c) = 0.05$.

(c) Estimation of X.

The r_c gave us the vacancy rate, but suppose we wish to know the total number of vacancies. Then, theoretically,

(11) $$\hat{X}_c = r_c Y$$

where Y (the total number of hotel rooms) is assumed to be known.

The variance of $\hat{X}_c$ is obtained by noting that $\hat{X}_c = r_c Y$. Thus

(12) $$V(\hat{X}_c) = Y^2 V(r_c) = \sum N_h^2 \frac{N_h - n_h}{N_h} \frac{1}{n_h} S_{ch}^2$$

The estimate, $\hat{V}(\hat{X}_c)$, is obtained by

(13) $$\hat{V}(\hat{X}_c) = Y^2 \hat{V}(r_c)$$

In terms of our illustration about hotel vacancies we have

$$\hat{X}_c = r_c Y = (33/135)135 = 33 \text{ rooms}$$

$$V(\hat{X}_c) = Y^2 V(r_c) = (135)^2 \left[\left(\frac{1}{135}\right)^2 (3)^2 \left(\frac{3-2}{3}\right)(1.04) \right] = 3.12$$

$$\sigma(\hat{X}_c) = 1.7 \text{ rooms}$$

Problems

1. Given the following hypothetical data answer the questions.

Hotels	N_h	X_{hi} (Vacancies)	Y_{hi} (Rooms)
Small	5	1, 2, 3, 3, 4	6, 7, 7, 8, 10
Medium	4	3, 4, 4, 5	14, 14, 18, 19
Large	4	5, 6, 8, 8,	30, 33, 40, 48

(i)   Find the population ratio of vacancies R.
(ii) Select a sample of $n_h = 3$ from each stratum and estimate R.
(iii) Calculate $V(r_c)$ from the population.
(iv) Using the sample selected in (ii), calculate $\hat{V}(r_c)$ and $s(r_c)$.
(v)   Calculate the population X and Y.
(vi) Calculate $\hat{X}_c$.
(vii) Calculate $\hat{V}(\hat{X}_c)$ and $s(\hat{X}_c)$.

2. Given the following data (in units of $1000), answer the questions.

Supermarkets	N_h	X_{hi} (May sales)	Y_{hi} (April sales)
Small	10	2, 4, 1, 3, 1, 5, 4, 4, 5, 3	3, 4, 2, 4, 2, 5, 4, 5, 6, 5
Medium	8	5, 6, 5, 7, 8, 8, 9, 11	6, 8, 6, 9, 11, 8, 10, 13
Large	5	11, 13, 15, 12, 18	13, 12, 18, 14, 24

(i)   Find the population ratio R of the May-to-April sales.
(ii) Select a sample of size $n_h = 3$ from each stratum and estimate R.
(iii) Using the sample selected in (ii), calculate $\hat{V}(r_c)$ and $s(r_c)$.
(vi) Calculate the population X and Y.
(v)   Calculate $\hat{X}_c$.
(vi) Calculate $\hat{V}(\hat{X}_c)$ and $s(\hat{X}_c)$.

(ii) Separate ratio estimate.

(a) Estimate of R.

In the separate ratio estimate, the numerator of $r = \hat{X}/Y$ (that is, $\hat{X}$) is estimated by repeated application of the ratio estimate method to each stratum, whereas Y is assumed to be known. Let us explain how $\hat{X}$ is found.

Let $r_h = x_h/y_h$ be the ratio estimate of stratum h. Then

(14)
$$\hat{X}_h = r_h Y_h = \frac{x_h}{y_h} Y_h$$

is the ratio estimate of the total for stratum h. Hence, the estimate for the total, X, is

(15)
$$\hat{X}_s = \sum \hat{X}_h = \sum r_h Y_h$$

where the subscript s indicates it is the total estimated by the separate ratio procedure. Hence, since Y is assumed to be known, r becomes

$$(16) \qquad r_s = \frac{\hat{X}_s}{Y} = \frac{\sum\limits_{}^{L} r_h Y_h}{Y} = \sum\limits_{}^{L} \frac{Y_h}{Y} r_h$$

where the subscript s shows that r_s is obtained by the separate ratio estimate method.

This method requires the calculation of r_h for each stratum and hence may be useful when this additional information is required. For example, besides the overall vacancy rate, we may wish to know the vacancy rates for the large, medium, and small hotels.

(b) $V(r_s)$

The sampling variance of r_s is

$$V(r_s) = \frac{1}{N^2} \frac{1}{\bar{Y}^2} \sum\limits_{}^{L} N_h^2 \frac{N_h - n_h}{N_h} \frac{1}{n_h} (S_{xh}^2 + R_h^2 S_{yh}^2 - 2R_h \rho_h S_{xh} S_{yh})$$

$$(17) \qquad = \frac{1}{N^2} \frac{1}{\bar{Y}^2} \sum\limits_{}^{L} N_h^2 \frac{N_h - n_h}{N_h} \frac{1}{n_h} S_{sh}^2$$

$$= \frac{1}{\bar{Y}^2} \sum\limits_{}^{L} N_h^2 \frac{N_h - n_h}{N_h} \frac{1}{n_h} S_{sh}^2$$

As shown, we need R_h for each stratum in this case. Also note that $N\bar{Y} = Y$.

Example 2. Using the illustration of hotel vacancies, let us calculate X_s and r_s. Let us first find the strata r_h.

n_h	x_{hi}	x_h	$\bar{x}_h$	y_{hi}	y_h	$\bar{y}_h$	$r_h = x_h/y_h$
2	1, 3	4	2	4, 6	10	5	4/10
2	3, 4	7	3.5	14, 16	30	15	7/30
2	5, 6	11	5.5	24, 26	50	25	11/50

Using the strata r_h, we may now find $\hat{X}_s$ and r_s.

Y_h	$r_h Y_h = \hat{X}_h$
15	$15 \times 4/10 = 6$
48	$48 \times 7/30 = 11.2$
72	$72 \times 11/50 = 15.84$
	33.04

$$\hat{X}_s = 33.04 \qquad r_r = \frac{33.04}{135} = 0.25$$

Let us next find the strata S_{sh}^2, and then calculate $V(r_s)$.

S_{xh}^2	R_h^2	S_{yh}^2	$R_h^2 S_{yh}^2$	ρ_h	$2R_h\rho_h S_{xh}S_{yh}$	S_{sh}^2
1	0.16	1	0.16	1	0.8	0.36
1	0.06	4	0.24	1	1.0	0.24
1	0.04	4	0.16	1	0.8	0.36

$$V(r_s) = \frac{1}{Y^2} \sum N_h^2 \frac{N_h - n_h}{N_h} \frac{1}{n_h} S_{sh}^2$$
$$= (1/135)^2 \times 1.44 = 0.00008$$
$$\sigma(r_s) = 0.0089$$

(c) Estimate of X.

The estimate of X is obviously

(10) $$\hat{X}_s = \sum r_h Y_h = \sum \frac{x_h}{y_h} Y_h = \sum \hat{X}_h$$

For example, when we wish to estimate the total number of vacancies, we find the r_h for the large, medium, and small hotels; find $\hat{X}_h = r_h Y_h$ for each stratum; and then sum the $\hat{X}_h$.

The $V(\hat{X}_s)$ is obtained by

(19) $$V(\hat{X}_s) = V(r_s Y) = Y^2 V(r_s) = \sum N_h^2 \frac{N_h - n_h}{N_h} \frac{1}{n_h} S_{sh}^2$$

Example 3. We see from Example 2 that

$$\hat{X}_s = \sum r_h Y_h = \sum \hat{X}_h = 33 \text{ rooms}$$
$$V(\hat{X}_s) = Y^2 V(r_s) = (135)^2 \times \left[\left(\frac{1}{135}\right)^2 \times 1.44 \right] = 1.44$$
$$\sigma(\hat{X}_s) = 1.2 \text{ rooms}$$

Problems

1. Using the data of Problem 1, p. 353,
(i)   Select samples of $n_h = 3$ from each stratum and calculate r_s.
(ii) Calculate $V(r_s)$ and $\sigma(r_s)$.
(iii) Calculate $\hat{V}(r_s)$ and $s(r_s)$.
(iv) Calculate $\hat{X}_s$.
(v)   Calculate $\hat{V}(\hat{X}_s)$ and $s(\hat{X}_s)$.

2. Using the data of Problem 2, p. 354, perform the same operations as in Problem 1 above.

(*iii*) *Allocation of the sample.*

Assuming a sample size n has been determined, we have the problem of allocating the n among strata. In Chapter 6 we discussed such methods as proportional allocation, optimum allocation, and Neyman's allocation.

Of these methods, the optimum allocation was theoretically the most logical method. It allocated the sample so that the variance was minimum subject to a given cost constraint. That is, we minimized

$$V(\bar{x}_{st}) = \frac{1}{N^2} \sum N_h^2 \frac{N_h - n_h}{N_h} \frac{S_h^2}{n_h}$$

subject to a linear cost constraint

$$c = c_0 + \sum n_h c_h$$

The result was

$$(20) \qquad n_h = \frac{N_h S_h / \sqrt{c_h}}{\sum N_h S_h / \sqrt{c_h}} \cdot n$$

And when we assumed $c_h = c_f = $ constant, that is, c_h is equal for all strata, then

$$n = \frac{c - c_0}{c_f}$$

and the sample size n became fixed—c was the total cost (or the budget for the survey), and c_0 was the fixed cost. This led to the Neyman allocation, which was

$$(21) \qquad n_h = \frac{N_h S_h}{\sum N_h S_h} \cdot n$$

Since the reasoning of n_h for (20) and (21) is the same (except for the additional factor of c_h in (20)), let us proceed with our discussion in terms of (21) for simplicity.

Let us first consider the combined ratio estimate, and then the separate ratio estimate.

(a) Combined ratio estimate.

The variance for r_c and X_c were

$$V(r_c) = \frac{1}{N^2} \frac{1}{\bar{Y}^2} \sum N_h^2 \frac{N_h - n_h}{N_h} \frac{1}{n_h} S_{ch}^2$$

$$V(\hat{X}_c) = \sum N_h^2 \frac{N_h - n_h}{N_h} \frac{1}{n_h} S_{ch}^2$$

Hence, to find n_h for the r_c case, by substituting in $S_{ch}/\bar{Y}$ for S_h of (21), we have

$$(22) \qquad n_h = \frac{N_h(S_{ch}/\bar{Y})}{\sum N_h(S_{ch}/\bar{Y})} \cdot n = \frac{N_h S_{ch}}{\sum N_h S_{ch}} \cdot n$$

And for the $\hat{X}_c$ case we get

$$(23) \qquad n_h = \frac{N_h S_{ch}}{\sum N_h S_{ch}} \cdot n$$

As shown, n_h is the same for both cases. The result indicates that smaller samples should be taken from the strata which are smaller and which have smaller variation as expressed by S_{ch}^2. But S_{ch}^2 will be small when the S_{xh} and S_{yh} are small and ρ_h is close to 1. This may be explained as follows: A small S_{xh} and S_{yh} mean that the dispersion of X_{hi} and Y_{hi} are small in the strata. Hence, only a small sample is necessary to estimate the variances S_{xh}^2 and S_{yh}^2. And when ρ_h is close to 1, only a small sample is necessary to estimate ρ_h.

(b) Separate ratio estimate.

For the separate ratio estimate, we have

$$V(r_s) = \frac{1}{N^2}\frac{1}{\bar{Y}^2} \Sigma \ N_h^2 \frac{N_h - n_h}{N_h}\frac{1}{n_h}S_{sh}^2$$

$$V(\hat{X}_s) = \Sigma \ N_h^2 \frac{N_h - n_h}{N_h}\frac{1}{n_h}S_{sh}^2$$

Hence, n_h will be the same for r_s and $\hat{X}_s$:

(24) $$n_h = \frac{N_h S_{sh}}{\Sigma \ N_h S_{sh}} \cdot n$$

The interpretation of this result is similar to that of the previous case.

(c) Proportional allocation.

The simplest procedure for allocating a sample is proportional allocation, which is given by

(25) $$n_h = \frac{N_h}{N} \cdot n$$

(iv) *Determination of the sample size.*

The procedure for determining the sample size is similar to that discussed in Chapter 6. Let us recapitulate the procedure of Chapter 6 for proportional allocation. We have

$$V(\bar{x}_{st}) = \frac{1}{N^2}\Sigma \ N_h^2 \frac{N_h - n_h}{N_h}\frac{S_h^2}{n_h}$$

and

$$n_h = \frac{N_h}{N} \cdot n$$

The basic formula for deriving the sample size was

$$d^2 = z^2 V(\bar{x}_{st})$$

from which we defined the desired variance as

$$V(\bar{x}_{st}) = d^2/z^2 = D^2$$

Setting this desired variance equal to $V(\bar{x}_{prop})$ and solving for n, we found

(26) $$n = \frac{N \ \Sigma \ N_h S_h^2}{N^2 D^2 + \Sigma \ N_h S_h^2}$$

In our present case, the variance is

$$V\left(\frac{\hat{X}_c}{N}\right) = \frac{1}{N^2}\sum N_h^2 \frac{N_h - n_h}{N_h} \frac{1}{n_h} S_{ch}^2$$

$$S_{ch}^2 = S_{xh}^2 + R^2 S_{yh}^2 - 2R\rho_h S_{xh} S_{yh}$$

and $n_h = (N_h/N)n$. Hence, we may find n by replacing S_h^2 in equation (26) by S_{ch}^2. We get

(27)
$$n = \frac{N \sum N_h S_{ch}^2}{N^2 D^2 + \sum N_h S_{ch}^2}$$

The sample size for the separate ratio estimate can be obtained in a similar manner. The result will be the replacement of S_{ch} by S_{sh} in (27).

Problems

1. Let the data of Problem 2, p. 354, be a pilot sample of size $n = 23$ from a population of size $N_1 = 200$, $N_1 = 160$, $N_3 = 100$. We have taken 5% of each stratum. Let the desired variance be $D^2 = 1$. Find the sample size n using equation (27).

(v) *Comparison of the two methods.*

Having developed the combined ratio estimate and the separate ratio estimate, the question is: which of the two methods should be used? This will be determined by assessing which of the two methods has the smaller bias, smaller variance, and other practical considerations. Let us start with a comparison of the biases first.

(a) Bias.

The bias of the separate ratio estimate is likely to be larger than the combined ratio estimate. This is especially true when the n_h from each stratum is small. The biases of the ratios from each stratum may cumulate, especially if they are all in the same direction, and thus cause the bias of the overall ratio to be substantial (relative to its standard error) even though the total sample size may be large. In a case where the n_h are small but $n = \sum n_h$ is large, the combined ratio estimate is less subject to bias.

Hansen, Hurwitz, and Madow recommend that when the n_h are 50-100 or more, the bias for the separate ratio estimate will be negligible.

When n_h are small, but so are the biases of the ratios of each stratum, the separate ratio may be used without fear of bias. This occurs when the regression line in each stratum passes through the origin (it was explained in subsection (i) of 13.3 that there would be no bias when the regression line passed through the origin).

(b) Variance.

The $V(r_s)$ is valid only if the n_h of each stratum is large. Hence, when n_h are small, the combined ratio method is recommended.

Another point is that the more R_h differs from stratum to stratum, the smaller $V(r_c)$ will be relative to $V(r_s)$. This may be shown by finding $V(r_c) - V(r_s)$ as follows:

$$V(r_c) - V(r_s) = \frac{1}{Y^2}\Sigma \ N_h^2 \frac{N_h - n_h}{N_h}\frac{1}{n_h}[(R^2 - R_h^2)S_{yh}^2 - 2(R - R_h)\rho_h S_{xh}S_{yh}]$$

$$= \frac{1}{Y^2}\Sigma \ N_h^2 \frac{N_h - n_h}{N_h}\frac{1}{n_h}[(R - R_h)^2 S_{yh}^2$$

$$+ 2(R - R_h)(2R_h S_{yh}^2 - 2\rho_h S_{xh}S_{yh})]$$

We have seen in subsection (i) of 13.3 that when $RS_y = \rho S_x$, the regression line goes through the origin and there is no bias. When the situation is such that this is approximately true of each stratum, then $2R_h S_{yh}^2 - 2\rho_h S_{xh}S_{yh} = 0$. Hence

$$V(r_c) - V(r_s) \propto (R - R_h)^2$$

This shows that when R_h differs from stratum to stratum, $(R - R_h)^2$ will tend to be large and $V(r_c)$ will be greater than $V(r_s)$. That is, it will be more efficient to use the separate ratio estimate under those circumstances.

(c) Additional points of comparison.

We know that $V(r_s)$ requires calculation of r_h for each stratum, but that this does not require a great deal of additional work. Furthermore, r_h may be of interest to the surveyor.

To summarize: When the n_h are small, the bias of the separate ratio method will be large (unless the regression line of each stratum goes through the origin), and the combined ratio method is therefore recommended. When the n_h are large (over 50), the bias will be negligible. If knowing r_h for each stratum is desired, and the n_h are large or the regression lines go through the origin, the separate ratio method is recommended. But when r_h differs greatly from stratum to stratum, the combined ratio method will be more efficient than the separate ratio method.

13.5 Cluster sampling case

Let us now consider the ratio estimate procedure when used with simple cluster sampling. We shall first recapitulate the essential points of simple cluster sampling and then show how the ratio estimate is merely an extension of the simple cluster sampling case.

(a) Simple cluster sampling.

The estimator of the total in simple cluster sampling was

$$(1) \qquad \hat{X}_{cl} = \frac{M}{m}\sum_i^m \frac{N_i}{n_i}\sum_j^{n_i} x_{ij}$$

and the variance of $\hat{X}_{\mathrm{cl}}$ was

$$V(\hat{X}_{\mathrm{cl}}) = M^2 \frac{M-m}{M} \frac{S_b^2}{m} + \frac{M}{m} \sum_i^M N_i^2 \frac{N_i - n_i}{N_i} \frac{S_i^2}{n_i}$$

(2)
$$S_b^2 = \frac{1}{M-1} \sum_i^M (X_i - \bar{X})^2$$

$$S_i^2 = \frac{1}{N_i - 1} \sum_j^{N_i} (X_{ij} - \bar{\bar{X}}_i)^2$$

The estimator of the population mean was obtained from (1) and (2) as:

(3)
$$\hat{\bar{X}}_{\mathrm{cl}} = \frac{\hat{X}_{\mathrm{cl}}}{N}$$

(4)
$$V(\hat{\bar{X}}_{\mathrm{cl}}) = \frac{1}{N^2} V(\hat{X}_{\mathrm{cl}})$$

Let us now extend these results to the ratio estimate.

(b) Ratio estimate.

The estimator of R is simply

(5)
$$r_{\mathrm{cl}} = \frac{\hat{X}_{\mathrm{cl}}}{\hat{Y}_{\mathrm{cl}}}$$

where $\hat{X}_{\mathrm{cl}}$ and $\hat{Y}_{\mathrm{cl}}$ are obtained by using equation (1) for X_{ij} and Y_{ij} separately.

The variance of r_{cl} is

(6)
$$V(r_{\mathrm{cl}}) = \frac{1}{Y^2}\left(M^2 \frac{M-m}{M} \frac{S_{1b}^2}{m} + \frac{M}{m} \sum_i^M N_i^2 \frac{N_i - n_i}{N_i} \frac{S_{2i}^2}{n_i} \right)$$

(7)
$$S_{1b}^2 = S_{xb}^2 + R^2 S_{yb}^2 - 2R\rho_b S_{xb} S_{yb}$$

(8)
$$S_{2i}^2 = S_{xi}^2 + R^2 S_{yi}^2 - 2R\rho_i S_{xi} S_{yi}$$

$$S_{xb}^2 = \frac{1}{M-1} \sum_i^M (X_i - \bar{X})^2$$

$$S_{xi}^2 = \frac{1}{N_i - 1} \sum_i^{N_i} (X_{ij} - \bar{\bar{X}}_i)^2$$

$$\rho_b = \frac{1}{M-1} \frac{\sum_i^M (X_i - \bar{X})(Y_i - \bar{Y})}{S_{xb} S_{yb}}$$

$$\rho_i = \frac{1}{N_i - 1} \frac{\sum_i^{N_i} (X_{ij} - \bar{\bar{X}}_i)(Y_{ij} - \bar{\bar{Y}}_i)}{S_{xi} S_{yi}}$$

The similarity between (2) and (6) is obvious. In fact, when $Y_{ij} = 1$, (6) reduces to (2).

In addition, it is easily seen that when $M = m$, (6) reduces to the combined ratio estimate of the stratified sampling case.

The sample estimate of $V(r_{\mathrm{cl}})$ is obtained by finding the sample estimate of the components of $V(r_{\mathrm{cl}})$. We get

$$\hat{V}(r_{\text{cl}}) = \frac{1}{\hat{Y}^2}\left(M^2\frac{M-m}{M}\frac{s_{1b}^2}{m} + \frac{M}{m}\sum^{m} N_i^2\frac{N_i-n_i}{N_i}\frac{s_{2i}^2}{n_i}\right)$$

(9)
$$s_{1b}^2 = s_{xb}^2 + r_{\text{cl}}^2 s_{yb}^2 - 2r_{\text{cl}}\hat{\rho}_b s_{xb}s_{yb}$$
$$s_{2i}^2 = s_{xi}^2 + r_{\text{cl}}^2 s_{yi}^2 - 2r_{\text{cl}}\hat{\rho}_i s_{xi}s_{yi}$$

where, for example,

$$s_{xb}^2 = \frac{1}{m-1}\sum^{m}(x_i - \bar{x})^2$$

$$s_{xi}^2 = \frac{1}{n_i-1}\sum_{j}^{n_i}(x_{ij} - \bar{\bar{x}}_i)^2$$

and likewise for the other terms.

As shown, there is a considerable amount of calculation involved, and any simplification would be welcome. Recall that in section 8.4, we simplified $\hat{V}(\hat{X}_{\text{cl}})$ for cases where $M \gg m$ by assuming $m/M \doteq 0$. In our present case, if the situation is such that we may assume $m/M \doteq 0$, (6) simplifies to

(10)
$$\hat{V}(r_{\text{cl}}) = \frac{1}{Y^2}\left(\frac{M}{m}\right)^2\left(ms_{1b}^2 + \frac{M}{m}\sum N_i^2\frac{N_i-n_i}{N_i}\frac{s_{2i}^2}{n_i}\right)$$
$$= \frac{1}{Y^2}\left(\frac{M}{m}\right)^2(ms_{1b}^2)$$
$$= \frac{1}{Y^2}M^2\frac{s_{1b}^2}{m}$$

We have seen in section 8.8 that the optimum allocation of the sample was given by

(11)
$$\bar{n} = \sqrt{\frac{c_1}{c_2}\frac{S_{2i}^2}{S_{1b}^2 - (S_{2i}^2/\bar{N})}}$$

and m was obtained by solving

$$c = c_1 m + c_2 m\bar{n}$$

where we assumed $\bar{n} = n_i$ for simplicity.

In our present case of ratio estimation, we can find m and $\bar{n}$ by replacing S_{1b}^2 and S_{2i}^2 with their corresponding terms in (7) and (8).

13.6 Cluster sampling with pps

We may easily extend our discussion to the case where cluster sampling is with pps. Recall from Chapter 9 that

(1)
$$\bar{x}_{\text{pps}} = \frac{1}{m\bar{n}}\sum^{m}\sum^{\bar{n}} x_{ij}$$

(2)
$$V(\bar{x}_{\text{pps}}) = \frac{1}{mN}\sum^{M} N_i(\bar{X}_i - \bar{\bar{X}})^2 + \frac{1}{mN}\sum^{M}(N_i - \bar{n})\frac{S_i^2}{\bar{n}}$$

(3)
$$S_i^2 = \frac{1}{N_i - 1} \sum^{N_i} (X_{ij} - \bar{X}_i)^2$$

For ratio estimate with cluster sampling with pps, these formulas become

(4)
$$r_{\text{pps}} = \frac{\bar{\bar{x}}_{\text{pps}}}{\bar{\bar{y}}_{\text{pps}}}$$

(5)
$$V(r_{\text{pps}}) = \frac{1}{\bar{\bar{Y}}^2}\left[\frac{1}{mN} \sum^{M} N_i(\bar{\bar{X}}_i - R\bar{\bar{Y}}_i)^2 + \frac{1}{mN} \sum^{M} (N_i - \bar{n})\frac{S_i^2}{\bar{n}}\right]$$

(6)
$$S_i^2 = S_{xi}^2 + R^2 S_{yi}^2 - 2R\rho_i S_{xi} S_{yi}$$

Recall also that we found the unbiased estimate of $V(\bar{x}_{\text{pps}})$ in section 9.3 to be

(7)
$$\hat{V}(\bar{x}_{\text{pps}}) = \frac{1}{m(m-1)} \sum (\bar{x}_i - \bar{x}_{\text{pps}})^2$$

In terms of the ratio estimate case, this becomes

(8)
$$\hat{V}(r_{\text{pps}}) = \frac{1}{\bar{\bar{Y}}^2}\left[\frac{1}{m(m-1)} \sum^{m} (\bar{x}_i - r_{\text{pps}}\bar{\bar{y}}_i)^2\right]$$

Notes and References

For further discussion of the ratio estimate, see Hansen, Hurwitz, and Madow (1953), pp. 158–178 and 189–200. They also explain the ratio estimate in connection with simple cluster sampling and stratified cluster sampling (Chapter 7), but it is discussed simultaneously with the other methods in these chapters. For an advanced discussion with mathematical proofs, see Cochran (1963), Chapter 6, and pp. 311–313. Also see Deming (1950), pp. 165–189; Yates (1960), pp. 159–162, 212–218; Cyert and Davidson (1962), Chapter 7.

At this point, the student may wish to read some case histories. For a delightful nontechnical discussion of case histories concerning the race track, mail order houses, worksampling in a department store, stock market forecasts, railroads, airlines, income-tax returns, inventory sampling, audits, market research, telephone business, accounts payable, quality control in a department store, and others, see Slonim (1960), pp 100–144. For other references of applications on a more technical level, see the various articles in the *Journal of the American Statistical Association*. A list of these articles can be found in the *Index to the Journal*, Vol. 35–50 (1940–1955), under the subject index "Survey, applications of," and the index to volumes 51–60 (1956–1965).

Chapter 14

Replicated Sampling

14.1 Introduction

Replicated sampling is a sampling procedure that was developed by Professor E.W. Deming, and a full account of it may be found in his book *Sample Design in Business Research* (1960). Professor Deming states in Chapter 6 that "The chief advantage of replication is ease in estimation of the standard errors" (p. 87). He further states in Chapter 11 that "Replicated sampling went under the name of the Tukey plan in my earlier papers and in my book *Some Theory of Sampling* (Wiley, 1950), in respect to my friend Professor John W. Tukey of Princeton, who in 1948 took the trouble to persuade me to use 10 interpenetrating subsamples in a certain application, to eliminate the labor of computing the standard errors. I have used no other method since." (p. 187).*

As we have experienced in the previous chapters, estimating the standard error was one of the major headaches, if not the major one in the sampling procedures. Hence, replicated sampling as developed by Professor Deming is a very important procedure for practicing statisticians.

As Professor Deming states, "This system of replicated sampling is now in regular use here and abroad in social and economic studies of many types, including estimates of acreage and of yield, in marketing research, and in studies of attitudes, in program-listening, in the appraisal of buildings and of other kinds of physical plant, in the testing of industrial materials, and in studies of accounting records." (p. 87–88).*

We shall in this chapter give only a simple explanation of the basic ideas of replicated sampling and advise the student to continue his study with Professor Deming's book.

We shall approach replicated sampling via the stratified sampling procedure which we studied in Chapter 6. As we shall see, by imposing certain

* Source: E.W. Deming (1960). *Sample Design in Business Research*, New York: John Wiley and Sons, Inc., p. 87, p. 187, pp. 87 ~ 88. By Permission of the author and publishers.

assumptions on the stratified sampling procedures, we shall obtain the basic results for replicated sampling. Let us first discuss the procedure for estimating the population total, and then discuss the variance of this estimator in section 14.3.

14.2   Estimation of population total

In stratified random sampling, the population total was estimated by

$$\hat{X}_{st} = \sum_{h}^{L} N_h \bar{x}_h \tag{1}$$

where L indicated the number of strata; N_h the number of sampling units in stratum h; and $\bar{x}_h$ was

$$\bar{x}_h = \frac{1}{n_h} \sum_{i}^{n_h} x_{hi} \tag{2}$$

and was the sample mean of the sample of size n_h taken from stratum h.

Let us now assume that each stratum is of the same size and set $N_h = \bar{N}$, and furthermore select the same size samples $n_h = \bar{n}$ from each stratum. Then (1) becomes

$$\hat{X}_{st} = \sum_{h}^{L} \bar{N} \bar{x}_h$$

$$= \bar{N} \sum_{h}^{L} \frac{1}{\bar{n}} \sum_{i}^{\bar{n}} x_{hi}$$

$$= \frac{\bar{N}}{\bar{n}} \sum^{L} \sum^{\bar{n}} x_{hi}$$

But

$$\sum^{L} \sum^{\bar{n}} x_{hi} = x$$

where x is simply the sample total. Hence, we may write

$$\hat{X}_{st} = \frac{1}{\bar{n}} \bar{N} x \tag{3}$$

as an estimate of the population total. We know that this is an unbiased estimate of the population total.

Let us now convert this result into Prof. Deming's replicated sampling procedure terminology. First, the strata will be called *zones*, and the number of sampling units in each zone (viz., $\bar{N}$) will be denoted by Z.

Second, the size of the samples selected from each zone (stratum) which is $\bar{n}$, will be denoted by k. Then (3) will become

$$\hat{X} = \frac{1}{k} Z x \tag{4}$$

in terms of Prof. Deming's notation. We shall follow his notation as much as possible so that the student may easily refer to his book.

At this point, however, a very crucial change in viewing the frame is introduced. Let us illustrate this with the following example: Suppose there are 4 classes (zones) with 5 students in each class, that is, $Z = 5$.

Zone	1	2	3	4	5	
1	x	⊗	x	⊗	x	01—05
2	x	⊗	x	⊗	x	06—10
3	x	⊗	x	⊗	x	11—15
4	x	⊗	x	⊗	x	16—20

Let $k = 2$. This means we select $k = 2$ students from each zone (class) Using the random number table and selecting 2 numbers between 01—05, suppose we got 2 and 4. Then we select the 2nd and 4th student in the 1st zone. We repeat this for each zone (class). However, for simplicity let us assume that the order of the students is random. Then, using the systematic sampling procedure, we may select the students from the subsequent strata by adding $Z = 5$ to 2 and 4. The result will be the following sampling table.

Sampling table

($Z = 5$, $k = 2$)

Zone	1	2
01—05	2	4
06—10	7	9
11—15	12	14
16—20	17	19

In terms of stratified sampling, there are $L = 4$ strata, and from each stratum we select samples of size $k = \bar{n} = 2$. In replicated sampling, however, we shall view the above sampling table in the following way. The 1st student selected from each of the 4 zones (strata) grouped together will be called the 1st *subsample*. Hence, (2, 7, 12, 17) is the 1st *subsample*. As is seen, we have selected $k = 2$ subsamples. And there are $Z = 5$ possible subsamples. Hence, we may say, we have selected a $k/Z = 2/5 = 40\%$ sample.

We may now summarize our discussion as follows. We have $L = 4$ zones; each zone has $Z = 5$ sampling units; and there are $k = 2$ subsamples. The total sample size is $n = kL = 2 \times 4 = 8$ students. The total population is $N = LZ = 4 \times 5 = 20$ students. Hence, the basic structure of replicated sampling may be shown by the following model:

(5)
$$N = LZ$$

(6)
$$n = kL$$

(7)
$$Z = \frac{N}{L} = \frac{N}{n/k}$$

(4)
$$\hat{X} = \frac{1}{k} Zx$$

$$x = \sum_{i}^{L} \sum_{j}^{k} x_{ij}$$

Example 1. Suppose that in the above illustration we wish to estimate the total number of books owned by the $N = LZ = 4 \times 5 = 20$ students. Let us assume that the students who have been selected according to the sampling table have the following number of books.

Sampling table

Zone	Subsamples		
	1	2	
01—05	5 books	3 books	
06—10	9	1	
11—15	4	8	
16—20	2	5	
	20	17	37

Hence, from equation (4), we have

$$\hat{X} = \frac{1}{k} Zx = \frac{1}{2}(5)(37) = 5 \times 18.5 = 92.5 \text{ books}$$

This simple example also illustrates how (4) may be interpreted. We may write

$$\hat{X} = \frac{1}{k} Zx = Z\frac{x}{k}$$

As shown, there are k subsamples. Hence, $x/k = 18.5$ books is the average number of books per subsample. Since there are $Z = 5$ sampling units (students) per zone, there are a total of $Z = 5$ possible subsamples from which we have selected $k = 2$ subsamples. Thus, an estimate of the total will be

$$\hat{X} = Z\frac{x}{k} = \frac{1}{k} Zx$$

One may also interpret equation (4) in terms of clusters. We may interpret the population to be grouped into $Z = 5$ clusters. We have selected $k = 2$ clusters and the average of these $k = 2$ clusters is x/k. Hence, an estimate of the total will be as given in equation (4).

As shown, the estimation procedure is very simple. But the essence of this simple sampling procedure is in the art of constructing an appropriate frame. This involves determining the sampling unit, Z, k, and n. In actual situations, we need to determine n first.

Example 2. Suppose there are

$$N = LZ = 3600 \text{ sampling units}$$

and we wish to select a sample of

$$n = kL = 200 \text{ sampling units}$$

Suppose we decide to select $k = 10$ subsamples—which means $k = 10$ sampling units from each zone. Then there will be

$$L = \frac{n}{k} = \frac{200}{10} = 20 \text{ zones}$$

and each zone will have

$$Z = \frac{N}{L} = \frac{3600}{20} = 180 \text{ sampling units.}$$

The population is partitioned schematically in the following manner:

	Zones			$Z = 180$	
$L = 20$ zones	1	1	2	$\cdots$	180
	2	181	182	$\cdots$	360
	$\vdots$		$\cdots$		
	20	3421	3422	$\cdots$	3600

From each zone we select $k = 10$ sampling units. Hence the sampling table may be shown schematically as follows:

Sampling table

	$k = 10$ subsamples				
Zone	1	2	3	$\cdots$	10
01—180					
181—360					
261—540					
$\cdots$					
3421—3600					

Example 3. Suppose there are $N = 20$ students and we wish to select a sample

of size $n = 8$ students to estimate the total number of books they have. Let $k = 2$. Then, since $n = kL = 8$, we need

$$L = \frac{n}{k} = \frac{8}{2} = 4 \text{ zones.}$$

And since $N = LZ$, we have

$$Z = \frac{N}{L} = \frac{20}{4} = 5 \text{ sampling units per zone}$$

Suppose the data is as follows:

Zones	1	2	3	4	5
01—05	7 books	⑤	1	⑥	2
06—10	2	①	6	④	8
11—15	2	②	8	③	5
16—20	6	⑧	5	⑦	2
	17	16	20	17	17

Since $k = 2$, we select $k = 2$ sampling units from each zone (stratum). Suppose the 2nd and 4th sampling units are selected. Assuming the students are randomly ordered, we use systematic sampling and select every $Z = 5$th student from the 2nd and 4th units of the 1st zone. Hence the students who are circled have been selected. This is summarized in the following table.

Sample

1st	2nd
5 books	6 books
1	4
2	3
8	4
16	17

As shown, there are $k = 2$ subsamples, and the subsample totals are

$$x' = 16 \text{ books} \qquad x'' = 17 \text{ books}$$

The total of the sample is thus

$$x = x' + x'' = 16 + 17 = 33 \text{ books}$$

Hence, the average number of books per subsample is

$$\frac{x}{k} = \frac{33}{2} = 16.5 \text{ books}$$

Since there are $Z = 5$ possible subsamples, an estimate of the total is

$$\hat{X} = Z\frac{x}{k} = 5 \times 16.5 = 82.5 \text{ books.}$$

The true total is $X = 87$.

Example 4. Suppose there is a small town with 6 blocks as shown in Fig. 14-1.

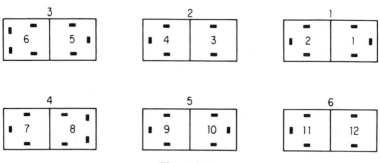

Fig. 14-1

We wish to estimate the number of dwelling units (d.u.) in this town. The procedure will be to divide the blocks into segments, and to select a sample of these segments to estimate the total number of d.u. These segments will be the sampling units, which may be 1/2 a block, or 1/3 of a block, or some other proportion. We construct a frame with these sampling units.

Suppose the town policeman tells us that there are about 6 d.u. per block. Using this information, we may set up the frame as follows:

Frame

Block	# of d.u. (by policeman)	Sampling units	Serial # for sampling units
1	6	2	1— 2
2	6	2	3— 4
3	6	2	5— 6
4	6	2	7— 8
5	6	2	9—10
6	6	2	11—12

We shall assume it has been decided to have about 3 d.u. per sampling unit (segment). This means that each block will be divided into $6/3 = 2$ segments (sampling units). Hence, we obtain the list of sampling units (that is, the frame) shown above.

As we can see from the figure, there are (for example) only 5 d.u. in the 2nd block. The data given by the policeman is merely a rough count that we have used to set up the sampling units. Also note that a serial number is given to each sampling unit (segment).

Assume we wish a 50% sample and that we want $k = 2$ subsamples. Each zone therefore needs $Z = 4$ sampling units, which means there will be $Z = 4$ possible samples. Then, $k/Z = 2/4 = 50\%$, which satisfies our requirement of a 50% sample.

The number of zones (strata) will thus be

$$L = \frac{N}{Z} = \frac{12}{4} = 3 \text{ zones}$$

This is shown diagramatically as follows:

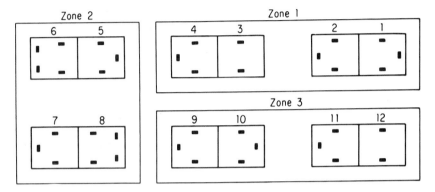

Fig. 14-2

The next step is to select the sample. Using the random number table, $k = 2$ sampling units are selected from each zone (for this, we select random numbers between 1 and $Z = 4$ without replacement). Let the result be shown as in the following table:

Sampling table

Zone	Random numbers		Serial number of sampling units	
	1st	2nd	1st	2nd
1	1	3	1	3
2	2	1	6	5
3	2	4	10	12

For zone 1, the random numbers we selected between 1 and $Z = 4$ are 1 and 3. Hence the corresponding segments (sampling units) are the 1st and 3rd, which are in the 1st zone. For zone 2, the random numbers between 1 and $Z = 4$ are 2 and 1. Hence, the corresponding segments are the $2 + 4 = 6$th and $1 + 4 = 5$th, which are in the 2nd zone. For zone 3, we have 2 and 4, and the corresponding segments are the $2 + (4 \times 2) = 10$th and $4 + (4 \times 2) = 12$th, which are in zone 3.

Having selected the sample, we now visit these segments (sampling units) and actually investigate the number of d.u. We find the following results:

| Zone | Segments | | Number of d.u. | |
	1st subsample	2nd subsample	1st subsample	2nd subsample
1	1st	3rd	3 d.u.	2 d.u.
2	6th	5th	4	3
3	10th	12th	3	2
			10	7

Hence, the estimate of the total number of d.u. we seek is

$$\hat{X} = \frac{1}{k}Zx = \frac{1}{2}(4)(10 + 7) = 34$$

The true total is $X = 36$.

Example 5. Suppose there is a town with 100 blocks and we wish to estimate the total number of dwelling units in this town. The policeman tells us there are about 12 d.u. per block. Suppose we wish to have about 3 d.u. per segment. Then each block is to be divided into $12/3 = 4$ segments (sampling units). Hence, we may construct the frame as follows:

Frame

Block	# of d.u. (by policeman)	Segments	Serial number of segments
1	12	4	1—4
2	12	4	5—8
3	12	4	9—12
...	...	...	...
100	12	4	397—400

Suppose we wish a 20% sample and $k = 5$ subsamples. This means each zone needs $Z = 25$ sampling units (segments), so that there will be $Z = 25$ possible samples. Then, $k/Z = 5/25 = 20\%$ as required.

The number of zones will be

$$L = \frac{N}{L} = \frac{400}{25} = 16 \text{ zones}$$

Hence, we have the following sampling table:

Sampling table

| Zone | Zone boundaries | Subsamples | | | | |
		1	2	3	4	5
1	1—25	18	1	8	23	11
2	26—50	43	26	33	58	36
3	51—75	68	...			
...		...				
16	376—400	393	376	383	398	386

Using the random number table, we select 5 numbers between 1 and 25 without replacement. Let the results be as shown in the sampling table for zone 1. We may repeat this for each of the remaining zones, but let us use systematic sampling. We shall add 25 to each of the numbers to obtain the serial numbers for the 2nd zone; then add another 25 to obtain the serial numbers for the 3rd zone, and so forth.

The next step is to visit these sampling units (segments) and investigate the number of d.u. There are $n = Lk = 16 \times 5 = 80$ segments to visit. Suppose we obtain the following results:

Sample data

Zone	1	2	3	4	5	
1	10 d.u.	12	10	14	11	
2	11	10	13	12	10	
...	...					
10	...					
	190	195	185	188	192	950 d.u.

Hence, an estimate of X would be

$$\hat{X} = \frac{1}{k} Zx = \frac{1}{5}(25)(950) = 4750 \text{ d.u.}$$

Problems

1. Suppose there are $N = 24$ students and we wish to select a sample of size $n = 8$ students to estimate the total number of books they own by replicated sampling. Let $k = 2$. Then there are $L = 4$ zones. Let the data be as follows where the figures show the number of books:

Zones				Books			
01—06	7	5	1	6	2	3	
07—12	2	1	6	4	8	5	
13—18	2	2	8	3	5	6	
19—24	6	8	5	4	2	4	

(i)   Calculate the total number of books X.
(ii) Estimate X by selecting a sample of $n = 8$ students by the replicated sampling procedure. Select $k = 2$ sampling units from each zone using random numbers.
(iii) Assuming the data are in random order, select the sample by systematic sampling and estimate X.
(iv) Show that the probability of any student being selected is $1/6$.

(v) Show that the probability of selecting a given sample is $(1/6)^8$ when sampling with replacement. What is the probability when sampling without replacement?

2. Suppose that in Problem 1, there are 25 students. In addition to the data in Problem 1, let the 25th student have 7 books.

(i) Give serial numbers 01—25 to the 25 students.

(ii) Define the sampling unit so that there will be $N = 24$ sampling units by letting the 1st sampling unit consist of the 1st and 25th student; and the 2nd to the 24th sampling units consist of 1 student each. Make a list of the sampling units.

(iii) Select a sample of $n = 8$ by letting $k = 2$, constructing $L = 4$ zones, and following the procedure used in Problem 1, using the random number table for each zone. Estimate X.

(iv) Show that the probability of selecting any student is $1/6$. Note that when the 1st sampling unit is selected, the 1st and 25th students are both selected.

(v) Show that the probability of selecting a sample is $(1/6)^8$ when sampling with replacement. What is the probability when sampling without replacement?

3. Suppose that in Problem 1, there are 23 students.

(i) Define the sampling units so that there will be $N = 24$ sampling units by adding a 24th sampling unit consisting of a blank (or a student without books). Make a list of the sampling units.

(ii) Select a sample of $n = 8$ by letting $k = 2$ using systematic sampling, and estimate X.

(iii) Show that the probability of selecting any student is $(1/6)$ when sampling with replacement.

4. Following the procedures of Problems 1, 2, and 3, consider the case where there are:

(i)   26 students.

(ii) 22 students.

5. Suppose there is a town with 8 blocks, and each block has a certain number of dwelling units as shown in the table.

Blocks	Dwelling units
1	18
2	15
3	16
4	13
5	17
6	23
7	20
8	14

Form groups (zones) of 3 blocks, where the blocks are the sampling units, Hence, we have 1—3, 4—6, 7—9 as zones, where the 9th block is a dummy block. Next, group the dwelling units into groups of 4. Hence, for the 1st block, we have 5 groups, where the last group has the 17th and 18-th d.u. and 2 blanks. Group the d.u. of the other blocks in a similar manner. Select 1 block from each of the 3 groups (zones) of blocks, then select 1 d.u. from each of the groups of d.u. in the selected block. Show that the probability of selecting a d.u. is 1/12 for all d.u.

14.3 The variance of $\hat{X}$

The variance of $\hat{X}$ may also be found by using the results of stratified sampling. In Chapter 6, we found that

(1)
$$\hat{V}(\hat{X}_{st}) = \sum_{h}^{L} N_h^2 \frac{N_h - n_h}{N_h} \frac{s_h^2}{n_h}$$

$$s_h^2 = \frac{1}{n_h - 1} \sum^{n_h} (x_{hi} - \bar{x}_h)^2$$

In terms of our present notation for replicated sampling, this becomes

$$\hat{V}(\hat{X}_{st}) = \sum_{i}^{L} Z^2 \frac{Z - k}{Z} \frac{s_i^2}{k}$$

$$= Z^2 \frac{Z - k}{Z} \frac{1}{k} \sum_{i}^{L} s_i^2$$

$$= Z^2 \frac{Z - k}{Z} \frac{1}{k} \sum_{i}^{L} \frac{1}{k - 1} \sum_{j}^{k} (x_{ij} - \bar{x}_i)^2$$

$$= Z^2 \frac{Z - k}{Z} \frac{1}{k} \frac{1}{k - 1} \sum_{i}^{L} \sum_{j}^{k} (x_{ij} - \bar{x}_i)^2$$

Assuming that $(Z - k)/Z = 1$, and

$$T^2 = \sum_{i}^{L} \sum_{j}^{k} (x_{ij} - \bar{x}_i)^2$$

we get

(2)
$$\hat{V}(\hat{X}) = \frac{Z^2 T^2}{k(k - 1)}$$

which is the basic equation for the estimated variance of $\hat{X}$.

For the special case where $k = 2$, we get

$$T^2 = \sum_{i}^{L} \sum_{j}^{2} (x_{ij} - \bar{x}_i)^2$$

$$= \sum^{L} \left[\left(x_{i1} - \frac{x_{i1} + x_{i2}}{2} \right)^2 + \left(x_{i2} - \frac{x_{i1} + x_{i2}}{2} \right)^2 \right]$$

$$= \sum^{L} \frac{1}{4} [(x_{i1} - x_{i2})^2 + (x_{i2} - x_{i1})^2]$$

$$= \frac{1}{2} \sum^{L} (x_{i1} - x_{i2})^2$$

Substituting this into (2) gives us

(3)
$$\hat{V}(\hat{X}) = \frac{Z^2}{2(2-1)} \frac{1}{2} \sum_{i}^{L} (x_{i1} - x_{i2})^2$$

$$= \frac{1}{4} Z^2 \sum^{L} (x_{i1} - x_{i2})^2$$

$$= \frac{1}{4} Z^2 R^2$$

where

$$R^2 = \sum_{i}^{L} (x_{i1} - x_{i2})^2$$

As shown, R^2 is merely the sum of the squares of the ranges in the L zones.

As shown in formula (2), the main computational task is to calculate

$$T^2 = \sum^{L} \sum^{k} (x_{ij} - \bar{x}_i)^2$$

where k is usually less than 10, but where L may become very large. Hence, it would be desirable if some scheme could be developed to reduce this computational task. This problem is considered in section 14.5 in our discussion of thin zones and thick zones.

But for the present, the procedure for calculating T^2 will be to first calculate the sum of squares of each zone and then over the L zones. This may be shown schematically as follows:

zone 1: $\quad \sum_{j}^{k} (x_{1j} - \bar{x}_1)^2 = \sum^{k} x_{1j}^2 - \frac{(\sum x_{1j})^2}{k}$

zone 2: $\quad \sum_{j}^{k} (x_{2j} - \bar{x}_2)^2 = \sum^{k} x_{2j}^2 - \frac{(\sum x_{2j})^2}{k}$

$\cdot$
$\cdot$
$\cdot$

zone L: $\quad \sum_{j}^{k} (x_{Lj} - \bar{x}_L)^2 = \sum^{k} x_{Lj}^2 - \frac{(\sum x_{Lj})^2}{k}$

$T^2 = \quad \left(\sum_{j}^{k} x_{1j}^2 + \cdots + \sum^{k} x_{Lj}^2 \right) - \frac{1}{k} [(\sum x_{1j})^2 + \cdots + (\sum x_{Lj})^2]$

With the use of electronic computers, T^2 may be easily programmed, and its computations will become relatively easy.

Example 1. Suppose there are $L = 3$ zones and each zone has $Z = 3$ students. The following table gives the number of books each student has. Select $k = 2$ subsamples and estimate X and $V(\hat{X})$.

Zones	1	2	3
1	5 books	3	1
2	1	4	3
3	3	2	5

(a) Select the sample. Suppose the 1st and 3rd student in the 1st zone are selected and the following sampling units are selected by systematic sampling. We get

Sample

	1	2
1	5 books	1
2	1	3
3	3	5
	9	9

(b) Estimate X.

$$\hat{X} = \frac{1}{k} Zx = \frac{1}{2}(3)(9+9) = 27 \text{ books}$$

(c) Estimate $V(\hat{X})$.

$$\hat{V}(\hat{X}) = Z^2 \frac{Z-k}{Z} \frac{1}{k} \frac{1}{k-1} \sum_{}^{L} \sum_{}^{k} (x_{ij} - \bar{x}_i)^2$$

$$= (3)^2 \frac{3-2}{3} \frac{1}{2} \frac{1}{2-1} \{[(5-3)^2 + (1-3)^2]$$

$$+ [(1-2)^2 + (3-2)^2] + [(3-4)^2 + (5-4)^2]\} = 18$$

$$s(\hat{X}) = \sqrt{18} = 4.2 \text{ books}$$

Example 2. Suppose the sampling units are selected by random numbers from each zone. Using the Kendall and Smith tables, we get:

Sampling table

	1	2
1	2	3
2	1	2
3	2	3

Hence our sample is:

Sample

	1	2
1	3 books	1
2	1	4
3	2	5
	6	10

$$\hat{X} = (1/2)(3)(6 + 10) = 24 \text{ books}$$
$$\hat{V}(\hat{X}) = 33/2 = 16.5$$
$$s(\hat{X}) = \sqrt{16.5} = 4.06$$

Example 3. Let us calculate $\hat{V}(\hat{X})$ using the computation scheme

$$T^2 = (\sum x_{1j}^2 + \sum x_{2j}^2 + \sum x_{3j}^2) - \frac{1}{k}[(\sum x_{1j})^2 + (\sum x_{2j})^2 + (\sum x_{3j})^2]$$

(a) For Example 1:

	1	2	$\sum x_{ij}^2$	$(\sum x_{ij})$	$(\sum x_{ij})^2$
x_{1j}	5	1		6	36
x_{1j}^2	25	1	26		
x_{2j}	1	3		4	16
x_{2j}^2	1	9	10		
x_{3j}	3	5		8	64
x_{3j}^2	9	25	34		
			70		116

$$T^2 = 70 - (1/2)(116) = 12$$
$$\hat{V}(\hat{X}) = (3/2)(12) = 18$$

which is what we found in Example 1.

(b) For Example 2:

			$\sum x_{ij}^2$	$\sum x_{ij}$	$(\sum x_{ij})^2$
x_{1j}	3	1		4	16
x_{1j}^2	9	1	10		
x_{2j}	1	4		5	25
x_{2j}^2	1	16	17		
x_{3j}	2	5		7	49
x_{3j}^2	4	25	29		
			56		90

$$\hat{V}(\hat{X}) = (3/2)[56 - (1/2)(90)] = (3/2)(11) = 33/2 = 16.5$$

which is the same as the result of Example 2.

Problems

1. Suppose there are 18 students and we wish to estimate the total number of books they own by replicated sampling. Select a sample of size $n = 9$ and let $k = 3$. Then $L = n/k = 9/3 = 3$. Let the data be as follows:

Zones	1	2	3	4	5	6
01—06	5 (books)	3	1	4	2	6
07—12	1	4	3	5	6	3
13—18	3	2	5	7	4	4

(i) Select $k = 3$ sampling units from each zone by random sampling and obtain a sample of size $n = 9$.

(ii) Using the sample, find $\hat{X}$. Also calculate X.

(iii) Using the sample, calculate $\hat{V}(\hat{X})$ and $s(\hat{X})$.

2. Suppose that in Problem 1, we have 17 students. Then, let the 18th student be a blank (that is, no books).

(i) Calculate $\hat{X}$ and $\hat{V}(\hat{X})$. Note that if the 18th student is selected, the number of books for that draw will be zero. The procedure for calculating $\hat{X}$ and $\hat{V}(\hat{X})$ is the same as in Problem 1.

(ii) What is the probability of selecting a sampling unit in Problem 1? What is the probability in this problem?

3. Using the data of Problem 1, p. 373, and using the sample that has been selected, calculate $\hat{V}(\hat{X})$ and $s(\hat{X})$.

14.4 The ratio estimate

In Chapter 13, we discussed the ratio estimate in connection with sampling procedures such as random sampling and stratified sampling. Since we have developed this replicated sampling as a variation of stratified sampling, we may use the results of the previous chapter concerning the combined ratio estimate and show how the ratio estimate may be obtained via replicated sampling.

The estimator of the ratio R by the combined ratio estimate method was

(1) $$r_c = \frac{\hat{X}}{\hat{Y}} = \frac{N\bar{x}}{N\bar{y}} = \frac{x}{y}$$

where x and y were sample totals. In our present case, we need merely find x and y, or $\hat{X}$ and $\hat{Y}$ by replicated sampling. We know how to find

$$\hat{X} = \frac{1}{k}Zx$$

so we may easily find x or $\hat{X}$, and likewise y or $\hat{Y}$ in order to estimate R.

The variance of r_c was found as

(2) $$V(r_c) = \frac{1}{Y^2} \sum_{}^{L} N_h^2 \frac{N_h - n_h}{N_h} \frac{1}{n_h} S_{ch}^2$$

(3) $$S_{ch}^2 = \frac{1}{N_h - 1} \sum_{}^{N_h} [(x_{hi} - \bar{X}_h) - R(y_{hi} - \bar{Y}_h)]^2$$

and an estimate of $V(r_c)$ was

(4)
$$\hat{V}(r_c) = \frac{1}{\hat{y}^2} \sum_i^L N_h^2 \frac{N_h - n_h}{N_h} \frac{1}{n_h} s_{ch}^2$$

(5)
$$s_{ch}^2 = \frac{1}{n_h - 1} \sum^{n_h} [(x_{hi} - \bar{x}_h) - r_c(y_{hi} - \bar{y}_h)]^2$$

In terms of the replicated sampling procedures, this becomes

$$\hat{V}(r_{rp}) = \frac{1}{\hat{Y}^2} \sum_i^L Z^2 \frac{Z - k}{Z} \frac{1}{k} s_{ci}^2$$

$$= \frac{1}{\hat{Y}^2} Z^2 \frac{1}{k} \sum_i^L \frac{1}{k-1} \sum_j^k [(x_{ij} - \bar{x}_i) - r_c(y_{ij} - \bar{y}_i)]^2$$

$$= \frac{1}{\hat{Y}^2} Z^2 \frac{1}{k} \frac{1}{k-1} U^2$$

where

$$U^2 = \sum_i^L \sum_j^k [(x_{ij} - \bar{x}_i) - r_c(y_{ij} - \bar{y}_i)]^2$$

and we have also assumed that $(Z - k)/Z = 1$.

We also know that

$$\hat{Y} = \frac{1}{k} Z y$$

Substituting this into the above equation gives us

(6)
$$\hat{V}(r_{rp}) = \frac{1}{[(1/k)Zy]^2} Z^2 \frac{1}{k} \frac{1}{k-1} U^2$$

$$= \frac{k}{k-1} \frac{U^2}{y^2}$$

which is the basic equation for the variance of the ratio estimate r_{rp}. We shall (for brevity) drop the subscript rp of r_{rp} in subsequent discussion.

Computation Scheme of U^2

As shown, U^2 is a major computational problem. Following is one of the various computational schemes that could be developed. First, U^2 may be expanded as follows:

$$U^2 = \sum_i^L \sum_j^k [(x_{ij} - \bar{x}_i) - r(y_{ij} - \bar{y}_i)]^2$$

$$= \sum_i^L \sum_j^k [(x_{ij} - \bar{x}_i)^2 + r^2(y_{ij} - \bar{y}_i)^2 - 2r(x_{ij} - \bar{x}_i)(y_{ij} - \bar{y}_i)]$$

$$= \sum_j^k x_{1j}^2 - \frac{(\sum x_{1j})^2}{k} + r^2 \left(\sum y_{1j}^2 - \frac{(\sum y_{1j})^2}{k} \right) - 2r \left(\sum x_{1j} y_{1j} - \frac{\sum x_{1j} \sum y_{1j}}{k} \right)$$

$$+ \sum_j^k x_{2j}^2 - \frac{(\sum x_{2j})^2}{k} + r^2 \left(\sum y_{2j}^2 - \frac{(\sum y_{2j})^2}{k} \right) - 2r \left(\sum x_{2j} y_{2j} - \frac{\sum x_{2j} \sum y_{2j}}{k} \right)$$

$$+ \cdots$$

$$+ \sum_j^k x_{Lj}^2 - \frac{(\sum x_{Lj})^2}{k} + r^2 \left(\sum y_{Lj}^2 - \frac{(\sum y_{Lj})^2}{k} \right) - 2r \left(\sum x_{Lj} y_{Lj} - \frac{\sum x_{Lj} \sum y_{Lj}}{k} \right)$$

We therefore need $\sum x_{ij}^2$, $(\sum x_{ij})^2$, $\sum y_{ij}^2$, $(\sum y_{ij})^2$, and $\sum x_{ij}y_{ij}$ for each zone. The worksheet for this may be set up as follows:

	x_{ij}	x_{ij}^2	$(\sum^k x_{ij})^2$	y_{ij}	y_{ij}^2	$(\sum^k y_{ij})^2$	$x_{ij}y_{ij}$	$(\sum^k x_{ij})(\sum^k y_{ij})$
$L=1$	x_{11}	x_{11}^2		y_{11}	y_{11}^2		$x_{11}y_{11}$	
	$\cdots$							
	x_{1k}	x_{1k}^2		y_{1k}	y_{1k}^2		$x_{1k}y_{1k}$	
	$\sum^k x_{1j}$	$\sum^k x_{1j}^2$	$(\sum^k x_{1j})^2$	$\sum^k y_{1j}$	$\sum^k y_{1j}^2$	$(\sum^k y_{1j})^2$	$\sum^k x_{1j}y_{1j}$	$(\sum^k x_{1j})(\sum^k y_{1j})$
$\vdots$								
$L=L$	x_{L1}	x_{L1}^2		y_{L1}	y_{L1}^2		$x_{L1}y_{L1}$	
	$\cdots$							
	x_{Lk}	x_{Lk}^2		y_{Lk}	y_{Lk}^2		$x_{Lk}y_{Lk}$	
	$\sum x_{Lj}$	$\sum x_{Lj}^2$	$(\sum x_{Lj})^2$	$\sum y_{Lj}$	$\sum y_{Lj}^2$	$(\sum y_{Lj})^2$	$\sum x_{Lj}y_{Lj}$	$(\sum x_{Lj})(\sum y_{Lj})$

$\sum x_{ij}^2$	$(\sum x_{ij})^2$	$\sum y_{ij}^2$	$(\sum y_{ij})^2$	$\sum x_{ij}y_{ij}$	$(\sum x_{ij})(\sum y_{ij})$
$\sum x_{1j}^2$	$(\sum x_{1j})^2$	$\sum y_{1j}^2$	$(\sum y_{1j})^2$	$\sum x_{1j}y_{1j}$	$(\sum x_{1j})(\sum y_{1j})$
$\vdots$					
$\sum x_{Lj}^2$	$(\sum x_{Lj})^2$	$\sum y_{Lj}^2$	$(\sum y_{Lj})^2$	$\sum x_{Lj}y_{Lj}$	$(\sum x_{Lj})(\sum y_{Lj})$
A	B	C	D	E	F

$$\therefore \quad U^2 = A - \frac{B}{k} + r^2\left(C - \frac{D}{k}\right) - 2r\left(E - \frac{F}{k}\right)$$

Example 1. Suppose there are $L = 4$ classes with $Z = 5$ students in each class. We wish to estimate the proportion of science books the students have. And for this, $k = 2$ subsamples are to be selected. Assume the sample is as follows:

Sample

X_{i1}	Y_{i1}	X_{i2}	Y_{i2}
Science books	All books	Science books	All books
2	5	1	3
3	9	1	1
1	4	4	7
0	2	2	5
6	20	8	16

(a) Estimation of the ratio

$$x = 6 + 8 = 14$$
$$y = 20 + 16 = 36$$
$$r = x/y = 14/36 = .39$$

(b) Estimate $V(r)$

	x_{ij}	x_{ij}^2	$(\sum x_{ij})^2$	y_{ij}	y_{ij}^2	$(\sum y_{ij})^2$	$x_{ij}y_{ij}$	$\sum x_{ij} \sum y_{ij}$
$L = 1$	2	4		5	25		10	
	1	1		3	9		3	
	3	5	9	8	34	64	13	24
$L = 2$	3	9		9	81		27	
	1	1		1	1		1	
	4	10	16	10	82	100	28	40
$L = 3$	1	1		4	16		4	
	4	16		7	49		28	
	5	17	25	11	65	121	32	55
$L = 4$	0	0		2	4		0	
	2	4		5	25		10	
	2	4	4	7	29	49	10	14

$\sum x_{ij}^2$	$(\sum x_{ij})^2$	$\sum y_{ij}^2$	$(\sum y_{ij})^2$	$\sum x_{ij}y_{ij}$	$\sum x_{ij} \sum y_{ij}$
5	9	34	64	13	24
10	16	82	100	28	40
17	25	65	121	32	55
4	4	29	49	10	14
36	54	210	334	83	133
A	B	C	D	E	F

$$U^2 = A - \frac{B}{k} + r^2\left(C - \frac{D}{k}\right) - 2r\left(E - \frac{F}{k}\right)$$

$$= 36 - \frac{54}{2} + \left(\frac{14}{36}\right)^2\left(210 - \frac{334}{2}\right) - 2\left(\frac{14}{36}\right)\left(83 - \frac{133}{2}\right) = 2.7$$

$$\hat{V}(r) = \frac{k}{k-1}\frac{U^2}{y^2}\frac{Z-k}{Z} = \frac{2}{2-1}\frac{2.7}{(14)^2}\frac{3-2}{3} = 0.0092$$

$$s(r) = 0.096$$

Problems

1. Suppose we wish to estimate the rate of room vacancies in hotels in a city where there are 78 hotels. We wish to select a sample of size $n = 30$. Let us set $k = 3$. Then $L = n/k = 30/3 = 10$ zones, and from each zone select $k = 3$ sampling units (hotels).

(i) Number the hotels serially from 01 to 80 where the 79th and 80th hotels are blanks. Since $L = 10$ zones, there are $Z = N/L = 80/10 = 8$ sampling units (hotels) per zone. The total population may be shown schematically as follows:

	Population							
Zones	1	2	3	4	5	6	7	8
01—08								
09—16								
.								
.								
73—80								

(ii) Assume the hotels are randomly ordered so that we may use systematic sampling. Suppose we find the random numbers 2, 5, and 7 from the random number table. Then the sampling table may be shown schematically as follows:

Sampling table

	Zones		k	
		1	2	3
1	01—08	2	5	7
2	09—16	10	13	15
.	.			
.	.			
.	.			
10	73—80			

Write out the complete sampling table.

(iii) Suppose the data is as follows:

Data

Zones	Total rooms Y_{ij}			Vacancies X_{ij}		
	Y_{i1}	Y_{i2}	Y_{i3}	X_{i1}	X_{i2}	X_{i3}
1	40	30	50	4	2	5
2	60	90	20	8	9	3
3	40	70	30	4	6	2
4	90	80	30	9	8	4
5	70	30	60	6	3	6
6	80	60	20	8	8	4
7	30	50	70	2	5	7
8	40	60	60	4	7	6
9	20	40	20	3	4	4
10	70	30	0	8	2	0

Estimate the vacancy rate r.

(iv) Estimate $V(r)$.

14.5 Thin zones, thick zones

As mentioned in 14.3, the calculation of T^2 is a major computational task. However, by combining several zones into thick zones, we may simplify calculations of $\hat{X}$ and $\hat{V}(\hat{X})$ further. Let us illustrate this schematically as follows:

(*i*) *Estimate of* $\hat{X}$.

Suppose there are $L = 6$ zones which we shall call *thin zones* to distinguish them from the combined zones which we shall call *thick zones*. There are $Z = 5$ sampling units per thin zone, and assume the order is random. Using systematic sampling, the 2nd and 4th sampling units of each zone are selected. We know that

Table 14-1

$L = 6$		Population					Sample		$\bar{x}_h$
	1	x	$\otimes$ x	$\otimes$	x		x_{11} x_{12}		$\bar{x}_1$
	2	x	$\otimes$ x	$\otimes$	x		x_{21} x_{22}		$\bar{x}_2$
	3	x	$\otimes$ x	$\otimes$	x		x_{31} x_{32}		$\bar{x}_3$
	4	x	$\otimes$ x	$\otimes$	x		x_{41} x_{42}		$\bar{x}_4$
	5	x	$\otimes$ x	$\otimes$	x		x_{51} x_{52}		$\bar{x}_5$
	6	x	$\otimes$ x	$\otimes$	x		x_{61} x_{62}		$\bar{x}_6$

(1)
$$\hat{X}_{st} = \sum_{h}^{L} N_h \, \bar{x}_h = \sum^{L} N_h \frac{1}{n_h} \sum^{n_h} x_{hi}$$

In terms of replicated sampling, this becomes

(2)
$$\hat{X}_{rp} = \sum_{i}^{L} Z \frac{1}{k} \sum_{i}^{k} x_{ij} = \frac{1}{k} Z \sum_{i}^{L} \sum_{j}^{k} x_{ij}$$
$$= \frac{1}{k} Z \sum_{j}^{k} (x_{1j} + x_{2j} + x_{3j} + x_{4j} + x_{5j} + x_{6j})$$

Let us now combine thin zones 1, 2, and 3 into the 1st thick zone and thin zones 4, 5, and 6 into the 2nd thick zone. This is shown as follows:

Table 14-2

$m = 2$	Population					Sample		
1	x	$\otimes$ x	$\otimes$	x				
	x	$\otimes$ x	$\otimes$	x		x_{011} x_{012}		$\bar{x}_{01}$
	x	$\otimes$ x	$\otimes$	x				
2	x	$\otimes$ x	$\otimes$	x				
	x	$\otimes$ x	$\otimes$	x		x_{021} x_{022}		$\bar{x}_{02}$
	x	$\otimes$ x	$\otimes$	x				

We denote the number of thick zones by $m = 2$. The x_{011} and x_{012} in the table are

$$x_{011} = x_{11} + x_{21} + x_{31}$$
$$x_{012} = x_{12} + x_{22} + x_{32}$$

(and likewise for x_{021} and x_{022}.) Then $\hat{X}$ becomes

$$\hat{X} = \frac{1}{k}Z\sum_{j}^{k}(x_{1j} + x_{2j} + x_{3j} + x_{4j} + x_{5j} + x_{6j})$$

$$= \frac{1}{k}Z(x_{11}+x_{12}+x_{21}+x_{22}+x_{31}+x_{32}+x_{41}+x_{42}+x_{51}+x_{52}+x_{61}+x_{62})$$

$$= \frac{1}{k}Z[(x_{11}+x_{21}+x_{31})+(x_{12}+x_{22}+x_{32})+(x_{41}+x_{51}+x_{61})+(x_{42}+x_{52}+x_{62})]$$

$$= \frac{1}{k}Z(x_{011} + x_{012} + x_{021} + x_{022})$$

$$= \frac{1}{k}Z\sum_{j}^{k}(x_{01j} + x_{02j}) = \frac{1}{k}Z\sum_{j}^{k}\sum_{i}^{m} x_{0ij}$$

$$\therefore \quad \hat{X} = \frac{1}{k}Z\sum_{i}^{m}\sum_{j}^{k} x_{0ij}$$

Note that the subscript Oij of x_{0ij} indicates that the ij are to be interpreted for the thick zones. That is, the i indicates the ith thick zone and j is the jth subsample of the ith thick zone.

Hence, we have

(4) $$\hat{X} = \frac{1}{k}Z\sum_{i}^{L}\sum_{j}^{k} x_{ij} \qquad L = 6 \text{ thin zones}$$

(5) $$= \frac{1}{k}Z\sum_{i}^{m}\sum_{j}^{k} x_{0ij} \qquad m = 2 \text{ thick zones}$$

where the difference is that x_{ij} shows the individual sampling units, whereas x_{0ij} is made up of $L/m = 6/2 = 3$ sampling units. Both are unbiased estimators of X.

As shown, (4) and (5) are general formulas which hold when the sampling units are selected by random sampling from each zone.

Example 1. Let us use the data of Example 1, section 14.2 to estimate X by combining 2 thin zones into 1 thick zone.

	Sample		
	1	2	x_{0i}
1	5 books	3	
	9	1	
	$14 = x_{011}$	$4 = x_{012}$	$x_{01} = x_{011} + x_{012} = 14 + 4 = 18$
2	4	8	
	2	5	
	$6 = x_{021}$	$13 = x_{022}$	$x_{02} = x_{021} + x_{022} = 6 + 13 = 19$

$$\hat{X} = \frac{1}{k} Z \sum_{i}^{L} \sum_{j}^{k} x_{ij} \qquad\qquad L = 4 \text{ thin zones}$$

$$= (1/2)(5)(37) = 92.5$$

$$\hat{X} = \frac{1}{k} Z \sum_{i}^{m} \sum_{j}^{k} x_{0ij} \qquad\qquad m = 2 \text{ thick zones}$$

$$= (1/2)(5)(18 + 19) = 92.5$$

(ii) $\hat{V}(\hat{X})$.

Let us now find $\hat{V}(\hat{X})$ for thick zones. For convenience, the scheme that was used in subsection (i) is reproduced below.

$m = 2$	1	2	3	4	5
1	x	$\otimes$	x	$\otimes$	x
2	x	$\otimes$	x	$\otimes$	x
3	x	$\otimes$	x	$\otimes$	x
	x	x_{011}		x_{012}	
4	x	$\otimes$	x	$\otimes$	x
5	x	$\otimes$	x	$\otimes$	x
6	x	$\otimes$	x	$\otimes$	x
		x_{021}		x_{022}	

The $L = 6$ thin zones have been combined into $m = 2$ thick zones. Our problem is to find the $\hat{V}(\hat{X})$ based on these $m = 2$ thick zones.

Let us first interpret these $L = 6$ thin zones as $L = 6$ strata. Then the variance for $\hat{X}$ (using the results of Chapter 6) will be:

$$(6) \qquad V(\hat{X}_{st}) = \sum_{h}^{L} N_h^2 \frac{N_h - n_h}{N_h} \frac{S_h^2}{n_h}$$

$$(7) \qquad S_h^2 = \frac{1}{N_h - 1} \sum_{i}^{N_h} (X_{hi} - \bar{X}_h)^2$$

$$(8) \qquad \bar{X}_h = \frac{1}{N_h} \sum^{N_h} X_{hi}$$

We shall also use the alternative definition

$$(9) \qquad \sigma_h^2 = \frac{1}{N_h} \sum_{i}^{N_h} (X_{hi} - \bar{X}_h)^2$$

and we have

$$(10) \qquad S_h^2 = \frac{N_h}{N_h - 1} \sigma_h^2$$

The unbiased estimator for $V(\hat{X}_{st})$ was found to be

$$(11) \qquad \hat{V}(\hat{X}_{st}) = \sum_{h}^{L} N_h^2 \frac{N_h - n_h}{N_h} \frac{s_h^2}{n_h}$$

(12)
$$s_h^2 = \frac{1}{n_h - 1} \sum_{i}^{n_h} (x_{hi} - \bar{x}_h)^2$$

(13)
$$\bar{x}_h = \frac{1}{n_h} \sum_{i}^{n_h} x_{hi}$$

In terms of replicated sampling for the $L = 6$ thin zone case, this becomes

(14)
$$V(\hat{X}) = \sum Z^2 \frac{Z - k}{Z} \frac{S_i^2}{k}$$

(15)
$$S_i^2 = \frac{1}{Z - 1} \sum_{j}^{Z} (X_{ij} - \bar{X}_i)^2$$

(16)
$$\bar{X}_i = \frac{1}{Z} \sum_{j}^{Z} X_{ij}$$

As in (9) above, we may define

(17)
$$\sigma_i^2 = \frac{1}{Z} \sum_{j}^{Z} (X_{ij} - \bar{X}_i)^2$$

(18)
$$S_i^2 = \frac{Z}{Z - 1} \sigma_i^2$$

The estimate of (14) was

(19)
$$\hat{V}(\hat{X}) = \sum^{L} Z^2 \frac{Z - k}{Z} \frac{s_i^2}{k}$$

(20)
$$s_i^2 = \frac{1}{k - 1} \sum_{j}^{k} (x_{ij} - \bar{x}_i)^2$$

(21)
$$\bar{x}_i = \frac{1}{k} \sum^{k} x_{ij}$$

Let us now combine $L = 6$ thin zones into $m = 2$ thick zones as shown above, and let us also assume the circled sampling units have been selected as the sample. For the 1st thick zone,

$$x_{011} = x_{11} + x_{21} + x_{31}$$
$$x_{012} = x_{12} + x_{22} + x_{32}$$
$$\bar{x}_{01} = \frac{1}{2}(x_{011} + x_{012})$$

and similarly for the 2nd thick zone. As shown, x_{011} and x_{012} may be considered as the subsample totals. How many such samples may be selected from the 1st thick zone?

Since we select 1 sampling unit from each thin zone which has $Z = 5$ sampling units, and there are $L/m = 6/2 = 3$ thin zones in each thick zone, there are

$$\binom{5}{1}\binom{5}{1}\binom{5}{1} = 125$$

possible samples (x_{011} and x_{012} are 2 of these 125 possible subsample totals.)

Let us now find the variance of these subsample totals. For the 1st thick zone, it will be:

$$(22) \qquad \sigma_{01}^2 = \frac{1}{M} \sum_j^M (X_{01j} - \bar{X}_1)^2$$

where

$$M = \binom{5}{1}\binom{5}{1}\binom{5}{1} = 125$$

$$(23) \qquad \bar{X}_1 = \frac{1}{M} \sum_j^M X_{01j}$$

There is a very important relation between σ_i^2 and σ_{0i}^2 which provides the link between the variances of the thin and thick zones. For our illustration of $m = 2$ thick zones, this is

$$(24) \qquad \sigma_{01}^2 = \sigma_1^2 + \sigma_2^2 + \sigma_3^2$$

$$(25) \qquad \sigma_{02}^2 = \sigma_4^2 + \sigma_5^2 + \sigma_6^2$$

which may be written as

$$(26) \qquad \sigma_{0i}^2 = \sum_i^{L/m} \sigma_i^2 \qquad (0i = 1, 2)$$

Using this relation, $V(\hat{X})$ in (14) becomes

$$(27) \qquad V(\hat{X}) = Z^2 \frac{Z-k}{Z} \frac{1}{k} \sum_i^L S_i^2$$

$$= Z^2 \frac{Z-k}{Z} \frac{1}{k} \frac{Z}{Z-1} \sum_i^L \sigma_i^2$$

$$= Z^2 \frac{Z-k}{Z} \frac{1}{k} \frac{Z}{Z-1} \sum_{0i=1}^m \sigma_{0i}^2$$

The remarkable thing about this formula is that whereas it is a formula for the variance of $\hat{X}$, it is in terms of σ_{0i}^2—which is in terms of x_{0ij}.

To find the estimate of $V(\hat{X})$ in (27), we need to find the estimate of σ_{0i}^2. Recall that for the 1st thick zone, there were $M = 125$ possible samples values of X_{0ij}. In our illustration we have randomly selected $k = 2$. Hence, an estimator of σ_{01}^2 would be

$$(28) \qquad s_{01}^2 = \frac{1}{k-1} \sum_j^k (x_{01j} - \bar{x}_{01})^2$$

where

$$\bar{x}_{01} = \frac{1}{k} \sum_j^k x_{01j}$$

In general, we have

$$(29) \qquad s_{0i}^2 = \frac{1}{k-1} \sum_j^k (x_{0ij} - \bar{x}_{0i})^2$$

Substituting this (29) into (27) to find the estimator gives us

$$(30) \qquad \hat{V}(\hat{X}) = Z^2 \frac{Z-1}{Z} \frac{1}{k} \frac{Z}{Z-1} \sum_i^m s_{0i}^2$$

$$= Z^2 \frac{Z-k}{Z} \frac{1}{k} \frac{Z}{Z-1} \frac{1}{k-1} \sum_i^m \sum_j^k (x_{0ij} - \bar{x}_{0i})^2$$

For simplicity, let us assume

$$\frac{Z-k}{Z} = 1, \qquad \frac{Z}{Z-1} = 1$$

Then (30) becomes

$$(31) \qquad \hat{V}(\hat{X}) = \frac{Z^2}{k(k-1)} \sum_i^m \sum_j^k (x_{0ij} - \bar{x}_{0i})^2 = \frac{Z^2 T^2}{k(k-1)}$$

where

$$T^2 = \sum_i^m \sum_j^k (x_{0ij} - \bar{x}_{0i})^2$$

which is the estimator we seek.

Let us summarize:

$$(32) \qquad \hat{V}(\hat{X}) = \frac{Z^2}{k(k-1)} \sum_i^L \sum_j^k (x_{ij} - \bar{x}_i)^2 \qquad L \text{ thin zones}$$

$$(33) \qquad \hat{V}(\hat{X}) = \frac{Z^2}{k(k-1)} \sum_i^m \sum_j^k (x_{0ij} - \bar{x}_{0i})^2 \qquad m \text{ thick zones}$$

Note carefully that in (27), the variance was equal for thin and thick zones. However, the estimates—(32) and (37)—are not equal.

Example 1. Suppose we have the following data:

m			
	1	2	3
1	2	0	1
	0	4	5
2	....		

Assume the above data shows the 1st 3 thin zones of the $L = 6$ thin zones which have been partitioned into $m = 2$ thick zones. Assume also that $k = 2$ subsamples are to be selected to estimate X. We wish to demonstrate relation (24)

$$\sigma_{01}^2 = \sigma_1^2 + \sigma_2^2 + \sigma_3^2$$

Let us first find

$$\sigma_1^2 = (1/3)[(1-2)^2 + (2-2)^2 + (3-2)^2] = 2/3$$

$$\sigma_2^2 = (1/3)[(2-1)^2 + (0-1)^2 + (1-1)^2] = 2/3$$

$$\sigma_3^2 = (1/3)[(0-3)^2 + (4-3)^2 + (5-3)^2] = 14/3$$

$$\therefore \ \sigma_1^2 + \sigma_2^2 + \sigma_3^2 = 6$$

The σ_{01}^2 was defined as

$$\sigma_{01}^2 = \frac{1}{M} \sum_j^M (X_{01j} - \bar{X}_{01})^2$$

where

$$M = \binom{3}{1}\binom{3}{1}\binom{3}{1} = 27$$

$$\bar{X}_{01} = \frac{1}{M} \sum_j^M X_{01j}$$

Let us first find the $M = 27$ samples. These are given in the Table 14.3.
As shown, we find

$$\bar{X}_{01} = (1/27)(162) = 6$$

Using this result, σ_{01}^2 is found to be

$$\sigma_{01}^2 = (1/27)(9 + 1 + \cdots + 4 + 9) = (1/27)(162) = 6$$

Thus

$$\sigma_{01}^2 = \sigma_1^2 + \sigma_2^2 + \sigma_3^2 = 6$$

Table 14-3

Sample			x_{01j}		$x_{01j} - \bar{x}_{01}$			$(x_{01j} - \bar{x}_{01})^2$
1	2	0	x_{011}	= 3	3 − 6 =	−3		9
		4	x_{012}	= 7	7 − 6 =	1		1
		5	x_{013}	= 8	8 − 6 =	2		4
	0	0	x_{014}	= 1	1 − 6 =	−5		25
		4	x_{015}	= 5	5 − 6 =	−1		1
		5	x_{016}	= 6	6 − 6 =	0		0
	1	0	x_{017}	= 2	2 − 6 =	−4		16
		4	x_{018}	= 6	6 − 6 =	0		0
		5	x_{019}	= 7	7 − 6 =	1		1
2	2	0	x_{0110}	= 4	4 − 6 =	−2		4
		4	x_{0111}	= 8	8 − 6 =	2		4
		5	x_{0112}	= 9	9 − 6 =	3		9
	0	0	x_{0113}	= 2	2 − 6 =	−4		16
		4	x_{0114}	= 6	6 − 6 =	0		0
		5	x_{0115}	= 7	7 − 6 =	1		1
	1	0	x_{0116}	= 3	3 − 6 =	−3		9
		4	x_{0117}	= 7	7 − 6 =	1		1
		5	x_{0118}	= 8	8 − 6 =	2		4
3	2	0	x_{0119}	= 5	5 − 6 =	−1		1
		4	x_{0120}	= 9	9 − 6 =	3		9
		5	x_{0121}	= 10	10 − 6 =	4		16
	0	0	x_{0122}	= 3	3 − 6 =	−3		9
		4	x_{0123}	= 7	7 − 6 =	1		1
		5	x_{0124}	= 8	8 − 6 =	2		4
	1	0	x_{0125}	= 4	4 − 6 =	−2		4
		4	x_{0126}	= 8	8 − 6 =	2		4
		5	x_{0127}	= 9	9 − 6 =	3		9
			x_{01}	= 162		0		162
			$\bar{x}_{01}$	= 6				

Example 2. Using the data of Example 1, let us find an estimate of σ_{01}^2 by selecting $k = 2$ subsamples from the 1st thick zone. Suppose we select

1	3
2	1
0	5
3	9

$$\bar{x}_{01} = \frac{1}{k} \sum^{k} x_{01j} = \frac{1}{2}(3 + 9) = 6$$

$$s_{01}^2 = \frac{1}{2 - 1}[(3 - 6)^2 + (9 - 6)^2] = 18$$

which is an estimate of $\sigma_{01}^2 = 6$.

As shown, $\sigma_{01}^2 = 6$, and $s_{01}^2 = 18$ and there is a large variation. This is mainly due to the fact that there is only $k - 1 = 2 - 1 = 1$ degree of freedom.

Example 3 Let us find $\hat{V}(X)$ for the data of Example 1 in subsection (i) above.

	Sample	
	1	2
	5	3
	9	1
	14	4
	4	8
	2	5
	6	13

$$s_{01}^2 = \frac{1}{2 - 1}[(14 - 9)^2 + (4 - 9)^2] = 50$$

$$s_{02}^2 = \frac{1}{2 - 1}\left[\left(6 - \frac{19}{2}\right)^2 + \left(13 - \frac{19}{2}\right)^2\right] = \frac{49}{2}$$

$$\hat{V}(\hat{X}) = Z^2 \frac{Z - k}{Z} \frac{1}{k} \frac{Z}{Z - 1}\left(50 + \frac{49}{2}\right)$$

$$= (5)^2 \frac{5 - 2}{5} \frac{1}{2} \frac{5}{5 - 1} \frac{149}{2} = 700$$

$$s(\hat{X}) = \sqrt{700} = 26$$

Recall that $\hat{X} = 92.5$ books.

Problems

1. The data in Problem 1, p. 373, concerning the number of books owned by students was as follows:

Zones			Books			
01—06	7	5	1	6	2	3
07—12	2	1	6	4	8	5
13—18	2	2	8	3	5	6
19—24	6	8	5	4	2	4

(i) Using the sample that has been selected in Problem 1, combine 2 thin zones into 1 thick zone. Construct a table.

(ii) Estimate X using the data of the 2 thick zones and check that it is equal to the result obtained from the 4 thin zones.

(iii) Calculate $\hat{V}(\hat{X})$ using the data of the thick zones. Assume for simplicity that $(Z - k)/Z = 1$ and $Z/(Z - 1) = 1$.

2. Using the data of Problem 1, p.382, estimate the total number of hotel rooms X by combining 5 thin zones into 1 thick zone and constructing 2 thick zones. Also estimate $V(\hat{X})$ using the thick zones.

Notes and References

As mentioned at the beginning of this chapter, the main reference of replicated sampling is Professor Deming's book. The student is recommended Chapters 6-10 for illustrations of replicated sampling applied to various cases.

In addition, the student is recommended Chapters 1-5 for a general discussion of the role of statistics and the statistician in planning a survey. Chapter 1, "Responsibilities in Planning a Survey," is especially recommended.

Deming, E. W. (1960). *Sample Design in Business Research*, John Wiley & Sons, Inc., New York.

APPENDIX

Table I. Random numbers

First Thousand

	1–4	5–8	9–12	13–16	17–20	21–24	25–28	29–32	33–36	37–40
1	23 15	75 48	59 01	83 72	59 93	76 24	97 08	86 95	23 03	67 44
2	05 54	55 50	43 10	53 74	35 08	90 61	18 37	44 10	96 22	13 43
3	14 87	16 03	50 32	40 43	62 23	50 05	10 03	22 11	54 38	08 34
4	38 97	67 49	51 94	05 17	58 53	78 80	59 01	94 32	42 87	16 95
5	97 31	26 17	18 99	75 53	08 70	94 25	12 58	41 54	88 21	05 13
6	11 74	26 93	81 44	33 93	08 72	32 79	73 31	18 22	64 70	68 50
7	43 36	12 88	59 11	01 64	56 23	93 00	90 04	99 43	64 07	40 36
8	93 80	62 04	78 38	26 80	44 91	55 75	11 89	32 58	47 55	25 71
9	49 54	01 31	81 08	42 98	41 87	69 53	82 96	61 77	73 80	95 27
10	36 76	87 26	33 37	94 82	15 69	41 95	96 86	70 45	27 48	38 80
11	07 09	25 23	92 24	62 71	26 07	06 55	84 53	44 67	33 84	53 20
12	43 31	00 10	81 44	86 38	03 07	52 55	51 61	48 89	74 29	46 47
13	61 57	00 63	60 06	17 36	37 75	63 14	89 51	23 35	01 74	69 93
14	31 35	28 37	99 10	77 91	89 41	31 57	97 64	48 62	58 48	69 19
15	57 04	88 65	26 27	79 59	36 82	90 52	95 65	46 35	06 53	22 54
16	09 24	34 42	00 68	72 10	71 37	30 72	97 57	56 09	29 82	76 50
17	97 95	53 50	18 40	89 48	83 29	52 23	08 25	21 22	53 26	15 87
18	93 73	25 95	70 43	78 19	88 85	56 67	16 68	26 95	99 64	45 69
19	72 62	11 12	25 00	92 26	82 64	35 66	65 94	34 71	68 75	18 67
20	61 02	07 44	18 45	37 12	07 94	95 91	73 78	66 99	53 61	93 78
21	97 83	98 54	74 33	05 59	17 18	45 47	35 41	44 22	03 42	30 00
22	89 16	09 71	92 22	23 29	06 37	35 05	54 54	89 88	43 81	63 61
23	25 96	68 82	20 62	87 17	92 65	02 82	35 28	62 84	91 95	48 83
24	81 44	33 17	19 05	04 95	48 06	74 69	00 75	67 65	01 71	65 45
25	11 32	25 49	31 42	36 23	43 86	08 62	49 76	67 42	24 52	32 45

Second Thousand

	1–4	5–8	9–12	13–16	17–20	21–24	25–28	29–32	33–36	37–40
1	64 75	58 38	85 84	12 22	59 20	17 69	61 56	55 95	04 59	59 47
2	10 30	25 22	89 77	43 63	44 30	38 11	24 90	67 07	34 82	33 28
3	71 01	79 84	95 51	30 85	03 74	66 59	10 28	87 53	76 56	91 49
4	60 01	25 56	05 88	41 03	48 79	79 65	59 01	69 78	80 00	36 66
5	37 33	09 46	56 49	16 14	28 02	48 27	45 47	55 44	55 36	50 90
6	47 86	98 70	01 31	59 11	22 73	60 62	61 28	22 34	69 16	12 12
7	38 04	04 27	37 64	16 78	95 78	39 32	34 93	24 88	43 43	87 06
8	73 50	83 09	08 83	05 48	00 78	36 66	93 02	95 56	46 04	53 36
9	32 62	34 64	74 84	06 10	43 24	20 62	83 73	19 32	35 64	39 69
10	97 59	19 95	49 36	63 03	51 06	62 06	99 29	75 95	32 05	77 34
11	74 01	23 19	55 59	79 09	69 82	66 22	42 40	15 96	74 90	75 89
12	56 75	42 64	57 13	35 10	50 14	90 96	63 36	74 69	09 63	34 88
13	49 80	04 99	08 54	83 12	19 98	08 52	82 63	72 92	92 36	50 26
14	43 58	48 96	47 24	87 85	66 70	00 22	15 01	93 99	59 16	23 77
15	16 65	37 96	64 60	32 57	13 01	35 74	28 36	36 73	05 88	72 29
16	48 50	26 90	55 65	32 25	87 48	31 44	68 02	37 31	25 29	63 67
17	96 76	55 46	92 36	31 68	62 30	48 29	63 83	52 23	81 66	40 94
18	38 92	36 15	50 80	35 78	17 84	23 44	41 24	63 33	99 22	81 28
19	77 95	88 16	94 25	22 50	55 87	51 07	30 10	70 60	21 86	19 61
20	17 92	82 80	65 25	58 60	87 71	02 64	18 50	64 65	79 64	81 70
21	94 03	68 59	78 02	31 80	44 99	41 05	41 05	31 87	43 12	15 96
22	47 46	06 04	79 56	23 04	84 17	14 37	28 51	67 27	55 80	03 68
23	47 85	65 60	88 51	99 28	24 39	40 64	41 71	70 13	46 31	82 88
24	57 61	63 46	53 92	29 86	20 18	10 37	57 65	15 62	98 69	07 56
25	08 30	09 27	04 66	75 26	66 10	57 18	87 91	07 54	22 22	20 13

Table I. Random numbers (*continued*)

THIRD AND FOURTH THOUSANDS

Third Thousand

	1–4	5–8	9–12	13–16	17–20	21–24	25–28	29–32	33–36	37–40
1	89 22	10 23	62 65	78 77	47 33	51 27	23 02	13 92	44 13	96 51
2	04 00	59 98	18 63	91 82	90 32	94 01	24 23	63 01	26 11	06 50
3	98 54	63 80	66 50	85 67	50 45	40 64	52 28	41 53	25 44	41 25
4	41 71	98 44	01 59	22 60	13 14	54 58	14 03	98 49	98 86	55 79
5	28 73	37 24	89 00	78 52	58 43	24 61	34 97	97 85	56 78	44 71
6	65 21	38 39	27 77	76 20	30 86	80 74	22 43	95 68	47 68	37 92
7	65 55	31 26	78 90	90 69	04 66	43 67	02 62	17 69	90 03	12 05
8	05 66	86 90	80 73	02 98	57 46	58 33	27 82	31 45	98 69	29 98
9	39 30	29 97	18 49	75 77	95 19	27 38	77 63	73 47	26 29	16 12
10	64 59	23 22	54 45	87 92	94 31	38 32	00 59	81 18	06 78	71 37
11	07 51	34 87	92 47	31 48	36 60	68 90	70 53	36 82	57 99	15 82
12	86 59	36 85	01 56	63 89	98 00	82 83	93 51	48 56	54 10	72 32
13	83 73	52 25	99 97	97 78	12 48	36 83	89 95	60 32	41 06	76 14
14	08 59	52 18	26 54	65 50	82 04	87 99	01 70	33 56	25 80	53 84
15	41 27	32 71	49 44	29 36	94 58	16 82	86 39	62 15	86 43	54 31
16	00 47	37 59	08 56	23 81	22 42	72 63	17 63	14 47	25 20	63 47
17	86 13	15 37	89 81	38 30	78 68	89 13	29 61	82 07	00 98	64 32
18	33 84	97 83	59 04	40 20	35 86	03 17	68 86	63 08	01 82	25 46
19	61 87	04 16	57 07	46 80	86 12	98 08	39 73	49 20	77 54	50 91
20	43 89	86 59	23 25	07 88	61 29	78 49	19 76	53 91	50 08	07 86
21	29 93	93 91	23 04	54 84	59 85	60 95	20 66	41 28	72 64	64 73
22	38 50	58 55	55 14	38 85	50 77	18 65	79 48	87 67	83 17	08 19
23	31 82	43 84	31 67	12 52	55 11	72 04	41 15	62 53	27 98	22 68
24	91 43	00 37	67 13	56 11	55 97	06 75	09 25	52 02	39 13	87 53
25	38 63	56 89	76 25	49 89	75 26	96 45	80 38	05 04	11 66	35 14

Fourth Thousand

	1–4	5–8	9–12	13–16	17–20	21–24	25–28	29–32	33–36	37–40
1	02 49	05 41	22 27	94 43	93 64	04 23	07 20	74 11	67 95	40 82
2	11 96	73 64	69 60	62 78	37 01	09 25	33 02	08 01	38 53	74 82
3	48 25	68 34	65 49	69 92	40 79	05 40	33 51	54 39	61 30	31 36
4	27 24	67 30	80 21	48 12	35 36	04 88	18 99	77 49	48 49	30 71
5	32 53	27 72	65 72	43 07	07 22	86 52	91 84	57 92	65 71	00 11
6	66 75	79 89	55 92	37 59	34 31	43 20	45 58	25 45	44 36	92 65
7	11 26	63 45	45 76	50 59	77 46	34 66	82 69	99 26	74 29	75 16
8	17 87	23 91	42 45	56 18	01 46	93 13	74 89	24 64	25 75	92 84
9	62 56	13 03	65 03	40 81	47 54	51 79	80 81	33 61	01 09	77 30
10	62 79	63 07	79 35	49 77	05 01	30 10	50 81	33 00	99 79	19 70
11	75 51	02 17	71 04	33 93	36 60	42 75	76 22	23 87	56 54	84 68
12	87 43	90 16	91 63	51 72	65 90	44 43	70 72	17 98	70 63	90 32
13	97 74	20 26	21 10	74 87	88 03	38 33	76 52	26 92	14 95	90 51
14	98 81	10 60	01 21	57 10	28 75	21 82	88 39	12 85	18 86	16 24
15	51 26	40 18	52 64	60 79	25 53	29 00	42 66	95 78	58 36	29 98
16	40 23	99 33	76 10	41 96	86 10	49 12	00 29	41 80	03 59	93 17
17	26 93	65 91	86 51	66 72	76 45	46 32	94 46	81 94	19 06	66 47
18	88 50	21 17	16 98	29 94	09 74	42 39	46 22	00 69	09 48	16 46
19	63 49	93 80	93 25	59 36	19 95	79 86	78 05	69 01	02 33	83 74
20	36 37	98 12	06 03	31 77	87 10	73 82	83 10	83 60	50 94	40 91
21	93 80	12 23	22 47	47 95	70 17	59 33	43 06	47 43	06 12	66 60
22	29 85	68 71	20 56	31 15	00 53	25 36	58 12	65 22	41 40	24 31
23	97 72	08 79	31 88	26 51	30 50	71 01	71 51	77 06	95 79	29 19
24	85 23	70 91	C5 74	60 14	63 77	59 93	81 56	47 34	17 79	27 53
25	75 74	67 52	68 31	72 79	57 73	72 36	48 73	24 36	87 90	68 02

SOURCE: This table is reproduced from M. G. Kendall and B. Babington Smith, Tracts for computers, No. XXIV, Tables of Random Sampling Numbers, Cambridge University Press, 1954, by permission of the authors and publishers.

Table II. Areas under the normal curve

Normal Deviate z	.00	.01	.02	.03	.04	.05	.06	.07	.08	.09
0.0	.5000	.4960	.4920	.4880	.4840	.4801	.4761	.4721	.4681	.4641
0.1	.4602	.4562	.4522	.4483	.4443	.4404	.4364	.4325	.4286	.4247
0.2	.4207	.4168	.4129	.4090	.4052	.4013	.3974	.3936	.3897	.3859
0.3	.3821	.3783	.3745	.3707	.3669	.3632	.3594	.3557	.3520	.3483
0.4	.3446	.3409	.3372	.3336	.3300	.3264	.3228	.3192	.3156	.3121
0.5	.3085	.3050	.3015	.2981	.2946	.2912	.2877	.2843	.2810	.2776
0.6	.2743	.2709	.2676	.2643	.2611	.2578	.2546	.2514	.2483	.2451
0.7	.2420	.2389	.2358	.2327	.2296	.2266	.2236	.2206	.2177	.2148
0.8	.2119	.2090	.2061	.2033	.2005	.1977	.1949	.1922	.1894	.1867
0.9	.1841	.1814	.1788	.1762	.1736	.1711	.1685	.1660	.1635	.1611
1.0	.1587	.1562	.1539	.1515	.1492	.1469	.1446	.1423	.1401	.1379
1.1	.1357	.1335	.1314	.1292	.1271	.1251	.1230	.1210	.1190	.1170
1.2	.1151	.1131	.1112	.1093	.1075	.1056	.1038	.1020	.1003	.0985
1.3	.0968	.0951	.0934	.0918	.0901	.0885	.0869	.0853	.0838	.0823
1.4	.0808	.0793	.0778	.0764	.0749	.0735	.0721	.0708	.0694	.0681
1.5	.0668	.0655	.0643	.0630	.0618	.0606	.0594	.0582	.0571	.0559
1.6	.0548	.0537	.0526	.0516	.0505	.0495	.0485	.0475	.0465	.0455
1.7	.0446	.0436	.0427	.0418	.0409	.0401	.0392	.0384	.0375	.0367
1.8	.0359	.0351	.0344	.0336	.0329	.0322	.0314	.0307	.0301	.0294
1.9	.0287	.0281	.0274	.0268	.0262	.0256	.0250	.0244	.0239	.0233
2.0	.0228	.0222	.0217	.0212	.0207	.0202	.0197	.0192	.0188	.0183
2.1	.0179	.0174	.0170	.0166	.0162	.0158	.0154	.0150	.0146	.0143
2.2	.0139	.0136	.0132	.0129	.0125	.0122	.0119	.0116	.0113	.0110
2.3	.0107	.0104	.0102	.0099	.0096	.0094	.0091	.0089	.0087	.0084
2.4	.0082	.0080	.0078	.0075	.0073	.0071	.0069	.0068	.0066	.0064
2.5	.0062	.0060	.0059	.0057	.0055	.0054	.0052	.0051	.0049	.0048
2.6	.0047	.0045	.0044	.0043	.0041	.0040	.0039	.0038	.0037	.0036
2.7	.0035	.0034	.0033	.0032	.0031	.0030	.0029	.0028	.0027	.0026
2.8	.0026	.0025	.0024	.0023	.0023	.0022	.0021	.0021	.0020	.0019
2.9	.0019	.0018	.0018	.0017	.0016	.0016	.0015	.0015	.0014	.0014
3.0	.0013	.0013	.0013	.0012	.0012	.0011	.0011	.0011	.0010	.0010

Table III

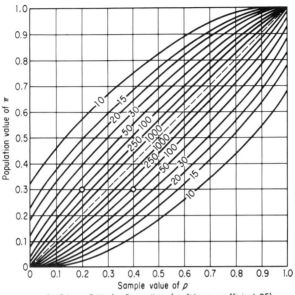

Confidence Belts for Proportions (confidence coefficient .95)

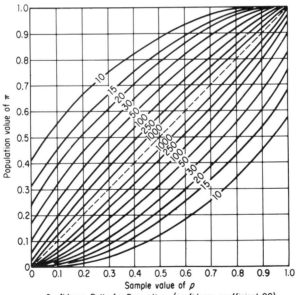

Confidence Belts for Proportions (confidence coefficient .99)

Table IV. Sample size for specified confidence limits and precision when sampling attributes in percent.

A. 95% confidence interval $(p = 0.5)^a$

Population size	Sample size for precision of					
	±1%	±2%	±3%	±4%	±5%	±10%
500	b	b	b	b	222	83
1,000	b	b	b	385	286	91
1,500	b	b	638	441	316	94
2,000	b	b	714	476	333	95
2,500	b	1,250	769	500	345	96
3,000	b	1,364	811	517	353	97
3,500	b	1,458	843	530	359	97
4,000	b	1,538	870	541	364	98
4,500	b	1,607	891	549	367	98
5,000	b	1,667	909	556	370	98
6,000	b	1,765	938	566	375	98
7,000	b	1,842	959	574	378	99
8,000	b	1,905	976	580	381	99
9,000	b	1,957	989	584	383	99
10,000	5,000	2,000	1,000	588	385	99
15,000	6,000	2,143	1,034	600	390	99
20,000	6,667	2,222	1,053	606	392	100
25,000	7,143	2,273	1,064	610	394	100
50,000	8,333	2,381	1,087	617	397	100
100,000	9,091	2,439	1,099	621	398	100
→ ∞	10,000	2,500	1,111	625	400	100

^{a} p—Proportion of units in sample possessing characteristic being measured; for other values of p, the required sample size will be smaller.

^{b} In these cases 50% of the universe in the sample will give more than the required accuracy. Since the normal distribution is a poor approximation of the hypergeometrical distribution when n is more than 50% of N, the formula used in this calculation does not apply

Table IV. (continued)

B. 99.7% confidence interval $(p = 0.5)^a$

Population size	Sample size for precision of				
	$\pm 1\%$	$\pm 2\%$	$\pm 3\%$	$\pm 4\%$	$\pm 5\%$
500	b	b	b	b	b
1,000	b	b	b	b	474
1,500	b	b	b	726	563
2,000	b	b	b	826	621
2,500	b	b	b	900	662
3,000	b	b	1,364	958	692
3,500	b	b	1,458	1,003	716
4,000	b	b	1,539	1,041	735
4,500	b	b	1,607	1,071	750
5,000	b	b	1,667	1,098	763
6,000	b	2,903	1,765	1,139	783
7,000	b	3,119	1,842	1,171	798
8,000	b	3,303	1,905	1,196	809
9,000	b	3,462	1,957	1,216	818
10,000	b	3,600	2,000	1,233	826
15,000	b	4,091	2,143	1,286	849
20,000	b	4,390	2,222	1,314	861
25,000	11,842	4,592	2,273	1,331	869
50,000	15,517	5,056	2,381	1,368	884
100,000	18,367	5,325	2,439	1,387	892
$\rightarrow \infty$	22,500	5,625	2,500	1,406	900

^{a} p—Proportion of units in sample possessing characteristic being measured; for other values of p, the required sample size will be smaller.

^{b} In these cases 50% of the universe in the sample will give more than the required accuracy. Since the normal distribution is a poor approximation of the hypergeometrical distribution when n is more than 50% of N, the formula used in this calculation does not apply.

Table V. Squares, square roots, and reciprocals

n	n²	$\sqrt{n}$	$\sqrt{10n}$	1/n	n	n²	$\sqrt{n}$	$\sqrt{10n}$	1/n
1	1	1.000	3.162	1.00000	51	2601	7.141	22.583	.01961
2	4	1.414	4.472	.50000	52	2704	7.211	22.804	.01923
3	9	1.732	5.477	.33333	53	2809	7.280	23.022	.01887
4	16	2.000	6.325	.25000	54	2916	7.348	23.238	.01852
5	25	2.236	7.071	.20000	55	3025	7.416	23.452	.01818
6	36	2.449	7.746	.16667	56	3136	7.483	23.664	.01786
7	49	2.646	8.367	.14286	57	3249	7.550	23.875	.01754
8	64	2.828	8.944	.12500	58	3364	7.616	24.083	.01724
9	81	3.000	9.487	.11111	59	3481	7.681	24.290	.01695
10	100	3.162	10.000	.10000	60	3600	7.746	24.495	.01667
11	121	3.317	10.488	.09091	61	3721	7.810	24.698	.01639
12	144	3.464	10.954	.08333	62	3844	7.874	24.900	.01613
13	169	3.606	11.402	.07692	63	3969	7.937	25.100	.01587
14	196	3.742	11.832	.07143	64	4096	8.000	25.298	.01562
15	225	3.873	12.247	.06667	65	4225	8.062	25.495	.01538
16	256	4.000	12.649	.06250	66	4356	8.124	25.690	.01515
17	289	4.123	13.038	.05882	67	4489	8.185	25.884	.01493
18	324	4.243	13.416	.05556	68	4624	8.246	26.077	.01471
19	361	4.359	13.784	.05263	69	4761	8.307	26.268	.01449
20	400	4.472	14.142	.05000	70	4900	8.367	26.458	.01429
21	441	4.583	14.491	.04762	71	5041	8.426	26.646	.01408
22	484	4.690	14.832	.04545	72	5184	8.485	26.833	.01389
23	529	4.796	15.166	.04348	73	5329	8.544	27.019	.01370
24	576	4.899	15.492	.04167	74	5476	8.602	27.203	.01351
25	625	5.000	15.811	.04000	75	5625	8.660	27.386	.01333
26	676	5.099	16.125	.03846	76	5776	8.718	27.568	.01316
27	729	5.196	16.432	.03704	77	5929	8.775	27.749	.01299
28	784	5.292	16.733	.03571	78	6084	8.832	27.928	.01282
29	841	5.385	17.029	.03448	79	6241	8.888	28.107	.01266
30	900	5.477	17.321	.03333	80	6400	8.944	28.284	.01250
31	961	5.568	17.607	.03226	81	6561	9.000	28.460	.01235
32	1024	5.657	17.889	.03125	82	6724	9.055	28.636	.01220
33	1089	5.745	18.166	.03030	83	6889	9.110	28.810	.01205
34	1156	5.831	18.439	.02941	84	7056	9.165	28.983	.01190
35	1225	5.916	18.708	.02857	85	7225	9.220	29.155	.01176
36	1296	6.000	18.974	.02778	86	7396	9.274	29.326	.01163
37	1369	6.083	19.235	.02703	87	7569	9.327	29.496	.01149
38	1444	6.164	19.494	.02632	88	7744	9.381	29.665	.01136
39	1521	6.245	19.748	.02564	89	7921	9.434	29.833	.01124
40	1600	6.325	20.000	.02500	90	8100	9.487	30.000	.01111
41	1681	6.403	20.248	.02439	91	8281	9.539	30.166	.01099
42	1764	6.481	20.494	.02381	92	8464	9.592	30.332	.01087
43	1849	6.557	20.736	.02326	93	8649	9.644	30.496	.01075
44	1936	6.633	20.976	.02273	94	8836	9.695	30.659	.01064
45	2025	6.708	21.213	.02222	95	9025	9.747	30.822	.01053
46	2116	6.782	21.448	.02174	96	9216	9.798	30.984	.01042
47	2209	6.856	21.679	.02128	97	9409	9.849	31.145	.01031
48	2304	6.928	21.909	.02083	98	9604	9.899	31.305	.01020
49	2401	7.000	22.136	.02041	99	9801	9.950	31.464	.01010
50	2500	7.071	22.361	.02000	100	10000	10.000	31.623	.01000

INDEX